Coopers
&Lybrand

The finan<

A guide to fi<

GUA1019186

Phil Rivett
Peter Speak

Foreword

The second edition of 'The financial jungle – a guide to financial instruments' is Coopers & Lybrand's flagship capital markets textbook. It is the result of detailed research into, and analysis of, the instruments available in the financial marketplace. The objective of the book is to promote the understanding of financial instruments and to identify their risks and benefits in a way which renders the subject accessible to both the designers and users of the instruments.

In the last few years, there have been a number of major problems resulting from companies and other organisations dealing in financial instruments without appreciating fully how the instruments have been put together, how they work from an accounting, taxation and regulatory perspective and, critically, their risks. As financial instruments have become increasingly complex, so, frequently have the timescales in which management is required to take major decisions reduced. It is essential to have at hand guidance which is comprehensive in scope and detailed in its analysis of the available instruments. 'The financial jungle – a guide to financial instruments' meets these criteria.

This book results from a collaborative effort by a large number of capital markets specialists in the member firms of Coopers & Lybrand. The skills of these accountants, taxation specialists and treasury consultants have been used to expand considerably the first edition, to include commentary on the individual European markets for financial instruments and to describe, in more detail, some of the basic techniques and methods of valuation. As for the first edition, the principal authors and editors are Phil Rivett, Chairman of the Coopers & Lybrand Securities and Commodities Industry Group and Peter Speak, a senior manager and member of that group. Both specialise in capital markets and have expertise in the use of financial instruments.

We believe 'The financial jungle' represents the best guide available today and hope that finance directors, treasurers, lawyers, accountants and financial advisors will find it invaluable.

Peter Smith
Head of Financial Services – Coopers & Lybrand

IFR Publishing
Aldgate House, 33 Aldgate High Street
London EC3N 1DL.

ISBN 1 873446 85 3

Typeset by BPC Digital Techset Ltd.
Printed and bound by BPC Wheatons Ltd.
Members of the BPC Group of Companies.

Preface

'Issuers and investors should seek to understand fully the risks of financial instruments both in the short and long term'. This cautionary note was struck in the Introduction to the first edition of 'The financial jungle'. Ironically the book was published only a few weeks before the Stock Market crash in October 1987 which made apparent some of the potential risks identified in that edition of 'The financial jungle'. Subsequently, many of the other risks identified in the book have become apparent as a result of developments in the financial marketplace and from recession in the economies of many countries.

Our main objective in preparing the second edition is to continue to promote the understanding of financial instruments. We have expanded the book to cover new instruments which have emerged since the first edition was published and have described in more detail some of the techniques and basic instruments as well as methods employed in their valuation. In addition, with the assistance of our colleagues in Coopers & Lybrand Europe we have expanded the book to include features of the principal European markets for financial instruments.

In the second edition we have raised once again questions on accounting and taxation which should be addressed by issuers and investors. With our European colleagues we have also provided a framework in which answers to the matters raised can be developed. For many instruments it will be necessary to understand the particular circumstances before a definite solution can be found. We hope that finance directors, treasurers, lawyers, accountants and financial advisors will find the analysis helpful in assisting their understanding of financial instruments and techniques.

The second edition of 'The financial jungle' represents a considerable amount of work by, and the cooperation of, our colleagues in seventeen European offices of Coopers & Lybrand. We are grateful for the efforts of the partners and staff in these offices who have assisted us by providing the information to make this book possible. Details of the European offices and partners concerned are given at the back of the book. We are also indebted to partners and staff in London for providing helpful and constructive comment and for their patience and commitment to read and check chapters of the book. In particular we would like to thank John Tattersall, Paul Reyniers, Douglas Paterson, Alastair Wilson and Elizabeth Willetts for their contributions and comments, as well as staff in the audit support department for reviewing the technical content of the book.

Preface

Finally, we are grateful to David Peck for helping pull the book together
and our secretaries for their patience with the many drafts.

Phil Rivett
Peter Speak
October 1991

Contents

Contents

How to use this book

The intention of this book is to enable the reader to enhance his understanding of the many different financial instruments which are now available for the raising of finance or the management of risk.

Structure of the book

This book is comprised of a general introduction, four main chapters and a final chapter in which the accounting and taxation in 18 European countries is explained. The four main chapters, which group financial instruments with similar characteristics, are:

- Chapter 2 – Debt instruments;
- Chapter 3 – Asset backed securities;
- Chapter 4 – Equity and equity linked instruments;
- Chapter 5 – Hedging instruments.

Although the groupings are fairly well defined, the distinctions between them can become blurred. For example, in recent years a number of instruments which can be described as debt/equity hybrids have been developed. These include instruments such as repackaged perpetual bonds which are debt instruments with some of the characteristics of equity, or other instruments such as convertible preference shares which are structured as equity issues but economically behave very much like debt.

Structure of each chapter

Each chapter has been structured to enable the reader to research one particular instrument or to read each chapter as a whole. The framework of each chapter is as follows:

- an overview summarises the format of the chapter and describes the key characteristics of, and current trends in, each group of instruments;

• the chapter is then divided by broad subcategory of instrument, usually with an introduction, which describes the function of groups of instruments. Firstly the basic or traditional instruments within the category are explained, together with a description of the more important markets in Europe where the instruments can be issued, purchased or traded. Following the discussion of the basic instruments, recent innovations and related products within each grouping are described;

• an analysis of the benefits, and risks and disadvantages for each group of instrument is followed by a series of accounting and taxation questions either related to a group of instruments or for a specific one. These questions will be relevant to issuers of, and investors in, these instruments based in most jurisdictions in Europe. The risks and disadvantages of each instrument are also identified from the users and investors viewpoint;

• each chapter has a section describing specific accounting and taxation issues affecting the instruments in a number of European countries. These very brief summaries do not attempt to answer all the questions which have been raised concerning each instrument in a particular chapter; rather they attempt to set the general framework within which these questions will be addressed in particular countries.

Country accounting and taxation framework

Chapter 6 explains the general accounting and taxation framework in 18 European countries. It is within this framework that the accounting and taxation treatment of a particular instrument will be established.

Introduction

Development of new financial instruments

There appear to be two main reasons for the explosive growth in new financial instruments in the 1980s. The first, and perhaps most important, is the process termed 'disintermediation'. Disintermediation, whereby borrowers raise finance directly from lenders rather than from banks, has itself been driven by a number of factors. The erosion of bank balance sheets following the lesser developed countries debt crisis made it more attractive for banks to earn fees from issuing bonds and other securities rather than interest income from lending. Banks could thereby improve their earnings without risking their capital and without exceeding regulatory restrictions on the amount of their 'risk assets'. Competition between the traditional lending banks and the newer investment banks which, for regulatory reasons, may not be able to lend money, has led to the development of instruments covering the whole range of maturities traditionally encompassed by bank overdrafts and syndicated loans. In addition, borrowers have become more sophisticated and better able to raise finance at reduced interest margins. Although disintermediation can reduce the direct cost of borrowing in the short term, as has been seen recently, it can create an overall increase in risk to the borrower and to the lender or investor.

The other main factor behind the growth in financial instruments has been the improvement in information technology. This improvement has enabled ever more complex financial instruments to be devised and more sophisticated financing techniques to be designed. Powerful personal computers have allowed individual bankers (the so called 'rocket-scientists') and investors to develop complex financial models and make intricate calculations. The ability to process large amounts of data has lead to the design of securities which combine and allocate cash flows from large pools of mortgage loans (or other homogeneous pools of assets) to investors with different investment objectives. Improvements in communication have enabled financial instruments to be traded on markets with no physical existence and simultaneously in different market places. These markets can either be computer based whereby transactions are matched by computer or over the international telephone networks.

However, if financial innovation has not quite become a dirty word, certainly recent events have made both issuers and investors more cautious. For disintermediation to be successful, the markets for bonds and other assets which replace traditional bank finance (eg commercial paper) have to be liquid and active at all times. The stock market crash in 1987 showed that liquidity can be eroded quickly, in even the largest markets, and at the very time it is most important to investors. The development of the junk bond market in the United States in the 1980s gave a small group of investment bankers the ability to threaten some of the world's largest corporations with takeover by means of leveraged buy-outs. Bonds issued by these corporations before the buy-out was announced, which had previously been regarded as very high quality investment grade securities, suffered a significant fall in value which has increased the general suspicion of financial innovation. The speed with which apparently sound companies which chose to 'shop around' for the cheapest source of funds and therefore often issued commercial paper can be forced into liquidation, demonstrates the need for good relationships with bankers. The recent financial difficulties of some corporations have demonstrated the importance of committed bank facilities which are not so susceptible to market sentiment.

Other techniques developed during the 1980s have also fostered this suspicion. The problems which occurred in the swap market in the United Kingdom when local authorities were judged to have acted in an *'ultra vires'* capacity can not have helped this market develop as widely and quickly as perhaps might have been expected. Major public companies which sought to avoid making provision for the extra interest payable to investors on 'premium put convertibles' have now realised the need to consider at the outset the potential disadvantages of the bonds rather than assuming that all will be well. Losses incurred by large corporations involved in option trading emphasises the need for management to understand the risks to which their treasurers are exposing the corporation. Such events can only increase the conservatism of borrowers and investors alike and make them more sceptical of complex financial instruments.

Despite these factors, it is inevitable that financial instruments and techniques will continue to develop. More innovation will be driven by the need to attract new investors, the requirement to eliminate or reduce risk and the requirement of banks to increase their scarce capital while still making returns for their shareholders.

Basle Convergence Agreement

The Basle Convergence Agreement reached by the Basle Committee of

Banking Regulations and Supervisory Practices (comprising representatives of the central banks of the Group of Ten countries or 'G-10'), to secure international convergence on the capital adequacy requirements of international banks will further increase the need for banks in some countries (notably the United States and Japan) to increase their regulatory capital or reduce their risk assets or both. The Basle Convergence Agreement has been implemented in European Community Directives, and member states are required to comply by 1 January 1993. Other G-10 members such as Switzerland, Japan and the United States are to comply by the same date.

The Basle Convergence Agreement, as well as making disintermediation more attractive to the banks, has also helped promote the development of new financial instruments in two areas:

● instruments which blur the distinction between debt and equity. This category of instrument can be of particular interest to banks seeking to increase their capital base. In particular, preferred shares which can increase 'core capital' (so called tier 1 capital) and debt equity hybrids which can qualify as 'supplementary capital' (tier 2 capital);

● asset backed securities which allow banks to sell large pools of assets and thus reduce their risk assets.

With the increasing likelihood of convergence of the capital requirements of banks regulated under the Basle agreement with those of the securities companies and investment banks regulated under different legislation, the process of innovation looks set to continue.

Hedging instruments

Many of the developments in financial instruments which occurred in the 1980s were designed to facilitate better management of liabilities and assets. Whilst within the European Community the European Monetary System ('EMS') may help to reduce the volatility of exchange and interest rates, fluctuations are allowed between the EMS currencies and there is always the risk of realignment. In addition, the EMS currencies are still exposed to exchange rate fluctuations with the major economies in the rest of the world such as the United States and Japan. Consequently it is likely that the trend set in the 1980s will continue, with hedging instruments being developed at a high rate.

New futures exchanges and contracts are established each year and it seems that a futures exchange is a prerequisite of any emerging financial marketplace. New contracts are introduced for traditional commodities to enable exchanges to compete for market share. In addition, exchanges have teams developing innovative contracts based on new underlying instruments (eg insurance premiums, real estate prices). However, these exchanges and contracts will only be successful if there is an underlying need for the contract which is sufficient to generate liquidity. It remains to be seen whether new contracts and exchanges can be sustained over the long term but new and innovative contracts are likely to be a feature of the 1990s. It also seems likely that there will be more over the counter instruments developed to provide a hedge against risks specifically affecting particular sectors of industry. These instruments are likely to be similar to existing instruments, but will be designed to overcome perceived (or actual) shortcomings or specific risks. Such products are intended to give their designer a competitive advantage in the marketplace, at least in the short term.

Hedging instruments can be extremely valuable if used properly to reduce or eliminate exposure to price movements. However, their use inevitably introduces new risks which management must understand and control. First, the use of hedging instruments creates exposure to counterparties which is often not properly evaluated or controlled. The ability (or rather inability) to offset payments and receipts arising under different hedging instruments is often not considered when reviewing credit limits and exposures. Offsetting, if it can be legally enforced, can reduce significantly credit exposure. However, this presupposes that proper credit procedures are instituted in the first place and that the transaction is properly documented. Hedging instruments can create an exposure to the counter-parties as a result of improper documentation which may result in legal disputes; problems could also result from the inability of the counterparty to enter into the contract (eg is it *ultra vires?*).

Second, as the users of hedging instruments get more sophisticated the level of activity increases, and the department arranging the transaction (eg the treasury) can be seen as a 'profit centre' rather than being responsible for reducing risk. This can be particularly true if substantial profits are made in the start-up phase. The profit centre concept almost inevitably leads to an increase in risk. Generating increasing levels of profit, to meet demanding budgets, may necessitate taking further positions which will increase rather than reduce the overall exposure. In addition, if the treasury is located offshore it may also be 'out of sight out of mind'. If the nature of the activity is not properly understood by senior management, corporations can find themselves with very large exposures to interest and foreign exchange rates. Often these exposures are considerably in excess of those originally identified as requiring to be hedged and sometimes result in losses greater than the profits generated from the entire operations of the corporation.

The objectives and policies for hedging must be clearly established by management. These policies must be regularly monitored. If the activities of a corporate treasury are treated as a profit centre, corporations need to appreciate that this may involve creating additional risks. Before such risks are taken proper controls must be designed and implemented and senior management must understand the level of risk to which the corporation is exposed. In recent years there have been a number of examples of what were perceived to be conservatively-managed corporations incurring substantial losses because they failed to appreciate, monitor and control the risks which were being created from the use of hedging instruments. Such problems give hedging instruments a reputation for increasing risk. However, hedging instruments are designed specifically to reduce or eliminate exposure to price movements and will achieve this when used properly.

A final word of warning regarding hedging instruments. It is important to establish the accounting and taxation treatment of hedging instruments at an early stage. Sometimes the accounting treatment which is specified in the corporation's normal accounting policies, and the relevant accounting standards, can create an anomalous result. Although the hedging instrument should reduce or eliminate the economic risk to which the corporation is exposed the accounting treatment can result in a spurious profit or loss (perhaps offset by a movement to reserves). These spurious results can usually be avoided if the economics of the transaction are understood and all aspects consistently accounted for. However, the taxation position is often less clear. In the United Kingdom the Inland Revenue have recently published proposals for the tax treatment of hedging instruments used for managing interest rate risk (see below), but the treatment of other instruments is less clear. In many countries in Europe however, the tax authorities have no defined policy for the taxation of any hedging instruments. Consequently, what may appear to be an economic hedge before taxation may not be so on an after tax basis because a gain is taxable and a loss is not deductible, or vice versa. It is therefore vital to ensure that the taxation position is carefully considered before the transaction is completed.

Accounting for financial instruments

It is generally recognised that the accounting for, and the taxation of, financial instruments can raise significant problems. When the problem of interpretation is viewed within the context of Europe the position becomes more complex. Comparisons between European countries both within the European Community and others highlights important differences in the accounting and taxation treatment of financial instruments. In 1978 and 1983 the European Community set in train the process of harmonisation of financial reporting with two directives; namely, the fourth directive (Company accounts) and the seventh directive (Group accounts). These directives are still in the process of being implemented in the various member states. However, even with such directives, harmonisation has not been achieved. In addition, other non European Community members have laws and practices which are different. This situation exists even though increasingly Europe is seen as being one financial marketplace.

One of the effects of these directives has been to provide a more uniform layout of the profit and loss account, balance sheet and notes to the accounts. However, whilst the layout of financial statements in all member states is now broadly similar, an examination of how other aspects of the directives have been implemented shows there is less agreement on the objectives of financial statements. Two distinct approaches are still apparent:

• financial statements where the emphasis is on reporting the stewardship of the directors. Such statements place an emphasis on the need to present a true and fair view of the results and financial position. Such financial statements tend to attach more importance to the profit and loss account and earnings per share;

• financial statements where the emphasis is on compliance with regulation and prudence. Such financial statements are drawn up on a more conservative basis with a tendency to understate profits and asset values.

A country which places considerable emphasis on the stewardship concept of financial statements is the United Kingdom where, historically a significant amount of capital for businesses has been provided through the mechanism of the Stock Exchange and venture capitalists. By contrast, in many other European countries the trend has been for institutions, typically the large commercial banks, to provide a considerably higher proportion of capital for businesses than in the United Kingdom. One consequence of these different means of financing businesses has been that financial reporting in the United Kingdom has had a greater regard for the true and fair measurement of a business's performance since for the providers of capital and for the operation of the capital markets, key factors are dividends and earnings per share. Investors will make decisions and switch between investments based on the quality of earnings, historically and prospectively. This tends to put the reporting of profit, including the correct identification of extraordinary items, as a priority before such matters as, say, minimising taxation liabilities through over-prudent accounting. In countries where capital has been raised from banks, there is less emphasis on the reporting of profit. This produces a tendency to report results on a conservative basis, particularly if the financial statements are also used as the basis for calculating taxation liabilities. This leads to conservatively presented balance sheets. The two concepts of reporting to different types of shareholders, are not in themselves mutually exclusive but, in general terms, they will tend to exert opposite pressures on financial reporting.

The term 'generally accepted accounting principles' or GAAP is a well known and frequently used expression in the context of financial reporting. The extent to which GAAP is written down or codified differs significantly from country to country. Certain countries have incorporated GAAP almost entirely in the law of the country while in other countries the law restricts itself to a statement of basic principles. These countries leave the development of GAAP to documents issued by other bodies, usually accountants, in the form of accounting standards.

It is against this diverse background that the most appropriate accounting treatment for any financial instrument and the extent of disclosure required must be determined. At first sight, many financial instruments appear to be highly complex and accounting for them seems difficult. Experience has shown that an understanding of the true economics of a financial instrument, in particular the taxation treatment, together with an understanding of the risks and rewards inherent in the instrument, will usually help determine the appropriate accounting treatment.

Many of the financial instruments in this book were not contemplated when company accounting legislation and standards were developed. Consequently, the appropriate accounting treatment may often need to be determined on an ad hoc basis. The recently published exposure draft from the International Accounting Standards Committee – 'Financial Instruments' will help this process. The exposure draft does not prescribe accounting treatments for particular instruments but provides a framework within which the appropriate accounting treatment can be determined. This framework should aid consistency between countries and types of instrument. It also has the advantage that by not being prescriptive it will be more difficult to design instruments to get round the rules.

Taxation

As with accounting, a distinction can be made between those countries where tax concepts are contained in a codified system of law and those countries where, although there are tax laws, heavy reliance is placed on case law and legal precedence. However, in most European countries the taxation position of financial instruments is not covered by legislation or case law. A key issue in determining the taxation of financial instruments and one which applies to many countries is whether the particular instrument is a trading or investment (capital) transaction.

In the United Kingdom, the Inland Revenue have published two consultative documents in 1991 which are relevant to financial instruments. In March 1991 'Foreign Exchange Gains and Losses' dealt with proposals for the taxation of foreign currency translation, and conversion profits and losses. More recently in August 1991 a consultative document was published which deals with the taxation treatment of financial instruments for managing interest rate risks. The main features of this document are:

● payments and receipts from such financial instruments should be taxed within an income regime. This should eliminate current anomalies when certain instruments are treated as capital (or 'nothings') while the underlying transaction is treated as revenue;

● the recognition of payments and receipts for tax purposes should follow commercial accounting principles;

● specific anti-avoidance provisions to cover matters such as payments to tax havens, and an arms-length test.

The proposals cover a wide range of instruments such as swaps (both interest rate and currency), caps, collars, floors, futures and forward rate agreements.

The future

It is likely that the development of financial instruments will continue. It also seems probable that, as investors and issuers become more sophisticated, the instruments will become more complex. However, many of the instruments which are most successful are simple in concept when they are explained and understood. Perhaps, therefore, increasingly complex instruments will be replaced by the more basic simple instruments, for which the benefits and risks can be identified easily. It will be necessary for corporations to ensure that the implications of all the instruments used are fully understood. In addition, management systems which monitor and control risk will be required and tighter controls designed, implemented and monitored. Management's strategy and policy for the use of financial instruments as well as the limits on exposure (overall, by instrument, intra-day etc) must be formulated.

Accounting standards and taxation legislation appears to be developing in a way which should provide a framework within which the appropriate treatment can be determined. The effects of stock market crashes and the economic downturn have brought into clear focus the need to develop robust solutions to the accounting problems posed by new instruments. It is no longer sensible to hope that circumstances will be such that the expected (or hoped for) outcome will occur – there must be more certainty. One important effect of these events seems to be a more conservative and prescriptive approach by the regulators. For example, in the United Kingdom the recent proposals from the Accounting Standards Board will, if implemented, require most originators to retain securitised assets on their balance sheet, even if they are affectively insulated against risk. However, it will be important that the regulators, by being prescriptive, do not inhibit the development of instruments which have a sound economic purpose and which provide issues and investors with significant benefits.

Chapter 2

Debt instruments

Debt instruments

2.1 Overview

A debt security can be defined as an instrument which is issued, usually in the form of a certificate, to evidence the contractual obligation to make payments of interest (coupon) and to redeem a stated principal amount on a stated future date or dates (the maturity date).

This chapter is concerned with the basic categories of tradeable debt securities and a number of the variants which have been developed. One important category of debt security is excluded from this chapter, convertible bonds and bonds issued with equity warrants. These are dealt with in chapter 4 – Equity and Equity Linked Instruments, because economically they behave more like equity than debt (except where there is a significant fall in the value of the issuer's equity). Asset backed securities are also dealt with in a separate chapter.

This chapter is divided into three sections. The first section deals with the basic debt instruments. These are:

- Bonds:
  - fixed rate;
  - floating rate.
- Short term debt instruments:
  - commercial paper;
  - euronotes;
  - negotiable certificates of deposit.
- Medium term notes.

The specific instruments which are described in the other two sections of this chapter are all variants on the basic structures of debt instruments. These instruments either have their future cash flows linked to the performance of currencies, commodities or indices ('Currency Linked and Index Linked Issues'), or involve a restructuring of the cash flows of the debt instrument, varying the relationship between interest and principal, or make use of options ('Other Bond Issues').

2.2 Debt markets

A brief description of the most important debt markets in Europe is contained in the sections on 'Bonds' and 'Short term debt instruments'. Both the long and short term debt markets are analysed as follows:

• The International or Eurobond market. This market originally developed to issue long term debt instruments but the Eurocommercial Paper market has developed very rapidly in recent years. This is an international market place but historically the market has been based in Europe (principally London) and a high proportion of the issuers and the majority of investors have been based in Europe.

• European countries' domestic debt markets are dominated usually by the government debt markets, the mechanism by which individual governments will raise funds by issuing publicly tradeable debt. Apart from government bonds, there are active domestic bond markets in several European countries. Bonds are usually issued in these markets by local or municipal authorities, domestic corporations and also by overseas entities who wish to tap the market of a particular country. Recent problems in the Eurobond market, particularly the perceived lack of liquidity arising from the unregulated secondary market and the crisis in the FRN market, has led to an increase in activity in domestic markets.

A feature of the debt markets in the United States in recent years has been the explosive growth of the high yield or 'junk' bond markets (the high yield bond is one of the specific instruments described in more detail in this chapter). These bonds, which pay higher than average coupons, were used to finance the highly leveraged takeovers ('LBOs') of increasingly large corporations, including the $26 billion purchase of R J R Nabisco. The use of high yield bonds has had a disturbing effect on the established debt market because the large increase in gearing resulting from an LBO will usually cause a downgrading of the target company's credit rating, with adverse implications for the price of existing debt. The market has yet to understand fully the impact ('event risk') of the effect of a leveraged takeover or buyout on the price of debt issued by blue chip corporations which may be vulnerable to takeovers. However, the junk bond market's development has been severely curtailed following defaults in the United States market and rising interest rates which have made LBOs unattractive. Recent debt issues incorporate covenants designed to protect the holders from event risk. The covenants usually allow the investors to put (or resell) the debt back to the issuer at par (or greater) if the stipulated event occurs, a so-called poison put. One impact of event

14

risk has been the widening of the spread between corporate and government bond yields.

2.3 Bonds

Bonds are long term debt instruments. Typically bonds have maturities of from five years up to thirty years, although there is no exact definition, and there have been bonds issued with maturities of less than five years and (very rarely) with maturities greater than thirty years.

When bonds are issued to the public, a bond indenture will be established which will specify the principal characteristics of the bond. The most important of these will be:

● the coupon, maturity and any call or sinking fund provisions;

● any protective covenants undertaken by the issuer. These could include limitations on the diversion of resources from payment of obligations arising from the bond, such as dividend payments to shareholders or excessive compensation to management, and limitations to prevent the issuer taking on additional obligations, such as setting limits on the issue of additional debt or a requirement to maintain agreed working capital ratios.

The issuer will be in default if he fails to meet interest or principal payments, or any indenture provision. When default occurs, the whole of the principal and arrears of interest will usually become payable immediately.

Bonds may be issued where the investors are given different degrees of security in the event of default:

● secured bonds – the bonds are backed by the specific pledge of certain assets as collateral. In case of default or bankruptcy of the issuer, the bondholder has first claim on the collateral usually exercised by trustees acting for the bondholders;

● negative pledge – no new debt can be issued which takes priority over the claim of the existing bondholders;

● unsecured bonds – issued against the general credit of the issuer. Effectively, the investor's security is all the assets of the issuer which have not been pledged as collateral for secured debt;

● subordinated bonds – bonds where the claims of the bondholders on the assets of the issuer are subordinated to the claims of holders of other debt securities;

● cross default – a covenant by an issuer in respect of itself its subsidiaries and guarantor (if any) under which each party will be in default in respect of the bond issue should the issuer, its subsidiaries and guarantor default on any payment under its other borrowings.

Often the whole of the par value of a bond is redeemed by the issuer on the maturity date of the bond. A debt security which is redeemed in this way is known as a 'bullet'.

Bond issues can pay either fixed or floating rates of interest. Fixed rate and floating rate bonds are described separately in the following sections.

Features and variations

● Bonds are often issued with options for the issuer to 'call' (ie redeem) the bond prior to its stated maturity. Such calls will usually be at a premium to the redemption price at maturity, and the size of the premium will decrease as the maturity date approaches. The call option can be attached to either fixed or floating rate bonds, but is particularly important with fixed rate issues to protect the issuer from paying in excess of market interest rates if they decrease after the bond has been issued.

● Bonds can also be issued with an option for the investor to 'put' (ie require redemption) the bond before the stated maturity. These puts will usually be at a premium to nominal value to compensate investors for a reduced coupon and are combined with a conversion feature. Such convertible bonds are dealt with in the Equity and Equity Linked chapter.

● The bullet feature of bonds can lead to a significant strain on the issuer's cash flow, as the full amount of the loan is repaid at maturity. To mitigate this, the issuer can either roll over the debt by making a new issue, using the proceeds of the new issue to pay off the principal of the old issue, or make use of a sinking or purchase fund provision. Sinking or purchase funds provide for the amortisation of the issue over its life. The word 'fund' is a misnomer; the issuer does not fund the provision by setting aside specific cash or other assets, but applies money periodically to redeem the bonds prior to their stated maturity. With a sinking fund, depending on the terms of the issue, the issuer may retire the bonds either by calling them by lot for redemption or by purchasing bonds in the open market. With a purchase fund, the issuer may purchase bonds in the open market, but only if the bonds are trading at a discount to their par value.

2.4 Price quotations

Prices in most markets are quoted 'clean'; that is, a purchaser will pay a price for the bond which is quoted exclusive of any accrued interest. The purchaser will pay to the seller the clean price (expressed as a percentage of par) and any accrued interest. Interest will normally accrue from the date of the previous coupon to the value date. Depending on the market, this can be based on the number of days calculated on an inclusive or an exclusive basis. Value date is usually the same day as the settlement date, but this is not necessarily the case.

'Dirty' prices are where the price quoted to the seller include the accrued interest. This method of quotation is now rare, but operates in some markets and for some types of bonds.

A bond may be quoted 'cum-div' or 'ex-div'. This is a reference to the calculation of accrued interest. If a bond is traded cum-div the accrued interest is the interest which has accrued between the previous coupon date and the value date. If a bond is traded ex-div, there is a period prior to the dividend date when the bond is traded without any entitlement to that dividend or coupon. Bonds which can go 'ex-div' at a stipulated date before the next coupon is due are usually registered bonds, where it is necessary to identify the recipient. Bearer bonds, where payment of a coupon is made following the presentation of a coupon, are always traded cum-div.

2.5 Calculation of accrued interest

The method for calculating accrued interest on any day between two coupon dates will differ depending on the basis used to calculate the number of days between the dates. Although the effect of these different bases is small in absolute terms, they can have a significant impact on the profitability of a transaction, particularly for dealers trading large amounts for small margins. This is particularly important in the swap market (swaps are described in chapter 5 – Hedging Instruments).

The variety of methods of calculation arise from the use of different conventions to determine both the number of days between the last coupon date and the value date, and the number of days which are assumed to be in one year.

The number of days between the last coupon date and the value date is calculated usually on one of the following bases:

● the 'actual' basis, which involves calculating the actual number of days between the two dates;

● the '30 days basis', which involves calculating the number of days assuming 30 day months. The method of calculating the number of days between two dates when 30 day months are used and there are 31 days in the month varies from market to market.

The number of days in a year are calculated according to one of the following bases:

● 365 day basis – actual number of days based on a 365 day year;

● 360 day basis – assumes a year of 360 days;

● actual basis – the number of days in the current coupon period multiplied by two. For a bond with a semi annual coupon, the year can range from 362 days to 368 days (as a coupon period can be from 181 to 184 days).

The Association of International Bond Dealers ('AIBD') method for quoting yields which is described in section 2.12 on fixed rate bonds is based on the accrual of interest on a 30/360 basis. The various combinations used in the European markets are set out in Table 2.1.

2.6 Bond markets

Bond markets in Europe can be analysed into the following categories:

● government bond markets;

● domestic bond markets;

● the international or Eurobond market.

Some of the key features of these markets across Europe are set out in Table 2.1.

2.7 Government bond markets

Governments use the bond markets as an alternative to raising funds through taxation or the sale of savings products directly to the public. The most important markets in Europe are described briefly below.

United Kingdom

The United Kingdom Government securities market is the oldest government bond market in the world. The structure of the market was substantially reorganised in 1987 as part of Big Bang and is now very similar to the United States Treasury bond market. Some of the more important characteristics of the United Kingdom government securities (or the gilt edged or 'gilts') market are as follows:

● gilts are issued through primary dealers, who have a direct dealing relationship with the Bank of England ('the Bank'). The Bank regulates the conduct of the primary dealers and monitors their compliance with net worth or capital adequacy requirements. There are currently 18 primary dealers;

● gilts are issued either through an offer for sale by tender, whereby dealers make bids for a new issue and bonds are allotted at the lowest price at which demand for the entire issue is met, or through a tap issue, where the Bank will gradually sell an issue on to the market. Following Big Bang, the Bank has experimented with auctions based on the system used in the United States Treasury market. In an auction, the issue is not underwritten by the primary dealers and investors can make direct bids without applying through a primary dealer. Investors can make either 'competitive' or 'non-competitive' bids. Competitive bids will only be successful if they are at or above the lowest accepted price. Non-competitive bids are allotted in full at a price based on an average of the successful competitive bids.

The following types of gilt-edged stock are available:

● conventional gilts – these are 'plain vanilla' fixed rate bonds and are by far the most common gilt-edged stock. They are analysed into 'shorts' (maturities up to five years), 'mediums' (five to 15 years), and 'longs' (maturities over 15 years).

● fixed coupon with variable redemption date – these bonds have a fixed maturity with an option to call at an earlier date;

● irredeemables – these bonds are in fact redeemable at par at the option of the Treasury but have no fixed maturity date. There have been no issues of irredeemables in recent years and the existing issues are low coupon bonds such as $3\frac{1}{2}\%$ War loan;

● convertibles – fixed coupon bonds which may be converted into

Table 2.1: **Characteristics of Debt Markets in Europe**

	Euro Market	United Kingdom	Ireland	France	Belgium	The Netherlands	Germany	Switzerland
Is government approval required for issue?	No	Notification only	Yes*	If over Ffr 500m notification to French Treasury	Yes	Notification only but prospectus approval needed	Yes (in future no)	Yes if in excess of SFr 10m
Is there a queuing system?	No	No	No	Yes	Yes (but informal)	No	Partly	No
Minimum maturity	None	5 years	Under 5 years	>7 years (currently under review)	Not specified - 5 years or more	None - usually 5 years	None	None
Coupon payments	Annual	Semi-annual	Semi-annual	Annual	Annual	Annual	Annual	Annual (Semi-annual if convertible)
Withholding tax on coupon payments	None	25%	None	None	25% pre 1 March 1990 10% post 1 March 1990	None	None except convertibles at 25%	Yes at 35% if Swiss domiciled issuer
Calculation of accrued interest	30/360	Actual/365	Actual/365	Actual/360	30/360	30/360	30/360	30/360
Standard settlement terms	7 days	1 day or Stock Exchange account period	Normally 1 day	1 day	2 days	7 days	2 days	3/7 days
Registered or bearer bonds?	Bearer	Registered	Registered	Registered with book entry transfer	Bearer	Bearer with book entry transfer	Bearer	Bearer

* All issues on primary market are through the government broker. All issues on the secondary market must be approved by the government broker.

This table is intended to show the characteristics of the majority of issues within a particular market. It is not intended to be definitive in all cases.

Table 2.1 (continued):   *Characteristics of Debt Markets in Europe*

	Austria	Sweden	Norway	Finland	Greece	Cyprus	Portugal	Spain
Is government approval required for issue?	Yes	Notification only	No	Yes	Yes	Yes	Yes if over Pte 494,912,000	If in local currency
Is there a queuing system?	No	No	No	No	No	No	Yes after approval	Yes
Minimum maturity	None	30 days	None	None	Over 1 year	None	Over 1 year	None
Coupon payments	Annual	Annual or quarterly	Annual or Semi-annual	Annual	Semi-annual or Annual	Semi-annual	Semi-annual	Quarterly or Semi-annual
Withholding tax on coupon payments	25%	None	None	None	None	None	20%	25%
Calculation of accrued interest	30/360	30/360	30/360	30/360	Actual/365	Actual/365	Actual/365	Actual/365
Standard settlement terms	2 days	5 days	3 days	5 days	Same day	Same day	2 days	7 days
Registered or bearer bonds?	Bearer	Registered	Registered	Registered	Bearer	Registered	Bearer	Bearer

This table is intended to show the characteristics of the majority of issues within a particular market. It is not intended to be definitive in all cases.

specified alternative gilt-edged stocks. They are usually short term gilts which are convertible into longer term issues;

● index linked gilts – bullet bonds whose coupon and redemption proceeds are linked to the Retail Price Index.

Gilts and the gilt market have the following features:

● gilts pay coupons semi-annually and interest is calculated on an actual/365 day basis. Interest is paid net of withholding tax except for holdings by non residents of certain 'A' or tax-free stocks;

● gilts become 'ex-dividend' (or ex-div) 37 days prior to interest payment. That is, the holder of the securities at the time the stock goes ex-div is entitled to receive the coupon net of the basic rate of income tax (currently 25%);

● primary dealers also act as market makers in the secondary market and are obliged to quote continuous two-way prices for agreed sizes of bargains. The primary dealers have access to the Inter Dealer Brokers ('IDBs') and may lend and borrow stock through approved Stock Exchange money brokers;

● IDBs enable the market makers to trade with each other whilst maintaining anonymity. IDBs can only deal with market makers;

● money brokers lend money and stock to primary dealers. This enables the primary dealers to fund their inventory and take short positions, which helps to maintain the liquidity of the market. To date, the Bank of England has not allowed the development of an active unregulated Repo market (which is the method used by primary dealers in the United States Treasury bond market to fund themselves. Repos are explained in chapter 5 – Hedging Instruments);

● settlement of transactions normally occurs on the business day after trade date, but same day or 'cash settlement' is possible in certain circumstances. Settlement of transactions between the major participants in the market is normally made through the Central Gilts Office which operates a computerised book entry system;

● gilts are usually registered securities, although a number of issues are in bearer form.

The Bank of England also issues Treasury Bills on behalf of the government which are short term instruments with a 91 day maturity. Treasury Bills are usually denominated in sterling but ECU issues have been made. Treasury Bills are issued at a discount and redeemed at par. The Treasury Bills are issued by a tender process and there is a very active secondary market. The bills are negotiable bearer documents.

France

The total outstandings in the French government bond market at the end of August 1989 was approximately FFr1,200 billion. The main types of bonds issued are as follows:

● Treasury bills	These have a maximum maturity of seven years. They pay a fixed rate of interest and cannot be issued at a discount or be redeemed earlier than the stated maturity date.
● *Obligations Renouvelables du Trésor* ('ORT')	Debt instruments on which interest is capitalised until either they are renewed (after three years) or repaid (six years).
● *Obligations Assimilables du Trésor* ('OAT')	New debt issues which are issued with characteristics (maturity, rate, etc) identical to existing issues (the only variable is the price). The new issue is then merged with the preceding issue.

Issuing procedures

Bonds are issued through an auction method which is modelled on the United States system (this is described in the section on the United Kingdom above). There are 15 *Spécialistes des Valeurs du Trésor* ('SVT') or primary dealers which are subsidiaries of large banks or other financial institutions. The primary dealers are allocated stock from certain issues on a non-competitive basis. They act as market makers in the issues but quote indicative rather than firm prices.

The Netherlands

The Dutch Government taps the guilder capital market by private placement and public bond issues, of which there are normally about 10 a year. Before 1986, in order to ensure an orderly market, the Government adopted a scheme of repayments over the life of the issue. As the size of the market increased this was no longer considered necessary and bullet repayment structures were adopted in 1986. In some instances the Government had the right to redeem the bonds prior to maturity and in the past some high coupon issues have been redeemed. Zero coupon bonds and medium term notes (maturity of two to five years) are also permitted.

Most bonds are issued in bearer form and have a maturity of five to eight years with an annual coupon. The conventional bullet structure and the strong Guilder have attracted foreign investors, but most bonds are still purchased by Dutch institutional investors such as pension funds and insurance companies.

Issuing procedures

Dutch Government bonds are issued by means of a tender. The agent of the Ministry of Finance will announce a new bond issue by means of prospectus and advertisements which state the maturity, the coupon and other conditions. The price or size of the issue is not publicised. In order to be flexible the Government has recently introduced an experimental issuing procedure which is a a combination of tender and auction.

Investors can subscribe to the issue either on a *'bestens'* (non-competitive) basis or by means of a competitive bid. The agent will then decide on the size and pricing based on the market conditions. The bestens bids and subsequent highest bids will be honoured up to the desired size of the issue. All investors will pay the same price and will be allotted bonds according to their bids. The domestic banks and security dealing firms are the principal distribution channels.

Secondary market

The secondary market is maintained by the major Dutch banks who act as market makers. The market makers are regulated by the Amsterdam Stock Exchange. Settlement is effected through a book entry system owned by a consortium of banks. Only the members of the clearing system can settle transactions in this way; third parties will settle their trades through the member banks. Membership is not restricted and foreign banks operating in the Dutch market have become members. The standard trading terms are for seven day settlement.

The Dutch Central Bank (*De Nederlandsche Bank*) has taken large positions in government bond issues for the purposes of intervention to help to maintain an orderly market. The market in recent issues is liquid because of the larger issue size (up to NGL 6 billion).

Germany

With the increase in public indebtedness that has taken place since the mid-seventies, the market for public debentures in Germany has expanded rapidly. Following the abolition of the *'Kuponsteuer'* (withholding tax on interest paid to foreigners) in 1984 there was an increase in the number of foreign investors. By the end of 1985 more than half of Federal bonds were in foreign portfolios.

The most important Federal fixed interest securities are described below:

● Government Bonds (*'Bundesanleihen'*). Fixed interest bearer government bonds normally with a ten year original maturity. At times of high demand twelve and fifteen year bonds have been issued. German 'Federal government bonds' have been issued as plain vanilla bullet fixed interest bonds and there have been no issues of variable interest and non-interest bearing bonds although this has been possible since 1985. The Federal Bond Consortium is responsible for the issue of the government bonds. All well-known German banks as well as many foreign banks are represented in the Federal Bond Consortium, which is regulated by the Deutsche Bundesbank;

• Public sector medium term notes ('*Kassenobligationen*') are bearer notes and have maturities in the two to six year range and are issued mainly by tender. The Bundesbank (which acts as the agent of the Ministry of Finance) permits only domestic banks to make bids. All trading is over the counter;

• Government Treasury Bonds ('*Bundesobligationen*') have been issued by the Federal government since 1979 with a fixed maturity of five years. The bonds can be issued only to private subscribers;

• Federal Savings Bonds ('*Bundesschatzbriefe*') are issued and can be subscribed for only by private investors. There are two types of federal savings bonds: Type A and Type B. Type A has a maximum duration of six years and pays interest every year, whereas type B has a maximum term of duration of seven years and accumulates interest until maturity. Both types offer a fixed rate of interest which increases each year and allows the investor to return the bond at the full value before maturity date. The investor's risk on *Bundesschatzbriefe* is very limited but the yield is relatively modest. The Federal government is subject to the risk that when interest rates are increasing rapidly the investors may redeem the federal savings bonds to finance the purchase of other securities;

• Treasury Notes ('*Finanzierungsschaetze*') are issued with a maturity of one or two years and can be subscribed for by private investors.

Switzerland

The Swiss government is the second largest issuer in the domestic bond market (after the domestic banks). Since 1980, federal bonds and some cantonal issues have been launched through procedures akin to the 'Dutch auction'. The borrower publishes in advance the total amount, interest rate and maturity of the issue, whereupon the subscribers submit bids specifying the amount they are prepared to buy and at what price. The issue is allocated to the highest bidders in descending order until the whole issue is covered; the price for the whole issue is that of the last number to receive an allocation.

In other respects the Swiss government market is similar to the domestic corporate market which is described below.

2.8 Domestic bond markets

The principal domestic bond markets in Europe are described below.

United Kingdom

A large number of non-gilt debt securities are listed on the International Stock Exchange of Great Britain and the Republic of Ireland ('The Stock Exchange') in London (in total comprising some 60% by number of all securities listed on the Exchange). However they account for only a small proportion of the total capitalisation of The Stock Exchange (approximately 10%) and an even smaller proportion of its daily turnover (2%). This is largely because the majority of debt securities listed in London (as of September 1990, £125 billion out of a total of £146 billion) are Eurobonds which are issued and traded on the international bond market.

Bonds issued in the domestic market are usually registered and pay semi-annual coupons net of the basic rate of income tax (currently 25%). In addition, they are often secured against the assets of the issuer. A sterling denominated bond issued by a foreign borrower in the United Kingdom domestic market is called a bulldog. Eurosterling bonds are usually unsecured and pay coupons gross on an annual basis. Eurosterling bonds have also been attractive to issuers because their yields tend to be lower than bulldogs. However, because Eurosterling bonds pay coupons gross rather than net of tax they are also attractive to investors. When sterling is strong overseas investors tend to invest in the Eurosterling market and yields can fall below the gilt yield.

The Bank of England has published guidelines for capital market issues in sterling. No timing consent for issues has been required since March 1989 but the Bank of England, on behalf of The Stock Exchange and the British Merchant Banking and Securities Houses Association, has established procedures for an exchange of information on new issues over £20 million. These new issue calendar arrangements are designed to prevent a clash between competing issues. There are no specific restrictions on the issue of sterling bonds with a maturity of less than five years other than the requirements of the Companies Act, Financial Services Act and regulations made by the Bank of England. Since March 1989 there is no objection to foreign public sector bodies issuing deep discount and index linked sterling bonds. To promote an orderly market the Bank of

England requires all sterling issues to be managed in the United Kingdom by a firm which has satisfied its requirements to act as an issuing house. The Bank of England must be notified of the main details of any issue over £20 million at the time it is made.

United Kingdom corporations

During the 1970s the United Kingdom corporate bond market contracted due to the low profitability of United Kingdom companies and high inflation. With the improvement in the United Kingdom economy in the 1980s, the domestic bond market became more attractive to issuers. In addition, the reduction in public sector borrowing has resulted in demand for long term fixed interest securities (from institutions such as pension funds and insurance companies) which cannot be met by the gilt market. Issues have traditionally been fixed rate but the floating rate market is growing. Issues generally have short maturity dates (usually five to seven years) but long term borrowing can be arranged to tap institutional demand. Minimum maturity of five years applying to the issue of sterling bonds has recently been amended by the Bank of England to permit the issue of medium term notes by corporates without contravening the Banking Act 1987 (see medium term notes section 2.50).

Issuing procedures

Issues in the United Kingdom domestic bond market may be listed or unlisted. Listed issues are preferred because of the reporting requirements imposed by The Stock Exchange and restrictions preventing certain types of investors holding unlisted securities. Issues of both domestic and Eurosterling bonds are usually arranged through a placing, and the managers of an issue distribute the issue to institutional investors rather than the bonds being offered to the public in an underwritten sale. The institutions who are the largest investors in a domestic issue often act as sub-underwriters whereas Eurosterling issues are syndicated by managers and co-managers for sale on to retail investors. Only a small proportion of bonds is offered to the public.

Secondary market

Approximately 10% of the debt securities listed on The Stock Exchange are quoted on the Stock Exchange Automated Quotation system ('SEAQ'). There are currently 10 registered market makers in these securities but they are not required to quote firm prices. The turnover is limited—the daily average in the period January to September 1990 was £106 million compared to £2 billion for gilts. In addition, domestic and Eurosterling issues are traded on the over the counter ('OTC') market.

France

At 31 December 1989 the total outstandings in the French domestic bond market (excluding government bonds) was FFr1,500 billion. Both fixed and floating rates issues are made with maturities generally over seven years. Bonds can be issued on the market by any type of company, whether they are listed or unlisted, state owned or private or banks or commercial operations.

The total outstandings analysed by issuer are as follows:

State owned companies and local authorities	50%
Industrial and commercial companies	13%
Financial institutions	36%
Other	1%
	100%

All the public issues must have a prospectus approved by the *Commission des Operations de Bourse* ('COB'), and follow a time schedule prepared by a committee representing the French Treasury, large banks and state owned financial institutions. Bonds are issued through an offer for sale by tender, or more recently, through auction procedures. Treasury consent is not required for issues of less than FFr1 billion.

The Netherlands

The principal issuers in the Dutch domestic bond market are major Dutch corporations, quasi-governmental bodies (*Nederlandse Waterschapsbank, Bank Voor Nederlandsche Gemeenten*) and banks and financial institutions. The issues have maturities ranging from five up to 25 years. The spreads over the Government bonds are relatively small for good quality credits. Most issues are amortised over the last part of the life of the security by the use of sinking funds.

Most issues are listed on the Amsterdam Stock Exchange. Managing and underwriting banks have to be registered with the Central Bank. The secondary market is sometimes illiquid due to the small issue sizes but the sponsoring bank for the issue will often try to maintain a market.

Germany

On 1 May 1985 within a framework for the liberalisation of the fixed interest securities market, the *Deutsche Bundesbank* granted approval to the issue of new financial instruments. As a result of this German issuers can offer FRNs, issues combined with swaps, bull and bear bonds and zero coupon bonds. The reaction to the liberalisation was on the whole favourable and a number of FRNs and zero coupon bonds have been issued. The most common types of securities issued in Germany are described below:

• Mortgage Bonds and Municipal Bonds (*'Pfandbriefe'*, *'Kommunalobligationen'*) are issued by public and private mortgage banks. The use of proceeds of these bonds is subject to legal regulation and the bonds are secured by mortgages. The maturity is on average between five and 10 years. *Kommunalobligationen* differ from *Pfandbriefe* as they are secured by claims against the local authorities (or government) to whom the mortgage has been granted;

• Bank Bonds (*'Bankschuldverschreibungen'*) are issued as bearer bonds and deposit certificates by banks and credit institutions. In contrast to mortgage bonds and municipal bonds the proceeds are not subject to legal regulations as with mortgage bonds and municipal bonds. Their yield and maturity correspond roughly to that of mortgage bonds and municipal bonds. Bank debentures can also be issued as FRNs and zero coupon bonds;

• Corporate Bonds (*'Industrieanleihen'*) are often secured by mortgages on the assets of the issuer or by negative pledge clauses. The issue of these securities requires government approval. To avoid the need for government approval and to minimise tax disadvantages, most recent issues of corporate bonds are offered for sale on the Euromarket by subsidiary companies. For these reasons corporate bond issues are relatively insignificant to the domestic fixed interest securities market;

• Deutschmark Bonds issued by foreign issuers are mainly offered as medium and long term domestic fixed interest securities. Among the issuers are national governments, supranational institutions, provincial and municipal councils, credit banks, mortgage banks and industrial companies. For a publicly offered bond there is a minimum maturity of five years and for a private placement three years;

• There are also certificates of indebtedness or promissory notes called *Schuldscheine* which are not securities in a strict legal sense. These are issued by the government, local authorities and some companies in the German domestic market and are widely available.

Secondary market

The fixed interest securities of the Federal government and of private issuers are traded in an identical manner on all eight German stock exchanges, of which Frankfurt is the most important in terms of trading volume. Trading on stock exchanges is not mandatory and over the counter market trading is more active. Net prices are quoted on the over the counter market so commissions are included in the price. The stock exchanges quote gross prices. The bonds are cleared by the banks' own system which is linked to Euroclear and Cedel. Settlement takes place two days after trade date.

Switzerland

The Swiss bond market has a long-standing history. As early as 1900 there were 93 domestic issues and 24 foreign bonds listed on the largest Swiss exchange. The Swiss franc is one of the major currencies used to issue bonds. As a truly international finance centre, Switzerland has few restrictions on capital transactions. Bonds issued in Switzerland are classified as foreign or domestic (the former being more significant in size) and public or private. Historically Swiss franc yields have been usually lower than yields in other currencies. However, this is no longer the case.

Interest is calculated on the 30/360 day method. In general terms, interest on domestic bonds is subject to a withholding tax of 35% whereas foreign bond interest is exempt from this tax. The effects of the 35% withholding tax may be reduced for foreign investors through tax treaty relief.

Domestic bonds

Most domestic bonds are fixed rate issues, but the number of equity linked bonds is increasing. The major issuers of bonds are the banks followed by the public sector. Issue size is generally between Sfr10 million and Sfr150 million although government issues can be as large as Sfr300 million. The securities are issued in denominations of Sfr1,000, Sfr5,000 or Sfr100,000. The issues generally have maturities of eight to 15 years.

Foreign bonds

The most popular types of foreign bond are bonds with warrants and straight bonds although there are some perpetuals, floating rate bonds and convertible bonds. The major issuing nation is Japan with many corporations wishing to issue equity linked bonds. In Switzerland the interest rate is generally linked to domestic capital market interest rates, unlike the Eurodollar market where it is linked to money market rates.

Issues are generally between Sfr50 million and Sfr200 million denominated in Sfr5,000 or Sfr100,000. Although there are no restrictions, maturity is typically eight to 15 years (until May 1986, the Swiss National Bank stipulated a minimum maturity of eight years). Permission is required from the Swiss National Bank for foreign issues exceeding Sfr10 million with maturities of a year or more.

Issuing procedures

Swiss Franc bond issues are offered for sale to the public by an ad hoc syndicate of banks or finance companies which have to be domiciled in Switzerland. The issue is conducted by a lead manager who concludes an underwriting agreement with the borrower and forms a syndicate by inviting other financial institutions to participate. The prospectus (which is available at the syndicate members), an extract of which is published in the leading daily papers, contains detailed information on the issuer, the terms of the bond and subscription period and payment deadline. By law, the issuers are liable for the correctness and completeness of the financial position as presented in the prospectus. By subscribing, the investor undertakes to purchase the number of bonds subscribed. If the issue is oversubscribed a reduced allocation will be made. There is also a 'grey market' and a 'premarket' as noted below.

Secondary market

In contrast to many other countries, Switzerland does not have any supervisory body with primary regulatory authority over the securities industry. The Swiss National Bank plays an important role complemented in specific areas by institutions and associations. Switzerland has also no rating agency for assessing the quality of bond issues.

The secondary market for publicly subscribed bonds is conducted on the Swiss securities exchanges. The major Swiss securities exchanges are located in Zurich, Geneva and Basel. Trading takes place on trading rings by open outcry. The floor traders consist exclusively of representatives of the banks (banks also act as brokers in Switzerland). A security may be traded officially only if it is admitted to the exchange. An electronic dealing system is expected to operate from the summer of 1991.

Switzerland also has a 'premarket' and over the counter trading. Premarket trading are transactions conducted before the official session opens. Newly issued securities may be traded for a few months on the premarket before printing and delivery of the certificates, which are required for a listing.

There is also a so-called 'grey market' in which a number of banks participate. This market is centred in Geneva and Zug and deals with the issues prior to the premarket trading which starts two days after the end of the subscription period. Grey market trading is not permitted in certain cantons such as Zurich.

Prices are quoted exclusive of accrued interest (clean prices) except for dual currency and zero coupon bonds.

Private Placements (PP)

These account for a significant proportion of bonds issued in Switzerland. The main participants are foreign borrowers. The instruments issued can take any form such as straight, convertible, warrant, floating rate, dual currency and zero coupon. The issue period is usually four to eight years and they are denominated in amounts of Sfr50,000. The sizes of the issues can vary substantially but are normally between Sfr50 million and Sfr200 million for foreign borrowers and Sfr20 million and Sfr50 million for Swiss borrowers. There is a 35% withholding tax deduction on interest on PPs of domestic borrowers.

Issues are usually underwritten by a single institution which offers the bonds to its private and institutional customers. There is a liquid secondary market with many market makers quoting prices for nominal amounts between Sfr250,000 and Sfr500,000. The PPs are very similar to public issues but there is no stock exchange listing. There is no restriction on placing eg only to professional investors.

2.9 The Euromarket

The Euromarket is an international capital market which, until recently, was concerned mainly with raising debt rather than equity capital. The term 'Euro' is an historical one deriving from the Eurodollar market; Eurodollars being US dollars held outside the United States. It is now more generally used to denote the issue of a security in a currency other than that of the country of residence of the issuer. The market's most important characteristic is that securities are sold internationally rather than within the confines of one particular country. The securities are also sold largely outside the country of residence of the borrower. The factors which account for the size and spectacular growth of this market are as follows:

• the market is international rather than being confined to a particular country and new security issues can avoid a great deal of national regulation which may involve onerous registration requirements. This can lead to a significant reduction in the cost of the issue. While prospectus requirements in the countries where the securities are promoted will normally have to be complied with, short form circulars or abridged particulars of the issue terms may be all that is required for certain categories of issuers or investors;

• the Euromarket has evolved an efficient and flexible distribution network which can sell or 'place' securities in large volumes and, for the most part, can ensure that the issue will be launched successfully and in an orderly fashion. This is because new issues are managed, underwritten, and sold by syndicates. These syndicates are dominated by the London-based Swiss, American and Japanese banks which have strong distribution networks;

● once securities have been issued through the syndicate ('the primary market'), they are traded on the secondary market. Securities are traded on an over the counter market by dealers over the telephone rather than on an exchange floor. This market is dominated by large firms of professional dealers who can act both as market makers and brokers on behalf of retail and institutional investors;

● the international marketplace gives borrowers access to a greater number and diversity of investors than would be possible within their own marketplace. This ability to tap different sources of finance can reduce overall interest costs.

2.10 Eurobonds

'Eurobond' is a general term for any long-dated debt security issued through the Euromarkets. The general characteristics shared by most Eurobond issues are as follows:

● Eurobonds are issued in bearer form – that is, investors do not have to be registered (as in the domestic United States bond market) and ownership is evidenced by physical possession. Interest is payable to the holder presenting the coupon to the paying agent for that particular issue. The coupon is detachable from the bearer bond. This can be an advantage to investors who wish to retain anonymity;

● interest is quoted on the AIBD (30/360) basis;

● Eurobond issues pay interest gross and the effect of any withholding taxes would be borne by the issuer;

● Eurobonds are long-term instruments with maturities in excess of five and up to 30 years;

● Eurobonds are usually issued in small denominations (often $1,000);

● borrowers are typically sovereign states, government-based institutions, supranational entities (such as the World Bank) and the larger multinational corporations – that is, issuers tend to be household names with high credit ratings;

● the issues are usually unsecured, reflecting the quality of the borrowers;

● Eurobonds will normally be listed on a stock exchange, although this is not a requirement. The listing will usually be on either the Luxembourg Stock Exchange or The Stock Exchange. Listings are undertaken to make issues more popular with investors, both because of the disclosure and reporting requirements of the stock exchanges and because some countries do not allow their residents to purchase unlisted foreign securities. Only a very small percentage of the trading in listed Eurobonds takes place on these exchanges;

● the standard terms of trade are for seven day settlement, and the majority of transactions are settled through two clearing houses, Euroclear and Cedel.

2.11 Fixed rate bonds

Fixed rate bonds are debt securities on which the coupon payments are fixed at the date of issue as a specified percentage of par value. These bonds will usually be issued and redeemed at par, although both premiums and discounts are possible. Traditionally, most long term public debt issues have been of this type. However, the volatility of interest rates in the early 1980s led to an increasing number of floating rate notes (section 2.19) being issued.

The cash flows arising on a plain vanilla fixed rate bond issued and redeemed at par can be shown diagrammatically as follows:

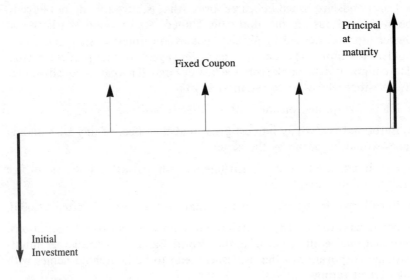

Diagram 2.1: Fixed rate bond

As the coupon is fixed, all the interest cash flows are for the same amount. The redemption of the principal at maturity will usually occur at the same time as the final coupon payment, but the space shown between the arrows in the diagram is for clarity.

The cash flows on a callable fixed rate bond can be shown as follows:

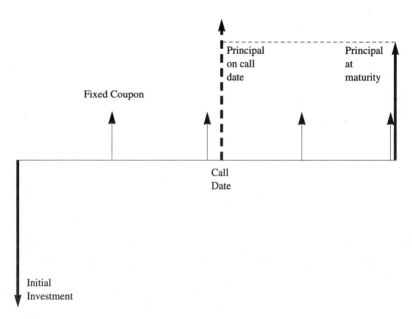

Diagram 2.2: Callable fixed rate bond

If the call option is exercised, the principal will be redeemed and there will be no further cash flows from the call date. The amount of the principal redeemed early is higher than at maturity to reflect the usual premium for early redemption.

2.12 Pricing of fixed rate bonds

The plain vanilla fixed rate bond pays a predetermined rate of interest at specified periods and has a defined maturity date. Therefore, all of the cash flows arising from the bond are known in advance, which makes the valuation of these securities simple – the fair value of the bond is the present value of all the principal and interest cash flows, which can be expressed as follows:

$$P = \sum_{t=1}^{t=n} \frac{C_t}{(1+r)^t} + \frac{R}{(1+r)^n}$$

Where:

P = price
R = principal amount at maturity
C_t = coupon payment at time t
r = required rate of return
n = number of periods to maturity

The most important assumption is the required or risk adjusted rate of return. This has two components:

• the risk free rate of return;

• the premium required over the risk free rate.

The risk free rate is usually taken to be the interest rate on the most actively traded government bond issue with a similar coupon and maturity date.

The premium required over the risk free rate is the amount required by investors to compensate for the perceived risk of the default of a particular issuer (the credit risk). The more creditworthy the borrower, the lower the required premium (or 'spread') over government bonds. In practice, spreads are determined in different ways in the various markets due to the differing perceptions of the investors – for example, the Eurobond market is very name conscious and there is high demand for bonds issued by corporations with 'household' names. Therefore, a well known company may be able to achieve finer terms on Eurobond issues than less well known corporations who may in fact be of greater credit quality.

The importance of these different perceptions has diminished in recent years due both to the development of the swap market (which has reduced anomalies between markets by arbitrage) and because of the increasing use in international capital markets of credit rating agencies, which originated in the United States domestic market. The most widely used agencies are Standard and Poors ('S&P') and Moody's. Credit ratings provide an independent benchmark for comparing the risk adjusted yields on debt instruments. The credit ratings which are assigned to borrowers range from AAA (S&P) or Aaa (Moody's) for the finest quality credits to C for the poorest quality. Generally, any issues rated below BBB (S&P) or Baa (Moody's) are not considered to be of 'investment grade'.

Current yield

As the cash flows arising on the bond are certain, changes in the price of the bond result from changes in the discount rate applied to the cash flows. This can be due to changes in how the borrower's credit status is perceived by the market (either favourable or unfavourable) or changes in prevailing market interest rates. The effect of changes in interest rates on the price of a bond can be seen by the effect on the current yield. The current yield is a simple way of estimating the return on a bond and is calculated by dividing the annual coupon by the purchase price. For example, if £100 nominal of bond is priced at £90 and pays an annual coupon of £9, the current yield is 10% (9/90).

If prevailing interest rates change, the price of a bond will change to yield the current market rate. If in the above example, interest rates rise to 15% the price of the bond will fall to £60 (a yield of 9/60 = 15%). Similarly, if interest rates fall to 6%, the price of the bond would rise to £150 (9/150 = 6%).

Yield to maturity

The current yield is used only as an approximation in calculating the return on a bond, as it does not take account of any capital appreciation or depreciation which may arise at maturity if the bond is priced above or below par, or the interest earned on the reinvestment of coupons received during the life of the security. Yield to maturity is the most widely used formula and involves equating the current market price to the discounted value of future coupon payments and the redemption value. The yield to maturity is the percentage which discounts all future payments of coupons and principal back to the current market price of the bond—effectively the internal rate of return. It is calculated from the following formula:

$$P = \frac{1}{(1+y)^f}\left[\sum_{i=1}^{n}\frac{gi}{(1+y)^i} + \frac{R}{(1+y)^n}\right]$$

Where:

y = yield to maturity as a percentage
P = current market price
R = redemption value
gi = coupon at time i
n = number of interest periods from next coupon date to maturity
f = fractional period to next coupon date

In order to calculate the yield to maturity a process of iteration (trial and error) must be used to find the value of y which solves the equation. In practice bond tables or bond calculators are used.

The formula will require modification for bonds which pay interest other than annually and where there are unequal coupon periods (eg leap years or if payment days fall on non-business days).

There is also simple yield to maturity which does not take account of the reinvestment of coupons received. The most important assumption made in the yield to maturity calculation is that coupons received can be reinvested at the yield to maturity. This assumption is important because reinvestment income can be a significant proportion of the total return on a bond over the course of its life, particularly in the case of high coupon bonds and bonds of longer maturities. This limitation was exploited by the large number of stripped Treasury bonds issues in the 1980s (see section 2.130).

2.13 Benefits – issuer

● With a fixed rate bond, an issuer knows the interest cost over the life of the security. This certainty will assist in planning and budgeting projects.

2.14 Benefits – investor

● The price of a fixed rate bond moves in an inverse relationship to a movement in interest rates, which gives the investor a greater opportunity for capital gain than with floating rate securities if market interest rates fall.

2.15 Risks and disadvantages – issuer

● If market interest rates fall after the bonds have been issued, the issuer can be locked into paying interest at above market rates. This risk can be mitigated by building call features into the bonds but, in return for the risk that the bond will be called, the investor will require a higher coupon.

2.16 Risks and disadvantages – investor

• Although there are greater opportunities for capital gains with fixed rate bonds, the investor can incur significant capital losses if interest rates rise.

• If the bond has a call option attached and the issuer exercises the call, the investor will have to reinvest the proceeds elsewhere. This can be unattractive to long-term investors such as pension funds as the call will be exercised usually when prevailing interest rates have fallen.

2.17 Accounting questions

• The accounting treatment of bonds for most countries is well established and is set out in sections 2.209 to 2.244 on accounting and taxation in various countries in Europe at the end of this chapter.

2.18 Taxation questions

The country sections (2.209 to 2.244) at the end of this chapter set out the basic tax considerations for various countries in Europe. However, in general the taxation treatment of fixed rate debt instruments will depend on the answers to the following questions:

On issue

• Is any premium tax free to the issuer?

• Can the issuer obtain tax relief on any discount?

• Is tax relief available on all issue costs?

• What are the VAT consequences (if any) of the issue?

• Are any other duties payable on issue?

On interest payments

• Is there withholding tax on interest and do different rules apply to interest paid to residents and non-residents?

● Is it possible to avoid withholding taxes, e.g. by arranging payment through a foreign agent?

● Is interest received by a foreign investor exempt under a double tax treaty or under specific statutory provisions or concessions in the country of issue?

● Will interest be taxed on an accruals or a received basis?

● How is any discount allowed or taxed?

● Is any premium on redemption taxable or tax deductible?

● Is interest payable an allowable tax deduction to the issuer on an accruals or a paid basis?

● What returns, if any, of interest paid must be made by the issuer or paying agent?

● Is an interest receipt a VAT exempt supply (to an EEC issuer) or zero-rated?

On sale/redemption

● Is any profit or loss made by the issuer on early redemption exempt from tax?

● Is any part of the sale proceeds taxable as income of the investor and if so how is this amount calculated?

● Is any profit or loss not taxed as income of the investor subject to other taxes?

● Are any capital or stamp duties payable on transfer?

● What, if any, are the VAT consequences of redemption at a premium ?

Other matters

● Are exchange gains/losses taxable/tax deductible for the issuer and if so on a realisation or translation basis?

For the investor

● Can a deduction be obtained for a write down if the market value of the bond, debenture etc has fallen below the investor's acquisition price?

● Are exchange gains/losses taxable/tax deductible for the investor?

2.19 Floating rate bonds

Floating rate bonds, commonly referred to as floating rate notes or FRNs, are debt securities whose coupon is refixed periodically on the 'refix date' by reference to some independent interest rate index. In the Euromarkets this is usually some fixed margin over London Interbank Offered Rate ('LIBOR') (usually six month LIBOR). FRNs traded in the Euromarkets offer the following features:

• they are long dated bonds with interest rates linked to short term money market indices;

• coupons are refixed, and coupon payments made, usually every six months, whereas fixed rate bonds will more commonly pay interest annually.

The cash flows arising on a plain vanilla FRN can be shown as follows:

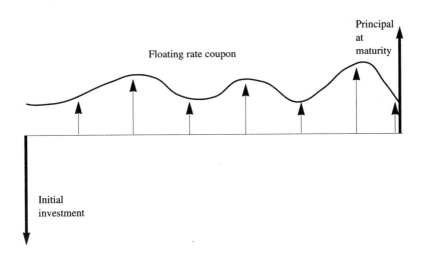

Diagram 2.3: Floating rate note (FRN)

This diagram is the same as for a fixed rate bond except that the coupons are represented by arrows of a different height over time indicating varying interest rates.

2.20 FRN market characteristics

Longer term FRN issues tend to be illiquid, and therefore more volatile, because banks (who are large investors in FRNs) prefer instruments with shorter maturities. The other principal determinant of relative price volatility is the frequency with which the interest rate is refixed—the more frequent the refix date, the less volatile the FRN.

Variations

Capped FRNs

Stipulate a maximum ceiling on the interest rate payable. For example, an FRN could be issued with a coupon of $\frac{1}{2}$% over LIBOR but on the basis that a coupon of no more than 13% would be paid. Typically, the spread over LIBOR would be higher than on a plain vanilla FRN and therefore the investor enhances his current yield in exchange for accepting a longer term risk. The issuers of capped FRNs often sell the cap to a third party using the proceeds of sale to reduce the overall cost of the issue to below a comparable plain vanilla issue. The cash flows arising on a capped FRN can be shown as follows:

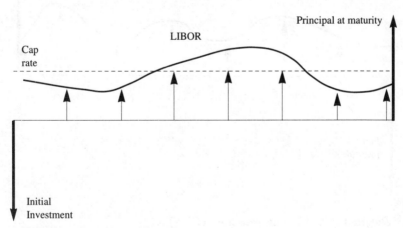

Diagram 2.4: Capped FRN

Convertible FRNs

Convertible at the investor's option into a fixed rate bond at any time during a stated period. The maturity of the long-term bond will be typically much longer than the original FRN.

Deferred Coupon FRN

FRN which pays no interest for a fixed period and then pays interest for its remaining life at a wide spread over the appropriate index. These issues have been popular with Japanese investors because the structure proved tax efficient.

Drop-lock FRNs

Automatically convert into fixed rate bonds when short term interest rates fall below a specified level (the 'trigger rate'). This can be shown as follows:

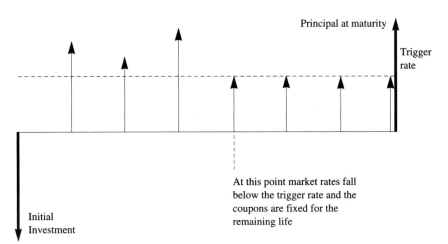

Diagram 2.5: Drop-lock FRN

Dutch Auction Notes

Issuers offer notes on which the coupon will be priced every 35 days at a 'Dutch Auction' (which means that investors bid for the notes so that they are sold at the lowest yield necessary to sell all of the notes). The auction process works by investors submitting bids for the notes every 35 days through brokers/dealers, who pass these bids on to the bank or trust company which acts as the auction agent. The agent calculates the new interest rate at the lowest yield necessary to sell all of the notes and, with the brokers/ dealers, arranges for the purchase and sale of the notes through the clearing system. Issuers hope to reduce long-term financing costs by paying short term rates. They provide longer-term money than commercial paper because the notes are repriced only every 35 days and not redeemed and resold as is the case with commercial paper. Investors in the United States market find these issues attractive because the market is liquid.

Dutch Auction Rate Transferable Notes	Variation of Dutch Auction Notes. Trade name of Salomon Brothers.
Extendible Notes	The interest rate is adjusted every two years to a rate linked to a two year market index. The investor can sell the bonds back to the issuer (a put option) at par every two years. The issuer can pay a rate above the index to encourage investors not to exercise their put options.
Fixed Interest Rate Short Tranche or Fixed Interest Rate Substitute Transaction (FIRST)	Two tranches of FRNs which result in the issuer paying a fixed rate of interest. The two tranches use different indices, the movement on which cancel to give a fixed rate. For example a floating rate tranche and an inverse floating rate tranche.
FRNs with issuer set rates	The borrower has the option to choose the index at each refix date from a number of alternatives. This allows the issuer to manage its liabilities but, because the issuer will opt for the index which minimises his funding costs, the investor will be exposed to a negative yield curve, which can make this instrument unattractive.
FRN with variable spread	The interest rate is determined by reference to the spread between two different indices. This structure has been used where the issuer wants to raise funds linked to a particular rate (eg the US Treasury bill rate) but wishes to link the price of the issue to LIBOR, which is more attractive to investors. Therefore the

interest rate would be determined by taking a percentage of the difference between LIBOR and the T-Bill rate.

Inverse FRNs

These pay interest in an inverse relationship to movements in the benchmark interest rate. For example, if LIBOR increases, the coupon on an inverse FRN will decrease, and vice versa. Usually the interest rate is computed by deducting LIBOR from a fixed rate. This can be shown as follows:

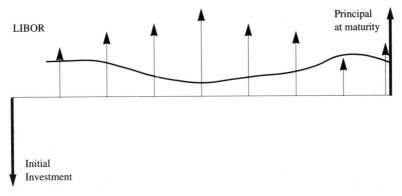

Diagram 2.6: Inverse FRN

Also called 'reverse' or 'bull' FRNs. This type of issue is attractive to investors who believe that interest rates will fall (but are potentially risky for issuers, if LIBOR falls), unlike conventional FRNs which are purchased by investors who believe that interest rates will rise and who wish to protect capital values.

Mini-Max FRNs

Have a lower limit of interest payable ('floor') as well as the cap described above. This type of issue affords both the investor and the issuer some protection against interest rate risk. As in the case of the Capped FRN described above, the issuers of mini-max FRNs will often sell the cap and the floor to third parties to reduce the cost of the issue. The cash flow arising on this type of issue can be shown as follows:

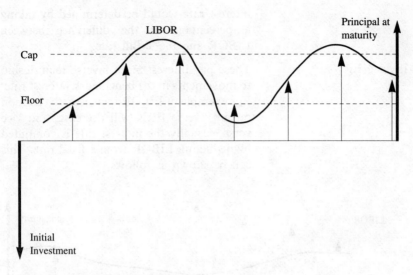

Diagram 2.7: Minimax FRN

	The coupons always remain within the upper and lower limits set by the cap and the floor.
Mismatch (or rolling rate) FRNs	Coupons are reset every month (usually based on three month LIBOR) but are only paid three or six monthly (as the average of the three or six settings). This results in the yields matching the short end of the yield curve and is beneficial to investors when short term interest rates are rising.
Money Market Notes	Variation of Dutch Auction Notes. Trade name of Lehman Brothers.
Serial FRNs	Have a mandatory amortisation. Unlike sinking fund securities which are redeemed by lot or purchased randomly, each individual note is amortised systematically with principal repayment coupons paid with interest coupons.
Step-up FRNs	FRN with interest paid at a spread over the relevant index which increases at a fixed date during the issue. This structure is used as a 'sweetener' in long term (eg 30 year) issues.
Step-down FRNs	FRN with interest paid at a declining spread over the index. After a period the note is callable at par.

Variable Coupon Renewable Note (VCR)	A form of frequently repriced debt instrument. After an initial period (typically one year) during which the coupon rate is reset based on an index rate, the issue is automatically renewed each quarter. If the investor chooses not to renew the notes the yield is lowered a predetermined amount and after three quarters at that yield the notes mature.
Variable Rate Note (VRN)	FRN where the spread over an index such as LIBOR will vary over the life of the issue, being fixed at the start of each coupon period by a remarketing process (eg Dutch auction). VRNs are usually issued with no maturity date or a five year maturity but longer fixed date issues have been made. A maximum coupon rate is also set if the remarketing should fail. On some issues the investors are given a put option to sell the VRNs back to the lead manager of the issuing syndicate at any interest payment date provided the interest margin has been agreed for the next period. The remarketing process is aimed at providing investors with a regular put option at par thus providing liquidity on what would otherwise be a perpetual issue (section 2.166) and unattractive to investors. A number of VRN issues have been made by banks as if they are undated and if correctly structured they qualify as regulatory capital.
Yield curve notes	See inverse FRNs.

2.21 Valuation of FRNs

The determination of the fair value of a floating rate note is more complex than for a fixed rate bonds because the cash flows arising on the note are not fixed in advance. Subject to any adjustment to investors' perception of the credit status of the issuer, the value at the beginning of the next refix date should be close to par because the coupon is adjusted to the market rate given by a particular index. The price at the refix date will be par if the final redemption is to be at par and the existing spread of the coupon over the interest rate index continues to compensate investors for their current perception of the risk of investing in the FRN. In this case, the price between refix dates will be such as to give a market return for the period to the next refix date based on the change in the capital value of the FRN (ie purchase price to par) and the coupon interest earned compared to the price and the accrued interest paid to the vendor on purchase. This can be expressed as follows:

$$\text{Return to refix date} = \frac{R + (C \times T/360) - (P + A)}{P + A} \times \frac{360}{t} \times 100$$

Where:

R = principal amount at maturity
C = current coupon rate
T = total number of days in current coupon period
P = flat purchase price
A = accrued interest on settlement date
t = time to refix in days

The value of FRNs may not, however, return to par at the refix date because the current credit risk assessment of the issuer demands a different margin over the index to that fixed at the issue date. Consequently in order to value the FRNs an estimate must be made of their price at that date. In the above formula this estimate is substituted for R.

The above calculation is useful when comparing an FRN with other money market instruments such as deposits or CDs (see section 2.45). However it is less useful when comparing FRNs as the time to the refix date will not be the same for different FRNs and the relevant return will vary depending on the current yield curve. FRNs may be compared using yields or margins. As for fixed rate bonds the current yield is a simple but very crude measure of return, because it ignores any capital return. FRNs whose coupons are based on the same index can be compared more satisfactorily by the 'Simple Margin', which adds the spread of the coupon over the interest rate index and the capital appreciation to redemption on an annual basis:

$$\text{Simple margin} = \frac{\dfrac{(R - P)}{T} + S}{P/100} \times 100$$

Where:

R = redemption price
P = current price
T = number of years to redemption
S = spread of coupon over the interest rate index

In practice it will also be necessary to allow for the carry on the FRN which is a one off effect arising in the current coupon period. The carry is the difference between coupon income and the cost of finance from settlement to refix date. The adjusted simple margin takes account of this carry.

2.22 Benefits – issuer

• Banks have been able to issue FRNs with a lower interest rate than they were receiving on their syndicated loan portfolios. FRNs pay interest in much the same way as syndicated credits and they enable banks to match interest income and expense.

• Non-bank borrowers who had previously raised finance through syndicated loans have found it cheaper to issue FRNs instead.

2.23 Benefits – investor

• The adjustment of coupons at regular intervals to reflect movement in market rates affords protection to the investor against significant capital losses in periods of interest rate uncertainty.

• The return on FRNs is linked to short term interest rates, which can be attractive when short term rates are at high levels.

2.24 Risks and disadvantages – issuer

• If interest rates rise after the FRN is issued, the issuer may incur greater costs than if a comparable fixed rate security had been issued.

• If the interest rate is set by an auction process (eg VRNs) the auction may fail. The rate will then be set at the margin specified in the issue documentation which may be very high and therefore unattractive.

2.25 Risks and disadvantages – investor

• There is far less opportunity for capital gain than with fixed rate instruments.

• The coupon is determined by reference to short term interest rates. This may not be the highest point on the yield curve, in which case investors will fail to maximise their return.

• If the bond has an action process designed to provide the investor with liquidity, and if the auction fails, the fall back margin may not compensate adequately for the lack of liquidity.

2.26 Accounting questions

• The accounting treatment of bonds for most countries is well established and is set out in sections 2.209 to 2.244 on accounting and taxation in various countries in Europe at the end of this chapter.

2.27 Taxation questions

• As for fixed rate bonds in section 2.18.

2.28 Short term debt instruments

The short term debt, or money market, enables both borrowers and investors to manage their working capital efficiently. Borrowers use this market to finance normal credit receivables and seasonal needs for funds – such as the stockpiling of production in advance of a peak selling period. The market is attractive to investors who wish to maximise their return from short term surpluses of funds.

Money market instruments are generally dealt in large amounts but can provide both borrowers and investors with an attractive alternative to bank finance:

● to the borrower, they will often be a cheaper source of finance than bank overdrafts;

● it is also useful for a borrower to have alternative sources of funds;

● investors can realise a higher yield than from depositing funds with a bank.

The borrower can obtain cheaper interest rates and the investor a higher yield on the instrument than on other similar forms of investment because the bank no longer acts as an intermediary. This is an example of securitisation or disintermediation. However, at times of financial pressure borrowers may find it more difficult to replace funding obtained through the money markets than with bank borrowings.

The principal money market instruments discussed below are as follows:

– commercial paper;

– Euronotes;

– negotiable certificates of deposit.

2.29 Commercial paper (CP)

Commercial paper issues are negotiable promissory notes with short term maturities. Their most important characteristics are:

● maturities are flexible and are fixed by the issuer at the time of issue and in most markets will range from a few days to a year;

● notes are issued usually in higher denominations than longer- dated securities – US dollar Eurocommercial paper issues, for example, are issued in $250,000 denominations compared with $1,000 for Eurobonds. This reflects the domination of markets by large and professional investors;

● the majority of commercial paper issues are unsecured. However, most commercial paper programmes are given ratings by the leading credit rating agencies in a similar way to bonds. Moody's ratings for commercial paper are from P1 to P3 and Standard and Poors range from A1 + to A3;

● commercial paper can be issued in interest bearing form, analogous to longer dated instruments (with a principal amount and bearing a stated interest rate). However, it is more usual for the paper to be issued at a discount to its face value. The yield on the instrument is reflected in the difference between the discounted price and the par value at which it will be redeemed;

● commercial paper is quoted in the secondary markets on a yield basis rather than at a price expressed as a percentage of par;

● commercial paper is issued in bearer form.

2.30 Commercial paper markets

The largest and most well established commercial paper market is the United States domestic market where, at the end of 1990, there was $564 billion of commercial paper outstanding. The principal markets in Europe are as follows:

● Eurocommercial Paper ('ECP');

● Sterling Commercial Paper ('SCP');

● French Commercial Paper;

● Dutch Commercial Paper;

● Switzerland;

● Other European markets.

There are also issues of commercial paper which are backed by a pool of assets owned by a special purpose company. These are dealt with in chapter 3 – Asset Backed Securities.

Eurocommercial Paper Market

The Eurocommercial Paper Market ('ECP') comprises US dollar denominated commercial paper issued outside the United States through the Euromarket distribution network. The profile of the dealers and the issuers is similar to that in the longer term Eurobond market. Investors are principally institutional investment managers, large corporations and banks. At the end of 1990 Euroclear reported that total outstandings of ECP amounted to some $70 billion. Some of the key features of ECP are:

● ECP market maturities can be from two to 365 days but are usually less than 180 days. Maturities are generally longer than in the much larger United States commercial paper market where maturities can be from one to 270 days, but are usually less than 90 days. In the United States a large amount of commercial paper is issued with a maturity of less than 30 days and often overnight. ECP rarely has an initial maturity of less than 30 days;

• interest on ECP is calculated on the AIBD basis (30/360) unlike the United States domestic commercial paper market which uses the actual/360 day basis;

• ECP is traded for spot (two day) settlement. Settlement is through Euroclear or Cedel two days after trade date;

• ECP issues are free of withholding taxes;

• ECP tends to be more actively traded than United States commercial paper where the paper is usually held to maturity (reflecting the shorter maturities).

Mechanics of issue

There are three methods under which ECP can be issued:

• through a tender panel;

• by dealership agreements;

• directly to investors.

Tender panel

Tender panels are used most commonly in connection with Euronote issues (see section 2.38). Under tender panels a group of agents is asked to make firm bids for the paper. These bids are satisfied in order of cost-effectiveness and no agent is assured of a winning bid in advance of the issue.

Dealership

Dealership agreements are now the most common arrangement for issuing ECP. Under this method an issuer will select either one dealer or a small group of dealers (usually investment banks) who will attempt, on a best efforts basis, to sell paper directly to investors in amounts and at a price which have been set by the issuer.

Direct issue

The issuer will undertake the dealership function himself and sell paper directly to investors. This approach is feasible only for the largest multinational corporations which have their own in-house finance and treasury functions.

Sterling Commercial Paper (SCP)

Prior to 1986 United Kingdom companies other than authorised banks were prohibited by the 1979 Banking Act (since repealed) from taking deposits in sterling. In April 1986 the regulations were amended to exempt issuers of sterling commercial paper from being classed as deposit takers. The requirements currently in force for SCP issues are set out in a Bank of England notice dated 11 January 1990. The methods of issue are the same as for ECP but issuers of SCP must satisfy the following conditions:

• minimum net assets of £25 million;

• the ordinary or preference shares of the issuer or its holding company or the company unconditionally guaranteeing the issue must be listed on The Stock Exchange or on the Unlisted Securities Market or another stock exchange included on the list of authorised exchanges published by The Stock Exchange;

• SCP must be issued and payable in the United Kingdom;

• banks and Building Societies authorised under the Banking Act 1987 are now permitted to issue SCP, providing that their SCP issues are not confused with their Certificates of Deposit issues. From 1 April 1990 certain local authorities were permitted to issue SCP;

• SCP must carry certain specified details and disclosures regarding compliance with listing regulations;

• SCP must be issued in amounts of at least £100,000 and with a maturity of at least eight days and not more than 365 days;

• SCP may carry put or call options at any time during its life;

• any repurchases of SCP by the issuer must be such as to ensure that a misleading or false market is not created.

The development of the SCP market has to date been restricted for two principal reasons:

• SCP falls within the prospectus requirements of the Companies Act. Issues have to be made by offshore subsidiaries with offers made only over the telephone or only to professional investors to avoid the requirement of the Companies Act that a prospectus must be published with every public offer of securities by a company and the prohibition on private companies making public offers;

• the SCP market has had to compete with the well established bankers' acceptance market as a source of short term funds.

The major clearing centre for SCP is First Chicago who offer same day settlement providing instructions are received before a specified time of day. The British Bankers Association has laid down standards for 'London Good Delivery' of SCP which cover printing (including security features) handling and paying. The standards are similar to those for sterling certificates of deposit. Issuers or their appointed agent, must notify the Bank of England at the commencement or extension of a SCP programme and monthly thereafter at the amount outstanding. By the end of 1990 there was some £5.3 billion of SCP outstanding from 190 programmes reported to The Bank of England.

Central Moneymarkets office

On 1 October 1990 The Bank of England inaugurated the Central Moneymarkets Office ('CMO') which will provide a central depository for safe custody and immobilisation of sterling money market instruments as well as book entry transfer of instruments between members and the creation of the associated payment instructions for same day settlement. The CMO will provide this service to its members in commercial paper as well as certificates of deposit (see below) and bills (Treasury, Local Authority, bank and trade). Participants may be direct members with input and receipt of instruments via a computer terminus and settlement through a bank which is a member of CHAPS (Clearing House Automated Payment System) or indirectly through a nominee who is a direct member.

French commercial paper

The domestic French commercial paper market started in late 1985 and as of August 1989 the total outstanding was approximately FFr 100 billion. French commercial paper is called *billets de trésorerie* to distinguish it from trade bills called *papier commercial*. Some of the more important characteristics of the market are as follows:

● issuers must have been incorporated in France for at least two years with audited financial statements but do not have to be listed;

● issuers require a minimum capitalisation of FFr 1.5 million;

● maturities can be from 10 days to seven years with a minimum denomination of FFr 1 million. Most issues are in the 20-40 day range;

● issuers are required to produce regular financial information including six monthly balance sheets, commentary on results and annual certified consolidated balance sheets;

● the *Agence d'Evaluation Financiere* (ADEF) provides ratings for each issuer, which range from T1 to T3. Rating is mandatory for issues with a maturity over two years;

- CP issues are distributed through dealerships rather than tender panels;
- the principal dealers are the large French banks although money brokers are also eligible;
- all issues with a maturity of less than two years must have underwriting agreements in place for up to 75% of the total issue.

Dutch commercial paper

The Dutch commercial paper market commenced in early 1986. The restrictions on issuance are minimal – there are no net worth or listing requirements and issuers do not have to be incorporated in Holland. However, the market remains small, principally due to competition from the efficient *Kasgeld*, (the short term money market) which enables corporate treasurers to obtain a competitive source of funds. Clearing of commercial paper transactions is effected through the Central Bank.

Switzerland

There is no short term money market as such in Switzerland, the main obstacle being a stamp duty imposed on transactions and a withholding tax of 35% on the interest. A special instrument is, however, the money market debt register claims of the Swiss Confederation.

The Confederation's debt register claims comprise short term paper with terms of 30, 90, 180 and 360 days. They are offered for subscription by way of a quasi-auction by the Swiss National Bank and allocated at a single price. Interest payments are subject to 35% withholding tax. The paper is denominated in units of Sfr10,000. There is no stamp duty on these transactions.

A similar system with book entry of so called payment rights (or Continuously Offered Payment rights or COPs) has been developed for some high quality foreign issuers. Due to the lack of transparency it is presently difficult to judge the success of this system. Some investors do not accept the book entry system, since the name of the investor will be disclosed and consequently anonymity is not retained as with normal bearer securities.

Other European markets

Finland

In Finland a domestic commercial paper market commenced in 1986. The restrictions on issuance are minimal, with no requirements for net worth or listing. Issuers have to be incorporated in Finland and the paper is distributed through dealerships comprising the larger Finnish banks.

Maturities are from one week to a year with most in the 45-90 day range.

Italy

In Italy the domestic commercial paper market commenced in 1985 and consists of a letter acknowledging a transferable corporate loan. There is no formal regulation of the market.

Norway

In Norway the commercial paper market was established during 1985 and there is little regulation. The commercial paper is not listed and the maturity cannot exceed 365 days. The paper is interest bearing. Dealing is carried out by banks and brokers (who have to be licenced).

Sweden

The commercial paper market or *Foretagscertifikat* in Sweden commenced in early 1983 and all programmes require approval with a prospectus for each programme giving the disclosures required by the Swedish stock exchange. The maturities are up to one year with an average of three months.

Spain and Turkey

There are also domestic markets in Spain for the issue of *pagares de empresa* or commercial paper (maturities no less than one month but few other restrictions) and Turkey (where issues are controlled by the Capital Markets Board which has rules regarding net worth, audited accounts and guarantees).

2.31 Benefits – issuer

• Issuers can obtain cheaper funds than through bank overdrafts or loan facilities.

• Flexibility – the issuer can tailor the maturity of the instrument either to meet his own funding requirements or to tap investor demand.

• With a dealership agreement issues can be made at very short notice (often within a day), which means that issuers can react quickly to favourable movements in interest rates and to strength of investor demand.

• The issuer is able to diversify sources of funds.

• A CP programme is usually cheaper than issuing Euronotes (see section 2.38) because the issuer does not have to pay underwriting fees.

• Unlike bankers' acceptances no underlying trade transaction is required.

2.32 Benefits – investor

• The wide range of maturities means that investors are better able to find an instrument that suits their specific requirements.

• If CP is issued through a dealership agreement the dealer(s) will be obliged to make a market in the issue. The investor will therefore always be able to sell his investment to the dealer if he wishes to liquidate his holding prior to maturity although this may be expensive.

• Prior to the development of CP and Euronotes, the main instrument in which short term funds could be invested was the Negotiable Certificate of Deposit which can only be issued by Banks (section 2.45). Purchase of CP allows investors to diversify out of bank risk.

• As the notes are repaid within one year (or usually less) the investor is exposed only to short term credit risks and therefore there is less risk to capital values than with FRNs.

2.33 Risks and disadvantages – issuer

• As CP is not underwritten, the issuer cannot guarantee that he will be able to place the paper with investors and raise the funds he requires. This restricts access to the market to large corporations with strong credit ratings and/or household names and presents particular difficulties for existing issuers whose credit rating declines suddenly.

• If companies wish to redeem the existing paper out of the proceeds of issuing new paper, a bank line of credit may be needed to ensure that the issuer obtains the funds. This may be expensive.

2.34 Risks and disadvantages – investor

● The investor is exposed to changes in the credit status of the issuer which may make the CP difficult to sell before maturity.

● ECP is usually unsecured and this may result in an increased exposure to defaults.

● Large denomination securities are unattractive to the small investor.

2.35 Accounting and taxation

The accounting and taxation treatment of debt issues which is set out in sections 2.209 to 2.244 on the accounting and tax treatment in various European countries at the end of this chapter is relevant to commercial paper. Some specific matters to be considered are set out below.

2.36 Accounting questions

Isssuer

● Where commercial paper is issued at a discount:

 – When should the discount be recognised in the profit and loss account? Should a straight line or yield basis be used?

 – Should the ultimate liability be shown in the balance sheet with the discount as an asset or is it more appropriate to show the net amount as a liability?

Investor

● Where the CP is held by an entity which actively trades in securities, is it appropriate to value CP at market value or at cost/adjusted cost?

● If valued at market prices can the market be said to be sufficiently liquid and active for market prices to be properly established?

2.37 Taxation questions

- Will costs of issue qualify for tax relief as a trading expense or as a cost of obtaining loan finance?

- What are the VAT consequences (if any) of the issue?

- Is any interest payable an allowable tax deduction to the issuer and if so on an accruals or paid basis?

- How is the discount taxed or allowed?

- Are exchange gains/losses taxable/tax deductable for the issuer and if so on a realisation or translation basis?

- Is there withholding tax on any interest paid?

- Is the profit/loss on disposal only taxable/allowable on realisation?

- Will any exchange gain or loss on redemption of CP be trading income or an allowable trading expense of the issuer?

- Will a financial trader as holder be taxed on profits on an accruals basis or only on sale or maturity?

- Are exchange gains/losses taxable/tax deductable for the investor?

- Will the investor's profit on sale or maturity be taxed as income or as a capital gain?

- Is a foreign investor exempted from tax in the issuing country by a double tax treaty or by concession?

- Is any sale or maturity proceeds an exempt supply for VAT purposes, regardless of the 'place of belonging of the counterparty'?

2.38 Euronotes

Once issued, Euronotes are essentially the same as commercial paper. The principal feature which distinguishes a Euronote issue from a commercial paper issue is that Euronotes are underwritten by an investment bank or banks, which ensure that the issuer will receive funds even if investors do not buy the paper – the underwriters will either buy the paper themselves or extend the use of a credit line to the issuer. The underwriting fee will make Euronotes more expensive than commercial paper. At the end of 1990 Euroclear reported that $19 billion of Euronotes were outstanding.

There are two other features which usually characterise a Euronote issue and are generally, though not necessarily, absent in an issue of ECP:

● Euronotes are issued usually in fixed maturities of one, three, or six months;

● Euronotes are issued usually through a tender panel, where a number of appointed dealers bid for the paper (on indications received from investors of what they are prepared to pay).

Types of Euronote Facility

Borrower's Option for Notes and Underwritten Standby (BONUS)	Two separate but related elements as follows: – an uncommitted note placement arrangement by tender – a committed standby facility
Note Issuance Facility (NIF)	A procedure for the issue of Euronotes agreed between the issuer and a bank. The issuer will normally have a revolving credit facility. The precise arrangements for the issue and the tender panel procedures will be set out in the documentation.
Revolving Underwriting Facility (RUF)	A variant of the NIF whereby the issue of the notes is underwritten by a group of banks. If the tender panel fails the underwriting banks are required to purchase the notes.
Revolving Acceptance Facility by Tender (RAFT)	A form of RUF but using eligible bank bills ('acceptances') rather than notes.
Short term Note Issuance Facility (SNIF)	A term used for a NIF with short term notes.
Multi Option Facility (MOF) or Multiple Option Funding Facility (MOFF)	A facility which grants the issuer the option to draw down on the commitment by the use of more than one type of instrument. The typical options are Euronotes, cash advances or bankers acceptances and the facility usually runs for five to seven years.
Securitised Note Commitment Facility (SNCF)	This is an FRN issue where the note holders are committed to buy Euronotes. If the commitment was not met the FRN was forfeited. Investors, rather than the banks, provide the backstop to the NIF.

Transferable Revolving Underwriting Facility (TRUF)	A RUF in which the investment banks' underwriting commitment is transferable.

2.39 Benefits – issuer

- Euronotes may be a cheaper source of funds than alternative sources of bank finance.
- As the notes are underwritten, the issuer has a guarantee that it will receive the funds.
- Where Euronotes are issued through a tender panel, the competitive bidding process will help to ensure that the paper is issued at the lowest cost.

2.40 Benefits – investor

- As for commercial paper in section 2.32.

2.41 Risks and disadvantages – issuer

- A Euronote facility is generally more expensive than commercial paper issues because of the fee which has to be paid to the underwriting banks.
- The underwriting fee and the front end management fee can make the issue expensive if not fully utilised.
- The lead time in the issue of notes under a tender panel agreement (usually two to three days) is generally longer than for commercial paper. This makes the mechanism less responsive to changes in market conditions and the lowest borrowing cost may not be achieved.
- The maturities of Euronote issues tend to be less flexible than for commercial paper.
- The tender panel means that the issuer may not know the cost of borrowing until the issue date.

• The tender panel members have no assurance that they will receive the paper they bid for. Consequently, there may be less incentive to develop an investor base.

2.42 Risks and disadvantages – investor

• With a tender panel the investor is not assured receipt of the paper bid for through the placement agent.

• Tender panel members are not obliged to make markets in the issuer's paper, and this can reduce the issue's marketability.

• There can be price inconsistency between the primary and secondary markets as tender panel members are not obliged to make markets.

2.43 Accounting questions

• As for commercial paper in sections 2.35 and 2.36.

2.44 Taxation questions

• Are Euronotes 'certificates of deposit' for VAT or United Kingdom income tax purposes?

• Other questions as for commercial paper in section 2.37.

2.45 Negotiable certificates of deposit (CD)

A negotiable certificate of deposit (CD) is an acknowledgement from a bank of a deposit of funds with that bank for a specified period at a specified interest rate. It is essentially a negotiable time deposit. The CD is the longest established money market instrument in the Euromarkets.

Features of the CD

● Maturities are generally up to one year. However, CDs can be issued with maturities of up to five years.

● Usually issued in bearer form.

● In the United Kingdom, CDs with maturities of less than five years pay interest free of withholding taxes.

● In the United Kingdom CDs can be settled through the Central Moneymarkets Office (see section 2.30).

Variation

Floating rate CDs (FRCD)	These are usually medium term CDs where the interest rate is fixed semi-annually by reference to a money market interest rate – usually London Interbank Bid Rate (LIBID).

2.46 Pricing of CDs

Certificates of deposit are quoted by reference to their yield. From the yield the price of sterling CDs with maturities of less than one year is calculated on a 365 day basis, as follows:

$$P = \frac{(M \times r/100) + 365}{(t + y/100) + 365} \times \text{Principal}$$

Where:

M = original maturity in days
r = interest rate on stated issue
t = time to maturity in days
y = quoted yield
P = price

US dollar CDs are priced on a 360 day basis.

CDs with maturities of more than one year

As with other fixed rate interest bearing instruments, the price is determined by discounting the cash flows (annual interest payments and principal at maturity) by the current yield. The actual number of days in each year should be used to calculate the interest.

Discounted CDs

Discounted CDs are quoted at a percentage discount on an annual basis. The price is therefore:

Price = P(1 − (D × t/365))

Where:

P = principal
D = discount rate
t = time to maturity in days

The yield is always higher than the discount rate and is calculated as:

$$\text{Yield} = \frac{D}{1 - (D \times t/365)}$$

US dollar CDs are priced on a 360 day basis.

2.47 Benefits – issuer

• Because the instruments are negotiable, the issuing banks can usually take deposits more cheaply than on the inter-bank market.

2.48 Benefits – investor

• There is an active secondary market in CDs so the instrument is liquid and relatively risk free.

• They are issued by banks with good credit ratings.

2.49 Accounting and tax questions

• There are no specific accounting questions for CDs. For tax questions see commercial paper section 2.37.

2.50 Medium term notes

Medium term notes (MTNs) are a hybrid instrument, sharing some of the features of commercial paper, Euronotes and Eurobonds. This is reflected in the maturity of these instruments, which is usually between one and five years (although the maturity has been up to 10 years). MTNs share the following features in common with short term instruments such as commercial paper:

● the maturity can be tailored to suit investor requirements;

● they are not normally underwritten;

● they are usually offered continuously through dealers, placement agents, or tender panels rather than issued in one tranche underwritten by a syndicate of banks.

MTNs share the following features with longer-dated bonds:

● they are issued usually in small denominations;

● they are interest bearing instruments and can be fixed or floating rate;

● interest is paid on a predetermined schedule regardless of the issue or maturity date;

● they are issued at par and priced at a percentage of par value rather than being quoted on a yield basis;

● in the secondary market, settlement is normally seven days after trade date, rather than same day or one day later, as with commercial paper.

Issuing procedures

There are two main structures through which MTNs are issued:

● Continuously Offered Long Term Securities (COLTS)

These programmes will usually be issued through multi-dealerships. Issuers will post a range of maturities and interest rates at which they will issue the notes which are then sold by the dealers on a 'best efforts' basis. The notes are usually offered for a range of maturities (eg one year to 18 months) but the investor can choose the actual maturity of each note.

● Multitranche tap notes

An alternative issuing procedure developed by Merrill Lynch as a response to concerns of Euromarket investors about liquidity. Under this structure the issuer has to issue one tranche of at least US $50 million of notes to provide a minimum level of liquidity. Notes with the same maturity will then be issued on a tap basis over the following six months.

2.51 MTN markets

The MTN market developed firstly in the United States but in recent years the number of issues in the Euromarket ('EMTNs') have increased substantially. In 1990 some 90 issuing programmes were signed bringing the total to nearly 400 of which some $22 billion was outstanding at the end of 1990. While the EMTN market originally comprised mainly US dollar denominated issues, Canadian dollars, deutschemarks, lira and yen have been used as well as the ECU. By mid 1990 the total outstanding were estimated at some $15 billion.

The principal differences between MTNs issued in the United States domestic market and the Euromarket are as follows:

• MTNs issued in the United States are usually registered in the name of the holder, whereas they are issued in bearer form in the Euromarket;

• interest on United States domestic MTNs is calculated on an actual/360 basis and in the Euromarket on an AIBD basis;

• EMTNs issued in the Euromarket are usually listed on either The Stock Exchange or the Luxembourg Stock Exchange. This is because many potential investors are not allowed to purchase unlisted securities.

United Kingdom

On 11 January 1990 The Bank of England announced changes to allow a United Kingdom corporation to issue MTNs denominated in sterling ('SMTNs'). The changes allow issues with maturities of up to five years. The announcement extends the exemptions from the Banking Act 1987 currently used for SCP issues. The requirements are as for SCP except for MTNs:

• the original maturity must be more than one year;

• put or call options can only be exercisable after one year from issue date.

Germany, France and The Netherlands

In June 1989 the *Deutsche Bundesbank* announced that it would allow public deutschmark MTN issues with two to five year maturities. To date foreign banks have been the most active issuers. In France the authorities have not yet clarified the legal status of French franc MTNs and it is possible that only French banks will be permitted to lead manage such issues, as for French franc Eurobonds. In the Netherlands there are currently approximately 15 outstanding MTN programmes which have been issued in the domestic market. The most active issues have been *Bank Nederlandse Gemeenten* and *Nederlandse Waterschapsbank*. Maturities range from two to 10 years and issues are made by the tap method. The typical denomination of the notes is NGL 100,000, reflecting the fact that investors are professionals and the larger institutions. No issuer is allowed to issue more than NGL 50m in one day. Transactions are cleared through the Dutch Central bank.

2.52 Benefits – issuer

● An MTN programme gives the issuer flexibility in the raising of longer-term funds.

● The flexibility of maturities enables lower rates to be obtained by matching investor demand.

● As the notes are not underwritten, there can be savings compared to the costs of a Eurobond syndication.

● The issuer has flexibility over the amount of notes to be issued at any one time. It is seldom economical to make Eurobond issues of less than $100 million, but MTNs can be issued in the $5–20 million range (albeit that the programme may be for a much larger amount).

2.53 Benefits – investor

● MTNs generally have a higher yield than other instruments which are available to medium term investors (such as medium term CDs and United States Treasury bonds).

2.54 Risks and disadvantages – issuer

• MTNs are priced according to money market rates and may be expensive when compared to long-dated instruments.

2.55 Risks and disadvantages – investor

• At present, the secondary market in these instruments is illiquid, which can make it difficult for the investor to dispose of a holding prior to maturity.

2.56 Accounting and tax questions

• The accounting treatment for MTNs for most countries is, as for fixed and floating rate bonds, well established and is set out in the sections 2.209 to 2.244 on accounting and taxation in various European countries at the end of this chapter. Section 2.18 on fixed rate bonds sets out the taxation questions for MTNs.

Currency linked and index linked issues

2.57 Introduction

This part of the chapter describes a variety of debt instruments which have developed in the Euromarket in recent years which have a common element – they are fixed or floating rate bonds where the amount of principal (and, in some cases, interest) is not fixed but is dependent on movements in exchange rates, interest rates, commodity prices or indices. These instruments can be divided into the following two main categories:

• Currency linked issues Redemption is made either in a currency different to that in which the bond is issued or in the original currency, with the amount to be paid being linked to exchange rate movements.

- Index linked issues   Redemption value is linked to a specified index. This can be an inflation index or the index of the price of commodities, bonds, shares or other goods and services.

2.58 Currency linked issues

The development of currency linked bonds was made possible by the development of the currency swap market and the related extension of the foreign exchange market to maturities of greater than one year. The development of the swap market (swaps are covered in chapter 5 – Hedging Instruments) led to the issue of Eurobonds in a wide range of currencies. Many of these bonds were issued in currencies which would appeal to investors and were not denominated in the desired currency of the issuer, hence the issuer had to enter into a currency swap in order to obtain the required currency. With such a wide range of currencies it was inevitable that investment banks would develop securities that combined the related currency swap with the issue of bonds, for example issues being made in one currency with interest payments in another. In addition, the options (often over a long term) granted by the investor over currencies in some of the structures could be bought by the investment bank (thus hedging the issuer) and sold to another party or used to hedge other transactions. The existence of the swap, the far forward foreign exchange markets and currency options meant that these issues could be tailor-made for specific investors. The use of swaps and other hedging transactions meant the issuer could obtain the debt profile which was required at a lower overall cost.

Currency linked issues were popular in the mid-1980s but the market for new issues virtually ceased due to the combination of a glut of issues and the increasing perception of investors that the redemption exchange rate was not reasonably priced. Recently currency option bonds (where redemption in another currency is optional and not mandatory) have become popular.

The majority of currency linked issues have been targeted at Japanese institutional investors, and in particular have exploited the regulations which prescribe the types of investments which can be made by those institutions. In the 1980s the influence of Japanese investors in the Euromarkets was increasing and whole issues were designed for one of the large investors and are in effect private placements. Consequently there is often little liquidity in the secondary markets for these instruments.

2.59 Index linked issues

The volatility of interest rates, commodity prices and stock exchange indices and the continuing development of futures and options markets have resulted in bonds which are linked to commodity prices, interest rates and stock exchange indices. These instruments can act as a hedge both for the issuer (such as the producer of a commodity) and for the investor (who may be a purchaser of the commodity). The issues in effect usually incorporate an option on interest rates, stock exchange indices or commodity prices in their terms.

2.60 Benefits – issuer

• The benefit of linked bonds to the issuer is a reduction in interest costs. In some cases this may be achieved by offering features which appeal to a particular category of investor, in others because the issuer has a source for the commodity or currency which forms the basis of the linking. Some of the instruments are designed in such a way that the movements in redemption values of different tranches offset each other so that the issuer is exposed to no overall risk. Other instruments rely on complex hedging operations and swaps to eliminate or reduce the risk to the issuer while still providing a reduction in interest costs.

2.61 Benefits – investor

• The benefit to the investor is the wide range of investment opportunities with risks and rewards based on different indices and exchange rates. In particular the currency linked issues often allow investors to include within their portfolio instruments that reflect their view of future foreign exchange movements. Often investors are precluded from including a naked forward foreign exchange contract due to its perceived risk, but would be allowed to hold an interest bearing listed investment such as a dual currency bond.

Debt instruments

2.62 Risks and disadvantages – issuer

• If the issuer does not own the underlying commodity or currency, and is not properly hedged, the expected overall interest savings may not arise since losses may be incurred if the index or currency rate changes in a manner other than expected. This may lead to higher payments of interest and/or principal.

• Investor demand may not be as expected, leading to a shortfall in funding. This may also make the issue more expensive than anticipated, reducing the effect of any interest savings.

• The instrument may be difficult to price as there may be no comparable investment.

• Complex hedging transactions result in long term exposure to the credit status of the hedge counterparty.

2.63 Risks and disadvantages – investor

• Unless the investor is hedged in some way or the linked investment forms part of a properly structured portfolio the investor is speculating on movements in rates or indices. If the currency rates or indices fluctuate in an unexpected manner the higher redemption values or interest receipts may not arise.

• It is not always possible to hedge fully such investments.

• The market in this type of investment may be illiquid making it difficult to dispose of the investment before maturity.

2.64 Accounting and taxation

There is a wide variety of securities included in this part of the chapter and the accounting and taxation questions for each issue will depend upon its particular terms. The general accounting and taxation treatment for debt instruments in various countries in Europe is set out in sections 2.209 to 2.244 at the end of this chapter. However, there are a number of general matters to consider with the securities dealt within this part of the chapter which are set out in sections 2.65 and 2.66 below.

2.65 General accounting questions

For the issuer

- If the redemption value of the debt instrument is linked to an index or exchange rate, the final liability will be uncertain unless a specific hedge is taken out. How should the issuer account for potential gains or losses on redemption? What is the amount of the liability to be included in the accounts at any intermediate date? How should any hedging transaction be treated?

- Should the interest savings compared with a straight debt issue by the same issuer with the same maturity be deferred to offset a possible increase in redemption value or future losses?

- If the redemption amount is based on a future foreign exchange rate which is not hedged should the liability be translated at the appropriate forward rate or the period end rate?

- Should the proceeds of the issue be allocated between the debt instrument and any contingent right? Should these amounts be offset in the balance sheet?

For the investor

- Should the investor mark the debt instrument to market? If so, is the market sufficiently liquid to provide reliable prices? If market values are not used can a formula based on the linkage be adopted?

2.66 General taxation questions

- It will be important to determine the treatment of exchange gains and losses with this type of instrument. In particular, are exchange gains/losses taxable/tax deductible for the issuer/investor and if so on a realisation or translation basis?

- Does the index-linked element represent income or capital for tax purposes?

• Other questions as for fixed rate bonds (section 2.18).

2.67 Dual currency bonds

Dual currency bonds are instruments whose cash flows arise, or may arise, in more than one currency. The relationship between the two currencies is fixed at the time of issue. The term 'dual currency bond' is a vague one and has at times been used to describe various issue structures, but the most common one is where the issue price is fixed in one currency, fixed coupons are paid in that currency but principal is redeemed in another currency. The cash flows will arise as follows:

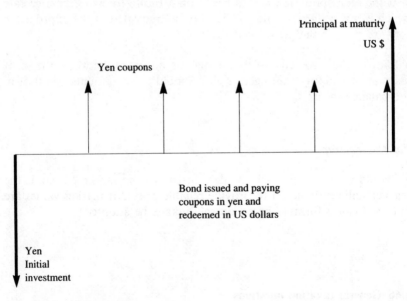

Diagram 2.8: Dual currency bonds

Dual currency bonds are usually issued and pay coupons in a currency with low interest rates (eg Swiss francs and yen), but at higher rates than would be normal on plain vanilla issues in that currency. The majority of these issues are redeemable in US dollars, at a rate higher than the spot rate at the date of issue but lower than the break even rate implied by the interest rate differentials between the two currencies, resulting in a cost saving to the issuer. This can be illustrated using the following hypothetical example:

A multinational French AA rated corporation wishes to raise approximately US$140 million for 10 years, paying interest at fixed rates. As an alternative to issuing a plain vanilla fixed rate bond the corporation issues a 20 billion yen dual currency bond paying a 6.5% annual coupon (in yen). The bond is to be redeemed in US dollars in 10 years time at a fixed rate of 115 yen/US dollar. The issuer will convert the yen proceeds of the issue into US dollars at the spot rate and will purchase forward in the foreign exchange market the yen required to pay the annual coupons.

The spot rate at the date of issue is 142.00. The one year Eurocurrency interest rate is 5.5% for yen and 8.75% for US dollars. For simplicity this example assumes that the yield curve from one to ten years is flat, and therefore that, for the purposes of calculating the forward foreign exchange rates, the interest rate differential between the two currencies is constant. A further simplifying assumption is that 10 year government bond yields in both the United States and Japan are equivalent to the one year Eurocurrency rate at the issue date.

If fees and transaction costs are ignored, the resultant cash flows are as follows:

Table 2.2: Dual Currency Bonds

Time (years)	Cash Flow	Yen(m)	FX Rate	US$(m)	Comparable US$ straight US$(m)
Spot	Issue proceeds	20,000.00	142.00	140.85	140.85
1	Coupon	(1,300.00)	137.76	(9.44)	(13.03)
2	Coupon	(1,300.00)	133.64	(9.73)	(13.03)
3	Coupon	(1,300.00)	129.65	(10.03)	(13.03)
4	Coupon	(1,300.00)	125.77	(10.34)	(13.03)
5	Coupon	(1,300.00)	122.01	(10.65)	(13.03)
6	Coupon	(1,300.00)	118.37	(10.98)	(13.03)
7	Coupon	(1,300.00)	114.83	(11.32)	(13.03)
8	Coupon	(1,300.00)	111.40	(11.67)	(13.03)
9	Coupon	(1,300.00)	108.07	(12.03)	(13.03)
10	Coupon	(1,300.00)	104.84	(12.40)	(13.03)
10	Redemption proceeds*	(20,000.00)	115.00	(173.91)	(140.85)
		Cost (excl fees)		9.08%	9.25%

*The Yen cash flow is notional only

If it is assumed that AA rated corporate bonds yield 50 basis points over government bonds, the investors in the dual currency bond will be earning 50 basis points over comparable fixed rate bonds denominated in yen (a coupon of 6.50% compared with 5.50% plus 50 basis points or 6%). However, because the redemption rate is higher than the forward foreign exchange rate implied by the interest rate differential (115 compared to 104.08), the issuer makes an overall saving of 17 basis points (9.08% compared to 9.25% or $239,445 per annum).

Such dual currency bonds were popular in the mid 1980s but became unpopular when investors came to appreciate the foreign exchange risks associated with the product.

Variations

Foreign currency bond	Bonds where the coupon is paid in a different currency than the issue proceeds, but where the amount paid is determined by the spot rate at payment date, and not fixed in advance. The redemption may be in the currency of issue or coupon at the investor's option, also at the spot rate of exchange.
Partly-paid dual currency bond	A partly-paid dual currency bond allows for the second tranche to be paid for in a choice of currency at the investor's option at a predetermined rate.
Reverse dual currency bond	Reverse dual currency bonds are issued and pay coupons in a currency with high interest rates. The bonds are redeemed at a predetermined rate in another currency. They are called 'reverse' dual currency bonds because the majority of dual currency bonds were denominated in yen and redeemed in US dollars, and the reverse issues have been mainly denominated in US dollars with redemption in yen. The cash flows on this instrument are as follows:

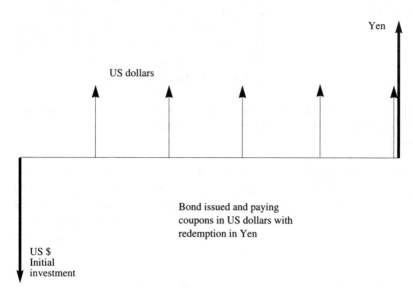

Diagram 2.9: Reverse dual currency bonds

Foreign Interest Payment Security (FIPS)	A perpetual reverse dual currency bond with a put option for investors every 10 years. Due to the unfavourable terms to investors there have been few such issues.
Currency-change bond	The interest is payable first in one currency then in another, the currencies being stipulated at the time of issue.
Heaven and hell bond	The redemption proceeds of the bond are linked to the deviation of the exchange rate at maturity from a predetermined rate. In general as the base currency appreciates the redemption proceeds increase and conversely as the base currency depreciates the proceeds decrease. The level of the redemption value is equivalent to the investor granting a call and purchasing a put currency option at the same strike price (see chapter 5 – Hedging Instruments).

Principal Exchange Rate Linked Securities (PERLS)	Securities which pay interest and are redeemed in US dollars but the redemption proceeds are based on the exchange rate between US dollars and another currency. Depending on the exchange rates at maturity the redemption amount will be greater or less than the nominal value.
Purgatory and hell bond (Capped heaven and hell bond)	Heaven and hell bonds, with a cap on the redemption proceeds.
Reverse forex linked bond (Or reverse heaven and hell bond)	Heaven and hell bonds linked to the exchange rate at maturity whereby as the base currency appreciates redemption proceeds decrease and conversely a depreciation in the base currency leads to an increase in redemption proceeds.
Marginal reverse forex linked bonds	Redemption will be at par unless the base currency appreciates strongly above a predetermined level.
Index Currency Option Notes (ICONs)	The coupon is fixed in dollar terms and the repayment of principal is at least par value but can increase depending on the exchange rate at maturity. The effect is that the investor receives a higher than normal coupon in return for granting a currency call option (see chapter 5 – Hedging Instruments).

2.68 Benefits – issuer

• The setting of the redemption proceeds at off market rates enables the issuer to reduce the costs of the issue.

• The far forward exchange and currency options implicit in the redemption amount can be sold to an investment bank (who for example could use the long term currency option for another transaction) to eliminate currency exposures and thus reduce funding costs of the issuer.

2.69 Benefits – investor

• Dual currency bonds offer investors the opportunity to speculate on future exchange rates. This can be attractive to investors who do not have access to the far forward or currency option markets.

• The high coupon can be attractive to investors who cannot distribute capital gains. This is particularly true of Japanese insurance companies, who were willing to assume the foreign exchange risk implicit in these instruments because they could distribute the coupon interest received to shareholders.

2.70 Risks and disadvantages – issuer

• While the pricing and predetermined exchange rates should result in lower funding costs, if exchange rates do not pass the break even point a relatively higher cost will have been incurred, unless the issue is properly hedged.

• Due to the specialist nature of the issues and the investors they attract it may be difficult to place fully an issue. As a result, most issues are for relatively small amounts.

• Credit exposure to the counterparty for any hedging transactions.

2.71 Risks and disadvantages – investor

• The redemption exchange rate is usually set to favour the issuer.

• While dual currency bonds will outperform similar plain vanilla bonds if exchange rate movements are favourable, it is possible to construct a portfolio of straight bonds (and options) which will perform at least as well without the foreign exchange risk of dual currency bonds.

● The market may be illiquid such that it is difficult to sell the investment before maturity.

2.72 Accounting questions

● How should the investor/issuer account for the related foreign currency transactions and the translation adjustments?

● How should the difference between the exchange rate at the issue date and the predetermined future redemption rate be treated? Should it be included as interest?

● See also general accounting questions in section 2.65.

2.73 Taxation questions

● See the general taxation questions in section 2.66. See chapter 5– Hedging Instruments for the taxation treatment of the related hedge transactions. However, the crucial question for any hedge transactions is whether the tax treatment mirrors that of the risk being hedged. If it does not the risk is not properly hedged on an after tax basis.

2.74 Currency option bonds

The principal and coupon of currency option bonds are fixed in one currency but the issuer has the option to redeem in another currency at maturity. The exchange rate at which the option may be exercised is fixed at the time of issue. The cash flows on this bond can be shown as follows:

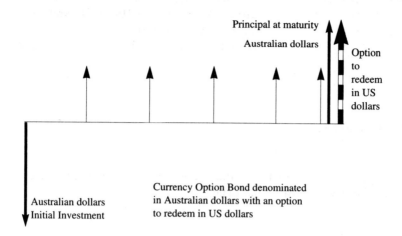

Principal at maturity
Australian dollars

Option to redeem in US dollars

Australian dollars
Initial Investment

Currency Option Bond denominated
in Australian dollars with an option
to redeem in US dollars

Diagram 2.10: Currency option bonds

Currency option bonds are a relatively recent innovation. Most of the issues to date have been denominated in high coupon currencies, such as Australian or Canadian dollars, with the issuer having the option to redeem in US dollars. As with the original dual currency structure, the investor receives a high coupon in return for the foreign exchange risk (effectively, the investors in this product write an in-the-money option for the issuer).

Variations

Covered Option Securities (COPS)	Short term dollar denominated securities that give the issuer an option to repay the dollar principal and interest in a foreign currency at an exchange rate agreed at the time of issue. In exchange for this option, the issuer offers the investor a substantial yield premium over comparable short term debt. The yield offered depends on the general level of interest rates, the foreign currency to which the instrument is linked and the prevailing market conditions. The investor, in effect, writes a put option on the foreign currency the additional yield representing the premium. To date, these issues have been made only in the United States domestic market.

Dual option bond   A bond, the redemption proceeds of which are expressed in two currencies and the investor may choose the currency in which to receive payment of coupons and redemption.

2.75 Benefits – issuer

● The long position in the in-the-money option enables the issuer to reduce the overall cost of the issue.

2.76 Benefits – investor

● Higher yields than for comparable plain vanilla bonds.
● Enables the retail investor, who does not have access to currency option markets, to write an option.

2.77 Risks and disadvantages – issuer

● If the option is unexercised the issuer will pay a higher rate of interest compared to a straight debt issue.

2.78 Risks and disadvantages – investor

● Not a liquid investment.
● The investor is effectively selling the currency option linked to the bond very cheaply. Larger investors who have access to the OTC option market could construct a similar position themselves at a lower cost.

2.79 Accounting questions

• At a balance sheet date how should the liability under the option be valued? Should the option premium implicit in the security be accounted for separately?

• At a balance sheet date how should the investor value the security?

• See also general questions in section 2.65.

2.80 Taxation questions

• Is all or part of the interest a deemed dividend?

• Can the investor be taxed on issue on a notional option premium by reference to the higher coupon received?

• See the general taxation questions in section 2.66. See chapter 5 – Hedging Instruments for the taxation treatment of any related hedge transactions. However, the crucial question for any hedge transactions is whether the tax treatment mirrors that of the risk being hedged. If it does not the risk is not properly hedged on an after tax basis.

2.81 Duet bonds

The redemption value and each interest payment of a duet bond are calculated by reference to a formula linked to the exchange rate between two currencies at the date of payment (eg the US dollar/yen exchange rate). Essentially payment is made on the difference in value between dollars and yen at the payment date. In the case of the duet bond issued by the Kingdom of Denmark, the formula used to calculate the payment of interest and principal was highly leveraged; a small percentage increase in the value of the dollar would increase significantly the return on the bond. The purchase of a duet bond is equivalent to purchasing a number of plain vanilla bonds in the bullish currency (US dollars in this case) and taking a short position in a bond denominated in the currency about which the investor has a bearish view (yen in this case).

2.82 Benefits – issuer

● Reduces financing costs by taking advantage of the disparity of interest rates in the two markets.

2.83 Benefits – investor

● Some investors do not have access to the far forward foreign exchange market and the duet bond can provide an alternative long term hedge against foreign currency movements.

● The duet bond structure is highly leveraged and if the exchange rate moves favourably this can lead to a large increase in the return on the bond.

2.84 Risk and disadvantage – issuer

● The reduction in financing costs may not be achieved if rates move unfavourably and the foreign exchange exposures are not hedged at the time of issue.

2.85 Risks and disadvantages – investor

● There are few such instruments and the markets are likely to be illiquid.

● The leveraged nature of the instrument means that if the exchange rate moves unfavourably the duet bond will significantly underperform against plain vanilla fixed rate bonds.

● Unless part of a hedging strategy the investor is exposed to significant foreign currency risks.

2.86 Accounting questions

● As for dual currency bonds in section 2.72.

2.87 Taxation questions

● See the general taxation questions in section 2.66. See chapter 5—Hedging Instruments for the taxation treatment of related hedge transactions. However, the crucial question for any hedge transactions is whether the tax treatment mirrors that of the risk being hedged. If it does not the risk is not properly hedged on an after tax basis.

2.88 Mixed dual currency bonds

Mixed dual currency bonds are repaid in two different currencies fixed at the time of issue. Interest payments on the bond are also linked to the two exchange rates. The percentage of the bond payable on redemption in each currency may vary, for example 20% of the value may be redeemed in one currency and 80% in the other. The interest payments will also be computed according to this split. The mixed dual currency bond is essentially a simultaneous issue of two bonds in different currencies which are not separately tradeable. The cash flows can be shown in the following example of a bond where 80% of the bond is denominated in yen and 20% in New Zealand dollars:

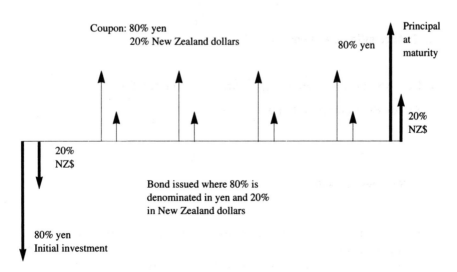

Diagram 2.11: Mixed dual currency bonds

2.89 Benefits – issuer

● Allows funding of assets and liabilities of relatively small amounts in different currencies.

● Can allow small amounts of currency to be raised more cheaply than through bank loans.

2.90 Benefit – investor

● May provide an opportunity to invest in currency assets and speculate on future exchange rates.

2.91 Risk and disadvantage – issuer and investor

● As for dual currency bonds in sections 2.70 and 2.71.

2.92 Accounting questions

● How should the currency exposure be accounted for?

● As for dual currency bonds in section 2.72.

2.93 Taxation questions

● See the general taxation questions in section 2.66. See chapter 5 – Hedging Instruments for the taxation treatment of the related hedge transactions. However, the crucial question for any hedge transactions is whether the tax treatment mirrors that of the risk being hedged. If it does not the risk is not properly hedged on an after tax basis.

2.94 Index linked bonds

Index linked bonds attempt to offer the investor a form of capital maintenance, by adjusting the redemption value and in some cases the interest for the movements in a specific index. The commonest form of indexed bonds are those issued by governments which are linked to movements in a retail price index or other similar measures of inflation. These issues tend to be made during times of high inflation. Corporate issues have usually been linked to the performance of specific indices (particularly stock exchange indices) rather than general price indices. Where there is a linkage to a price index the interest rate is usually adjusted to provide a specific real rate of return. In other types of issues the interest rate is predetermined but at a higher than normal rate to compensate the investor for the risk that redemption value is unknown (and may be less than par if indices move unfavourably).

Variations

Treasury indexed notes	The redemption value is linked to the price of a long term (usually 30 years) United States treasury bond. The redemption value will be more or less than par depending on the bond price at maturity. The redemption formula can be such that the value will increase or decrease with rising bond prices.
Inflation – indexed bonds (or Real yield bonds – REALS)	A bond which is linked to a consumer price index paying a fixed rate over increases in the index ('the real yield'). If the change in the index is negative the coupon is set at a floor level.
Stock Performance Exchange Linked (SPELs)	Redemption value linked to the NYSE Composite Index with a guaranteed redemption at par and an additional amount if the index rises. The annual coupon is set at just below the dividend yield on the shares.
Standard and Poors Indexed Notes (SPINs)	Similar to SPELs but linked to the Standard & Poors 500 index.
All-Ordinaries Share Price Riskless Index Notes (ASPRINs)	A zero coupon issue with a redemption value linked to the All-Ordinaries Index of the Sydney Stock Exchange, the minimum redemption amount being par.

Swiss Market Index
Liierte Emission
(SMILE)

A bond in which the redemption value is fixed and the coupons are linked to the Swiss Market Index (SMI). After an initial period, the coupon rate is fixed for the remaining term of the bond according to the level of the SMI. The higher the SMI, the higher the interest rate of the coupon. Minimum and maximum interest rates are fixed at the date of the issue. SMILES will be quoted on the Swiss Stock Exchanges.

2.95 Benefits – issuer

• The issuer may be able to reduce his financing cost by selling the options granted by the issuer over the specified index to an investment bank.

2.96 Benefits – investor

• Offers exposure to an index without the associated transaction costs.

• Bonds linked to stock exchange indices have a minimum redemption value of par and offer a substitute for equity (the coupon being similar to equity returns) with the risk of capital loss limited to the bond's value as a straight debt instrument.

2.97 Risks and disadvantages – issuer

• The issuer is exposed to an unknown redemption value unless the issue is properly hedged.

• It may not be possible (or economical) to hedge completely all aspects of the exposure either due to the nature of the exposure created by the issue (eg no offsetting hedging transaction exists) or due to a lack of liquidity in the related hedging instrument (eg due to the size of the issue).

In addition, it may be difficult to unwind any hedging transaction if the issue is to be called.

• It may be necessary to hedge all aspects of the issue (eg principal and interest) which can be complex and result in significant administration over the life of the issue.

• Credit exposure to the counterparty for any hedge transactions.

2.98 Risk and disadvantages – investor

• The expected return arising from the increase in the index may not materialise.

2.99 Accounting questions

• Should any interest saving be deferred to offset the additional redemption amount?

• Do any hedging transactions meet the criteria to qualify as a hedge (see chapter 5 – Hedging Instruments)?

• What is the amount to be included in the issuer's accounts if the redemption value is unknown?

• How should both the investor and issuer account for changes in the underlying index value?

• See also general accounting questions in section 2.65.

2.100 Taxation questions

• See the general taxation questions in section 2.66. See chapter 5 – Hedging Instruments for the taxation treatment of the related hedge transactions. However, the crucial question for any hedge transactions is whether the tax treatment mirrors that of the risk being hedged. If it does not the risk is not properly hedged on an after tax basis.

2.101 Commodity linked bonds

Commodity linked bonds are those bonds in which the redemption value and in some cases the coupon is linked to a commodity price or a commodity index. If redemption is linked to a commodity produced by the issuer, such bonds can offer a relatively cheap means of raising finance to fund increased requirements for working capital particularly during periods of inflation. Investors are offered an instrument that will rise in value in line with the underlying commodity whereas the return on equity in a similar company is dependent on other factors. Such bonds effectively offer investors a form of royalty on the production of the issuer. Bonds linked to gold, silver and oil have been issued.

Variation

Oil indexed bond   A zero coupon bond with a redemption value
                              linked to oil prices.

2.102 Benefits – issuers

• Providing the issue is properly hedged funding costs may be reduced considerably, as investors may accept a lower coupon in return for the potentially higher returns arising from the link to commodity prices.

• If the issuer owns or produces the underlying commodity the issue may offer a means of hedging the future sale value at advantageous prices.

2.103 Benefits – investors

• A security linked to a commodity index (eg gold) is attractive to investors since commodity prices may perform better than stock market prices.

• May enable investment in a market not otherwise available to the investor.

• If the investor is a consumer of the commodity, the purchase of a commodity linked bond will act as a hedge against future purchases.

• Allows investment in a market without the associated transaction and storage charges.

2.104 Risk and disadvantages – issuer

• If commodity prices may rise by more than the premium built into the issue, the issue will be expensive relative to alternative methods of raising funds.

• Investors may be prohibited by local legislation from investing in such instruments.

2.105 Risk and disadvantage – investor

• If commodity prices fall the rate of return will be lower than on a plain vanilla fixed rate bond.

2.106 Accounting questions

• What is the amount to be included as a liability in the issuers' accounts if the redemption value is unknown?

• Do any hedging transactions qualify for treatment as hedges?

• See also general accounting questions in section 2.65.

2.107 Taxation questions

• See the general taxation questions in section 2.66. See chapter 5 – Hedging Instruments for the taxation treatment of the related hedge transactions. However, the crucial question for any hedge transactions is whether the tax treatment mirrors that of the risk being hedged. If it does not the risk is not properly hedged on an after tax basis.

2.108 Bull and bear bonds

These instruments are fixed rate bonds where the repayment of principal is linked to a stock index or commodity price. The bonds are issued in two tranches with different redemption values based on the index or price at maturity giving investors the opportunity to take a view on the future movements of the index. The 'bull' bond has a redemption value which increases as the index or commodity price rises, the 'bear' bond's redemption value increases as the index or commodity price falls. Usually the redemption amounts are calculated in such a way that the increase in the value of one of the tranches will be offset by a fall in the value of the other. There is usually an upper and lower limit on redemption values. The two tranches are sold to different types of investors; the bear bonds being useful to investors wishing to hedge falls in the value of the underlying index particularly over the long term. The bull bonds may be of interest to investors who want exposure to movements in stock market prices while receiving a fixed annual coupon. The overall redemption value may be less than the principal received on issue. Issues of bull and bear bonds have usually been linked to stock market indices but United States treasury bond prices and gold prices have also been used.

2.109 Benefits – issuer

● The issuer will be able to reduce financing costs as the issue will be at a lower overall cost than the equivalent plain vanilla fixed rate bond.

● The movement in redemption value of the tranches usually cancel so there is no risk to the issuer from increases in redemption values; increases in one tranche will be offset by a reduction in the other.

2.110 Benefits – investor

● The securities provide a long term interest bearing hedge against a portfolio of the underlying instruments or commodities.

● If regulations do not permit a bearish investor to hold short positions, the 'bear tranche' may provide an alternative means of reflecting the investor's view.

Chapter 2

2.111 Risks and disadvantages – issuer

• If the tranches do not cancel the issuer is exposed to an unknown redemption value unless the issue is properly hedged.

• It may not be possible (or economical) to hedge completely all aspects of any exposure (eg currency) either due to the nature of the exposure created by the issue (eg no offsetting hedging transaction exists) or due to a lack of liquidity in the related hedging instrument (eg due to the size of the issue). In addition it may be difficult to unwind any hedging transaction if the issue is to be called.

• It may be necessary to hedge all aspects of the issue (eg principal and interest) which can be complex and result in significant administration over the life of the issue.

• If demand for the issue is misjudged the issuer (or the investment bank) may be left with part of one tranche, and therefore in an unhedged position.

2.112 Risks and disadvantages – investor

• The expected return resulting from the increase or reduction in the index or commodity price may not materialise. Given that the issue will only be made if it lowers funding costs this must increase unfavourably the cost of the investment for at least one tranche of investor.

2.113 Accounting questions

• If the tranches do not cancel how and when should any additional principal be provided?
• As for fixed rate bonds (section 2.17).

2.114 Taxation questions

See the general taxation questions in section 2.66. See chapter 5 – Hedging Instruments for the taxation treatment of the related hedge transaction.

However, the crucial question for any hedge transactions is whether the tax treatment mirrors that of the risk being hedged. If it does not the risk is not properly hedged on an after tax basis.

2.115 Performance indexed paper (PIPs)

Performance indexed paper is currency linked commercial paper which has similar maturities and denominations to commercial paper but the return to the investor is linked to a specific currency. In effect the issuer of the commercial paper issues plain vanilla single currency notes with a fixed rate of interest agreed with the investment bank arranging the transaction. The investment bank then agrees a minimum and maximum rate of return to the investor based on a range of future exchange rates for the currency chosen by the investor. The issuer makes all payments directly to the investor so the issuer and investment bank then enter into a side agreement to hedge the issuer's foreign exchange risk. Thus the investor obtains a rate of return linked to the chosen currency but the issuer has a fixed rate liability in the base currency.

As with Participating Forward Contracts which are described in the Hedging Instruments chapter, the investor can choose the minimum acceptable rate of return and the investment bank will set the maximum. The lower the minimum return which the investor will accept, the greater the maximum return possible. The investor is exposed to exchange rates but only within the range of return chosen at the outset. PIPs are a product of Salomon Brothers.

2.116 Benefits – issuer

● The addition of a foreign currency element can make the issue more attractive to the investor allowing the issuer to reduce overall costs.

● There is no foreign exchange exposure for the issuer.

2.117 Benefits – investor

● This issue has the attractive short term maturity and denomination features of commercial paper, but if exchange rates move favourably the return is greater.

● The downside risk is limited to the minimum return specified at the outset.

● From the investor's viewpoint the foreign currency risk is assumed by the issuer so no additional credit risk is assumed.

2.118 Risks and disadvantages – issuer

● The issuer cannot benefit from any favourable exchange rate movements.

● The issuer is exposed to the credit status of the investment bank providing the hedge against the foreign exchange exposure.

2.119 Risks and disadvantages – investor

● Risk is borne effectively by the intermediary, in the event of currency appreciation, or by investors, in case of currency depreciation, but both can mitigate their risks by hedging.

● There is no active secondary market.

2.120 Accounting questions

As for dual currency bonds in section 2.72.

2.121 Taxation questions

● See questions on commercial paper in section 2.37. However, the crucial question for the hedge transactions is whether the tax treatment mirrors that of the risk being hedged. If it does not the risk is not properly hedged on an after tax basis.

Other bond issues

2.122 Introduction

Earlier in this chapter plain vanilla debt instruments were described. The currency and index linked bonds in the previous sections were variations on plain vanilla debt where the principal and or coupon was varied by reference to a different currency or index. This part of the chapter includes bonds where the principal and or interest is restructured or where bonds are combined with options. These instruments can be analysed into two categories.

● *Restructuring of the principal and interest cash flows.* These issues vary the structure of a plain vanilla bond where interest payments are made semi-annually or annually and the full amount of the principal is repaid at maturity. At one extreme is the zero coupon bond, when one payment is made at maturity and there are no interest payments made during the life of the issue, and at the other is the perpetual bond, where there is no repayment of principal and interest payments are made for perpetuity. Care is needed when analysing these instruments and in comparing their returns with the yield obtainable on plain vanilla debt instruments. Whereas cash flows may be described in the issue terms as principal and interest, economically the distinction can become blurred.

● *Bonds combined with options.* The options may be in the form of warrants (which are detachable and can be traded separately from the host bond) or embedded in the bond. The most common type of option to be issued with debt instruments is the option to convert into the equity of the issuer, either in the form of equity warrants, or convertible bonds. As stated in the overview, these are dealt with in chapter 4 – Equity and Equity Linked Instruments. This section describes other types of options that have been attached to bond issues.

2.123 Deep discounted bonds

Deep discounted or zero coupon bonds (ZCB) are bonds that make no periodic interest payments and are therefore sold at a large discount ('deep discount') to their nominal value. Instead of interest payments the buyer of such a bond receives as a return the difference between the purchase price and the higher redemption proceeds. There are only two cash flows which arise on a zero coupon bond, the proceeds at the date of issue (which if the bond is to be redeemed at par, will be at a substantial discount to par value) and the payment on redemption date. These cash flows can be shown as follows:

Principal at maturity

Initial Investment

Diagram 2.12: Zero coupon bond

The issue will be priced at a larger discount to par value the longer the life of the zero coupon bond. The price of the bond in the secondary market will gradually appreciate as the maturity date approaches.

Zero coupon bonds became popular in the early 1980s as issuers wished to reduce the cost of borrowing at a time of high and volatile interest rates by exploiting the wish of investors to reduce or eliminate reinvestment risk. With normal interest bearing debt, the yield or return on an instrument which is held to maturity depends upon not only the purchase price and stated interest or coupon rate, but also the ability to reinvest coupons at the same yield to maturity prevailing at the time the bond is acquired. The calculation of the yield to maturity at the time of acquisition assumes that all interest payments will be reinvested at the then yield to maturity (see section 2.12). If interest rates fall after the bond is issued, this will not be possible and the investor will suffer a reduced actual yield to maturity. With zero coupon bonds, this reinvestment risk is eliminated if the bond is held to maturity as there are no coupons to reinvest. This can be particularly attractive to investors such as pension funds and insurance companies who require certainty as to their returns to be able to fund anticipated liabilities. This elimination of reinvestment risk induced investors to pay more for the bonds which reduced issuers' financing costs.

An additional reason why zero coupon bonds became attractive was the advantageous taxation treatment in certain countries. In some cases, issuers are able to obtain a tax deduction for imputed interest charges over the life of a zero coupon bond even though the issuer makes no payment until maturity. Elsewhere, for example in Japan, investors were not taxed on imputed interest proceeds but merely on the capital gain arising on the difference between the purchase price and the proceeds received at redemption. This was attractive because capital gains were taxed at a lower rate than taxes on income, which could persuade investors to pay a premium to purchase the bond.

Many projects require funding up front, but are unlikely to give rise to an income stream to service interest costs for some period of time. A typical example would be a building project, in which substantial cash outlays would be needed for construction, whilst income either from rentals or the sale of the building would be received much later. Zero coupon bonds (or other deep discount bonds) can be useful sources of funding for such projects as they help to match cash flows.

Variations

Biennial Bond	Interest paid after two years.
Deep Discount Stepped Interest Loan Stocks	A low coupon is payable but it increases in steps every five years.
Deferred Coupon Bond	No interest is paid for the first few years (usually four) and the accrued interest is paid as a lump sum in the fifth year. These bonds were designed to be attractive to investors whose capital gains are tax free. The interest element in the first few years being treated as capital rather than income. However, a number of countries including the United Kingdom have introduced legislation to prevent such income being treated as capital.
Deferred Interest Bond	As for deferred coupon bond.
GAINS (Growth and Income Securities)	Zero coupon bonds which convert on a prescribed date into a conventional interest bearing bond. This structure allows the issuer to defer interest payments for a significant portion of the issue.

Serial Zero Coupon bonds	Bonds which do not pay interest but make a series of repayments of principal commencing a number of years after the issue was made. For example a 30 year $100 million issue made in 19X1 could make five repayments of $20 million commencing in 19Y5.
Zero Coupon Convertible	Zero coupon bonds convertible at maturity into the equity of the issuer – see convertible bonds in chapter 4 – Equity and Equity Linked Instruments.

2.124 Benefits – issuer

● Issuers may raise funds without needing an immediate income to service interest costs. The cash flow advantages are further helped by tax deductions for accrued interest or discount which are not paid until maturity.

● Investors who receive a favourable tax treatment may accept a lower effective yield.

● For a ZCB there are no annual coupons to administer and therefore paying agent fees and administration are reduced.

● Cashflow and currency management of coupons is not required for a ZCB.

2.125 Benefits – investor

● The investor in a ZCB is certain of his return if held to maturity. The actual return to maturity on a regular bond is affected by interest rate movements.

● Certainty of yield allows a ZCB to be used to hedge a future payment by locking in the cost.

● Certainty of yield may be attractive to investors in times of volatile interest rates. If interest rates drop, the ZCB investor will benefit most as the price will tend to rise more than that for normal debt.

● The investor may be able to defer recognition of taxable income to a period of lower tax rates or benefit from the cash flow advantage of later tax payments.

2.126 Risks and disadvantages – issuer

• If interest rates fall, the issuer is locked into paying a high fixed return on the bond. Although call features could be included to limit this risk this would increase the initial cost.

• The issue costs are based on nominal values which may make them expensive when compared with actual proceeds received.

2.127 Risks and disadvantages – investor

• When interest rates rise, the value of ZCBs will fall more than that of normal bonds because of the locking in of the yield to maturity. Consequently, prices tend to be far more volatile than for normal interest bearing securities.

• The risk of default by the issuer may be greater as funds must be available to pay off the entire 'interest' and principal at maturity. If a change occurs in the credit status of the issuer, the value of a ZCB is likely to fall more than that of a normal debt issue.

2.128 Accounting questions

• How should the discount be treated in the profit and loss account? Should a straight line or yield basis be used to amortise the discount?

• Should the full nominal value be treated as a liability and the discount as an asset or should the net amount be shown as a liability?

• If the net amount is included what disclosure is required in respect of the commitment to repay the nominal amount?

2.129 Taxation questions

● Will a 'bank or financial services company' be taxed on discount on an accruals basis or only on sale or maturity?

● Is there specific tax legislation in the issuer's country which relates to ZCBs (eg deep discount/deep gain legislation in the United Kingdom)?

● Will tax relief for the discount be allowed to the issuer immediately on issue, an accruals basis or on redemption?

● At what exchange rates is amortised discount in a foreign currency ZCB converted into the issuer's currency in calculating tax relief?

● At what exchange rate is the discount on a foreign currency ZCB converted into the investor's currency in calculating tax liabilities?

● Is the investor deemed to receive income on maturity of a ZCB even if the issuer is in default?

2.130 Stripped treasury certificates

Stripped treasury certificates are a type of zero coupon bond, but they are not issued directly by corporations or other entities to raise funds. They are usually created by investment banks buying blocks of long-term securities issued by a government ('treasury stocks') and separating ('stripping') the future coupon payments and principal redemption values. Usually a special purpose vehicle (SPV) is set up to carry out the stripping. Zero coupon bonds are then issued by the SPV with maturity values determined by, and secured on, the coupons and redemptions of the underlying treasury stocks. Thus a series of zero coupon bonds are created with a range of maturities matching the date of payment of coupons on the bonds and their final redemption. The treasury stocks are held in trust by a custodian bank which collects the coupons to pay off each tranche of zero coupon bonds. Although the investor does not hold securities issued by a government, the custodian arrangements ensure that the redemption of the certificate is collateralised by the treasury stock so there is minimal default risk.

There are two principal reasons why these stripped treasury issues have been successful:

● the stripping process created securities which were attractive to investors but which were not previously available;

- the first stripped treasury issues exploited a limitation in using the yield to maturity as an effective measure in valuing and comparing different bonds. The yield to maturity is a single interest rate which is applied to all the cash flows arising from a bond. This does not take account of the interest rate implied by the yield curve at the time of these cash flows. The yield curve which does take account of the current interest rate at the time of the cash flows is called the 'spot rate yield curve' (it is also known as the zero coupon yield curve or the theoretical term structure of interest rates). This yield curve plots the yield to maturity of a zero coupon bond of that maturity date. Where the yield curve is positive (that is, interest rates are rising the longer the maturity), the spot rate yield curve will rise more steeply than the conventional yield curve. This feature enabled investment banks to make a profit, by retaining the difference between the yield to maturity on the conventional treasury bullet bond and the higher yield on the stripped instruments which were priced effectively by reference to the spot rate curve. After the initial stripped treasury programmes, arbitrage removed this advantage.

Trade Names

Merrill Lynch created the first such instrument in August 1982 called TIGRs (Treasury Income Growth Receipts). Similar instruments have also been issued by other investment banks including:

CATS   – Certificates of Accrual on Treasury Securities (Salomon Brothers)

COUGRs – Certificates of Government Receipts (A.G. Becker)

LIONs   – Lehman Investment Opportunity Notes (Lehman Brothers)

ZEBRAs – Zero Coupon Eurosterling Bearer or Registered Accruing Certificates (S.G. Warburg). United Kingdom Government Gilt-edged Stocks stripped by an offshore SPV.

There are also DOGs, GATORs, EAGLEs, and STARs which all represent trademarks of the different investment banks.

The United States government has also become directly involved in the market for stripped treasury securities through a Separate Trading of Registered Interest and Principal Securities (STRIPS) programme. This programme allows the separate trading of interest and principal of designated issues to create zero coupon treasury securities which are direct obligations of the United States government. The separate trading of treasury receipts (TRs) is conducted through the book entry system operated by the Federal Reserve. By assigning the same CUSIP numbers (identification numbers issued by the Committee on Uniform Securities

Identifying Procedures) to TRs with the same maturity date, generic TRs were created from the different underlying issues of treasury securities allowing secondary market liquidity for stripped treasury certificates.

2.131 European markets

United Kingdom Government Bonds have been used on the basis of stripped treasury programmes such as the ZEBRAS referred to above. In Germany although the *Bundesbank* has opposed the issue of such zero coupon bonds, two issues have been arranged offshore, for the *Bundespost* and *Bundesbahn* respectively. These issues have been made through a trust formed in the Channel Islands, Euro DM Securities Limited. These issues were backed by *Schuldscheine*. In May 1991 the French government announced that French government bonds could be repackaged into stripped securities. Stripping will be carried out by *Sicovam*, the French stock registry centre, together with a primary dealer (see section 2.7). The stripped securities will carry a government guarantee. The securities are likely to be based on the OAT bonds which have the longest maturity dates. Some Dutch Government Bond issues have also been stripped.

2.132 Benefits – issuer

• Stripped treasury securities offer government backed stocks to investors in a different, possibly more attractive form, hence accessing a wider group of investors.

• Investment banks do not return all the stripped interest and principal to investors and therefore make a profit on these arrangements as well as commission income on secondary sales to customers.

2.133 Benefits – investor

• A low credit risk instrument useful for long-term investment by institutional investors such as pension funds where income needs to be matched with obligations over the long term.

● Stripped treasury securities are useful for hedging the 'cost' of a long term liability.

● As for zero coupon bonds in section 2.125.

2.134 Risks and disadvantages – issuer

● The issuer or SPV is required to fund the ZCB at a stated rate of return and it may be necessary to reinvest coupon receipts prior to redemption of the ZCB. In practice it may be difficult to ensure that the required reinvestment rate is achieved.

2.135 Risks and disadvantages – investor

● There has been a poor secondary market for stripped securities associated with particular investment banks.

● As for zero coupon bonds in section 2.127.

2.136 Accounting questions

● If an SPV is set up for the issue should its accounts be consolidated with those of the backing issuer?

● Should purchase of treasury securities and proceeds from stripped securities be netted off in the balance sheet of the SPV?

● How is any profit (eg. from favourable reinvestment) arising in the SPV to be treated and who bears any loss?

2.137 Taxation questions

● Is the SPV a separate entity issuing securities or a 'see through' vehicle?

● Should the investor be regarded as having a direct interest in the underlying securities?

● If the SPV is a separate entity, is it taxed as a trader or investor?

- Is a foreign SPV holding securities a non-qualifying offshore fund?
- Will the discount on an issue be taxed in the investor's hands on an accruals basis or a realisation basis?
- Will tax relief for the discount be allowed to the issuer on an accruals basis or only on redemption?
- Does redemption of the issue create a supply by the investor for VAT purposes?
- Is the VAT treatment of any supply on redemption by reference to the place of belonging of the SPV or of the issuer of the underlying securities?

2.138 Partly paid bonds

Bonds are issued with only part of the issue price payable immediately and the remainder due in one or more instalments. These bonds are particularly popular in the United Kingdom domestic and Euro sterling market. Interest is accrued only on the fraction paid up until the nominal value of the bond is fully paid. If the issue is structured correctly, the borrower can swap all of the proceeds on issue date even if only a small proportion (say 10%) is paid up. This can lead to a significant reduction in the cost of the issue.

The cash flows arising on a bond where the principal is to be paid in three equal instalments can be shown as follows:

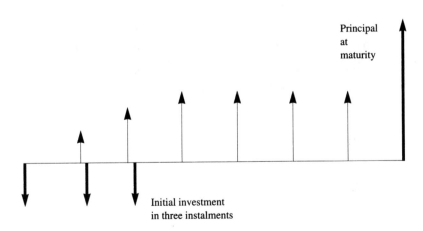

Diagram 2.13: Partly paid bonds

Variation

Deferred payment bond A bond issued in fully paid form but the payment date is deferred. This can help to reduce costs if the issue is linked to a swap.

2.139 Benefits – issuer

• Issuers hope to reduce funding costs by offering a lower coupon which will be attractive to investors who can lock in the rate on the whole of the nominal value.

2.140 Benefits – investor

• A partly paid bond initially offers the investor more leverage than a plain vanilla fixed rate bond. For a small initial investment a coupon has been locked in on the total nominal value offering the opportunity to make significant gains if interest rates fall.

2.141 Risks and disadvantages – issuer

• Issue costs will all be payable on the issue date and calculated on the nominal value which could be more than the cash received.

• If interest rates fall a high funding cost may be incurred on cash received in the future.

2.142 Risks and disadvantages – investor

• Interest rates may rise making the liability for future instalments unattractive as well as suffering losses on the original investment.

• Substantial losses may be incurred if instalments are not met.

• The secondary market is illiquid, because of the small number of outstanding issues of this type and the difficulty of comparing the return on these instruments with yields on plain vanilla securities.

2.143 Accounting questions

• What liability should be incorporated in the issuer's accounts before the bond is fully paid? Should the gross liability and a receivable be included or the net proceeds?

• As for fixed rate bonds the accounting treatment for most countries is well established and is set out in sections 2.209 to 2.244 on accounting and taxation in various countries in Europe at the end of this chapter.

2.144 Taxation questions

• See questions on fixed rate bonds in section 2.18.

2.145 Increasing rate debt

A debt instrument that initially matures in a short period (eg 90 days) but which can be extended at the issuer's option for an additional period at each maturity date until final maturity. The interest rate on the bond increases a specified amount each time the note's maturity is extended.

Variations

Extendible bonds	Bonds with a fixed redemption date at which time the investor can opt to have the bond redeemed or to hold the bond for a further period, usually at a higher coupon rate.
Stepped-up coupon puttable bonds	A hybrid between debt with warrants and extendible bonds/notes. After a specified period investors can either put the bonds back to the issuer or hold the bonds for

	a stated period with higher (stepped-up) coupons.
Retractable bonds	Bonds which pay coupons fixed for five years after which the issuer chooses the coupon rate for the next five years and the investor has the option to redeem. The issuer may also choose to redeem at the reset date.

2.146 Benefits – issuer

• The option at each redemption date increases the alternative sources of funding and the ability to achieve lower overall funding costs.

• The issuer will pay potentially a lower rate for long-term financing due to the short term feature of the instrument.

2.147 Benefits – investor

• The investor will generally receive a higher rate than normal short term securities and be protected by the increasing rate if the maturity is extended.

2.148 Risks and disadvantages – issuer

• The expected interest savings may not materialise, particularly if interest rates in general do not increase, and if short term rates are at higher levels or there is a change in the credit status of the issuer.

2.149 Risk and disadvantages – investor

• If market interest rates increase more than the scheduled increase in coupon rate a loss will result.

2.150 Accounting questions

• How should the periodic interest cost be determined?

• Should the securities be reflected as a current or long-term liability particularly if a maturity date falls just after the balance sheet date?

• If the debt is repaid at par before its expected maturity, how should any excess interest accrued be accounted for?

2.151 Taxation questions

• Is the extension of the instruments treated as a redemption of the old instrument and the issue of a new one?

• As interest rates increase will any part of the coupon be a deemed dividend or trigger any other anti-avoidance legislation?

• Is the issue capable of a life exceeding 364 days? If it is, see taxation questions on fixed rate bonds (section 2.18). If not, see taxation questions on commercial paper (section 2.37).

2.152 Annuity notes

The bond, which pays a fixed rate of interest, is structured so that the investor receives equal cash flows each year (being interest and principal) over the life of the issue. In effect the annual payments comprise an increasing amount of principal and a corresponding decreasing amount of interest.

From the issuer's point of view the bond is similar to a fixed rate bond with a sinking or purchase fund. However, the investor is assured of an annual redemption and is not relying on a possible market purchase or drawing of lots to receive an early redemption to reduce the average life.

2.153 Benefits – issuer

• The repayment of capital can be financed out of regular operating cash flows. There is no 'bullet' repayment of capital at maturity to be funded or refinanced.

● An issue of annuity notes can be linked with the issue of a zero coupon bond. The issuer has effectively issued a synthetic plain vanilla fixed rate bond, but the different issues can be targeted at specific demand from investors, enabling the overall cost of the issue to be reduced.

2.154 Benefits – investor

● These issues can be attractive to investors such as pension funds and insurance companies who need to finance regular payments to policy holders.

2.155 Risks and disadvantages – issuer

● If this issue is linked with a zero coupon bond issue, there will usually be increased costs associated with two separate issues.

2.156 Risks and disadvantages – investor

● The structure of this instrument can make it difficult to price relative to plain vanilla bond issues.

● There is no active secondary market which makes it difficult for the investor to liquidate his holding prior to maturity.

2.157 Accounting question

● How should the annual interest charge be calculated and reflected in the issuer's profit and loss account?

2.158 Taxation questions

● Is the analysis of annual repayments between principal and interest acceptable for tax purposes?

● How is any gain on the principal calculated and where and how is it taxed?

● Is there withholding tax on the principal and/or interest element of the annual repayments?

● Will the interest element in the annual repayments be tax deductible for the issuer?

2.159 High yield bonds

High yield bonds (also called junk bonds) have high interest rates and are issued by lower credit rated companies or companies with no credit rating. They will often be issued to finance the takeover of a company in a leveraged buy out ('LBO'). Typically in an LBO, the company will have positive cash flow which is used to service the high coupon on the bonds. Asset sales are identified to provide a means of repayment of the bonds. The majority of junk bond issues have been structured as plain vanilla fixed rate bonds. However, recent innovations include payment in kind ('PIK') bonds whereby interest is paid by way of additional bonds (see also Bunny bonds section 2.188) in the early part of the instruments life.

To date, junk bond issues have mostly been confined to the United States domestic market. In the United Kingdom, mezzanine debt (high yielding debt placed with institutions usually with some form of equity participation) has been used to finance takeovers and other leveraged transactions but no significant public issues have been made of high yield bonds. The development of a junk bond market in Europe has been made less likely following the number of well publicised defaults in the United States market and the consequent collapse in prices and liquidity.

2.160 Benefits – issuer

● Although these bonds pay a high coupon, this will often be lower than the rate which would be paid on bank finance, which may be the only other source of funds available to a company of this type, and the issue, because it is widely distributed, will usually raise more cash than the banks are willing to lend.

● Although the interest rate is high, the potential of the new project which the bonds will be used to finance, may be such that it is an acceptable cost.

● Call features can be included so that the debt can be redeemed out of sales of assets following restructuring of the company's operations.

2.161 Benefits – investor

● The higher than normal yield on the bonds. Research in the United States has been used to claim that, even after allowing for the higher than average defaults expected with these bonds, high yield portfolios can perform better than other fixed income portfolios as any defaults are more than compensated for by the higher coupons. However, subsequently commentators and researchers have argued that with a rising level of defaults returns are no better (and possibly considerably worse) than a portfolio of higher credit rated bonds.

2.162 Risks and disadvantages – issuer

● The projected cash flow may not materialise causing possible defaults or forced asset sales.

● Proceeds from anticipated asset sales out of which early redemption of the debt was intended to be made may not arise or may fall short of the anticipated amounts, resulting in the higher interest rates being incurred for longer than originally intended.

2.163 Risks and disadvantages – investor

● The high coupon and the highly leveraged nature of the companies issuing these bonds increases the possibility of default. In practice, investors may hold a portfolio of high yield bonds so that the potential effect of a loss on the default may be reduced and offset by the higher than normal yield on the portfolio (but see comments above).

2.164 Accounting treatment

• Sections 2.209 to 2.244 at the end of this chapter set out the accounting treatment for debt instruments in various countries in Europe which is relevant to high yield bonds.

2.165 Taxation questions

• Will any part of the coupon be a deemed dividend or will the high interest rate trigger any other anti-avoidance legislation?

• Other questions as for fixed rate bonds (section 2.18).

2.166 Perpetual bonds

Perpetual bonds are bonds which are issued with no fixed redemption date. Perpetuals paying interest at fixed rates have been issued in the past (particularly by governments – for example the British Government's War Loan issues) but most recent perpetuals have been FRNs. Perpetual FRNs have been issued principally by banks as many Central Banks have allowed these securities to rank as capital for capital adequacy purposes. In addition, they have been issued by quasi – governmental agencies (particularly in France) which are not able to issue equity but who want to strengthen their balance sheets. In December 1986 the Perpetual FRN market collapsed – the prices of most issues fell considerably and liquidity was reduced significantly. This was principally due to a glut in the market following a large number of issues of this type, and because of the perception by investors that the interest margin over LIBOR was insufficient to compensate for the risks involved in holding what is in economic terms similar to preferred equity.

Variations

Puttable perpetual FRNs	A perpetual FRN which is repayable at the option of the investor after a specified period has expired. These issues have been popular in the United States because the United States tax authorities treat non-puttable Perpetual Bonds as equity and disallow the coupon interest.
Undated Variable Rate Note	A VRN issued with no stated maturity. The remarketing process is designed to provide the investor with adequate liquidity at each auction date. See also section 2.20 on FRNs.

2.167 Valuation of Perpetuals

The theoretical fair value of a perpetual FRN is similar to a conventional FRN dealt with earlier in this chapter (section 2.21), except that the margin over LIBOR is not adjusted because the amortisation of the discount or premium takes place over an infinite period.

2.168 Benefits – issuer

• The equity-like features of the perpetual can strengthen the issuer's balance sheet.

• The issuer does not have to finance repayment of principal.

2.169 Benefits – investor

• Most perpetual FRNs pay interest at a greater margin over LIBOR than conventional FRNs.

2.170 Risks and disadvantages – issuer

• Due to the loss of confidence in the perpetual FRN market any new issues would have to pay a very high coupon to attract investors.

2.171 Risks and disadvantages – investor

• The absence of a maturity date increases the exposure to a deterioration in the credit quality of the issuer. Receipt of principal is dependent upon onward sale in the secondary market or redemption only at the issuer's option.

• The secondary market remains very illiquid.

• The exposure to the deterioration in credit quality over a potentially infinite period increases the difficulty of determining a fair price for these securities.

• For some issues, the position of the investor in the event of a liquidation of the issuer (or guarantor) is the same as the holder of a preference share (ie ranking after all other debt).

2.172 Accounting question

• How should the perpetual bonds be reflected in the balance sheet of the issuer? If they are not to be redeemed should they be included in or alongside shareholders' funds?

2.173 Taxation question

• Are the bonds treated as debt or equity? If debt see taxation questions on fixed rate bonds (section 2.18). If equity see chapter 4 – Equity and Equity Linked Instruments.

2.174 Repackaged perpetual bonds

Repackaged perpetuals (or instantly repackaged perpetuals as they are usually called) have been issued as a response to the collapse of the Perpetual FRN market. They have also been called 'Credit Enhanced Undated Floating Rates Notes' (the word 'perpetual' being avoided). These issues appear similar to perpetual FRNs but they offer the investor an arrangement whereby principal will be repaid. These issues have been structured in one of the following ways:

• a company issues undated floating rate securities which pay a LIBOR linked rate of interest for a certain number of years and then a negligible rate (0.00001%) thereafter. The company makes an immediate prepayment of interest into a trust. This prepayment is calculated as the principal value of the FRNs discounted to the interest reduction date. The prepayment is invested by trustees in zero coupon bonds (ZCBs) with a maturity value at the interest reduction date equal to the nominal value of the FRNs. The trustees grant put options to investors whereby they will repurchase the 'perpetual FRNs' from the investors at the issue price on or after the interest reduction date, if the investors exercise their put options. For example, a company issues perpetual notes with a face value of $100 million paying interest at LIBOR + 1/8% per annum for 15 years, and at 0.0001% from that date. The investors have a put option which is exercisable 15 years from the date of issue. The issuer makes an immediate payment of $20 million out of the proceeds into a trust and the trustees use these funds to purchase a $100 million zero coupon bond maturing in 15 years time. After 15 years, the investors will exercise their put option and the trustees will repay the principal out of the proceeds of the ZCB. These cash flows can be shown in the following way:

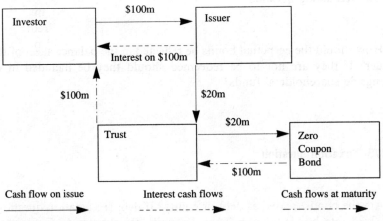

Diagram 2.14: Repackaged perpetual FRN

- alternatively the terms of the undated FRNs are identical to those above except that the interest rate is fixed significantly above the normal borrowing rate and there is no prepayment. Once again the investors have the ability to redeem the bonds on or after the interest reduction date by putting them to trustees. The extra interest margin is paid to the trustees to be invested such that they have adequate funds to redeem the 'perpetual FRNs' at the interest reduction date.

Economically the transactions described above are identical in that the issuer repays principal and pays interest. When the issuer elects to make a prepayment then the combination of the prepaid amount being no longer available to the company to invest, and the fact that interest is payable on the whole of the nominal value, means that economically the issuer repays both interest and principal over the period to the interest reduction date (as in an annuity note – section 2.152). Similar considerations apply where the rate of interest paid up to the interest reduction date is in excess of normal interest rates for the same borrower. Consequently, in substance, the instrument is debt which is repayable in instalments (annual/semi-annual etc) up to the interest reduction date.

2.175 Benefits – issuer

- In certain circumstances the apparent equity like features of these issues can be used to strengthen the issuer's balance sheet.

- In certain countries the initial payment made into the trust may be an allowable deduction against taxes on profits which can reduce the overall costs of the issue below that of a plain vanilla bond of similar effective maturity.

2.176 Benefits – investor

- Unlike the conventional perpetual FRN, the put option means that the investor is, in effect, able to redeem the issue.

- These issues may pay a higher than normal coupon.

2.177 Risks and disadvantages – issuer

• The structure of the issue means that interest is paid on the total value of the issue prices despite the fact that a proportion of the funds are paid to trustees. Therefore, the overall cost of the issue can be expensive if tax deductions for the initial payment are not available or tax legislation changes.

2.178 Risks and disadvantages – investor

• The secondary market is illiquid.

2.179 Accounting questions

• Should an element of the annual interest payment or the prepaid amount (depending on the structure) be treated as a return of principal to result in a more appropriate cost of funding?

• How should the issue be reflected on the balance sheet of the issuer? Should the issue be disclosed as a borrowing, as part of equity or alongside minority interests? What happens at the interest reduction date?

• Should the prepayment be netted from the proceeds of issue or shown as a deferred asset?

2.180 Taxation questions

• Is the prepayment tax deductible for the issuer?

• Do withholding tax rules apply to the prepayment?

• Could tax deductions be denied under 'abuse of law' or other anti-avoidance legislation?

• Other questions as for perpetual bonds (section 2.173).

118

2.181 Bonds with bond warrants

A bond is issued with a warrant attached which entitles the investor to buy more bonds of the same issue or a new issue. The warrants can usually be exercised after a span of two years.

Bonds with bond warrants usually take the form of a fixed rate bond with immediately detachable warrants (although floating rate notes with immediately detachable warrants have also been issued). The bond warrant usually entitles the warrant holder to purchase a bond of a lower coupon than that of the original issue. To limit the potential outstanding debt of the issuer, warrants may be issued which permit either the call of an equal amount of the existing issue (harmless warrants) or the issue of new bonds only when the existing bonds are surrendered with the warrant (wedding warrants). Thus there is no increase in the total outstanding debt following conversion of the warrants. For further details of warrants see chapter 5 – Hedging Instruments. For bonds with equity warrants see chapter 4 – Equity and Equity Linked Instruments.

2.182 Benefits – issuer

• The warrant provides the investor with a 'sweetener', and therefore he should be prepared to expect a lower coupon, reducing the cost of the issue.

• The premium payable for the warrant is received by the issuer at the inception of the issue.

2.183 Benefits – investor

• The warrant offers the investor a considerable degree of leverage because a relatively small investment in the warrant can lead to a large potential profit if market interest rates move favourably.

2.184 Risks and disadvantages – issuer

• The issuer may face an increase in outstanding debt.

• The premium received on issue due to the warrant feature may be less than the cost of any new debt if market rates fall more than expected.

2.185 Disadvantages and risks – investor

• The warrant may expire worthless if interest rates do not move as expected.

• With harmless warrants, while the exercise or onward sale may result in a profit, the original debt may be called, leading to a reduction in coupon income.

• The exercise of a wedding warrant will lead to the investor owning a bond with a lower coupon.

2.186 Accounting questions

Issuer

• Is part of the issue price relating to the warrant a liability/ deferred credit to be used to match an increased interest cost in future periods? How is this portion of the issue price determined?

• How and when is credit taken for the portion of the issue price relating to the warrant? Can all the credit be taken if the warrants become worthless due to a rise in interest rates?

• Should the amount attributable to the warrant be taken through the profit and loss account or directly to reserves? Is it a distributable profit?

• If the amount attributable to the warrant is recognised in the profit and loss account should it be spread or taken as a lump sum?

• Should the income statement reflect the full normal interest cost for a similar issue to provide an amount to offset any increased cost if interest rates fall below those of the bond into which the warrant can be exercised?

• How are contingencies in respect of the exercise of the warrant treated and disclosed in the financial statements?

Investor

- How are the warrants to be valued in the accounts? Should they be marked to market or the cost amortised over the remaining life?
- If ex-warrant bonds are held which may be called at a fixed price by the issuer when warrants are exercised how should they be valued?

2.187 Taxation questions

- Is any price payable for the warrant taxable on the issuer (eg as if it was an option) and, if so when is any tax due and payable?
- Does expiry of the warrant give the investor a capital loss?
- Does attribution of part of the issue price to the warrant bring the bond within any special deep discount rules?

2.188 Bunny bonds

A bunny bond (or multiplier) is a fixed rate bond which permits investors to reinvest the interest income into bonds with the same terms and conditions as the host bond. Economically, if interest rates fall, the bunny bond behaves like a zero coupon bond. This is because reinvestment risk is eliminated – the investor will exercise his option to subscribe for the additional bonds as they are yielding above market rates. If interest rates rise, the issue will behave like a plain vanilla fixed rate bond (because investors will not exercise their options and will receive coupons in the normal way).

Variation

Pay in kind debenture (PIK)	A bond in which interest is paid in additional PIK debentures in the initial years and thereafter in cash. The additional bonds are known as baby bonds.

2.189 Benefits – issuer

- The reinvestment feature can be attractive to investors so the issuer can pay a lower coupon.

- If investors choose to reinvest the interest payment, this will have a beneficial effect on the issuer's cash flow.

2.190 Benefits – investor

- The option to reinvest interest at the original yield can be attractive to long term investors such as pension funds, who wish to avoid the risk of reinvesting interest at lower yields which can make it difficult for them to meet future commitments.

2.191 Risks and disadvantages – issuer

- If interest rates fall, the issuer may have to issue additional debt at above market rates, because investors would choose to reinvest interest income in the bond. This not only increases the interest charge above market rates but also the amount of outstanding debt on which the interest arises.

2.192 Risks and disadvantages – investor

- If interest rates rise, a bunny bond will probably lose its value more quickly than a plain vanilla fixed bond because the option to reinvest will be out of the money and therefore will not compensate the investor for the low coupon.

2.193 Accounting question

- For both issuers and investors, how is the interest to be accounted for? If the interest is reinvested in the bonds, then does part of the redemption proceeds (as with the zero coupon bond) represent rolled-up interest?

2.194 Tax questions

● Could new bonds issued constitute a deemed dividend?

● Will the investor be subject to income tax on the full value of bonds issued, even if that exceeds the nominal amount of interest due?

● If withholding tax is required on the bonds issued instead of coupons, how is it satisfied?

2.195 Flip flop notes

A flip flop note is a bond which gives the investor the option to convert into another type of debt instrument and to reconvert back to the original bond at some later date. The option can change the maturity of the issue and the interest rate profile. For example, a floating rate note may give investors the option to convert to a short term note, an intermediate fixed rate bond or perpetual notes and then back to the FRN. This structure has most commonly been used with perpetuals as it gives the investor an option to redeem the security.

The cash flows arising on a flip flop note with this structure would be as follows:

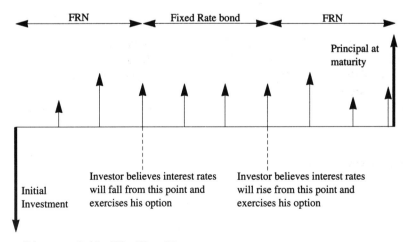

Diagram 2.15: Flip Flop Notes

Debt instruments

2.196 Benefits – issuer

● The conversion option can persuade investors to accept lower interest rates and thus reduce the cost to the issuer.

2.197 Benefits – investor

● The conversion feature increases the investor's options in the event of movements in interest rates.

2.198 Risks and disadvantages – issuer

● There is uncertainty as to maturity dates and interest rates.

2.199 Risks and disadvantages – investor

● The lower interest rate accepted may not be offset by the benefit of the conversion features.

2.200 Accounting question

● Should the debt be classified as short or long term in the accounts of the issuer?

2.201 Taxation questions

● Is the exchange treated as a redemption of the old instrument and the issue of a new one?

- Does conversion trigger receipt/payment of accrued interest?

- Other questions as for fixed rate bonds (section 2.18).

2.202 Bonds with put options

Bonds are issued whereby the borrower grants the investor an option to sell the bonds back to the issuer (a put option) at a fixed price at a fixed future date or dates. Such put are usually combined with a conversion feature ('Premium Put Convertibles' – see chapter 4 – Equity and Equity Linked Instruments). The effect of the put can be seen in the following cashflow diagram:

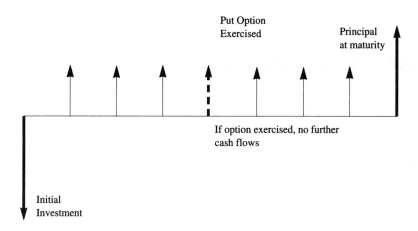

Diagram 2.16: Bonds with put options

2.203 Benefit – issuer

- The addition of a put can reduce the costs of the issue as the investor may accept lower interest rates because he has the option to sell back at a predetermined price.

2.204 Benefit – investor

• The put option offers protection for the investor if interest rates move adversely. If rates increase after the bond is issued, it can be sold back and the proceeds reinvested at current market rates.

2.205 Risk and disadvantage – issuer

• If interest rates increase and the put is exercised, the issuer may have to issue another bond to redeem the existing bond (and to continue to fund his operations). As the new issue will have to be at the new (higher) market rate, funding costs in the long term will increase.

2.206 Risks and disadvantages – investor

• If the exercise of the put is uneconomical, investors have given up some yield which in other circumstances would have been available.

• The issuer may be forced to redeem the bond earlier than its stated maturity, consequently the credit status of the issuer (and particularly the ability to generate cash) will be particularly important with this type of issue.

2.207 Accounting questions

• How is the put option accounted for? Should a liability be created in the issuer's accounts and if so how is it calculated? For the investor should any value be attributed to the put option?

• If the option is not exercised how is the release of any provision made by the issuer treated?

• For the investor does any amount attributed to the option form part of the acquisition cost of the new bond or is it an expense?

2.208 Taxation questions

- Is any price payable for the option taxable on the issuer?

- When is any such tax due and if the put option is not exercised can it be recovered?

- Does expiry of the put option give investors a taxable loss?

- How should the exercise of the option be dealt with for tax purposes?

- Does a payment for the option bring the bond within any special deep discount rules?

- Other questions as for fixed rate bonds (section 2.18).

Debt instruments—country accounting and taxation

United Kingdom

2.209 Accounting treatment

The Companies Act 1985 ('CA 1985') and other United Kingdom GAAP requirements for an issuer of bonds are as follows:

- the outstanding par value of the bonds should be included on the balance sheet in creditors, split between amounts payable within one year and after more than one year;

- there must be a separate analysis of creditors due after one year between:

– amounts payable other than by instalments and falling due after the end of five years from the balance sheet date; or

– amounts payable by instalments any of which fall due for payment after five years, in which case the aggregate amount falling due after five years must also be shown.

This requirement is particularly relevant to bonds with sinking or purchase fund provisions.

- the terms of repayment and interest rates for each type of bond (ie each issue) must be disclosed in a note to the accounts unless, in the opinion of the directors, this statement would be excessively long, in which case a general indication of repayment terms and interest rates will suffice;

● if any bonds are secured on the assets of the company, the aggregate amount secured and a general indication of the nature of the security must be disclosed in a note to the accounts;

● foreign currency issues will have to be translated at closing rates of exchange, with exchange differences normally being taken to the profit and loss account. Statement of Standard Accounting Practice 20 prescribes the treatment of any translation differences which, in certain circumstances, may be offset by translation differences on long term investments and taken directly to reserves;

● interest payable (gross) must be disclosed separately in the profit and loss account analysing interest, usually in a note to the accounts, between that payable on:

– loans not repayable by instalments and due for repayment within five years;

– loans repayable by instalments the last of which falls due within five years;

– loans of any other kind.

Companies listed on The Stock Exchange are required to provide a more detailed analysis.

● the expenses of, and commission paid on, an issue should be written off immediately;

● CA 1985 (section 130) permits the expenses of, the commission paid or discount allowed on the issue of debentures (the term used by the CA 1985 for a written acknowledgement of a loan, which includes a bond) to be applied against the share premium account. However, it is generally considered that the application directly to share premium is not intended to include the large discounts on zero coupon and other deep discounted issues. These instruments and other instances where the discount is essentially a yield adjustment are discussed further below (see deep discounted bonds). CA 1985 does not allow the expenses of any commission on any issue of shares or debentures to be treated as an asset;

● if a company issues debentures, then it must disclose in a note to the accounts:

– the reason for making the issue;

– the classes of debentures issued;

– for each class, the amount issued and the consideration received for the issue;

• profits or losses on retirement of bonds should be reflected in the profit and loss account immediately.

Variable rates of interest

TR 677 (see chapter 6 for details of the status of technical releases which provide guidance and are not mandatory) considers that where a bond is issued with a variable rate of interest (eg interest linked to retail price index or LIBOR), and the reference period used to calculate the interest payable is not materially different from the reporting period, the interest payable is a fair charge against the profits for the period, as the accounts should reflect external events outside management's control which have an impact on the enterprise and occur in the reporting period.

Currency and index linked bonds

The most important accounting issue concerning such instruments is how to account for the future cash flows arising from the bond (both principal and interest). As the amounts payable are linked to a variable index, the ultimate liability will be uncertain at any reporting date prior to payment or maturity. TR 677 states that where the amount of principal to be repaid is adjusted by an index, an annual charge should be made if the movement in the index during the period would increase the liability of the enterprise; if that rate was to prevail at the maturity of the instrument. The technical release states that the charge should be calculated from the movement in the relevant index during the year even if the liability to repay has not yet arisen. However, the technical release does not provide detailed guidance on two questions which arise when this approach is adopted:

• while it would be normal to use the movement in the index during the year it is possible that an adjustment to reflect the movement in the index concerned during the year (such as inflation measured by the RPI) may not be appropriate (for example if there is an upper limit or the movement in the index is out of line with expectation). It may be more appropriate for a proportion of the estimated total movement in the index to maturity to be written off each year. This would require an estimate based on actual movements to date together with likely future movements, and a computation of the effective rate of interest over the life of the instrument which would be implied by this estimate. The charge for the year would then be calculated by reference to this effective rate of interest as described below in the treatment of bond issues with non-standard cash flows;

• if the movement in the index is favourable to the issuer, and would lead to a reduction in the liability if that rate prevailed at maturity, should the benefit be anticipated and reflected in the profit and loss account through a reduction in the effective interest rate? This would probably be appropriate only if the risk that the trend in the movement of the index would significantly reverse again prior to maturity, was considered to be remote.

TR 677 addresses only accounting questions arising for issuers rather than investors in these instruments. However, the accounting treatment to be adopted by investors would appear to be less problematical; the probable overall gain or loss on the instruments should be assessed at each reporting date, and whether or not this should be recognised will depend on the individual enterprise's reason for the holding investment and its accounting policy.

Bond issues with non-standard cash flows

Many of the variations from the plain vanilla bond structure discussed in this chapter involve a restructuring of the cash flows arising from the bond and varying relationship between interest and principal. Two of the general principles which TR 677 seeks to establish as applicable when accounting for complex capital issues concern the accounting for such issues:

● where the cost of repaying debt exceeds the proceeds of the issue the difference should be charged against profits on a systematic basis over the life of the instrument;

● the total charge to the profit and loss account in any particular year in respect of a debt issue should be based on an effective annual rate throughout the whole period of the loan. In practice this would involve making a charge against profit based on the yield to maturity of the instrument and not directly based on the cash flows which arise in a particular year. This calculation may involve making estimates of future events.

TR 677 illustrates the application of these principles with respect to two types of instrument:

● Stepped bonds (Increasing Rate Debt);

● Deep discounted bonds.

Increasing Rate Debt

TR 677 states that it is not appropriate for earlier years to benefit from the lower rate of interest and the effective rate over the life of the instrument should be charged against profit. This approach has not been accepted by certain industries, for example investment trusts which have made these types of issues. The Association of Investment Trust

Companies has argued that the use of an effective annual rate of interest would not be appropriate for an investment trust as the income derived from the issue proceeds will increase over the period of the investment, and charging interest on a 'stepped' basis against profit will serve to match income and expense. TR 677 would permit departure from the principle of charging an effective annual rate of interest if there are good economic reasons for a different approach to be adopted. It is doubtful if this special pleading falls within the good economic reasons.

Deep discount bonds

In substance the discount is 'rolled up' interest and should be charged against profit each year on an appropriate basis, and described in the accounts of the company as interest payable.

Two other issues discussed in TR 677 which arise in the United Kingdom with deep discount bonds (and particular zero coupon bonds) are as follows:

• some companies have taken advantage of section 130 of CA 1985 to write off the discount directly to the share premium account. TR 677 states that this is not appropriate and that the discount (interest) should be charged through the profit and loss account to show a true and fair view. The technical release does allow, however, that a transfer between share premium account and distributable reserves could subsequently be made after the discount has been charged through the profit and loss account in the first instance;

• CA 1985 requires that assets and liabilities should not be offset, and also allows the discount on a debt issue to be shown as an asset. TR 677 states that if the loan can be repaid early at less than par it is preferable for the liability under a zero coupon issue to be shown net (ie the gross redemption value less the unamortised discount). If the terms of the issue are that the issue is repayable at par (either at the end of a set period or, in specific circumstances, on an earlier date) it would be appropriate to show the liability at par and the unamortised discount as an asset.

2.210 Taxation treatment

Interest on debt instruments will be allowable normally as a deduction on a paid basis regardless of the accounting treatment (unless paid to a United Kingdom bank or a United Kingdom branch of a foreign bank in which case the accruals basis applies). Where interest is index linked (for example index linked bonds) these rules apply to the total interest payable or paid including indexation.

Discount is allowable as a deduction on an accruals basis if incurred wholly and exclusively for trade purposes. Discounts not so deductible may be allowable as a deduction from total profits (as a charge on income) if they qualify under the deep discount legislation. To qualify the bond must be:

• issued by a company;

• issued after 13 March 1984;

• issued at a discount of more than 1/2% for each complete year of the security's life.

The company obtains a deduction as a charge on income for the income elements in each income period ending in an accounting period (the income element is calculated according to a formula provided in the legislation). Zero coupon bonds will automatically fall within the deep discount legislation.

Bonds which do not fall within the statutory definition of a deep discount security because they incorporate variable features (for example a floating rate coupon or uncertain redemption proceeds) may be caught by the 'deep gain' rules. Under these rules all the profit from a transaction (including any related foreign exchange gain) is taxed as income in the hands of the investor. In addition the issuer is usually unable to obtain a tax deduction for any premium paid on redemption. However, index linked and convertible securities are not caught by the new rules. The characteristics of a 'qualifying indexed security' and a 'qualifying convertible security' are complex requiring the security to meet a number of tests as regards the issue date, listing particulars and other terms of issue. The new rules, introduced in 1990 are considerably more restrictive than appeared to be promised by the government in June 1989 and may make certain types of convertible bonds (eg premium puts) uneconomic to a UK issuer.

Withholding tax of 25% will generally apply to payments of yearly interest on debt instruments unless payable on quoted Eurobonds or where prior authority is obtained to pay gross under the terms of a relevant double taxation treaty. Whilst withholding tax may apply to interest there is no withholding tax on discounts. The incidental costs of raising debt finance may be deducted as a trading expense, or as a management expense of an investment company, when paid, if the interest on the debt finance raised is an allowable deduction either in calculating trading profits or from the company's total profits.

If debt instruments are denominated in foreign currency the treatment of exchange gains and losses on them gives rise to a number of complications. The main problem is that a United Kingdom company cannot obtain tax relief for an exchange loss arising on a foreign currency borrowing which is considered to be capital in nature. In March 1989, a consultative document was issued by the United Kingdom Inland Revenue on the tax treatment of exchange gains and losses which examined the scope for comprehensive legislative reform and also identified a number of areas where businesses have found particular difficulties. A second Inland Revenue consultative document was issued in March 1991 taking the consultative process one stage further by setting out proposals for legislation which would greatly reduce the difference between trading and non-trading treatment of foreign currency transactions. One of the key features of the proposals is that tax relief would be provided for all exchange gains and losses on foreign currency borrowing and lending (and taxation of corresponding gains). Foreign currency financial instruments such as forward contracts, currency options and currency swaps would also be brought into the scheme. It does seem that the government now intend to legislate in this complex area to remove some, at least, of the anomalies which exist under the current tax law.

Channel Islands

2.211 Accounting treatment

The accounting treatment follows closely best practice adopted in the United Kingdom.

2.212 Taxation treatment

Resident companies

A Jersey company obtains relief at the time of payment of interest by deducting tax at 20% therefrom regardless of the residence status of the lender. No further Jersey tax is due by the lender. Guernsey rules are similar except that interest is paid gross to Guernsey residents.

In the case of a debt instrument issued by a Jersey or Guernsey bank interest is paid gross and relief is obtained on an accruals basis. Non resident lenders are concessionally exempt from Jersey tax and statutorily exempt from Guernsey tax in respect of interest paid by a bank.

There is no specific legislation dealing with discounts. The tax authorities take the view that tax relief is not available to the borrower in respect of any discount granted on issue or premium paid on redemption. The authorities will however seek to tax the lender directly on the discount/premium received.

Exchange gains or losses in relation to loans and other debt instruments will normally be treated as capital items, although in appropriate circumstances the tax authorities will accede to a request to treat exchange differences on a revenue basis.

The expenses in connection with the issue of debt instruments are not allowable except in the case of a bank where the issue forms part of its normal business activities.

Non-resident companies – ('Exempt' companies)
Exempt companies are treated as non-resident for tax purposes and are exempt from local income tax except in certain very limited circumstances. Interest on loans is paid gross and is exempt from Jersey/Guernsey tax in the hands of a non-resident lender. Discounts/premiums are similarly exempt.

Isle of Man

2.213 Accounting treatment

● The accounting treatment follows closely best practice adopted elsewhere in the United Kingdom.

2.214 Taxation treatment

● Interest is allowed as a deduction when accrued and there is no difference between the tax treatment of interest and discount.

● The general rate of withholding tax on interest is 20% when paid to non-residents. There are no double taxation agreements covering interest paid.

● All fees for raising finance are not tax deductible.

• Exchange gains and losses are only taken into account where a trading company incurs gains/losses on circulating (rather than fixed) capital.

Republic of Ireland

2.215 Accounting treatment

The legislative framework for accounting for debt instruments in the Republic of Ireland are the Companies Act 1963 and the Companies Amendment Act 1986. The provisions of these Acts mirror closely the UK Companies Act 1985. The guidance issued by the English Institute of Chartered Accountants in the form of TR 677 is not mandatory in Ireland but is indicative of best practice. The accounting treatment in Ireland is in line with that set out in the United Kingdom section (the Companies Acts references are obviously different). In addition, particulars of redeemed debentures which the company has the power to reissue must be provided. Unlike the UK there is no need to disclose the reason for making an issue of debentures.

2.216 Taxation treatment

• Interest payable is allowable for tax purposes in one of two ways depending on how the borrowings are used. Interest on borrowings used for business purposes is allowable on an accruals basis. Otherwise interest may be allowed, subject to certain conditions, on a paid basis.

• Interest which is treated as a distribution is not tax deductible. Interest categorised in this way includes interest related to the borrowing company's profitability, interest in excess of a commercial rate, and interest paid to a non-resident 75% parent or fellow subsidiary. An international financial services company paying interest to an affiliate resident in a tax treaty country may elect to have the interest treated as not being a distribution.

• Borrowings of companies eligible for the 10% corporation tax rate are frequently structured as 'Section 84' loans so as to render the interest payable a distribution. This results in cheap borrowing due to the fact that distributions are tax exempt to the lending bank. Foreign banks may also benefit by setting up an Irish subsidiary as a Section 84 lender. Recent legislation has, however, restricted the scope of Section 84 lending for Irish banks.

● The general rate of withholding tax on interest is 30% subject to reduction under the terms of any double taxation agreement where interest is paid to a non-resident. Interest paid abroad by Shannon companies and international financial services companies is not subject to withholding tax.

● There are no specific provisions dealing with fees incurred for raising finance. Fees incurred in raising fixed capital are regarded as capital expenditure and are not allowable for tax purposes. Fees incurred in raising finance other than fixed capital (ie working capital) are regarded as a trading expense and are allowable when accrued in the accounts.

France

2.217 Accounting treatment

The accounting treatment for most debt instruments is set out in the New Accounting Chart (1981), statements of the accounting bodies and *Commission des Operations de Bourse* recommendations.

The key requirements are as follows:

● outstanding debt issues are included in a specific caption on the balance sheet, analysed between long and short term debt and interest payable. Characteristics (such as maturity, guarantees, analysis by maturity, interest rates) are described in a note to the accounts;

● debt issues are recorded at their repayment value at maturity. Premiums and discounts are recorded on balance sheet as separate debtors or creditors and are amortised over the life of the debt;

● debt issued in foreign currencies (or repayable in foreign currencies) are converted at each balance sheet date at the closing exchange rate. The revaluation is recorded on the asset or liability side of the balance sheet as a 'conversion difference account' and a provision is established in the case of a non-hedged loss;

● the issue costs may be immediately written off or amortised over the life of the debt.

Debt with debt warrants (*OBSO*)

• Upon issue, warrants are recorded as deferred income.

• Specific information on warrant characteristics is given in the notes to financial statements (issuance amounts, number of warrants).

• If warrants are exercised, income is spread over the life of the debt.

• At the redemption date, income resulting from warrants which have not been exercised is recorded in the income statement.

Debt with stock (*equity*) *warrants* (*OBSA*)

• On issue, warrants are not recorded.

• Specific information on warrants is included in notes to financial statements, explaining the warrants' characteristics and the potential capital increase.

2.218 Taxation treatment

• Interest is allowed as a deduction on an accruals basis, and not on a cash or paid basis.

• No clear definition of discount exists for tax purposes but a discount is only likely to be taxable if it falls within a category of ordinary commercial income, eg discount on a letter of credit.

• Special rules exist for premiums paid in connection with bond issuance which allows a tax deduction to be spread over the term of the bond.

• Since June 1987 the general rate of domestic withholding tax on interest is 45% but there is no withholding tax on interest on finance obtained from outside France.

• If borrowings are denominated in a foreign currency, realised gains or losses will be taxed or allowed as they arise. In addition, unrealised translation gains and losses are brought into account at the end of each financial year in determining taxable profits.

• The cost of raising funds, including commissions and underwriting fees, may be taken into account in determining taxable profits either on a cash basis or capitalised and depreciated over a maximum period of five years.

Luxembourg

2.219 Accounting treatment

● The disclosure requirements and accounting treatment for issues of plain vanilla bonds are similar to the United Kingdom, except for the treatment of expenses and commissions which can be treated as an asset and amortised over the life of the bond.

● Investors in debt instruments are required to carry their holdings in the balance sheet at the lower of cost or market value. This applies both to banks and other corporates. Investment Funds are required to carry investments at market value.

2.220 Taxation treatment

● Interest payable is deductible for tax purposes on an accrual basis and discount is similarly treated.

● There is no withholding tax on interest paid from Luxembourg.

● Expenses of raising finance are usually deductible on a paid basis but an immediate payment of a disproportionate amount of fees may lead to the tax administration enforcing amortisation over the life of the debt.

● Exchange gains and losses are taxable as well as capital gains and losses.

● Unrealised gains are not taxable.

Belgium

2.221 Accounting treatment

The accounting treatment for debt instruments is covered by the provisions of the Royal Decree of 1976 and the guidelines issued by the Commission on Accounting Standards. In general, when new debt instruments require by virtue of their terms and conditions specific accounting treatment, generally accepted practice in countries more familiar with the type of debt instrument is adopted provided the basic accounting postulates required by law, which are set out below, are followed.

- The amount of debt outstanding is shown split between that due in less and more than one year.

- Debt issues in foreign currencies are converted at closing rates of exchange. Exchange gains or losses are usually charged to income but gains may be deferred in accordance with prudence concept.

- When capitalised, issue costs are written off over a period which should not exceed the life of the debt.

- Premiums or discounts are written off over the life of the related debt instrument.

- Long term interest free (or low interest) debt is shown at face value except when used to acquire fixed assets when the related discount is deducted from the acquisition cost and is amortised over the life of the loan.

- Loans are disclosed in the notes to the accounts and classified on the basis of the remaining maturities being less than one year, between one to five years and over five years.

2.222 Taxation treatment

- Interest payable on debt is tax deductible on an accruals basis. In principle, interest is subject to the standard rate of withholding tax of 10% for loan agreements concluded after 1 March 1990 (and prior to that date 25%). Among other exceptions to this rule, no withholding tax arises on a loan not represented by a security, to resident lenders or to non-resident lenders having an establishment in Belgium. The withholding tax can be deferred if accrual is made by provision for interest and not by direct credit to the lender's account. For Belgian resident companies, Belgian withholding tax may be offset against the income tax liability and any excess reimbursed.

- Interest paid in the form of discount is accrued rateably over the life of the instrument and withholding tax is normally due at the time of loan repayment. If the debt is sold before maturity the withholding tax will be due on the interest accrued.

- Exchange gains are, in principle, taxable only when realised and the rollover of an existing loan is not considered in itself a realisation.

Exchange losses are tax deductible when realised and can also be deductible when they are written off if unrealised.

● Fees for raising finance are tax deductible when accrued. They can also be amortised over a maximum of five years or the life of the bonds.

The Netherlands

2.223 Accounting treatment

The accounting treatment for debt issues is set out in Title 9 of Book 2 of the Dutch Civil Code and in the guidelines for annual reporting issued by the Council for Annual Reporting. In general the requirements are:

● outstanding debt is included in a specific caption on the balance sheet analysed between long term (maturing after more than one year) and short term debt;

● disclosures such as maturity, guarantees and interest rates are included in the notes to the accounts as well as the amount of debt repayable after more than five years;

● outstanding debt is usually included at amortised value whereby the difference between issue price and redemption value is taken to income over the term of the debt;

● issue costs are usually written off immediately;

● foreign currency debt issues are translated at closing rates of exchange, with exchange differences being taken to the profit and loss account. However, unrealised gains on long term debt are deferred.

Currency linked and index linked issues

In The Netherlands there is no detailed guidance for the reporting of these instruments. In addition to the general guidelines noted above the following applies to index linked bonds:

● the movement of the index during the year will in general be recognised in the profit and loss account, unless it is more appropriate to amortise the movement over the remaining term or to account for it through reserves;

● details of the issue including interest and repayment schedules as well as the index on which the ultimate liability is dependent will have to be disclosed by the issuer in the accounts.

2.224 Taxation treatment

• Interest is deductible on an accruals basis. Differences between the face value of a loan and the actual cash received should be expensed over the life of the loan. If a Dutch company lends at a discount, the amount of discount should be recognised as income on an accruals basis.

• Fees for raising finance should be capitalised and amortised over the life of the loan. Expenses incurred in financing the acquisition of foreign participations are not deductible if the participation is exempted from corporation tax.

• Realised and unrealised exchange gains or losses are taxable/tax deductible as ordinary income. However, long term unrealised exchange gains can be deferred until actually realised.

• The Netherlands does not levy any withholding tax on interest payments.

• In The Netherlands it is important to ensure that a debt instrument is not treated as equity under tax law. Four basic characteristics may be identified to help distinguish debt from equity:

– the manner and extent to which the investor shares in profits and losses of the issuer, with the sharing of possible losses being a crucial criterion;

– whether income on the instrument depends on profit;

– the life of the instrument. If an issue has a very long life or if repayment terms are not stated the instrument could be regarded as equity;

– control over the company. In certain circumstances, eg thin capitalisation, a loan from a shareholder could be considered as equity for fiscal purposes.

Germany

2.225 Accounting treatment

• Bonds are carried in accordance with the German Commercial Code as a separate balance sheet item '*Anleihen*' (bonds) at their redemption amount. *Anleihen* includes long term liabilities obtained on the public capital market in the form of:

- bonds;

- convertible bonds;

- bonds with warrants attached;

- participating bonds;

- profit participation certificates.

• Profit participation certificates can be similar to equity capital and then are normally carried as a separate balance sheet item 'Profit Participation Capital'. Details have to be provided concerning the nature and number both of existing profit participation rights as well as those which have been issued during the fiscal year of the company.

• In the case of '*Aktiengesellschaften*' (public limited companies) there is a legal obligation to provide information concerning conditions attaching to convertible bonds or subscription rights. The nominal value of such bonds or rights must be carried in the balance sheet.

• Liabilities due within one year and those due after more than five years have to be shown in the balance sheet and in the notes to the financial statements respectively. For both items the maturities can be shown in a breakdown of liabilities either in the balance sheet or in the notes to the financial statements.

• The total liabilities which are secured by means of liens and similar rights also have to be shown in the notes to the financial statements according to type and form of security.

• Foreign currency liabilities are valued at the greater of the value on the date of the transaction or the exchange rate effective at the balance sheet date. This is a result of the obligation to value liabilities in accordance with the prudence principle.

• If the redemption amount of a bond is higher than the issue price, the difference (discount) is carried on the asset side of the balance sheet (compulsory for tax purposes) under prepaid expenses. If the reverse is the case and the redemption amount of a bond is lower than the issue price, the difference (premium) is to be carried on the liabilities side of the balance sheet under deferred charges and amortised over the life of the bond.

• The premium on the issue of convertible bonds and bonds with warrants attached is included in a capital reserve. For example, if a bond with warrants, is issued at par value and because of the warrants carries a rate of interest lower than the market rate, the amount paid by the purchaser for the receipt of the warrants should be included in the capital reserve and is not to be treated as income.

• The inclusion of redemption value in the balance sheet causes a problem in cases where zero coupon bonds ('*Null-Coupon-Anleihen*') are involved. According to a statement made in 1986 by the *Institut der Wirtschaftsprüefer* zero coupon bonds are to be carried in the balance sheet of the issuer at the amount equivalent to that owed to the bond creditor as at the balance sheet date. The interest charge in each period is added to the issue price so that at maturity the zero coupon bond will be shown at its full redemption amount.

2.226 Taxation treatment

• Interest may be deducted as accrued. Annual interest paid can be deducted immediately as a business expense in the year of payment.

• For trade income tax purposes, the interest on borrowings can be deducted only as to half the amount.

• Generally, a discount cannot be deducted immediately in full as a business expense, but can be spread rateably over the terms of the loan.

• Withholding tax of 25% applies to interest on convertible bonds subject to reduction under the terms of any relevant tax treaty.

• Exchange gains form part of taxable income assessable upon realisation. However, a reserve must be set up for unrealised expected exchange losses.

• Fees paid to third parties for raising finance are tax deductible at the time of payment.

Switzerland

2.227 Accounting treatment

Issuers

Bonds – General

• The Swiss Code of Obligations requires that bonds issued by a company have to be recorded under liabilities as a separate heading at the full amount repayable. A discount ('*disagio*') may be treated as an asset but has to be amortised by annual depreciation prior to the maturity date.

● A premium ('*agio*') may be used to offset the cost of the bond issue. Any excess amount can be accrued and released to income over the period of the bond issue.

● It is recommended that interest rates, maturity and the amount due within one year be disclosed by way of note to the accounts.

● If the issue conditions allow, repurchased bonds can be cancelled and accordingly the liability in the balance sheet reduced. Any profits on bonds repurchased at a value below the repayment value can be taken to income if the bond liability is reduced or if the bonds on hand are shown under deferred or other assets.

Zero coupon bonds

● As noted above the law requires the redemption amount to be included as a liability. It therefore follows that the discount is an asset which is amortised (interest expense) over the life of the bond. Amortisation can be on a straight line method but a better method is to use a compound interest formula.

Extendible bonds

● The interest charge should be determined on a prudent basis. It might be appropriate to spread the total maximum interest charge evenly over the original term before extension. However, the treatment will depend on the terms of the issue.

Investor

● Quoted bonds can, but need not be, valued at market prices; if not they are valued at the lower of cost and market value. Unquoted bonds have to be valued in accordance with the principle of prudence at the lower of cost and estimated realisable value.

● Long term investments are to be valued at cost less, where appropriate, provision for a permanent diminution in value.

2.228 Taxation treatment

General

As explained in chapter 6 – Country Accounting and Taxation Framework, the taxation treatment follows in general the accounting treatment.

Issuer

• Issue expenses are tax deductible expenses.

• Interest expense (including accrued interest) is always a tax deductible expense.

• Exchange gains and losses are considered a taxable income or a taxable expense as the case may be.

• Also any premium or discount is taxable income or expense.

Investor

• It should be noted that even though traded bonds can be valued at market rates there is no requirement to do so if cost is lower. For tax purposes a valuation at the lower of cost or adjusted cost value is possible.

• Profits or losses on securities and exchange gains or losses are treated as regular income or expense if the investor is a corporation. Interest can be accounted for on a cash or accruals basis.

• For transactions between related parties it is required that the coupon rate is determined at arm's length basis.

Zero coupon bond

• Special tax questions arise in the case of a zero coupon bond. The discount is considered to be interest, however, the treatment for federal and state taxes can vary depending on the state. For federal tax purposes the interest becomes due only at maturity and any profits realised by intermediary holders is considered a capital gain (this distinction is important only for individuals). Consequently the Swiss withholding tax of 35% paid by the issuer and deducted from the gross interest paid is to be recouped by the holder at maturity. This treatment means that a stripped instrument is from a tax point of view favoured by certain investors. The canton of Zurich, for example, has a different treatment. The interest component during any holding period is taxed as such in the respective period if the bond is sold. Tax practice accepts that a corporation keeps a zero coupon bond at cost in its books until maturity.

Austria

2.229 Accounting treatment

Issuer

• According to Austrian legal regulations bonds issued by a company have to be carried in the balance sheet of the issuer under long term liabilities as a separate heading. Bonds have to be recorded at the full amount repayable.

• A discount (*'disagio'*) has to be treated as an asset under prepaid expenses and amortised over the life of the bond.

• A premium (*'agio'*) on issue of bonds is taken to a capital reserve and is not treated as income.

• A premium on the issue of convertible bonds is carried in a separate capital reserve. When conversion rights are exercised the related part of this reserve is transferred to a capital reserve. After expiry of the conversion rights that part of the separate capital reserve which related to conversion rights and is not used is treated as income.

• Terms of the bonds issued such as maturity, interest rates and amounts due within one year are disclosed by way of a note to the accounts.

• Bonds issued in foreign currency have to be translated at original exchange rates or higher exchange rates at the balance sheet date.

Investor

• Bonds have to be valued at the lower of cost or market value at the balance sheet date.

• Profits or losses on foreign exchange or market valuation as well as interest are treated as regular income or expenses.

2.230 Taxation treatment

• Interest payable is allowed as a deduction as accrued and, for tax purposes, there is no difference between the treatment of interest and discount.

• Fees and other expenses for raising finance normally have to be amortised over the life of the loan.

Sweden

2.231 Accounting treatment

The Accounting Act 1976 together with the disclosure rules in the

Companies Act 1975 set out the relevant accounting treatment for debt issues in Sweden. The specific requirements are set out below:

Issuer

• The par value of the bonds must be included in the balance sheet in creditors, split between amounts payable within one year (current liabilities) and after more than one year (long term liabilities).

• Any premium or discount of an issue is usually amortised over the life of the instrument.

• Where not directly recorded as an expense, expenses relating to issues of long term liabilities may be amortised over the life of the issue.

• Foreign currency issues have to be translated at closing rates of exchange. Unrealised gains on long term liabilities denominated in foreign currencies should be deferred and credited to a 'foreign currency reserve'. Movements on this reserve are reflected as an appropriation in the income statement and an untaxed reserve in the balance sheet.

• Interest rates, plans of redemption, maturity dates and any other details must be disclosed by way of a note to the accounts.

Investor

• Bonds are stated at cost. The difference between the cost and the par value is spread over the life of the bond on a straight line basis or a compound interest method.

2.232 Taxation treatment

• All companies report and are taxable on interest income and expenses on an accruals basis. Individuals are taxable on interest on a cash basis. For companies there is no difference between the tax treatment of interest and discount.

• There is no withholding tax on interest.

• Companies report currency fluctuations under Swedish generally accepted accounting principles. For taxation purposes no adjustment of reported profit or loss is required. However, a company that has established a foreign currency reserve has to impute income amounting to 54% of the reserve multiplied by the interest rate for a standardised treasury bond. For individuals realised gains and losses are taxable and treated as capital gains, taxed at the preferential 30% rate rather than as ordinary income, taxed at 30-51%.

• If a company wants to amortize the front end fee for a bond issue over the life of the issue, this is deductible.

Norway

2.233 Accounting treatment

The Norwegian Companies Act 1976 and other Norwegian requirements for treatment of plain bonds (debentures) are as follows:

Issuer

• The outstanding par value of the bonds should be included on the balance sheet in creditors, split between amounts payable within one year and after more than one year.

• Foreign currency liabilities are valued at the greater of book value and the exchange rate at the balance sheet date. Exchange differences will normally be taken to the profit and loss account and recorded as financing items. Translation differences may be offset by corresponding differences on investment in the same currency.

• Norwegian generally accepted accounting principles allows direct expenses of and the commission paid or discount allowed on the issue of debentures to be included on the balance sheet and be written off in instalments over the life of the bond.

• If a company issues debentures, then it must disclose in a note to the accounts:

– information on the currency risk involved and what hedging has been undertaken;

– the total amount in long term investment and long term debts in each currency and the corresponding amount in Norwegian kroner;

– an analysis of any translation differences included on the balance sheet;

– information on the effect of changes in currency rates after the balance sheet date;

– if bonds are secured on the assets of the company, the aggregate amount secured and a general indication of the nature of the security must be disclosed.

Investor

● Investors holding debt instruments are required to include their holdings at the lower of cost and market value. For banks and insurance companies, under certain conditions, bonds can be carried at par value even if market value is lower. However, the Norwegian Stock Exchange has recommended that such companies adopt a policy of lower of cost and market value.

● Investment funds include debt instruments at market value.

2.234 Taxation treatment

● With a few exceptions, interest is allowed as a deduction as it accrues.

● Special rules cover the exchange gains/losses on long term loans (including debt instruments). Unrealised exchange losses on receivables are set off against unrealised exchange gains on loans denominated in the same currency. Unrealised exchange losses on loans are set off against unrealised exchange gains on receivables in the same currency. Receivables cannot be valued at a lower exchange rate than the lower of the rates at the end of the accounting year and the time of acquisition. Loans cannot be valued at a higher exchange rate than the higher of the rates at the end of the accounting year at the time of establishing the loan.

● Fees for raising finance are normally tax deductible when incurred.

● For banks and insurance companies realised gains or losses on debt instruments are taxable/tax deductable as ordinary income. For most other corporates, gains or losses are not taxable/tax deductable.

Finland

2.235 Accounting treatment

The general Finnish accounting treatment for most debt issues is set out in the Accounting Act and in special accounting instructions for banks given by the Finnish Banking Inspectorate. The Finnish accounting practice is to some extent tax related, and tax regulations also have some reflections on the Finnish generally accepted accounting principles ('GAAP').

The Finnish GAAP requirements concerning debt instruments are as follows:

Issuer

• The outstanding par value of the bonds should be included in the balance sheet in creditors, split between amounts payable within one year and after more than one year.

• Details of the bonds issued must be specified in a note to the accounts.

• Foreign currency issues have to be translated at closing rates of exchange.

• The expenses of, and commissions on, an issue of bonds should be written off immediately.

• Profits or losses on retirement of bonds should be reflected in the profit and loss account immediately.

• The premium or discount on an issue should be amortised over the life of the instrument.

Investor

• The investor has to treat the amounts invested in debt instruments as either trading or investment assets according to whether the instruments have been taken into the portfolio for trading purposes or if they are going to be held in the portfolio until maturity.

• At the balance sheet date the trading assets have to be revalued at the lower of cost or market value.

• The investor is allowed to make an extra charge for a provision following the revaluation of trading assets. For example in 1990 a provision of 10% of the revalued closing value of trading assets was allowed.

• Debt instruments held for the long term by an investor are allowed to be kept at their acquisition cost. However, the difference between the acquisition cost and the par value of the instrument should be amortised over the life of the instrument. The investor is allowed to make a provision (5% in 1990) after the revaluation of investment assets. This relates only to banks and insurance companies.

• The above provisions for trading and investment assets are made primarily for tax purposes, and according to the Finnish Trade Tax Act the charges have to also be made on the accounts.

2.236 Taxation treatment

● Interest is in general treated as a deduction from income as accrued. The discount on a zero coupon bond is treated in the same way as interest.

● Interest paid to non-residents is usually tax exempt on deposits, bonds, debentures and foreign loans which are not regarded as capital investments.

● Fees for raising finance are usually tax deductible when paid.

● Currency losses may be expensed at the tax payer's choice either when the exchange rate has changed or at a later stage. Currency losses must be expensed by the end of that fiscal year during which the amount corresponding to the loss was paid.

● Unrealised currency losses on loans may be partly expensed and partly activated. Where one instalment of the loan is paid, the currency loss on that part of the loan is realised and must be expensed.

Greece

2.237 Accounting treatment

Issuers

The Greek Uniform Code of Accounts provides for bonds to be shown as a separate item under long term liabilities. Bonds which are issued at their face value with coupons are treated for accounting purposes as normal loans and the interest is accrued for in the normal way.

Bonds which are issued at a discount are also accounted for at their face value and the discount (interest) is applied initially to a suspense account and transferred to interest expense as it accrues. Such bonds are issued only by the Central Bank of Greece.

Investors

The Greek Uniform Code of Accounts provides that investments in bonds be stated separately under the category 'Investments' distinguishing between Greek bonds and foreign bonds.

Investors usually record bonds at their actual purchase price and record the interest earned as it accrues. Some companies, especially insurance companies, revalue their investments to market value each year where official market values exist.

2.238 Taxation treatment

• Interest is allowed for tax purposes as it accrues. There is no difference in the tax treatment of interest and discount.

• There is no withholding tax on interest paid to a bank operating in Greece. Interest paid to a foreign lender is liable to withholding tax of 46% unless reduced by a double tax treaty.

• The taxation of exchange gains and losses to a great extent generally follows accounting principles.

• Fees for raising loan finance are tax deductible for tax purposes on an accruals basis provided that they are supported by sufficient documentation.

• Interest income from debt instruments issued by banks, the Greek state and state owned authorities, (eg Public Power Corporation, National Telecommunication Authority etc) is not subject to income tax.

Cyprus

2.239 Accounting treatment

• The accounting treatment normally follows the practice in the United Kingdom as the legal and accounting standards are similar. The Cyprus Companies Law provides that the commission paid or discount allowed on issuing debentures may be applied against the share premium account. The legal requirements are supplemented by the International Accounting Standards.

2.240 Taxation treatment

• As a general rule interest is deductible in the year in which it becomes a legal liability of the company. If the interest is income then it becomes taxable in the year in which the company has a legal right to collect it. Interest on bonds issued at a discount is usually taxable as income or expense at maturity.

• The general withholding rate applicable to on-shore entity interest payments in the absence of a double tax treaty is 42.5%. In the case of payments under a treaty the withholding tax is usually reduced to either 10% or zero. Payments of interest by off-shore companies are not subject to any withholding tax.

• Exchange differences arising from loans denominated in currency other than the company's reporting currency are allowed or taxed as the case may be if they are realised.

• Fees incurred for raising finance, the interest charge on which is of a revenue nature are deductible when incurred. If the interest charge is not of a revenue nature, neither are the fees relating to it.

Spain

2.241 Accounting treatment

Ordinary bonds

Issuer

• The liabilities of the company that result from issuing bonds and debentures are recorded in the 'debenture and ordinary bonds account' and are stated at their redemption value. When they are issued at a premium, the premium should be recognised when the bonds are issued. Repayment premiums are also recognised at the time of issue of the bonds or debentures.

• A company's issuing expenses may be charged to expense or, alternatively, they may be recorded as deferred expenses in the balance sheet. These expenses must be written off within five years.

• In compliance with the accruals principle, annual interest expense payable to debenture holders must accrue evenly (recorded under 'interest payable not yet due') over the term of the bond, regardless of when interest is actually paid. This treatment also applies to zero coupon bonds.

Investor

• Bonds are stated at cost. This price comprises the total amount paid to the seller, including subscription rights, and expenses arising from their acquisition.

● Interest income is recorded under 'Short term investment income' as recommended in the General Accounting Plan.

2.242 Taxation treatment

● Interest is allowed as a deduction on an accruals basis. In principle, there is no difference between the tax treatment of interest and discount.

● The general rate of withholding tax on interest is 25% subject to the terms of any relevant double taxation agreement. With regard to discount, withholding tax also applies to the difference between the amount received at the time of amortisation or sale and the amount paid at the time of subscription or purchase, except for certain financial instruments issued by the Treasury or Bank of Spain.

● Fees for raising debt finance can be deducted when paid or may be amortised over the life of the debt.

● Exchange losses can be booked each year at the rate of exchange prevailing at the end of the period but, in any event, they must be taken to profit and loss for the year in which the debt is settled.

Italy

2.243 Accounting treatment

The accounting treatment and the disclosure requirements for debt issues are set out in the Civil Code (*'Codice Civile'*) and the Italian accounting standards issued by the professional accounting bodies.

Civil Code

The Civil Code states that a discount on an issue of bonds can be included as an asset in the balance sheet and amortised in accordance with the repayment terms of the bonds. Convertible bonds cannot be issued at a discount and the conversion rates of such bonds must be determined in advance.

Accounting standards

The accounting standards expand further on the accounting treatment laid down in the Civil Code. The more important requirements are the following:

• bonds are to be analysed between long and short term;

• a company can purchase its own bonds on the open market provided such a clause has been included in the deeds of issue. In cases where the company's own bonds are purchased with the intention of holding until maturity or for early redemption the par value of such bonds is shown as a deduction from the balance of bonds outstanding. The profit accruing on the purchase of any bonds below par value, after taking into account any discounts on the original issue, is credited to the profit and loss account;

• the issue costs are amortised over the life of the debt. Premiums on an issue of bonds are written off to the profit and loss account over the life of the bonds;

• information regarding the number and nominal value of bonds, their repayment terms, interest rates, terms of any conversion, any bonds repurchased and discounts and premiums capitalised is disclosed by way of note to the accounts.

The accounting principles are general in nature and do not include any specific regulations regarding the more sophisticated instruments, such as zero coupon bonds, deep discount bonds and other non-standard issues.

2.244 Taxation treatment

Interest expense

Generally interest expense of an Italian company is deductible on an accruals basis. A discount cannot be deducted immediately in full but can be spread ratably over the duration of the loan.

There are rules disallowing part of a company's interest costs and general expenses where the company has tax-exempt interest income.

Interest income

Generally interest is subject to withholding taxation at source. Applicable rates of withholding tax are:

– Interest from securities	30% for newly issued securities – lower rates exist for some securities issued under old legislation.
– Interest on loans paid by a company to an individual or to a non resident company or individual	15% subject to the provisions of any relevant treaty.
– Interest on loans paid between resident companies	0%

The above tax at source is exempt from further taxation in the hands of the recipient when the recipient of the interest is an individual or a partnership. However, where the recipient is a company, the tax at source is withheld on account of corporate income tax (IRPEG). In the latter case the interest is also subject to local income tax (ILOR).

Chapter 3

Asset backed securities

Asset backed securities

3.1 Overview

The distinctive feature of asset backed securities is that the return on the securities is derived from the performance of specific assets (although this performance may be supported by various forms of guarantee). In an issue of asset backed securities, specific assets both serve as collateral for the securities and generate the payment streams which are used to finance the payment of interest and principal to the investors in the security. This compares with a corporate bond where payments to investors are made out of cash flows derived from the entity's operations as a whole (albeit that some bonds may be secured by charges on assets in the event of a default).

This distinction can be illustrated by the difference between a corporate bond backed by mortgages and a mortgage backed security.

• The corporate bond will be secured by mortgage loans held by the issuer and in the event of a default the trustees acting for the bondholders will be able to sell the mortgage loans and use the proceeds to repay principal to the investors. However, in other circumstances, the issuer will pay interest and principal due on the bonds out of general corporate funds and not specifically using the cash flow received on the mortgage loans.

• In the case of a mortgage backed security investors will have the same rights to the mortgage loans in the event of a default. However, the interest and principal repayments received by the issuer from the mortgage loans will be the only source of payments of interest and principal to the investor. These 'securitised' assets comprise the primary collateral supporting the cash flows of the securities although credit enhancement techniques and insurance policies may also be used. Typically the issuer cannot easily convert into cash those assets which are used to collateralise asset backed securities (such as mortgages and leases) by other means.

In common with other capital markets, there is some confusion over the nomenclature for the various financial instruments used in the asset backed securities markets. This is particularly true with the term 'asset backed securities' which is used both for the market as a whole and as a generic term for receivables backed by assets other than mortgage loans. In this chapter we use the term 'structured receivables financing' to refer to the latter, reserving asset backed securities as a term for the market as a whole.

3.2 Development of asset backed securities

The first type of assets to be securitised and sold on to investors were residential mortgage loans. This market developed in the United States, when in the early 1970s governmental and quasi-governmental organisations such as the Government National Mortgage Association (GNMA or 'Ginnie Mae') pooled residential mortgage loans and either issued or guaranteed the issue of 'participation certificates' or 'pass through securities'.

The mortgage backed security market developed in the United States largely to correct structural problems in the United States residential mortgage market. Prior to the development of this market, the United States mortgage market was very localised. Savings and Loan associations ('S&L's) acted in a similar way to the United Kingdom building societies but regulation meant their activities were confined to particular states or even smaller jurisdictions. As a result, the market was very inefficient, with excess savings arising in some parts of the country which could not be matched with mortgage queues in other areas. In an effort to remove these inefficiencies and to promote home ownership, United States Government sponsored organisations began purchasing pools of mortgage loans from S&Ls and selling 'pass through' securities collateralised by the mortgage loans to investors with a return derived from the cash flows resulting from those mortgage loans.

In addition to pass through securities, another type of asset backed security which has been developed is the Collateralised Mortgage Obligation ('CMO'). The flexibility of the CMO structure has led to a rapid growth in this market since its introduction in 1983 in the United States. The CMO structure is explained later in this chapter.

In recent years there has been a considerable increase in the number of organisations which have issued or sponsored asset backed securities, and in the variety of assets which have been used to back the security. As well as residential mortgage loans, securities have been issued which have been backed by automobile and computer leasing receivables ('CARs' and 'CLEOs'), credit card receivables ('CARDs') and export credit receivables. Asset backed issues have not developed as fast in Europe as in the United States. In part, this has been due to their unfamiliar and complex structure and also the legal and regulatory frameworks in place in each country. Asset securitisation in Europe has, to date, followed the trend set by the United States, beginning with the securitisation of residential mortgages, with more issues backed by other financial assets developing gradually thereafter. The position in various countries in Europe is described in sections 3.64–3.98 dealing with 'Securitisation in Europe' at the end of this chapter.

3.3 How asset backed securities work

The most important characteristics of asset backed securities are as follows:

• the original lender ('the originator') will typically sell the assets which are to back the securities to a trust or another form of special purpose vehicle ('the intermediary' or the 'SPV') in return for cash;

• the intermediary finances this purchase by issuing securities to investors in return for cash;

• the investors will receive income and return of capital from the assets via the intermediary over the life of the securities;

• the securities held by the investors will be collateralised by the assets. This is attractive to investors as the assets themselves will usually be collateralised. For example residential mortgage loans taken out to purchase property would be secured on that property;

• a proportion of the cash flows received by the intermediary will be paid as servicing fees to the agent who administers the assets throughout their remaining life. This is usually the originator. The role of the servicer is described further below. The intermediary will also retain a certain percentage of the cash flows to ensure it can meet all its obligations. This amount retained by the intermediary is known as a 'residual interest'.

These factors can be shown in the following cash flow diagrams. The first diagram shows the sale of the assets by the originator and the issue of the securities by the SPV.

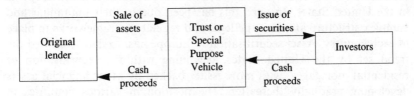

Diagram 3.1: Issue of securities by SPV

The second diagram shows the cash flows arising during the life of the asset backed securities issue. The servicer is compensated for administering the receivables by a service fee, which is usually calculated as a percentage of the interest received from the borrowers. The interest, and therefore the service fee, declines in absolute terms during the life of the issue due to the amortisation of principal.

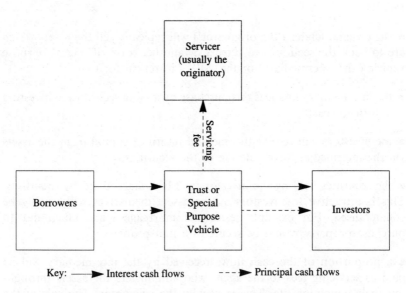

Key: ——▶ Interest cash flows   - - -▶ Principal cash flows

Diagram 3.2: Cash flows arising from asset backed securities issue

The servicer

The principal functions performed by the servicer are:

• to collect the monthly payments from the borrowers and to account for these collections;

- reinvesting the funds received from the borrowers and other available funds;

- calculating the interest and principal payments due to the holders of the securities and arranging payment;

- enforcing the terms and conditions of the mortgage or lease agreement made with the borrower (including the recovery of arrears or repossessions);

- paying the operating expenses of the intermediary;

- administering and maintaining any insurance policies or other form of guarantee which enhances the collateral of the issue.

Profit extraction

The profit on the transaction is essentially the net present value of the difference between the interest rate earned on the receivables and the rate paid on the securities issued to investors by the SPV, net of expenses. These expenses comprise servicing fees and the cost of enhancing the collateral of the receivables to a degree sufficient to obtain the required credit rating together with issue costs. The originator will want to retain as much of the profit as possible. There are a number of ways in which this can be achieved:

- payment of dividends, if the originator owns ordinary or preference shares in the SPV. However, in many jurisdictions ownership of shares in the SPV will require the originator to consolidate the accounts of the SPV into their accounts;

- the use of an interest rate swap whereby the originator will pay the SPV the interest rate payable on the securities in exchange for the interest received on the mortgage loans;

- payment of servicing fees and other management fees;

- payment of interest on a subordinated loan;

- the sale of the residual interest in the issue as a separately tradeable security. This is a popular method used in connection with multi-tranche collateralised mortgage obligation issues in the United States market, as is described further in section 3.21.

Each of these methods will have different tax consequences which will have to be carefully considered by the originator.

3.4 Asset backed security structures

Different structures have evolved for issuing asset backed securities to take account of the varied requirements of both issuers and investors.

The two basic forms of asset backed securities are:

- where investors are regarded as having an interest in the underlying assets, usually through a trust;

- where a special purpose vehicle (SPV – usually a company) issues to investors negotiable securities whose value is derived solely from and secured on the assets held by the vehicle.

In the United Kingdom, the first technique is commonly referred to as 'unitisation' and the second as 'securitisation'. In the United States the first form is usually referred to as an issue of 'pass through' certificates and the second as an issue of 'pay through' bonds.

Pass through certificates

A pass through certificate or security is one which passes income from the debtor to the investor, usually via a trust acting as intermediary. Pass through securities represent undivided interests in specific pools of assets which are sold to investors who receive participation certificates. The payments of interest, amortisation of principal and prepayments from the pool of assets are passed through directly (albeit with a payment delay) to the owners of the certificates or securities by the firm servicing the mortgage payments.

Pay through bonds

The issue of pay through bonds is structured as a financing transaction. Debt securities are issued which are backed by collateral (eg mortgage loans), held by the issuer. In a pay through bond the cash flows generated from the assets will not be passed directly through to investors as in a pass through certificate, but in the event of a default a trustee may attach and sell the collateral in order to meet the investors' claim.

The cash flows required to pay interest and principal to investors are in theory derived from general corporate funds, as with normal corporate bonds described earlier in this chapter; the difference is that the SPV will be very thinly capitalised and will have few assets other than the collateral, and therefore in practice the cash flows will be derived from the collateral.

The terms of the trust deed or bond indenture relating to the issue of the securities will usually restrict the activities of the SPV and prevent it undertaking many activities typical of most corporations. The restrictions will usually prescribe that the SPV cannot:

- establish any subsidiaries;

- dispose of any assets except to support the securities;

- pay any dividends prior to discharging all its obligations to the investors in the securities;

- incur any indebtedness other than the securities.

Collateralised mortgage obligations

The collateralised mortgage obligation developed as a special form of a pay through bond. The cash flows generated from the pool of assets are not passed directly to investors, as in a conventional pass through certificate, but are restructured through the issue of multiple tranches of bonds backed by the same pool of mortgages, and are used to pay interest on the bond and redeem principal payments on the different tranches in a predetermined sequence. There is no reliance on the general corporate funds of the originator.

3.5 Enhancement of collateral

The collateral is enhanced to reduce the following risks to investors:

- credit risk – that borrowers will default on their obligations;

- liquidity risk – that borrowers will not make timely repayment of interest and principal;

- reinvestment risk – usually there is a delay between payments being made by borrowers and payments of interest to investors in the securities. During this period, the funds will be invested. If interest rates fall, there could be a shortfall in the amount required to meet the obligation to investors.

There are a number of ways in which credit enhancement can be achieved. The most widely used methods, and the risks which they address, are as follows:

- *Pool insurance (credit risk).* For a fee, an insurer will agree to underwrite any defaults over a certain percentage on the underlying pool of assets.

- *Letter of credit (credit risk).* Obtained usually from a bank, whereby the bank agrees to guarantee a set percentage of the receivables from arrears and defaults.

• *Overcollateralisation (credit risk).* In this case, the cash flows provided by the collateral are considerably in excess of what is required to fund the cash flows on the securities issued to investors. Over collateralisation is typically achieved by the use of a senior/ subordinated issue structure. The pool of assets will act as collateral for both the senior and subordinated class of securities, but only the senior class would be offered to investors, with the subordinated class being sold to the originator (or retained by the issuer). Within predetermined limits, the rights relating to the subordinated securities will be junior to the rights of the holder of the senior class in the event of default. The subordinated class of securities are sometimes sold to investors (with a higher yield than the senior class) but are often purchased by the originator.

• *Spread account (credit risk, liquidity risk).* Part or all of the spread between the average rate of interest paid on the assets and the coupon on the securities issued to investors (after servicing fees) is placed in escrow, to be used in the event of default (and sometimes delayed payment) by borrowers. Once the securities have been redeemed, the balance remaining on the spread account will usually revert to the issuer or the originator. Providers of insurance will often require the establishment of a spread account to reduce their exposure.

• *Liquidity insurance (liquidity risk).* An insurance company will guarantee timely payment in the event of a delay.

• *Guaranteed investment contract or 'GIC' (reinvestment risk).* A bank or insurance company will guarantee that funds invested with it will earn a stated rate of interest.

With the exception of overcollateralisation, all of these techniques involve some form of guarantee from a third party (either a bank or an insurance company). In addition to being expensive, this has the consequence that the credit rating of the securities will be to a considerable extent dependent on the credit rating of that third party. During the 1980s the credit ratings of many banks deteriorated, and recently there have also been concerns about the credit quality of major composite insurers offering credit enhancement insurance policies. As a result of these concerns, the use of overcollateralisation and the senior/junior issue structure has become more popular. However, if the subordinated class of securities are retained by the originator, this could prejudice the transfer of the assets off balance sheet, as the originator is effectively still exposed to most of the credit risk.

The use of guarantees provided by 'monoline' insurance companies such as Financial Security Assurance is becoming more prevalent, particularly in the United States. These companies engage exclusively in providing financial guarantees and will provide unconditional assurance of timely payment of principal and interest. However, such a guarantee will not be provided unless the issue has adequate forms of credit enhancement using one or several of the other techniques described above. Effectively, this transfers the responsibility for performing detailed credit analysis of the often very complex structure from the investor to the insurer, and the comfort this provides to investors is the main benefit of this arrangement to the originator.

3.6 Assets suitable for securitisation

In general, many forms of assets can be securitised providing they have a contractual cash flow. To be successfully packaged and sold to investors they must exhibit most of the following characteristics:

• the cash flows should fall due in accordance with a predetermined schedule. Such a schedule would be laid down in for example a mortgage agreement or a lease agreement;

• the cash flows must be regular and predictable. To a certain extent the regularity of the cash flows would be ensured by the predetermined schedule referred to above. However most mortgage and lease agreements allow for the possibility of prepayments. For example, someone who purchases a house by using a residential mortgage loan may at a later date want to move house, either because the property no longer suits their needs, or because they have to move to a different part of the country. In this instance the mortgagor will often repay the whole of the original mortgage loan and take out a new mortgage. In addition, if the mortgage loan or lease bears a fixed rate of interest, the borrower may wish to prepay the loan if interest rates fall to refinance the liability at a lower interest rate. This prepayment risk is the most significant risk to the investor in an asset backed security except the risk of default. If a borrower prepays at a time when interest rates are falling the investor would have to invest the cash proceeds from the prepayment at the prevailing (lower) rate of interest, thus suffering a lower rate of return. Therefore, to make one of these securities attractive, the expected rate of prepayments for the mortgages or other assets which are being securitised should be predictable. In the United States, there is a large amount of statistical information available which shows the expected prepayment rates for mortgages taken out by different classes of borrower in different areas of the country. This enables the investor to have some degree of assurance as to the expected life of the securities;

167

• there should be a statistical history available of the loss experience of the assets involved. This would include the previous experience of default by the borrowers concerned;

• homogeneity – the assets must be sufficiently similar for them to be pooled together;

• there should be a large enough pool available of these similar types of assets to enable them to be economic to issue securities derived from the cash flows in the capital markets;

• the assets should be of good saleable quality with a low credit risk.

3.7 Benefits – issuer/originator

• Depending on the structure of the transaction, the originator may be able to improve balance sheet ratios by excluding both the original assets and the securities (debt) created by the transaction from its balance sheet. This can be particularly important to regulated institutions (such as banks) which have to conform to capital adequacy requirements. Assets such as mortgages and leases attract risk weightings and the consequent charges against capital. Securitisation can therefore have a leveraged effect on regulatory capital by both reducing borrowings and removing the risk weighted assets from the originator's balance sheet.

• The removal of assets from the balance sheet and the consequent reduction in gearing can enable the originator to generate more business and therefore more income.

• The originator can generate cash from the assets immediately rather than over a number of years, enabling funds to be redeployed in other projects.

• Profit on the sale of the assets can be crystallised and locked in, removing any possible loss due to interest rate mismatches (if, for example, the originator had previously to fund the long term receivable by short term liabilities).

• The originator can improve the risk profile of its earnings by substituting fee income from servicing in place of income from lending with the consequent exposure to the credit of the borrower.

• Asset backed securities can often attract a better credit rating than may be possible for the originator on the original form of financing (eg loans etc). Whereas the specific assets may be of good quality, there may be general economic or other reasons why the originator's credit rating is deteriorating. This is particularly true for banks whose credit ratings have suffered during the 1980s due to problems with LDC debt and other exposures. Thus a profit can be made from the lower interest costs of financing the portfolio of assets to help defray issue and other costs.

• The use of the asset backed securities market can provide an alternative source of funds to the conventional public debt market or bank finance, thus increasing the options available for the originator to obtain the cheapest cost of funds.

3.8 Benefits – investor

• These instruments have a relatively low credit risk (given that the securities are generally secured by good quality collateral) and offer a high yield when compared with other low risk investments such as government stocks.

• The investor buys an interest in a specific set of assets with a known amount of risk. This is safer than lending to a company whose cash flow can be dependent on a number of sources and whose circumstances can change.

3.9 Risks and disadvantages – issuer/originator

• Once the assets have been securitised, the originator has crystallised its profit, and will have foregone any opportunity to profit in the future from any favourable movements in interest rates.

• To make the securities attractive to investors, the originator may have to incorporate recourse provisions in the event of default into the structure of the issue. The originator could suffer losses if widespread defaults occur on the underlying assets. Alternatively, some form of credit enhancement may be required, but this increases the cost of the issue.

• The company responsible for administration of the underlying assets (normally the originator) will typically have the responsibility for setting interest rates on the securitised assets. Consequently, the originator may have to:

    – advance funds or otherwise make good any shortfall of interest paid on the security to that received from the underlying assets. This may be particularly apparent with floating rate mortgages where the rate setting on the mortgages may be prone to political influences when the rate on the security is linked to the money markets;

– account for the risk that the cash received, either from prepayments or other sources, may have to be reinvested at or below the current rate payable on the securities issued.

These risks can be reduced by the use of swaps or other hedging instruments.

• The structure of the transaction may preclude the removal of the assets and liabilities from the balance sheet (see the 'General accounting questions' section 3.11 below).

3.10 Risks and disadvantages – investors

• The extent and timing of cash flows are uncertain. The cash flows generated from the assets may arise earlier than scheduled (such as where prepayments are made on a mortgage) which leads to an earlier than expected redemption of the security. There may be a higher risk of prepayment if the underlying assets are based on fixed rather than floating rates of interest (and thus more responsive to interest rate fluctuations).

• In the event of a default on the underlying assets, investors may not have recourse to the originator, or, depending on the terms of the issue, such recourse may be limited to a fixed percentage of the value of the assets.

3.11 General accounting questions

The principal accounting issues to be addressed with respect to asset backed securities are:

• Should the assets which have been securitised be removed from the balance sheet of the originator? That is, should the transaction be deemed to be a sale of assets or a financing transaction collateralised by the receivables?

• Should the originator's profit from the sale be recognised immediately, amortised over the redemption period or deferred to the redemption date?

• Can the originator take excess service fees or excess interest to profit immediately?

On or off balance sheet?

For originators the most important accounting question is usually whether the securities issued and the assets which have been securitised can be deemed to have been sold and excluded from the balance sheet. The answer will depend on the structure of the transaction. The methods adopted to issue the securities could be:

• the issue of securities by the entity which originally owned the assets;

• a sale of pass through certificates or the issue of collateralised bonds;

• the sale or loan of the assets to an SPV which issues the securities. If an SPV is created it could be either a subsidiary or an entity which is unassociated with the originator.

Depending on which option is selected, the following issues should be considered:

• Are both the legal form and the substance of the transaction such that:

– there is a sale of assets which can be excluded from the balance sheet? In substance have the principal benefits and risks of ownership been passed on to the buyer of the securities?

– it is a financing transaction (borrowings collateralised by the assets) which should be retained on the balance sheet?

• Should the SPV which has been formed to issue the securities be consolidated into the accounts of the issuer? If not, what information about the SPV should be provided, and how can profits be remitted by the SPV?

• Is it appropriate to offset the collateral against the related borrowings?

• Is there any profit on the sale (either directly to investors or to the SPV), and if so, is it a realised profit?

In general, to determine the appropriate accounting treatment in particular instances, the following are among the issues which will require consideration:

• Does the investor have any recourse to the original owner in the event of default?

• Are the securities sold with either put or call options which enable the debt to be redeemed prior to the realisation of the assets which back the issue?

- Does the originator have any residual interest in the cash flows generated from the assets?

- Are any benefits and related risks remaining with the originator of a kind that are best indicated by retaining the assets on its balance sheet?

- Does the transfer satisfy the terms and conditions of the underlying asset with all necessary consents being obtained?

- Does the transfer of the assets mean that if any renegotiations take place the buyer not the originator would be subject to these negotiations?

- What are the arrangements to fund any shortfall in interest if the coupon on the securities exceeds the rate on the underlying assets?

Profit on sale?

As to whether the profit on sale should be recognised immediately is largely dependent on whether or not the transaction is accounted for as a sale for balance sheet purposes – if the transaction is a sale, all of the profit is generally recognised immediately.

Excess service fees

The role of the servicer is usually taken by the originator, and the service fees can be one method by which the originator extracts profit from the SPV. 'Excess' service fees arise where the fees are in excess of a normal market rate. There is no guidance available on the treatment of the excess fees in the United Kingdom or the rest of Europe, nor is there a definitive accounting standard in the United States. However, the United States Emerging Issues Task Force ('EITF'), a body set up by the Financial Accounting Standards Board to recommend appropriate accounting practice on significant new issues, has stated that the net present value of the excess servicing fees should be recognised immediately on sale of the receivables in the profit and loss account of the originator, providing certain conditions are met. The EITF also offers guidance on the most appropriate discount rate to be used to calculate the net present value.

The accounting guidance available in different countries is set out in section 3.64 to 3.98 dealing with securitisation in Europe at the end of this chapter.

3.12 General taxation questions

- Is there a tax disposal of the underlying assets on transfer to a SPV or is the SPV regarded as transparent for tax purposes? If there is a disposal, what is the consideration for the disposal, and will this be an income or a capital transaction?

• Will the SPV be included in a tax group with the owner of the original assets?

• Will capital duty or transfer taxes be payable on the issue of the securities or the sale of the assets?

• Can and should the SPV be separately registered for VAT purposes?

• Will any disposal of assets be a taxable supply for VAT purposes? Can such VAT be recovered by the SPV or by investors?

• Can the SPV qualify as an onshore vehicle with special treatment?

• Is an offshore SPV subject to other anti-avoidance legislation?

• Will income of the SPV be taxable currently in the hands of investors, regardless of any distribution by the SPV?

• Will any profit or loss on sale by the investor be taxable as income or as a capital gain?

• Will distributions from the SPV be treated as taxable income or tax free allocations of already taxed income?

3.13 Mortgage backed securities

3.14 Mortgage pass through securities

A mortgage pass through security grants an undivided interest to investors, usually in the form of participation certificates, in a pool of residential mortgages. The interests are undivided in that each investor has a proportionate interest in each cash flow generated from the pool of assets. Payments of interest and principal are 'passed through' directly to investors (net of servicing fees) without any restructuring of the cash flows. Usually payments are made monthly.

The nature of the cash flows passed through to the investors will depend on the structure of the underlying mortgage. With a traditional annuity mortgage structure (which has a fixed term, and equal repayments made each month by the borrower), each payment made by the borrower (and consequently, the amount passed through to the investor in the security) contains a mix of interest and principal. The amount of principal redeemed in each payment increases over the life of the loan until the final payment on maturity is almost entirely principal. This feature of mortgage pass through securities differentiates them from the more traditional bullet structure of bonds, where only interest is paid over the life of the instrument and the full amount of the principal is redeemed on maturity.

A typical pass through structure may be shown by the following diagram:

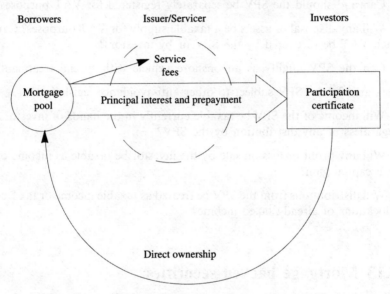

Diagram 3.3: Mortgage pass through security

Pass through certificates were the first tradeable securities to be issued in the secondary mortgage market in the United States, and still represent the largest value of outstanding mortgage debt. The majority of these issues have been made or sponsored by governmental or quasi-governmental organisations who guarantee the certificates to differing extents. The organisations and the extent to which certificates are guaranteed are as follows:

	Extent of guarantee
Government National Mortgage Association (GNMA or Ginnie Mae)	Full and timely payment of principal and interest
Federal Home Loan Mortgage Corporation (FHLMC or Freddie Mac)	Timely payment of interest and eventual repayment of principal

Federal National	Full and timely payment of
Mortgage Association	interest and principal
(FNMA or Fannie Mae)	

In addition to the pass through certificates backed by these agencies, private entities such as banks have issued these securities, which are known as either 'Conventional' or 'Private' Pass Through Certificates. In general, it is usually more attractive for the originator to sell the mortgages to either FNMA or FHLMC, and the growth of the conventional issue market has largely grown to enable originators to sell mortgages which are not eligible for purchase by the quasi-governmental bodies. Typically, this is because the mortgage loans are 'jumbo' loans which have balances greater than permitted by the FNMA or FHLMC standards. In the absence of a guarantee from one of the agencies, the collateral is usually enhanced by either pool insurance or over collateralisation.

In most issues of mortgage pass through securities, the pool of mortgages is sold to a grantor trust. The trust is not taxable under United States legislation and the investors in the securities issued by the trust are deemed to have an interest in the underlying assets (the mortgages). Prior to the United States Tax Reform Act of 1986, a grantor trust could only retain tax transparency if one class of securities was issued, which meant that the certificates had to mirror the attributes of the underlying mortgages. The Tax Reform Act introduced the Real Estate Mortgage Investment Conduit ('REMIC') which allowed multi-class certificates to be issued. This has allowed pass throughs to be issued with accrual bonds, residuals and other features previously issued using the CMO structure.

Pricing of pass through securities

One of the most important factors in the pricing of pass throughs is the analysis of prepayments. There is a large amount of data available on historical rates of prepayment of mortgages in the United States. The most significant determinant of prepayment rates are the interest rates payable on the loans compared to current mortgage loan rates, but other factors such as inflation, the relative affluence of different areas and demographic factors such as population trends are important. Investment banks in the United States have developed sophisticated models to attempt to predict prepayment rates. There are a number of conventions which have been developed in the market to provide benchmarks to assist in quantifying the effect of prepayments. The most important of these are the Conditional Prepayment Rate ('CPR') and the Public Securities Association ('PSA') Standard Prepayment Model.

Asset backed securities

Conditional Prepayment Rate

This measure assumes that a constant percentage of outstanding principal is prepaid in each period during which repayment is expected (normally monthly). The model is 'conditional' in the sense that prepayments are measured conditional on the previous period's outstanding balance. The rate of prepayment arising from this assumption is expressed as an annualised percentage. This model is attractive because it is easy to understand and use in price and yield calculations.

PSA Standard Prepayment Model

The PSA standard was originally developed for the analysis of CMOs, but is also sometimes used for pass throughs. 100% PSA is equivalent to a series of CPR assumptions – 0% CPR in month zero, 0.2% per year in the first month, increasing by 0.2% monthly until month 30 and at 6% CPR thereafter. The PSA Model was developed to reflect the fact that prepayment rates increase as a mortgage pool ages.

Yield calculations

Quoted yields on mortgage pass through securities are calculated by reference to a 'prepaid life', where all the prepayments in a mortgage pool are assumed to occur at one average point in time. The market convention for quoting yields assumes a 12 year prepaid life. The quoted yield is a very inaccurate measure to use to estimate the actual return on a pass through security because it is not a realistic model of the actual distribution of prepayments during the life of a security.

Valuation methods have been developed to calculate the yield on a pass through based on the net present value of cashflows generated using period-by-period prepayment assumptions such as the CPR and the PSA, known as the 'cash flow yield'.

If an investor purchases a pass through at par, prepayments do not affect the yield on the security (although of course there will be reinvestment risk or any principal repaid early) because interest is earned on the residual unamortised principal at the original coupon rate. However, prepayments will increase the yield on a pass through purchased at a discount, because by shortening the life of the security, prepayments reduce the amount of time required to earn the discount. Conversely, prepayments will reduce the yield on a pass through purchased at a premium.

3.15 Benefits – issuer/originator

● Issuing costs may be lower than for CMOs which tend to have a more complex structure than pass throughs.

3.16 Benefits – investor

● The principal attraction of pass throughs is the high yield when compared with the credit quality, as described in the overview. In addition, the greater uncertainty of the timing of cash flows on pass throughs can lead them to be issued with comparatively greater yields than asset backed bonds such as CMOs.

3.17 Risks and disadvantages – issuer/originator

● Due to the difference in the structure of the cash flows, with monthly repayments of both interest and principal, it is difficult to compare the yield to maturity of pass through securities with other debt securities such as government stocks and corporate bonds. This can lead to difficulties in pricing the issue.

3.18 Risks and disadvantages – investor

● There is a greater risk of prepayment with pass throughs than with CMOs, as there is no restructuring of the cash flows prior to being paid through to investors. This makes these issues unattractive to institutional investors who normally wish to avoid prepayment, which would mean having to reinvest in other instruments, probably at a lower yield (prepayment of fixed rate mortgages will tend to increase as interest rates fall).

● Pass through securities usually incorporate a payment delay. This is the time difference between the date on which the underlying assets are scheduled to make payments and the date on which interest is paid to the holders. Payment delays will reduce the yield.

- For pass through securities mortgage yield is usually quoted. This is based upon simplifying assumptions as to prepayment rates and servicing fees and is the same for all securities regardless of the age of the underlying assets. Consequently, quoted yield may be misleading, and the more accurate cash flow yield is difficult to calculate.

3.19 Accounting questions

- See section 3.11.

3.20 Taxation questions

- Are investors in a 'pass through' security taxed only on net income received or will they be taxed on gross income of the SPV with an allowance for certain expenses?
- See also the taxation questions in section 3.12.

3.21 Collateralised mortgage obligations (CMO)

CMOs are multi-tranche pay through bonds collateralised by a pool of mortgages. The fundamental difference between the CMO structure and the pass through certificate is the legal ownership of the underlying assets. In a pass through structure, the security holders have pass through certificates which represent a pro rata undivided ownership interest in the underlying assets. In a collateralised structure the originator will set up a special purpose vehicle ('SPV') to hold separately on trust, or to acquire the assets which are then pledged to an independent trustee. This vehicle will then issue the securities. Accordingly, the SPV owns the underlying pool of assets; the investors own a debt security which is collateralised by the pool of assets.

The first CMO was issued by the United States Federal Home Loan Mortgage Corporation in 1983 but the market developed because investment banks purchased in the secondary market large pools of pass through certificates issued by the governmental agencies. The investment banks restructured the cash flow from the certificates to make them more attractive to investors.

There are two reasons why pass throughs were unattractive to investors:

- the amortising structure of cash flows;

- the prepayment risk.

Mortgages and leases generally have what is known as an amortising structuring of repayment. This is, each payment includes an element of interest and an element of repayment of principal. The amount of repayment of principal included within each payment would increase over the life of the security. This can be shown graphically as follows:

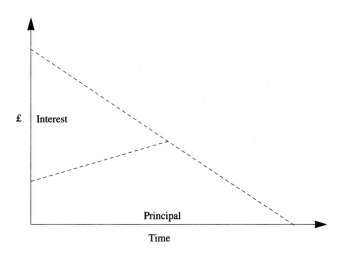

Diagram 3.4: Repayment of principal and interest

However, the majority of instruments traded in the capital markets have what is known as a 'bullet' structure whereby interest is paid over the life of the security and the full amount of the principal is repaid at maturity. The different structure of mortgage bonds made it difficult for investors (particularly institutional investors) to compare their return with other securities of comparable maturity.

The prepayment risk attached to mortgages securities meant that investors demanded a higher rate of return than they would on other securities with similar maturities. Therefore it was more expensive to issue this kind of security relative to similar instruments which did not have a prepayment risk. With a CMO issue, the cash flows relating to the repayment of principal are allocated to the holders of different securities in sequence, which has the effect of reducing the uncertainty arising from prepayments.

A typical CMO structure may be shown by the following diagram:

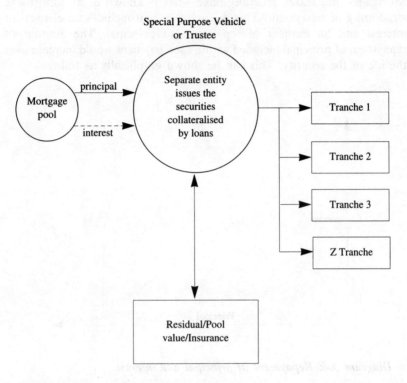

Diagram 3.5: Typical CMO structure

This structure enables the SPV to issue different tranches of securities with each tranche having a different maturity and rate of return. This compares with pass through securities where investors receive pro-rata distributions of interest and principal in each payment, depending on the structure and the remaining life of the underlying mortgage. With a CMO or other types of asset backed bonds, once sufficient funds have been received to pay interest to all investors, any further cash flow generated by the assets is applied to redeem the principal on different tranches in a predetermined order. For example, the diagram below illustrates the cash flows on the various tranches of an hypothetical CMO up to and including the redemption of the first tranche:

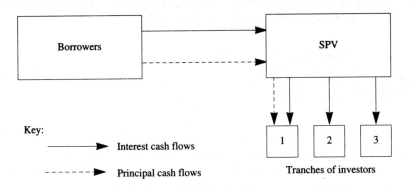

Diagram 3.6: Cash flows on a CMO

Once the first tranche is redeemed the cash flows would be as follows:

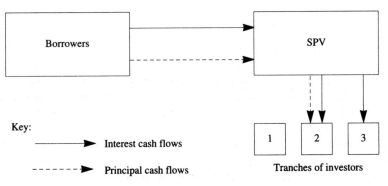

Diagram 3.7: Cash flows on a CMO

This process would continue until all the tranches had been redeemed.

CMO structures

CMOs offer great flexibility to issuers in devising different tranches and bonds to attract different types of investors. Some of the most common are as follows:

Planned Amortisation Classes (PACs)

This is essentially a scheduled sinking fund mechanism which virtually assures the investor of fixed payments over a predetermined period except at times of very high prepayments. It is typically the second tranche of a CMO issue. Whilst it produces cash flow certainty for the PAC investor it will increase the uncertainty for investors in the other tranches. These bonds are also known as Planned Redemption Obligations (PROs) and Stabilised Mortgage Reduction Terms (STRMs).

Targeted amortisation classes (TACs)

Similar to PACs except that the investor receives no protection against high rates of prepayment.

Z tranche or accrual bonds

These are zero coupon CMO tranches. They receive no payments until earlier tranches are paid in full but the coupon attributable to them is accrued and added to the principal balance ('negative amortisation') whilst the earlier tranches are still outstanding. Once the earlier tranches have been retired, the coupon interest plus prepaid principal is paid to the investor. From this point it behaves as a pass through bond. The accrual feature of the Z tranche tends to make all other tranches less volatile.

Residuals (or CMO equity)

The residual is entitled to the cash flows which arise from the difference between the cash flows contributed by the collateral (less servicing fees) and the cash flows required to fund the other CMO tranches. The fixed rate residual (where the underlying mortgages pay interest at a fixed rate) is essentially a bear market instrument. The majority of the income of the residual is derived from excess interest, the spread between the coupon on the collateral and the coupon paid on the CMO bonds. If interest rates rise, there will be fewer prepayments and the CMO's average life will increase, thus earning more excess interest. Residuals are highly responsive to changes in prepayment rates and are therefore extremely volatile.

Pricing of CMOs

Complex computer models have been developed by issuers and their investment bankers to price CMOs. Principally the value of these securities is a function of current interest rates, levels of prepayment made, reinvestment rates achieved, the underlying credit risk and the level of ongoing expenses of the issue.

While some elements, such as current interest rates, are certain others such as the prepayment rates and reinvestment rates must be estimated. As with pass through securities, models have been developed in order to analyse prepayment and default histories of mortgage loans. While reinvestment rates are particularly difficult to predict, this risk may be reduced through the use of interest rate swaps or a substitution clause, whereby the issuer is committed, under certain circumstances, to apply principal moneys received from borrowers in purchasing substitute mortgage loans.

CMOs are often issued at a discount to their expected net present value because the issuer will retain the residual interest in the pool of assets which is taken into account in the pricing of the issue.

CMO bonds are priced at a spread over comparable United States treasuries securities or other government bonds. Comparable treasury bonds will have a maturity close to the average life of the CMO bond. The average life is calculated as the average time to the receipt of principal, weighted by the amount of principal. The most important factors which determine the size of the spread over treasuries are the quality of the collateral, and the volatility of the prepayment rates on the underlying mortgage loan pools.

3.22 Benefits – issuer/originator

• The ability to issue different tranches with different structures means that packages can be tailored to meet the requirements of each investor. For example, fixed and floating rate tranches can be issued with differing maturities, and the 'Z' tranche appeals particularly to investors (such as pension funds and other institutional investors) who wish to reduce the risk of prepayment and the consequent need to reinvest funds elsewhere. The ability to tap a broad range of investors can reduce the costs of the issue.

• The assets are securitised into bonds, with regular coupon payments and a series of bullet redemptions. Such structures facilitate the calculation of the security's yield and comparison with other instruments and therefore the pricing of the issue.

3.23 Benefits – investor

• There are usually a large number of mortgage pools which are assembled as the collateral for CMO bonds. As a result, the mortgage portfolio is diversified, which can reduce default risk and lead to a more predictable pattern of prepayments.

• The segmentation of the paydown of the principal of the CMO bonds reduces the prepayment risk for each tranche compared to pass through securities. This is particularly the case with PACs and Z tranche bonds.

• The issue of securities with varying terms and maturities allows the investor to choose a security that best suits his investment needs.

• Most CMO bonds are liquid securities with an active secondary market.

3.24 Risks and disadvantages – issuer/originator

• If the issue is made through an SPV, this entity will have to be capitalised even if only to a minimal extent, which will increase the costs of the issue.

• Because the cash flows generated from the assets are restructured in this type of transaction, the securities usually have to be sold at a discount because the timing and value of future payments are uncertain and the value of residual interest, which usually accrues to the issuer, cannot be quantified precisely.

• The monthly proceeds which are received from typical mortgages have to be reinvested to fund the interest and principal payments to the investors. The interest payments to holders of the CMO bonds are usually made quarterly or semiannually. If the proceeds cannot be reinvested at the required rate, a shortfall may arise.

• The investor may require some sort of insurance for defaults, which will increase the costs of the issue.

3.25 Risks and disadvantages – investor

• For CMOs, normal bond measures of return such as yield to maturity or average life will be affected by prepayments. The historical data, which will form the basis of the assumptions as to average life in the issue documentation, while indicative of the possible average life, is unlikely to be matched in practice by the specific pool of assets being securitised.

• Although the risk of prepayment is reduced when compared with pass through securities future prepayments may not match the models used to predict the average life of the security. This could lead to different maturities than expected particularly for the Z tranche and means that yield calculations will not be truly comparable with other bonds.

3.26 Accounting and taxation questions

• The accounting and taxation questions for CMOs are set out in sections 3.11 and 3.12. For tax questions relating to CMOs issued in the Euromarkets see section 2.18 dealing with Eurobond issues in chapter 2 – Debt Instruments. Tax questions relating to the Z tranche are as for stripped securities in section 2.137.

3.27 Stripped mortgage backed securities

Stripped mortgages backed securities, which are also known as interest only/principal only mortgage backed securities (IOPOs), are a hybrid between asset backed securities and stripped treasuries/zero coupon bonds. The interest elements of the cash flows from the mortgage backed securities are stripped from the principal element and separate Interest Only (IO) securities backed by these cash flows are issued. The securities backed by repayment of principal are known as Principal Only (PO) bonds.

The structure of IOs and POs causes them to react differently to movements in interest rates than most other fixed income securities and in completely opposite ways to each other. When interest rates rise, the rate of prepayments tends to decrease (as the mortgagor will now be paying interest at below market rates and will not wish to refinance the mortgage). This means that the income stream on the IOs will continue longer than originally anticipated and therefore their price will rise (despite the fact that interest rates are now higher which on normal fixed rate bonds leads to a fall in price). However, the repayment of principal will now be slower so the holders of the POs will have to wait longer for redemption, and consequently the price of these securities will decrease. However, as market interest rates have risen and the final maturity has been extended, the fall in price will be greater than with a comparable stripped treasury or zero coupon bond. Consequently, IOs and POs are very sensitive to movements in interest rates and their prices are extremely volatile.

An example of the dangers for both the issuer and investor in this type of complex security occurred in May 1987 when Merrill Lynch in the United States disclosed that they had suffered US$250 million in trading losses through dealings in PO securities. While the blame for this loss has been placed on unauthorised trading activity, it appears that the original problem may have occurred through an apparent mispricing of an issue of US$1.7 billion IOPOs in the previous month. As a result, the underpriced IOs were sold quickly and the bank was left holding US$900 million in overpriced POs. Subsequent price movements and additional purchases of POs resulted in the reported trading losses.

3.28 Benefits – originator

• The novel features of these instruments means that different types of investors can be attracted. This may be particularly true for very active issuers of asset backed securities (such as GNMA in the United States) who may have saturated investor demand in the plain vanilla market.

3.29 Benefits – investor

• The distinct way in which IOPOs react to movements in interest rates may make them attractive to fund managers as a hedge against other components of a fixed interest portfolio.

3.30 Risks and disadvantages – originator

• Whilst it may be possible to issue these securities at relatively low interest rates, the unusual nature of the two portions of the issue, their sensitivity to interest rates and the lack of comparable instruments makes pricing difficult. If the two tranches are incorrectly priced relative to each other the issuer may not be able to sell one type of bond and thus be exposed to the volatile price movements.

3.31 Risks and disadvantages – investor

• The extreme volatility of these securities can lead to significant losses if interest rates move unfavourably.

• It is difficult to hedge the interest rate risk of these securities other than by holding IOs to hedge POs and vice-versa.

3.32 Accounting questions

• The accounting questions are set out in the section 3.11.

3.33 Taxation questions

• Is a PO bond a stripped security similar to a zero coupon bond with the issuer's option for early redemption at par? If so, is the investor deemed to receive income on an accruals basis? (See also questions on deep discounted bonds in section 2.129).

• Is the investor's profit on early repayment (ie where it is in excess of discount amortised to date) or sale regarded as income or capital gain?

• Should an IO bond be taxed as an annuity under United Kingdom tax law?

• Can the investor obtain any tax relief for amortisation of cost of purchase against income received, or loss on sale of an IO bond?

3.34 Sterling mortgage backed floating rate notes

The only market for asset backed securities of any size in Europe is sterling mortgage backed floating rate notes (FRNs). Between 1989 and June 1991, 85% of the asset backed securities issued in Europe have been backed by United Kingdom sourced mortgages. They have significant structural differences from United States mortgage backed securities, which are described elsewhere in this chapter. The development of the market and legal and technical features which issuers and investors have to address are described in section 3.65 below on securitisation in the United Kingdom.

By far the largest proportion of securities which have been issued backed by United Kingdom Residential Mortgages have been FRNs which reflects the fact that virtually all of the mortgages issued in the United Kingdom are variable rate. To date, all the sterling mortgage backed FRNs which have been issued have been collateralised by endowment mortgage loans. A mortgagor who takes out an endowment mortgage loan pays interest on the outstanding principal (usually monthly) but does not repay principal on an amortising basis, as would be the case with an annuity mortgage; instead the mortgagor makes regular payments into an endowment life policy taken out with an insurance company. When the policy matures, the proceeds are used to repay the outstanding principal on the mortgage. Therefore, in contrast to United States mortgage backed securities, the FRNs backed by these mortgages have a bullet rather than an amortising structure. This can be illustrated as follows:

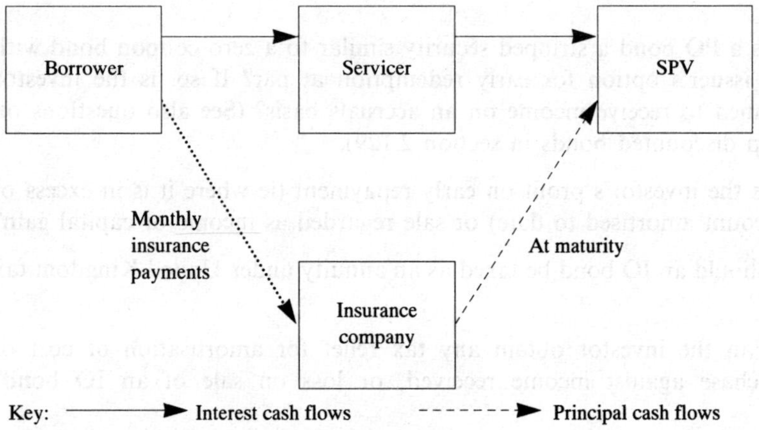

Diagram 3.8: UK mortgage backed issue

Other significant features of these securities are as follows:

- because the underlying mortgages pay interest at variable rates, the rate of prepayment is much lower than on fixed rate United States mortgages and is more predictable because it does not fluctuate with movements in interest rates;

- the majority of these securities pay interest at a margin over LIBOR with the coupon being set quarterly. As the mortgagors will typically pay interest monthly, the servicer is usually required to reinvest the mortgage repayments to ensure that the issuer has sufficient funds available to make payments to the bondholders;

• the collateral available to secure the FRNs has most commonly been enhanced by pool insurance, whereby an insurer has agreed to underwrite losses of up to 10% of the balance of the pool of mortgage loans. In addition, the mortgagor is usually required to take out insurance covering physical damage to his property and (less often) a mortgage indemnity policy to insure a proportion of the mortgage loan in the event of default;

• the rate of interest on the mortgages is set by the servicer (who is also usually the originator of the mortgages). The servicer can have a potential conflict of interest. To maintain goodwill amongst mortgagors and to generate more business the servicer may wish to keep the mortgage rate as low as possible, although if the rate is too low in comparison to LIBOR the interest could be insufficient to fund the issuer's obligations to the bondholders. To prevent this, most issues provide that the servicer has either to set a minimum mortgage rate sufficient to pay interest to bondholders, or commit to make good any shortfall;

• historically, there have been periods in the 1980s when LIBOR has been higher than the average rate of interest on endowment mortgage loans, which creates the possibility of a shortfall. Some issues have incorporated liquidity insurance purchased from insurance companies, together with recourse to the originator in the event of a shortfall.

3.35 Benefits – issuer/originator

• As for asset backed securities generally – see section 3.7.

3.36 Benefits – investor

• The rate of prepayment on these securities is usually stable and predictable, and less sensitive to changes in interest rates.

• Sterling mortgage backed FRNs usually have a high yield relative to conventional FRNs. They are particularly attractive to banks who can finance the investment in the interbank market and lock in an interest rate spread.

• The securities are collateralised by United Kingdom residential mortgages, which have historically offered a high quality of security with a low default rate (although rising interest rates in the United Kingdom in the late 1980s and early 1990s have increased significantly the default rate).

3.37 Risk and disadvantages – issuer/originator

• The risk of a funding shortfall can lead to the originator having to make advances to the issuer if this is prescribed by the terms of the issue. This could prejudice attempts to account for the transfer of the assets as a sale as the issuer retains some of the risks of ownership of the assets.

• The purchase of pool insurance and possibly liquidity insurance can be expensive.

3.38 Risk and disadvantages – investors

• The possibility of a funding shortfall can mean that the investor has a credit risk to the originator unless liquidity insurance has been purchased.

• Issues can incorporate pool insurance, and liquidity insurance and the underlying mortgages may be partially secured on mortgage indemnity and building insurance, in addition to the maturity of the endowment policy. Therefore the investor is to some extent exposed to the credit-worthiness of the insurer over the life of the issue. This risk is increased if the same insurance company provides all the insurance associated with the issue.

3.39 Accounting questions

• Does the potential of having a funding shortfall (if the interest rate on the mortgage loans exceeds LIBOR) mean that the originator should consolidate the accounts of the issuing SPV in its accounts?

• The other accounting questions are set out in section 3.11.

3.40 Taxation questions

● See taxation issues for floating rate bonds in Section 2.27.

3.41 Commercial property schemes

A natural progression for the techniques used in the securitisation of residential mortgages has been the development of commercial property schemes (CPS). A major factor in this development has been the size of commercial property transactions and developments. Commercial property transactions are moving beyond a size that can be financed comfortably by a single insurance company or pension fund (the traditional financiers in this market). In addition, the lack of liquidity in the property market makes securitisation more attractive. Single properties can usually only be sold following protracted negotiation. The uncertainty surrounding the valuation of properties is also reduced if securities are publicly traded.

There have been a number of issues of rated commercial mortgage bonds (RCMBs) in the United States market. RCMBs are bonds backed by mortgages on single commercial properties. The bonds are rated on the basis of specific criteria for rating commercial property loans which have been developed by the major credit rating agencies. Despite this, the market has remained very small, partly because of investors' perceptions of the high risks involved in commercial property.

United Kingdom

During the 1990s a number of single property schemes were developed in the United Kingdom. However, none of these were successful, partly due to taxation problems, but also because of the condition of the property market. In the late 1980s the shares of property companies were trading at discounts to their assets values and the situation has deteriorated during the current economic recession in the United Kingdom, which has affected the commercial property sector particularly severely.

The schemes which were developed were as follows:

● *Property Income Certificates (PINCs)* – PINCs are stapled certificates entitling investors to voting rights in the management company managing the property ('the management company'), in addition to a share of the rental income and capital gains.

● *Single Property Ownership Trusts (SPOTs)* – SPOTS enable investors to acquire units in a trust established to acquire a single property. Unlike PINCs, SPOTs were not able to obtain tax transparency. The Inland Revenue would not agree to treat SPOTs as authorised unit trusts. Therefore, in addition to the SPOT being liable to capital gains tax (CGT) on the disposal of the property, the investor would also be liable to CGT on the sale of his unit.

● **Single Asset Property Companies (SAPCO)** – A SAPCO is a company formed to acquire a single property, funding the purchase by issuing conventional securities (ordinary shares, preference shares and bonds). The only public issue to date, by Billingsgate City Securities Plc, was not well received by the market.

The Stock Exchange requirements

In May 1987, The Stock Exchange issued rules for the listing of commercial (or single) property schemes.

The most important requirements which need to be considered for a listing for a CPS on The Stock Exchange are as follows:

● the scheme must own the freehold of the property or a long leasehold interest (110 years or more);

● the value of the property must be at least £10 million;

● the annual rental on the property must exceed annual expenditure;

● all the earnings of the CPS must be fully distributed to investors except for 'reserves to finance prudent estate management';

● the CPS must maintain a 'log book' giving various disclosures about the scheme and the property (such as the nature of the title to the property and the structure of the building);

● the prospectus for the issue must include reports by accountants, solicitors and surveyors;

● an annual report and other information must be submitted to The Stock Exchange.

In addition, in 1990 the Department of Trade and Industry and the Securities and Investments Board issued draft regulations concerning the operation and marketing of authorised property unit trusts (APUTs), which could allow large institutional holders of property such as pension funds to unitise parts of their portfolios.

Belgium

There has been a market for property certificates ('certificates immo-biliers/vastgoedcertificaten') in Belgium since the 1960s. These certificates represent rights to the proceeds of the rent and of the sale of a property owned by the company issuing the certificates. The holder of the certificates has usually the right to receive a proportional share in the following:

• a fixed annual amount corresponding to the amortisation of the capital invested; this portion is in general equivalent to the depreciation allowances on the property held by the issuing company, computed on a straight line basis;

• annually an amount of income corresponding to the rentals less running costs and depreciation allowances received by the issuing company;

• the capital gains (if any) realised by the issuing company at the time of the sale of the property.

The certificates are transferable and are classified as investments.

The Belgian tax authorities treat the income received by the holders (ie the portion of the annual payments corresponding to share of rental income and capital gains on sale referred to above) as investment income. This has the main consequences that:

• withholding tax on interest (at the rate of 10%) may be due;

• payments when made on an arm's length basis are tax deductible.

The value of property certificates outstanding at 30 August 1990 amounted to approximately BEF 32.5 billion. 86 property certificates have been issued and property certificates relate mainly to shopping centres (45%) or office premises (50%). The average annual returns in 1990 range from −20% to +22.7%.

3.42 Benefits – issuer/originator

• CPS provide a new source of equity finance for the issuer, in particular giving the owner of the property the opportunity for a partial sale.

• The issuer can dilute his level of risk in the ownership of the property by attracting other investors.

3.43 Benefits – investor

• CPS allow investors to make small investments in large properties. The returns on capital on larger properties are in general considerably higher than from smaller properties.

• CPS introduce liquidity into the property market, reducing the lead time between the decision to invest and the completion of the transaction.

• The valuation of large buildings for direct investment is often very uncertain. Where these properties are traded in securitised form, a valuation is available in the form of the market price of the security.

• Where the issue contains both debt and equity, the ordinary equity holders are often entitled to the proportion of the capital increase in the property value that would have otherwise been attributable to the debt holders. Such an entitlement considerably increases the gearing of the ordinary equity holder. Preferred equity holders are entitled to a proportion of the total rental income exclusive of expenses such as running costs, corporate taxation and the risk of shortfall.

3.44 Risks and disadvantages – issuer/originator

• The issuer may forego some or all of the capital gain on the property if the price rises.

3.45 Risks and disadvantages – investor

• The value of the investor's holding is dependent on the value of the underlying property and will fall if property values fall. Any reduction will be further compounded by the level of gearing in the equity holding.

• Where the preferred equity holder is entitled to an exclusive proportion of the rentals, then these additional costs are usually born by the ordinary equity holder. As a result, the return on investment of the ordinary equity holder may be reduced significantly.

3.46 Accounting questions

The accounting issues will depend on how the CPS is structured and its relationship to the original owner of the asset. The questions will include:

• Should the CPS be consolidated into the accounts of the original owner?

• When will the CPS recognise and distribute profits arising from the ownership of the property?

• Is any profit made from the sale to the CPS realised and distributable?

3.47 Taxation questions

• The PINCs Association has obtained confirmation from the United Kingdom Inland Revenue that the entity itself would be tax transparent, that is, it would not attract tax and the tax liability of each investor be determined by the tax status of that investor. The PINCs holders are entitled to the profit rental which the financial intermediary makes under the terms of the leases, the payments made to the PINCs holders being annual payments paid under deduction of basic rate income tax. Investors will be liable to tax on capital gains on any disposal of PINCs.

• The United Kingdom tax position of SPOTs is less clear:

– Will the trust be a unit trust for tax purposes so that it is itself taxable on income?

– Can the trust become an authorised unit trust so that any gains on sale by it will be tax free?

– Will transfers of units be subject to stamp duty?

3.48 Structured receivables financing (SRF)

This is a general term for the securitising or unitising of assets other than mortgages or property, such as leasing receivables or other short to medium term receivables. The assets must have some or all of the features described in section 3.6 above. These securities can be unitised (pass through securities) or securitised as collateralised financing transactions (asset backed securities).

Amongst the issues that have been made, and the assets used to back them, the most significant are CARs (certificates of automobile loans) and CARDs (certificates of amortising debts). These are discussed separately in sections 3.51 and 3.57 respectively. Other issues which have been made include:

CLEOS – Collateralised Lease Equipment Obligations

In March 1985, Sperry Lease Corporation offered the first public issue of securities which were backed by computer leases. The issue was conducted using a 'pay through' structure which paid monthly principal and interest. The issue made use of a minimum amortisation schedule in order to assist investors determine the potential life of the note. Additional security was provided by a bank providing a letter of credit for 10% of the issue.

Particular complexities which confront the issuer of this type of security include the choice of lease quality, the annuity payment structure of most leases and the use of upgrading and maintenance agreements. The most likely issuers of this form of security would be companies with relatively low credit ratings but with a good portfolio of high quality leases. This could enable these companies to obtain funding at rates below their normal unsecured borrowing rate.

FRENDS – Floating Rate Enhanced Debt Securities

Mezzanine finance, combining features of both debt and equity, was increasingly used to fund management buy outs and leveraged buy outs during the 1980s. A natural progression from this is the securitisation of the issued mezzanine (or working capital financing) debt. Mezzanine debt in the United Kingdom has traditionally taken the form of short term notes or more recently loans with equity warrants attached. Securitised junk bonds have yet to appear.

In 1988, Continental Illinois launched a repackaged bond issue collateralised against senior loans from United States LBOs. Two floating rate tranches were used. The senior tranche was listed on the Luxembourg Stock Exchange and achieved a BBB credit rating, while the junior tranche remained unlisted and unrated (but was issued at a significant premium over LIBOR). As with a CMO structure, the issued securities are repaid as the underlying loans amortise. In effect, the purchase of these securities would create a ready made diversified loan portfolio.

Credit For Exports (CFX)

The first securitisation of export credit receivables in the United Kingdom

196

took place in 1984, through a special purpose vehicle called Credit For Exports plc. This securitisation arose from the rescheduling of Brazilian export debt that had been guaranteed by the United Kingdom Export Credit Guarantee Department ('ECGD'). This rescheduling was funded though the issue of unsecured floating rate notes designed to match the underlying cash flows of the loan.

Particular features of the structures used in order to issue these securities include the use of an SPV, a specified delay in payment of principal and interest (although this has been eliminated in the more recent issues), and a revolving credit facility to ensure prompt payment. The guarantee of the export credit receivable by a government agency such as the ECGD will usually ensure a high credit rating.

PARRs – Purchased Accelerated Recovery Rights

PARRs are an example of the wide range of receivables that may be considered for securitisation. PARRs involve the securitisation of the anticipated cash flows from recoveries on written off bank loans. In January 1986 First City Bank Corporation of Texas sold the rights to the first US$20 million of future recoveries on written off loans.

In addition, securities have been issued backed by leases, consumer marine loans (boat loans), manufactured housing loans, and commercial mortgage loans.

3.49 Benefits, disadvantages and risks

The benefits and disadvantages and risks for these securities are as for either mortgage pass throughs or CMOs, depending on which structure is adopted (see sections 3.15 to 3.18 and 3.22 to 3.25).

3.50 Accounting and taxation questions

● The accounting and taxation questions are set out in sections 3.11 and 3.12.

3.51 Certificates of automobile receivables (CARs)

CARs (an acronym devised by Salomon Brothers which is now commonly used to describe the market) are created by the repackaging of automobile loan receivables into tradeable securities. The first public issue of CARs was made by Marine Midland in May 1985 for US$60 million. Since that date, the market has grown substantially. As of 31 May 1991, public issues of CARs with a total value of US$50 billion have been made in the United States, representing 39% of the United States non-mortgage asset backed market.

Most issues of CARs have been by finance subsidiaries of automobile companies. The most active issuers in the market have been General Motors Acceptance Corporation (GMAC), Ford Motor Credit Corporation and Chrysler Financial Corporation. CAR issues tend to be very large and issue sizes in the range of US$1 billion to US$5 billion are not uncommon. The structures used to issue CARs have included both pass through securities and variations of the CMO structure.

The assets backing CAR issues have high depreciation rates compared to other assets such as mortgages. However, the collateral backing these issues is usually of a high quality, due to the following factors:

• in the United States, automobile receivables have a relatively low default rate compared with other types of consumer lending;

• borrowers are usually required to make downpayments to protect the lender against any decline in value of the collateral;

• lenders will normally require the borrower to insure the vehicle fully against damage or loss.

As a result, and due to the enhancement of the collateral by the use of pool insurance, CAR issues in the United States have generally attracted an AAA or AA rating.

Compared to mortgage backed securities, CARs exhibit stable cashflows for investors and have lower rates of prepayment. This is principally for two reasons:

• the stated maturity of CARs issues is usually between three and five years, compared to 20 or 30 years for mortgage backed securities. Due to the faster amortisation of principal of the underlying receivables, the prepayments represent a smaller percentage of the total payment of principal;

• the prepayment rates on car loans are much less sensitive to changes in interest rates. Due to the high depreciation rates of motor vehicles, it is difficult to refinance car loans if interest rates fall. Lenders usually charge a premium for loans secured by used cars.

Most issues of CARs have been made in the domestic United States market. The first issue in the Euromarket was made in 1986 by GMAC and raised US$276 million. The issue was structured a pass through. Euromarket investors have shown resistance to this type of investment due to the monthly payment structure, prepayment risk and concerns about the liquidity of the secondary market. The first issue of CARs backed by United Kingdom sourced loans was originated by Chartered Trust and lead managed by Goldman Sachs in June 1990. The principal features of the issue were:

- a special purpose company (Cardiff Automobile Receivables Securitisation (UK) plc) was set up to acquire the receivables;

- the issue was partly guaranteed by a 15% letter of credit, which together with the quality of the underlying collateral was sufficient to earn the issue a triple A credit rating;

- the term to maturity was five years, although on each interest date prior to June 1993 there is the option to revolve in new loans to replace those which have matured. This will allow the average life of the deal to be extended;

- the interest rate exposure is reduced via interest rate swaps taken out whenever the SPV acquires receivables from Chartered Trust.

Pricing of CARs

CARs issued in the United States using the pass through structure are priced in a similar way to mortgage passes through securities – at a spread over United States Treasury instruments with a maturity comparable to the average life of the CARs issue. The model most commonly used to predict prepayments is the Asset Backed Security (ABS) Model (also known as the Absolute Model).

The ABS model measures prepayments in each month by assuming that a constant percentage of the original number of loans in the pool prepay each month, unlike CPR and PSA (see section 3.14) where each month's prepayments are expressed as a percentage of the outstanding loans at the end of the previous month. For example, with a 1.3% ABS rate (which characterises most car loan pools), one would expect that 13 out of every 1,000 loans originally in the pool would repay each month. The ABS model has been found to correspond more closely than other models such as CPR and PSA to the historical prepayment characteristics of car loans.

Asset backed securities

3.52 Benefits – issuer/originator

• The lower prepayment risk means that CARs can be issued with a coupon set at a lower spread over the rate offered on government securities with similar maturities than is possible for mortgage backed securities.

• The spread between the interest rate payable on automobile loans and the rate offered on CARs is very wide compared to mortgage backed securities, which therefore increases the excess interest earned by the originator.

3.53 Benefits – investor

• The relatively low prepayment rates give investors greater cash flow certainty than mortgage backed securities.

• The average lives and maturities of CARs can make them particularly attractive to medium term investors such as insurance companies.

• CARs offer a high yield compared to other debt instruments with similar credit ratings and maturities.

3.54 Risks and disadvantages – issuer/originator

• As for asset backed securities – see section 3.9.

3.55 Risks and disadvantages – investors

• Because of the high depreciation rates of motor vehicles, the quality of the collateral is highly dependent on the credit terms offered by, and the due diligence procedures undertaken by, originators. These should be described in the issue prospectus.

3.56 Accounting and taxation questions

• The accounting and taxation questions are set out above in sections 3.11 and 3.12.

3.57 Certificates of amortising revolving debts (CARDs)

CARDs (a trade name of Salomon Brothers) is one of the most recent developments in the securitisation of receivables. The first public issue backed by credit card receivables (by Republicbank Deleware) did not occur until early 1987. Since that date, the market has grown very quickly. As of 31 May 1991, US$53 billion of credit card receivables had been securitised in publicly issued asset backed securities, representing 42% of the non-mortgage asset backed market in the United States.

The structure of CARDs is significantly different from mc⁻ᵗ ɔther forms of asset backed securities, due to the nature of the assets which back the issue. Credit card receivables are revolving consumer credit facilities and are usually unsecured. Revenue is generated mainly from interest charges and from annual fees charged for having the credit card.

CARD issues have been made using both the pass through and pay through structure. Some of the more distinctive features of CARDs issues are:

• credit cards are revolving facilities so the repayment of principal is (within certain limits) at the discretion of the cardholder. CARD issues incorporate a specified 'revolving' period when the principal on the CARDs is not amortised. The issuer will retain the principal received from the cardholders and reinvest the proceeds in additional receivables to maintain the level of principal outstanding on the CARDs. After the revolving period, the principal will be repaid relatively quickly, and therefore the average life of a CARDs issue is largely determined by the length of the revolving period;

• the originator will generally dedicate a specified set of cardholder accounts to the CARDs issue. Generally, this will include considerably more receivables than are allocated to the CARDs investors. This allows for substitution during the revolving period, to take account of the seasonality of credit card use (which will tend to peak during holiday periods) and attrition when accounts are discontinued. The pool of accounts is frozen at the end of the revolving period;

● most United States CARDs issues have incorporated rapid pay out clauses to protect the investors, whereby amortisation will occur prematurely if a prescribed 'pay out event' occurs (such as the bankruptcy of the issuer or losses on the credit card portfolio above defined levels);

● the credit card receivables are unsecured so the level of guarantee or insurance obtained for a CARDs issue is generally higher than with other asset backed securities. However, the number of the receivables dedicated to the CARDs issue and the diversification of risk due to the large number of accounts involved will also help to reduce the risk for the investor.

The majority of credit cards are provided by banks, mainly using the Visa and Mastercard systems, and as a result most of the CARDs issues have been based on bank originated receivables. However, there have also been a number of issues backed by credit cards offered by retailers (store cards).

Most CARDs issues have taken place in the domestic United States market but the number of deals being offered in the Euromarkets is increasing. The largest issue in the Euromarkets to date has been a US$1.25 billion issue for Citicorp launched in June 1990. All of the issues in the Euromarkets to date have been backed by receivables sourced in the United States. Some of the issues have been for subsidiaries of European corporations. For example, the Spiegel Charge Account No.1 (SCAT 1) a US$150 million issue was made in December 1988 for Spiegel Inc, a United States retail mail order merchant which is a subsidiary of Otto Versand. The issue was underwritten by Deutsche Bank.

Variation

CARDs with controlled amortisation	CARDs structure whereby the principal is repaid at a constant predetermined rate following the end of the revolving period. This structure is made possible by the purchase of a guaranteed investment contract from an insurance company, which ensures that principal received can be reinvested at the required rate until it is paid to investors.

Pricing of CARDs

Because of the revolving period, the cash flows for most of the life of CARDs securities are stable and predictable, which makes them more like conventional bonds than with most asset backed securities where principal is repaid on an amortising structure. The principal difference to a conventional bond (apart from the fact that interest is usually paid monthly) is that principal is repaid over a period, although this period is usually fairly short. As a result, the spread over comparable United States Treasuries on CARDs is usually narrower than for other asset backed securities.

3.58 Benefits – issuer/originator

• Because of the reduced prepayment risk CARDs issues can generally be sold at a lower yield than other asset backed securities.

3.59 Benefits – investor

• The use of the revolving period when there is no amortisation of principal substantially reduces the prepayment risk compared to other forms of asset backed securities.

3.60 Risks and disadvantages – issuer/originator

• The use of a 'buffer' of receivables dedicated to the CARDs and the possible need for recourse to the issuer due the receivables being unsecured may prejudice the removal of the receivables from the originator's balance sheet.

3.61 Risks and disadvantages – investor

• The use of 'pay out events' to protect investors may create an early maturity of the CARDs and therefore investors should assess the possibility of a pay out event occurring.

• The investor is generally exposed to reinvestment risk in the limited period when the principal is repaid following the revolving period.

3.62 Accounting questions

• Investors in CARDs have an interest in a pool of accounts, but the issuer or originator will retain the excess. In addition, the investors percentage interest on the pool constantly changes. Do these facts preclude off-balance sheet treatment by the originator?

• How are payments of principal allocated to investors during the amortising period? If a percentage of all principal payments of the pool is allocated to investors, rather than a percentage based on their residual participation balance, can this be treated as a sale by the originator?

• How should any gain or loss on sale be calculated by the originator? Should it include only a calculation of the spread on the receivables which exist at the inception of the transaction, or is it reasonable to include an estimate of the spread on the receivables to be purchased during the revolving period?

3.63 Taxation questions

• See section 3.12.

3.64 Securitisation in Europe

The market for asset backed securities in Europe is far smaller and less well developed than in the United States for a number of reasons, the most significant of which are:

• legal and regulatory restrictions or the absence of a legal framework to enable the market to develop;

• resistance by European investors to unfamiliar and complex instruments;

• the existence of developed markets which offer competing sources of funds and investments. This is particularly true in the mortgage loan markets, where mortgage lenders have access either to large retail savings markets (as in the United Kingdom) or to mortgage bond markets (such as the '*Pfandbriefesystem*' in Germany and Switzerland or the mortgage bond market in Italy).

The only market of a significant size which has developed during the 1980s has been in sterling mortgage backed securities, backed by United Kingdom sourced residential mortgage loans. However, there have recently been developments in other countries, and there have been examples of securitisation in France, Sweden, Italy and Spain. Local regulation means that these securities have often been issued offshore, or structured as private placements or syndicated loans.

It is likely that the market will continue to expand over the next few years. This trend will be given a significant impetus because credit institutions in the EC will have to comply with the capital adequacy requirements set out in the Basle Convergence Agreement from 1 January 1993. The requirement for credit institutions to comply with the 8% capital to risk weighted asset ratio will make it more attractive to banks and other institutions to use securitisation to remove assets from their balance sheet (indeed, this was the primary motivation for the introduction of the 'Titrisation' legislation in France to provide a legal framework for securitisation). However, the EC directive assigns a risk weighting of 50% to mortgage loans. Therefore, the securitisation of other consumer loans, such as car loans, leases and credit card debts, which attract a 100% risk weighting, may be more attractive.

One aspect of the EC directives may to some extent inhibit the development of the securitised mortgage loan market. Investments in mortgage backed securities attract a 100% risk weighting (despite the fact that the underlying mortgage loans would only attract a 50% weighting on the balance sheet of the originating bank). The majority of asset backed securities issued to date in Europe have been FRNs. As the most active investor in the FRN markets are banks, the implementation of the directives would make these assets less attractive. When the Bank of England implemented the directives for banking companies in the United Kingdom in January 1991, the yield on sterling mortgage backed FRNs increased by approximately 20-30 basis points reflecting the increase in risk weighting from 50% to 100%.

The following sections briefly describes the status of the market and the legal and regulatory framework in different European countries. Of course, one of the crucial restraints on securitisation in a particular country is the extent to which assets which have been securitised can be taken off balance sheet by the originator. The guidance available in different European countries is also discussed in these sections. For EC countries, the implementation of the 7th Directive on group accounts has had a significant impact. The concept of 'subsidiary undertaking' is defined in the Directive largely on the basis of control, rather than legal ownership. Therefore, originators and their advisors need to consider carefully the structure of any transaction using a special purpose vehicle.

3.65 United Kingdom

3.66 Mortgages

To date, the largest asset backed market in Europe has developed from the securitisation of United Kingdom residential mortgages. The residential mortgage market is dominated by building societies, whose principal activity is to make residential mortgage loans which are funded by deposits taken from retail investors. During the 1980s the building societies have faced increased competition in the mortgage market from United Kingdom and overseas commercial banks, insurance companies and 'Specialist Mortgage Lenders' (SMLs). The majority of mortgage backed securities issues in the Euromarkets to date have been issued by the SMLs with some issues being made by insurance companies and commercial banks (principally overseas banks). SMLs use securitisation as their principal source of funding, as, unlike building societies and banks, they do not have access to alternative sources of funds such as retail investors or the wholesale market. The most active of the SMLs have included The Mortgage Corporation plc (a subsidiary of Salomon Brothers) and The Household Mortgage Corporation plc.

Building societies have not yet entered the mortgage backed securities market, mainly due to regulatory restrictions but also because the majority of societies have not been restricted by capital constraints. In addition, the margin on mortgage lending over the cost of funds makes conventional mortgage lending profitable. It is also possible that the building societies have not wished to assist competitors in the mortgage market such as SMLs by helping to develop the market on which the SMLs mainly rely as a source of funds.

The structure of bond issues backed by United Kingdom residential mortgages is discussed in sections 3.34 to 3.40. In summary, some of the more important characteristics of the United Kingdom mortgage market which affect the mortgage backed security market are:

• unlike the United States, the majority of United Kingdom residential mortgages pay interest at variable rates, with the rate being set by the lender;

• to date, only mortgage loans sourced in England and Wales have been securitised – there are important differences between the Scottish and English legal systems and there are a number of legal issues (particularly

206

relating to the transfer of mortgages) which would have to be resolved before Scottish mortgages can be securitised;

• borrowers who take out a loan for a qualifying purpose (which includes the purchase of a property for primary residence) can obtain tax relief on interest paid on principal up to £30,000 by making net interest payments to mortgage lenders who recover the deducted amounts from the Inland Revenue. This 'Mortgage Interest Relief At Source' (MIRAS) system can be operated only by qualifying lenders, who in practice are normally resident in the United Kingdom. Due to the difficulty of a non-United Kingdom resident becoming a qualifying lender, it is often more practical for an SPV issuing mortgage backed securities to be resident in the United Kingdom;

• there are two methods by which the transfer of a mortgage debt and the related security can be effected; a legal assignment or an equitable assignment. Legal assignments in England and Wales are governed by the 1925 Law of Property Act (for unregistered land) and the 1925 Land Registration Act (for registered land). The registration fees and other costs can make the legal transfer of registered land expensive and administratively complex and for this reason an equitable assignment can be more attractive. However, this method of transfer means that the assignee has a less secure position and the originator remains the lender of record.

3.67 Consumer Loans

Legislation relating to consumer loans will extend to securities backed by, inter alia, automobile loans, credit cards, and agreements. The most important legislation in this area is the 1974 Consumer Credit Act. Some of the constraints which this legislation imposes on the securitisation of United Kingdom consumer loans are as follows:

• the legislation currently extends only to loans with a limit of £15,000;

• if loans are sold to an SPV which issues securities, the SPV may fall under the definition of an 'ancillary credit business' which will require it to be licensed under the Consumer Credit Act;

• if, for example, an originator sells credit card receivables to an SPV, the originator may have joint and several liability with the SPV in an action brought by the borrower.

In summary the provisions of the Consumer Credit Act and other consumer legislation such as the Sale of Goods Act have to be carefully considered prior to issuing securities backed by such receivables.

Partly due to these legal constraints, the market for securities backed by consumer loans such as car loans and credit card receivables have not developed in the United Kingdom to the extent of the secondary mortgage market. The first non-mortgage sterling denominated securitised issue in the United Kingdom was made in June 1990, managed by Goldman Sachs. This is described further in section 3.51.

3.68 Regulation in the United Kingdom

In addition to the general legal and accounting framework which particularly address the conditions under which assets may be removed from the originator's balance sheet, many of the potential originators of asset backed security issues are subject to regulation. In the next few paragraphs, the following are discussed:

- building societies;

- the Bank of England;

- The Stock Exchange;

- general accounting requirements.

Building societies

The activities of building societies are subject to the Building Societies Act ('BSA') and they are regulated by the Building Societies Commission. Section 18 of BSA States that a building society cannot invest in a corporation unless that is a body designated by statutory instrument. In July 1989, an 'Appropriate Mortgage Company' (or 'AMC') was designated as a body in which a building society may invest. AMCs must have the following characteristics:

- be limited by shares and registered in the United Kingdom;

- maintain systems similar to those required by building societies for the safe custody of documents and for assessing the adequacy of security;

- secured loans made by the AMC must be capable of being transferred without the borrower's consent;

- the company may make a secured loan only in circumstances where the building society itself would have had the power had the borrower been a member of the building society.

The use of an AMC would enable a building society both to purchase mortgage loans made by other lenders and to make mortgage loans which could subsequently be transferred to an SPV and securitised. The use of the AMC would avoid the complications arising due to the membership rights of borrowers from building societies.

Before the commission made the 1989 Amendment Order it sought assurance from the Building Societies Association that societies would comply with a code of practice on certain aspects of the transfer of mortgages. The main requirements of this code are:

• that a borrower from a society or an AMC which is making a loan on terms which enable it to be transferred without further intervention by the borrower should understand, before the mortgage is completed (or, by agreement, at some later time), that it might be transferred;

• the implications of such a transfer for the borrower's membership of the building society should be fully explained at the time of the transfer;

• where a loan is transferred to an AMC, the borrower must be made aware that the AMC is a separate legal entity;

• the borrower should be clear as to who is administering the loan after any transfer;

• the borrower should be notified of certain information available to the society or the AMC concerning the transferee's policies which may affect the terms of the loan after transfer.

Building societies are subject to capital requirements imposed by the BSA, and the requirements relating to off balance sheet transactions are set out in Prudential Note 1988/2. The basic requirement is that capital is not required so long as the society is absolved from any continuing credit or interest rate risk, and that in practice it will not feel compelled to support the scheme if it is in difficulty – the Note states that this may be the case with an SPV established by the society.

The Bank of England

In response to the growth in securitised products, the Bank of England issued policy notice BSD/1989/1 on 'Loan Transfers and Securitisation' in February 1989. The policy notice covers both the sale of single loans and the packaging, securitisation and sale of loan pools. It also covers the transfer of risk under subparticipation agreements. The requirements of the policy notice are binding on all institutions regulated under the Banking Act, regarding their prudential and statistical returns to the Bank of England.

The purpose of the Bank's policy was to ensure that:

• loan sales and packaging achieve their intended effect of passing rights and obligations from the seller to the buyer;

• all parties fully understand their responsibilities and risks;

• any material risks are properly treated in the Bank's supervision of banks.

The Bank of England distinguishes between three different types of loan transfer, novation, assignment and subparticipation, and sets out conditions where the transfer leads to assets being excluded from the seller's risk asset ratio.

In all transfers the seller must have transferred its rights and obligations and not have any residual beneficial interest, nor can the buyer have any formal recourse to the seller for any future losses arising. The seller may retain an option (but not an obligation) to repurchase the loan provided the loan remains fully performing. Where the transfer involves the packaging or pooling of loans and the seller remains as the servicing agent, then the administered assets may be excluded for risk ratio purposes only if the special purpose vehicle is perceived as independent from the seller. Accordingly, the following additional conditions will apply:

• the transferring bank may not own any share capital in the vehicle or scheme;

• the board of directors of the vehicle must be independent although the transferring bank may have one director representing it;

• the transferring bank must satisfy its auditors and legal advisors that the terms of the scheme protect it from any liability to investors in the scheme other than from negligence;

• the transferring bank must also be able to demonstrate that it took all reasonable precautions to ensure that it is not obliged nor feels impelled to support any losses suffered;

• the vehicle or scheme may not include any reference to the transferor in its own name.

The Stock Exchange

In June 1990 The Stock Exchange changed certain of its listing requirements, and permitted the issue of securities backed by financial assets to be listed in London provided that they conform with the requirements of Section 7 Chapter 2 of The Yellow Book (see chapter 4 – Equity and Equity Linked Instruments). There are a number of detailed requirements concerning the description of the assets used to back the securities and the structure of the transaction and the anticipated flow of funds.

3.69 Accounting requirements

In the United Kingdom, guidance on the most appropriate accounting treatment has been given by:

- Companies Act 1989;
- ED 49 'Reflecting the substance of transactions in assets and liabilities'.

Companies Act 1985

The Companies Act 1985 does not address the issue of securitisation specifically but the 1989 Companies Act has amended the 1985 Companies Act by widening the definition of subsidiary to base it on control rather than legal ownership of an entity's share capital. The 1989 Act implements most of the provisions of the EC's 7th Directive with regard to the definitions of subsidiary undertaking. An undertaking may be a subsidiary of a parent undertaking where the parent:

- holds a majority of the voting rights;
- is a member of the undertaking and can appoint or remove directors having the majority of the votes on the board;
- has a right to exercise a dominant influence (that is, can control its operating and financial policies) over the undertaking by virtue of provisions either in its memorandum or articles, or in a 'control contract';
- is a member of the undertaking and exercises control via an agreement with other shareholders;
- owns a participating interest in the undertaking and actually exercises a dominant influence or operates unified management.

SMLs such as the National Home Loans Corporation who had developed securitisation programmes prior to the implementation of the 1989 Companies Act have used vehicles in which they had control of the board and all the ordinary shares (but only 50% or less of the equity, with other parties holding preferred shares). It appears that these securitisation vehicles could well become subsidiary undertakings under the new definition.

Exposure Draft 49

ED 49 was issued in May 1990. It sets out high level principles to identify when assets and liabilities, transactions and arrangements should be recorded in an entity's balance sheet. Specific guidance is also given on certain arrangements, including mortgage securitisation and loan transfers. The statement sets out what maybe interpreted as best practice. However it is not mandatory, and may be amended, in whole or in part, prior to being issued as an Accounting Standard. According to the published work programme of the Accounting Standards Board, a financial reporting standard on off balance sheet finance is planned for issue later in 1991.

The general principle set out by ED 49 is that assets and liabilities should be recognised in the balance sheet where certain 'recognition criteria' are met. Recognition would normally be required where an entity carries substantially all the economic risks and rewards of ownership.

The specific guidance contained in ED 49 for securitised mortgages and loan transfers is summarised below.

Securitised mortgages

ED 49 contains a guidance note referring to arrangements for the securitisation of mortgages involving the setting up of a special purpose vehicle. The ED sets out various conditions which must be assessed to determine the most appropriate accounting treatment. If the transfer of mortgages fails to satisfy any of the four conditions, then for accounting purposes it is not an effective sale by the originator. Consequently, the assets should be retained in the originator's balance sheet, and any sales proceeds recorded as a liability. The conditions in ED 49 are:

• the transfer does not contravene the terms and conditions of the underlying mortgages;

• the originator has no residual beneficial interest in the principal amount of the mortgages and the issuer has no formal recourse to the originator for losses;

• the originator has no obligation to repurchase the mortgages at any time;

• the arrangements of the transfer are such that if mortgages are rescheduled or renegotiated the issuer, not the originator, is subject to any revised terms.

If the originator is the parent of the SPV either specifically under the terms of the Companies Act 1985 or exercises control as a 'quasi-subsidiary', the SPV should be accounted for as a subsidiary. A quasi subsidiary is a term which has been introduced by ED 49, despite the introduction in the Companies Act 1989 of new control based definitions of a subsidiary undertaking. A quasi-subsidiary is defined in the ED as any enterprise where a company has, in substance, the same degree of control over it, and receives the same benefits and risks as though it were legally a subsidiary, and proposed accounting practice is that the company should consolidate such an enterprise. This is essentially an anti-avoidance measure, because some off balance sheet vehicles may not fall within the new definition in the Companies Act.

The ED recognises that, with some schemes, the originator's interest in the vehicle is confined to the residual cash flow or profit, and that it may be more relevant for the originator's accounts to focus on the net cash flows rather than the gross cash flows of the issuing vehicle as a source of benefits available to the originator. Whether or not this treatment is appropriate depends on the extent to which the originator is insulated from the risks attaching to the SPV's assets and liabilities. If the securitisation is structured so that the risk that the originator will bear any losses incurred by the issuing vehicle or its investors is effectively removed, a net presentation in the originator's accounts will be more appropriate. If a securitisation arrangement meets all of the six conditions listed below, then the net presentation is acceptable, otherwise the SPV is deemed a quasi-subsidiary, and should be fully consolidated in the accounts of the parent (the originator). These conditions (as extracted from the ED) are as follows:

• the originator does not bear any of the ongoing expenses of the scheme. However, it may make a one-off contribution to enhance the creditworthiness of the issuer. It may also lend on a long-term subordinated basis to the issuer provided that the loan is repayable only following winding up of the scheme. Any transactions under these headings must be undertaken at the initiation of the scheme;

• apart from finance permitted under the condition set out above, the originator does not fund the issuer and in particular does not provide temporary finance to cover cash shortfalls arising from delayed payments or non-payments of mortgages which it services;

• the originator does not intentionally bear any losses arising from the effect of interest rate changes on the scheme. However, it may enter into interest rate swap agreements at market prices with the issuer. There should be provision for unintended temporary losses arising from normal administrative delays in changing mortgage rates to be recovered by the originator as soon as possible;

• except for the duration of a start-up period of no more than three months, the originator is under no obligation to replenish the mortgage portfolio by transferring additional assets to the issuer;

• the originator does not retain an option to repurchase (or refinance) the mortgages except where the mortgage portfolio has fallen to less than 10% of its maximum value and the option extends only to fully performing mortgages;

• the originator is protected under the terms of the scheme from any liability to investors in the issuer, save where it is proved to have been negligent. The arrangements for servicing the mortgages and financing the issuer are of sufficient quality and flexibility to satisfy the standards of commercial behaviour expected of the originator. Furthermore, the latter has taken all reasonable precautions to ensure that it will not feel impelled to support any losses suffered by the issuer or its investors.

If the transaction meets these conditions and the originator can in effect legitimately exclude the transferred mortgages from its balance sheet, the proposals require note disclosure to explain the nature of the company's interest and any income arising therefrom. As a minimum, the note should include a summary balance sheet and profit and loss account of the SPV, details of any income recorded in the transferor's own accounts and an indication of how long this income will continue to be received.

The conditions set out above do not seek to determine whether the originator should consolidate the SPV by reference to control, in the sense of directing operational and financial policy, because the agreements which are put in place when the vehicle is set up usually determine these matters. Instead, they concentrate on the extent to which the originator enjoys the benefits and is exposed to the risks of the assets and liabilities.

Most of the conditions set out in the Application Note to ED 49 would allow many of the issues of securities backed by assets which have been originated by United Kingdom corporations to remain off balance sheet, providing that the provisions of the Companies Act concerning equity participation and the composition of the board of directors were complied with. Indeed, the Application Note seems to be inconsistent with some of the main principles of the ED itself. In particular:

• if the originator is allowed to lend funds to the issuing SPV on a subordinated basis (this would presumably include a subordinated loans) and the purchase of the junior notes in a senior issuing structure. In this case, the originator will directly be exposed to the risk of loss on the mortgages;

• the originator is allowed to enter into an interest rate swap with the issuer, providing this is at market rates. Effectively, the originator will be able to extract the residual profit from the underlying assets, although

ED 49 states that an asset should only cease to be recognised as an asset when a transaction or event occurs which deprives the enterprise of future benefits or takes away its control.

However, two of the conditions in particular would have an adverse impact on the typical securitisation structure. These are:

• the requirement that the originator should not have an obligation to repurchase the mortgage at any time. In most securitisations, the originator is required to repurchase mortgages if defects are discovered. This condition appears to be unduly restrictive, and perhaps it would be more appropriate for a standard to allow repurchase in strictly defined circumstances;

• the requirement that the originator does not replenish the portfolio after an initial period. This condition is particularly relevant if these conditions were to be applied to issues backed by assets other than mortgages, such as credit cards, where substitution is an important part of the structure. Perhaps this condition should be restricted to preventing substitutions of delinquent assets (unless this arose as a result of a breach of warranty), rather than those which have matured or have been repaid.

In October 1991 the Accounting Standards Board (ASB) issued further proposals regarding the accounting treatment of securitisations. These proposals depart from the approach set out above and note that there are two key issues; first whether the transfer of assets constitutes a sale for accounting purposes, and secondly whether the relationship between the issuer and originator is such that the issuer should be consolidated with the originator. The proposals state that a sale will not have ocurred if the originator guarantees the performance of the securitised assets in some way (eg where the issuer has recourse to the originator for losses, or provides subordinated debt or a reserve fund from which losses are deducted). This is substantially similar to the conditions proposed in ED 49. Second, the proposals in the ASB statement are that if the residual benefit of the net assets of the issuer accrue to the originator the issuer should be consolidated. This approach contrasts with the proposal under ED 49 under which a net presentation of the investment in the residual benefit is acceptable. This proposal is likely to result in the securitised assets of existing issues having to be included in the consolidated accounts. The ASB propose that securitisation issues should have separate disclosure on the face of the balance sheet. It remains to be seen whether these proposals are implemented and, if so, whether new structures are designed to overcome the 'residual benefit of the net assets' test.

Loan transfers

A further guidance note deals with schemes not involving the establishment of an SPV. These circumstances would include the transfer of mortgages or other loans to a trust which issues participation certificates (pass through securities). Only if a loan transfer or subparticipation satisfies all of the criteria set out can the loan be eliminated from the lender's balance sheet, together with the related funds received by way of consideration. If one or more of the conditions set out ceases to apply then the loan would be retained on the balance sheet of the originator, and the consideration received be shown as a liability. Provision should also be made for any loss arising. The conditions set out on the ED are similar to those for securitised mortgages.

Additional disclosure is also required of the amounts of any loans outstanding at the balance sheet date which have been netted against a subparticipation, and the amount of any interest receivable on loans subparticipated.

3.70 Tax considerations

Tax status of the SPV

Under United Kingdom tax rules, the preferred route for a securitisation transaction is through an incorporated SPV, as the rules in relation to trusts can be particularly complex. In order for the SPV to obtain tax relief for its expenditure, including its cost of funds, it must either be a trading company or an investment company for tax purposes. In September 1991, the United Kingdom Inland Revenue issued a guidance letter to, amongst others, the Institutes of Chartered Accountants in England and Wales and in Scotland. This letter makes clear that the United Kingdom Inland Revenue will not normally accept that a company which has entered into arrangements which make it impossible for it ever to enjoy a profit is a trading or an investment company. An SPV may be regarded as trading but trading company status is likely to be difficult to achieve unless the SPV intends to originate new business, which may be undesirable from a commercial viewpoint, or to deal in mortgages or other debts. A company is likely to be regarded as an investment company if its principal activity can be shown to be the making of investments and it can be shown to be operating on a normal commercial basis with a view to making a profit. If the SPV is regarded as neither a trading nor an investment company then the SPV is not entitled to tax relief for either management expenses or interest paid.

Tax issues

Where the SPV is regarded as an investment company the following problems may arise:

- investment companies cannot get a deduction for short (on borrowings of less than 12 months) interest paid to someone other than a United Kingdom bank, discount house or a Stock Exchange member, although interest on debt capable of exceeding one year (annual interest) is deductible;

- it would be desirable for the SPV to pay interest gross on its borrowings, which can be achieved by issuing quoted Eurobonds, provided either the beneficial owners are not United Kingdom resident or the bonds are held in a recognised clearing system;

- it is possible that cash flow problems may result because interest may be received net under the MIRAS arrangements but interest payments to investors will be gross;

- if a Eurobond is denominated in sterling it may also be regarded as a qualifying corporate bond on which any capital gains arising on disposal are exempt. However, United Kingdom resident investors may be chargeable to tax on income on an amount representing interest accrued on the bond at the time of disposal;

- the SPV may not get a deduction for insuring its assets, since only expenses incurred in making and managing investments are deductible, so it could instead 'insure' its liability to make payments to its lenders (ie a guarantee premium), since it is possible to get a deduction for incidental costs of obtaining loan finance;

- any bad debts would be capital losses (provided they are realised) and therefore only allowable against current and future capital gains;

- if mortgages within the MIRAS arrangements are transferred to the SPV it will be desirable to stay within MIRAS arrangements and therefore United Kingdom Treasury approval for the SPV to be a 'qualifying lender' will be required. It should be noted that arrangements under which beneficial entitlement to mortgage interest is apportioned amongst more than one person cannot be accommodated within the MIRAS system;

- if the originator and the SPV are not within a 75% tax group the transfer of assets could be deemed to be at market value;

- if the SPV pays dividends to the originator it will have to account for ACT unless a group income election is in force;

- if interest payable is a function of the SPV's surplus for the period it is likely that any interest in excess of a market rate will be treated as a distribution and hence not be tax deductible;

• the nature of any transfer of assets and the structure of the transaction will have VAT, stamp duty and withholding tax implications.

Given some of these often onerous tax burdens in the United Kingdom on securitisation structures, it may be beneficial for them to be constituted off-shore.

3.71 Channel Islands

The market for the securitisation of mortgage loans has recently been developed in the Channel Islands. Credit Suisse First Boston and Skandinaviska Enskilda Banken (SEB) issued in November 1990 a US$160 million mortgage backed FRN issue undertaken by a Jersey registered company. The issue was the first European securitisation of mortgage loans outside the United Kingdom. The issue was backed by mortgage loans originated in Sweden and the terms of the issue are described further in Section 3.87. In such cases it is usual for an orphan company to be established by the credit institution which originated the assets and for the Jersey registered company to be held under the terms of a trust established under Jersey Law by an instrument of trust on a discretionary basis.

Under current Jersey law payments made in respect of notes issued for asset backed securities will be made without withholding tax or duties or charges and Jersey income tax is not deducted from any interest paid by the Jersey company to a holder not resident in Jersey for taxation purposes. It is also usual for the Jersey company to obtain exempt company status under the Finance (Jersey) Law 1989. Exempt companies are treated for any year of assessment and for all purposes of the income tax (Jersey Law 1961), as amended, as not resident in Jersey and are not liable to Jersey income tax in respect of their profits.

Special provisions for Jersey and Guernsey were negotiated in connection with the entry of the United Kingdom into the European Community. Under the arrangements concluded, none of the fiscal provisions in the Treaty of Rome apply to Jersey and Guernsey and there is no obligation to follow any harmonisation of taxation the Community might adopt.

A French bank and other banks have also used a Jersey company owned by a trust to issue a series of variable interest limited recourse secured notes with a 25 to 30 year maturity. There have been a number of such issues through Jersey.

In some cases the establishment of Jersey Companies will require registration under the Collective Investment Funds (Jersey) Law 1988. A similar law applies in Guernsey. The Jersey and Guernsey authorities will discuss draft proposals for such schemes and are well versed in the operation and approval of such schemes.

3.72 France

3.73 Mortgage loans

As in the United Kingdom, mortgage loans form the largest non corporate domestic credit market. Mortgage loans can be subsidised or undertaken on the free market. The legal framework of the mortgage loan market derives from two laws dating from 1966 and 1969, which were amended in 1985. The market is regulated by the *'Credit Foncier de France'* (CFF). This is a commercial company whose shares are listed on the Paris Stock Exchange. The state does not directly own any shares but it does nominate the directors. The principal objective of the CFF is to facilitate the refinancing of mortgage loans, providing that they meet certain criteria; they must be loans with a maturity between 10 and 20 years, and be made for house purchase or home improvement. CFF also provides loans directly to individuals with a total value in excess of Ffr 200 billion, which represent about 11% of the total market. The market is very secure and French mortgages have historically been very safe assets with a low incidence of default.

Historically, the majority of French residential mortgages pay interest at a fixed rate. However, in response to the high level of prepayments following the sharp fall in interest rates in 1986 most new mortgages are contracted at floating rates.

For several reasons, it is unlikely that a large market will develop for the securitisation of French mortgages. The most important of these are as follows:

• French mortgages are to a large extent 'non standard' (particularly due to low start mortgages and subsidies), making them difficult to package and securitise;

- mortgages are priced at a very narrow spread over the cost of wholesale funds.

3.74 Consumer loans

France has experienced a high increase in consumer loans during the second half of the 1980s. The end of credit restraint in 1986 led to a 33% increase in consumer lending in 1986 and 100% from 1986 to 1988. Despite this, France has a high savings rate compared to most developed countries, mainly due to the residual effect of credit restraints from 1982 to 1986 and relatively high interest rates. Therefore, the market still has a great potential for growth: consumer loans represented only 4% of the total loans in the French economy in 1986, rising to 6.5% in 1988.

The most important legislation relating to consumer loans is the 1978 consumer credit law known as 'Loi Scrivener'. This regulates all credit granted to private consumers, with a maturity in excess of three months and principal of Ffr100,000 or higher. The borrower can ask the court to suspend his interest payments for up to two years. The interest rates are freely negotiable within certain constraints as follows:

- they are maintained below a level defined every six months by the Banque de France;

- they are not more than 25% higher than market rates for loans of the same maturity.

More than half of this market is originated by French banks; the remainder by specialised lenders like leasing companies. As is explained further below, most leases and corporate trade receivables cannot be securitised, although this is possible for car loans. These are particularly attractive because of the large spread over the cost of funds.

3.75 Legal framework

In France it is the government rather than the market that has determined the structure of securitisation transactions. French securitisation is regulated by a law dated 23 December 1988; this legislation is specifically aimed at securitising the assets of banks. The main incentive in favour of securitisation is to shrink balance sheets and overcome the constraints on the issue of new shares by some banks (like the state owned Banque

Nationale de Paris, 'BNP'). Financial institutions are often thinly capitalised in France, particularly in relation to the rules proposed by the EC Capital Adequacy Directives to implement the Basle Convergence Agreement.

At the end of 1989 France's three largest banks – Societe Generale, Credit Lyonnais and BNP – had an average capital ratio of 8.7%. According to January 1990 estimates, the securitisation of 1% of credit institutions' consumer loans (Ffr36 billion) could mean a Ffr 1.5 billion – 3 billion decrease in capital requirements.

Titrisation

Prior to 1988, the assignment of debt was possible under French law, but there was no mechanism to create a negotiable instrument. The law of December 1988 made securitisation ('*titrisation*') possible by creating the framework for the '*fonds commun de creances*' (FCC), the equivalent of the SPV. However, as is explained further below, the FCCs are not incorporated entities and have some distinctive characteristics.

The creation of an FCC is simple in theory. A bank which wants to securitise a pool of receivables will create an FCC whose only purpose will be to purchase receivables from a credit institution and to issue securities, each representing a share in the pool of receivables. In addition to the FCC, the titrisation structure requires the establishment of a management company and depositaire. Their roles are explained further below.

Management company

The management company ('*Societe de Gestion*') is responsible for all aspects of the management of the FCC. The *Societe de Gestion* is regulated by the COB (the French Stock Exchange Commission) and must be able to establish sufficient financial net worth or adequate guarantees.

Moreover it will:

- establish rules of the FCC regarding:

  - protection against non payment of receivables;

  - future use of funds;

  - length of the financial year.

- appoint an auditor and commission an evaluation of the project by a rating agency;

- make an agreement with the seller explaining the way the management company will manage the collection of receivables;

- be responsible for the FCC against third parties;

- be responsible for the production of the audited accounts for the year;

- confirm every six months the existence of the underlying assets;

- control the amount of shares held by units trusts.

The Depositaire

The *Depositaire* collects funds due to the FCC from the receivables and distributes the sums received. It also acts as a depository for the assets of the FCC. The *Depositaire* does not have to be a company (so public bodies can act as a *Depositaire*). It has the following power in relation to the management company:

- ensuring the legality of the decisions of the management company;

- controlling the biannual inventory of the FCC assets carried out by the management company;

- it may request the court to dismiss the directors of the management company.

The law requires that the following guarantees are provided for the holders of FCC units against the nonpayment of the receivables:

- a guarantee provided by a credit institution or an insurance group;

- the purchase of additional receivables that may be required to be substituted for delinquent assets. However, substitution is not allowed for receivables which have been repaid;

- the issue of equity and debt whose claims are subordinated to those of the holders of FCC units. These assets cannot be purchased by unit trusts or individuals.

The creation of an FCC must comply with the following rules:

- only assets with a maturity date of more than two years can be securitised;

- an FCC can only purchase loans originated by financial institutions;

- the repurchase of securities by the FCC is allowed;

- an FCC cannot borrow money;

- an FCC does not have a 'legal personality' in the sense that action cannot be brought against it in law;

- the loan portfolio has to be valued and rated by a credit rating agency;

- the FCC can issue securities which have different rights with regard to principal and interest, and with different maturities;

- no more than 5% of the securities issued by an FCC can be placed with unit trusts managed by the originating bank (in order to avoid self-securitisation);

- an FCC can be created in such a way that it pays a terminal bonus.

To date, 19 issues have been launched for an estimated total of Ffr 12 billion. The relatively small volumes is because, as the legislation currently operates, there are a number of significant disadvantages for issues using the titrisation structure. These include:

- substitution is not possible: this substantially reduces the average life of issues and so lowers the economic advantage of securitisation;

- the maturity of the underlying assets is limited to two years: this eliminates the possibility of securing many types of consumer loan, such as credit card receivables;

- loans originated by leasing companies cannot be secured. (Leasing companies in France are part of the '*Societes Financieres*' system and are not considered to be financial institutions).

Because of these restrictions, it is likely that many future issues will take place offshore. In the first securitisation of car loans originated in France (in January 1990), the SPV was domiciled in Guernsey in the Channel Islands to avoid the necessity to comply with the regulations introduced by titrisation. The loans were originated by DIAC, the finance subsidiary of Renault. 21,000 consumer loans with a value of Ffr 500 million were sold to the SPV. The structure allows for the possibility of substitution.

3.76 Accounting requirements

The French National Accounting Council has issued a recommendation relating to special purpose vehicles created by the loan securitisation.

- The mortgage loans are recorded by the FCC at nominal value; the difference between this value and the purchase price is recorded in a special asset account and the difference is amortised over the life of the loans (pro-rata to capital repayment or using an actuarial method).

- Shares are recorded at their nominal value and any issue premium is recorded in a special liability account. The premium is amortised through the profit and loss account in a similar way to the premium on mortgage loans.

FCCs established under the titrisation legislation do not normally have to be consolidated by the originator. However, the French Banking Commission has recently required that entities such as unit trusts have to be consolidated if they are majority owned by a bank.

3.77 Tax considerations

● FCCs are exempt of income tax and VAT.

● Interest on FCC shares may bear a withholding tax upon the buyer's request of 25% for shares with over five years maturity, and 32% for others.

● Profit on the disposal of shares is taxed at a 16% rate for shares with over five years maturity and 32% for others.

3.78 Germany

3.79 Mortgages

There are 26 privately owned mortgage banks in Germany, regulated by the Mortgage Bank Act 1899, which was last amended in 1988. Some mortgage banks are incorporated under public law (the Act Regarding Mortgage Bonds and Related Bonds of Public Law Banking Institutions 1926, as last amended in 1986). Both types of banks restrict their operations exclusively to the extension of long term loans secured by mortgages and the granting of loans to municipalities and other public institutions. They refinance themselves either by issuing mortgage bonds (*pfandbriefe*) secured by mortgages which the banks have taken as security, or by municipal bonds, backed by their claims on the municipalities or other public bodies. The bonds have par values of DEM 100, pay interest annually, typically at fixed rates and have maturities that range up to 30 years. There are no restrictions on purchases by non-residents in either the primary or secondary markets.

Both mortgage and communal bonds may be issued in registered or bearer form. The redemption terms may specify repayment in full at maturity by drawings or by repurchase in the market. Mortgage bonds are issued directly by the borrowing institution without using a banking consortium, though banks may act as placing agents. Mortgage bonds are listed on stock exchanges and there is an active and liquid secondary market.

3.80 Scope for securitisation

At present there is no market for asset backed securities in Germany. By using factoring or forfeiting techniques, German companies can achieve similar results to securitisation. This is principally because of the attractive conditions offered by banks and the competition in the factoring and forfeiting market. In addition, German banks do not have a great incentive to securitise their assets, as they are generally better capitalised than many of their competitors in Europe, whilst the mortgage bond market provides an attractive source of funding for mortgage loans.

However, the asset backed securities market could develop in Germany in the near future. There are no legal restrictions to prevent the development of this market, except that the Bundesbank seeks to control the issue by foreign borrowers of deutschmark bonds on the Euromarket. The Bundesbank issued guidelines in 1986 stating that such issues should have a minimum maturity of two years, and be lead managed by a German financial institution. The lead manager should notify the Bundesbank of the terms of the transaction prior to the issue. Regulations which require government permission for the issue of bonds will be cancelled in 1991. The cancellation of withholding tax on interest income in 1990 and the reduction in the minimum maturity of Euro deutschmark bonds has improved the conditions for issue of asset backed securities.

Receivables, like automobile loan receivables and credit card receivables, are suitable for securitisation. They provide good quality collateral to the investors because of their 'spreads' (difference between interest rate in loans and interest rate of the securities). In addition, there is a ready supply of data on default and prepayment rates. There are no restrictions in creating tradeable securities which are secured on mortgage and consumer loans. As the market for these types of loans is very extensive, securitisation could take place on a large scale.

To date, the following issues of securities backed by assets originated in Germany have been made using offshore vehicles:

● KKB Bank, a subsidiary of Citibank, issued DEM 230 million of

Schuldschein notes backed by consumer loans in December 1990, using a Cayman Islands vehicle called Consumer Loan Finance No1. The notes pay interest at 0.3125% over LIBOR, and have an average life of 16 to 18 months with a maximum maturity of six years. The issue obtained an Aaa rating from Moody's and the collateral was enhanced by a letter of credit and a reserve deposit. The transaction was structured as a private placement, possibly to avoid the requirement for Bundesbank approval.

• Europaiche Hypothekenbank, a Luxembourg mortgage bank formed by Deutsche Bank, issued a five year DEM 100m bond in June 1990 carrying a coupon of 7.75%. This is not a securitisation, but an attempt to introduce an offshore market for the German *Pfandbriefe* system (mortgage bonds).

3.81 Accounting requirements

The requirements for companies to prepare consolidated accounts are set out in section 290 of the German Commercial Code ('the Code'). Where enterprises are within a group under the uniform control of a company (the parent) which is incorporated in Germany, and the parent owns a participating interest, the parent is required to prepare consolidated accounts. A participating interest is defined in section 271 of the Code as holdings in other enterprises designed to serve the business through creation of a long term connection to that other business. For these purposes it is of no consequence whether the shares take the form of certificates or not. In case of doubt, it shall be assumed that holdings in an enterprise whose nominal value exceeds in total a fifth of the nominal capital of the enterprise are participations.

3.82 Taxation considerations

The transfer of assets from the originator to the SPV is a taxable event for the originator. Other taxation issues are similar to those set out in chapter 2 – Debt Instruments.

3.83 Switzerland

There has been a mortgage backed bond (*Pfandbriefe*) market in Switzerland since the 1930s. The bonds are issued by two private specialist mortgage bond issuing companies ('*Pfandbriefebank Schweiz Hypothekarinstitute*' and '*Pfandbriefebank der Kantonalbanken*') who are authorised under Swiss Federal Law. The law also specifies other matters such as the rights and duties of the specialist companies, the issue of the bonds, and the control over security and valuation of the mortgaged properties.

The activity of these specialist companies is restricted to issuing Pfandbriefe. However, the companies have their own employees and they are not dedicated to the issue of one particular type of securities and will issue bonds into the market on a regular basis. The companies issue bonds and lend the proceeds to the banks participating in the system. The banks use the proceeds to finance their mortgage lending business. The mortgage loans remain the property of the banks who continue to administer the loans and remain liable for any defaults. Therefore the assets remain on their balance sheet. They are required to keep a register of the loans and store the mortgage deeds securing the loans separately. The amount of mortgage backed bonds which the companies can issue is limited by the requirement that their total liabilities (including the bonds) cannot exceed fifty times their equity.

This is an attractive source of funding for the banks. The role of the specialist companies and the legal requirements and controls, leads investors to accept lower yields than would be the case with debt issued directly by the banks themselves. The current legal framework in Switzerland does not allow banks to securitise their own mortgage loan books.

3.84 Sweden

3.85 Mortgages

The Swedish mortgage loan market is dominated by six mortgage lending institutions who are supervised by the Swedish Bank Inspection Board. This dominance is due to the fact that finance companies and insurance companies are not permitted to issue bonds in the Swedish bond market to finance mortgage lending, and banks are restricted as to the amount they can lend to borrowers at fixed rates for periods over a year. However, with the exception of the large Urban Mortgage Bank, most mortgage institutions are owned by banks and insurance companies.

The majority of residential mortgage loans in Sweden bear a fixed rate of interest and are partially amortising with a maturity of five years. When the loan matures, the borrower will normally refinance the loan with the same mortgage lender at a new fixed rate. In the last two years there has been an increase in the number of floating rate mortgages. Mortgage institutions are not allowed to lend more than 85% of the valuation of the property, and in practice they do not normally lend more than 75%. The *Statens Bostadsfinansieringsaktiebolag* (SBAB), which is a government owned mortgage lender, makes subsidised loans for new homes in excess of the amounts which the mortgage institutions are allowed to lend.

3.86 Consumer loans

There has been a large increase in consumer lending during the 1980s. To date the losses on these loans have been moderate, but these losses are now expected to increase significantly. This increase is mainly due to a tougher economic climate, falling prices in the real estate and stock markets and changes in the tax system regarding the deductability of interest.

Typically consumer loans have a five year maturity, with annuity amortisation schedules. If the loans are made by a bank, they are legally only for one year at a time. The agreements often enable the lender to 'adjust' the interest rate periodically to market levels. In substance, the loans bear interest at floating rates. At present, the quality, maturity and interest structure makes consumer loans unsuitable for securitisation.

3.87 Issue of securities

Any public debt instrument issued in Sweden has during the post war period required the permission of the Swedish Central Bank. The general perception is that the Central Bank has not been in favour of the issue of asset backed securities. It is expected that the requirement for Central Bank permission will be lifted in 1991. However, the creation of asset based companies, will most likely be regarded as 'finance companies'. This means that those companies would have to meet the same type of capital adequacy requirements as the banks, which would eliminate the reasons for establishing such companies. A limited number of Swedish companies (e.g. Volvo) have issued asset backed securities through their subsidiaries abroad.

The first Swedish mortgage backed security was issued offshore (in 1990) and secured on mortgage loans originated by *Svenska Fastighetskredit* (SFK), a mortgage lending institution which is a subsidiary of Skandinaviska Enskilda Banken. The issue was placed with investors outside Sweden. The issue was an FRN with a face value of US$ 160 million, using an SPV registered in Jersey. Interest is payable quarterly in arrears at a margin of 0.3% over LIBOR, with an expected maturity of four years. The mortgage loans in the portfolio pay interest at fixed rates and are partially amortising being denominated in Swedish kronor. The borrowers do not have any right to prepay their loans prior to maturity except in certain circumstances following the death of a borrower. SFK is not under any obligation to refinance the mortgage loans at maturity. To enable the issuer to make payments of interest and principal, the issuer has entered into a currency coupon swap (see chapter 5 – Hedging Instruments) and has arranged a liquidity facility and pool insurance.

Due to the domestic restrictions, it is likely that future issues will also take place offshore. An increase in the interest for this type of security is likely to develop as the new tax system coupled with the high level of prevailing interest rates is expected to increase the demand for high quality interest rate instruments. In addition the banks are eager to reduce their on balance sheet lending, due to the requirement to conform with the Basle Convergence Agreement.

3.88 Accounting requirements

Under Swedish GAAP assets can be offset against liabilities if a short term loan in a foreign currency is financing certain assets, and if the following conditions are met:

● the receivable is without credit risk;

● the receivable and the payable are 'packaged' (the payable is collateralised by the receivable);

● the receivable and the payable are of equal amounts;

● the receivable and the payable have the same due dates;

● the currency risk of the payable is effectively hedged.

The above criteria have been laid down in a pronouncement by the

Swedish Institute of Authorised Public Accountants. The pronouncement specifically states that it should not be applied in other situations which may be similar. Nevertheless, in the absence of definitive guidance on the general question of off-balance sheet financing there are some similar arrangements where netting of assets and liabilities have been made in restricted circumstances.

The Swedish Companies Act stipulates that where a company directly or indirectly holds more than half of the votes attached to the shares of another enterprise, or exercises a dominant influence over the enterprise and has a considerable share in its earnings, the company is a parent company and the other enterprise is a subsidiary. An option through which one company would control more than half of the votes of another enterprise would not create a parent subsidiary relationship. According to the Companies' Act, a company which exercises decisive influence over an enterprise and in which the company has a share in its result, is a parent company and the other enterprise a subsidiary. In practice, however, such enterprises are seldom consolidated unless the investing company holds more than half of the votes.

3.89 Taxation issues

The transfer of the assets from the originator to the SPV is a taxable event within the originator's ordinary business. Gain or loss will be included in the taxable income of the originator in the year of transfer. No transfer tax or similar duty is imposed on the transfer.

If the SPV is located in a low tax area and is at least 10% owned by the originator and at least 50% by other Swedish residents they will be taxed on their share in the operating profit (if any) of the SPV.

Since financial services are exempt from VAT no such tax will be payable or recoverable as a consequence of the transfer.

3.90 Spain

In Spain, asset backed securities have only been developed in connection with the mortgage market. The secondary market was established under Act 2/1981 of 24 March 1991, expanded by Royal Decree 685/1982 of 17 March 1991. The purpose of the Act was to create a market for mortgage securities in order to promote the building and construction sector and to lower financing costs. The Spanish investor has not yet appreciated the credit quality of this type of security. Therefore their interest rates need to be competitive with other higher risk securities.

There are three kinds of mortgage security in Spain: *'Cedulas'* (Bonds) *'Bonos'* (Debentures) and *'Participaciones'* (Participations).

Cedulas

The main participants in the secondary mortgage market are the *Banco Hipotecario de Espana*, official credit institutions, savings banks, credit cooperatives, private banks, *Caja Postal de Ahorros* (Postal Bank) and mortgage credit companies. Mortgage *Cedulas* are the most typical and widespread security in the mortgage market. *'Cedulas Hipotecarias'* represents the most attractive type of security for the issuer, as they require neither registration on the 'Property Register' nor the setting up of a 'Bondholder's Syndicate'. However *cedulas* have now lost the tax advantages they previously enjoyed. The capital and interest of the *cedulas* are specially guaranteed by means of a mortgage on all *cedulas* registered in favour of the issuing company at any time, without prejudice to that company's overall capital requirements. *Cedulas* can be issued either as a public offer or a private placement.

Bonos

The capital and interest of the *Bonos* are especially guaranteed according to terms set out in the deed of insurance, and the effect of this is clearly stated in the Property Register. The value of the issued *Bonos* is restricted to the credit they represent.

When the *Bonos* are issued in a series, a 'Syndicate of Holders' must be set up, and the issuing Institution must appoint a Commissioner to ensure compliance with the issue deeds on behalf of the investors. The appointment of the Commissioner should be ratified by the 'Assembly of Holders'. He will be the Chairman of the Syndicate and in addition to the authority conferred upon him in the deed of issue or attributed to him by the Assembly, he will be the legal representative of the Syndicate. The complexity of the Bonos issuing process has been the principal cause of their very scarce utilisation.

Participaciones

Mortgage participaciones is the assignment of mortgage credit in full or in part. The buyer assumes the risk of default on the loan, in proportion to the percentage of capital and interest he holds. It is possible to insure this risk.

Participaciones (participations) are currently issued very rarely, although it is expected that new regulations will be introduced which will make them more attractive. It is expected that the new regulations would classify participations as 'off balance sheet' for the issuer, and therefore they would not be taken into consideration when calculating capital adequacy requirements for financial institutions.

The management of the mortgage is generally carried out by the issuer, although the investor has certain rights to ensure a proper management. The maturity of the participation can not surpass the maturity date of mortgage loans and the interest rate on the participation can be no higher than the rate attaching to the mortgage.

Mortgage secondary market

The main characteristics of the mortgage secondary market are as follows:

• pursuant to Spanish Law, the securities may be transferred without requiring endorsement by a public attending officer (unlike other securities);

• the securities are admitted to official listing on the Stock Exchange once they have been issued, and compliance with the appropriate regulations only has to be evidenced subsequently;

• funds for the regulation of the mortgage market have been created, the purpose of which is to secure a sufficient degree of liquidity. The institutions issuing the securities participate in these Funds on a voluntary basis.

3.91 Italy

3.92 Mortgages

There is no specific law in Italy regulating the mortgage loan market, and there are no restrictions on the maturity of loans or loan to value ratios. In practice, however, loans are made up to 75% of property values and their maturities vary from five years to 15 years but may in some cases be extended up to 25 years. Loans are both fixed rate and floating rate, but the latter prevails for maturities over five years. Borrowers have a legal right to prepay the loans. An amortising structure is generally used.

The major issuers in the market are autonomous divisions of commercial and savings banks and specialised credit institutions. At present, finance companies have no significant role. Credit institutions are regulated by the Italian central bank, the Banca d'Italia.

Specialist mortgage lenders finance their activities through issuing mortgage bonds, and as of March 1990 there were bonds with a value of LIT 12,000 billion outstanding.

Italy still has one of the highest savings rates in the world, but this is now declining rapidly. However, nearly two out of every three car purchases are financed by loans, with approximately LIT 4,800 billion of loans being made every year. The total size of the market has been estimated at LIT 110,000 billion. Car loans usually pay interest at fixed rates. The finance subsidiaries of major car manufacturers currently control nearly one third of the car loan market. The other main lenders are commercial banks and finance companies.

Other types of consumer loans are mainly for the purchase of durable and nondurable goods.

3.93 Scope for securitisation

At present there are a number of obstacles to the development of an asset backed securities market in Italy. These include:

• high rates of interest are available on Italian government debt. In addition, the withholding tax on government debt is less onerous than on other securities (currently 30%). It is likely that the Italian government will not reduce the withholding tax on bonds issued by private companies (including asset backed securities) to protect government funding;

• Italian institutional investors are conservative and may not find instruments with complex structure attractive;

• securitisation structures have no status in Italian law. In addition, the Italian Civil Code does not allow companies (except for credit institutions and other institutions specifically authorised by law) to issue debentures with a value in excess of their share capital, unless the excess is secured on the company's real estate (up to two thirds of its value) or government bonds;

• the mortgage bond market (where the issuers are specialist mortgage lending institutions) is a well developed source of funds for financing mortgages in Italy.

Despite these factors, it is expected that asset backed securities will develop in the near future. In particular, the requirement to implement the Basle Convergence Agreement by 1993 will make securitisation attractive to banks (most Italian banks are generally thinly capitalised compared with the 8% ratio which will be required).

The first major transaction with securitisation features which was backed by Italian receivables took place in April 1990. The transaction was a syndicated loan rather than a public issue for LIT 210 billion (US$170m) in two tranches of roughly equal size, one of 12 months and the other of four years. The borrower was Chariots Limited, a Cayman Islands vehicle. The loan is indirectly backed by car loan receivables originated by Citicorp Finanzaria SA. The proceeds of the issue were passed to Citicorp through Banca Commerciale Italiana to refinance an existing loan secured on the car loans.

3.94 Accounting requirements

At present, the presentation of consolidated financial statements is not requested by Italian law. However, consolidated financial statements are expressly required by CONSOB, the stock exchange regulatory authority, in the event of quoted companies having controlling interests in subsidiaries of significant size.

The accounting principles for the preparation and presentation of the consolidated financial statements are explained in Document No.8 issued by the Italian Accounting Bodies. Such principles comply with those issued by the International Accounting Standards Committee.

The bill which introduced the 4th and the 7th EC Directive relating to financial statements and consolidated group accounts respectively is expected to become effective during 1991. As concerns the consolidated financial statements, the criteria for the drawing up included in the text presently under discussion are substantially similar to those issued by the International Accounting Standards Committee.

3.95 Other countries

In most other European countries, legal restrictions or the size of the market in the underlying assets restrict the development of the asset backed securities market. Brief summaries of the current position are set out below.

3.96 Republic of Ireland

There is no market in Ireland for collateralised securities at present. The commercial banks and, in particular, the building societies are reviewing the possibility of securitising part of their home mortgage book. Most recently Allied Irish Bank have acquired approximately US$100 million of mortgages from their United States subsidiary First Maryland Bank. This has been a form of securitisation arranged within the group to manage liquidity in the United States.

There are no official rules covering securitisations other than the general power of the Central Bank to regulate such transactions. This power is most tightly defined in the Building Societies Act whereby a building society entering such a deal would require specific permission from the Central Bank. In the case of commercial banks, securitised transactions do not require direct approval. The accounting rules are similar to the United Kingdom.

3.97 Belgium

Like many other financial techniques developed in the United States and the United Kingdom, securitisation will probably infiltrate the financial and banking community in Belgium. However, the legal structure in Belgium is not appropriate yet for this type of transaction, and amendments to the existing legislation are presently contemplated in order to facilitate the emergence of securitisation in Belgium.

There is a market for property certificates in Belgium. This is described further in section 3.41 on Commercial property schemes.

3.98 Luxembourg

There is currently no asset backed securities market in Luxembourg and due to the size of the country it is very unlikely that a significant market could develop in the field of mortgages, car loans and credit cards and other forms of consumer loans. However, Luxembourg investment funds are currently being used as vehicles to securitise various assets from foreign groups and this activity is likely to grow in the future.

The regulatory and accounting rules relating to such asset backed securities are those currently affecting investment funds in Luxembourg. Other rules and constraints arising from the countries where these assets are located must also be considered.

Equity and equity linked instruments

Equity and equity linked instruments

4.1 Overview

As an alternative to raising funds by means of debt securities a corporation may issue equity or some form of debt which may subsequently be converted or exchanged into equity. This provides an additional range of instruments to corporations although equity issues tend to face additional legal considerations when compared with debt.

'Equity' is a general term for the basic form of capital raised by a business, which will take different forms in different legal jurisdictions. Ordinary shares in the United Kingdom, 'common stock' in the United States, '*action*' in France and '*aktien*' in Germany have important differences between them, but share common characteristics; in particular, they are usually more permanent than other forms of capital and imply some form of ownership in the business, unlike debt. In its most basic form, equity capital in most countries has some or all of the following features:

● voting privileges with respect to the management of the business;

● a share in the profits of the business, payable by way of dividend;

● limited liability in the event of a winding up;

● a proportionate share of the assets of the business in the event of a winding up (after the claims of creditors have been accounted for);

● subscription privileges in the event of a new issue of shares (pre-emptive rights);

● limited access to the books and records of the business.

The distinction between debt and equity is becoming increasingly blurred as companies and their advisers seek to design instruments with the benefits of equity (such as the reduction in gearing and the improvement of capital ratios) but without the associated disadvantages (such as the non tax deductibility of dividends). The ability to achieve the desired result will depend upon taxation, legal and accounting considerations in the country of issue as well as the country of incorporation of the company (or its holding company). Further complications may arise if the company's shares are quoted and traded in other countries. There are features which help distinguish debt and equity although economically they may appear very similar. Equity usually ranks behind debt on the liquidation of the issuer and normally debt does not entitle the holder to be treated as a member (or owner) of the issuer.

The recently published exposure draft from the International Accounting Standards Committee on financial instruments makes the following statement regarding issues which seek to blur the distinction between debt and equity.

'A financial instrument may contain many features that are common to both liabilities and equity, such as voting rights, rights to return on capital in the form of interest or dividends, and liquidation priorities. One feature is critical in differentiating a financial liability from an equity instrument – the contractual obligation of one party to the underlying financial instrument (the issuer) to deliver cash or another financial asset to the other party (the holder) or to exchange another financial instrument with the holder under conditions that are potentially unfavourable to the issuer. When such a contractual obligation is a feature of a financial instrument, that instrument meets the definition of a financial liability regardless of the form in which the contractual obligation is settled. When such a contractual obligation is not a feature of a financial instrument, that instrument is an equity instrument. The holder of an equity instrument may be entitled to receive a pro rata share of any dividends or other distributions out of equity, but the issuer has no contractual obligation to make such distributions'.

The exposure draft then comments that the substance of the instrument should govern its balance sheet position rather than its legal form.

Although there are variations in the taxation, company law and accounting frameworks in different countries, there are three basic types of instruments with the characteristics of equity which are found in all countries. These basic types comprise:

- ordinary shares;
- preferred shares;
- convertible debt instruments.

All of the instruments in the 'Specific instruments' section of this chapter fall within one of the above categories. The majority of the instruments in the 'Specific instruments' sections of this chapter have been issued either in the United States (particularly many of the preferred stock variants) or in the Euromarkets (particularly by United Kingdom quoted companies). Whilst there are no legal restrictions in most jurisdictions to prevent issuing most of these variants, particular local features (particularly the tax treatment) may make them unattractive. For example, the requirement for United Kingdom tax resident companies to pay advance corporation tax on dividends makes the issue of many of the preferred shares unattractive. Consequently most of these issues (which have been made for United Kingdom based corporations) have been made by a fully guaranteed offshore finance subsidiary. Many of the preferred stock issues described in this chapter take advantage of United States taxation legislation and would not be as attractive to issuers and investors in most jurisdictions in Europe. They have been included because they may be of interest to European companies with operations in the United States.

Due to the increasingly global nature of the business of multinational corporations, and particularly in anticipation of the removal of most trade barriers between member states of the European Community with the creation of the single market at the end of 1992, cross border mergers have become increasingly common. This has focused the attention of investors on the different regulations relating to takeovers and mergers within each country, and these are briefly discussed in the 'Equity markets in Europe' sections of this chapter. In addition, cross border mergers have led to innovative shareholding structures being devised to make the equity of the merged corporation attractive to investors domiciled in both the countries of origin of the parties to the merger.

4.2 Euro and international equity issues

Since the mid 1980s an increasing number of large companies, particularly those based in Europe, have arranged for their equity to be listed on stock exchanges outside their country of incorporation. These multiple listings have resulted from changes in the trading structure of markets. Investors are more sophisticated and have an international outlook, and increasingly efficient settlement systems and international quotation systems have enabled markets to become more international.

It is possible for shares to be listed and issued on a domestic stock exchange and offered internationally simultaneously. Such global (or 'Euro-equity') issues are usually underwritten by a syndicate of banks in much the same way as Eurobond issues. The shares may then be traded on the international telephone markets as well as on the various stock exchanges where they are listed. Two methods of distributing Euro-equity issues have developed. A Euro-equity syndicate is formed and the shares are distributed like a Eurobond or, alternatively, a geographically targeted syndicate is formed. With a geographically targeted syndicate, syndicate members may seek to sell shares only in a particular geographical area. This procedure was introduced to achieve the widest geographical distribution and thus prevent 'flow back' of the shares to the domestic market. It also helps prevent potential investors being solicited by more than one syndicate member. Flow back may lead to an oversupply of shares on the domestic market which could depress the share price. To avoid flow back, the syndicate should be comprised of banks with strong retail distribution networks.

The advantage of broader geographical ownership is that the range of shareholders can be wider which could help make the company less vulnerable to a hostile takeover. If the issue is not an initial public offering there is also the possibility of issuing shares at a higher price than an offer to existing shareholders who may expect a substantial discount to current market values. However, issuers will have to ensure that any pre-emption rights of existing shareholders are preserved.

4.3 Secondary markets

The ability of a company to raise finance by means of an equity issue, and the price which investors are willing to pay, is dependent on the existence of an active secondary market, to provide sufficient liquidity to enable the investors to feel confident that they can dispose of their holdings when they want to. The secondary market will usually be the domestic stock market of the issuer together with any international markets on which listings have been obtained. These exchanges should also provide a regulatory framework for the protection of investors. The procedure for obtaining a listing and trading on a particular exchange are described in sections 4.99 to 4.163 dealing with equity markets in Europe.

4.4 Depository receipts

Trading and investing in foreign equities can be difficult for investors due to taxation issues and difficulties in dealing with foreign registrars. American Depository Receipts (ADRs) were developed by United States investment banks to remove this problem for United States investors and to enable foreign companies to gain easier access to the United States capital markets. With ADRs the investor purchases a certificate which represents an interest in the equity of a company. The equity is purchased by an investment bank or broker and is held in trust by a bank which issues the ADR to acknowledge that it holds the underlying equity. The ADR is then freely traded between investors and brokers. The trustee bank will collect the dividends paid on the shares and make payments to the ADR holders. ADRs are priced and dividends paid in US dollars (the depository bank undertaking the necessary foreign exchange transactions) and ADRs will be held in a book entry transfer system. ADRs are usually, but not necessarily, sponsored by the company and registered under the United States securities legislation.

ADRs are traded on the United States stock exchanges or on the National Association of Securities Dealers Automated Quotations System ('NASDAQ'). Some of the ADRs can now be traded on the London Stock Exchange. There also are similar instruments traded in The Netherlands and Sweden.

4.5 Ordinary shares

Ordinary shares normally allow the investor full rights to participate in the control of the company and its profits – either in terms of dividends, or the surplus on a winding up (liquidation) of the company after all prior interests are satisfied (creditors and preference shareholders). In some jurisdictions, companies can issue more than one class of ordinary shares, for example Class A and Class B shares which may differ in terms of nominal values, voting rights and entitlement to dividends or distributions in the event of a winding up. The rights of different classes of equity will be set out in the company's written constitution. Dividends on ordinary shares are not predetermined but are determined by the directors and, in general, approved by the shareholders in a general meeting. Dividends are usually restricted by law to the amount of the company's accumulated realised profits.

Ordinary shares are the most basic form of investment in a company and in most countries provisions concerning them are fundamental to company law. Every company has to have some ordinary shares in issue. In most jurisdictions there are rules concerning the following:

• whether shares have to be registered or can be in bearer form;

• the treatment of premiums on the issue of shares, and whether issues at a discount are possible;

• the maintenance of capital contributed by ordinary shareholders. In most countries, there are rules which restrict the circumstances in which ordinary shares can be repurchased or redeemed. In addition, there are rules regarding the action required of shareholders should the level of capital fall below a minimum amount or percentage of original capital;

- there are requirements for companies to have a minimum amount of share capital in some countries;

- whether different classes of ordinary shares with different rights can be issued.

The legal framework relating to European countries is discussed further in sections 4.99 to 4.163 of this chapter dealing with Equity Markets in Europe.

4.6 Issue of ordinary shares

There are five main ways in which shares can be issued:

- 'initial' or 'primary' public offering;

- rights issue;

- scrip or bonus issue;

- in consideration for an acquisition;

- on conversion of other forms of investment.

Initial public offering

In most jurisdictions, there are strict rules designed to protect investors governing the sale of shares to the public. A company will usually have to satisfy stock exchange requirements to obtain a listing on the stock exchange or to be quoted on unlisted markets designed for smaller companies. The requirements in European countries are set out in sections 4.99 to 4.163 of this chapter.

Rights issues

In most countries, ordinary shareholders have pre-emption rights and companies already listed who wish to raise new equity will often do so by way of a 'rights issue'. A rights issue entitles existing shareholders to subscribe for new shares at a fixed price in proportion to their existing holdings (ie 'their right'). This price will usually be at a discount to the prevailing market price (although in most countries it must be in excess of the par value of the shares), to make the issue attractive to shareholders. In most cases, the shareholders are entitled to sell their rights if they do not wish to subscribe to more shares.

Scrip issues

A scrip issue is an issue of new shares to existing shareholders in proportion to their existing holding; unlike a rights issue, no payment is made for the shares. Instead, the company will capitalise a proportion of its undistributed profits. There is no increase in the cash investment and consequently there is no change in the overall value of the company, but there will be a change in the price of individual shares. One reason for scrip issues is to reduce the price per share, to make the shares more marketable. In some jurisdictions, companies can make arrangements for their shareholders to elect to receive dividends in the form of additional shares rather than cash (known as a scrip dividend or a stock dividend).

In consideration for an acquisition

A company may issue new shares as consideration for the acquisition of shares in another company. This is often attractive to companies whose shares have a high value relative to the rest of the market. The following matters will normally arise in most jurisdictions in connection with such share issue:

• existing shareholders normally have pre-emption rights so they will have to agree to waive these rights to enable the shares to be issued;

• the shares to be issued will have to be valued. This will normally be the fair value of the shares acquired (based on the market value of the company), which may require the acquiring company to create a non-distributable reserve representing the excess valuation of each share above the nominal value of the shares. In some countries, special 'merger relief' rules may apply (providing certain conditions are met) enabling the shares issued in connection with a merger to be recorded at their nominal value.

On conversion of other forms of instrument

Shares may be issued on the exercise of the conversion option embedded in a convertible bond or on the exercise of a share warrant. These instruments are discussed later in this chapter.

Variations

Share warrants — Where a country's law and the company's constitution permits, a company may issue warrants in respect of issued and fully paid up shares in the company. The share warrant is a negotiable bearer instrument transferable by delivery. It should not be confused with equity warrants (described later in this chapter and in chapter 5 – Hedging Instruments)

245

which are essentially an option to subscribe for shares. The bearer of the share warrant is entitled to a specified number of shares and it may also provide for the payment of future dividends. Future dividends may be provided by means of coupons for which payment is obtained by the bearer presenting the coupons to the issuer's agent bank. If share warrants have been issued it will be necessary to advertise dividend rates in national newspapers. Coupons are also used to claim entitlement to rights or bonus issues. In certain countries share warrants are viewed unfavourably by the regulators and the investment exchanges because they are not registered and can be used to build up undisclosed holdings in companies. For example, in the United Kingdom, The Stock Exchange limits the amount of shares which can be issued in the form of warrants and specific shareholder approval is required.

Deferred shares

These are ordinary shares issued with restrictive rights (for example, no votes and no dividends rights). Some such shares, including 'Founders shares', are often associated with the promotion of the company and allow promoters to have a limited stake in the enterprise but leave the majority of the equity available to other investors. At an appointed time or event, rights in the shares may be activated such that the shareholdings are equivalent to ordinary shares (or preferred shares). In the United Kingdom such shares have been issued for tax reasons on the transfer of shares in a family-owned company to the next generation or to save duties or tax payable on an acquisition or merger.

Multi-currency shares

Most countries do not permit companies to denominate their share capital in foreign currencies but it is possible in the United Kingdom, Ireland and The Netherlands. Several United Kingdom subsidiaries of foreign banks have changed the capital to the currency of their parent. The Scandinavian Banking Group plc (SBG) changed its capital from sterling to a basket of currencies (US dollars, sterling, deutschmarks and Swiss francs). The share capital is divided into shares of each currency but, whilst SBG was a public company, they could be bought and sold together only as a complete 'unit'. Dividends are declared in sterling and reserves allocated to each currency.

4.7 Valuation of ordinary shares

The return from an investment in ordinary shares is subject to much greater uncertainty than, say, the return on a fixed rate bond. There is usually no fixed redemption date and future dividends are dependent on future cash flow, profitability and also the dividend policy of the company (which is usually at the discretion of the directors). For this reason the valuation of ordinary shares is often referred to as being more of an art than a science.

Formal valuation models of ordinary shares are based on the expected future cash flows (dividends) arising from the investment. For example, the 'Gordon growth model' makes a simplifying assumption that future dividends will grow by a constant percentage. The return on an equity investment is given by the following equation:

$$R = \frac{D(1 + g)}{P} + g$$

where

R = return on equity

D = most recent dividend

P = current share price

g = constant percentage growth in dividends

The prediction of future dividends is difficult and is usually based on an analysis of previous performance, although in practice there is no consistent trend in constant earnings and dividend growth – this is dependent on the investment success of a company and the quality of its management.

There are two ratios which are most often used to measure the historical performance of a company, the price-earnings (P/E) ratio and the dividend yield. These can be defined as follows:

$$\text{P/E ratio} = \frac{\text{market price of one share}}{\text{net earnings per share}}$$

$$\text{Dividend yield} = \frac{\text{dividend per share}}{\text{market price per share}}$$

These measures are available in most countries but the following factors are significant:

• the P/E ratio will be affected by the markets perception of the future earnings potential (through the market price of the shares);

• the net earnings per share is dependent both on accounting conventions peculiar to different countries and on accounting judgements;

• the comparison made between the yield on shares in different countries may have to be adjusted for differences in tax treatment. In particular, the effect of taxation using an imputation system, where taxpayers will receive a tax credit for the corporation tax suffered by the company, will have to be adjusted for to give a comparable yield to that of companies taxed under the classical system;

• different companies may have different dividend policies – some companies may reinvest a higher proportion of their profits, thus potentially increasing future returns. The dividend cover, or the ratio of dividends paid to earnings per share, is significant in estimating the potential for future increases in dividends.

4.8 Benefits – issuer

• A source of long term finance for which the return can be set in the light of the current circumstances facing the company.

• If shares are already listed, it is easy to establish the appropriate price.

• Listed shares may help the company make acquisitions more easily, for example enabling acquisitions to be on a share for share basis if the company's shares are attractive to investors.

• The listing of shares provides the issuer with publicity.

4.9 Benefits – investor

• Shares offer the opportunity to participate in the long term prosperity of the company.

• If the company performs well or in periods of rising stock market prices substantial capital gains can be made.

- Listed shares are liquid and easily saleable.

- It is possible to make small investments.

4.10 Risks and disadvantages – issuer

- The share issue may not be well received in the market. Investor expectations can be swayed at short notice, with the result that not all shares are subscribed for. The issue can be underwritten (which would be usual), but underwriting fees increase the issue cost. The underwriters may also be unwilling to agree to a high issue price.

- There will be an expectation that regular and increasing dividends will be paid.

- For any listed company, there is a possibility that shareholdings may be accumulated until such time as enough shares are held to make a bid for all the shares in the company. Legislation in most jurisdictions provide that shareholdings over a certain limit must be disclosed.

- Once shares are issued, it may be difficult to cancel them or repurchase them.

- If shares have to be offered to existing shareholders, they may have to be issued at a discount to market value, thus lowering the amount that might otherwise be received and possibly diluting earnings.

- There may be regular reporting requirements under the rules set by the exchange on which the shares are listed.

- Companies may have to notify the exchange on which the shares are listed of significant events which may affect the share price. In addition, certain transactions may have to be reported in accordance with the rules of the exchange.

- Large issues may reduce the market price of the company's shares.

- The number of shares which can be issued may be restricted by legislation (such as pre-emption rights) law or domestic share issue controls exercised by central banks.

- Earnings per share and hence market capitalisation and share prices may be affected by conversion rights or options on unissued shares.

4.11 Risks and disadvantages – investor

• The value of the shareholding may fluctuate significantly particularly over the short term since share prices are influenced by many factors other than those relating to the company's specific performance. Debt security prices reflect market interest rates, and are not affected by perceptions about the company's performance except if it affects the credit standing.

• In certain circumstances, a stock exchange may suspend the listing of a company's shares, making it difficult for the investor to dispose of his holding.

• Ordinary shareholders will be the last to recover any value on their shares in the event that the company is wound up, and full recovery of even the nominal value of the share (which is likely to be considerably less than the acquisition cost) is not assured. The potential recovery for a particular class of shares in a liquidation is governed by the rights given to that class in the company's written constitution.

4.12 Accounting questions

The issuer

• How should any premium (excess of issue price over nominal value) on any issue of shares be accounted for? Does it form part of capital or is it distributable?

• Should the expenses and commission on a share issue be transferred directly to reserves or pass through the profit and loss account in the first instance?

• Should earnings per share calculations be amended to reflect conversion rights or options on unissued shares?

• If the shares are issued in relation to an acquisition of another company are there special rules for merger accounting? If so, at what value should any shares be recorded – the nominal value or the fair value of the consideration?

• Where a company pays a scrip dividend, should the bonus issue be made out of capital reserves or distributable reserves?

• Should the financial statements include provision for only dividends paid or should declared dividends also be included?

250

The investor

• For the corporate investor, is the investment a current or fixed asset?

• How should the investment be valued in the accounts?

• Do acquisition costs form part of the carrying cost of the investment?

4.13 Taxation questions

• Is VAT chargeable on the fees relating to the share issue?

• Is any such VAT recoverable by the issuer?

• Can any of the costs of the share issue be claimed as a deductible expense for taxation purposes?

• Does redemption or repurchase of shares at a premium by the issuer create a distribution? If so, does this have any adverse taxation consequences?

• Can the company obtain clearance from the relevant tax authorities so that its purchase of own shares does not create distribution for tax purposes?

• Is there a withholding tax requirement on the payment of a dividend and, if appropriate, can advance clearance from the tax authorities be obtained to pay gross?

• Does a double tax treaty allow a foreign investor to recover all or part of any taxation credit attaching to a dividend?

• Can an investor be subjected to tax on redemption or repurchase on deemed income greater than the real profit?

• Is a bonus issue in lieu of dividend taxable income to the investors?

• Are the terms of any bonus issue of ordinary shares such as to make the issue a distribution?

• What is the investor's base cost of the shares for capital gains purposes?

• Is the issue subject to any duty or other taxes such as stamp duty or capital duty?

• Can shareholders obtain clearance that any profit on sale of shares by an investor to the company is a capital gain rather than income?

• Will a pension fund investor be caught by anti-avoidance legislation on sale of shares to, or redemption by, the company?

• Is a share warrant subject to 'bearer stamp duty' on issue?

• For bearer shares or share warrants, must a dividend statement from the company identify the recipient?

• Should the company obtain any prior clearance from the tax authorities before issuing shares?

• Will the issue affect the taxation position of employee shareholders?

4.14 Preferred shares

Preferred (or preference) shares are shares which have defined but usually limited rights to the profits and distributions of capital of the company. Preferred shares usually have the following features:

• a dividend computed by reference to predetermined factors which is payable before dividends on ordinary shares;

• restricted voting rights – usually only available in a situation where the rights attaching to the preferred shares are being amended or if dividends are in arrears;

• repayment of nominal value (or such greater amount as provided for in the company's written constitution) before ordinary shares on a winding up;

• preferred shares are generally not callable at the option of the issuer.

Preferred shares typically pay dividends at a fixed rate but recently a number of preferred shares have been introduced which pay floating rates of dividends. These are dealt with in sections 4.57 to 4.63 below.

Dividends on preference shares can be cumulative, in which case any arrears of dividends have to be paid before dividends can be paid on other classes of shares or non-cumulative. On non-cumulative shares if a dividend payment cannot be made (for whatever reason) it is not made up at a later date.

In most jurisdictions, dividends on preferred shares are paid out of post tax profits and are not tax deductible. Consequently, they can be unattractive to issuers by comparison with raising capital by means of fixed or floating rate debt on which the interest is tax deductible. However, preferred shares rank as capital and banks and other credit institutions have issued preferred shares to boost capital. The requirement of credit institutions in the EC to comply by 1993 with the directives implementing the Basle Convergence Agreement concerning capital adequacy requirements (see chapter 1 – Introduction) has made this type of instrument and its variants more attractive to this sector of the market. The directives allow perpetual non-cumulative preferred shares (whether redeemable or not) as 'tier 1' or core capital and perpetual cumulative preferred shares within 'tier 2' or supplementary capital.

In addition, in some jurisdictions, the taxation treatment for investors receiving dividends can allow preferred shares to be issued with lower coupons than would be the case for a similar debt security, which can make these issues beneficial. This may be particularly the case for companies with low taxable income who do not necessarily need a taxation deduction for interest. This is the case in the United States where many of the variants of preferred stock referred to in this chapter have originated.

Variations

Participating preference shares	A preferred share which has some further right to a share of profits in addition to the fixed dividend as well as a share of any surplus on a winding up.
Cumulative preferred shares	A preferred share where any unpaid dividends accumulate and have to be paid before any dividends can be paid on ordinary shares.
Convertible preferred shares	A preferred share which is convertible into a predetermined number of ordinary shares of the company at some future specified date. Similar considerations which are appropriate for convertible debt instruments also apply to such shares. These instruments have also incorporated premium puts (described under premium put convertibles in sections 4.78 to 4.84).
Redeemable preferred shares	A preferred share which is redeemable at a future date either at the option of the company or the investor. Redeemable shares are not permitted in all jurisdictions and the method by which redemption is achieved can vary. Redemption of shares in various European countries is dealt with in sections 4.99 to 4.163 below.

Preferred stock with a dividend holiday	Preferred stock where the issuer does not pay dividends for a specified period after issue. These offer a fixed reinvestment rate for a specified period to investors (similar to deep discounted bonds) and have cash flow benefits for issuers.
Increasing rate preferred stock	Preferred stock paying dividends which increase to normal market levels over a period of time. To compensate for the lower dividends the stock is issued at a discount to par values.

4.15 Valuation of preference shares

Economically, preference shares are similar to fixed rate debt – the investor receives a fixed return at regular intervals. However, there are two significant differences:

• preference shares rank after debt securities in the event of liquidation. In addition, the company does not have to pay a preference dividend, unlike an interest payment. Consequently, investors will demand a higher rate of return than for comparable debt securities to compensate for these additional risks;

• many preference shares do not have fixed redemption dates and therefore their cash flows are effectively perpetuities.

In certain jurisdictions, care must be taken when comparing the return on preference shares with other fixed income securities, due to the different ways in which they are taxed. In countries which operate the imputation system (such as the United Kingdom, France and Finland), a taxpayer who receives a preference dividend also receives a tax credit which can be offset against their tax liability. This has to be taken into account in assessing the overall return on the security.

4.16 Benefits – issuer

• A way of raising equity finance at a set cost without diluting ordinary shareholders' rights.

• Preference shares may not be subject to any pre-emption requirements of company law providing certain criteria are met, eg in the United Kingdom, if they are not participating or convertible.

4.17 Benefits – investor

• A way of investing in a company with a fixed minimum return and specified rights in a winding up.

• In certain jurisdictions, some investors (eg United Kingdom Corporations) may not be liable to pay tax on dividend receipts.

4.18 Risks and disadvantages – issuer

• There is a fixed requirement to pay dividends and possibly make up arrears if cumulative preference shares are issued. This does not provide the issuer with any discretion on distribution of profits.

• Listing requirements will have to be fulfilled if a stock exchange listing is obtained to make them attractive to investors.

• The shares may be difficult or expensive to cancel or repurchase.

• In most jurisdictions, the dividend payment will not be tax deductible.

4.19 Risks and disadvantages – investor

• Unlike ordinary shareholders, the preference shareholder does not share in the growth in the earnings, and the value, of the company.

• In the event of a winding up, preferred shareholders will receive a refund of their share capital before ordinary shareholders but there is no guarantee that there will be full recovery of the nominal value or issue price which may be less than acquisition cost.

• If the preference shares are non cumulative and dividends are not paid the investor will not receive a payment at a latter date when (if) dividends are paid subsequently.

4.20 Accounting questions

● In general as for ordinary shares in section 4.12.

● What disclose is required in the accounts in relation to the rights attaching to the shares?

4.21 Taxation questions

● Will participating preference shares be treated as ordinary shares for tax purposes?

● Will holders of preference shares be 'equity holders' for group relief anti-avoidance legislation?

● Other questions as for ordinary shares in section 4.13.

4.22 Convertible debt instruments

A convertible debt security (convertible bond or debenture) has the features of a normal fixed rate bond (for example, periodic coupons and repayment of principal at maturity) but is convertible into shares of the issuer or its holding company. The conversion right cannot be separated from the debt.

The coupon rate on the convertible bond is always less than the rate for the same borrower in the fixed rate debt market. The price at which the bond is convertible into shares is stipulated at the time of issue and will be at a premium to the market value of the shares at the issue date. The coupon rate and level of premium are interlinked; the higher the coupon the higher the premium.

Convertibles originally evolved to enable small, growing companies to issue what was in effect deferred equity. Such companies need to raise fresh capital but can find it difficult to raise equity at a reasonable cost due to the lack of a track record and because investors perceive them to be of high risk. In addition, such a company may not have adequate distributable profits to make non tax deductible dividends. Equally, their poor credit ratings would make debt expensive. Convertible debt was a means of overcoming these problems by providing the investors with a fixed return while retaining the future ability to convert to equity if the company is successful. However, convertible debt securities are now issued by large corporations, both in domestic markets and the Euromarkets. The domestic markets within Europe are discussed in sections 4.99 to 4.163 below. Issues in the Euromarkets are made for similar reasons to straight debt issues – to attract foreign investors, avoid stringent issuing requirements and gain access to an international distribution network.

Significant features of convertible bond issues include the following:

• to exercise the conversion option, the investor must surrender the bonds in return for the shares. No cash is exchanged;

• the conversion option can be exercised by the investor at either one future date or within a range of dates (known as the 'window period') which usually commences a few years after the issue date;

• the initial conversion price, which is the price which the investor would pay for the shares if he exercised the conversion option, can be expressed in terms of the conversion ratio. The conversion ratio is the number of ordinary shares into which the nominal value of the bond converts. For example, if the conversion ratio of a bond is 20, each £1,000 nominal value converts into 20 shares. The conversion ratio stays fixed throughout the life of the issue although the conversion price will move over time due to movements in the price of the bond;

• the issuer will typically have a call option enabling it to redeem the securities at a price specified at the date of issue. Once the issuer has exercised the call option, investors usually have the choice of either converting into equity or redeeming the bond at a stipulated price (in addition some issues have incorporated put options – these 'premium put convertibles' are described further in section 4.78).

Variations

Zero coupon convertibles	A convertible bond issued at a large discount to par value and having no coupon.
LYONS	Liquid Yield Option Notes – a zero coupon convertible.
Exchangeable debt	A bond issued which is exchangeable into shares in another company. These shares are held by the issuer either as part of an

investment portfolio or from a strategic stake possibly built up during a failed takeover. If these shares were to be sold directly into the market, they would probably have to be sold at a large discount to their current value. The attraction to the issuer of an issue of exchangeable debt is that funds can be raised at competitive rates while still being able to benefit from any increase in the value of the shares. The dividends received on the shares may be non taxable while the interest payments will be tax deductible, which allows the issuer to reduce the cost of funding the investment. Unlike an issue of a convertible, no dilution of the issuer's equity occurs.

4.23 Valuation of convertible bonds

The complexities described above make convertible bonds difficult to value. There are two models which are used fairly widely, the 'income differential' model (also known as the 'cross over' or 'discounted cash flow' model) and the 'bond plus option' model (or 'binomial' model). These models attempt to determine a theoretical fair value of the conversion option, which can be used by investors to attempt to determine whether the market price of an instrument is cheap or expensive. In addition, they can be used by issuers when pricing an issue, as it is important to ensure that ordinary shareholders are not disadvantaged by underpricing of a convertible bond, and particularly that pre-emption limits are not breached. In the United Kingdom, the Pre-Emption Group (a lobby group of powerful institutional investors) has issued guidelines to limit the acceptable discount on a cash issue or vendor placing of shares (including convertibles) to 5%. Therefore, if we assume issue fees of $2\frac{1}{2}\%$, any opening premium above $2\frac{1}{2}\%$ could breach these guidelines.

Determinants of value

Valuation models for convertible bonds must take account of the factors

258

which influence their price in the market. The most significant of these are as follows:

• the share price of the issuer. If the convertible bond is trading at only a modest premium to the share price, there will be a strong positive relationship between the share price and the price of the bond. However, if the convertible bond is trading at a high premium (where, for example, there has been a significant fall in the share price, such as occurred to most shares in October 1987), the price of the convertible bond is usually very insensitive to the share price, and is dependent on the yield of the bond;

• interest rates. When a convertible bond is 'out of the money', or trading at a high premium to its conversion value, it is effectively priced as a fixed rate bond, and therefore the most significant determinants of its value are movements in interest rates. The impact of interest rates on the price of the convertible bond reduces as the premium decreases;

• volatility of the share price. Convertible bonds are usually more valuable if the price of the underlying share is volatile, because high volatility increases the probability that the share price (and, therefore, the value of the conversion option) will increase significantly. Volatility is particularly important because, although the investor can benefit from upward price movements, the downside risk is limited to the bond value of the convertible;

• dividend yields. The importance of the differential between the yield on the convertible bond and the dividend yield varies in different markets. In the United Kingdom, one of the main reasons why investors are prepared to pay a premium for a convertible bond is the income and yield advantage over an investment in the underlying shares. The lower the dividend yield relative to the coupon on the convertible bond, the higher the premium investors will pay. In other markets, such as Japan, dividend yields have (historically at least) been less significant than expected capital growth;

• call and put options. Generally, call options will reduce, and put options increase, the value of convertible bonds.

Income differential model

This model assumes that investors will hold the convertible bond until the income differential between the fixed coupon and the increasing dividend stream on the ordinary shares is eroded. The point at which the dividend yield (multiplied by the conversion ratio) exceeds the bond yield (the 'crossover point'), is when the investor will convert into the underlying shares. The net present value of the income differential (ID) can then be used to determine the fair value of the convertible bond as follows:

Convertible price = Conversion ratio × (current share price − ID)

The income differential model has traditionally been used by United Kingdom investors to value convertible bonds, and by issuers and their advisors to set the issue price. However, there are a number of weaknesses in the model:

● it takes no account of the volatility of share prices and the value of the option embedded in a convertible bond;

● it assumes that the changes in the share price will occur only in conjunction with changes in expectations about dividend growth, which does not always happen in practice;

● it ignores the case where the value of the issuer's equity has fallen and the convertible is priced similarly to a fixed rate bond. In addition, it assumes that conversion will take place;

● it cannot take account of call and put options;

● the discount rates used to determine the net present value of the income differential must be chosen somewhat arbitrarily, as it will involve discounting mixed cash flows (better debt and equity) at the same rate.

For those reasons, models incorporating option valuation techniques are becoming more popular.

Bond plus option model

This model analyses the value of a convertible bond into its constituent elements, as can be shown in the following equation:

value of convertible bond = value of equivalent fixed rate bond ('bond value') + value of option to convert into equity ('conversion option').

Bond value

The bond value of a convertible bond effectively sets the lower limit for its value (ie where the conversion option is worthless). It is the value of a fixed rate bond of the issuer with the same maturity and coupon rate as the convertible bond. This can be estimated by comparing the coupon with the redemption yield on a similar fixed rate bond. For example, a

260

10 year convertible bond with a coupon of $7\frac{1}{2}$% would be compared to the yield on a fixed rate bond with a 10 year maturity issued by a similarly rated company. If the yield to maturity on this bond was 10% then the bond value of the convertible bond is the value which using a $7\frac{1}{2}$% coupon and a 10 year maturity gives a yield to maturity of 10%, which is 84.6% of par or a price of 84.6.

Conversion option

The valuation of options is discussed in chapter 5 – Hedging Instruments and the option 'embedded' in a convertible bond can be valued in a similar way using option valuation models. There are, however, significant differences which make a convertible bond a more complex instrument to value than a plain vanilla option. These are:

• due to the range of possible conversion dates which are usually offered with a convertible bond, an adjustment must be made in respect of dividends expected to be paid before the option is exercised. With traded options, this adjustment is relatively straightforward, as only one or two dividends will have to be forecast. With a convertible bond, the period to be forecast is considerably longer;

• with a traded option, cash equal to the exercise price has to be paid by the holder to be able to exercise the option. However, in the case of a convertible bond, the bond is surrendered in return for shares, and no cash is exchanged. The exercise price is effectively the value at the date of conversion of the fixed rate bond which has been surrendered. Therefore the option model has to estimate the bond value at the optimal conversion date.

This model is more powerful than the income differential model but is complex to use and also has a number of limitations similar to those of option models (eg relating to volatility). In practice, the valuation adopted by issuers and investors is not always scientific and depends in part on such factors as market sentiment and investor preferences.

When the share price reaches a certain value most issuers will exercise their call option to force conversion. This results in the issue of equity which may have been the primary motive behind the issue and prevents bond holders in effect having all the advantages of equity but with a coupon rate which is in excess of the dividend yield. Consequently, convertible bonds tend to trade at only a modest premium to conversion value. However, the price of the convertible bond is limited by its value as a fixed rate instrument. Consequently, as the price of the underlying share falls the value of the convertible bond will fall less rapidly and is limited by its value as a bond. This is illustrated in the graph below.

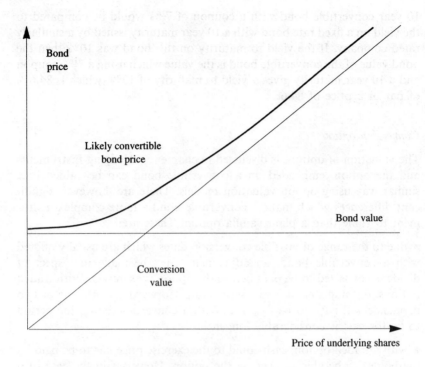

Bond
price

Likely convertible
bond price

Bond value

Conversion
value

Price of underlying shares

Diagram 4.1: Convertible bond price

Convertible debt issues are typically for much smaller total amounts than fixed rate bond issues because of restrictions on the amount of dilution existing shareholders will be prepared to suffer and the relatively small size of the market. Issues also tend to have long maturities, typically 15 years. The initial conversion premium is usually in the range of 15% to 25% and it is one of the most important factors in pricing an issue. A very high initial premium will require a good previous record of share price rises and excellent future prospects. As previously noted, most issues incorporate call provisions to force conversion. These are usually in two parts. In the early years no call will be possible. This period will be followed by a number of years when calls can be made at a premium to par value (usually around 5%) but only if the bond has been trading for a given period well above its par value (typically 120% – 130%). After a further period calls can be made, usually at a premium which reduces over time, without any conditions on the market price of the bond.

A new issue of convertible bonds will be subject to the normal procedures for a fixed rate bond issue but there usually will be additional requirements because of the ultimate need to issue equity on conversion. Shareholder pre-emption rights and listing arrangements will have to be considered and these will result in higher costs. Underwriting fees are also usually higher.

4.24 Benefits – issuer

• Convertible debt always pays a lower interest rate than straight debt, improving cash flow and undiluted earnings per share in the short term.

• Where the issue is callable, the issuer can force conversion by calling the debt issue for redemption if the market value of the underlying shares increases sufficiently in the future, thus controlling the cost of funding.

• Convertible bond issues usually have a longer stated maturity than fixed rate debt, although their actual maturity is usually shorter because most issues will be converted or called before maturity.

• The initial strike price of a convertible is at a premium to the market price of the equity, which can enable the issuer to avoid issuing equity at a discount as would usually be the case in a conventional rights issue. This is particularly true for highly geared companies with a depressed share price.

• There is no immediate dilution when the convertible bond is issued, so it is less likely to depress the share price of a company than issuing equity directly.

• The issuer can retain some control over who obtains equity by issuing the debt into new markets.

• May allow by-passing of pre-emption rights in some jurisdictions.

• While unconverted the interest payments will, unlike dividends, usually be tax deductible.

4.25 Benefits – investor

• The option to convert into shares allows the investor the opportunity to share in the performance of the ordinary shares while receiving a fixed return which is usually higher than that on the ordinary shares.

• With falling share prices, convertible bonds are better investments than the underlying equity as price falls are limited by the debt features. Consequently, in a falling market they usually offer greater income and suffer less capital loss.

• Convertible debt will give greater protection than equity in the event of a liquidation as it will usually rank ahead of ordinary and preferred shares.

• Convertible debt in the Euromarkets is in bearer form so that a form of equity can be held with anonymity.

4.26 Risk and disadvantages – issuer

• The share price may appreciate more than expected, which may make the issue of equity when the bonds are converted more expensive than a rights issue. A debt issue redeemed by a rights issue may, with hindsight, be cheaper. The imperfections of the equity markets make it difficult to predict future share prices, increasing the risk of the issuer underpricing the convertible bond issue.

• If the debt is converted, a cheap source of finance may be replaced by relatively expensive dividends which are not tax deductible.

• There may be a requirement to comply with the pre-emption rights of existing shareholders.

• There may be a requirement to disclose the effect of dilution on earnings per share.

• Before conversion, the convertible bond will rank as debt and therefore increase gearing.

• A failure to be able to force conversion (because share prices have not risen enough) may make subsequent issues of equity or debt more difficult.

• If conversion is not forced, the issuer faces uncertainty over cash flow forecasting.

• The bond and equity may be denominated in different currencies leading to a currency exposure.

4.27 Risks and disadvantages – investor

• If the share price does not appreciate as expected, the overall yield on the debt will be lower than that obtainable from other forms of debt.

• In a rising share market the capital appreciation may be less than that of the underlying equity.

• Investors should consider the risk of default by the issuer since convertible debt is usually subordinated to other debt issues.

• No interest is paid upon conversion from the last interest payment date. Where possible, conversion should therefore be timed with coupon and dividend dates.

• The bond and the underlying equity may be denominated in different currencies leading to an exposure and making value more difficult to assess.

• In the event of a takeover bid the terms of issue may provide for conversion to equity which can then be used to take up the bid options. This may not be attractive if the bonds were trading at prices reflecting a conversion premium.

4.28 Accounting questions

• Should the conversion option receive separate accounting recognition at the time of issue?

• Should the costs of conversion be accrued in the accounts and, if so, at what rate?

• Should premiums payable on redemption be accrued as part of the interest cost even if conversion (rather than redemption) is considered likely? Can the issuer avoid the need to do this by having the issue of new shares on conversion underwritten?

• Is the excess over nominal value which is received on conversion a distributable profit or part of the capital?

• What is the effect on fully diluted earnings per share? How should these be calculated and disclosed?

4.29 Taxation questions

- Is the issue itself (or any part of it) a distribution?
- Are the costs of the issue eligible for tax relief?
- Is transfer of convertible debt subject to duties or taxes, eg in the United Kingdom, stamp duty or stamp duty reserve tax?
- Will issue or conversion trigger a charge to capital duty?
- Will conversion be regarded as a taxable disposal by the investor?
- Is the interest on a convertible issue (or any part of it) a distribution?
- Must the issuer withhold income tax at the basic rate from interest payments?
- Will the issuer obtain tax relief for the excess of the worth of the shares issued over the par value of the debt?
- What is the investor's base cost in the shares?
- Is the recipient allowed to claim credit for any tax withheld from the interest payments?
- Is the interest payable on the debt tax deductible?
- Is the interest on the debt taxable in the hands of the recipient?
- Other questions as for ordinary shares in section 4.13.

Specific instruments

4.30 Participation certificates

Participation certificates are becoming increasingly popular in the Euro-markets. The holder of a participation certificate, which is usually a bearer document, has a right to share in the profits of the company and, if the terms are such, any surplus on a liquidation. Participation certificates carry no votes or other rights which other shareholders hold. Participation certificates are in effect non-voting shares.

Participation certificates developed in Switzerland partly as a means of enabling Swiss companies to split their equity into more manageable portions (Swiss companies' shares must have a nominal value of at least SFr100) and to help prevent the companies falling under foreign control. The issue of participation certificates therefore increased the company's equity without changing the current control of the company. The entitlement to profits can be pari passu to the ordinary shares or at a higher rate with a guaranteed minimum yield. Participation certificates have also been issued in Germany, Austria, The Netherlands and France.

In some jurisdictions (eg Germany and France) it is possible to structure participation certificates as debt, where the 'dividends' are deductible for tax purposes even though economically they are like equity. Participation certificates may be convertible into ordinary shares and can be redeemable at any time for the payment of market value.

Variations

Investment Certificate (IC)	A French company may issue ICs. They divide the rights attached to ordinary shares and represent the rights to dividends and profits. The voting rights are represented by a Voting Right Certificate (VRC). In France participation certificates are more like perpetual debt.
Non-voting shares	In the United Kingdom it is possible to issue shares which carry no votes enabling further equity to be raised without existing shareholders losing control. Non-voting shares can be listed on The Stock Exchange providing they are clearly designated non-voting.

4.31 Benefits – issuer

• Enables the company to raise equity without suffering any potential for change in control.

• In some jurisdictions, it may be possible to structure the participation certificate so that the 'dividends' are tax deductible.

4.32 Benefits – investor

• Enables participation in the profits of a company when this may not be available in the form of ordinary shares.

4.33 Risks and disadvantages – issuer

• The issue may not be well received by the market and may impact on the price of the ordinary shares.

• As for ordinary shares in section 4.10.

4.34 Risks and disadvantages – investor

• Participation certificates have no votes so a holder will have no control over the actions of the company, although there may be remedies in the event that ordinary shareholders do not exercise control in a proper manner.

• The value of the investment may fluctuate over the short-term and may not be related to movements in the share price.

4.35 Accounting questions

• Should participation certificates be included in the balance sheet as equity or debt?

• What is the effect on earnings per share?

• If the dividends are tax deductible should they be shown as dividends or interest in the accounts? Where is the tax credit included in the accounts?

4.36 Taxation questions

• Are the 'dividends' payable on the participation certificates deductible for tax purposes?

• Other questions as for ordinary shares in section 4.13.

4.37 Stapled stock

A 'stapled stock' arrangement is one where an investor purchases two different instruments, typically an ordinary share in the parent company of a group and a non voting preference share in a local subsidiary. These stock units are stapled together in the sense that they cannot be split and transferred separately. They are traded in the market as a single unit.

This shareholding structure has been designed specifically to mitigate the problems which can arise for companies and their shareholders following cross-border mergers. As a result of a cross-border merger, the shareholders of one of the merged companies will normally hold shares in a parent company located overseas, which can have disadvantageous tax consequences when dividends or other distributions are made. The stapled stock arrangement allows foreign investors to receive distributions from a domestic source while still retaining their investment in the parent company and without the parent company suffering any dilution in control of its foreign subsidiaries. Some of the potential problems that can arise from a cross border merger are shown by the example below.

Since laws relating to the incorporation and regulation of companies, and to the taxation of profits earned by companies, vary significantly from country to country, it is not usually possible to 'merge' companies from different countries. In some countries, such as the United Kingdom, it is not always possible to merge domestic companies. Therefore, cross-border mergers can only be carried out by using an acquisition structure (ie one company buying the other company or a new vehicle buying both). If UK PLC and Germany AG decide to merge without using a special merger vehicle, one of these companies has to acquire the other, for example, by offering to purchase the shares of the other company in exchange for its own shares. If Germany AG was to acquire UK PLC, it would offer its shares to the shareholders of UK PLC in exchange for shares in Germany AG. Prior to the merger, the structure of the two companies is as follows:

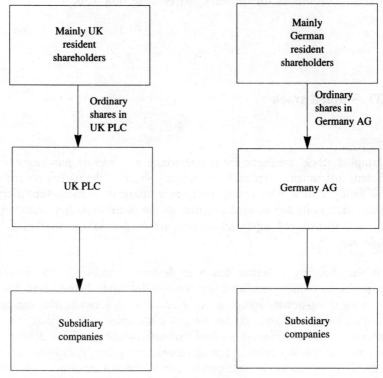

Diagram 4.2: Shareholding structure before merger

Following the merger, the corporate structure of the merged group would be as follows:

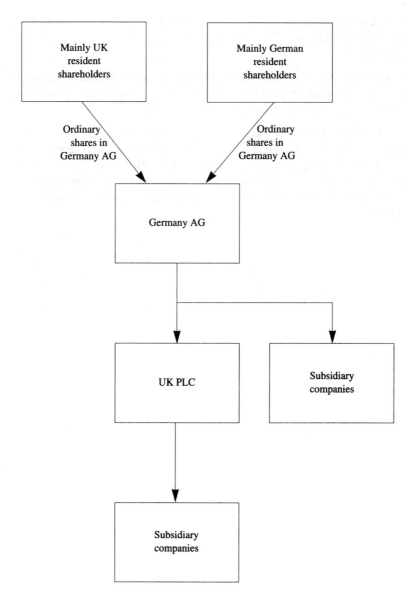

Diagram 4.3: Shareholding structure after merger

With this structure, the United Kingdom shareholders would receive dividends from the German parent, which would be disadvantageous for two reasons:

- the investor would be subject to 15% German withholding tax; and

- the United Kingdom investor would not be entitled to a local tax credit, as would be the case if the dividend was paid by a United Kingdom company.

In addition, the group structure may create a tax inefficient structure for the new group which could be improved by paying dividends to shareholders of a company other than Germany AG.

A stapled stock structure could be used as an alternative. The United Kingdom investor would receive an ordinary share in Germany AG and a non voting preference share in UK PLC; the investor could elect to receive a dividend from UK PLC by foregoing the dividend from Germany AG. The corporate structure would be as follows:

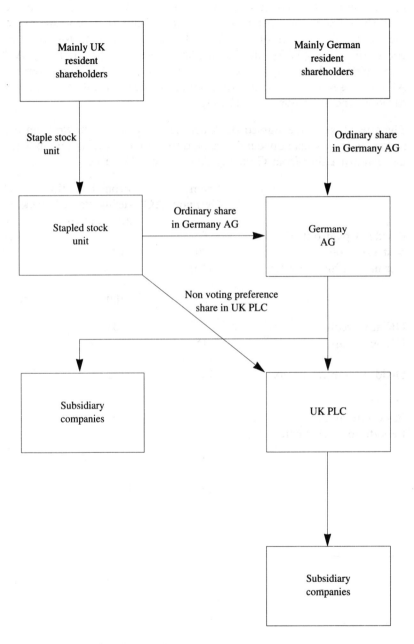

Diagram 4.4: Stapled stock structure

Alternatively, if the corporate structure had been reversed, with UK PLC as the parent, the foreign subsidiary could pay dividends direct to the local shareholders. Accordingly, the stapled stock structure would avoid the potential problem of UK PLC having to account for advance corporation tax (ACT) on the dividends paid to the Germany AG shareholders which may prove to be unrecoverable. Any unrecoverable ACT would have to be written off leading to a decrease in the company's earnings and the value of its shares.

The advantage of the stapled stock arrangement can be shown from the following table where dividends are paid to the United Kingdom individual investor either from Germany AG or from UK PLC:

	From Germany AG	From UK PLC (using stapled stock arrangement)
Dividend paid out of post tax profits	£ 100	£ 100
German withholding tax	(15)	–
	85	100
UK tax credit	–	33
UK gross up	15	–
Dividend subject to tax	100	133
UK tax		
Basic rate at 25% — 25		(33)
Less double tax credit — (15)		
	(10)	–
	£90	£100
Tax – UK	10	33
Tax – German	15	–
	£25	£33
Net receipt	£75	£100

Similar structures to this one were used in the takeover of Wedgewood plc by Waterford Glass Group plc, and in the initial public offering of shares by Eurotunnel plc.

4.38 Benefits – issuer

• Stapled stock schemes can eliminate additional fiscal costs which can be incurred by cross-border dividend flows.

• The use of this structure can make the issue of shares a realistic alternative to a cash offer for the acquisition of a company resident in a different country.

• The structure can encourage shareholders to accept the terms of a cross border acquisition or merger.

• The holding company does not have to suffer dilution of control of its foreign subsidiaries.

4.39 Benefits – investor

• The investor can receive dividends from a national source rather than a foreign source, thus avoiding withholding tax problems and in some jurisdictions receiving a tax credit.

• The exchange rate exposure may be removed.

• The investor usually has the choice of jurisdiction from which to receive dividends.

4.40 Risks and disadvantages – issuer

• If the shareholder can elect which jurisdiction it can receive a dividend from, the company has to some extent surrendered control of its dividend planning as it may not be able to predict how much of the total dividend will be payable in each jurisdiction.

• The structure of the shareholdings may have to be cleared in advance with the tax authorities in both jurisdictions to avoid the risk that it could be challenged. This can be time consuming.

• The issuer may suffer onerous tax consequences from legislative changes in the future; however, this could be mitigated to an extent by the parent company reserving the right to suspend or terminate the stapled stock scheme.

4.41 Risks and disadvantages – investor

• An investor may be exposed to a foreign exchange risk if the value of the dividend is set in another currency.

4.42 Accounting questions

• How should preference dividends paid by the subsidiary be disclosed in the group accounts?

• How is the minority interest in the subsidiary disclosed in the group accounts?

4.43 Taxation questions

• Does the issue of the stapled stock constitute a taxable receipt in the hands of the investor?

• If the parent company funds the dividend payments made by the subsidiary on the non voting preference shares, do such dividend payments constitute distributions by the parent company?

• Does the stapled stock scheme require tax clearance by the relevant tax authorities or other Government bodies?

• Is there specific legislation to counteract a stapled stock scheme?

• Is there a capital gains disposal and related tax liability on the exchange of shares by the investor for the stock unit?

4.44 Equity commitments

Equity commitments is in effect a mandatory convertible. Equity commitments comprise a fixed rate note issue accompanied by detachable contracts for the purchase of ordinary shares. The owners of the contracts are required to buy shares to the principal amount of the fixed rate note. The price of the shares is within a range set at the date of issue. Unlike a normal convertible bond, the holder is compelled to convert. These instruments were not popular but the concept was taken further by the equity contract note described below.

Variations

Equity contract note

A contract is exchangeable for ordinary shares having a market value equal to the principal amount of the fixed rate notes. If the holder chooses not to take up the equity, the issuer sells them in the market to redeem the notes. If the equity cannot be sold the holder is required to take up the shares.

Equity commitment notes

Unlike the Equity commitment and Equity contract note the note holders are not obliged to purchase the equity with the notes. The issuer is committed to redeem the notes with the proceeds of an equity issue at some future date.

4.45 Benefits – issuer

• The issuer is guaranteed to raise equity at a future date.

• The interest on the commitment is tax deductible until forced conversion.

• For banks, regulators have been prepared to allow such issues to count towards capital ('Tier 2' capital as defined by the Basle Convergence Agreement).

Equity and equity linked instruments

4.46 Benefits – investor

● The investor earns a fixed rate of return prior to the date of the mandatory conversion which should be in excess of the dividend yield on the shares.

4.47 Risks and disadvantages – issuer

● If the share price rises more than expected the issuer may forego some of the rise.

● Credit rating agencies will treat the issue as debt so there is no improvement in capital ratios.

4.48 Risks and disadvantages – investor

● If the share price does not perform the mandatory conversion may not be attractive.

4.49 Accounting questions

● Should the proceeds be included in the balance sheet as equity or debt?

● What is the effect on earnings per share and how is it calculated if the number of shares to be issued is unknown?

4.50 Taxation questions

● Will the investor be liable to any chargeable gain arising on the disposal of the contract?

- Other questions as for convertible debt instruments in section 4.29.

4.51 Puttable stock

Stock (shares) is issued where the issuer grants the buyer a put option allowing the investor to return the stock at a fixed price in the future either on a specific date or during a set period. The issues were introduced after a number of new equity issues had run into difficulties in the market. Such an issue is in effect a redeemable share where the investor has the redemption option. The option is not separable from the stock. This type of issue is also known as 'stock with married put'. Some issues are repayable in cash, debt or common stock at the issuer's option.

In most countries in Europe, there are legal restrictions which may limit the possibility of repaying or redeeming equity capital, and as a result the issue of puttable stock may not be possible or only possible within certain limits. These legal restrictions are discussed further in sections 4.99 to 4.163 dealing with equity markets in Europe.

Variations

Superstock	This was a Drexel Burnham Lambert innovation in the United States where stock was packaged with a separate right to sell the stock back to the issuer. In certain circumstances the issuer had the option to finance the repurchase by the issue of 10 year senior subordinated debt.
Retractable Preferred shares	Retractable preferred shares have been issued in Canada which require the issuing company to refund the investment on a predetermined 'retraction' date.

4.52 Benefits – issuer

- If exercised, the right or option given to the investor to return the stock results in a 'free' or reduced cost of capital during the issue period. The cost saving depends on the dividends paid.

4.53 Benefits – investor

• If stock prices fall the right or option makes the equity more like debt but, if prices rise, it has all the benefits of equity.

• If stock prices fall and the option is exercised it may be difficult to fund the redemption.

4.54 Risks and disadvantages – investor

• If the stock price rises the exercise of the put will be uneconomical and the investor will have paid for an option/right which was unnecessary.

• If the investor wishes to exercise the put, it is likely to be because the company is unsuccessful and therefore it may be unable to honour the put and a substitute security may have to be accepted.

4.55 Accounting questions

• How should the amount related to the option or right be treated in the issuer's accounts? Is it a component of equity or a liability?

• If the option/rights are repurchased in the market how should they be accounted for?

4.56 Taxation questions

• Does the redemption at a premium create income or a capital gain for the investor?

• Is the premium deductible for tax purposes for the issuer?

• Does the redemption constitute a distribution?

• Is the option a separate asset for tax purposes?

• Is the redemption subject to any duty or other taxes?

280

4.57 Floating rate preferred stock

These are preferred stocks with floating or variable dividends and are principally issued in the United States markets. They have become a large proportion of the preferred stock market since their introduction in the early 1980s. The intention, as with FRNs, was that the stock should trade at close to par at the refix date.

The rate of dividend is determined by reference to some external measure (eg treasury bill rate, commercial paper rate) or by an auction process. In the United States this type of stock is often issued by low or zero tax paying companies who would obtain no benefit from the tax deduction available for interest payments on debt issues. The preferred stock is intended to behave like floating rate debt but, because of United States tax legislation (the 80% dividend received deduction by which part of the income is not taxable to the recipient), the investor is willing to receive a lower nominal rate of 'interest' which will give a similar or greater after tax yield than a similar debt issue. Most of these types of issues incorporate call or other features so that the issuer has flexibility in the event of its tax position changing.

Recently United Kingdom companies have issued floating rate preferred stock in the United States market taking advantage of the well developed market and as of December 1990, 12 companies had issued securities with a total value in excess of US $3.3 billion. Due to the taxation treaty between the United Kingdom and the United States, the issues are attractive to the United States investors while being at an equivalent cost to commercial paper which they replace. However, part of this attraction may be because they are being compared with commercial paper when in fact legally (and hence in terms of security) they are equity.

Variations

There are many variations of floating rate preferred stock. Some of the more common ones are set out below.

Auction market preferred stock (AMPs)	Preferred stock with a floating dividend rate set by auction every 28 days. It is a product of Merrill Lynch. In the auction, investors bid for the securities which are then sold at the lowest yield necessary to sell the entire issue. Most of the issues made in the United States market by United Kingdom companies have been in this form.

Adjustable rate preferred stock (ARPs)	Preferred stock with a floating dividend rate, normally related to the United States Treasury bill rate. It was issued by banks as it qualified as regulatory capital. The dividend rates may be adjusted every two weeks and most issues have caps and collars to give maximum and minimum rates.
Money Market Preferred stock (MMPs)	Issuers offer preferred stock where the dividend rate will be reset every 49 days via a Dutch auction. The 49 day rotation allows United States corporate investors to claim the 80% dividend exclusion for tax purposes and allows the issuer a short-term interest rate. In effect this is a long-term share issue, paying 'short-term' interest rates.

There are several other variations of the money market preferred product:

Exchangeable Money Market Preferred stock (EMMPs)	MMPs for a set period after which the issuer can opt to exchange it for Money Market Notes.
Convertible Money Market Preferred stock (CMMPs)	MMPs convertible at the investors option into common stock.
Money Market Notes	Debt securities with interest set by auction every 35 days.

All the MMP investments are products of Lehman Brothers.

Remarketed Preferred (RP)	RP stock is similar to money market preferred stock. With RP, investors have the option of investing for seven days or the traditional 49 days after the first 49 day period has expired. The investor can change his investment to alternate between the two periods as required. This issue is repriced through a remarketing process rather than a Dutch auction. Therefore, RP stock relies on the dexterity of a remarketing agent to establish dividend yield, while the money market preferred stock relies on the investors themselves through the auction process. This is a product of Merrill Lynch.

There are also other variations including the following which are all similar:

DARTS – Dutch Auction Rate Term Securities;

CAPS – Convertible Adjustable Preferred Stock – (convertible after a dividend refix);

CAMPS – Cumulative Auction Market Preferred Stock;

CMPs – Capital Market Preferred Stock;

MAPs – Maturing Adjustable Preferred Stock;

STARs – Short-term Auction Rate Preferred Stock;

MARPs – Market Auction Rate Preferred Stock.

4.58 Benefits – issuer

- A method of raising long-term finance at a low cost. The reference rate or auction process should ensure the lowest cost.

- Depending upon the structure, the stock can have a perpetual life as investors may have no put options.

- Flexible call or other features can be included so that the stock can be redeemed or changed to debt if circumstances change.

- The issue of floating rate preferred stock as an alternative to FRNs or commercial paper will improve gearing ratios.

- If the stock is perpetual and non-cumulative, an issue by a credit institution would rank as Tier 1 capital under the terms of the Basle Conversion Agreement.

- The yield is lower than on ordinary equity or other forms of preferred equity.

- No dilution of control for existing ordinary shareholders.

4.59 Benefits – investor

- The effective yield on preferred stock may be greater than comparable commercial paper or floating rate debt.

• The stock may be registered under local securities law (eg in the United States, the Securities Act of 1933), to provide investor protection.

• As the stock has a floating rate it should trade at or around par value.

4.60 Risks and disadvantages – issuer

• If the dividend rate is set by an auction process the auction may fail. The rate will then be based upon some composite rate (eg commercial paper) which may not be attractive. This has happened to several issues recently due to investors' concerns about the credit status of particular issues or more general economic concerns. Apart from increasing the cost to the issuer, the failure of an auction can lead to bad publicity for the issuer.

• If the auction fails the publicity could be embarrassing.

• The dividends are fixed by market forces and therefore the company may have less control over dividend policies, particularly if interest rates rise.

• The redemption of the preferred stock may result in a reduction of distributable profits if there is a legal requirement to maintain capital (eg in the United Kingdom).

• If the stock has to be registered under local securities law, it may increase the cost and will impose regular reporting requirements on the issuer. However, the scope for making private equity placements in the United States has improved recently due to amendments to SEC regulations which allows issues to large institutions without prior SEC registration.

4.61 Risks and disadvantages – investor

• The stock may be called at the issuers option with no put option for the investor.

• The return may be less than a similar debt issue if the auction process (or reference rate) results in a low dividend rate.

• The market may be illiquid making it difficult to dispose of the stock.

• The dividend on the stock is linked to interest rates. Does the yield take account of the fact that the stock is a form of equity (ie in a liquidation it will be repaid after all debt)?

4.62 Accounting questions

- Is the dividend really interest and should it be shown as such?
- If the substance of the preferred share is that of debt where should it be included in the balance sheet of the issuer?

4.63 Taxation questions

- Must the issuing company have 'earnings and profits' (E&P) in order for payments made with respect to the stock to be classified as dividends and qualify for any dividend received deduction?
- Must a United States investor hold the stock for more than 45 days to qualify for the dividend received deduction?
- If the issuing company has no E&P can it pay dividends to foreign investors without withholding tax? How will the receipt by the investor be taxed?
- Other questions as for preferred shares in section 4.21.

4.64 Convertible exchangeable preferred stock (CEPs)

Convertible exchangeable preferred stock is convertible at the option of the investor into ordinary shares of the issuer and exchangeable at the issuer's option for the issuer's convertible debt. Issued by United States corporations which have significant tax losses carried forward to offset future taxable profits, CEPs allow the issuer to maximise its after tax profit. In the periods when tax losses are available dividends are paid which, due to the dividend deduction rules for investors in the United States, can be at a lower rate than interest on debt. Once the tax losses are used up, the issuer can exchange the CEPs into convertible debt to obtain a tax deduction for the interest.

Variations

Convertible Adjustable Preferred Stock (CAPs)	Rate on preferred stock is set by reference to treasury bill rate. The conversion is to

	equity stock or cash at the investors option in the period following the refixing of the dividend. The dividend setting formula can be varied by the issuer to discourage conversion.
Convertible Money Market Preferred Stock (CMMPs)	Rate on preferred stock is set by an auction process. Conversion to equity by the investor is possible at any time.

4.65 Benefits – issuer

• Useful to companies about to become profitable who do not need the tax deduction for interest now but will in the near future. The CEPs should reduce funding costs in the short term when tax deductions for interest are of no current benefit.

• The conversion rights can be at a large premium to the current share price.

• Such issues provide considerable flexibility to corporate treasurers.

• As with all convertible issues the effective cost of funding should be lower than a similar plain vanilla issue.

4.66 Benefits – investor

• Provides the investor with the flexibility of a fixed return but the option to convert into equity.

4.67 Risks and disadvantages – issuer

• May be difficult or expensive to redeem the stock if the company's situation changes.

• There may be legal restrictions preventing the exchange of equity for debt.

286

- A higher effective interest cost may have to be offered to compensate the investor for the risk that exchange into debt may take place.

4.68 Risks and disadvantages – investor

- The issuer may force the exchange to a debt security when the conversion feature (by which an equity investment could be retained) is unattractive to the investor.

- The lower return may not be compensated if the conversion premium is not matched by an increase in the price of the underlying equity.

4.69 Accounting questions

- Should CEPs be included in shareholders' equity or debt?

- What is the effect on earnings per share calculations?

4.70 Taxation questions

- Are the options separate assets for tax purposes?

- Other questions as for convertible debt instruments in section 4.29.

4.71 Convertible stock note

These are bond issues which pay coupons and principal in the form of ordinary shares of the issuer rather than cash. They have been issued by financially restructured companies.

Equity and equity linked instruments

4.72 Benefits – issuer

• Convertible stock notes are attractive to newly reorganised companies which cannot generate cash to service debt.

• Will increase the capital base of the issuer.

4.73 Benefits – investor

• The notes will provide an equity investment with a higher yield than that typically available on ordinary shares.

4.74 Risks and disadvantages – issuer

• May prove to be expensive compared with dividends on ordinary shares.

4.75 Risks and disadvantages – investor

• The issuer's share price may not perform particularly well if the company has just been restructured.

4.76 Accounting questions

• How should the instrument be shown on the issuer's balance sheet? Should it be included as debt, equity, or somewhere in between?

4.77 Taxation questions

• Is the 'coupon interest' payable in the form of shares taxable on the recipient and, if so, when?

• Other questions as for convertible debt instruments in section 4.29.

4.78 Premium put convertibles (debt with 'premium puts')

In addition to the ability to convert into equity these convertible bonds allow the holder to require the issuer to redeem the bond for cash at a future date at an amount substantially in excess of par value (the 'premium put'). The put is usually exercisable after about a third of the bond's life at a premium such that the yield is equivalent to a normal fixed rate bond of similar maturity from the same issuer. For example, assume that an AA rated company issues a convertible bond with maturity in 10 years time and an annual coupon of $7\frac{1}{2}\%$. At the date of issue, the yield the market would expect on a 3 year fixed rate bond from an AA issuer is 9.25%. The terms of the issue provide that the holders of the bond can put it back to the issuer in three years time at a price of 105.75, which if exercised would give the investor a yield of approximately 9.25%. This put arrangement offers the investor protection by allowing him to obtain a fixed rate return equivalent to market rates if the share price does not appreciate sufficiently to make conversion attractive. However, in practice the yield which the investor would obtain would be lower than market rates to take account of the value of the option.

After expiry of the put the bond is usually callable by the issuer at decreasing amounts until redemption at par. The call option provides the issuer with a safeguard if the share price performs well and the investors do not convert because of the attractive coupon (either in absolute terms or relative to the dividend on the shares).

Several United Kingdom companies issued convertible bonds with premium puts prior to the stock market crash in 1987. Following the crash, it became apparent that conversion was far less likely to be attractive to the investors. In addition, the performance of some of the issuers have deteriorated, with the result that they may have difficulty in redeeming the bond at the premium if investors exercise their put option. The problem faced by these issuers indicates that, because they expected the share price to continue to rise (which would lead the holders of the bonds to exercise the conversion option), they priced the put options too cheaply.

Variation

Convertible bonds with rolling put	Premium put convertibles with a series of put options extending over a number of

years at an increasing level of premiums. The level of the premium is calculated to give a yield at each put date equivalent to a normal fixed rate bond of similar maturity. The rolling put is designed to make conversion into equity more likely as the investor does not have to make a put decision at one date but can wait while being protected by the ability to ultimately require redemption at a premium. These issues have been popular with United Kingdom companies, some of whom have treated the issue proceeds as part of shareholders' funds on the grounds that redemption was unlikely.

4.79 Benefits – issuer

• The put feature should lower the coupon when compared with a normal convertible and providing the share price rises above the conversion premium at no cash cost.

• The call feature can help force conversion to reduce funding costs.

• As for convertible debt instruments in section 4.24.

4.80 Benefits – investor

• Provides protection if the share price does not exceed the conversion premium. The premium on the put will compensate for the lower coupon rate (providing the company has adequate resources to meet the liability if the put is exercised).

4.81 Risks and disadvantages – issuer

• If the share price does not exceed the conversion premium the put could make the issue expensive and will require significant cash resources to redeem the bond at the premium. With a 'rolling put' arrangement the liability which results from the put can be significant when compared to the issue price of the bond.

• If holders exercise the put option the expected gearing ratio will not be achieved.

4.82 Risks and disadvantages – investor

• If the put is to be effective the investor must be confident that the issuer will be able to repay not only the principal but also the premium. The possibility of default risk should be taken into account in assessing the value of the put option.

• As for convertible debt instruments in section 4.27

4.83 Accounting questions

• How should the premium be accounted for? Is it an adjustment to the interest charge or a one-off cost on issue or exercise? At what stage does an accrual become unnecessary? Can the uncertainty relating to the put be removed by the issuer taking out a put option for the placement of shares which would have been issued on conversion?

• On conversion should any premium which has been charged to income be treated as a profit or a reserve movement?

• If conversion is likely can the proceeds be included as shareholders' funds?

• What disclosures are required in the financial statements?

4.84 Taxation questions

• Is the premium a distribution?

• Does the redemption constitute a distribution?

• Are the options separate assets for tax purposes?

- Does the premium put make the issue a deep discount security?

- If the debt is a deep discount security, does conversion to shares create deemed receipt of the premium as income in the hands of the investor?

- Is the premium deductible for tax purposes for the issuer?

- Does redemption give rise to a disposal for capital gains tax purposes?

- Other questions as for convertible debt instruments in section 4.29.

4.85 Convertible bonds exchangeable into convertible preferred shares

These bonds are issued with a very low nominal (redemption) value compared to issue price (eg $1 compared with $1,000) but they can be exchanged, at the investor's option, into convertible preferred shares of the issuer. The convertible preferred shares convert into the ordinary shares of the issuer. The coupon is paid by reference to the issue price not nominal value.

The low redemption value of the bonds means that it is unlikely that the bonds will be redeemed and that conversion into preference shares is virtually certain. The investor receives back the original investment by exchange into preferred shares which are redeemed immediately, or converts into the ordinary shares through the conversion feature of the bond. In substance these instruments are identical to convertible preferred shares. However, legally, these bonds are debt until exchange or conversion takes place, which should enable the issuer to treat the coupon payments as interest which will be deductible from profits for tax purposes. The exchange into preferred shares (rather than the normal redemption of the bonds at maturity) is designed to assist in the bonds being treated as some form of equity in the issuer's balance sheet. The bonds are very unlikely to be redeemed (and if they were, the amount involved is very small) but it is virtually certain that some form of equity will be issued (either ordinary shares from conversion or preference shares from exchange). Consequently, it is argued that it is not appropriate to treat such instruments as debt. However, as the preference shares are immediately redeemed the instrument shares many of the features of convertible debt.

These issues were attractive to United Kingdom issuers as they appeared to offer the gearing benefit of convertible preference shares (if the argument that they are not debt is accepted by directors and auditors) while structured such that the interest payments should be tax deductible.

In addition such interest payments are not treated as dividends attracting advance corporation tax which, if irrecoverable, could increase the cost to the issuer. However, as the amount to be repaid on the debt is only a nominal amount it is possible that the interest on the whole of the issue proceeds may not be tax deductible.

Variation

Convertible capital bonds

The convertible capital bond structure evolved in the United Kingdom from convertible bonds exchangeable into preferred shares. Convertible capital bonds are convertible debt instruments issued by a non United Kingdom company (usually Jersey) which is resident in the United Kingdom for taxation purposes. The bonds are convertible into preference shares of the issuer or exchangeable into the ordinary shares of the issuer's United Kingdom parent company which are listed on The London Stock Exchange. The structure was designed to have the accounting benefits of convertible bonds exchangeable into preference shares but to avoid any dispute that the coupon payments were interest and therefore tax deductible. In addition, the use of a non United Kingdom company to issue the debt and preference shares avoids the Companies Act requirements in the United Kingdom to maintain capital following the redemption of shares.

4.86 Benefits – issuer

● The coupons should be a tax deductible expense.

● It may be permissible to exclude the issue from the debt section of the balance sheet and treat it as either equity or a special category in the balance sheet between debt and equity thus reducing gearing.

4.87 Benefits – investor

• A way of investing in a company with a fixed minimum return, specified rights in a winding up but with the opportunity to share in the performance of the ordinary shares.

• With a falling share price the instrument will be a better investment than the underlying equity as price falls are limited by the coupon rate.

4.88 Risks and disadvantages – issuer

• The accounting treatment may not permit the issue to be included as some form of equity.

• The coupons may not be wholly tax deductible and may be treated as dividends.

4.89 Risks and disadvantages – investor

• There may be legal restrictions on the redemption of the preferred shares, such as a requirement to maintain capital, which may prevent redemption.

• In a winding up the instrument will only repay nominal value unless converted into preferred shares which will then rank after all other debt.

4.90 Accounting questions

• Should the instrument be included as debt, equity or somewhere in between?

• If it is not treated as debt, should the coupons be treated as interest or dividends?

• Should the conversion option receive separate accounting recognition at the time of issuance or exchange?

• What is the effect on earnings per share?

4.91 Taxation questions

- Are the coupons a tax deductible expense? If not, do they represent a distribution?
- Other questions as for convertible debt instruments in section 4.29.

4.92 Debt with equity warrants

Debt is issued with warrants to subscribe for equity in the issuer or its parent company. The issue is similar to convertible debt except that the conversion feature is in the form of a separately tradeable warrant. The equity warrants may also entitle the purchase of shares in a third party. Unlike a convertible bond the exercise of the warrant will normally increase the total capital of the issuer as the debt is not replaced by equity but the equity is issued in addition to the debt which is redeemed independently at its stated maturity. In addition, the warrant has a constant strike price, unlike the convertible bond whose strike price varies with the market value of the bond.

The maturities of the warrants can be 15 years but shorter maturities are more usual (less than five years). The warrant's exercise period usually starts shortly after issue. More details of warrants are given in chapter 5 – Hedging Instruments.

Variation

Redeemable warrant   A warrant with a fixed redemption amount as well as conversion rights.

4.93 Benefits – issuer

- Reduced funding costs as the investor may accept a lower yield in the anticipation of a profit on the exercise of the warrant.
- Additional equity capital when the warrant is exercised at a premium over current market prices as well as the amount received from the issue of the warrant.

4.94 Benefits – investor

• A low cost way of participating in the equity of the company.

• Warrants generally offer a longer expiry period than traded options.

• The warrants are highly geared and a small increase in the share price leads to a large increase in the value of the warrant.

4.95 Risks and disadvantages – issuer

• If the share price appreciates to a great extent over the exercise price, less capital would be raised by the issuer than from another form of equity issue of the same number of shares.

4.96 Risks and disadvantages – investor

• As they are highly geared the price of warrants can be extremely volatile and often have large bid/offer spreads.

• The warrant bears no coupon to offset holding costs.

• While the market is fairly liquid the volatility of the market may make it difficult to sell the warrants.

• The warrant may expire worthless.

4.97 Accounting questions

• Should the issuer allocate the proceeds between the debt and the warrant?

• If so, how should the amount attributed to the debt warrant be determined?

• Should the amount attributable to the debt be determined using market rates for straight debt of the same issuer or by valuing the warrant?

• If an amount is attributed to the warrant where should it be included in the balance sheet of the issuer?

• If the warrant is exercised should the attributed amount be transferred to share premium?

• If the warrant expires unexercised how should the attributed amount be treated?

• What is the effect on fully diluted earnings per share? How should any dilution be calculated?

4.98 Taxation questions

• Should the issue price be allocated between the debt and the warrants by both the issuer and the investor? If so, does the allocation make the issue a deep discount security?

• Is the issue price of the warrant a capital gain from the grant of an option? If so, when is the tax due?

• Does exercise of the warrant alter any such gain?

• Does the expiry of the warrant give the investor a capital loss?

• Is capital duty payable on the issue or exercise of the warrant?

• What is the investor's base cost in the shares if the warrant is exercised?

• Is issue or transfer of the warrant subject to any duty or taxes (eg VAT or stamp duty)?

• Is the issue of the warrant a distribution?

• Will a taxation deduction be available for all payments made under the terms of issue (such as supplementary payments made under the terms of issue) if the warrants are not exercised?

4.99 Equity markets in Europe

4.100 United Kingdom

In the United Kingdom the issue of shares is governed by the Companies Act 1985 ('the Companies Act') as amended by the 1989 Companies Act and, in the case of listed shares, by regulations issued by the International Stock Exchange of Great Britain & the Republic of Ireland ('The Stock Exchange') pursuant to the Financial Services Act 1986. The provisions of the Companies Act are detailed but a summary of the more important or unusual ones relevant to equity or equity linked products is set out below:

• shares are required to have a positive nominal value;

• shares may be issued at a premium (for cash or otherwise), in which case the excess over nominal value must usually be transferred to a non distributable share premium account. There are exceptions to this where shares are issued at a premium in connection with a merger (provided that the Companies Act requirements for a merger are met) or during a group reconstruction. In these cases, the premium arising does not have to be transferred to the share premium account;

• use of the share premium account is governed by statute. It can be used only to:

– pay up bonus shares;

– write off preliminary expenses;

– write off expenses of, or commission paid or discount allowed on, any issue of shares or debentures of the company;

– provide for premiums payable on redemption of debentures (and, in certain circumstances, redeemable shares) of the company (not other categories of shares);

• bearer shares are not permitted;

• United Kingdom companies may issue shares and prepare accounts in currencies other than sterling (although the Registrar of Companies will only accept the accounts if the rate of exchange to sterling at the balance sheet date is shown in the accounts). Recently companies have issued shares in multiple currencies. Shares issued as part of multi-currency issues must be denominated in one particular currency which cannot be varied, although different shares can be denominated in different currencies. Such share capital is effectively used to hedge the company's non-sterling assets. In the case of a public company a minimum amount of tue share capital must be denominated in sterling (see below);

• it is illegal to issue shares at a discount to their nominal value.

4.101 Private and public companies

United Kingdom company law distinguishes between private and public companies. Only a public company may offer shares and debentures (debt) to the public. It is possible for shares in a private company to be widely distributed but it is a criminal offence to offer shares in a private company to the public except in limited and specified circumstances such as a private placing with no offer to the public.

There are specific provisions in the Companies Act governing public companies which are more stringent than those for private companies. These include:

• the company's name must end with the words 'public limited company' (or equivalent in Welsh);

• the nominal value of allotted share capital must be at least £50,000;

• at least 25% of the nominal value of the allotted share capital and all the share premium must be paid up;

• there are provisions governing the issue of shares for non-cash consideration;

• there are also provisions dealing with:

– maintenance of capital;

– distribution of profits;

– loans to directors;

– purchase of own shares;

– financial assistance for acquisition of shares;

– pre-emption rights on allotment of shares.

A public company may offer some of its shares to the public but first has to comply with the prospectus requirements of the Companies Act or, if the shares are to be listed on The Stock Exchange, the requirements of the Financial Services Act 1986. At present these requirements do not extend to shares which are quoted on the Unlisted Securities Market

(USM) of The Stock Exchange, but this is likely to change in 1991. Shares on the USM are, by definition, not listed even though they are quoted.

As noted above, when shares are issued to the public a prospectus (referred to as listing particulars when in connection with a listing on The Stock Exchange) is required, setting out the history of the company and its activities. The costs of this, the legal formalities, accountants reports and publicity, and underwriting costs can be significant. This may make a public share issue an expensive way of raising finance.

4.102 Redeemable shares

Under Section 159 of the Companies Act a company, whether public or private, has the power to issue redeemable shares provided it is authorised to do so by its Articles of Association (which, if they do not provide for this, can be amended by a special resolution). The other requirements of the Companies Act for redeemable shares are:

● any class of ordinary or preferred shares may be redeemable and redemption at a premium is possible;

● redeemable shares may not be redeemed unless they are fully paid;

● redemption may be at the option of either the company or the shareholders; the precise conditions for redemption will be subject to the provisions in the company's Articles of Association;

● after redemption, the company must still have non-redeemable shares in issue.

The general rule is that shares can be redeemed only out of either distributable profits (as defined in the Companies Act) or the proceeds of a fresh issue of shares made for the purposes of redemption. Any premium payable on redemption must be paid out of distributable profits except in circumstances where a new issue of shares is made where special rules may apply. Private companies, if authorised by their Articles of Association, may redeem shares out of capital providing detailed procedural requirements are followed.

4.103 Purchase of own shares

In general, private and public companies are prohibited by the Companies

Act from purchasing their own shares (whether by purchase or subscription). A company can only purchase its own shares in certain circumstances which are set out in the Companies Act and any other purchase of shares is void and there are criminal sanctions available against the company and its officers for breach of Companies Act requirements. The circumstances are complex but can be summarised as follows:

• a company can acquire its own fully paid shares otherwise than for valuable consideration (eg bequest or gift). A public company must dispose of or cancel such shares within three years. A company can acquire shares as a result of forfeiture or surrender of shares as a result of a failure to pay amounts due in respect of those shares. A public company which acquires shares by forfeiture must dispose of them within three years;

• a company may purchase its own shares if the rules in Sections 162 to 181 of the Companies Act are followed. These rules are similar to those for the redemption of shares noted in section 4.102 above. Once purchased the shares must be treated as cancelled and the issued capital reduced; they cannot be held in 'treasury' to be reissued. After purchase there must be at least one member of the company holding non-redeemable shares, and at least two members;

• a company may acquire its own shares under a scheme of reconstruction or amalgamation resulting in a reduction of capital. Confirmation of the court may be required for such schemes;

• a company may acquire its own shares as a result of a court order.

4.104 Market characteristics

The Stock Exchange is the main stock market in the United Kingdom and is based in London. It is divided into two tiers, the Main Market, and the Unlisted Securities Market ('USM'). Shares in public companies not listed or quoted on either of the above markets may in practice only be traded on a matched bargain basis 'over the counter' by certain specialised securities dealers under The Stock Exchange's Rule 535(2). The USM was originally established to provide a market suitable for the smaller company. However, in recent years the differences in the requirements of the Main Market and the USM have been eroded.

The Stock Exchange has no physical trading floor. Market makers who are authorised to quote prices in certain shares, indicated bid and offer prices on SEAQ (The Stock Exchange Automated Quotations System) and other market makers, dealers and agency brokers contact the market maker on the telephone to execute a transaction. These transactions are then reported thought the SEAQ system to provide price/deal transparency. Securities listed or quoted on The Stock Exchange are rated in bands according to their 'Normal Market Size' (NMS). The NMS of each security is calculated by reference to its daily turnover in the previous twelve month period, and is indicative of its liquidity. It forms the basis of regulations such as the minimum size of transaction for which market makers are required to quote two-way prices and whether these are firm or indicative prices.

The market place is governed by two main authorities. The Council of The Stock Exchange ('the Council') is the authority empowered under the provisions of the Financial Services Act 1986 to make listing rules. The Securities and Futures Authority is the self-regulatory organisation formed under the provisions of the Financial Services Act for the purpose of investor protection which regulates the activities of market makers, brokers and dealers in securities.

Settlement of transactions

Trading in shares listed on The Stock Exchange in London normally occurs within a two week 'account period'. Settlement day, when shares are transferred from seller to buyer and paid for, is normally six business days after the end of the Stock Exchange account. Settlement between Stock Exchange members is primarily through the central clearing service Talisman. The Stock Exchange proposes to amend the settlement terms to rolling settlement, but as yet there are no detailed proposals or timetable in place.

All transfers of equity securities outside (and into and from) the Talisman system is currently by the physical exchange of share certificates. The implementation of TAURUS (which is expected to occur in 1993) will introduce a book entry system for recording the ownership of most securities ('dematerialisation') and it is anticipated that this will simplify settlement procedures.

Admission to listing

The admission of securities to listing on the Main Market of The Stock Exchange is governed by the rules issued by the Council of The Stock Exchange in their publication 'Admission of Securities to Listing', more generally referred to as 'The Yellow Book'. The Yellow Book sets out the regulations that all applicants for a listing are required to satisfy. The regulations address such matters as the application procedure, the minimum size of applicants, the contents of the formal listing particulars (which must contain sufficient information about their history, prospects

302

and financial condition to form a reliable basis for market valuation) as well as the period of trading under the present management. The admission of securities to the USM is governed by a separate set of rules known as 'The Green Book'.

The principal requirements for obtaining a listing on the Main Market or a quotation on the USM are:

- a member firm of The Stock Exchange has to sponsor the company's application;

- the applicant must accept the continuing obligations imposed by the Council to listed companies (see below);

- the minimum market value of the shares to be listed must be £700,000 or £200,000 for debt securities (there are no equivalent minima for the USM). However, the Council may admit securities of a lower value if it is satisfied that there will be an adequate market;

- the shares must be freely transferable;

- the company must have published accounts for at least three years preceding the application;

- the directors of the company must be satisfied that there is adequate working capital;

- at least 25% of each class of shares issued (10% for the USM) must be available to the public by the time of admission. The public in this instance means persons not associated with the directors or major shareholders;

- listing particulars or, in the case of the USM a prospectus or particulars card, must be published. The requirements for the information to be included in this document are detailed, and may be summarised under the headings listed below:

– names of directors and professional advisors;

– details regarding the shares being issued;

– information on the issuer's equity and debt capital;

– description of the issuing group's activities;

– financial information on the issuer, including its audited accounts for at least three years prior to the issue (two years for the USM);

– information on the issuing company's management;

– details of the issuing company or group's indebtedness, a review of recent developments and future prospects (a profit forecast may be made but is not required);

– details of material contracts.

Compliance with certain of the requirements for listing shown above may be waived by the Council in special circumstances, and by the same token, satisfaction of these requirements is not of itself sufficient to guarantee the admission to listing, as the Council retains the right to accept or reject applications at its absolute discretion.

The most common method for bringing securities to listing is by means of a public offering, although other methods may be allowed by concession in certain circumstances. A public offering may take the form of an offer at a fixed price or a tender offer, and there are detailed rules governing the procedures which must be followed for each permitted issuing method.

Continuing obligations for listed companies

One of the principal objects of the continuing obligations imposed by the Council on listed companies is to secure the immediate release of information which can reasonably be expected to have a material effect on market activity and prices of listed securities. For this reason companies are required to notify developments affecting them as soon as possible to The Stock Exchange. The detailed requirements for specific information to be notified to the exchange are extremely broad and are contained in The Yellow and Green Books. The guiding principles are that all users of the market should have simultaneous access to the same information, and that therefore any information which is expected to be price sensitive should be released immediately it has been the subject of a decision.

Companies are also required to notify (and/or seek approval from) shareholders, by means of a circular, the details of transactions or proposed transactions of a significant size in relation to the company, or transactions involving directors or substantial shareholders of the company. Significant size in this respect generally means 15% or more (35% for the USM) of the assets or profits of the company or of the market value of its equity capital – such transactions are called 'Class 1'. Transactions taking place within a short period of time may be aggregated for the purposes of the 15% test. Transactions where the relevant percentage defined above is 25% (75% for the USM) ('Super Class 1') or more require the approval of shareholders in general meeting. Smaller acquisitions or disposals still need to be notified to the exchange. More stringent notifications and approval requirements apply to transactions in which directors or major shareholders are involved ('Class 4').

The Council also imposes a number of regulations concerning the contents of the company's annual accounts and special requirements exist for non United Kingdom companies listed on the exchange. The Council expects listed companies to prepare their accounts in accordance with United Kingdom Accounting Standards and requires the directors to state in the annual report the reasons for any departure from such standards. Listed companies are also required by the Yellow Book to publish a half yearly report on the group's activities and profit or loss for the first six months of each financial year as well as a 'preliminary announcement' of the full years results and activities. Detailed requirements relating to the contents of half yearly reports are set out in The Yellow Book.

Overseas companies seeking a listing

For overseas companies, The Stock Exchange has in recent years relaxed many of the requirements which are applicable to United Kingdom companies to encourage such companies which already have a listing in their home country to seek a secondary listing on the exchange. For overseas companies there are very few requirements to be met which are additional to those faced in their home country; the principal requirement is that financial information included in listing particulars and in subsequent annual accounts is to have been prepared under United Kingdom or United States standards (generally accepted accounting principles) or to International Accounting Standards, and to have been audited to a comparable standard.

Equity capital raising

Companies who propose issuing securities for cash having an equity element are required by the Companies Act 1985 to offer those securities to existing equity shareholders in proportion to their existing holdings, unless shareholders approve the terms of another type of issue. This has the effect that most equity capital raising by United Kingdom listed companies is done by means of rights issues at a discount to the market price of the shares. Shareholders not intending to take up the rights may sell them on, and these rights are normally traded on The Stock Exchange. This requirement for companies listed on The Stock Exchange does not necessarily apply to non United Kingdom companies (depending on the laws of their country of registration) but any issue of shares which results in significant dilution of the interests of existing shareholders, or otherwise detracts from the interests of these shareholders, would require shareholders' approval before being accepted by The Stock Exchange.

Takeovers and mergers

The regulations concerning takeovers and mergers for public and certain other companies are set out in 'The City Code on Takeovers and Mergers and The Rules Governing Substantial Acquisitions of Shares', published by the Panel on Takeovers and Mergers. This publication is widely known as 'The City Code' or 'The Blue Book'. The principal purpose of the City Code is to ensure fair and equal treatment of all shareholders in relation to takeovers. The provisions of The City Code do not have legal status but are intended as a code of best business standards and are generally accepted as such by the investment community. In addition to The City Code, procedures to be adopted during a proposed merger are set out in the Fair Trading Act 1973, as amended by the Companies Act 1989.

Failure to comply with The City Code on the part of directors, shareholders and professional advisors will prejudice their ability to continue to carry on in business within the investment community in the United Kingdom. The City Code lays down a number of rules to be observed in the conduct of a takeover or merger. In order to avoid any ambiguity as to the application and meaning of the detailed rules, the general principles on which the rules are based are also set out. In addition to The City Code rules, the Companies Act contains some provisions regarding restricting stakebuilding of shares in a company. The more important rules and regulations of The City Code and the Companies Act are:

• an equity stake of 3% or more of the issued share capital must be disclosed to the company within two business days of its acquisition, and the company is required to notify the stake to The Stock Exchange within one further day;

• the acquirer of a stake totalling 30% or more of the issued share capital of a target company must (except in certain circumstances) either reduce its stake or make an offer (usually at the highest price paid for the previous acquisition) for all the remaining shares; such an offer may only be conditional on acquiring more than 50% of the share capital or on Government approval of the takeover;

• once it has acquired 90% or more of the target's share capital, the offerer may compulsorily acquire the shares of the remaining minority. Conversely, the minority may demand to be bought out by the offerer.

Planned takeovers or mergers of United Kingdom listed companies are reviewed by the Office of Fair Trading (OFT) where either the gross assets of the target exceed £30 million or the combined market share in the United Kingdom of target and offerer exceeds 25%. The OFT considers competition policy aspects of a proposed transaction and may recommend to the Secretary of State for Trade and Industry that the proposed transaction is referred for investigation by the Monopolies and Mergers Commission (MMC). The MMC will then recommend whether the transaction should proceed or whether it should be prohibited, principally on the grounds that the merger would have an adverse affect on competition and therefore would not be in the best interest of the public. The Secretary of State is not required to accept the recommendation of the MMC, but usually does.

4.105 Specific issues to be considered in the United Kingdom

Strict regulatory framework in the United Kingdom

United Kingdom equity markets are characterised by a strict regulatory framework. Raising equity by way of a listing on The Stock Exchange can be expensive for all but the largest issuers.

There is a possibility that shareholdings may be accumulated until such time as enough shares are held to make a bid for all the shares in the company. However, anyone who acquires more than 3% of the issued ordinary shares must, in accordance with the Companies Act, declare this fact to the company. If the terms of the Act are not complied with, the Secretary of State for Trade and Industry has the power to impose a restriction order on the shares, which, inter alia, suspends rights to vote in shareholders meetings and receive dividends.

The amount of additional shares which may be issued for cash at any one time is governed by company law. Pre-emption rights ensure that a public company may only issue new shares to new shareholders in limited circumstances. Pre-emption rights may be set aside by the shareholders in a general meeting but there is usually a limit of 5% placed on such share issues. Any issues in excess of this limit have to be approved by the shareholders. In addition, the 'Pre-emption Group' which is composed of members from the Investment Protection Committees of the Association of British Insurers and the National Association of Pension Funds, representing a large proportion of institutional investors, have issued a guideline of 5% issued share capital. Issues for cash in excess of the pre-emption waiver must be approved by shareholders who may require clawback provisions to enable them to participate in the issue. Non cash issues (ie share for share exchanges) are not subject to pre-emption but in the case of a listed company will be governed by the continuing obligations of The Stock Exchange.

Once shares are issued, it may be difficult to cancel them. There are two possible routes:

• purchase of own shares – Private companies may purchase their own shares thereby reducing the amount of capital available for creditors to call on providing certain conditions are met (including court approval), and the shareholders agree to this at a general meeting. Public companies may purchase their own shares but may not reduce their capital (that is, the amount of share capital and non-distributable reserves) without the consent of the court. Shares do not have to be 'redeemable' for this to happen. Shares purchased are cancelled;

- issue redeemable shares – Redeemable shares may give the investor the right to force the company to redeem the shares. In respect of redeemable shares, the shareholder has the right to sue the company for failure to repurchase shares at the specified date. However, if there are insufficient distributable profits the company cannot be required to redeem the shares. The company may have to raise new finance to finance the redemption of redeemable shares (if it has insufficient distributable profits) and this may be expensive. Redeemable shares may be redeemed at a price which is below their market value.

4.106 Accounting treatment

The accounting requirements relating to equity and equity linked instruments contained within the Companies Act and SSAPs are relatively straightforward. As noted in section 4.100 consideration received from equity issues is allocated between share capital and share premium. For equity linked issues in the form of convertible debt the requirements are as for debt instruments in general (see section 2.209) with the notes to the financial statements describing the terms of the issue.

Disclosure requirements

The Companies Act prescribes the position of equity within the balance sheet format, and there are rules relating to the information which has to be disclosed in notes to the accounts. The most important rules relate to:

- the number and aggregate nominal value of each class of share allotted, called up and fully paid;

- details of options on unissued shares;

- details of redeemable shares;

- details of shares issued during the period;

- disclosure in respect of business combinations.

Share premium account and merger accounting

The Companies Act sets out conditions where merger relief can apply – that is where a company need not comply with the requirement of Section 130 of the Companies Act to transfer any premium over the nominal value of the shares to a share premium account. The situations in which companies can obtain merger relief under the Companies Act are those in which the transaction satisfies the following three conditions:

• a company (known either as the issuing company or the acquiring company) secures at least 90% of the nominal value of each class of the equity share capital of another company (the acquired company) as a result of an arrangement;

• the arrangement provides for the allotment of equity shares in the issuing company. (Such allotment will normally be made to the acquired company's shareholders);

• the consideration for the shares so allotted is either the issue or the transfer to the issuing company of equity shares in the acquired company or the cancellation of those of the equity shares in the acquired company that the issuing company does not already hold.

There are detailed rules in the Act to determine where the conditions set out above apply.

In addition, SSAP 23 sets out further conditions under which merger accounting may be applied. The conditions for merger accounting in both the Companies Act and SSAP 23 are more restrictive than are conditions for merger relief. There may be occasions where a transaction qualifies for merger relief, but acquisition accounting must be used in preparing the group accounts in order to comply with SSAP 23. In these circumstances, the company may record its investment in the subsidiary at nominal value. SSAP 14 and the Companies Act both require the group to use fair values for the net tangible assets acquired and consideration given in the group accounts.

Group reconstructions

The Companies Act disapplies merger relief where an acquisition forms part of a group reconstruction. However, section 132 of the Companies Act allows group reconstruction relief in certain circumstances and sets out detailed rules for the calculation of the amount of share premium. In general terms, where such a group reconstruction takes place it will not be necessary to set up a share premiums account and the distributable reserves of the group will not be affected by the reconstruction.

Equity and equity linked instruments

Redeemable shares

The main requirements of the Companies Act for the issue and redemption of shares are set out in section 4.102. There are also detailed accounting rules relating to the redemption of shares. Briefly, the main points are:

• where the redemption is wholly out of the profits of the company an amount equal to the reduction of the issued capital is required to be transferred to the 'Capital Redemption Reserve';

• when the redemption is wholly or partly out of the proceeds of a fresh issue and the aggregate amount of the proceeds is less than the nominal value of the shares redeemed the amount of the difference is required to be transferred to the capital redemption reserve;

• the capital redemption reserve may only be applied for a bonus issue of new capital.

Convertible bonds

The appropriate accounting treatment to be adopted following an issue of convertible bonds is set out in TR 677 'Accounting for Complex Capital Issues'. TR 677 makes a distinction between convertible loan stock issued with no variation of rights (fixed terms) and those with variation of rights (conversion or redeemable options).

Convertible bonds with fixed terms

Convertible bonds with fixed terms normally carry a coupon rate of interest which is less than the prevailing market rate and are convertible into equity at the end of their lives. In practice, very few publicly issued convertibles have such inflexible conditions as investors do not find them attractive. The economic effects of such an issue are that a company's equity shareholders allow shares to be taken up in the future at less than full value. This will, therefore, dilute their future shareholdings in exchange for a reduction of interest costs in the intervening period.

For example, the particulars of a convertible loan stock with fixed terms are as follows:

Convertible to equity after 10 years or redeemable at par

Issue amount £100,000 at par with 6% interest

Current market rate of interest for this borrower on plain vanilla debt 10%.

Using the principles of TR 677 the market rate of interest (that is, 10%) for the bond should be charged to the profit and loss account. Conse-

310

quently, in addition to the 6% interest paid to the investors each year, an additional 4% would be accrued over the life of the bond (ie 10 years). TR 677 states this is necessary in order to show a true cost of capital. The difference between the market rate charged in the profit and loss account and the rate of interest paid should be treated as a capital reserve and disclosed separately as part of shareholders' funds. When the shares are issued, the additional interest (of 4% per annum) that has been built in the capital reserve (in this example accumulating at £4,000 per annum) should be treated as proceeds of the issue of those shares. It is not clear whether it should be included in the share premium account, or whether from a legal point of view the amount is distributable.

TR 677 does not discuss the situation where the investors do not exercise their option and the bond is redeemed at its par value. Presumably, the additional interest which has been built up in the capital reserve could be considered to be distributable once the liability to the investors had been extinguished.

Convertible bonds with redemption and conversion options

Convertible bonds that are issued with alternative redemption or conversion options would normally give the stockholder the choice of either redeeming the stock for cash at a future specified date, or range of dates, or opting for conversion into equity shares. The accounting treatment suggested by TR 677 can be illustrated in the following example. The particulars of the stock are identical to those in the previous example, except that the investor has a redemption option, as well as an option to convert.

Convertible to equity after 10 years at £2 per share (that is, convertible into 50,000 shares) or redeemable at par.

Issue amount £100,000 at par with 6% interest.

Redeemable at the investors option at a premium in five years to give a 10% return.

After five years the investor has the opportunity to redeem the stock at an amount above par that will give him a 10% return on his investment ('the put option'). If the share price after five years is below the £2 price per share, logically the investor will take the early redemption option.

As in the previous example, TR 677 recommends that the difference between the quoted interest rate and the true cost of finance (the yield which the investor is guaranteed by the redemption option which presumably approximates to the market rate at the time of issue) should be accrued over the life of the redemption option as a redemption reserve. If the investor opts for conversion rather than redemption, the redemption reserve should then be credited to the share premium account, as in the first example.

Where conversion is considered likely, some companies have in the past not accrued the additional interest guaranteed to the investor by the put option. However, the Urgent Issues Task Force (UITF) of the Accounting Standards Board issued a pronouncement in August 1991 stating that in future the 'supplemental interest/premium' (ie the cost of redeeming at the premium put value) should be charged to the profit and loss account annually from issue along with the coupon interest. The reason for the treatment is that:

• if the bond is redeemed, the cost to the company includes the premium payable on redemption. If the bond is converted, the effective consideration for the shares issued is equal to the proceeds of redemption forgone by the bondholders, being the amount of the company's liability in respect of the bonds which is thereby extinguished which includes the cost of the amount of the premium put at the conversion date. A company should, therefore, accrue the supplemental interest/premium regardless of the likelihood of conversion;

• a bondholders choice between conversion and redemption will depend on many factors including interest rates and the price of shares and bonds, which are inherently unpredictable. It is not appropriate to use predictions of such factors in determining whether or not a convertible bond, including any supplemental interest or premium, constitutes a liability for accounting purposes.

While pronouncements of the UITF do not have the status of accounting standards they should be viewed as mandatory as they could be the basis of an enquiry or action by the newly created Financial Reporting Review Panel. This panel has the power to order directors to amend the accounts. The treatment suggested in the pronouncement is consistent with that in TR 677 and the pronouncement is likely to force those companies which have not provided for the premium put to reconsider their accounting policy. It will also invalidate the assumption that a 'rolling put' which is designed to make conversion more likely (see section 4.78), enables companies not to provide for the cost of the extra interest/premium.

Convertible Capital Bonds

Many of the instruments discussed in this chapter seek to blur the distinction between debt and equity. This is particularly true of

Convertible Capital Bonds and convertible preference shares issued by a subsidiary company, and the accounting treatment sometimes adopted for these instruments is controversial. This controversy arises mainly from the treatment of the instrument on the consolidated balance sheet. Some companies have shown the proceeds (or the major part thereof) of the issue as part of shareholders' funds in the group accounts from the date of issue on the grounds that conversion into equity is likely. In some cases issuers have included the difference between the nominal value of the shares and the issue value of the bond as share premium. However, this treatment assumes that conversion has taken place (as share premium can only arise on an issue of shares) when as a matter of fact conversion is contingent upon the investor exercising the conversion option at a future date. However valid the assumption regarding conversion may be, it does not seem appropriate for any of the proceeds to be included in the share premium account until the shares are actually issued. In addition, the stock market crash of October 1987 and the subsequent difficulties faced by companies who issued premium put convertibles has shown the danger of reflecting assumptions about future events (particularly the behaviour of the share price) in financial statements.

An alternative accounting treatment which some companies have adopted is to show the bonds alongside or as part of minority interests. This treatment has been adopted on the grounds that conversion into preference shares is certain in cases where the option to convert into ordinary shares is not exercised by the investor. Therefore some form of equity will be issued (even if only as a means of redemption in some cases – see section 4.85). In addition, if there is a reasonable probability that conversion into ordinary shares will occur, it is argued that the instrument is not debt. Consequently, including capital bonds in the balance sheet alongside minority interests perhaps shows best the true nature of such hybrid debt/equity instruments. Such a treatment indicates that these instruments are neither debt nor equity. However, this will be a departure from the Companies Act disclosure requirements so the directors (and auditors) will have to be satisfied that this is the only appropriate disclosure.

The International Accounting Standards Committee's recently published exposure draft on financial instruments would suggest that until conversion all debt instruments which may result in repayment should be included in the balance sheet as a liability. The Urgent Issues Task Force of The Accounting Standards Board is also considering the most appropriate accounting treatment for such instruments. Issuers will need to consider, in the light of these factors, the effect such instruments are likely to have on gearing in the future if a requirement to treat them as debt is introduced.

Equity and equity linked instruments

Debt with equity warrants

TR 677 states that where a company issues bonds with equity warrants which are detachable and can be separately traded, the proceeds should be split between the bonds and the warrants and accounted for separately. The proceeds allocated to the warrant should be treated as capital, and if the warrant is exercised treated as part of the proceeds of the issue of shares. However, if the warrant is allowed to lapse, the amount previously treated as capital can be taken to the profit and loss account.

TR 677 does not discuss how the proceeds to be allocated to the warrant should be calculated, but presumably it should be based on the relative fair values at the time of issue. Where the issue is widely traded and has reasonable liquidity, this should be obtainable by reference to market prices.

4.107 Taxation treatment

Payment of dividends

In the United Kingdom there is a requirement for companies to pay advance corporation tax (ACT) on dividends. At current rates of tax, for every £75 dividend paid the company is required to pay over to the Inland Revenue £25 ACT. The £75 dividend is tax exempt in the hands of a United Kingdom corporate shareholder. Other shareholders are treated as receiving £100 income and the £25 will be credited against payment of their income tax liability. The paying company will be able to treat the ACT as a payment on account of its corporation tax liability for the year in which the dividend is paid, for any of the preceding six years, or for future years, or alternatively it can surrender it to its subsidiaries providing it owns at least 51% of the equity of those subsidiaries. No ACT needs to be accounted for on dividends paid by a 51% owned subsidiary to its parent if an appropriate election is submitted to the Inland Revenue. If the group has no liability to corporation tax the ACT, as well as being a cash flow disadvantage, can also be a cost as the ACT asset will have to be written off if there is no likelihood of recovery. If the group has a significant level of overseas earnings and hence little or no United Kingdom corporation tax, irrecoverable ACT can be a major problem.

Relief for withholding tax on dividends received by a United Kingdom company from overseas can be obtained by offset against its corporation tax liability, and where the United Kingdom company owns more than 10% of the foreign company, relief can usually be obtained for underlying tax suffered on the foreign company's profits. A non-United Kingdom resident receiving a dividend from a United Kingdom company may be entitled to a repayment of part of the tax credit (ACT) under the terms of a relevant double tax treaty.

Issue and redemption of shares

In certain circumstances, the issue and redemption of shares may be deemed to be a distribution for tax purposes. However, a purchase of its own shares by an unquoted company is not a distribution if certain conditions are satisfied.

Issue related expenses are not tax deductible as they relate to a capital transaction.

VAT and capital duty

The issue or transfer of any share or warrant to United Kingdom or EC persons is exempt from VAT, whilst to non-EC persons it is zero rated. The receipt of a dividend on shares is outside the scope of VAT. VAT on costs associated with the issue of shares up to the point when the decision to make the issue could be made is treated as relating to the issuer's normal business activities. VAT on later costs will only be recoverable if the issue is to a non-EC person.

There is no capital duty on the issue of shares although stamp duty of $\frac{1}{2}$% is payable when a company repurchases its own shares. Stamp duty (or stamp duty reserve tax, as appropriate) of $\frac{1}{2}$% is generally payable on share transfers subject to certain exceptions, but there are plans to abolish this charge.

Except for movements of capital within the EC, it is illegal for a United Kingdom company to permit a non-United Kingdom company that it controls to issue shares (or debentures) or for a United Kingdom company to dispose of any shares (or debentures) in a non-United Kingdom company that it controls unless consent is obtained, although many classes of transactions are covered by 'general consents'.

Capital gains tax

United Kingdom resident companies and individuals are subject to capital gains tax on any gain made on the disposal of shares subject to relief for inflation (indexation relief). The tax is payable at the shareholder's relevant corporation tax or income tax rate. Rollover of the gains is available in respect of certain reorganisations of share capital, share for share transactions, and intra-group disposals of investments.

Convertible debt instruments

The tax legislation applicable to convertible debt instruments is extensive and extremely complicated. For example, if a debt satisfies a series of detailed conditions it will be treated as a qualifying convertible security. Broadly speaking, the overall return on a qualifying convertible is separated into an income element and a capital element. The income element is chargeable to tax in the hands of the investor and relief is available to the issuer. Some bonds which fail to meet the strict conditions for qualifying convertibles may be taxed as deep gain securities. In this case the investor still suffers an income tax charge but no relief is available to the issuer.

Interest on debt instruments will normally be allowable on a paid basis (unless paid to a bank in the United Kingdom in which case the accruals basis applies).

4.108 Channel Islands

In Jersey the raising of capital is currently governed by a Borrowing Control Law whilst the issue of shares is governed by the Law (1861) on Limited Liability Companies (as amended). A draft Companies (Jersey) Law to replace the old Law has been approved by the States of Jersey and it is anticipated that it will receive Royal Assent and be in operation by mid 1991. The more important aspects of the draft Law relevant to equity are as follows:

• shares may be denominated in any currency;

• shares may be issued at a premium in which case the excess over nominal value must be transferred to a non distributable share premium account;

• The share premium account can only be used to:

– pay up bonus shares;

– write off preliminary expenses;

– write off the expenses of, commission paid, or discount allowed on any issue of shares;

– provide for premiums payable on redemption of any redeemable preference shares.

In Guernsey the position is substantially the same with the raising of capital governed by the Control of Borrowing Ordinances and the issue of shares governed by the Companies (Guernsey) Laws 1908-1973.

A company has the power to issue redeemable preference shares provided it is authorised to do so by its Articles of Association. A company may also convert the whole, or any particular class, of its preference shares into redeemable preference shares. The principal provisions regarding redeemable preference shares include:

• shares may not be redeemed unless they are fully paid;

• shares can only be redeemed out of:

– The profits of the company which would otherwise be available for dividend; or

– The proceeds of a fresh issue of shares made for the purposes of the redemption;

• the premium, if any, payable on redemption must have been provided for out of profits or the share premium account;

• where shares are redeemed otherwise than out of the proceeds of a fresh issue there must be a transfer out of profits which would otherwise have been available for dividend to a Capital Redemption Reserve Fund a sum equal to the nominal value of the shares redeemed.

Typically redeemable preference shares are issued by Collective Investment Schemes which therefore assume the character of 'open ended' companies. This is usually achieved by issuing shares at a substantial premium with the nominal value of the shares being say 1p or such other currency in which the company may choose to denominate share capital.

Collective Investment Schemes are now regulated by the Collective Investment Funds (Jersey) Law 1988 and the Protection of Investors (Bailiwick of Guernsey) Law 1987. These Laws were established principally to enable Jersey and Guernsey to obtain Designated Territory Status under the United Kingdom Financial Services Act 1986 so as to permit schemes to continue to be marketed in the United Kingdom. Certain Schemes established in the form of open ended companies, have obtained listings on the International Stock Exchange of the United Kingdom and are governed by the Rules referred to in relation to that country.

Apart from Collective Investment Schemes the number of publicly owned companies is limited. There is no Stock Market but certain brokers, who are member firms of the International Stock Exchange, make a market in the shares of those companies which have made issues to the public. Such dealing is made on a matched bargain basis and dealings are usually recorded under Rule 535(2) of The Stock Exchange. Such companies will usually abide by United Kingdom practice and in particular The City Code on Takeovers and Mergers.

4.109 Isle of Man

In the Isle of Man the issue of shares is governed by the Companies Act 1931-1986 ('the Companies Acts') and, in the case of listed shares, also the Stock Exchange Listing Agreement (see section 4.104). The provisions of the Companies Acts are detailed but a summary of the more important or unusual ones relevant to equity is set out below:

• shares are required to have a positive nominal value;

• shares may be issued at a premium, in which case the excess over nominal value must be transferred to a non distributable share premium account;

• the share premium account is governed by statute and the permitted uses are as for the United Kingdom (see section 4.100);

• bearer shares are permitted;

• Isle of Man companies may issue shares in currencies other than their domestic currency (sterling);

• it is illegal to issue shares at a discount to their nominal value.

Private and public companies

Isle of Man company law distinguishes between private and public companies. Only a public company may offer shares and debentures (debt) to the public. It is possible for shares in a private company to be widely distributed but is is a criminal offence to offer shares in a private company to the public except in limited and specified circumstances such as a private placing with no offer to the public. There are specific provisions in the Companies Act governing public companies which are more stringent than those for private companies.

A public company may offer some of its shares to the public but first has to comply with the prospectus requirements of the Companies Act and the Financial Supervision Act 1988. For the shares to be listed, the requirements of the relevant exchange will also have to be met.

Redeemable shares

A company, whether public or private, has the power to issue redeemable shares provided it is authorised to do so by its Articles of Association and the detailed rules are similar to those in the United Kingdom.

Purchase of own shares

Private and public companies may not purchase their own shares.

Market characteristics

There is no Isle of Man based Stock Exchange, Isle of Man companies who require a stock exchange listing will tend to use the United Kingdom or other overseas markets. The companies are, of course, subject to the listing requirements of the exchange on which they are listed including rules relating to takeovers and mergers.

4.110 Accounting treatment

The accounting requirements relating to equity securities contained within the Companies Act and SSAPs are similar to the United Kingdom (see section 4.106).

4.111 Taxation treatment

In the Isle of Man dividends are treated as a charge against the company's profits for tax purposes. For example, a company making a profit of £100 and which distributes £60 by way of dividend pays tax only on the undistributed £40. There are complications in the opening and closing years.

4.112 Republic of Ireland

In the Republic of Ireland the issue of shares is governed by the Companies Act 1963 ('the Companies Act') and, in the case of listed shares, also The Stock Exchange Listing Agreement. A Companies Act was passed in 1990 but has not yet been brought fully into commencement. The provisions of the 1990 Act have been included below. The provisions of the Companies Act are detailed but a summary of the more important or unusual ones relevant to equity or equity linked products is set out below:

- shares are required to have a positive nominal value;

- shares may be issued at a premium, in which case the excess over nominal value must be transferred to a non distributable share premium account;

- the share premium account is governed by statute and can only be used for the same purposes as is permitted by United Kingdom legislation (see section 4.100);

- shares may only be issued at a discount if they are of a class already in issue and court approval is obtained;

- bearer shares are prohibited under Irish law;

- shares can be issued in currencies other than the Irish Punt.

Redeemable shares

Under Section 64 Companies Act 1963 a company, whether public or private, has the power to issue redeemable shares provided it is authorised to do so by its Articles of Association (which can be amended by special resolution). The requirements are very similar to those set out in the United Kingdom legislation (see section 4.102).

Legislation to become effective in 1991 will provide for the purchase by a company of own shares. The mechanism to be followed will provide for the purchase of shares and the cancellation of those shares to take place in two separate steps. It will be possible under this legislation to cancel shares or hold them in treasury for reissue.

Public issue of shares

A public company may offer its shares to the public providing that the prospectus requirements of the Companies Act are met. If the shares are listed, the requirements of the relevant exchange will also have to be complied with.

The main stock market in the Republic of Ireland is the Irish branch of The Stock Exchange. The Stock Exchange is divided in three tiers: The Listed Securities Market, The Unlisted Securities Market (USM) and, The Smaller Companies Market (SCM). A listing on the USM, SCM or The Third Market may be more advantageous for a company because of the lower costs involved in the flotation and less stringent requirements imposed by The Stock Exchange.

The market is governed by two main authorities. The Council of The Stock Exchange is the authority empowered to make listing rules. The Securities and Futures Authority is the self-regulatory organisation formed under the provisions of the United Kingdom Financial Services Act 1986 for the purposes of investor protection and regulates the activities of brokers and dealers in securities. Members of the Irish Exchange are all members of, and regulated by, The Securities and Futures Authority.

Admission to listing

The admission of securities to listing on the exchange is governed by the rules issued by the Council of The Stock Exchange in their publication 'Admission of Securities to Listing', more generally referred to as 'The Yellow Book'. There are certain minor amendments to the Rules set out in The Yellow Book for companies seeking a listing on the Irish Exchange.

The principal requirements for obtaining a full listing are as for the United Kingdom (section 4.104) except as follows:

● the minimum market value of the shares to be listed must be IR£700,000;

● the company must have published accounts for at least three years preceding application for listing.

Continuing obligations for listed companies

The continuing obligations for Irish companies listed on The Stock Exchange are similar to those for United Kingdom companies (see section 4.104).

Equity capital raising

Irish law requires companies proposing to issue securities having an equity element to offer those securities to existing equity shareholders in proportion to their existing holdings, unless shareholders approve the terms of any other type of issue. This has the effect that most equity capital raising by Irish listed companies is done by means of rights issues at a discount to the market price of the shares. Shareholders not intending to take up the rights may sell them on, as these are often traded on the market.

Takeovers and mergers

The regulations concerning takeovers and mergers are set out in 'The City Code on Takeovers and Mergers and The Rules Governing Substantial

Acquisitions of Shares', published by the Panel on Takeovers and Mergers. Whilst primarily a United Kingdom guideline 'The City Code' is followed by companies listed on the Irish Branch of The Stock Exchange.

Legislation introduced in early 1991 has introduced into Irish company law provisions in relation to stakebuilding in public companies similar to that set out in the City Code.

Settlement of transactions

Trading in shares on The Stock Exchange in Dublin normally occurs within a two week 'Stock Exchange' account period. Settlement day, when shares are transferred from seller to buyer and paid for, is normally six business days after the end of the Stock Exchange account. Settlement between Stock Exchange members is primarily through the central clearing service Talisman.

4.113 Specific issues to be considered in the Republic of Ireland

• Redeemable shares may give the investor the right to force the company to redeem the shares.

• In respect of redeemable shares, the shareholder has the right to sue the company for failure to repurchase shares at the specified date (however, if there are insufficient distributable profits the company cannot be required to redeem the shares).

• The company may have to raise new finance to fund the redemption of redeemable shares and this may be expensive.

• There is a possibility that shareholdings may be accumulated until such time as enough shares are held to make a bid for all the shares in the company. However, anyone who acquires more than 5% of the issued ordinary shares must, in accordance with the Rules of The Stock Exchange and the 1990 Companies Act, declare this fact to the company.

• Once shares are issued, it may be difficult to cancel them. There are two possible routes:

– purchase of own shares; or

– issue redeemable shares;

• Redeemable shares may be redeemed at a price which is below their market value.

• The company may have insufficient distributable profits out of which to make redemption of redeemable shares.

4.114 Taxation treatment

In the Republic of Ireland there is a requirement for companies to pay advance corporation tax (ACT) on dividends. At current rates of tax, for every £72 dividend paid the company is required to pay over to the Revenue Commissioners £28 ACT. The £72 dividend is tax exempt in the hands of an Irish corporate shareholder. Other shareholders are treated as receiving £100 income and the £28 will be credited against payment of their income tax liability. The paying company will be able to treat the ACT as a payment on account of its corporation tax liability for the year in which the dividend is paid, so that the ACT should not be an actual tax cost (although there is a cash flow disadvantage).

Stamp duty of 1% is payable on all share transactions.

Irish resident companies and individuals are subject to capital gains tax on any gain made on the disposal of shares. The tax is payable at rates of 30%, 35% or 50% depending on the period of ownership of the shares.

4.115 Accounting questions

• How is the share premium calculated where shares are issued for non cash consideration? Must such premium be recognised by a private company issuing shares?

• Where merger accounting under SSAP 23 is employed, are the 'preacquisition' profits distributable under Section 149 (5) of the Companies Act 1963?

• Has the company properly determined distributable profits when redeeming redeemable shares?

• Have the appropriate disclosures been made in the accounts in respect of redeemable shares, convertible debt, warrants, options, etc?

• Have debt/equity hybrids been properly classified in the balance sheet?

• Has a capital redemption reserve been correctly calculated and set up to provide for the redemption of redeemable shares?

• How are income flows, pension, discounts etc to be calculated? Should discounting be applied in apportioning income on expenses?

4.116 Taxation questions

• If the shares are redeemable, does their issue constitute a 'distribution'?

• Can ACT on dividends be offset currently or against prior years' tax liabilities?

• Can ACT be surrendered to offset subsidiaries' tax liabilities?

• Should the company obtain any prior clearance from the tax authorities, e.g. section 63 Finance Act 1982?

• Irrecoverable ACT attributable to dividends on preferred shares will be an absolute cost and will affect 'earnings per share' calculations. Where such irrecoverable ACT exists, earnings per share will be calculated on two bases, the 'net' basis and the 'nil' basis which assumes no dividends and therefore no irrecoverable ACT.

4.117 France

4.118 Legal requirements

In France, the issue of securities is governed by the *'Loi sur les sociétés commerciales'* enacted on 24 July 1966, which is periodically updated. This law categorises various types of securities as follows:

• *Actions*: ordinary shares;

• *Certificats d'Investissement*: ordinary share without the voting right, which has been separated, and a voting right certificate;

• *Certificats d'Investissement Privilégiés*: *'certificats d'investissement'* with a preference dividend;

• *Action à dividende prioritaire sans droit de vote*: non voting shares with a cumulative preference dividend; after three years where a dividend had not been paid, these shares recover their voting rights until the dividends in arrears are paid;

- *Obligations*: debentures;

- *Obligations convertibles*: convertible debentures.

Warrants can be issued in combination with all of these securities.

The issue of all of these securities (except for the debentures) must comply with the following requirements:

- the issue must be approved by a general meeting of shareholders with a majority of two thirds;

- all existing shareholders have a pre-emptive right to subscribe for the new securities unless there is a resolution passed by shareholders to cancel this right.

If a company wants to issue a security which does not fall within the categories governed specifically by law, and if the holders of this new security are entitled to a share of the net assets of the company, such issue must also comply with the above rules.

The most significant legal requirements relating to equity issues are as follows:

- par value must be positive and denominated in French francs;

- shares may be issued at a premium, but cannot be issued at a discount;

- ordinary and preferred shares are not callable by the issuer, and have no maturity date.

4.119 Equity markets

There are three different markets where equities are traded:

- the official list (*'Cote Officielle'*) which deals only in the securities of the largest issuers;

- the second market (*'Second Marché'*) which is designed for small/medium size firms;

- the over-the-counter market (*'Marché Hors-Cote'*).

There are two ways in which equities can be traded:

- on the Monthly Settlement Market ('*Marché à Réglement Mensuel*)'): trading is usually executed in lots with payment and delivery made seven days prior to month end;

- on the cash market ('*Marché au comptant*'): any quantity may be negotiated for immediate settlement and delivery.

The '*Sociétés de Bourse*' have a monopoly on securities trading in France. Members are subject to French law and are authorised to trade by the '*Conseil des Bourses de Valeurs*', which is the body responsible for regulating the securities market in France. All *Sociétés de Bourse* are members of the '*Société des Bourses Francaise*' which acts as their representative body, and they have a collective responsibility for the operation of the securities markets.

Since November 1984, French securities have been dematerialised except for bonds with sinking funds which are redeemable by drawing securities numbers by lot. Thus securities are paperless and the most active securities are traded by SICOVAM (clearing house) transfer orders.

Listing

When a company offers shares to the public, the issue and all related information given to the public has to be authorised by the '*Commission des Opérations de Bourse*' (COB), which is the body which determines and regulates the disclosure requirements relating to a public offering. The COB enacts rules that may cover accounting and legal matters as well as the issue and trading of securities. If companies do not conform to COB requirements (annual reports, prospectuses, press release), the COB has the power to impose punitive damages.

Companies can make a public offering and obtain a listing without having published accounts for prior years or a trading history. For listing on the Second Market, consolidated accounts are not required during the first three years.

Takeovers

A purchaser whose stake in a listed company crosses the 5%, 20%, 33.3%, 50%, 66.7% limit of voting rights must notify to the target company (within 15 days) and to the *Société des Bourses Francaise* (within five days) the numbers of shares which it owns. If notifications are not made in due time, the acquired shares are deprived of their voting rights for two years after notification has been made.

When a block of more than 20% of the issued shares of a company is acquired, the investor must notify the target company, the COB and the *Société des Bourses Francaise*, and make a press release about its intentions concerning the target company during the next 12 months. The purchaser of a controlling stake in a quoted company must publicly offer to purchase all the remaining shares at the same price for 15 business days.

It is expected that the *Conseil des Bourses de Valeurs*, will introduce new rules concerning takeover bids such as the obligation for an acquirer of a 33.3% stake to make an offer so as to get at least a 66.7% stake.

Taxation of dividends

French shareholders are granted a tax credit (*'avoir fiscal'*), equal to 50% of the gross amount of the dividend paid by a company. The avoir fiscal is credited against a taxpayer's personal income tax, and if it exceeds the tax liability will be refunded in cash by the French Treasury. Depending on tax treaties, foreign companies and individual foreign shareholders may also be entitled to the avoir fiscal.

Dividends together with *avoir fiscal* are revenues liable to taxation, except for parent companies holding at least 10% of the distributing company. Dividends received by these parent companies are not taxable and are not entitled to reclaim the *avoir fiscal*.

4.120 Accounting questions

• The accounting treatment for equities issued subject to the '*Loi sur les sociétés commerciales*' is prescribed by the law and COB regulations. What is the accounting treatment for equity issues not subject to this law?

4.121 Taxation questions

• The '*Code General des Impots*' (Tax Laws) sets out the taxation of dividends subject to the '*Loi sur les sociétés commerciales*'. What taxation rules should be applied to equity issues not subject to this law?

4.122 Luxembourg

Legal framework

In Luxembourg the issue of shares is governed by the 1915 Commercial companies law and, in the case of listed shares, also by Grand Ducal decree of 28 December 1990 whose object was to introduce the EC Directive 80-390 in respect of stock exchange listings into Luxembourg legislation.

Main characteristics of shares

The main provisions of the law on commercial companies relating to equity and equity linked products of *'sociétés anonymes'* (most commonly used type of public companies) are set out below:

● shares may be issued in a registered or bearer form. Bearer shares are freely transferable. Shares not fully paid must be registered;

● shares do not need to have a fixed nominal value but must have a value of at least LuxFr 50;

● several classes of shares can be issued. Common (ordinary) and preferred shares are permitted. Shares having a preferential right to the payment of dividend or to the distribution of capital upon liquidation have limited voting rights; the issue of preferred shares is limited to 50% of the share capital;

● shares may be issued in any currency;

● shares may be issued at a premium.

Issue of shares

The law distinguishes between authorised, issued and paid-up capital. The issued capital should be set up at a minimum of LuxFr 1.25m (at least 25% paid-up) for the *'sociétés anonymes'*.

A public company may offer some of its shares to the public but first has to comply with the prospectus requirements of the Grand Ducal decree of 28 December 1990. For the shares to be listed, additional requirements will also have to be met.

Redemption of shares

Under normal circumstances, a *société anonyme* is not allowed to acquire its own shares. However a company is authorised to acquire its own shares under the following conditions:

- a shareholders' meeting gives the company authorisation for the acquisition;

- this authorisation cannot exceed 18 months;

- the authorisation is limited to the acquisition of 10% maximum of the subscribed capital;

- only the acquisition of fully paid-up shares is authorised.

A company may also, under article 49-8 of the law on commercial companies, issue redeemable shares provided it is authorised to do so by its Articles of Association (which, if they do not provide for this, can be amended by special resolution). For redeemable shares the following rules are relevant:

- any class of ordinary or preferred shares may be redeemable and redemption at a premium is possible;

- redeemable shares may not be redeemed unless they are fully paid;

- redemption may be at the option of either the company or the shareholders; the precise conditions for redemption will be subject to the provisions in the company's Articles of Association.

The general rule is that shares can be redeemed only out of distributable profits (as defined in the law) or the proceeds of a fresh issue of shares made for the purposes of redemption. Any premium payable on redemption must be paid out of distributable profits.

4.123 Market characteristics

The majority of the instruments listed on the Luxembourg stock exchange are Eurobonds. However, the Luxembourg stock exchange also lists a significant number of equities, mostly investment funds and unit trusts.

The market operates on an open outcry basis, which means that securities to be dealt in are announced by a registrar of the Stock Exchange. In 1987, the Luxembourg Stock Exchange launched a market making system for the most active Eurobonds. The securities concerned are marked by one or two stars in the Official Price List. One star means that the security is traded by a 'bid' market maker while two stars indicate that the market maker is a 'bid and asked' market maker.

Any Stock Exchange member who is willing to act as a market maker for a particular security is required to register with the Stock Exchange authorities. His commitment to deal in the securities specified remains compulsory until he repeals it at his own discretion.

The Stock Exchange is organised in the form of a '*société anonyme*' and is supervised by the '*Commissariat aux bourses*'.

Since April 1991, the Luxembourg Stock Exchange's member banks and brokers progressively began to use a new computer assisted trading system to deal in listed securities.

Admission to listing

The admission of securities to the listing on the Luxembourg Stock Exchange is governed by the Grand Ducal decree of 28 December 1990. Anyone making an application for admission to the Luxembourg Stock Exchange official Price List of securities (or willing to proceed to a public offer of securities) has to inform the '*Société de la Bourse de Luxembourg*' at least 15 days in advance by submitting an application.

The application file to be submitted consists of three different parts:

• Part 1 covers the prospectus;

• Part II covers the following supplementary information:

– any additional information, the inclusion of which is foreseen in the prospectus but which does not yet appear in the draft submitted;

– any information which should have appeared in the prospectus but for which a waiver has been requested; any request for a waiver must be justified;

• Part III covers the documents supporting the information contained in the first two parts of the file. In principle, only the following documents are required to be submitted:

– the statutory documents;

– agreements, such as the underwriting agreement, the trust indenture, trust deed and the agreement relating to the issue of bearer certificates representing registered shares (deposit agreement);

– the annual reports for the last two fiscal years;

– the draft of the legal notice to be filed with the Chief Registrar of the District Court in Luxembourg.

Documents such as statutory documents and annual reports, already submitted to the stock exchange in connection with a previous listing, need not be submitted to the extent that, in the intervening period, they have not been amended. The stock exchange may however request any other document which it deems necessary, according to particular conditions and nature of the transaction and the financial position of the issuer.

Equity capital raising

Luxembourg law requires companies proposing to issue shares for cash, to offer those securities to existing equity shareholders in proportion to their existing holdings, unless shareholders approve the terms of any other type of issue. Shareholders not intending to subscribe may sell their rights.

4.124 Accounting treatment

Accounting requirements are laid down in the law on commercial companies and may be summarised as follows:

• presentation of capital and other equity accounts in the balance sheet follows the law of 1984 whose object was to introduce the EC 4th directive into Luxembourg legislation;

• disclosure requirements include:

– subscribed and paid-up capital (amount and number of shares);

– list of shareholders having not fully paid-up their shares;

– number and (nominal) value of shares subscribed during the period for each of existing classes of shares;

– existence of '*parts beneficiaires*' (founders' shares), convertible bonds and other similar securities.

4.125 Taxation treatment

Luxembourg companies without holding company or investment company status are subject to income, municipalities and net worth tax at a combined rate of 39.39% on income and 1% on net worth. The investor is not allowed to credit any of these taxes against their tax liabilities. However, for corporate investors, the '*affiliation privilege*' provides for an exemption of income received from affiliated companies and the corresponding part of net worth if some conditions are met (essentially participation rate and permanence of investment). This affiliation privilege is coupled with exemption from withholding tax for dividends paid to EC corporations; conditions for this exemption are similar, but not identical. Any other dividend payment is subject to withholding tax at a standard rate of 15%. This withholding tax is generally reduced under tax treaties, especially in the case of significant participation.

Luxembourg holding companies and investment funds/companies are tax-exempt entities that do not suffer tax on income and net worth in Luxembourg except for:

- subscription tax (0.2% annually on the 'company's value' or paid-up capital for holding companies and 0.06% annually on the net asset value for investment funds/companies);

- registration duty (1% of paid-up capital for holding companies at incorporation or capital increase by contribution; LuxFr 50,000 for investment funds/companies at creation).

No withholding tax is levied on distributions by such entities.

4.126 Belgium

Legal framework

In Belgium the issue of shares is mainly governed by the Companies Coordinated Law of 30 November 1935 and by Royal Decree No 185 regulating the issue of securities in companies limited by shares. Some of the more important provisions are:

- shares may be issued at par or without a par value and can be in registered or bearer form. In practice, most shares are issued in bearer form;

- from the date of incorporation a company must have paid up capital to a minimum value of BEF 1,250,000;

- each share must be paid up to at least one quarter of their par value. However, share premium must be fully paid up;

There are two major categories of shares, shares which comprise the capital of the company ('capital shares') and shares which do not form part of capital but are entitled to dividends and possibly a share of the proceeds on liquidation (beneficiary shares).

Capital shares

These shares are issued for a capital contribution in cash or in kind. They may be issued at or without a par value. They may have common or privileged rights. Privileged shares may give, for example, a preferred right to dividends or liquidation proceeds. They also may be issued with a fixed dividend (which may or may not be cumulative), or with a variable dividend. Bonus shares may be distributed free to the holders of capital shares whose nominal value has been paid up. Each capital share issued has the right to one vote. However, one shareholder is not entitled to cast more than 20% of the total votes in issue or 40% of the votes of members present at a general meeting.

Beneficiary shares

These shares do not form part of the capital of the company but their owners are entitled to vote and share in the profits of the corporation. There are several types of beneficiary shares:

● founders shares – they are given to the founders in exchange for their investment and for the initial efforts in the development of a company;

● *'actions de jouissance'* (a kind of profit sharing certificate). These are shares for which the original capital investment has been repaid in full;

● dividend shares – these shares have only a secondary right to earnings and liquidation proceeds. This type of share is seldom used.

Equity linked instruments

There have been some issues of convertible bonds and warrants in Belgium. They are not common, although they have been used recently as defensive measures against possible takeover bids. The issue of convertible bonds and warrants is strictly regulated.

Purchase of own shares

A corporation may only acquire its own shares or beneficiary shares through purchase or exchange following authorisation by a general shareholders' meeting. The general meeting shall establish:

● the maximum number of shares to be acquired;

● the duration for which the authorisation will be granted (it may not exceed 18 months);

● the minimum and maximum price payable.

The following provisions also apply to the purchase by a company of its own shares:

- the par value of the shares acquired may not exceed 10% of the total subscribed capital of the company;

- the shares must be redeemed out of distributable profits;

- the shares repurchased must be fully paid up;

- the offer to acquire the shares must respect the equality of all shareholders;

- until the shares are sold or cancelled, a non distributable reserve equal to the value of the shares acquired has to be established and the shares have to be carried as an asset in the balance sheet;

- the shares acquired must be transferred within two years of acquisition or sold to the new shareholders for whom the shares were acquired within a period of 12 months from the date of acquisition.

If these provisions are not complied with, the shares are void.

Issue of shares

A capital increase requires the authority of a general shareholders' meeting. This authority requires 80% of the votes present and 50% of the total votes of the company. However, the board of directors may also be authorised by the Articles of Association to increase share capital up to a an authorised amount. The authorisation will only be valid for five years from the date of publication of the Articles of Association or amendment to the bylaws of the company. It may be renewed for a maximum of five years duration.

The issue of shares below par has to be authorised by a general shareholders' meeting. The Board of Directors has to present a detailed report to the meeting, including the price of the share issue and the financial consequences for existing shareholders.

The issue of new capital shares must first be offered to existing shareholders in proportion to their existing rights. The right of preferential subscription may be exercised during a period which may not be less than 15 days. The subscription right is transferable during the whole of the subscription period.

The bylaws of the company may neither eliminate nor restrict the preferential rights of shareholders. Nevertheless, they may authorise the Board of Directors to reduce or override it in the interest of the company. This requires a special report to the members in which the Board justifies its decision. In addition, the shareholders in a general meeting may also waive or limit the pre-emption right.

4.127 Market characteristics

The operation of financial markets is governed by a law of 4 December 1990. The main stock market in Belgium is the Brussels Stock Exchange. Trading activity is supervised by the *Commission de la Bourse* (Stock Exchange Committee), which is a self regulating organisation of dealers and brokers. These dealers and brokers effectively enjoy a monopoly of trading on the exchange. Since January 1991, the dealers and brokers are required to operate as incorporated entities.

The markets may be classified according as follows:

- the official market, where quoted securities are listed. The official market consists of both the main market and a secondary market for smaller and medium sized companies;

- a supplementary market for non-listed securities.

The official market consists of a spot market (marché au comptant) and a forward market (*marché du terme*). Trading on both markets is principally by open outcry.

Spot market

All officially listed securities are traded on the spot market. The spot market consists of a ring and a floor market. Only one price is established during each trading session on the floor market, which is for less actively traded securities. There are no minimum transaction sizes or margin requirements on the spot market.

Forward market

The Stock Exchange Committee determines which securities are traded on the forward market. In practice these are only shares in the largest companies. By far the largest proportion of the turnover on the Brussels Stock Exchange takes place on the forward market, which is dominated by institutional and professional investors. There are minimum transaction sizes on the forward market, which are prescribed by the Stock Exchange Committee for each security, depending on their market value. There are also margin requirements on the forward market, generally up to 25% of the value of the transaction with a minimum of BEF 2,000.

Admission to listing

The Listings Committee of the Stock Exchange Commission is responsible for ruling on the admission of securities to listing, suspension of listing and the reporting requirements of listed companies. The members of this committee are appointed by the Minister of Finance. However, clearance of listings, takeovers and mergers is required from the *Commission Bancaire*, which has responsibility for the issue of shares, the regulation of capital markets, and the protection of the funds of retail investors. In practice, the Listings Commission will often merely confirm a decision of the *Commission Bancaire*.

Takeovers

Regulations concerning takeovers are contained in a law of 2 March 1989 and in a Royal Decree of 8 November 1989. This legislation has two main objectives:

• to ensure adequate disclosure of information by companies and equal treatment for all shareholders;

• to ensure that transparency and the proper functioning of the market.

The more important provisions of the law are as follows:

• the offerer must inform the *Commission Bancaire* and file a draft of the bid prospectus;

• the *Commission Bancaire* will publicise the offer the day after the filing;

• as from the date of notification of the Commission, the target company cannot increase its capital, make an issue of new equity, or dispose of significant assets without the approval of a general meeting;

• the *Commission Bancaire* has to inform the Board of Directors of the target company of the intended bid and the latter must give its opinion on the adequacy of the offer;

• the prospectus must be approved by the *Commission Bancaire* before being made public;

• the bid must remain open for a minimum and a maximum period of respectively 10 and 20 days from the date the prospectus is made public;

• the price of any counter offer must exceed the initial offering price by at least 5%. The notification concerning the counter offer must be rendered public two days before the closing of the initial offer.

There are currently no specific regulations with regard to mergers in Belgium, although a draft bill is being prepared by the Ministers of Finance and Justice.

4.128 Accounting treatment

The accounting requirements relating to equity securities are set out in a Law of 1975 concerning the financial accounts of companies, as amended by subsequent Royal Decrees and practice recommended by the Commission for Accounting Standards. In general, they do not depart from internationally accepted accounting practice.

Disclosure requirements

The following matters concerning the equity capital of a company have to be disclosed in a note to the accounts:

- the amount of share capital issued, less any uncalled portion;

- movement during the year (in both the number and value of shares);

- a list of the names of the shareholders for the amounts uncalled, or, if called, still unpaid;

- own shares held either by the company or by groups companies;

- information about shares issuable on the conversion of debt instruments;

- authorised capital still available for issue.

Share premium account

When a share premium account is raised there is a need to specify the amount as not available for distribution in order to avoid corporate taxation. This is purely a technicality. Subsequently, the share premium can be capitalised, used to offset losses through the appropriation account or paid back to shareholders just like share capital. The share premium account can also include the proceeds of the issue of warrant or scrips.

4.129 Taxation treatment

Capital contributions and issue of shares

Capital contributions are subject to a 0.5% registration duty. This duty is not payable in case of mergers, share splits or a capital contribution by an EC company to a Belgian company.

The issue of shares does not give rise to stamp tax or VAT, unless the shares are publicly issued (stamp tax of 0.035% with a maximum of BEF 10,000 per transaction).

Transfer of shares

There is no VAT or transfer tax on the disposal of shares by a Belgian individual or company. Stamp tax is due on any transfer of securities which is made through a broker or a bank (stamp tax of 0.017% with a maximum of BEF 10,000 per transaction).

Withholding tax on dividend distributions

Withholding tax is due at the rate of 25% on dividends distributed by a Belgian company to its shareholders. This rate may be reduced by application of double taxation treaties concluded by Belgium with the country of which the shareholder is a recipient (in general, the reduced tax rate is equal to 15% or 5% in case of significant shareholdings).

Tax treatment of dividends received by a Belgian resident

Either 85% or 90% of dividends received by a Belgian resident company from a Belgian or foreign company may be excluded from taxable income under the participation exemption regime provided the shares have been held on a long term basis by the recipient company (in principle, one year) and provided the distributing company has been subject to income tax on its profits (a transparency rule exists with respect to foreign holdings and financial companies, as well as investment companies). Additional requirements may be imposed after the enactment of a new Tax Reform Act in the summer of 1991.

Dividends received on investments which do not meet the long term holdings requirement give rise to a tax credit which is equal to 43% of the net dividends received for Belgian source dividends and to 15/85 of the net dividends received for foreign source dividends. This tax credit is included in the taxable income of the Belgian recipient company and offset against its overall tax liability; the excess may not be refunded.

For Belgian individual shareholders, the 25% Belgian withholding tax on dividends received is the final tax liability; if dividends have not been subject to Belgian withholding tax, the shareholders should declare their dividends which will then be subject to a 25% tax (plus local surtax).

4.130 The Netherlands

Legal framework

In the Netherlands the issue of shares is governed by the Civil Code. Shares have a nominal value in Dutch Guilders, but they may be issued at a premium (*'agio'*). The share premium reserve is part of stockholders' equity. The share premium reserve may be distributed and for tax purposes may be considered as a return of capital and not be taxed. Companies are not permitted to issue shares at a discount to their nominal value, except to pay commission to the issuing bank.

All shareholders of the same class should be treated equally. It is possible to issue different classes of shares, such as:

- preferred shares;

- cumulative preferred shares;

- priority shares, with special voting rights.

Existing shareholders at all times have a pre-emptive right to subscribe when new shares are issued.

The law distinguishes between public companies (NV) and private companies (BV). A BV can only issue registered shares whereas an NV can also issue bearer shares. The NV is the common form of organisation for listed companies. The minimum paid up capital is NLG 100,000. Companies can be listed on the stock exchange in Amsterdam or on the *'parallellmarkt'*, where it is easier to meet the regulations. The *parallellmarkt* is suitable for smaller companies.

The regulating body of the Amsterdam Stock Exchange controls the securities business transacted on the exchange. There is extensive regulation by law to supervise the securities business transacted outside the Stock Exchange. Insider trading is an offence. In 1991 a new law on investment funds came into force, aiming to protect the public from malicious trading and hazardous financial structures.

The Dutch Civil Code limits the acquisition of its own shares by an NV to 10% of the capital. The minimum capital and reserves of the NV must be sufficient to cover the amount paid for the shares. These rules do not apply to investment companies.

An increasing number of listed companies and larger non-listed companies have issued 'certificates of shares'. The shares (with the voting rights) are held by a foundation, and the certificate holders have only financial rights (ie to dividends and repayment of capital). The voting rights of these shares are exercised by the foundation, whose board may include representatives of management. Through this structure it is difficult to make a hostile take-over of the company.

For large corporations (which may be either BV or NV) the board of directors has a number of powers which are normally the preserve of shareholders, such as the adoption of the annual accounts, declaration of dividends and the appointment of managing directors.

4.131 Market organisation

The market is organised around the market makers ('*hoekman*'). Market makers maintain positions in a few issues and will quote two way prices. Brokers will act on clients' requests.

The settlement of transactions is arranged by means of a type of book entry system called '*Negicef*'. The *Negicef* is a custodian for the members of the stock exchange and will deliver the securities by means of book entry. The cash settlement is arranged separately, either direct or by the '*Kasassociatie*'. The *Kasassociatie* acts as banker to a number of stock exchange members. In the near future a fixed seven days settlement is to be adopted for securities transactions.

4.132 Accounting treatment

The most important accounting matter is the distinction between equity and debt (or provisions). The stockholders' equity must be shown separately as follows:

• paid up capital by type of shares;

• premium at issue (share premium reserve);

• revaluation reserves;

• statutory reserves;

• other reserves;

• undistributed profits, after tax;

• other restricted reserves.

The restricted reserves may not be distributed as dividends. The law prescribes a restricted reserve in special cases, such as revaluations of unrealised gains. All movements in any section of equity must be shown separately. Certain transactions with shareholders must be certified by an auditor.

Information must be disclosed on options, warrants, convertible bonds, limitations of rights for certain shares, priority shares and owners of these shares.

4.133 Taxation treatment

Any payment to shareholders is non-deductible for corporation tax. Dividends are paid net of tax (at 25%), with special rules for parent companies. Foreign shareholders are taxed according to the tax treaty with the relevant country. The Netherlands have tax treaties with most countries in the world.

In the Netherlands, companies pay corporation tax (approximately 35%) on profits and in addition the income tax of individual shareholders on dividends (double taxation). However if the owner of the shares is an NV or BV, the parent company pays no tax on the dividend received. This rule applies if the parent owns more than 5% of the subsidiary.

For the individual taxpayer there is no capital gains tax in the Netherlands, except for those who own more than one third in an NV or BV (this includes individuals and related parties).

Only the nominal value of a bonus share received by individuals is taxable. A bonus share which was issued out of the share premium reserve is considered a repayment of capital and is not taxed. This form of distribution of profits is quite popular in the Netherlands.

Warrants issued by the company, which give the right to subscribe to new shares at a certain prefixed price, are taxable income. The interest on convertible bonds is considered to be interest rather than a dividend. The payment on preferred stock is regarded as a dividend.

4.134 Germany

The German Company Act ('*Aktiengesetz*') allows companies to issue more than one class of shares. The most important equity securities allowed by the German Company Act ('Company Act') are:

- ordinary shares ('*Stammaktien*');

- preferred shares ('*Vorzugsaktien*');

- participation certificates;

- convertible securities.

The majority of shares are issued in bearer ('*Inhaber*') form and registered ('*Namen*') shares are rare.

Some of the significant provisions of the Company Act are as follows:

- dividends payable are restricted to the amount of retained profits;

- companies are not allowed to denominate their shares in foreign currencies (the Company Act prescribes that they have to have a par value in deutschmarks);

- shares must have a nominal value of at least DEM 50. Companies cannot issue shares at lower amount than their nominal value;

- shares may be issued at a premium. In this case the excess over nominal value must be transferred to a non distributable capital reserve;

- in general a company is not permitted to purchase its own shares (section 71, Company Act). There are, however, some exceptions mentioned in section 71, subsection 1, Company Act. A company can acquire its own shares:

– to offer them to its employees;

– if necessary to preserve it from serious difficulties;

– if the shares are purchased to compensate shareholders.

Ordinary shares

All shares must grant the same rights to shareholders and it is not possible to have different classes of ordinary shares. Ordinary shares allow the investor full rights to participate in the control of a company and its profits.

In Germany, minority shareholders have special rights. Holders of 5% of ordinary shares or capital with a nominal value of DEM 1 million can demand extraordinary shareholders meetings, the inclusion of specific matters on the agenda for shareholders meetings or the appointment of a special auditor. Holders of 10% of the ordinary shares or DEM 2 million of share capital can demand that the company does not waive its right to compensation claims, propose members of the board of directors and demand a special meeting to propose the dismissal of directors.

Preferred shares

German law permits preferred shares to be issued either with or without voting rights, but the latter must carry a preferential right to cumulative dividends when profits are distributed. Preferred shares without voting rights may comprise up to only 50% of the nominal value of a company's share capital. Preferred shares do not ensure payment of a dividend at a predetermined rate but the dividend is determined by the directors and approved by the shareholders at the annual general meeting. If the company's constitution states that preferred shares provide for additional rights to the profits and that unpaid dividends accumulate and have to be paid prior to any payments for ordinary shares there may also be a provision in the company's constitution excluding the voting right (paragraph 139, Company Act). The voting right of preferred shares is revived if the shareholder has not received any dividend for at least two years.

Approximately 20% of the shares traded on German stock exchanges are preferred shares.

Participation certificates

Participation certificates ('*Genussscheine*') can be issued which do not grant voting rights or other rights which shareholders would normally be entitled to. Participation certificates can be structured as debt or as equity. They are structured as equity if they form part of the residual assets after liquidation. They are structured as debt if they do not participate in the liquidation proceeds and the 'dividends' are tax deductible for corporation tax and partly trade income tax purposes. Banking law recognises that participation certificates issued by banks which are legally structured as debt can rank as equity for regulatory purposes if certain conditions are met (eg participation in losses).

Convertible debt instruments

The provisions concerning convertible debt securities are laid down in paragraph 221 of the Company Act. In Germany, convertible bonds must be issued in deutschmarks. Very few convertible bonds have been issued in Germany. In total, only about 25 convertible bonds are listed on the Frankfurt Stock Exchange.

Equity warrants

Provisions concerning debt issues with equity warrants are laid down in paragraph 192 and 221 of the Company Act. In contrast with convertible debt instruments, equity warrants are very popular in Germany and there are more than 200 issues listed on the Frankfurt Stock Exchange.

4.135 Market characteristics

Germany has no comprehensive legislation governing the issue of and the trading in securities but there is statutory and case law with respect to certain important aspects. As a result of the German 'universal banking system' most banks participate in transactions concerning securities such as trading, brokerage, settlement, underwriting and custodian business.

Stock Exchanges

There are eight stock exchanges in Germany; Berlin, Bremen, Düsseldorf, Frankfurt, Hamburg, Hannover, München and Stuttgart. They are all organised by private entities, usually the local Chamber of Commerce. Frankfurt, being by far the most important of the exchanges, has been organised as a private corporation since January 1991.

The legal basis for the organisation and admission to the stock exchanges is the 1896 Stock Exchange Act (latest amendment August 1989). As all of the exchanges are subject to this legislation they are very similar in structure. Stock Exchanges are supervised by state commissioners appointed by the local estate government. The internal rules and procedures are stipulated by a Stock Exchange Board. Other bodies of the stock exchanges are the 'Admission Board', which supervises the listing of securities (see Admission to the Stock Exchange below), the Board of Arbitration settling disputes between exchange members and the Chamber of Brokers representing the '*Kursmakler*' who are 'official brokers' having the function to arrange transactions between dealers and to establish official quotations. Other admitted members of the exchanges are representatives of banks and unofficial brokers ('*Freie Makler*').

Stock Exchanges are open from Monday until Friday. Trading hours are between 10.30 am and 1.30 pm. Stock exchange rules require that settlement of cash transactions (payment and delivery of securities) must be effected within two business days.

Market segments of the Stock Exchange

Besides the official listing two other markets exist on all German stock exchanges: The Regulated Market and the Free Market (or Unofficial Market). The Regulated Market requires an admission procedure (see Admission to the Stock Exchange below) which is laid down in the Stock Exchange Act and the Rules and Regulations of each stock exchange. The admission requirements are less strict than for an official listing. Mainly medium sized and smaller firms choose listing on the regulated market. The Free Market is exclusively governed by rules adopted by the local association of security dealers of each exchange. The degree of formal requirements is at the Court level of all market segments.

Admission to the Stock Exchange (Official Market)

In May 1987, the German Federal Government adopted the Stock Exchange Admission Regulation providing for the details of the admission of securities to official trading as well as other obligations of the issuers of securities. This regulation covers official trading only. Admission to either the regulated or the free market is subject to different requirements as noted above. Admission requirements for the regulated market are detailed in the Rules and Regulations of the Frankfurt Stock Exchange. Free Market trading of securities must comply with the Rules for the Free Market but there is no admissions procedure.

Requirement for Stock Exchange Listing (Official Market)

Admission to the Official Market requires:

• that the issuer publishes a correct and complete prospectus disclosing all factual and legal circumstances which are of substantial relevance for the assessment of the securities;

• that establishment and articles of association of the issuer conform to the national laws of the issuers country of incorporation;

• that the market value of the shares to be admitted is at least DEM 2.5 million;

• that the issuing enterprise has existed for at least three years and has published its annual financial statements for the last three years in accordance with the national laws of the issuer's country of incorporation;

• that the securities are issued in accordance with the laws applicable to the issuer;

• that the securities are freely negotiable;

• that the denomination of the securities takes the requirements of stock exchange trading into account;

• that the application for admission comprises all shares of the same class (limitation may be accepted in the case of shares serving to maintain a dominant influence on the issuer if the limitation and the reasons therefore are stated in the prospectus);

• that the printing of the securities provides sufficient protection against forgery;

• that if the shares are officially listed in another country they are sufficiently distributed among the public of that country (at least 25% purchased by the public).

Prospectus requirements

The prospectus must be submitted in German and has to be signed by the issuer and one bank admitted to participate in stock exchange trading. The underwriters are liable for incorrect or incomplete statements. The prospectus must contain detailed information on:

• the persons or companies taking responsibility for the contents of the prospectus;

• the securities to be admitted (the Regulations provide a list of about 30 points to be observed in this respect);

• the issuer of the securities (general information; information on capital business, assets, finances, profits, accounting practices, subsidiaries and affiliates, net income and dividend per share, management and supervisory bodies of the issuer);

• the audited annual accounts of the issuer.

The information on the capital of the issuer must include the names of any person/company holding directly or indirectly at least 20% of the subscribed capital or 20% of the voting rights.

Admission procedure

Admission requires a written application including a draft of the prospectus and supporting documents required for the examination of the admission requirements. The Admissions office may in particular request submission of:

• a certified excerpt from the Commercial Register of its current status;

• the Charter of Incorporation or the Agreement of Association in its current version;

• the documents of authorisation or the establishment of the issuer, the conduct of its business or the issue of the securities requires governmental authorisation;

• the annual financial statements and the business reports for the three business years preceding the application, including the reports of the auditors;

• evidence of the legal basis of the issue of the securities;

• in case of individually printed certificates a sample certificate for each nominal value of the securities to be admitted (bond certificate and coupon sheet);

• in case of a global certificate a declaration by the issuer to the effect that:

– the global certificate has been deposited with a securities depository bank (*Wertpapiersammelbank*);

– the issuer will exchange the global certificate required by the holders of the securities.

Continuing obligations

The issuer of admitted securities must make available to the public and the paying agent the annual financial statements (immediately upon approval) and a business report.

In addition, the issuer must publish within two months after the end of a reporting period semi-annual interim reports. Disclosure is also required of significant changes in shareholding of more than 25% of the subscribed capital or voting rights, modifications of the rights of securities, shareholders meetings as well as notices regarding the payment of dividends, the issue of new shares and the exercise of exchange and subscription rights.

Takeovers and mergers

Paragraph 20 of the Company Act states that a company holding over 25% of shares in a listed company, or a majority shareholding, must inform the company about the shareholding at the time of acquisition. Paragraph 23 of the Act against Restraints of Competition (GWB) rules that a merger of companies must be disclosed to the Federal Cartel Authority if the companies achieve a dominant position in the market.

4.136 Accounting treatment

Shares

Companies are required by law to account for expenses and commission on a share issue through the profit and loss account.

Investors have to value investments in shares at the lower of cost of acquisition and market value. Cost of acquisition includes related costs, (commission and fees).

Convertible debt

The conversion option must be accounted for separately as the amount attributed to the option has by law to be transferred to a capital reserve. The amount by which the exercise price exceeds the nominal value of the shares on conversion is not a distributable profit but a part of capital.

The conditions for exercising the conversion option must be disclosed in the notes to the accounts together with the terms of conversion, such as the exercise price and whether the shares will be bearer or registered shares.

Costs of conversion must not be accrued in the accounts.

Debt with equity warrants

The proceeds of the issue must be allocated between the debt and the warrant. The determination of the amount attributed to the warrant depends on the type of warrant issue. There are two types:

• debt issues with warrants on which the normal market interest is paid. In this case, an *agio* (premium) has to be paid on the warrant. This premium is the amount attributed to the warrant.

• warrant issues on which interest is paid at a lower rate than on the market. In this case, the value attributed to the warrant is the difference between the interest rate payable on the bonds and the market rate.

The amount attributed to the warrant must not be reflected in the profit and loss account but has to be transferred to the capital reserve. If the warrant expires unexercised, the attributed amount remains in the capital reserve.

4.137 Taxation treatment

Issue of shares

Any costs of a share issue are deductible expenses. Since 1984 there has been no limit to those costs.

In principle, a bonus issue of ordinary shares must be treated like a distribution. Except in case of a capital increase by conversion of retained earnings, the bonus issue is not taxable income. A redemption of shares at a premium by the issuer may be deemed to be distribution of profit .

There is no VAT on fees paid by the issuing company relating to the share issue.

Taxation treatment of dividends

The distributing company is required to deduct a 25 % withholding tax from the amount of dividends payable to shareholders. Shareholders subject to unlimited tax liability can offset the tax withheld against their liability from income or corporation tax. The same holds for the 36 % corporation tax or the company's distributed profits.

Shareholders who are not subject to unlimited tax (foreign shareholders) can neither offset the 25 % withholding tax nor the 36 % corporation tax. However, they can apply for a refund according to the provisions of the relevant double taxation treaty because in some tax treaties the withholding tax rate on dividends is limited to 15 %. In such a case the tax withheld in excess of 15 % is refunded to the foreign shareholder on application.

4.138 Switzerland

In Switzerland, an issue of shares is governed by the Swiss Code of Obligations. Discussions in Parliament regarding a change of certain paragraphs are at present reaching a final stage, however, implementation is not expected to be before 1993.

Swiss law requires shares to have a par value of at least Sfr. 100 at the time of issue. It is possible to issue ordinary or preference shares, and, in addition, participation (profit sharing) certificates. These latter securities do not grant the investors the rights of shareholders, but may give rights to share in profits or in the proceeds of liquidation, or rights to subscribe to new shares.

Shares cannot be issued at a discount. Where shares are issued at a premium, the excess of the issue price over the par value of a share shall (after deduction of issue expenses) be allocated to the legal reserve to the extent that it is not used for depreciation or for employee benefits. There are also requirements to allocate to legal reserves 5% of profits (until it reaches 20% of equity) and 10% on dividends exceeding 5% of the capital. The legal reserve is only distributable to shareholders to the extent that it exceeds 50% of the capital.

The shareholders cannot, without their consent, be deprived of the rights which they have acquired by virtue of their position as shareholders. Among these rights are the right to take part in the general meetings of shareholders, voting rights, dividend rights and rights to a share of the liquidation proceeds.

The shareholders exercise their voting rights in proportion to the total par value of their shares. The voting power may, however, be limited in the company's statutes. The statutes may also provide for a voting right based on the number of shares held by each shareholder irrespective of the par value, so that each share has one vote. A so-called 'voting power share' can also be created. These are shares with a lower nominal value than the other classes of shares and which therefore have a stronger voting power relative to their par value. Such voting power shares must, however, be fully paid up, registered shares.

Swiss shares can be issued as bearer or registered shares. A combination of both types of shares is often used to prevent unwanted foreign ownership or other hostile takeover because the registered shares can have a lower nominal value (see above) and therefore allow a controlling vote with a relatively low investment. Furthermore, the statutes of a company may provide that transfers of registered shares (entry in the company's share register) can only take place after approval by the company's board. Depending on the statutes, a transfer can be refused without disclosure of the reasons for the refusal. Traditionally, many statutes provide that no foreign owner may be entered in the register of shareholders. In the past few years some large quoted companies like Nestle have ceased this practice.

Shares cannot be issued in foreign currencies.

Purchase of own shares

Generally, a company is not allowed to buy its own shares or to receive them in pledge. There are exceptions to this rule, but even in the circumstances where these exceptions apply, the company is required to sell the shares as soon as possible or to reduce capital.

Issue of shares

The public issue of shares and participating certificates is similar to that of bonds. Public issues are underwritten by syndicates after the existing shareholders have approved the increase in the company's share capital to be offered to the general public. Shareholders can waive their rights to subscribe to the shares at a general meeting. There is a stamp tax of 3% on the issue of new shares. If there is to be a public offer to subscribe for shares, a prospectus must be published giving details of the issue and the issuing company. Historically, issues of new shares and participation certificates of listed companies have been below market price, but companies are increasingly issuing new securities at the market price or with only a slight discount.

4.139 Stock exchanges

The main Swiss stock exchanges are located in Zurich, Geneva and Basle, but there are several others. In Zurich, the stock exchange comprises 5 trading rings or circular counters where the dealers meet; membership is restricted to the 'ring banks' ie those banks which are member firms of the Stock Exchange. Shares are generally traded in lots having a par value of Sfr 5,000 and the prices are fixed at the price per share, which takes into account the accrued dividend. Trading charges comprise mainly brokerage fees and federal transfer tax, both of which are are higher for foreign shares. About 70% of the shares traded on the Zurich Stock Exchange are traded on a 'cash basis', with settlement and delivery terms of 10 to 30 days after the trade date.

Foreign companies can obtain a listing on Swiss Stock Exchanges. Certain conditions must be fulfilled to receive the required approval by the local Stock market authorities. These include that the shares of the company to be listed must be frequently traded in a major or well known stock exchange and that a number of shares must be held by investors through banks in Switzerland. As a guideline it can be said that at least 250 clients of the banks should hold such shares and the value of the held shares should exceed Sfr. 10 million. Also some disclosure (such as publication of results) is required by the listed companies.

4.140 Taxation treatment

Dividends distributed are subject to a 35% withholding tax which can be recouped in full by a Swiss individual or a Swiss corporate shareholder. Foreign shareholders can recoup it partially or fully depending on the double taxation treaty with the country concerned.

4.141 Austria

The Austrian Company Act ('*Aktiengesetz*') allows companies to issue more than one class of shares. The most important equity securities allowed by the Austrian Company Act are:

• ordinary shares ('*Stammaktien*');

- preferred shares (*'Vorzugsaktien'*);

- participation certificates;

- convertible securities.

The majority of shares are issued in bearer (*'Inhaber'*) form and registered (*'Namen'*) shares are rare.

Some of the significant provisions of the Company Act are as follows:

- dividends payable are restricted to the amount of retained profits;

- companies are not allowed to denominate their shares in foreign currencies (the Company Act prescribes that they have to have a par value in Austrian Schillings);

- shares must have a nominal value of at least AS 100. Companies cannot issue shares at lower values than their nominal value;

- shares may be issued at a premium. In this case the excess over nominal value must be transferred to a non distributable capital reserve;

- in general a company is not permitted to purchase its own shares. There are, however, some exceptions mentioned in section 65 subsection 1 of the Company Act. A company can acquire its own shares:

- if the issue is necessary to preserve it from serious difficulties;

- if the shares are purchased on a commission basis in the normal course of business (for example, by a bank acting for its customer).

Ordinary shares

All shares must grant the same rights to shareholders and it is not possible to have different classes of ordinary shares. Ordinary shares allow the investor full rights to participate in the control of a company and its profits. Minority shareholders have certain special rights.

Preferred shares

Austrian law permits preferred shares to be issued either with or without voting rights, but the latter must carry a preferential right to cumulative dividends when profits are distributed. Preferred shares without voting rights may comprise up to only 50 % of the nominal value of a company's ordinary shares. Preferred shares do ensure payment of a dividend at a predetermined rate.

Participation certificates

Participation certificates (*'Genussscheine'*) can be issued. These do not grant voting rights or some other rights which shareholders would normally be entitled to. Participation certificates can be structured as debt or as equity. They are structured as equity if they form part of the residual assets after liquidation. They are structured as debt if they do not participate in the liquidation proceeds and the 'dividends' are tax deductible for corporation tax and partly trade income tax purposes. Banking law recognises that participation certificates issued by banks which are legally structured as debt can rank as equity for regulatory purposes if certain conditions are met (eg participation in losses).

Convertible debt instruments

The provisions concerning convertible debt securities are laid down in paragraph 174 of the Company Act. In Austria, convertible bonds must be issued in Austrian Schillings. Very few convertible bonds have been issued in Austria.

4.142 Accounting treatment

Shares

Companies are normally required by law to account for expenses and commission on a share issue through the profit and loss account. However if shares have been issued at a premium the costs of the share issue have to be accounted for through a non distributable capital reserve.

Investors are required to value investments in shares at the lower of cost of acquisition and market value. Cost of acquisition includes related costs, (commission and fees).

Convertible debt

The conversion option must be accounted for separately as the amount attributed to the option has by law to be transferred to a capital reserve. The amount by which the exercise price exceeds the nominal value of the shares on conversion is not a distributable profit but a part of capital.

The conditions for exercising the conversion option must be disclosed in a note to the accounts together with the terms of conversion, such as the exercise price and whether the shares will be bearer or registered shares.

Costs of conversion must not be accrued in the accounts.

4.143 Taxation treatment

Issue of shares

Any costs of a share issue are deductible expenses.

In principle, a bonus issue of ordinary shares must be treated like a distribution. Except in the case of a capital increase by conversion of retained earnings, the bonus issue is not taxable income. A redemption of shares at a premium by the issuer may be deemed to be distribution of profit.

There is no VAT on fees paid by the issuing company relating to the share issue.

Taxation treatment of dividends

The distributing company is required to deduct a 25 % withholding tax from the amount of dividends payable to shareholders. Shareholders subject to unlimited tax liability can offset the tax withheld against their liability to income or corporation tax.

Shareholders who are not subject to unlimited tax (foreign shareholders) cannot offset the 25 % withholding tax, but they can apply for a refund according to the provisions of the relevant double taxation treaty.

4.144 Sweden

In Sweden there are three main types of equity instruments or shares in addition to ordinary shares:

- depository receipts;
- preference shares;
- convertible bonds.

The most important of these (in terms of trading volumes as well as new issues) is the convertible bond.

Ordinary shares

In Sweden the issue of shares is governed by the Companies Act 1975 ('the Companies Act'). Some of the more important provisions are as follows:

354

• shares should have a positive nominal value. The nominal value may be reduced under certain conditions as stipulated in the Companies Act;

• shares may be issued at a premium, in which case the excess over nominal value must be transferred to a statutory reserve, which is restricted for dividend purposes;

• a reduction of a statutory reserve requires a decision at a General Shareholders' Meeting and may be made only for the following purposes:

– to cover losses which cannot be covered by non-restricted equity;

– to increase the share capital through a bonus issue;

– for any other purpose provided that the court has given their consent;

• shares can be transferred on a bearer basis or as registered instruments. Shares have to be registered to enable voting rights to be exercised; ;companies cannot issue non-voting shares. However, shares can be divided into 'free' and 'restricted' shares (or 'A' and 'B' shares) with the restricted shares carrying restricted voting rights. No share may have a voting right that exceeds ten times the voting right of another share (although there are some exceptions to these rules relating to old share issues such as Ericsson 'B' shares). Restricted shares can only be purchased by Swedish citizens. Foreigners can purchase free shares, but foreign ownership in companies owning real estate is restricted to 40% of the share capital and 20% of the votes. Permission is required from the government for significant foreign shareholdings (usually measured as 10% of the share capital or voting rights);

• generally a company may not acquire, or receive as collateral, its own shares. Shares may be acquired in connection with takeovers or business reorganisations, but have to be sold within a period of two years (although the Government may give permission for a longer period). Holdings of the company's own shares shall be shown in the balance sheet as assets with nil value but their total nominal amount shall be disclosed;

• Shares may not be issued in currencies other than Swedish kroner.

Depository receipts

This type of security was developed and established in Sweden to facilitate trading and investing in foreign shares. Depository receipts are traded on the Stockholm Stock Exchange and represent shares in foreign companies. The original share certificates are usually deposited at a Swedish bank, because of exchange restrictions. The receipts are issued by VPC (the organisation which maintains the shareholders' registers of the largest 500 companies in Sweden).

The maturities of these receipts can vary and usually there is no fixed redemption date. Dividends are paid by VPC to those owners who are registered with the depository bank at a fixed date. Deduction for taxes is made before payment. When a receipt is traded it must be sent to VPC to be exchanged to a new receipt in the new owners name.

There are at present nine foreign companies' shares in Sweden which are represented by depository receipts.

Preference shares

These shares have a long history in Sweden. The main reason for issuing preference shares was to attract investors who wanted to reduce their risk. These securities have priority concerning dividends in comparison with other types of shares. Dividends are usually fixed. The shares are traded and cleared on the Stockholm Stock Exchange and VPC in a similar way to ordinary shares. The outstanding value of preference shares as well as the trading volumes have declined during the last ten years. At present there are only five companies who have preference shares listed on the market.

Convertible bonds

The first issues of convertible bonds in the Swedish market occurred in the 1980s. Maturities vary from one up to about five years, but is rarely longer than three years. However, a special kind of convertible bond with maturities of between twenty and forty years exists and the interest rate on this type of bond is linked to the value of the dividend paid by the company.

There are two principal types of investors in these securities:

• employees (including management). These investors are invited to buy convertibles at favourable terms. They effectively form part of the remuneration package and are intended as an incentive;

• the second type of investors are the usual investors in other types of security. Quite often, the convertibles are purchased as part of a 'package' of securities, issued in connection with a merger and/or an acquisition.

The secondary market is as for ordinary shares and bonds. The registers of owners are administrated by VPC. All convertible bonds are registered instruments.

In 1989 there were about thirty convertibles issued by companies and quoted on the market in Sweden.

4.145 Obtaining a listing

The admission of securities to listing on the Stockholm Stock Exchange is governed by Government decree. The aim of the decree is to ensure that all applicants for listing are of a certain minimum size, and set out in formal listing particulars sufficient information about their history, prospects and financial condition to form a reliable basis for market valuation.

The principal requirements for obtaining a listing are:

• share capital not less than SEK 2 million;

• total equity not less than SEK 4 million.

For the primary official list (A:I) the above requirements are SEK 10 and 20 million respectively.

At least 10 % of the shares of the applicant company must be held by the public. In practice, the stock exchange encourages at least 15 % to be held by the public. There should also be a certain number of shareholders at the time of the listing, each holding shares totalling a minimum value. These requirements are presently under review and will in the future probably be more in line with EC requirements.

The financial performance, systems for management reporting and control of applicant are also reviewed by the stock exchange council, as well as standards for external reporting and disclosure.

Application for the listing of shares is to be made by the board of the company whose shares are to be listed. The application should in summary be accompanied by:

• the company's articles of association;

• a declaration that the company's share capital is fully paid up;

• information on the shares' approximate market value and their circulation among the public, together with an account of ownership;

• certain detailed information on the shares and, if the company has issued 'free' shares, details regarding the number of such shares;

• annual reports and auditors' reports for the past five accounting years (unless there are specific reasons to allow a shorter period);

• an undertaking, in compliance with a form ('the listing agreement') prescribed by the Council, to make public all pertinent information regarding the company and to give assistance to the Council in fulfilling its duties.

Takeovers and mergers

The regulations concerning takeovers and mergers are set out in an appendix to the listing agreement. The principal purpose of these regulations is to ensure fair and equal treatment of all shareholders in relation to takeovers. Unlike the rules in many other countries, there is presently no obligation for an acquirer of a stake totalling 30% or more of the issued share capital of a target company to make an offer for the remaining shares. This issue is however under consideration. Once 90 % or more of the target company's share capital, representing 90 % or more of the voting power, has been acquired, the owner has a right, according to the Companies Act, to acquire the remaining shares. There are special rules to determine the price at which the shares will be acquired. Up to this point the minority shareholders have a number of rights, including the right to appoint one auditor.

4.146 Accounting treatment

General

Shareholders' equity is generally divided between two subheadings; restricted equity and non-restricted equity or accumulated deficit. Restricted equity includes share capital, legal reserve and revaluation reserve. Non-restricted equity includes non-restricted reserves (retained earnings brought forward and net income for the year).

Share capital

Where the company's share capital is divided into several classes of shares, the amount of each class should be disclosed. The number of shares and the face value of each share should also be reported. All movements in each category equity since the preceding balance sheet should be disclosed in a note to the balance sheet. Regulations relating to the disclosure of a single entity's equity also apply to consolidated accounts, where appropriate.

Restricted reserves

Two kinds of restricted reserves may appear in a limited company's balance sheet, the statutory reserve and the revaluation reserve.

Statutory reserve

The following allocations must be made to the statutory reserve:

• at least 10 % of the net income for the year after deduction of any deficit brought forward. Such allocation must continue until the reserve equals 20 % of the share capital;

• any amount received in excess of the nominal amount at issue of shares;

• any amount paid by person whose shares have been declared forfeited;

• any amount according to the articles of association or approved by the general meeting.

Revaluation reserve

This reserve arises as a result of the revaluation of non-current assets. It may only be used for the following:

• a necessary write-down of the value of non-current assets;

• for a bonus issue of shares;

• to cover an accumulated deficit appearing in a balance sheet adopted by the general meeting, provided that the loss cannot be covered by available unrestricted equity. A decision to utilise the revaluation reserve to cover a deficit requires consultation with the auditors. Such a decision prevents the company from dividend declaration for a period of three years unless the share capital is increased by an amount not less than the deficit covered by the revaluation reserve, or if the court gives their consent.

Restriction on distributions

Dividends paid to shareholders may not exceed distributable reserves or, for a parent company, the distributable reserves disclosed in the consolidated balance sheet. Distributable reserves include the net income for the year, retained earnings brought forward and non-restricted reserves less reported loses, less amounts allocated to restricted equity and amounts which the articles of association require to be used for other purposes.

Dividends may not be paid to such an extent that, because of the company's or the group's cash needs or financial position, the distribution would be contrary to good business practice.

The general meeting may not declare a dividend which is higher than the dividend proposed or approved by the board of directors unless otherwise provided in the articles of association of the company.

A company may not grant cash loans to a person who owns shares in the company or who is a member of the board or managing director of the company or of another entity in the same group. The same rule applies to persons who are relatives to or otherwise closely related to a shareholder, to a member of the board or to the managing director of the company.

Untaxed reserves

Untaxed reserves are the result of tax appropriations. All tax appropriations, many of which imply asset undervaluation, are reported in a specified caption in the income statement. These appropriations are increases in untaxed reserves. These reserves should be viewed as a mixture of equity and deferred tax. As from 1991 the tax proportion of such reserves is 30%. Untaxed reserves cannot be used for dividend distribution. To pay dividends they have to be transferred to the income statement and become taxable income. Examples of untaxed reserves are inventory reserve, investment reserves, accumulated excess depreciation and, from 1991, the tax equalisation reserve.

4.147 Taxation treatment

Sweden still adheres to the 'classical' system for taxation of companies and their shareholders. Profits are taxed firstly in the hands of the company and secondly, when distributed, in the hands of the shareholder. Dividends are generally not deductible when calculating the taxable income of the distributing company, with one exception. Dividends paid on shares issued at the incorporation of a company or at an issue of new shares (other than a bonus issue) are deductible within certain limits. This deduction is however only available for dividends paid to shareholders who pay Swedish income or withholding tax on the dividend.

For resident shareholders dividends are as a general rule included in the taxable income. For corporate shareholders exemptions are applicable for operational holdings. Special rules apply to investment companies and unit trusts. Non-resident shareholders are subject to a withholding tax amounting to 30% of the gross dividend, unless a tax treaty provides for a lower or a zero rate.

Certain stamp and transfer duties are imposed on the issue and transfer of shares. For an issue of new shares for cash the duty is 2% of the share capital, and also of any premium if the issue is for cash. When shares are transferred Swedish buyers and sellers are subject to 0.5% transfer duty.

A sale of shares at a gain gives rise to taxation at the rate of 30% if the seller is a Swedish resident (individual or corporate). Roll-over relief can be used for share-for-share exchanges.

4.148 Norway

In Norway the issue of shares is governed by the Companies Act 1976 and in the case of listed shares, also the Stock Exchange Act 1988 and the detailed regulations of the Oslo Stock Exchange. The provisions of the Companies Act are detailed but a summary of the more important or unusual ones relevant to equity or equity linked products is set out below:

• shares are required to have a positive nominal value;

• a minimum share capital of NOK 50,000 is required for all limited companies;

• bearer shares are not permitted;

• shares may only be issued in Norwegian kroner;

• detailed regulations exist concerning appropriations to a restricted legal reserve fund from companies' profits.

Quoted and unquoted companies

Norwegian company law does not distinguish between quoted and unquoted companies. However, those companies defined as large companies have a greater disclosure requirement than small companies. Shares which are to be made freely available to the public require a stock exchange listing.

4.149 Stock exchanges

Although there are several provincial stock exchanges the Oslo Stock Exchange is by far the leading stock exchange in Norway. The most significant activity on the exchange is trading in equities and bonds. The Oslo Stock Exchange is a self-owned non-profit organisation which is regulated by the Ministry of Finance.

Main laws

The Stock Exchange operations are governed by the following major laws:

• the Companies Act, effective from 1977;

• the Accounting Act, effective from 1978;

• the Stock Exchange Act, effective 1988.

Apart from these laws there are rules of conduct imposed and enforced by the Stock Exchange Council as well as recommendations for generally accepted accounting practice. These standards are largely self-regulatory. As a corporate body the Stock Exchange Authority exercises control over members. The Stock Exchange Act includes regulation of stock exchange management, its members and representatives as well as the quotation system and penalties for breach of the regulations.

Authorisation system

The listing requirements for Norwegian companies are differentiated between the main list (*'Bors 1'*) and the secondary list (*'Bors 2'*). It is quite common that a new company listing is made on *Bors 2* with a later transfer to *Bors 1* when the company satisfies the more stringent listing requirements of the main list. It is also possible for a company which no longer satisfies the *Bors 1* requirements to be transferred to *Bors 2* instead of being delisted.

Foreign companies can qualify for listing in Oslo if, in addition to the requirements for Norwegian companies, they have significant operations in Norway or can provide evidence of significant Norwegian interest in its shares. Additionally, the shares must be listed on the official stock exchange in the country where the company has its corporate headquarters. Otherwise the continuing obligations of a foreign listed company with respect to information are the same as for Norwegian companies. Information may be provided in English.

Market rules

Rules governing the organisation of the market are found in the Companies Act 1976 (which imposes the statutory requirements), The Accounting Act 1977 (which provides minimum requirements for financial information) and the Stock Exchange Act 1988 (which gives the framework within which securities operations and dealings can be effected). The Stock Exchange Act includes regulation of Stock Exchange management, its members and representatives as well as the quotation system and penalties for breach of the regulations. The Securities Trading Act 1985 regulates trading practice, misuse of confidential and price sensitive information in securities trading, requirements for related parties to report their securities transactions and the listed companies' duty to provide information. Stock Exchange members are generally free from intervention by government departments because they are under the authority of the Stock Exchange. Powers of regulation and control are effectively delegated to the Stock Exchange Council.

Council powers

The Council's powers are wide and cover all matters relating to the association and the market. The Council can make both individual and general decisions. The Rules and Regulations of the Stock Exchange determine the general conditions for membership, dealing in securities, admission of securities to the Exchange etc. The Stock Exchange is bound by law to perform a number of surveillance and control functions with respect of the securities market. This is largely carried out by a separate department known as 'Stock Watch' which continually monitors all market activities as well as having responsibility for dissemination of information to the market.

Company prospectus and information requirements

The Stock Exchange has issued separate sets of rules on prospectus requirements for *Bors 1* and *Bors 2*. The Stock Exchange also imposes its own requirements relating to company information which have recently become more stringent.

A prospectus must be issued for any new stock exchange listing and this must be made available to prospective shareholders. The Stock Exchange also issues regulations covering information to be provided to the exchange.

The 1976 Company Law sets out reporting rules for the acquisition of significant blocks of shares or acquisition by a company of its own shares through merger or other means. An acquisition of 10% or more of the share capital or voting rights of a listed company must be reported. In addition, acquisition offers or merger proposals must be reported to the Stock Exchange no later than the general release or publication of this information. Additionally, where a listed company becomes aware that an official offer will be made or that a listed company decides to propose an offer to a third party the listed company has a duty to inform the Stock Exchange.

Securities registration

The Norwegian Registry of Securities (VPS) was established by law in 1985 and is a private, independent and self-financing institution. In general terms the VPS is a computerised registration system in which the ownership of, and all transactions related to, Norwegian publicly traded equity securities are normally recorded. The recording of a transaction in the VPS will normally be decisive in determining the legal rights of parties towards the company and towards a third party claiming an interest in the shares. Certificates representing shares are no longer issued.

VPS has a duty to provide the Bank Inspectorate with information necessary for its activities and additionally certain information can be demanded by the tax authorities in respect of individual persons' holdings of securities as well as dividend and interest payments.

Foreign investment in Norwegian shares and bonds

Norwegian law regulates the amount foreigners may buy in each separate company. The amounts are limited by several different laws under which maximum foreign ownership is restricted to:

- 15% of share capital in financial institutions;
- 20-33% of share capital in industrial firms;
- 40% of share capital in shipping companies.

Other limitations may be imposed by the constitution of individual companies. Several companies have obtained official permission to have a greater percentage of foreign ownership than prescribed by law.

As of 1989 foreign investors are also allowed to purchase Norwegian Government bonds which were previously only available to domestic investors.

Unlike Norwegians, foreigners can register shares through a nominee. Neither the unnamed shareholder nor his nominee will have voting rights. The nominee must be licensed as such by the Ministry of Finance and must register as a nominee in the company's share register. On request from the company or the authorities the nominee must state who is the real owner of the share.

4.150 Finland

In Finland the issue of shares is governed by the Companies Act 1978 and, in the case of listed shares, also the Securities Markets Act 1989. The securities markets are supervised by the Banking Inspectorate, which has the right to issue legally binding regulations concerning the markets.

A public company may offer some of its shares to the public but first it has to comply with the prospectus requirements of the Securities Markets Act. For the shares to be listed, the requirements of the Stock Exchange will also have to be met.

Redeemable shares

The Companies Act sets out the circumstances in which a company has the power to issue redeemable shares provided it is authorised to do so by its Articles of Association. These kinds of shares, however, cannot be listed either on the Helsinki Stock Exchange or on the OTC market.

Purchase of own shares

Subject to certain exceptions, companies may not purchase their own shares In addition subsidiaries may not purchase the shares of their parent company.

4.151 Market characteristics

The market is governed by two main authorities. The Banking Inspectorate which supervises the activities of the Stock Exchange and the brokers and the Council of the Stock Exchange which is the authority empowered to grant the brokers the right to deal on the Stock Exchange.

Admission to listing

The listing rules are governed by the Securities Markets Act. The Council of the Stock Exchange decides on the admission of securities to be listed on the exchange.

The principal requirements for obtaining a listing are:

• the applicant must agree to comply with the regulations of the Stock Exchange;

• the applicant must have at least 500 shareholders;

• the shares must be freely transferable;

• listing particulars must be published; the requirements for the information to be included in listing particulars are regulated by the Securities Markets Act and the regulations of the Stock Exchange.

Continuing obligations for listed companies

One of the principal objects of the continuing obligations imposed by the Securities Markets Act on listed companies is to secure the immediate release of information expected to have a material effect on market activity and prices of listed security. Listed companies are also required to publish, in addition to the annual report, a report on the financial position of the company at least once during each financial year (six month report).

Equity and equity linked instruments

Equity capital raising

The Companies Act in Finland requires companies proposing to issue securities having an equity element to offer those securities to existing equity shareholders in proportion to their existing holdings, unless shareholders approve the terms of any other type of issue. Because of this most equity capital raising by listed companies is by means of rights issues at a discount to the market price of the shares.

Takeovers and mergers

The regulations concerning takeovers and mergers are set out in the Securities Markets Act. The principal purpose of the regulations is to ensure fair and equal treatment of all shareholders in takeover. The purchaser of shares in a listed company must disclose his stake in the company, when his share of the voting rights exceeds or falls below the limits named in the Securities Markets Act (10%, 20%, 33.33%, 50% or 66.67%). The shareholder whose stake exceeds two thirds of voting rights in the company must make an offer for the remaining shares.

Settlement of transactions

The settlement day, when shares are transferred from seller to buyer and paid for, is normally five business days after the end of the Stock Exchange account.

4.152 Taxation treatment

A stamp duty of 1.0% is payable on share transactions on the Stock Exchange. Otherwise the stamp duty is 1.6% on share transactions.

An imputation system operates in Finland. The corporate tax paid on the profits, from which the dividends are paid, is credited against the shareholders' tax liability. An individual shareholder will have a taxable income equivalent to the 'gross' dividend, that is the amount received as dividends plus the attaching corporate tax credit. If the individual shareholder is paying tax at a rate which is lower than the corporate tax rate attributable to the distribution, then the excess is refunded. Likewise, if the shareholder is paying tax at a higher rate, the individual will be liable to additional tax.

In assessing the shareholders' liability to tax, it is assumed that the company has suffered tax equivalent to the corporate tax credit attached to the dividend. In practice, however, the company's liability to pay tax can be lower than the amount imputed to dividends. As a result a so called 'supplementary tax' has also been introduced. When a company's corporate tax based on taxable income is less than tax (at 42 %) imputed to profits paid out as dividends, the 'supplementary tax' will become payable by the company. This is to ensure that the dividend paid to the shareholders has been subject to corporate tax at a rate of 42 % (in 1990).

Shareholders who are non-profit foundations and organisations are outside the imputation system. Dividends received are tax exempt and no credit for corporate tax paid is granted.

The imputation system does not apply to non resident shareholders. Existing tax treaties will need to be amended before shareholders resident in tax treaty countries can claim a tax credit. If the foreign country allows a corresponding credit to Finnish shareholders, Finland will allow an equivalent credit to foreign shareholders. This means that it will be impossible to allow a credit to shareholders who live in a country which uses classical or dividend deduction methods to avoid double taxation of corporation and shareholders. For the present it seems that Finland will allow a credit to shareholders in the United Kingdom and France.

The new imputation system has a great impact on the tax treatment of dividends derived abroad by a Finnish corporation. Before the introduction of the imputation systems, dividends received from countries with which Finland had concluded a treaty for the avoidance of double taxation were tax exempt. Because of the reform, Finland will have to renegotiate these treaties.

The rules concerning dividends in the tax treaties have yet to be revised. The Business Income Tax Act included a temporary section to be in force for the two years 1990 to 1991 which states that a dividend distributed by a foreign corporation is not taxable income for Finnish corporations if Finland and the other country have a tax treaty and if the Finnish corporation owns at least 10 % of the total foreign corporation's voting stock.

4.153 Greece

In Greece, the issue of shares is governed by the Companies' Act 1920 as amended and modified by subsequent legislation. A company established under this act is called an '*Anonymous Etairia*' (AE) and is similar to a United Kingdom public limited company or a French *société anonyme*.

Share capital

Some of the more important legal provisions relating to shares are as follows:

• a company may not normally acquire its own shares except under certain specific circumstances provided for in law. In addition a company may not accept its own shares or the shares of its subsidiaries as a security for loans granted by it;

• companies are prohibited from providing financial assistance for the purchase of their own shares by third parties;

• issues of new shares must first be offered to existing shareholders in proportion to their existing shareholding;

• there are also provisions in the Companies' Act relating to maintenance of capital, distribution of profits, loans to directors and reduction of capital.

An AE must have a minimum share capital of Greek Drs. 5,000,000, although this limit is expected to be increased to Greek Drs. 30,000,000 in the near future. There are higher minimum capital requirements for certain kinds of AE such as insurance and banking companies. The capital of an AE must be equally divided into shares, with a maximum par value of Greek Drs.30,000, and a minimum of Greek Drs.100.

There are three types of shares which are found in Greece:

• capital shares;

• preferred shares;

• founders shares.

Capital shares (ordinary shares)

Capital shares may be either bearer shares or registered shares. The shares of certain kinds of companies (eg banking, insurance, railway, aviation), and any shares which are not fully paid up, must always be registered.

Preference shares

Company statutes may also provide for the issue of preference shares, with or without voting rights. Preference shares are entitled to the payment of dividends and, in case of liquidation, to the repayment of capital which has been invested by the shareholders, in priority to ordinary shares. Dividends may be accumulated and preferred shareholders may have the right to participate in whole or in part in the remaining profits of the company in addition to the fixed preference dividend. The holders of preference shares without voting rights may be granted, in addition to the above privileges, the rights to the payment of a fixed rate of interest in the absence or insufficiency of profits.

Founders shares

The statutes of the company may also create founders' shares. Such shares are issued in consideration for services rendered in connection with the formation of the company, or, more unusually, in the return for contributions in kind. They may confer on their holders the right to share in the company's profits. However, as these shares do not have a par value, they do not confer on their owners the right to participate in the administration of the company and/or to share in the company's assets on liquidation. Such shares should not exceed, in number, 10% of the number of the company's ordinary shares.

Ownership and transfer of shares

Bearer shares are freely transferable and transfer is effected by delivery of the shares. Registered shares are also freely transferable unless their transfer is conditional, by a provision in the company's statutes, on either the board or general meeting's approval. Transfer of registered shares is recorded in the register of the company and requires the signature of both parties or their legal representatives. After every such transfer a new certificate is issued by the company, or the transfer is noted on the old certificate together with the name, address, occupation and nationality of both the transferor and the transferee. Transfer of registered shares of companies listed on the Athens Stock Exchange within the administrative district of Athens is effected by endorsement of the share certificate by the transferor in favour of the transferee in the presence of a broker. However, the use of a notary is required for the transfer of shares in a company listed outside the administrative district of Athens.

There are no restrictions on the ownership of shares by foreigners except for shares in companies owning property in certain border areas. Regulations restricting the repatriation of capital and dividends to foreign shareholders have been considerably relaxed in recent years. However, there are still certain requirements which must be observed by foreign companies or individuals acquiring shares in Greek companies to secure the right to repatriate dividends and capital. The approval of a government department or, depending on the shareholders' residence, the Bank of Greece is required before shares with repatriation rights can be transferred. A valuation by state appointed auditors may also be required. A Greek resident who sells shares to a foreign resident must repatriate the sales proceeds into Greece.

4.154 Market characteristics

Although the Athens Stock Exchange has existed for many years, until fairly recently turnover was low and markets in most individual shares was thin. As a result, its role in raising finance was marginal and most companies looked to bank financing to raise capital. It is fair to say that until recent years, the main attraction of the stock exchange for the relatively few companies that sought to be listed was the favourable tax regime offered to listed companies. In the overwhelming majority of cases quoted companies are controlled by relatively small groups of shareholders (usually family members of the founders) and ownership is generally much less dispersed than in more sophisticated markets.

The Greek Stock Exchange has been much more active in the last few years. Increased interest by companies seeking to obtain listings is due both to high domestic interest rates which make loan finance prohibitively expensive, and also to a significant rise in investor demand resulting in much higher share prices and P/E ratios. This demand is partly due to the interest of foreign investors following the recent liberalisation of dividend and capital repatriation rules. Partly, however, it is also due to the limited range of alternative investment opportunities in Greece, especially since exchange rate instability has discouraged the export of capital and increased demand for domestic shelters for surplus funds which can act as a hedge against inflation.

In general, the market still lacks sophistication and depth and its administrative infrastructure needs to be overhauled if the Stock Exchange is to assume its proper role as the principal source of investment capital in Greece. Moves are under way for the modernisation and upgrading of trading practices, in light of the move towards free capital flows within the EC after 1992. A fairly recent development is the establishment of a second tier market with less stringent listing requirements than the Stock Exchange, although the activity on this market is still very limited.

Admission to listing

To be listed on the Stock Exchange, a company must have minimum equity capital of Greek Drs.50 million and must have published accounts showing satisfactory financial results for at least the 5 previous years. The decision on whether the application for a listing will be accepted is made by the Governing Committee of the Athens Stock Exchange.

The company seeking a listing must undertake to increase its share capital by at least 25% by the issue of new shares to be made available to the public. The public offering must be underwritten by a bank which sets the issue price. To ensure a reasonable dispersal of ownership, the underwriter must provide the Stock Exchange Committee with a list of the new shareholders indicating that the new shares were taken up by at least 100 different persons.

Companies seeking a listing must issue a prospectus, the contents of which must be approved by the Governing Committee of the Stock Exchange. The information to be disclosed in the Prospectus includes:

• history of the company;

• financial analysis of its operating results for the previous five years;

• balance sheets, profit and loss accounts and cash flow statements for five years;

• market data and marketing plan;

• production facilities;

• management;

• dividend policy;

• names of directors and principal shareholders;

• details of insurance cover.

In addition to the prospectus, the company seeking a listing must file details of its history, legal and financial status, and share capital with the Stock Exchange Committee.

Suspension or cancellation of listing

The Chairman of the Stock Exchange may suspend dealings in a company's share if there are sudden and unwarranted fluctuations in its price, or if he believes this to be in the interests of investors, or to safeguard the smooth operations of the market.

A company may be deprived of its Stock Exchange listing if:

• the Capital Markets Committee decides that it is not possible to maintain normal dealings in its shares;

• its capital falls to below Greek Drs.50,000,000;

• it fails to comply with the decisions of the Capital Markets Committee or Stock Exchange regulations;

• for three consecutive years the company fails to distribute the minimum dividend provided for in the Companies' Act (6% on the nominal value of its share capital);

- trading in its shares amounts to less than 1% of the number of its listed shares in any one year.

Disclosure requirements – financial information

Companies must file accounts with the local *Prefecture* in which they have their head office. In addition, the accounts must also be published in the Government Gazette and two local newspapers. The accounts published in this manner usually comprise a balance sheet, an income statement, an appropriation account and the report of the auditors. Companies quoted on the Stock Exchange must also publish half yearly statements comprising of a balance sheet and a profit and loss account.

Disclosure requirements have been made more comprehensive in recent years. All companies must prepare a directors' report and additional explanatory notes. The format of published financial statements has to conform to the National Chart of Account.

In spite of recent improvements, extreme caution should be exercised when interpreting the information contained in Greek financial statements. They are usually of very limited use for financial analysis and may be seriously misleading for those who are accustomed to international accounting standards of presentation and disclosure. Accounting principles are poorly defined and inconsistently applied; in general, financial statements are tax-driven and tend to be legalistic in their interpretation of accounting rules. As a result, foreign investors investigating the possibility of investing in Greek companies are advised to request the Greek company in which they are interested to provide them with a set of financial statements that are restated so as to conform to international accounting standards and disclosure requirements. In the case of cross-border mergers or acquisitions, this restatement is often the first prerequisite of the due diligence process.

Takeovers and mergers

There is no specific legislation governing the procedures to be followed intakeovers, although there may be requirements imposed by the articles of association of the target company. Similarly, certain procedures may be required by the purchase of shares in a company in a border area.

The regulations relating to trusts, monopolies etc are contained in Law 703/1977 relating to 'the control of monopolies and oligopolies and the protection of free competition'. This Law which was based on some of the EC requirements is at present being revised and new legislation to cover all EC requirements in this is expected shortly.

In respect of mergers, legislation relating to mergers of AE companies is included in the Companies Act which was last amended in 1987. In particular, articles 68-80 of the Act contain a virtual translation of the relevant provisions of the third EC directive. This legislation contains provisions concerning both the absorption of one or more AE by another AE and the merger of two or more AE to form a new AE.

4.155 Cyprus

In Cyprus the issue of shares is governed by the Companies Law Chapter 113 which is essentially a replica of the old 1948 United Kingdom Companies Act. The more important provisions of the Companies Law are as described for the United Kingdom in section 4.100.

A public company may offer its shares to the public through a prospectus which must satisfy the requirements of the Companies Law. The prospectus must contain specified information including inter-alia, the history of the company, its activities, particulars of its directors, its financial position and the use to which the proceeds of the share issue will be put.

Preference shares

These shares are entitled to preferential treatment when dividends are declared. Preference shares do not carry the right to participate in any surplus profits of the company unless the articles so provide. In the repayment of capital on winding up usually preference shares have priority over ordinary shares, either by the articles or terms of issue.

It should be noted that dividends on preference shares are not allowed as a deduction for tax purposes and consequently such shares are not very common. Debenture interest is an allowable deduction and a company in Cyprus is therefore more likely to issue debentures which are very similar to redeemable preference shares, at least from the investor's viewpoint.

Redeemable preference shares

The Companies Law provides for the issue of redeemable preference shares, and the provisions of the relevant sections are similar to the United Kingdom legislation.

Purchase of own shares

A company cannot be a member of itself (it cannot purchase its own shares) because such a purchase would amount to a return of capital to shareholders. This would be a reduction of capital which requires the consent of the court. As an anti-avoidance measure, there is a specific provision in the law which renders it illegal for a company to provide financial assistance for the purchase of its own shares.

Stock market

There is no official Stock Exchange in Cyprus as yet but trading in the shares and debentures of some 40 public companies takes place through brokers who publish bid and offer prices in the press. However, a draft bill setting up an official stock exchange and providing as to its manner of operation, is now ready and is expected to be enacted during 1991.

4.156 Spain

Issue of shares

In Spain, the issue of shares (except for listed shares) is regulated by the Companies Act. The issue of listed shares is governed by the Securities Market Act.

The principal requirements for an issue of shares are:

• it needs the approval of the shareholder's meeting and the modification of company by-laws;

• at least, 25% of the value of each share issued must be paid up.

In case of a public offer, the subscription will be included in a register with the following requirements:

• corporate's name and address and the mercantile register inscription data;

• name, address, nationality and residence of the subscriber;

• number and nominal value of the subscribed shares;

• the subscriber's payment;

• date and subscriber signature.

The new Companies Act allows the issue of shares without vote, if the nominal value is less than 50% of paid-up capital.

Purchase of own shares

The reform of Spanish company law allows the creation of treasury shares but sets their limit at 10% of share capital. The Commercial Code states that corporations may only acquire their own shares with shareholders funds, in order to reduce capital. At the same time, it prohibits corporations to borrow using their own shares as guarantee. In addition, Company Law requires that the acquisition of shares by the company itself without cancellation is only allowed in cases of extreme need, and with the authorisation of the shareholder's meeting.

4.157 Market characteristics

The Stock Exchanges in Spain has branches in Madrid, Barcelona, Bilbao and Valencia. Like other financial institutions, the Stock Exchange operates under the jurisdiction of the Ministry of Finance, and is governed by the 1988 Securities Market Act.

The stock exchange is divided into two categories: that of officially admitted companies and that of non officially admitted companies (secondary market) reserved for medium sized companies.

The amount of business transacted through the Stock Exchange and the number of corporations listed is still small compared with other European countries but there has been rapid growth in the last two years. With more companies seeking quotations on the Stock Exchange and the widespread interest shown recently by overseas investing institutions, this growth should continue in the future.

Admission to listing

A Stock Exchange listing is not particularly common for Spanish companies (only about a third of the country's 300 largest companies are listed) principally for the following reasons:

● there is reluctance by entrepreneurs to disclose information on their activities;

● there are company and shareholder tax considerations;

● companies do not want to lose control over the business;

● Spanish companies tend to be small and do not have the adequate size for entering the Stock Exchange.

Principal requirements for obtaining a listing

The application for admission must be made to the appropriate Stock Exchange Council. All essential circumstances relating to the security must be included. This is particularly important because there are no statutory restrictions to the free transmission of securities or their rights. Shares or bonds and similar securities can be listed.

Shares issues

● The company must have a minimum capital of 200 million pesetas, not including capital held by shareholders who directly or indirectly own an amount of shares equal to or greater than 25% of the total.

● Profits earned during the previous two, or during three non-consecutive years in the previous five years must have been sufficient to cover at least a 6% dividend on paid-up capital, after making provision for Corporate Income tax and allowing for legal or mandatory reserves.

Issue of bonds and similar securities

● The total nominal amount of a security issue must be a minimum of 100 million pesetas.

● If the issue is not secured by mortgages or government securities (State, Autonomous Communities, Local Corporations, and their branches) or by a Private or Savings Banking Syndicate, the conditions relating to prior years profits as described for share issues above will be required.

Takeovers and mergers

Spain is enjoying a period of rapid economic growth and, concurrently, of economic restructuring. Legal and regulatory reforms to bring in systems of regulation appropriate to this level of activity have been enacted. The Spanish Government has implemented this legislation in order to stimulate investment. Direct foreign investment is now almost completely liberalised, with only certain areas of strategic importance and of national interest remaining protected. In addition, investment authorisation procedures have been simplified.

Mergers are permitted by Spanish Company law and are accorded specific tax treatment by law. Such a merger results when two or more companies amalgamate their assets and shareholders into one company, upon prior dissolution of all the merging companies and the creation of a new company, or dissolution of all except one company, which absorbs the others. The resulting company must be a joint stock company ('*sociedad anonima*'), whether quoted or not. The merger proposal must include, as a minimum, the name and address of the companies involved in the merger and the new company, the method of share exchange and the exchange value, and the rights of each party to the merger.

Takeover bids are governed by the Securities Market Act. Persons intending to obtain a significant interest in the capital of a company, may not do so without launching a public bid addressed to all that company's shareholders. The regulations establish:

• the participation considered as significant;

• the rules and terms for its calculation taking into account direct and indirect interests;

• the terms on which the bid shall be irrevocable;

• the method of administrative control under the responsibility of the National Securities Market Commission.

Any person who acquires a number of shares admitted for trading on a Stock Exchange representing over 50% of the total votes of the issuing company may not amend that company's by-laws, except for the particulars to be provided by regulation, without launching a public bid for the purchase of the remaining voting shares admitted for trading.

Another important issue in merger and acquisitions operations is the vendor's tax position. In Spain, the capital gain to the private individual owners (as opposed to corporations) will be taxed at ordinary personal income tax rates, which reach 56% on earnings above Ptas. 8 million (about US$75,000). There are a number of possibilities for easing the seller's tax burden:

• the sale of assets rather than shares;

• international tax planning. One method that could be used by vendors is the use of foreign holding companies;

• to ensure that the merger qualifies under a special regime for (virtually) tax free mergers or spin-offs. However, this treatment is difficult to obtain.

4.158 Tax rules for securities transactions

The transfer of securities is exempt from Transfer Tax and from VAT except in the following cases which are subject to Transfer Tax:

• transfer of securities representing part of the share capital or capital of companies, funds, associations or other institutions where at least 50% of the assets consists of real estate located in Spain, when as a result of such transfer the purchaser obtains full ownership of such capital or at least a position enabling it to exert control over such institutions;

• in the case of commercial companies, such control shall be deemed to be obtained when an interest of over 50% in the share capital is reached;

• when determining the 50% of the assets consisting of real estate property (except for land), the net assets of companies whose sole corporate purpose is construction or real estate promotion shall not be taken into account;

• transfers of shares or interests in companies received through the contribution of real estate on the incorporation of companies or the increase of their share capital, when one year has not elapsed between the date of the contribution and that of the transfer.

4.159 Italy

Legal framework

The issue of shares in Italy is governed by the Civil Code, as amended in particular by a law of 7 June 1974. Some of the more important provisions are:

• shares cannot be issued at a lower amount than their nominal value, but it is possible to issue shares at a premium;

• shareholders have the right to subscribe for newly issued shares. New shares (as well as convertible debentures) must be offered firstly to existing shareholders to the company in proportion to the number of shares owned, at a fixed price. Shareholders must be given at least 30 days from the date of publication of the offer to exercise their option;

• shares cannot be issued in currencies other than lira.

There are three different types of shares in Italy; ordinary shares, preferred shares and savings shares. The characteristics of these different instruments are described further below.

Ordinary shares ('azioni ordinarie')

Ordinary shares are registered and confer voting rights at ordinary and extraordinary shareholders meetings, and rights to the dividends and the reimbursement of capital on liquidation. Ordinary shares must amount to at least 50% of a company's share capital.

Preferred shares ('azioni privilegiate')

Preferred shares are registered, and confer voting rights only at extraordinary meetings. The amount of preference dividend is established by the memorandum of association of the company, and they can be cumulative.

378

Savings shares (*'azioni di risparmio'*)

Savings shares were introduced by law in 1974; they can only be issued by companies listed on the Stock Exchange, and are bearer shares (however, upon request, they can also be converted into registered form). Savings shares do not have voting rights. They have a right to a preference dividend which can be cumulative for two years. The dividend must be equal to at least 5% of the nominal value of the savings shares, and it must exceed dividends paid to other categories of shares by at least 2% of the nominal value. Any losses incurred by the company are suffered by other categories of shares before affecting the holders of savings shares.

Purchase of own shares

The purchase of its own shares by a company is regulated by Articles 2357 and 2358 of the Civil Code. The most significant regulations can be summarised as follows:

• it is forbidden for the company to subscribe to its own shares;

• a company can only purchase shares which are fully paid up;

• a company can only purchase its own shares out of its distributable profits as disclosed in the most recently approved financial statements;

• the purchase must be approved by a shareholders' meeting in which the duration of the purchase transaction (in any event not exceeding 18 months), the maximum number of shares which can be purchased, and the minimum and maximum purchase price are disclosed;

• the nominal value of the shares purchased must not exceed 10% of the total share capital of the company;

• where shares are purchased in contravention to the above rules, they must be sold within a year, according to the terms to be established by the shareholders' meeting. If those conditions are not complied with, the shares must be cancelled and the share capital of the company reduced accordingly;

• a non distributable reserve, equal to the amount of shares purchased held as an asset in the balance sheet, must be maintained until the shares are either transferred or cancelled.

There are some circumstances where a company can purchase its own shares without following all the procedures set out above, such as following forced acquisition to settle a debt owing to the company.

4.160 Equity markets

There are 10 stock exchanges in Italy. By far the most important in terms of the number of listed shares and the volume of transactions is the Milan Stock Exchange. The others, in order of importance, are Rome, Turin, Genoa, Bologna, Florence, Naples, Palermo, Trieste and Venice. Admission to the stock exchanges is strictly controlled by laws and regulations. At present approximately 250 companies are listed on the Italian stock exchanges.

In Italy, there are three types of equity market: in addition to the stock exchanges there are the 'Restricted Market' and the so-called 'Third Market'.

Restricted Market

The restricted markets are strictly controlled although their operation is much simpler than the Stock Exchanges. These markets were established to create markets in the shares of medium sized companies, with less onerous requirements than those necessary to be admitted to the official listing on the stock exchanges. At present, there are six restricted markets. The market in Milan has the greatest volume of transactions and the highest number of quoted shares (approximately 40). Many of the shares quoted on the market are in banks (mainly credit cooperative banks), whose transfers of shares are restricted thus preventing their listing on the Stock Exchange.

Third Market

The Third Market is an over the counter market and is unregulated. Shares awaiting listing in a regulated market are traded in this way, as well as those shares temporarily suspended from the official listing and awaiting readmittance, and the shares of those companies which, although having all the prerequisites to be admitted in the Stock Exchange or the 'Restricted Market', do not wish to gain admission to the listing.

Requirements for admission to listing on the stock exchange

The following are the more important requirements that a company must meet to be admitted to the listing in the Stock Exchange:

● the net equity of the company to be admitted should amount to at least lira 10 billion (lira 50 billion in the case of banks or insurance companies);

● presentation of financial statements for the last three years;

380

- the last year's financial statements should be audited;

- at least 25% of the amount of each category of shares for which admission is requested must be made available to the public;

- there should be no limits to the transfer of the shares subject to admission.

The following are among the requirements for the 'Restricted Market':

- the net equity of the company asking admission should amount to at least lira 1 billion;

- presentation of financial statements for the last year;

- appointment of a firm to audit the financial statements;

- shares available to the public must represent at least 10% of the company's shares;

- there should be no restriction on the transfer of the shares subject to the admission.

The above requirements also have to be met to retain a listing. If one or more requirements are not met, CONSOB (the National Commission for Listed Companies and the Stock Exchange) can suspend or cancel the listing of the company concerned. A company can be admitted to listing upon request or be admitted if CONSOB decides that admission will safeguard the shareholders. Savings shares have an automatic right of admission to listing.

Issue of shares

The following procedures must be carried out before a listed company can issue new shares:

- delivery to CONSOB a notice of the meeting of the Board of Directors of the company to effect the capital increase: the notice must be sent at least 10 days before the meeting is held;

- at the board meeting the directors should:

– approve a report to be sent to CONSOB describing the aims of the transaction and the use of the funds;

– call an extraordinary meeting of shareholders to approve the capital increase;

– prepare the information which has to be published in the *Gazetta Ufficiale* (Official Gazette) and in the press;

- after the extraordinary meeting of shareholders the company should

381

deliver to CONSOB (within 30 days) the resolutions adopted regarding the capital increase;

• a prospectus has to be prepared containing information relating to the issuer, information on the broker/dealer sponsoring the issue and information relating to the shares and offer terms. The prospectus must be deposited in the archives at CONSOB;

• a formal request has to be made to the Treasury Ministry and to the Bank of Italy for authorisation to increase share capital if the total amount of the proceeds, (inclusive of any premium) exceeds lira 10 billion (taking into account similar transactions in the previous 12 months);

• a request has to be made for authorisation to the Bank of Italy if newly issued shares are to be listed on the Stock Exchange or distributed through credit institutions;

• the Treasury Ministry and the Bank of Italy must be notified that the capital increase has taken place.

Settlement of transactions

The majority of transactions in listed securities on the stock exchange are in the forward market and are settled monthly in accordance with the stock exchange calendar. Transactions in the restricted market are usually settled 10 days after the trade date, and transactions in the third market are usually settled in cash after three days. Delivery and withdrawal of shares is effected through a centralised custody and administration system run by Monte Titoli SPA. Transfers between system participants (banks and stockbrokers) is made by book entry.

4.161 Convertible debentures

There are several different types of convertible debentures that can be issued in the Italian market:

• 'direct' convertibles (when convertible debentures can be converted into the shares of the company issuing the debentures). On conversion, the issuing company would issue new shares;

• 'indirect' convertibles (which can be converted into shares of a different company than the company issuing the bond);

• totally convertible debentures (when the entire nominal value of the convertible debenture can be converted into shares);

• partially convertible debentures (when at the time of the conversion, a portion of the nominal value of the debenture is converted with the balance being repaid to the investor in cash).

The Civil Code only addresses debentures convertible in newly issued shares through the direct method. Where the issue of convertible debentures is intended to result to an increase in share capital, the Code requires that:

• approval at an extraordinary shareholders' meeting setting out the capital increase for an amount equal to the nominal value of the shares obtainable from the conversion, the conversion ratio and the time and terms of conversion;

• convertible debentures, as with the requirements laid down regarding the issue of shares, cannot be issued at an amount lower than nominal value;

• convertible debentures shall be offered to the shareholders of the company proportionally to the number of shares owned.

4.162 Accounting treatment

The main requirements of the two Italian professional bodies are described in outline below.

Purchase of own shares

An amount equal to the cost of the shares purchased should be transferred from retained earnings to a non-distributable reserve.

Shares should be carried in the balance sheet at cost. In the event of sale at an amount higher than cost, the gain should be taken directly to retained earnings, although it is acceptable to record the gain in the income statement as an extraordinary item, with appropriate disclosure in the notes to the financial statements. Following the sale, the non-distributable reserve should be re-credited to retained earnings. The same treatment applies if the shares are sold at a loss.

In the event of cancellation of own shares purchased, share capital shall be reduced by the nominal value of the shares. If the shares are purchased for more than their nominal value, the excess should be purchased out of retained earnings. Where the nominal value is greater than cost of purchasing the shares, the difference should be taken to share premium reserve. The non-distributable reserve should be re-credited to the retained earnings.

Convertible debentures

The most important regulations on the accounting treatment are as follows:

• at the time of issue and until the option right is exercised, the convertible bond should be accounted for in a similar way to other debt securities;

• at the time the option right is exercised, the amount of debentures converted should be taken out of liabilities and recorded as share capital at an amount corresponding to the nominal value of shares issued;

• if the nominal value of shares issued to convert debentures is lower than the value of debentures, the difference shall be credited to the share premium reserve;

• if the convertible debentures are issued above par, the premium should be recorded in the liabilities section of the balance sheet. When the debentures are converted, the share of the related premium should be credited to the share premium reserve. Where the debentures are repaid in cash, the premium should be credited to the income statement.

The disclosure required notes to the financial statements are similar to other debt instruments and the following additional information should be disclosed:

• conversion ratio of debentures into shares;

• time and terms of the exercise of the conversion right;

• significant amounts relating to profits on conversion of debentures.

4.163 Taxation treatment

Capital gains

As noted in chapter 6 – County Accounting and Taxation Framework, from 28 January 1991 the capital gains realised on sales of equity holdings by individuals and non-commercial enterprises, are subject to taxation being calculated on different bases depending on whether the taxpayer opts for a detailed or index based method of determining the capital gains.

In the former case, tax will be paid once a year on filing the income tax return, at a rate of 25% applied to the total of capital gains realised by the person in the tax period, determined as the difference between the sales proceeds and the price paid on purchase net of any loss calculated according to the same criterion.

In the latter case, the appointed intermediaries (stockbroker or bank) will apply a withholding tax of 15% on the capital gains deriving from each individual transfer, the determination of which varies according to whether the disposal concerns listed or unlisted shares.

Dividends on ordinary and preferred shares

In Italy dividends and profits on ordinary and preferred shares distributed under any form to shareholders are subject to a 10% withholding tax, except for total or partial distribution to shareholders of the share premium reserve which is tax exempt.

Dividends are taxed using the imputation system, to avoid double taxation of the same income. On completing the income tax return, the owner of ordinary or preferred shares must include the amount of the gross dividends received from Italian corporations increased by a tax credit equal to 9/16 of the gross dividend. The total tax due is then calculated by applying the appropriate tax rate to this gross income. From the total of tax due, the following amounts should be deducted:

- the 10% withholding tax levied upon distribution of the dividends;

- the tax credit (9/16 of the gross dividends).

Dividends on savings shares

Dividends on savings shares are subject to a 15% withholding tax, although holders of registered savings shares are entitled to elect for 10% withholding tax, they expect to be able to reclaim the tax.

Tax on transfers of shares

A 0.14% stamp duty (calculated by reference to the transfer price) is payable on all transfers of shares. This duty decreases to 0.1% in transactions between a bank and an individual, or through an intermediary such as a stockbroker.

Chapter 5

Hedging instruments

Hedging instruments

Overview

5.1 Introduction

The aim of hedging is either to offset or to minimise the risk of losses that an enterprise is exposed to due to the effect of price changes on its assets, liabilities, revenue and expenses or future commitments.

This chapter is concerned with the financial instruments which are available for this purpose, and is divided into three parts:

• the first part concerns the traditional hedging instruments – forward, futures and option contracts;

• the second part deals with a number of instruments which are hybrids of forwards, futures and options which have been developed as hedges against currencies and interest rates;

• the third part concerns financing techniques, particularly swaps and repurchase agreements which are often used to hedge any exposures resulting from an instrument described in this or an earlier chapter of the book.

5.2 Traditional instruments

The three basic types of hedging instrument are as follows:

• *the forward contract* – the purchase or sale of a fixed amount of a commodity or financial instrument at a price fixed at the contract date, with delivery and settlement at a fixed future date;

• *the futures contract* – similar to a forward contract except that purchase or sale is of a standardised amount (or lot) of a specified quality for standardised delivery dates. Trading of the contracts takes place on an organised exchange;

- *the option contract* – which conveys the purchaser right but not the obligation to purchase (call) or sell (put) a futures contract, a commodity or other financial instrument and may be in standardised lots traded on an organised exchange. The purchaser pays the seller (writer) a non-refundable premium.

These basic types of instruments have been developed to fulfil the hedging requirements of different enterprises. The forward contract allows specific known assets, liabilities or commitments to be hedged. The futures contract is standardised, and is traded on an organised exchange which regulates the transactions made between its members. As a result, the futures market is highly liquid and is generally cheap and efficient to use and exposes the user to minimal credit risk. However, price movements may not prove to be as closely correlated with the actual commodity as with the forward contract. The option is attractive to an enterprise which has a commitment which is not certain; for the amount of the premium, the purchaser of the option buys the right (but not the obligation) to hedge future price movements of the commitment.

Hedging instruments are available to enable enterprises to hedge against, and speculate in, movements in prices of four principal markets:

- physical commodities (such as precious metals and foodstuffs);

- currencies;

- money and credit (eg short and long term interest rates);

- stocks and shares.

The earliest forward, futures and option markets to develop were to hedge against movements in physical commodity prices and until relatively recently they were by far the largest of the markets. Traditionally the uncertainty of both supply and demand for physical commodities has made these markets volatile which has stimulated the development of hedging. However, the growth in importance of hedging instruments in recent years is mainly due to the increased volatility of exchange rates and interest rates following the breakdown of the Bretton Woods Agreement in the early 1970s (which had fixed the rates of exchange between leading currencies). This volatility has exposed corporations to the risk of losses from movements in exchange and interest rates and hence increased the importance of hedging as a risk management tool. To the extent that hedging is successful, a company can implement its planned operations without profits being at risk from fluctuations in rates over which the company has no control. Continuing innovation in this area is partly driven by the need to reduce the cost of hedging.

The importance of hedging currencies and interest rates has led to the growth of treasury departments within larger companies. In many cases they now operate as separate profit centres within the company, actively trading in the markets as well as hedging the company against risks of price movements. In effect they have become similar to the treasury or money market operations of privately owned banks.

5.3 Forwards, futures and options products

In addition to stimulating the development of the traditional hedging products, the increased volatility of interest rates and exchange rates has led to the development of a variety of products which are hybrids and combinations of the traditional products. In general terms, these products have developed as companies have been reluctant to use options, because of the difficulty in justifying the cost of the premium (often payable in advance) and due to the perception of options being speculative rather than hedging instruments. This perception appears to be largely due to the fact that if a purchased option expires unutilised the whole of the premium is lost and the event for which it was purchased to reduce or eliminate the risk of price movements is over looked. Despite this, there is a demand for an alternative to forwards and futures which, while locking in a fixed price, remove the possibility of participating in any favourable movements in rates.

5.4 Swaps and repos

A swap is more in the nature of a financing technique than an instrument. However, swaps have had a great impact in the financial markets in recent years and are often used in conjunction with instruments covered in other chapters of this book. For example, a high proportion of Eurobond issues during the 1980s were swap driven; a corporation may issue a fixed rate bond but want floating rate funds, and if the swap was not available, the issue would not have taken place.

Repurchase agreements (repos) are also financing transactions. While the legal form may be a sale and repurchase, in substance the seller borrows the proceeds from the purchaser and deposits securities with the purchaser as collateral. The difference between the purchase and sale price represents the interest. Many of the issuers and users of instruments described in this book will use the United States Treasury bond repo market, which forms a significant part of the money market in the United States, to hedge exposures to dollar interest rates.

5.5 Hedging or trading

The financial instruments discussed in this chapter can be used for speculative and trading purposes as well as for hedging. Indeed, the liquidity of the futures markets is largely dependent on speculators who trade in the market to make a profit. Investment banks and securities dealers may make markets in hedging instruments, taking positions so as to be able to service the needs of their clients. These institutions also use the same instruments to hedge the risks incurred by taking positions, as well as other items in their balance sheets.

5.6 General accounting questions

There are a number of general questions which must be considered in determining whether, and how, hedge accounting can be applied to a financial instrument:

• Is the transaction clearly identified as a hedge? Amongst the criteria which have to be considered are:

– Is the enterprise exposed to price movements and does the transaction eliminate or reduce substantially the exposure to risk from movements in prices?

– Was it designated as a hedge at the time it was entered into?

– Does the enterprise apply its criteria of designating transactions as hedges on a consistent basis?

– If the transaction was entered into to hedge a future commitment, is there a reasonable certainty that the commitment will actually arise?

– Is there a high correlation between the price of the hedging instrument and the price of underlying asset, liability or future commitment ('the underlying transaction')?

Whilst it may be possible to match hedges exactly with the underlying transaction, this is often extremely difficult in complex environments. For example, securities dealers and investment banks may use a variety of instruments to hedge their entire trading portfolios of securities. At one time particular hedging instruments may be designated as hedges but at a later date be trading assets (which are hedged by other positions), and vice versa. It may not always be possible to match the hedges with the individual elements of the portfolio. Although it can be difficult to determine exact criteria for what qualifies as a hedge, the economic reality may be that the enterprise has successfully hedged its risk to adverse price movements on its portfolio.

• Once an asset or transaction has been designated as a hedge, generally accepted accounting principles require that it should be accounted for in compliance with the accruals or matching concept. That is, the profits and losses which arise on the hedge should be accounted for in the same accounting period or periods as those arising on the underlying transaction. The questions to be addressed are:

– Has the underlying transaction been recorded in the accounting records at the balance sheet date?

– Is the underlying transaction a commitment at the balance sheet date which will be reflected in the accounting records at a future date?

• How hedge accounting will be applied in practice will depend on the accounting policies of the enterprise which apply to the underlying transaction. For example, if an asset which is being hedged is carried in the balance sheet at the lower of cost and market value, any profit or loss arising on the hedge will have to be taken into account in determining the market value of the asset. If assets and liabilities are stated at market value (as is usually the case with securities dealers and banks), then the hedging instruments should also be marked to market.

• Hedge accounting can apply only while the instrument is being used to hedge an identifiable risk and so long as it remains an effective hedge. As soon as this is not the case or where transactions do not qualify as hedges, the instruments should either be marked to market or carried at the lower of cost or market value, depending on the accounting policy of the enterprise. In any event, any losses on transactions which are not hedges should be provided for as soon as they are foreseen.

• Sections 5.140 to 5.173 at the end of this chapter set out the accounting treatment for hedging instruments in various countries in Europe.

5.7 General taxation questions

• The crucial question to be asked of any hedging transaction is whether the tax treatment of the hedge mirrors that of the risk being hedged. If it does not, the risk is not properly hedged on an after tax basis.

• Does the tax treatment follow the accounting treatment, in other words are profits taxable on an accruals or realisation basis?

• Do special tax rules apply and do these present problems in practice?

• Does the tax treatment differ if the underlying transaction being hedged is of a capital nature rather than of a trading nature?

• Is the tax treatment different for long-term and short-term hedging?

• If hedging instruments are entered into regularly will such activities be regarded as a separate trading activity in their own right? If so does this have adverse tax consequences?

• Do any withholding tax rules apply to the hedging instruments?

• Do any special returns need to be made to the tax authorities?

• Are there any exchange control regulations which may restrict the use of hedging instruments?

• What VAT or other indirect tax liabilities need to be considered?

• Are there any capital taxes or other duties to be considered (for example trade taxes)?

• Sections 5.140 to 5.173 at the end of this chapter set out the basic tax considerations for hedging instruments in various countries in Europe.

5.8 Traditional hedging instruments

5.9 Forward contracts – overview

A forward contract is an agreement between two parties to exchange a specified amount and type of commodity or financial instrument at a fixed future date at a fixed price. Any type of commodity or financial instrument can be bought and sold in this fashion – the most developed markets are in commodities (such as precious metals, base metals, foodstuffs and petroleum products) and in the purchase and sale of loans and deposits in currencies. These markets are described in more detail below. They exhibit the following features in common:

- they are OTC markets, where dealers transact business over the telephone and usually not through an organised exchange;

- the markets are largely unregulated;

- the markets will trade both in spot, forward and swap contracts. Spot contracts are for immediate delivery rather than a date in the future.

Variation

Basis contract	Rather than fixing a future contract price as in a forward contract a basis contract locks in the spread between the current spot price and the price at which the purchase or sale will take place in the future.

5.10 Forward commodity contracts

Forward commodity contracts are binding contracts to deliver or receive a specific amount and type of commodity at an agreed price at a specified future date. The delivery date, location, and the quantity and quality of the commodity are specified at the time the contract is struck. Unlike futures contracts, forward contracts usually result in actual delivery of the commodity in the condition and location specified in the contract. The contracts are not dealt with on a recognised exchange and will, by their nature, be illiquid. Although the market itself may be active with a large number of contracts traded, individual contracts will not usually be sufficiently interchangeable to be tradeable. The level of speculative activity in forward contracts is limited, and the major participants in the market are generally end users and suppliers/producers who deal through commodity traders. The gold market is an exception to this and the market is very liquid with major centres in London and Zurich.

5.11 Forward foreign exchange contracts

A forward foreign exchange contract is a binding contract to purchase or sell a specified foreign currency at an exchange rate determined on the date that the contract is made, but with payment and delivery at a specified future date. These contracts are traded on an OTC market in which most major banks participate. Contracts can be for maturities up to 10 years in the most popular currencies but the most liquidity is in contracts with a maturity of less than one year.

A survey published by 20 central banks in 1989 of the global foreign exchange market confirmed that the level of transactions has increased substantially since the previous survey in 1986. The market remains centred in London, New York and Tokyo with smaller markets in other European countries. The average daily turnover of the various major locations established by the survey were:

	$ *billion*
London	187
New York	129
Tokyo	115
Zurich	57
Paris	26
Amsterdam	13

The most important characteristics of the European markets are set out below.

London

● The market is dominated by United Kingdom and overseas banks resident in London – typically between 80% and 90% of all transactions in the market are interbank rather than with end users (mainly large companies). Some 27 banks each have more than 1% of the London market.

● Spot transactions account for 64% of the market, forward contracts 24%.

● The largest international banks make markets in all the major currencies. These are mainly the United Kingdom clearing banks and the United Kingdom branches and subsidiaries of major United States, Japanese and European banks.

● The London branches or subsidiaries of the major banks of a particular country tend to specialise as market makers in the currency of the country of their parent bank.

● There are a number of large brokers in the market who provide quotations to market professionals and large corporations. The brokers are an important source of liquidity and enable market makers to deal 'blind' without disclosing their position to other market professionals.

● The US dollar remains the most important currency in the market and most transactions will be executed against US dollars (approximately

90% in the 1989 survey) rather than 'cross currency'. For example, if a company places an order with its bank to sell sterling and buy Swiss francs, the bank will usually sell sterling against US dollars and buy Swiss francs against US dollars to cover the position. However, the volume of cross currency trading is increasing (up from 3% to 9% between 1986 and 1989) as a reflection of the relative decline in importance of the US dollar to other currencies such as the yen and the deutschmark.

• Prices quoted by market makers are indicative rather than firm and binding. This is dictated by the volatility of the market.

Zurich

• The market is dominated by Swiss and overseas banks and the majority of transactions are interbank. There are market makers for various currencies. There are a number of large brokers in the market who will provide quotations to market professionals and large companies. The brokers are an important source of liquidity.

• All major currencies are dealt with, however the US dollar and the deutschmark are the major currencies traded.

• Many transactions are now effected through the means of electronic dealing systems which has lead to a substantial volume increase in the recent few years.

• Slightly more than half of the transactions are spot transactions and over 70% of the transactions are entered into with foreign counterparties.

• Dealings are not regulated by the authorities. However, every bank will have its own daily and overnight limits for currencies as well as maximum limits for counterparties and currencies. These limits must be laid down in the bank's regulations which in turn must be approved by the Swiss Federal Banking Commission.

Paris

• The market is dominated by the large French and foreign banks resident in Paris. 85% of transactions are interbank transactions, of which one half is made through brokers. Six banks account for 50% of the total turnover.

• Spot transactions account for 58% of the market, forward contracts 36% and options and futures 6%.

• The US dollar is the most important currency (72%) and transactions are usually executed against US dollar. The second most active currency is the deutschmark (US dollar – deutschmark transactions account for

27% of US dollar transactions) and between 8% and 10% of transactions are in deutschmarks.

• Dealings are not regulated by the authorities but banks have to monitor foreign exchange positions as compared to capital and reserves.

Amsterdam

• Interbank dealings account for over 90% of transactions.

• Most currencies are quoted against the US dollar however cross currency trading between Dutch guilders and the deutschmark accounts for 19% of the market.

• In excess of 50% of the transactions are for spot settlement.

• There are market makers for each currency and foreign brokers have a leading position in quotes against the US dollar.

5.12 Pricing of foreign exchange contracts

Spot rates

Although domestic markets may have local practices which may differ (eg in Switzerland where most currencies are quoted in terms of 100 units to the Swiss franc) internationally spot rates are quoted as follows:

• most currencies are quoted in terms of the unit of currency to the US dollar (eg a deutschmark rate of 1.73 means you can buy DEM 1.73 in exchange for US$1);

• the exceptions are currencies such as sterling, Irish punt and Australian and New Zealand dollars, which are quoted in term of the US dollar to the unit of currency;

• rates are quoted in terms of the price at which the bank will sell US dollars and buy US dollars; a quotation of 1.8495–1.8505 for deutschmark means that the bank will buy US$1 for DEM 1.8495 and sell US dollars for DEM 1.8505.

Forward rates

• Forward rates are quoted at a premium or discount to spot rates.

• Premiums and discounts are quoted in terms of points or pips which, for most currencies, are 1% of the smallest basic unit of currency. If one month deutschmarks are quoted at a premium of 54–51 this means 54–51 one hundredths of a pfennig and this premium should be deducted from the spot price. If the spot rate is 1.8495–1.8505, the one month bid rate will be 1.8441 (1.8495–0.0054). Conversely, if a currency is at a discount to the US dollar the discount will be added to the spot rate to derive the forward rate.

• Forward rates can be determined arithmetically by applying the interest rate differential ruling between the two currencies in question to the spot rate. The process of arbitrage will ensure that the linkage between interest and exchange rates is maintained. If the rates were not linked it would be possible to borrow money in one currency, convert it and deposit it in a different currency and cover the foreign currency exposure with a forward contract and make substantial profits. The process of arbitrage keeps the rates in line such that any potentially large profits are rapidly eliminated. Forward rates can therefore be calculated from the prevailing interest rates. For example:

$$\begin{array}{ll} \text{US dollar interest rate} & 6\tfrac{3}{4}\% \\ \text{Sterling interest rate} & 11\tfrac{1}{4}\% \\ \text{Spot exchange rate} & 1.95 \end{array}$$

If £1m is borrowed for one year and immediately converted into $1.95m and deposited for one year the forward exchange rate for one year forward can be found by equating the two amounts as follows:

$$\frac{1.95 \times 1.0675}{1 \times 1.1125} = 1.8711$$

At this rate the maturing deposit of $2.08m could be converted to give £1.1125m to repay the loan and no arbitrage profit will arise.

• The majority of interbank transactions in the forward market are foreign exchange swaps (not to be confused with capital market swaps dealt with in sections 5.97 to 5.112). A foreign exchange swap is the simultaneous purchase and sale of a given currency at two different dates. Usually a swap will combine a purchase or sale in the spot market with a forward transaction. The swap rate or swap price is the differential between the rates quoted for the two dates of the swap. Where one leg is a spot transaction, the spot price is equivalent to the forward premium or discount.

• The interest rates used to determine the forward rates are the rates ruling in the interbank deposit market, which is described further below.

5.13 Interbank deposit market

The interbank deposit market based in London is one of the largest money markets in the world. It is often referred to as the Eurodollar or Eurocurrency market, the prefix 'Euro' meaning that the funds are held outside their country of origin, and beyond the regulation of that country's central bank. The Eurodollar deposit market is an OTC market with the main participants being United Kingdom clearing banks and the London branches and subsidiaries of the major international banks. The size of the market, the number of participants and the fact that participation is limited to large professional players has led to the development of a very efficient and liquid market. This, and the fact that the market is not for the most part subject to distortions arising from regulation, is why the foreign exchanges price forward rates from the interest rates quoted in the Eurodollar deposit market.

5.14 Benefits

• An institution can use the forward markets to hedge, or lock in the price of, commitments to purchase or sell a commodity in the future. For example, if a farmer knows that he will have to sell 300 tonnes of his wheat harvest in six months time, he can sell this wheat crop forward now and lock in his sale price, which will enable him to plan without the uncertainty as to the future price movements of wheat.

• Unlike the futures market, where standard types and amounts of a commodity are traded with standard delivery terms and locations, a forward contract can be tailored to the individual requirements of the parties involved – for example, if the farmer wanted to sell 305 tonnes of wheat at a location convenient to him, a forward contract could be negotiated with terms mutually agreed between the parties.

• Unlike futures contracts there is usually no initial margin or variation margin to be paid nor is there an option premium.

5.15 Risks and disadvantages

• The main drawbacks with outright forward contracts is that they do not enable the holders to derive any profit from favourable price movements. For forward foreign exchange contracts this has led to a proliferation of financial instruments which seek to combine the advantages of the protection against adverse currency movements afforded by forward contracts and their low cost to the holder with the profit potential of conventional options which permit gains to be made from favourable movements. The major instruments in this category and the main features of each are outlined in the sections below dealing with forwards, futures and options products.

• By entering into a forward contract, risk of exposure is created if the future commitment under the contract (eg to deliver or receive the commodity) cannot be met. For example, if the wheat farmer had contracted to sell his harvest forward and the crop failed, he would still be committed to selling 300 tonnes of wheat and would therefore have to purchase this amount on the open market. If the crop failure was general, the price would probably have risen to compensate for the shortfall in supply, which could expose the farmer to considerable loss (in addition to that arising from the crop failure).

• Forward commodity contracts deal in physical commodities and are not traded in standardised terms on recognised exchanges. These markets are generally less liquid than futures markets. Consequently, if one party wishes to close out a contract (that is, enter into a spot sale which exactly matches a forward purchase, or vice versa), they may not be able to find a counterparty on reasonable terms.

• A forward contract exposes the holder to a credit risk if the counterparty cannot perform his obligations on the delivery date. There is no organised exchange or clearing organisation to guarantee performance as in the case with futures contracts. On the settlement of a forward foreign exchange contract the credit risk (delivery risk) is increased as a payment instruction may have been given prior to receipt of the funds from the counterparty due to time differences in the two countries of settlement. For a commodity contract a substitute counterparty may have to be found and in this case the exposure is limited to any price movement between the contract price and the current market price.

5.16 Accounting questions

• If the forward contract can be identified as a hedging transaction, is this a hedge of an asset or liability which has already been reflected in the accounting records? Forward contracts should be matched with the asset or liability for the purposes of recognising profits and losses and for balance sheet valuation. For example, a United Kingdom company may have sold its products in the United States, and invoiced its customer in US dollars, but under the terms of the contract the customer would not make payment for six months. The sale would have been recognised in the accounts once the contract had been made with a debtor for the US dollar receivable. If the company had sold the US dollar receivable forward for sterling, at any intervening balance sheet date generally accepted accounting practice requires that the receivable is translated at the exchange rate ruling in the contract rather than the spot rate (as would otherwise be the case).

• For forward foreign exchange contracts how should any premium or discount to the spot rate on the date of the transaction be treated? Is it part of financing costs?

• If a forward contract has been 'rolled over' to match the maturity date with the underlying transaction how should any profits or losses on the rollover be treated?

• How should forward contracts other than forward foreign exchange contracts be treated? Should gains and losses at a balance sheet date be deferred and included in the cost of the underlying transaction?

• Has the forward contract been entered into to hedge a future commitment which has not yet been reflected in the accounting records? Is there a reasonable certainty that the commitment will materialise? If so, any profit or loss on the forward contract should be deferred until the anticipated transaction occurs. Alternatively, if it becomes doubtful whether the commitment will occur, the profit or loss should be treated as if it was a speculative transaction.

• If the transactions do not qualify as hedges what is the treatment of any unrealised gains arising on valuation at the balance sheet date? Can these be taken to the profit and loss account or must they be deferred?

• For transactions with maturities considerably in the future, should profits and losses be discounted to their present value?

• Sections 5.140 to 5.173 at the end of this chapter set out the accounting treatment of forward contracts in various countries in Europe.

5.17 Taxation questions

• Should profits and losses on forward contracts against non-trading positions be treated as capital, trading or other income?

• How regularly must forward contracts be entered into before becoming treated as a trading activity in their own right?

- Should profits and losses on forward purchases be recognised only on sale of the contract or on the sale of the asset purchased?

- Should forward sales be recognised as taxable events when made or when delivery takes place?

- If inventory is matched against a forward sale, should its net realisable value be taken as the forward sale price or the current spot price?

- Should matching forward purchases and sales be regarded as closed out, so that any profit or loss locked in is regarded as realised?

- Are there special taxation rules which apply to certain types of organisation, for example pension funds?

- What is the appropriate VAT treatment?

- See also general taxation questions in section 5.7.

5.18 Futures contracts – overview

A futures contract is an exchange traded agreement to buy or sell a standard amount of a specified commodity, currency or financial instrument at a fixed price at a fixed future date. There is a wide variety of futures contracts in many commodities and currencies as well as other financial instruments ('financial futures'). The different groups of futures contract are dealt with separately below.

The most important characteristics of futures contracts are that:

- the terms of the contract are standardised;

- trading is conducted on, and regulated by, a centralised exchange.

Contract terms

The following terms will typically be standardised:

- the quantity of the commodity;

- the dates on which the commodity can be delivered;

- the last date on which the contract can be traded;

- the minimum price movement;

- the location of delivery and the quality and type of commodity or financial instrument that can be delivered at expiry of the contract.

For some financial futures delivery is either difficult or impossible (for example stock index futures which have no physical existence). For these the contract is settled by cash payment. In other instances (for example government bond futures) there are a range of different instruments which may be delivered to settle a contract, and a formula is used to determine the quantity of a particular bond which is to be delivered (this is explained further below). With the exception of these government bond futures (whose delivery terms create effectively the opportunity for arbitrage), the standardised nature of the contracts means that price is the only variable. Consequently a futures contract is a fungible asset, unlike the underlying commodity, currency or financial instrument.

5.19 Features of futures exchanges

Each futures exchange will have its own rules and distinctive features, but the most important characteristics, which are shared by most exchanges, are:

• trading takes place on the floor of the exchange by the dealers who are members of the exchange. Dealers buy or sell contracts usually by 'open outcry' in trading pits. Automated Trading Systems have recently been developed (for example, by London FOX (see section 5.21 below) for some of its contracts) as a rival to floor trading, and there is considerable controversy as to which is the most efficient and transparent method of trading. This controversy has been fuelled by allegations of price fixing amongst dealers on the major Chicago exchanges. Some new futures exchanges (such as SOFFEX and the Deutsche Terminbörse – see sections 5.22 and 5.30 below) operate screen based trading only. In addition, established exchanges are developing screen based alternatives to open outcry; for example, the Automated Pit Trading (APT) system implemented by LIFFE for trading various contracts outside exchange hours. The exchanges in Chicago are developing a screen based alternative (Globex) also to extend trading hours;

• exchanges have different categories of members, only some of whom are 'floor' members (that is able to deal in the trading pit), or are able to clear trades on behalf of other members. In addition, most exchanges have 'local' members who are specialised traders who deal on the floor for their own account, but who cannot execute trades on behalf of clients (other than floor members). Members of exchanges have to satisfy certain conditions (the most important of which is to demonstrate a minimum net worth) and the conditions for being a floor or clearing member are more stringent;

- memberships, or 'seats' are usually limited in number, and can be sold or leased by the member, providing that the purchaser or lessee can satisfy the requirements for membership determined by the exchange;

- dealers execute trades on behalf of themselves and (except in the case of locals) for customers. Customers' orders are transmitted from the members offices to the floor of the exchange for execution by the dealers;

- the exchange uses the services of a clearing house to settle all transactions between members. Members report transactions to the clearing house which matches them with instructions from the other party to the contract. Normally, the clearing house then becomes the counter-party to the member's transactions. Matched transactions are confirmed to the parties concerned and unmatched transactions reported to the members concerned to be resolved;

- performance of transactions executed on the exchange which have been confirmed (that is, where both parties accept the validity of the contract) are guaranteed by the clearing house. This eliminates any credit risk in respect of dealings between members of the exchange and the only credit risk is with the clearing house;

- to limit exposure arising from its guarantee of performance of contracts, and to maintain the integrity of the market, the clearing house will operate a system of initial and variation margins. Parties to a futures contract must deposit a fixed amount per contract, known as 'initial margin' or 'deposit margin' as soon as the contract is executed. The initial margin is designed to protect the clearing house from movements in the price during one day's trading. The contract will then be marked to market each day to calculate the 'variation margin' which is payable to the clearing house by the party showing a loss and credited to the party showing a gain.

The standardised nature of the contracts and the centralised trading on regulated exchanges make most futures contracts liquid. This liquidity is enhanced by locals and by speculators who are drawn to the market by the standard terms and ease of execution.

While the terms of the futures contract are standard, there are a range of delivery locations and quality/type of commodity or financial instrument which are specified in the standard terms. As a result of this range and the ease of executing an off-setting transaction, very few futures contracts (less than 5% on most exchanges) are settled by delivery of the underlying commodity or instrument but are closed out prior to the delivery date. The actual commodity or instrument is then purchased (or sold) in the required location and condition in the spot or forward market, with the profit or loss made on the futures hedge counteracting the price movements over the period of the contract ('hedging').

5.20 Types of futures contracts

There are two basic types of futures contracts, namely physical commodity futures and financial futures. The principal variations of financial futures are as follows:

- currency futures;

- stock and stock index futures;

- interest rate futures (futures on fixed income securities or time deposits).

The different types of futures, and the principal futures exchanges are described below. The range of futures contracts is increasing every month and recent contracts include property futures in London and a proposed health insurance future in Chicago.

5.21 Commodity futures

There are futures contracts in many commodities including foodstuffs (wheat, coffee, etc), precious metals (gold, platinum, etc), non-ferrous metals (copper, zinc, etc) and petroleum products (crude oil, fuel oil etc). There are also meat and meat product futures and a number of other products (frozen orange juice, plywood and eggs).

London commodity futures exchanges

The principal commodity futures exchanges in London are summarised below.

- Non-ferrous metals are traded on *The London Metal Exchange* (LME). The contracts are more like forward contracts with standard terms and the exchange has used a clearing house only since 1987 following the implementation of the 1986 Financial Services Act (this was a requirement for the exchange to be approved as a Recognised Investment Exchange). A much higher percentage of LME contracts result in physical delivery because of the non-degradable nature of the commodity and the greater number of end users/producers using the market. Contracts executed between members of the exchange on 'the Ring' are now settled through the International Commodities Clearing House (ICCH) which guarantees performance and operates a system of initial and variation margins in the usual way. The terms of the futures contracts traded on the LME are set out in Table 5.1.

• *The London Futures and Options Exchange* (London FOX) was formed in 1987 following the reorganisation of the London Commodity Exchange which had itself been formed out of the various 'terminal markets' trading in soft commodities. London FOX has introduced a number of new contracts and these make use of automated trading systems (Fast Automated Screen Trading 'FAST') rather than being traded by open outcry. A number of new contracts are expected to be developed in the next year or so and London FOX has already introduced futures based on indices of property prices such as the Nationwide Anglia Building Society 'all houses index' and the Investment Property Databank Capital Value Property Index. The ICCH clears London FOX contracts and guarantees performance between its members. In 1991 London FOX merged with the Baltic Futures Exchange – see below. The terms of the futures contracts traded on London FOX are set out in Table 5.2.

• *The International Petroleum Exchange* (IPE) was founded in 1980 to trade in petroleum products (eg gas oil and crude oil) and its first contract (gas oil) was introduced in April 1981. ICCH acts as the clearing house for trading on IPE. IPE has developed Exchange of Futures for Physicals (EFP) which allows participants in the markets to exchange a futures position for a physical position. EFP allows buyers and sellers who want to deliver their futures contract but who find the standard conditions of the contract inconvenient to choose a counterparty for physical delivery. The parties execute offsetting futures transactions and swap their cash market and futures positions. The terms of the futures contracts traded on the IPE are set out in Table 5.3.

• *The Baltic Futures Exchange* (BFE) was formed in 1987 following the merger of the Baltic International Freight Futures Exchange (BIFFEX), the London Grain Futures Market (LGFM), the London Potato Futures Exchange (LPFM), the London Meat Futures Association (LMFA) and the Soyabean Meal Market (SMM). The merger occurred principally to avoid duplicating the administrative and regulatory costs of compliance with the 1986 Financial Services Act. The exchanges are still separate for trading purposes. Business on each exchange is conducted by open outcry. In 1991 BFE merged with London FOX. The ICCH is the clearing house for the BFE, except for grain, which has its own clearing house (The Grain and Feed Trade Association Clearing House). The terms of the futures contracts traded on BFE are set out in Table 5.4.

French commodity futures exchanges

The other significant commodity futures exchanges in Europe are in France where three forward commodity markets exist in Paris (white sugar, cocoa and coffee) Le Havre (coffee) and Lille (potatoes). Contracts are standardised and the clearing house for the markets is the MATIF, (see financial futures markets – section 5.22). Members of the MATIF are allowed to trade on the commodities market and commodities brokers who have sufficient net worth are automatically members of the MATIF. The terms of the commodity futures contracts in France are set out in Table 5.5.

Other European commodity futures exchanges

There is also a commodity futures exchanges in Amsterdam which has contracts in pork (live hogs) and potatoes. The terms of the contracts are set out in Table 5.6.

Exchanges outside Europe

Trading in commodity (and other futures) contracts is dominated by the Chicago markets, which account for over three quarters of the total of all futures contracts traded worldwide. The three principal futures exchanges in Chicago are the Chicago Board of Trade (CBOT), the Chicago Mercantile Exchange (CME) and the Mid–American Commodity Exchange. These exchanges have contracts in a wide range of commodities including most of those traded in London plus many others. In the United States there are also commodity futures exchanges in New York, the New York Mercantile Exchange (NYMEX – oil products, platinum and palladium), the New York Commodity Exchange (COMEX – gold and base metals) and the Coffee, Sugar and Cocoa Exchange (CSCE). Outside the United States, there are many commodity exchanges in Japan (for example Tokyo Commodity Exchange which has contracts in cotton, wool, precious metals and rubber), as well as Winnipeg in Canada (Grains) and Sydney in Australia (wool and cattle).

5.22 Financial futures

Currency futures

A currency futures contract is a contract to buy or sell a standard amount of a foreign currency on one of a predetermined series of specified future dates and delivery locations. The underlying rates of exchange will be almost identical to forward rates. The most important currency futures contracts available are the US dollars against sterling, deutschmark, Swiss franc, yen, French franc, Dutch guilder and Canadian dollar. The contract size is usually much smaller than the normal size of a forward foreign exchange contract. The largest market in currency futures is on the Chicago Mercantile Exchange which trades the largest volume of futures contracts in the world.

Stock index futures

These are futures contracts whose price varies with the movement of a 'basket' of shares underlying a well established stock market index. The underlying 'instrument' has no physical existence and there can be no physical delivery on settlement date. Any outstanding contracts which have not been closed out are settled for cash. Stock index futures are used to hedge portfolios of securities, although a perfect hedge could be achieved only if the portfolio matches exactly the securities comprising the index and if sales and purchases could be made instantaneously. The larger the number of the shares in the basket which are held in the portfolio, the more likely that the values will move in line with the index. The stock index futures traded on European futures exchanges are described further below. Important stock index futures traded outside Europe include:

Future	*Exchange on which traded*
Standard & Poors composite 500 index	Chicago Mercantile Exchange (CME)
New York Stock Exchange composite index	New York Futures Exchange (NYFE)
Nikkei 225 stock average	Osaka Securities Exchange
Tokyo Stock Price Index (Topix)	Tokyo Stock Exchange

Complex trading strategies have been developed which take advantage of time lags between the movement in price of the underlying stocks and shares and that of the futures contract on the index. By using computers to monitor the prices of the underlying stocks and shares, arbitrage opportunities can be identified and the stocks making up the index bought or sold at the same time as the futures contract is entered into. This 'basket trading' or 'program trading' was popular on Wall Street prior to the stock market crash of October 1987. This program trading is based upon relatively small price differences and, in order to generate a significant return, results in large values of shares being bought and sold. The futures contracts are held until maturity when they are settled for cash and the actual shares liquidated for the same value as the index giving rise to an overall profit.

The large amounts traded in these programs have resulted in dramatic falls in the stock prices on the maturity date of the futures and options contracts – the so-called 'triple witching hour'. The extent to which program trading was responsible for the 1987 stockmarket crash is still a matter of debate. At times of price volatility firms conducting these transactions on their own account have ceased trading on a temporary basis, although usually such transactions are still executed for customers.

Interest rate futures

Futures on fixed income securities or time deposits are primarily used as a hedge against future movements in interest rates and the pricing of the contract is a function of prevailing interest rates. For example, if three month Eurodollar interest rates are 9% a three month Eurodollar futures contract of similar maturity would be priced at 91 (100–9). If interest rates were 12%, the contract would be priced at 88 (100–12).

In the cash market the equivalent of the sale of a futures contract would be borrowing by taking a deposit or taking a short position on a fixed income security (depending on the type of futures contract). Equally, the equivalent of purchasing a futures contract would be placing a deposit or purchasing a fixed income security. To hedge against a fall in interest rates an investor would buy futures, which is known as a long hedge. To hedge against rising interest rates, one would sell futures (a short hedge).

As a simple example of a short interest rate hedge, assume that bank A has taken a 3 month $1 million Eurodollar deposit which it will have to roll over on 20 June. The interest payable on the loan is currently 8%. If on 21 March, the bank determines that interest rates are likely to rise in the near future it can sell one LIFFE Eurodollar 3 month contract. The futures price is 92 (reflecting an 8% yield). At 20 June, the spot interest rate is 10%, which enables the bank to buy back the contract at 90. The profit made on the futures contract will offset the additional borrowing costs. This can be shown as follows:

	$
Interest payable on new 3 month deposit	
$\$1,000,000 \times 10\% \times \dfrac{90}{360}$	25,000
Profit on futures trading	
$\$1,000,000 \times \dfrac{(92-90)}{100} \times \dfrac{90}{360}$	(5,000)
Effective interest cost	$20,000

The effective cost of $20,000 is equivalent to an annualised interest rate of 8%. Therefore, the use of the futures contract has enabled the bank to lock into the interest rates prevailing in March.

Delivery terms

The delivery terms of interest rate futures vary depending on the nature of the underlying instrument. There are two methods by which delivery is effected:

• Cash settlement. This will occur where physical delivery would be difficult (for example with LIFFE's Japanese Government Bond Future) or where there is no uniformity in the credit quality of the issuers of the underlying instrument. If there was physical delivery in the three month Eurodollar contract, for example, this would result in time deposits taken by the worst quality credits permitted by the contract terms being 'delivered'.

• Physical delivery of a range of securities. This method of delivery is adopted for most futures contracts on government bonds (where there is no variation in the credit quality of the issuer). The various deliverable bonds, which have different coupons and maturities, are brought on to a common basis for delivery by use of a price factor which is determined for each bond by the futures exchange . The amount deliverable or the 'invoicing amount' is calculated as follows:

$$\text{Invoicing amount} = (\text{Delivery Settlement Price} \times \text{Price Factor} \\ \times \text{Unit of Trading}) + \text{Accrued Interest}$$

The Delivery Settlement Price is the market price of the contract determined by the exchange at expiry. For example, assume that at the expiry of the March 1989 LIFFE German Government Bond Contract, the 6.375%, 20 January 1998 German Government Bond is to be delivered (on 10 March 1989) with 50 days of accrued interest. The Delivery Settlement Price on 7 March (the last trading day of the contract, three days before settlement day) is 98.50, the price factor for this bond is 1.024889 and accrued interest is DEM2,213.54. The unit of trading (or lot size) of the contract is DEM250,000 nominal. Therefore the invoicing amount per contract is:

$$\frac{(98.50}{100} \times 1.024889 \times \text{DEM250,000}) + \text{DEM2,213.54} = \text{DEM254,592.46}$$

The choice of the bond issue to be delivered rests with the seller of the futures contract, and therefore to assess the fair price of the contract buyers must anticipate the delivery of the bond which will maximise the profit (or minimise the loss) of the seller. This bond is known as the cheapest to deliver (CTD) bond.

Financial futures exchanges in Europe

As stated in the overview to this chapter, financial futures have developed in response to the volatility of exchange rates and interest rates in recent years. This has led to the formation of an increasing number of financial futures exchanges both in Europe and elsewhere. The most important financial futures exchanges in Europe are as follows:

- **The London International Financial Futures Exchange** (LIFFE). LIFFE was formed in 1982, and has approximately 180 members. LIFFE distinguishes between general and individual clearing members (general clearing members have the rights to clear other members' transactions as well as their own) and non-clearing members. Non-clearing members have to clear their transactions through a general clearing member. General clearing members have to meet minimum net worth requirements and other conditions set by the exchange and the ICCH, which acts as the clearing house for LIFFE. The terms of the financial futures contracts traded on LIFFE are set out in Tables 5.7 to 5.9.

- **The Marché à Terme International de France** (MATIF) was founded in 1986. The market operates under the authority of the *Conseil du Marché à Terme* (*'CMT'*) which establishes and monitors the rules and regulations. The MATIF has approximately 200 members of which only a small number are non-clearing members. MATIF SA provides the clearing service and will operate the Globex electronic trading system. In addition to the organised market, MATIF members conduct transactions on an over the counter basis at the beginning and end of the trading sessions. These transactions are cleared by MATIF SA at the next official trading session. The terms of the financial futures contracts traded on the MATIF are set out in Table 5.10.

- **The Irish Futures and Options exchange** (IFOX) opened in May 1989. The IFOX trading system is fully automated with no open outcry. The automated trading system feeds directly into the clearing system which is also part of the exchange and which guarantees the contracts. The financial futures contracts traded on IFOX are set out in Table 5.11.

- **The German Futures exchange** (*Deutsche Terminbörse 'DTB'*) commenced operation in 1990. A stock index contract ('DAX-Future') and an interest rate contract based on long term government bonds ('Bund Future') were introduced in November 1990 after equity options (see section 5.30) were introduced in February 1990. The DTB is a fully computerised futures and options exchange and has no floor. Liquidity of the market should be ensured by market markers who have to establish binding prices throughout the trading day. DTB is both an exchange and a clearing house. The terms of the financial futures contracts traded on DTB are set out in Table 5.12.

- **The Swiss Options and Financial Futures Exchange** (SOFFEX see section 5.30 below) has a stock index futures contract based on a Swiss Market Index (see Table 5.19).

- There are also financial futures exchanges in Stockholm (*Stockholm Options Market* – Table 5.13 see also section 5.30), Amsterdam (*Financiele Termijnmarkt* – Table 5.14), Barcelona (*Mercado Espanol de Futuros Financiers* – Table 5.15), Copenhagen (*Guarantee Fund for Danish Options and Futures* – Table 5.16) and Helsinki (*Finnish Options Brokers* – Table 5.25).

Financial futures exchanges outside Europe

Many of the more important futures on fixed income securities are traded outside Europe. Some of the more important are:

Future	Exchange
US Treasury Bonds	Chicago Board of Trade (CBOT)
US Treasury Notes	CBOT
US Treasury Bill	Chicago Mercantile Exchange (CME)
Eurodollar deposits	CME
12 year GNMA pass through security	CBOT
Japanese 10 year T-bonds	Tokyo Stock Exchange (TSE)

Other significant Financial Future Exchanges include the Singapore International Monetary Exchange (SIMEX), the Tokyo International Financial Futures Exchange (TIFFE), the New York Futures Exchange (NYFE) and the Sydney Futures Exchanges.

5.23 Pricing of futures contracts

Futures contracts are priced by reference to prices in the cash market – if prices in the futures market and the cash market move out of line, arbitrage trading will correct this. An arbitrageur will buy in the cash market and sell the future (a strategy which is known as a 'cash and carry'), if futures are expensive relative to the cash market (where the futures market is 'rich') or sell in the cash market and buy the future if futures are cheap relative to the cash market.

The difference between the cash price and the futures price is known as the 'basis'. As the delivery date of the futures contract is approached, the cash price and futures price will converge and the basis will move towards zero. Prior to the delivery date, the most important factor influencing the basis (assuming that the cash and future are identical) is the prevailing interest rate. Interest rates will determine whether or not it is cheaper to invest in the cash market (which has to be financed) or in the futures market (where, except for margins, financing is not required). The fair price of a future can be determined by calculating the theoretical futures price as a function of the spot price in the cash market and financing costs.

For example, if the spot price of gold is US $370, and one year interest rates are 10%, one would expect the one year gold futures price to be equivalent to the cost of buying spot and holding the gold for one year, or $407 $(370 + (370 \times 10\%))$. If the futures price were higher, say $430, then one could buy in the cash market and sell in the futures market realising a profit of $23 $(430 - 407)$. Conversely, if the futures price was lower (say $390), one could sell in the cash market and repurchase in the futures market. The proceeds of the cash sale could be invested at 10%, enabling a profit of $17 to be earned $(370 + (370 \times 10\%) - 390)$. For simplicity, this example ignores the impact of the cost of margins, transaction costs and warehousing costs.

For short term interest rate futures the theoretical futures price is calculated by determining the 'forward-forward rate' for the delivery date of the future using spot market rates. For example, on 30 October the fair price for the LIFFE three month Eurodollar futures contract, which has a delivery date of 20 December, should be the equivalent to the price which would be offered in the cash market for a three month time deposit commencing in 50 days time (ie 20 December) and maturing in 140 days time. The following mid point rates are being quoted in the interbank Eurodollar market (which is the 'cash market' in this case):

50 day Eurodollar = 10.3%

140 day Eurodollar = 10.5%

Therefore, the 90 day forward-forward rate commencing on 20 December can be calculated as follows:

$$\left(\frac{1 + (0.105 \times 140/360)}{1 + (0.103 \times 50/360)} - 1\right) \times \frac{360}{90} = 0.1046 \quad \text{or} \quad 10.46\%$$

The Eurodollar futures contract is priced off LIBOR (the offered rate). One half of the bid-offer spread of 1/8% (0.0625) has to be included in the interest rate. Therefore, the theoretical futures price is 89.48 $(100 - (10.46 + 0.0625))$.

The difference between the theoretical futures price and the actual price is called the 'value basis'. This should not be confused with the basis which compares the actual futures price with the spot cash market price.

For interest rate futures with a range of deliverable bonds, the price of the future is closely linked to the price of the CTD (cheapest to deliver) bond (to prevent the possibility of arbitrage). The CTD bond is calculated by reference to the implied repo rate, which measures the rate of return implicit between the differences in the spot and futures prices by assuming that a cash and carry is undertaken for each deliverable bond. The CTD bond is the bond with the highest rate of return on a cash and carry. Changes in the cash market can lead to a switch in the CTD bond, with a consequent effect on the futures price.

5.24 Hedging with futures contracts

The example of a short hedge with a Eurodollar futures contract set out above assumed that a perfect hedge was possible. In practice, this is rarely so and a hedger can be exposed to basis change risk. That is to say the risk that the relationship between the cash market price and the futures contract may change (other than for changes in interest rates). This is particularly true in commodity markets where raw material and product prices are often not related directly to futures prices. Thus basis can change over time and can impair the effectiveness of a hedge. It can also occur with interest rate futures where the future used to hedge an instrument is related to, but different from, the instrument underlying the future. This could occur, for example, where a government bond future is used to hedge against a position in non-CTD government bond, or where a government bond future is used to hedge against a corporate bond. Where the bonds have the same maturity and coupon this is known as a cross hedge. If the maturity and coupons are different (which is usually so), a 'weighted hedge' would have to be constructed. In practice, weighted hedges are calculated by using mathematical models employing duration analysis techniques and the historical volatility of the spreads between the different instruments.

5.25 Benefits

● Corporations can use the futures market to hedge, or lock in, the price of commitments to purchase or sell a commodity in the future, thus avoiding any fluctuation in the spot price before the commitment matures.

● The contracts are traded on a recognised exchange and with standard contract terms which promotes liquidity and tighter pricing. The liquidity enables participants to close out their positions at any time before maturity.

• The existence of a liquid market ensures that futures positions may be easily and readily valued.

• The clearing houses guarantee the performance of contracts between members of the exchange. This reduces the credit risks associated with forward contracts and when dealing in a volatile market.

• When the contract is taken out only an initial margin is paid so futures contracts may offer lower initial costs and therefore higher gearing than an equivalent option. The premium on an option may have to be paid at the inception of the contract.

• Futures contracts, unlike forward contracts, can be easily rolled forward at maturity.

5.26 Risks and disadvantages

• As with forwards, the use of futures contracts to hedge a future commitment may create an exposure if the commitment does not materialise.

• If futures contracts are used as hedging instruments, any potential profit from favourable price movements which may occur before maturity will be foregone. By definition hedging with futures means a willingness to forgo any favourable price movements.

• Variation margin may be called at the end of any trading day, depending on movements in the market price of the future. As well as a cash flow disadvantage, the administrative burden of monitoring futures positions on a daily basis may make futures contracts uneconomic for some corporate investors and hedgers.

• Futures contracts are traded only for certain commodities, currencies and instruments and are in standard denominations. It may not be possible to match exactly a future commitment as may be the case with a forward contract.

• While the clearing house guarantees performance of contracts between members of the exchange, non-members are exposed to the credit status of their broker or clearing agent.

5.27 Accounting questions

• Where futures contracts are being used as a hedge, as for forward contracts in section 5.16.

• How should brokers' fees or commissions be accounted for if futures contracts are used to hedge future commitments?

• Sections 5.140 to 5.173 at the end of this chapter set out the accounting treatment for futures contracts in various countries in Europe.

5.28 Taxation questions

• Should a bank or other financial services company (or an organisation which regularly undertakes futures contracts) seek prior approval from the tax authorities to marking to market as an acceptable accounting policy for tax purposes?

• Should the sale of a futures contract be recognised as taxable when made, on closing out against a purchase, on settlement or on some other basis?

• If spot purchases are hedged against sales of futures contracts, is the net realisable value of the spot position the current spot value or the value of the futures contract?

• Are any futures contracts arranged purely to achieve taxation advantages such as to jeopardise tax relief for losses?

• If futures transactions are not part of a trading activity are profits/losses taxable as capital gains/losses?

• Are there special taxation rules which apply if futures contracts are dealt with on a 'recognised exchange'?

• What is the appropriate VAT treatment?

• See also general taxation questions in section 5.7.

5.29 Options – overview

An option contract conveys the right, but not the obligation, to either buy or sell a commodity or financial instrument (eg equity, stock index, currency, bond, futures contract etc) at a fixed price at either a fixed future date or at any time during a fixed future period. An option to purchase is a call option; an option to sell is a put option. The price at which the option can be exercised is known as the strike or exercise price.

The purchaser (or taker) will pay a premium for the right to exercise the option. In exchange for the premium, the purchaser will limit his downside risk to the price volatility of the underlying commodity or financial instrument ('the underlying transaction') to the amount paid for the premium, whilst retaining unlimited potential to profit if price movements are favourable. The writer of the option grants the purchaser the rights under the contract and in return for taking on this unlimited risk receives the premium.

Where the market value of the underlying transaction increases the price of a call option will increase. With a put option, a favourable price movement is where the market value of the underlying transaction falls. Where it would be advantageous for the holder to exercise the option, the option is said to be 'in-the-money'. An option is 'out-of-the-money' if the exercise would not be advantageous. An option is 'at-the-money' where the market value of the underlying transaction is equal to the strike price.

Rights to exercise

A number of different types of option have developed. The two most common are:

- European Option   This option can be exercised only at the fixed date at which the option expires or a short period just beforehand.

- American Option   This option can be exercised at any time up to expiry.

American options are always more valuable than European options (due to the possibility of early exercise) except in circumstances where early exercise would not take place, in which case they would have equal value.

Variations

Boston Option (or deferred premium option)   This is an American option for which the payment of the premium is postponed by rolling it up into the strike price if exercised. If the option is not exercised the premium is payable on expiry. The Boston option is also known as a capitalised option or a forward reverse option.

Asian Option (Average rate option)	This is an option whose strike price is determined from average prices over a specific period rather than on a specific spot price.
Lookback Option	This option differs from conventional options in that its strike price is determined at the time of exercise of the option rather than at purchase. The strike price is any price which has existed during the term of the option (which is most favourable to the purchaser of the option).
Double Option	A combination of a call and put option, giving the purchaser the right to sell or buy the underlying transaction.
Bearer Exchange Rate Option (BERO)	A small denomination (£5,000) US dollar/sterling and US dollar/deutschmark currency option marketed by Barclays Bank.
Quantity adjusting option (QUANTO)	A currency option marketed by Goldman Sachs which allows the amount of foreign currency to be varied to meet changes in requirements.

5.30 Option markets

Options which are listed on, and traded through, a recognised exchange are known as traded options. A traded option can be sold before maturity on a recognised exchange and they are often traded on the same exchanges as futures contracts. Many of the traded options on such exchanges are settled by delivery of the related futures contract. Normally contracts are traded at a range of fixed strike prices. These ranges are called 'series' and new contracts are added to the series as the price of the underlying commodity or financial instrument moves by a set amount. Banks will also write customised, tailored options for their customers. These are known as over the counter options (OTC) and are not tradeable instruments and can be cancelled only by agreement with the writer.

The types of traded options available are:

Stock options	– Options on equity securities.
Stock index options	– Options on a stock index.
Currency options	– Options to exchange two different currencies at a specified rate.

Interest rate options   – Options on interest rates.

Commodity options   – Options on commodities.

Most traded options are traded on the principal future exchanges mentioned in sections 5.21 and 5.22 on futures contracts. The option contracts available on the leading European commodity and financial futures and options exchanges covered in sections 5.21 and 5.22 are set out in Tables 5.26 to 5.31.

In addition to the futures exchanges dealt with above which also have option contracts there are the following option exchanges in Europe:

• **The London Traded Options Market** (LTOM) was established in 1978 as part of the International Stock Exchange (ISE). The options are for UK publicly listed equities and options on the FT-SE 100 index. The contract size for equities is usually for 1,000 shares and contracts are traded by open outcry. Premiums must be paid on the day following the trade and all bargains except for currency options are registered and settled at the London Options Clearing House Limited ('LOCH'). LTOM is in the process of merging with LIFFE (see section 5.22). Details of the contracts traded on LTOM are set out in Table 5.17.

• **Foreign currency OTC options** in the interbank market in London are usually traded on BBA terms for the London Interbank Currency Option Market (LICOM). When granted, a LICOM option can be designated as European or American.

• **The European Options Exchange** (EOE) in Amsterdam. The EOE has traded options on equities, currencies, government bonds, bond and stock indices and bullion. The trading cycle is quarterly with options for the closest two months available for currency options in Dutch gilders against sterling and the US dollar. All bargains are cleared through the European Option Clearing Corporation (EOCC) which is owned by the EOE and which guarantees the commitments and monitors the margin requirements of the EOE. Details of the option contracts traded on the EOE are set out in Table 5.18.

• **Swiss Options and Financial Futures Exchange** (SOFFEX). In May 1988, SOFFEX, a fully integrated electronic trading and clearing system for options commenced operations in Switzerland. SOFFEX trades options on the Swiss market index as well as a number of equities of major Swiss companies. The standard size of a contract is for five shares (due to the high price of most Swiss shares). The options are American with a maximum life of six months. There are standard expiry dates with an option expiring on the Saturday after the third Friday in any of the three months following the month of creation of the option. Details of the contracts traded on SOFFEX are set out in Table 5.19.

• *Deutsche Terminbörse* (DTB). In Germany options on major German and foreign stocks and options on German government bonds are traded on the Frankfurt and Dusseldorf stock exchanges, although the volume is low. In 1990 the DTB (see section 5.22) commenced trading equity options in a standard size of 50 shares. Details of the option contracts traded on DTB are set out in Table 5.20.

• *The Stockholm Options Market* (SOM) was established in 1985. The SOM offers options on Swedish and Norwegian shares, on an equity index (OMX) and currency options and futures denominated in deutschmarks and Swedish kroner, both against the US dollar. The 55 members of the SOM execute transactions on an electronic system which automatically clears the trades. The SOM has grown substantially with the OMX being one of the most liquid European stock index options. The SOM is owned by Swedish banks and futures and options brokers and its shares are listed on the Stockholm Stock Exchange. OM London, a wholly owned subsidiary of SOM, also trades the OMX option contract. A real time computer link with SOM means that the two exchanges (London and Stockholm) operate as a single marketplace with the contract having the same liquidity in each. OM London also trades Swedish and Norwegian equity options. Details of the option contracts traded on SOM are set out in Table 5.21.

• In France options on interest rates, white sugar and deutschmarks are traded on the MATIF (see Table 5.22). In addition the *Marche des Options Negociables de la Bourse de Paris* (MONEP) trades options on French equities (usually in 100 share lots) as well as the CAC 40 index. Details of the option contracts traded on MONEP are set out in Table 5.23.

• There are also option exchanges in Copenhagen, (*Guarantee Fund for Danish Options and Futures*) with contracts in mortgage bonds, government bonds, a stock index as well as options on Danish equities. In Helsinki the *Finnish Options Brokers* exchange has equity options and an index option. Details of these option contracts are set out in Tables 5.24 and 5.25 respectively.

Exchanges outside Europe

Options are traded on the leading United States futures exchanges and on the Chicago Board Options Exchange (CBOE), which is devoted solely to trading in options.

421

5.31 Option strategies

Options are versatile instruments and can be combined with themselves and the transaction which underlie them both speculatively and as hedges. The profit profile of such option strategies can be illustrated by diagrams which show how the profit made on an option at the exercise date varies with the price of the underlying transaction. The profit made on the option contract is given on the vertical axis and the price of the underlying transaction is shown on the horizontal axis. Set out below is the profit diagram for a purchased or 'long' call option.

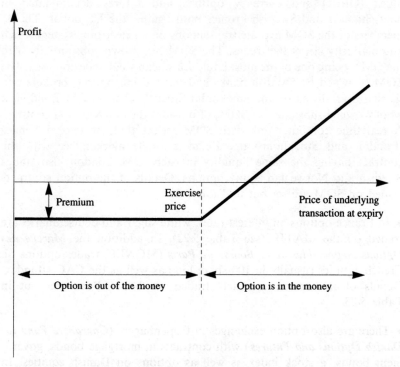

Diagram 5.1: Purchase of a call option

The diagram demonstrates that, while the option is out of the money (the price of the underlying asset is lower than the exercise or strike price) the loss of the investor is fixed at the premium paid. If, at the expiry date, the price of the underlying transaction is below the strike price, the option is out of the money and will not be exercised as the purchaser can buy the asset in the open market more cheaply than if he exercises the option. If the price of the underlying transaction rises above the strike price, the option is in the money and the purchaser will exercise the option and make a profit by buying the underlying transaction more cheaply than he can sell it in the open market (or will sell the option at a profit). The higher the price of the underlying transaction, the more profit the purchaser has made. By purchasing call options the holder has more leverage than buying the underlying transaction as a small increase in price of the underlying transaction will lead to a large increase in value of the option.

The profit profile of a written (or short) call is the inverse of the profile for the purchaser of the call. This can be shown as follows:

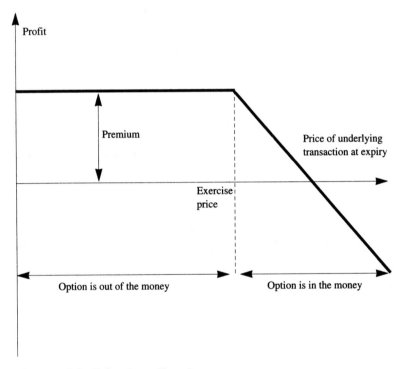

Diagram 5.2: Sale of a call option

The position of the writer of a 'naked' (or uncovered) call option on stock is unique in the sense that whereas the amount of income is fixed (the premium received), the potential downside is unlimited. This high risk strategy will generally be adopted by investors as an alternative to taking a short position in the underlying equity, where the investor does not consider that the anticipated fall in value of the equity will be sufficient to make going short profitable (the anticipated fall in value of the equity being less than the premium received). Writing a put option is a high risk strategy but the downside is limited to the value of the underlying transaction falling to nil.

The profiles for a long put option and a short put option are as follows:

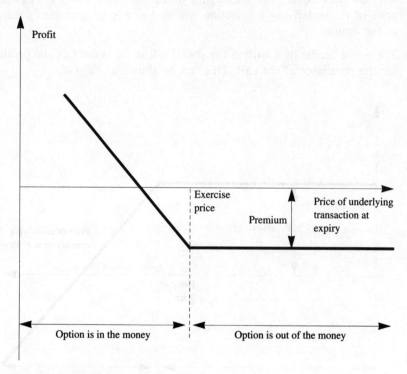

Diagram 5.3: Purchase of a put option

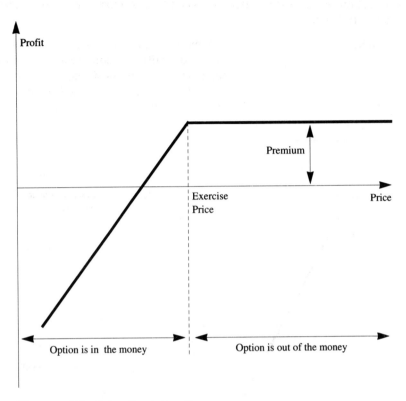

Diagram 5.4: Sale of a put option

If the underlying transaction price is higher than the strike price the purchaser will not exercise the option but will sell in the market, and lose the premium (which will be profit to the writer of the option). If at expiry the option is in the money (the market value of the underlying transaction is lower than the strike price) the purchaser can sell the asset for more than it will cost him to buy in the market. The profit is the difference between the market value and the strike price less the premium paid. The typical speculative purchaser of the put option has a bearish view on the equity price but does not want the exposure to price increases in the underlying transaction that arise from going short. The put writer is often a potential investor in the equity who expects the price of the stock to fall slightly so that he can buy it more cheaply.

These are the profit profiles for the basic positions which can be taken in options. These can be used as 'building blocks'; different option positions can be combined with each other or with the underlying transaction to develop 'strategies'. Amongst the most typical strategies are the following:

A simple hedge   A commodity producer knows that he will have a quantity of a commodity to sell in the market (a long position). To protect himself from falls in the market price of the commodity he buys a put option.

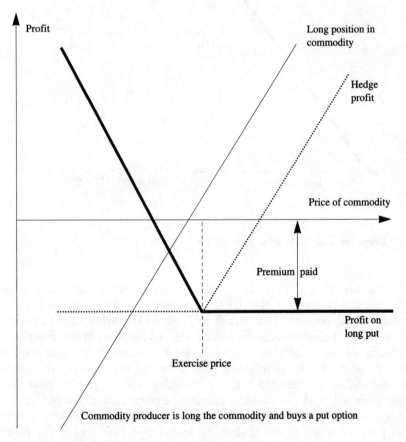

Diagram 5.5: A simple hedge

This strategy illustrates an important property of options: a position can be constructed in options and/or the underlying transaction to be equivalent to another position. In this example, the commodity producer has a long position in the underlying commodity (the production) and is long the put. The resulting profit profile is equivalent to being long in the call option. This strategy could be adopted by investors in other assets (eg shares) as a risk reduction strategy. However, (subject to any tax considerations) it would usually be more profitable to buy a call option (giving the same upside profit potential) and invest the cash, otherwise used to buy the shares, in high yielding debt securities.

Covered call   The purchase of the underlying trans-action (usually a share) and the sale of the related call option. The call option premium provides the investor in the underlying transaction with a degree of

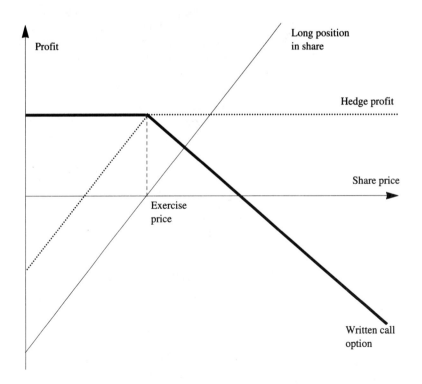

Diagram 5.6: A covered call

protection against a fall in price, but at the expense of limiting the potential profit if the price rises. Investors may use this strategy to enhance the short term yield on shares to be held long-term (by earning the premium) when they believe the market price is stable. As long term holders they are not interested in the appreciation in the value of the underlying transaction over the price of the option.

Synthetic future

This strategy exploits the equivalence of option positions referred to above by creating a combination of options which is equivalent to a position in the underlying transaction. For example, a synthetic long position can be created in ICI shares by buying the call option and selling the put option. If the market value rises, the investor takes his profit by exercising the call. If the market value falls, the holder of the put will exercise his option to put the shares to the writer of the option. Thus the investor has simulated all the economic conditions of buying the underlying ICI shares (other than the entitlement to a dividend). The cost of holding this position is minimal compared to the holding cost of the shares (being equal to any excess of the call option premium over the premium on the put). The difference between the synthetic position and owning the shares is the yield obtainable on the funds (which would otherwise be invested in the shares) if they were invested in a short term debt instrument, less the dividend yield on the underlying stock. Similarly, the investor can create a synthetic short position by selling the call option and buying the put.

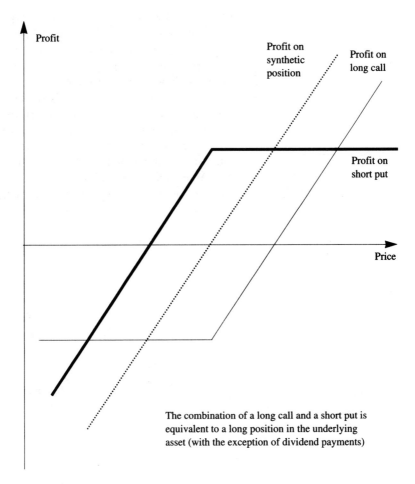

Diagram 5.7: A synthetic long position

Zero cost option

A variant on the synthetic future described above, whereby the investor equalises his positions in puts and calls so that the premium payable on the long position is equal to the premium receivable on the short position. This strategy enables banks to offer customers forward contracts at variable rates (such as Range Forwards dealt with in section 5.72) without an up-front premium. The bank will use American options which expire on or around the date of the forward contract.

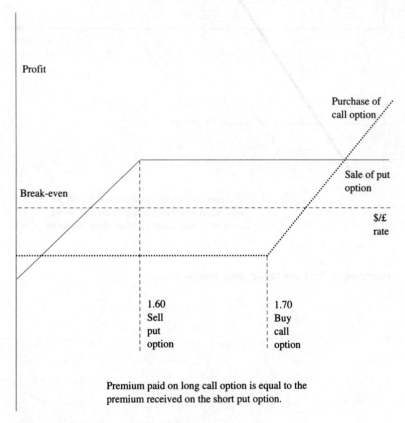

Premium paid on long call option is equal to the premium received on the short put option.

Diagram 5.8: Zero cost option strategy

Long straddle

The simultaneous purchase of a call option and a put option with the same strike price and expiry date. This strategy will be appropriate where the investor believes that the market is extremely volatile and liable to move considerably in either direction. If there is not a large price movement, this strategy will not be successful because the investor has purchased two options and at least one is virtually certain to expire worthless, with the resulting loss of the premium.

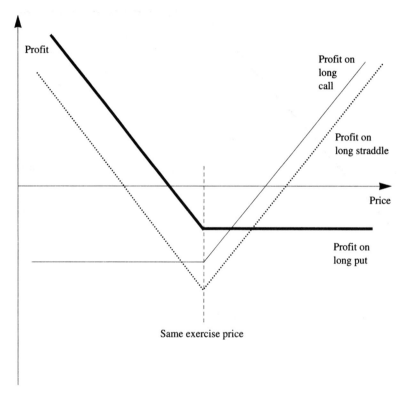

Diagram 5.9: A long straddle

Short straddle

This is the opposite of the long straddle, the sale of a call option and a put option with the same exercise and expiry terms. A user of this strategy would be expecting only small price fluctuations, that is, low volatility. The strategy is most profitable if the price of the underlying asset is equal to the strike price of the options on the expiry date.

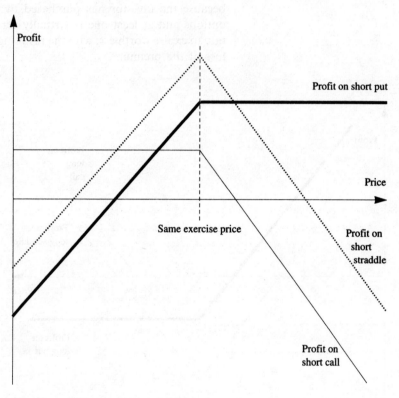

Profit

Profit on short put

Price

Same exercise price

Profit on short straddle

Profit on short call

Diagram 5.10: A short straddle

Options strategies involving the combination of two or more positions at different strike prices or for different expiry dates are called spreads.

Bull spread

The purchase of a call option with a relatively low exercise price and the sale of a call option with a relatively high exercise price. This strategy would be adopted by an investor who is only moderately bullish.

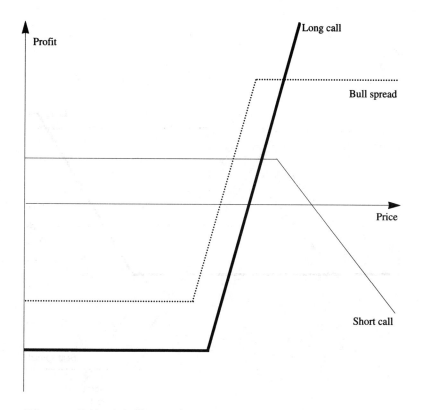

Diagram 5.11: A bull spread

Bear spread

The sale of a call option with a low exercise price and the purchase of a call option with a high exercise price. This strategy would be used by an investor who wants to earn the premium for writing a call option but wants to limit the downside risk. As the investor profits if prices fall this is known as a bear spread.

433

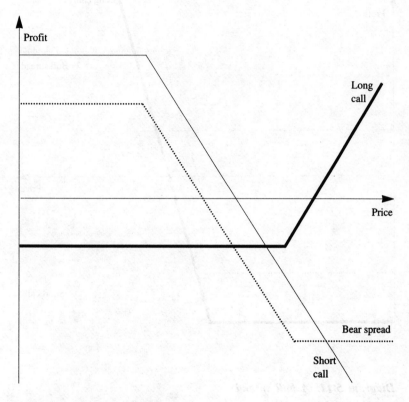

Diagram 5.12: A bear spread

Butterfly spread

By combining a bear spread and a bull spread the investor can take advantage of a market which he expects to remain close to the present market price, whilst limiting the risk of loss from large price movements.

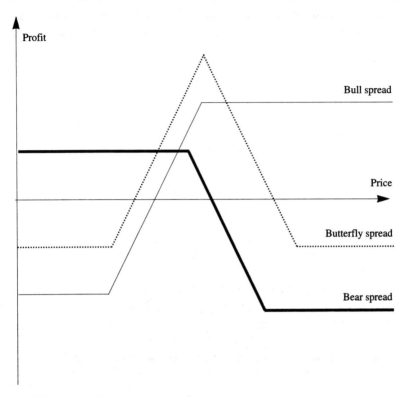

Diagram 5.13: A butterfly spread

There are also long and short strangles, and ratio spreads, as well as more complex strategies based on combinations of options and futures.

5.32 Pricing of options

The overall price of an option is the sum of its intrinsic value and its time value.

Intrinsic value

The intrinsic value of an option is the benefit to the holder if he were to exercise the option immediately. At the time of expiry of the option the value of the option is its intrinsic value and will be determined from a comparison of the difference between the market value of the underlying transaction and the exercise price of the option. For in the money options, the intrinsic value of the option is the difference between the market value of the underlying transaction and the strike price of the option.

For a call option, this can be shown as follows:

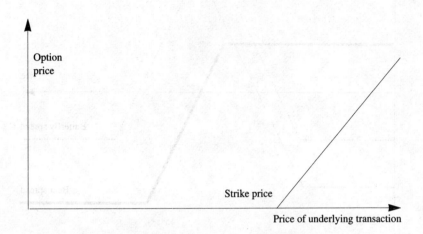

Diagram 5.14: The intrinsic value of an option at expiry

For at the money or out of the money options the intrinsic value is nil. The intrinsic value of an option can never be less than nil. For example, when the market price is below the strike price a call option will not be exercised and the owner of such an option will obtain no benefit.

Time value

The time value is the difference between the market value of the option and its intrinsic value. For an in the money call option, the time value can be calculated as follows:

Call option time value = option price + strike price
– price of underlying transaction.

For example, if the market value of ICI ordinary shares is 360p, and the market value of the ICI January 350p call option on the London Traded Options Market is 30p, the time value is 20p (30 + 350 – 360). Alternatively, the time value can be described as the call option price (30p) less the intrinsic value of 10p (360 – 350). For an out of the money option, the time value represents the whole of the value of the option premium as the intrinsic value is nil. Amongst the factors which determine the time value of an option are:

• The proximity of the market value of the underlying transaction to the strike price of the option. At any time an option will have the greatest time value if the price of the underlying transaction is equal to the strike price of the option and it will decrease if the option moves either deeply in to or out of the money. This is illustrated in the following diagram of the time value of a call option for a range of different values of the underlying transaction:

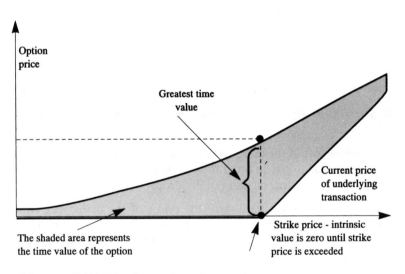

Diagram 5.15: The time value of an option

• The remaining life to expiry – the time value of an option will decrease over its life as the risk of the writer of the option diminishes. At expiry, the time value will be nil. The rate of decay of the time value increases the closer the option comes to expiry, as can be seen in the following diagram:

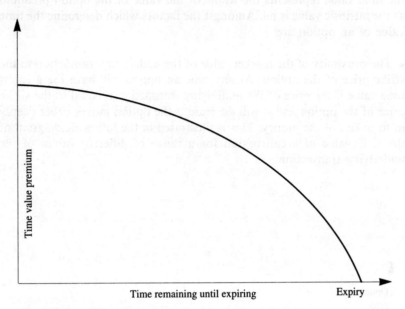

Time remaining until expiring   Expiry

The diagram assumes that the price of the
underlying transaction remains constant.

Diagram 5.16: The rate of decay of the time value of an option

● The holding cost of the underlying transaction – the amount of interest
that the writer has to pay in order to cover the option, net of any receipts
from the underlying transaction (eg dividends or coupons).

● The perceived future volatility of the prices of the underlying transaction – the greater the volatility, the higher will be the premium demanded by the writer of the option to compensate for the greater risk of
unfavourable price movements.

Option pricing models

In practice, investment banks and professional investors will use computer models to value options, based on differing option valuation
theories and volatility factors. These models attempt to determine the 'fair
value' of an option. This fair value is used as a basis for pricing an OTC
option which a bank or options dealer offers to its customer as well as
a method of calculating whether or not a traded option is under or
overpriced (the market price of a traded option will be determined by
supply and demand factors operating in the market). If an option is
underpriced relative to its fair value, buying the option will usually be the
best way to establish a position in the underlying asset. If the option is

438

overpriced, the sale of the option (either on a covered or an uncovered basis) should provide the investor with a better return than through taking a position in the underlying asset or through purchasing options.

Black-Scholes model

The option pricing model which has gained widest acceptance in the market was developed by F Black and M Scholes for the valuation of European call options (1973 'The Pricing of Options and Corporate Liabilities' Journal of Political Economy) . This model was developed for the valuation of options on shares, and is still widely used. This and other models which have been developed subsequently are based on the concept of the riskless or neutral hedge. This concept is derived from the risk equivalence of the combinations of positions in options and the underlying transaction which was shown in section 5.31 on option strategies. The riskless hedge concept requires that, subject to a number of assumptions, a perfectly hedged position consisting of a long position in an underlying stock and a short position in options on that stock (or a long position on the options and a short position in the stock) can be constructed. This position is perfectly hedged because, for a range of stock prices close to the current price, any profit resulting from the increase in price of the stock would be offset by a loss on the option, and vice versa. In this way, options can completely eliminate market risk from a stock portfolio. If there were no transaction costs, the hedged position could be amended constantly to keep the portfolio risk-free. Therefore, the option premium at which the hedge yields a pretax rate of return equivalent to the risk free rate is the fair value of the option.

Example of Black-Scholes model

The Black-Scholes model is mathematically complex, but the riskless hedge concept can be shown using the following example:

Suppose that the ordinary shares of ABC plc are trading at £5 per share, and the price of the shares can rise or fall in each year by only £1. An investor wishes to establish the fair value a European call option with a strike price of £3 which expires at the end of the year. To construct the riskless hedge, a portfolio long one share and hedged by short positions in call options has to be constructed. The number of calls required to do this is calculated as follows:

> The price of the share is currently £5. At the end of the year the price can rise to £6 or fall to £4. If the price rises to £6, the writer of the option will lose £3 (6-3). If the price falls to £4 the writer will lose £1. The number of calls required ('C') for a riskless portfolio can be calculated by equating the two possible price movements:

$6 - (C \times 3) = 4 - (C \times 1)$

Therefore, the number of calls (C) = 1

This portfolio is riskless because if the share price rises to £6, the total value of the portfolio will be £3, that is equal to the value of the share (£6), less the loss on the call option of £3. Similarly, if the share price falls to £4, the value of the share of £4 will be offset by a loss on the call option of £1, a total value for the portfolio of £3. If the share price remains at £5 the total value of the portfolio is also £3 (share price £5 less loss on call option of £2 (5-3)).

As this portfolio is risk free, it must earn the equivalent of the risk free rate of interest (if it did not, arbitrage would bring it into line).

Therefore the portfolio must have a value at the beginning of the year equal to its closing value discounted at the risk free rate of interest. However the cost of the portfolio is also equal to the price paid for the share less the premium received for the call option ('P'). If the risk free rate of interest for the period is 10% the premium for the option can be calculated as follows:

$$\frac{3}{1.10} = (5 - P)$$

Therefore, P, the premium on the call is £2.27

The most important assumptions which have been made in the above example are:

• the call option has European exercise terms and no dividends are paid on the underlying share;

• transaction costs have been ignored;

• a single risk free interest rate for the period to expiry of the option is used. Investors cannot usually borrow and lend at the same rate.

The example can be expanded to cover more time periods and by making these periods very short the result would be continuous price changes rather than discrete movements. This is the basis of Black-Scholes model. However the model still assumes that:

• share prices are a random variable in continuous time, and that the percentage of change in price has a normal probability distribution (or more exactly lognormal). However, empirical evidence indicates that share price distributions are not normal;

• future price behaviour (or 'volatility') can be predicted from past price changes (ie, volatility is stable). In practice, the quality and relevance of

440

the volatility assumptions and the historical data used are the key features which distinguish different option models.

Other option pricing models

Various other models (eg Cox's constant elasticity of variance diffusion formula) have been developed to attempt to overcome the perceived limitations of the Black-Scholes model. These models make use of different processes to simulate price behaviour but on the whole they provide no better predictions. The Black-Scholes model provides accurate prices for near or at the money options with medium or greater maturity. It is less good for pricing out of the money or in the money options, those with short maturities and when there are changes in volatility.

The models also provide measures of how option premiums vary over the short term with changes in the price of the underlying transaction, its volatility and the maturity of the option. These measures are all mathematical derivatives of the pricing formula and include:

- Delta

  The change in the premium given a one unit change in the price of the underlying transaction (ie the derivative of the premium with respect to price of the underlying transaction). Delta can range from 0 (deep out of the money options) to 1 (deep in the money options) for calls and from 0 (deep out of the money options) to −1 (deep in the money options) for puts.

- Gamma

  This is the derivative of delta with respect to the underlying transaction price (or the second derivative of the premium) and indicates how quickly delta changes with price movements.

Pricing of options on debt instruments and currency options

The basics of option pricing described above was for options on shares. The assumptions used in the models have to be amended when considering options on other assets. In particular:

- Options on debt instruments. Most debt instruments unlike ordinary shares have a fixed or finite life. Therefore, it cannot be assumed that the prices of debt instruments are random variables as a bond's price will move towards par (assuming the issuer's credit status is not in question) as it approaches its maturity date. In addition, price movements are dependant on interest rates, and this has to be taken account of in calculating price volatility.

- Currency options. The assumption that currency price distributions are lognormal is difficult to maintain in many circumstances, particularly where central bank intervention affects exchange rates. In addition, the existence of a very liquid forward foreign exchange market has an impact on currency option prices.

5.33 Benefits – purchaser

• Options are highly geared instruments. If market movements are favourable, speculative purchasers can make considerable profits on the basis of a small investment (the premium) and limit their potential loss to the non-recovery of the premium.

• Options are attractive to users who are attempting to hedge future commitments which are uncertain. The hedger can, for the price of the premium, retain more control over the hedge. If the future commitment does not materialise and the price moves unfavourably, the purchaser can avoid creating an exposure by allowing the option to expire at the cost of the premium. However, should the price move favourably a profit can be made to offset the cost of the premium.

5.34 Benefits – option writer

• A holder of the underlying commodity or financial instrument can increase returns at no additional up-front cost by writing a covered call option. The premium received is additional income and providing any price increase of the underlying instrument over the strike price is less than the premium, there will be increased income and no loss of capital gain.

• If the market moves as expected, and the option remains out of the money until expiry, the writer of a naked option will make a profit (the amount of the premium) without having made any capital outlay.

5.35 Risks and disadvantages – purchaser

• Whilst investors in other assets such as equity and debt may lose a proportion of their capital if the market value of the asset falls, they are

442

unlikely to lose all their capital except in the event of the issuer becoming insolvent or being in serious financial difficulty. However, an option can lose all its value (the premium paid), if it is out of the money at or near its expiry date.

- The premium has to be paid up front giving a cash flow disadvantage. This may be reduced by 'delta' margins now operated by some clearing houses.

- If rates move favourably the premium will be a cost for which, with hindsight, no benefit has been obtained.

5.36 Risks and disadvantages – option writer

- Where an investor writes a covered call or put option and subsequently the market moves so that the option is in the money, the holder of the option will exercise the call or put. This means that the writer of the option will forego the opportunity to benefit from movements in the price of the underlying transaction beyond the strike price.

- If the market moves to a significant extent the writer of a naked call or put can suffer substantial losses. Where the investor has written a naked call, and the underlying price rises substantially above the strike price, to satisfy the commitment under the call the asset will have to be purchased in the market at the current market price. Similarly, where the investor writes a put and the price of the underlying asset falls below the strike price, there will be a commitment to purchase the asset from the holder of the option at above the new market price.

- With an American style option there will be uncertainty as to the exercise date which could give rise to a problem in meeting the commitment if the underlying instrument is not readily available.

5.37 Accounting questions

- The market value of an option contract is the sum of the intrinsic value and time value. The price correlation with the underlying transaction which is being hedged is reflected in the intrinsic value. The time value is the cost to the hedger of insuring over the life of the option against any loss in value of the underlying transaction. Is it more appropriate to amortise the time value over the life of the option or to recognise profits and losses arising from the changes in the whole of the market value of the option at the same time that profits and losses on the underlying transaction are recognised?

● Assets and liabilities which are being hedged may be carried at market value or at the lower of cost and market value, depending on the nature of the asset or liability and the accounting policies adopted by the enterprise. Is it appropriate to amortise the time value of an option where the underlying asset or liability is carried at market value, or should the whole of the option be marked to market?

● Where an option contract is closed out prior to the maturity of the underlying transaction, should any unamortised amount of time value be taken to the profit and loss account immediately or should it be treated as an adjustment to the value of the item being hedged? If the contract is closed out, does this mean that the hedge is no longer required (and that hedge accounting treatment is no longer appropriate)?

● Where an option contract is closed out prior to the maturity of the underlying transaction, should the profit or loss arising be taken immediately, spread over the remaining life or deferred until the maturity of the underlying transaction?

● Correlation between the price of the underlying asset and the option is reflected in changes in the intrinsic value of the option. Where an option is out of the money (and therefore does not have any intrinsic value), is it still appropriate to apply hedge accounting?

● One of the uses of options is to hedge contingent events. On the assumption that there is a high probability of the underlying transaction occurring, is it prudent to carry forward the option premium or should the whole of the premium be written off immediately? What is the appropriate treatment if the probability of the underlying transaction occurring reduces?

● Is hedge accounting appropriate for written as well as purchased options?

● Where an enterprise marks to market its assets and positions, is this treatment appropriate for OTC as well as for traded options? Are option pricing formulae or models used for the OTC options a reliable substitute for market prices obtained in the liquid markets for traded options?

● What is the most appropriate accounting policy for premiums received on options written? Should they be deferred, amortised or immediately recognised as income or some combination of these?

● Sections 5.140 to 5.173 at the end of this chapter set out the accounting treatment for options in various countries in Europe.

444

5.38 Taxation questions

• Do special tax rules apply if options are quoted on a recognised exchange?

• If the option is not part of a trading activity are profits taxable as capital gains?

• Is a tax deduction available for the cost of an option if it is not exercised?

• Should a synthetic future be treated as a future or as separate option contracts?

• Do matching put and call options create an immediate disposal for tax purposes?

• Should other synthetics created by a combination of options be treated according to their economic effect or on their constituent parts?

• Should a bank or other financial services company (or an organisation which regularly undertakes option contracts) seek prior approval of the tax authorities to marking to market as an acceptable accounting policy for tax purposes?

• If a bank or other financial services company adopts a 'realisation basis' should receipts for writing options be recognised as taxable income on receipt or on an amortisation basis?

• Can a non-financial services company adopt its accounting treatment for tax purposes, or must profits and losses be adjusted onto a realised basis?

• What is the appropriate VAT treatment?

• See also general taxation questions in section 5.7.

5.39 Warrants

Warrants confer on the holder the right, but not the obligation, to purchase or sell a fixed amount of an underlying asset at a fixed price and at a fixed future date. They are similar to over the counter options in many respects, but have the following distinguishing characteristics:

• options, particularly traded options, are generally for a shorter maturity than warrants. Generally warrants have one to three year exercise periods although longer periods are possible;

• options usually grant rights over assets which are currently available;

For example, the exercise of a traded ICI call option requires the writer of the option to purchase existing shares on the open market to satisfy the contract; it does not lead to the creation of new equity. The exercise of a warrant issued by a company will usually lead to the creation of new equity capital in that company. Consequently, the existing shareholders may suffer dilution as a result of the exercise of warrants.

In recent years there has been a considerable increase in the range of warrants available. Many are attached to Eurobond issues as 'sweeteners' to persuade investors to accept low yields on the bonds. Eurobond warrants can be similar to either European options (exercisable only at one specific time) or American options (exercisable at any time). They can also have delayed exercise terms where the investor is prevented from exercising the warrant until a specified date (a European exercise period followed by a period of American exercise). More recently investment banks have issued warrants on stock exchange indices, baskets of equities, currencies and commodities (eg oil).

Types and variations of warrants

Detachable warrants	Detachable equity and debt warrants were the most common type of warrant. They are issued as part of a host bond and are detachable immediately and can be traded in the secondary market as separate instruments. These warrants entitle the holder to purchase new equity or debt of the issuer and act as a 'sweetener' to the investor to reduce the cost of debt. The cost of debt is reduced because the original investor in the bond will accept a lower coupon in return for a separately tradeable asset. These warrant issues are dealt with further in chapter 2 – Debt Instruments and chapter 4 – Equity and Equity Linked Instruments.
Window warrants	Warrants which can be exercised only during a specified period in the life of a host bond (the 'window').
Harmless warrants	Warrants are issued with a host bond and are exercisable into new debt of the issuer. These warrants are described as harmless because they will be exercisable only up to the date that the host bond is callable, allowing the issuer to avoid a permanent increase of the total debt outstanding. The bond can be callable at the end of or during the exercise period. In addition, the bond into which the

warrant can be exercised usually carries a lower coupon than the original host bond. For example, a company issues a five-year 12% bond callable in three years with warrants which can be exercised in the three year period to the call date into a new five-year, 10% bond. The warrants could be detached and sold to investors who believe that in three years interest rates will have fallen to below 10%. The issuer has the option to call the host bond in three years time only if the warrants are exercised. The issuer can use the proceeds of the warrants to reduce the cost of the issue, but the option to call the debt and refinance at the call date if interest rates have fallen is relinquished.

Wedding warrants	Similar to a harmless warrant except that prior to the call date on the host bond, the warrant can be exercised only if the host bond is also surrendered. The concept was introduced because most harmless warrants were issued with American exercise terms which could result in an increase in the issuer's outstanding debt for the period from exercise of warrant to the call date for the host bond.
Puttable warrants	Puttable warrants give the investor the right to put (or sell) the warrant back to the issuer at a fixed price enabling the risk to be limited. They are also known as redeemable warrants.
Income warrants	Income warrants pay interest based on the issue price of the warrant up to the date of exercise.
Money back warrants	The investor has the option to put the warrants back to the issuer at either a percentage of, or the full amount of the issue price. The warrant can be priced higher on issue as the investor has greater security. The issuer reduces the borrowing cost on the host bond by having the use of the warrant proceeds interest free until the warrant is either exercised or put back to the issuer.
Naked warrants	Such warrants are issued separately and not as part of a bond issue. Naked warrants can be issued either by investment banks (see 'currency/interest rate/commodity warrants' below) or by corporates to reduce the borrowing costs of earlier issues, where the warrants have an exercise period which corresponds to the call feature of that earlier issue. For example, Company A has an outstanding bond issue with a 12% coupon which is to

mature in 1995 and is callable from 1991. Sometime after the bond issue Company A could issue a warrant which is exercisable from 1991 into 10% bonds which mature in 1995. If interest rates do not fall below 10%, Company A has in effect reduced its borrowing costs by the amount of the proceeds of the warrant issue.

Cross currency warrants

Warrants which allow the investor to convert from the original bond issue into an issue in a different currency. This type of warrant, also termed a dual currency warrant, offers investors a hedge against the risk of currency depreciation.

Covered warrants

Covered warrants are not issued by a corporate as part of a bond or equity issue but are usually issued by investment banks and grant the investor the right to purchase equity or debt in a third party. The investment bank guarantees to the investor that the assets (eg shares of a company or a group of different companies so called 'basket warrants') will be made available on exercise of the warrant. The financial standing of the issuer of such warrants is therefore crucial. The consent of the third party will not necessarily have been obtained. These instruments are also called conversion equity warrants.

Currency/ interest rate/ commodity warrants

Currency/interest rate/commodity warrants entitle the holder to acquire a currency at a fixed rate, a fixed interest security (usually government securities) or a specific commodity at a future date. These warrants are similar to traded options in that they have standardised terms (premiums, strike prices and expiry periods) but transactions are conducted OTC rather than through a recognised exchange. In addition, they generally have longer periods to expiry than conventional options. These warrants have become popular with a number of issues each month. They are usually issued by investment banks who will hedge their commitment and there are an increasing range of these warrants. The profit to the investment bank is the difference between the proceeds of the issue and the cost of the hedge. Such warrants may also be callable by the issuing investment bank at a fixed price ('callable warrants') and may be issued with offsetting put and call tranches.

Equity index warrants

These warrants are similar to the currency/interest rate/commodity warrants above except that they are based on a stock exchange equity index. Such warrants have been developed for countries where there is no exchange traded option contract.

5.40 Pricing of warrants

Warrants are usually priced using the models developed for options (section 5.32). However, due to the differences between warrants and options noted above these models are less useful particularly where warrants have long maturities. The longer maturities of warrants mean that assumptions regarding dividend and interest rates can be unrealistic.

5.41 Benefits – investor/purchaser

• Warrants are bearer instruments which gives the investor the advantage of anonymity.

• Warrants are highly geared instruments and the profit potential can be a large multiple of the initial capital outlay if the warrants move into the money. This can make warrants very attractive to investors as a speculative tool.

• Some warrant markets are very liquid enabling the ready realisation of gains.

5.42 Benefits – issuer/writer

• The issue of a warrant can reduce the costs of a debt issue, both by providing the investor with a 'sweetener' which will usually lower the coupon rate, and from the use of the proceeds received from the warrants.

• The issue can raise additional funds by granting a contingent right which can either be hedged with other instruments or satisfied by an issue of debt or equity in the future.

• If properly hedged (or there are offsetting tranches) the issuer (writer) can make a profit from the pricing of the warrants (eg bid offer spread) by providing the investor (purchaser) with an option which would not otherwise be available. An active market can also result in additional income from trading profits and commission.

5.43 Risks and disadvantages – investor/purchaser

• The volatility of warrant prices can cause them to lose value very quickly once out of the money. Price movements can be very large within one day and the bid/offer spread is wide.

• Many warrants have European exercise terms which may make them inflexible.

• Except for income warrants, an investor does not receive any income to fund the investment in a warrant.

• The holder of an equity warrant foregoes any dividend payments and the warrants will become less valuable as dividends grow and the higher the dividend yield.

• As for options in section 5.35.

5.44 Risks and disadvantages – issuer/writer

• Warrants are bearer instruments and therefore potential predators could use equity warrants to build up a large undisclosed stake in the enterprise issuing the warrants prior to a takeover bid. Such a stake could also be used to prevent or restrict a corporate restructuring.

• The risks with warrants (particularly currency and interest rate warrants) may not be easy to hedge.

• It may be difficult to judge in advance of the issue how saleable the warrants attached to a bond issue will be. This could lead to the issue being mispriced.

• Existing shareholders may suffer dilution of earnings following the exercise of equity warrants.

• As for options in section 5.36.

5.45 Accounting questions

Issuer

• See bonds with bond warrants – chapter 2 – Debt Instruments.

• See debt with equity warrants – chapter 4 – Equity and Equity Linked Instruments.

• As for options – see section 5.37.

Investor

• As for options – see section 5.37.

5.46 Taxation questions

• See bonds with bond warrants – chapter 2 – Debt Instruments.

• See debt with equity warrants – chapter 4 – Equity and Equity Linked Instruments.

• See questions on options in section 5.38.

Forwards, futures and options products

5.47 Introduction

With increasingly volatile interest and exchange rates and a rapid expansion in international trade, banks have been seeking to offer products to their customers which have the benefits of forwards, futures and options but with fewer risks and disadvantages.

The problem for users of forwards or futures contracts is the risk that prices (rates) may move favourably and that if they lock into a forward contract they will have lost the opportunity for increased profits. The obvious answer would appear to be the option contract but this involves a premium, often payable in advance. If rates move favourably then the treasurer will be accused of incurring unnecessary costs in addition to having to justify the adverse cash flow consequences of payment of the premium up front. Consequently while, in effect, such a premium is an insurance and perhaps should be treated as a necessary expense, it is not always viewed that way.

Banks have designed a range of products derived from forwards, futures and options contracts principally to be used to hedge against foreign currency exposure. Many of these products are sold with no premiums payable and allowing participation in potential gains. All have a cost, usually in the eventual price (exchange or interest rate) given to the user. Before using such a product users should ensure that they understand the product and confirm that it matches their needs. In general terms, if rates are expected to move in the company's favour use an option (or option product) to protect the downside and if they are expected to move against, use a forward contract to lock in the price. Options should be used only if the expected movement is more than the option cost but out of the money options with little or no cost could provide a degree of insurance particularly against large adverse movements.

In the following sections a number of the products designed by banks to overcome the problems are explained. In most cases they are combinations of forwards and/or options sold in a convenient packaged form. Forward rate agreements, and interest rate caps, floors and collars are all designed to hedge against movements in interest rates. The other products are hedges against currency fluctuations.

5.48 General accounting questions

A number of general accounting questions apply to the products in the following sections:

• Should any premium paid at the time of the purchase of an option be spread over the life of the instrument, written off at the time of purchase or written off at the date of exercise or expiry?

• How should the price received by the writer be taken into income? Is part of the price an arrangement fee rather than a premium? Should the income be deferred to be set off against any losses at expiry or amortised over the life of the option ?

• For currency related products should they be analysed into their currency parts so that the interest rate related component be treated as a financing cost?

• For interest rate products, is the price an expense or an adjustment to interest charges or income?

• Should the products be marked to market if traded and, if so, how should market prices be determined?

5.49 General taxation questions

A number of general taxation questions apply to the products in the following sections:

• Section 5.7 sets out general taxation questions for hedging instruments. The crucial question is whether the tax treatment of the hedge mirrors that of the risk being hedged. If it does not the risk is not properly hedged on an after tax basis.

• Does the taxation treatment of any premium follow the accounting treatment?

• When is income recognised for tax purposes?

• Are the costs of entering into such agreements tax deductible, particularly to special category companies (eg holding companies)?

5.50 Forward rate agreement (FRA)

A forward (or future) rate agreement (FRA) is similar to an interest rate future in that it is a contract in which two parties agree the interest rate to be paid on a notional deposit of specified maturity on a specific future date. The deposit is purely notional and no borrowing or lending takes place. The contract enables the purchaser to fix interest costs for a specific (usually short) future period. At the settlement date, which occurs at the inception of the period of the notional deposit for sterling and two days later for US dollars, the seller pays the purchaser for any increase in rates over the agreed rate and if rates have fallen the purchaser pays the seller. The amount of the settlement is discounted (at the interest rate ruling at value date) because payment occurs at the beginning of the deposit period. The principal amounts subject to the agreement are not exchanged. The amount payable on settlement is calculated from the following formula:

$$S = \frac{P \times (L - R) \times D}{100 \times B} \times \frac{1}{\left(1 + \dfrac{L \times D}{B \times 100}\right)}$$

453

where:

S = Settlement amount

P = Notional deposit

L = LIBOR on settlement date for the deposit period

R = Contract interest rate

B = Days used to calculate interest (365 for sterling, 360 for US dollars and other currencies)

D = Number of contract days of notional deposit

For example Company A wishes to hedge the interest rate payable on a six months loan of $5 million which it has to take out in six months time (on 1 July 19X1). On 1 January 19X1, Bank B sells a six-twelve FRA (six months LIBOR in six months time) to Company A at 10%. On the settlement date, 1 July 19X1 six months LIBOR is 12%, Bank B pays Counterparty A the interest rate differential which is calculated, using the above formula, as follows:

$$\$5 \text{ million} \times \frac{12-10}{100} \times \frac{181}{360} \times \frac{1}{1 + \frac{12}{100} \times \frac{181}{360}} = \$47,417$$

Conversely, if 6 months LIBOR on 1 July was 8%, Company A would pay $48,334 to Bank B.

Variations

Interest rate future	See financial futures section 5.22.
Forward/forward deposit	One party contracts to make a deposit with the other party at a future date at a predetermined rate. Unlike a FRA, principal is exchanged.
Forward Spread Agreement (FSA)	A contract to hedge the spread between comparable rates in different currencies one of which is the US dollar. The transaction is similar to a currency swap and its simpler documentation may make it more useful in the short term market. The FSA is intended to hedge the risk of rising interest rates in the currency in which a liability is denominated with a decrease in which an asset is denominated.

Long Dated Forward Rate Agreement (LDFRA)	A FRA entered into to fix interest costs for future dates in excess of periods normally available in the FRA market. This instrument is an alternative to the forward swap. The LDFRA is a recent development and the market is illiquid.
Serial (or strip) FRAs	A series of FRAs to lock in an interest rate over a number of interest rate reset dates. The effect of the transaction is the same as an interest rate swap.
Interest Rate Guarantee (IRG)	An IRG is effectively an option on an FRA. The buyer of an IRG pays a fee in exchange for the right but not the obligation to fix an interest rate in a future interest period. See also interest rate cap in section 5.56.

5.51 The FRA market

Some of the more important characteristics of the FRA market are as follows:

• unlike interest rate futures contracts, FRAs are traded on an OTC market. The FRA is used widely in the interbank market, and increasingly by corporate customers;

• the market is centred in London (which accounts for some 40% of the market), principally due to its close links with the Eurodollar deposit market. New York is the second largest market;

• the largest market is in US dollar FRAs (some 60% to 70%) and the second largest is in sterling. There are also active markets in deutschmarks, yen and Swiss francs and FRAs in Australian dollars, New Zealand dollars, French francs and ECU are also available;

• most contracts are in the one month to one year period, although it is possible to get quotations up to five years (see LDFRAs above);

• there are only a small number of banks who quote two way prices in FRAs on a continuous basis (mainly the larger United Kingdom 'clearing' and United States 'money centre' banks). Most banks will quote prices for FRAs to their corporate customers. FRAs are also available from brokers;

455

- the market has an annual turnover estimated at $400 to $500 billion;

- the average contract size (based on the value of the notional principal) is approximately $10 million in the US dollar market and £5 million in the sterling market, and contracts as small as $1 million and as large as $1.5 billion have been arranged. The most liquid market is in FRAs with standard size and maturity (whole months). The bid/offer spread is 5 to 10 basis points;

- the British Bankers Association have specified standard contract terms for FRAs (FRABBA terms) and these apply to all contracts in the interbank market unless the counterparties explicitly agree otherwise. The use of standard contract terms has assisted the liquidity of the market;

- FRAs are priced by reference to the nearest available futures contract and the price reflects the cost of hedging in the futures or cash markets. The prices are quoted as an interest rate and no premium is payable;

- FRAs are quoted in terms of six-twelve, three-six etc, where the first date is the start date (settlement date) and the second the maturity date of the notional deposit. A six-twelve FRA starts in six months time and runs for six months.

5.52 Benefits

- Simple and flexible way of fixing future interest rates.

- Unlike financial futures contracts there are no margin calls to be made, and therefore no funding costs are involved in using FRAs.

- Use of an FRA avoids the administrative costs of monitoring margin calls which is required for financial futures contracts.

- The user of an FRA is not exposed to any basis risk (the difference between prices in the cash and the futures market).

- The instrument can often be tailored to the user's precise requirements in terms of settlement date, maturity date, principal and interest rate to be hedged and, unlike a futures contract, is not standardised.

- FRAs are available in currencies in which there are no financial futures contracts.

- An FRA does not involve the movement of principal and therefore is efficient in the use of capital and credit lines and the credit risk is limited to the interest differential payment. A FRA does not appear on the balance sheet.

5.53 Risks and disadvantages

• FRAs are not transferable and there is no central market place so liquidation is possible only by agreement to cancel or by an offsetting transaction.

• Compared with financial futures contracts the spread in bid and offer rates can be wide although increasing competition has reduced spreads.

• There is a risk that the counterparty may not perform at the maturity of the contract. Unlike financial futures contracts, there is no clearing house to guarantee performance. However, the credit risk is limited to the interest differential payment as principal is not exchanged.

• FRAs are not available in all currencies (although it may be possible to create one using a different currency FRA and a forward foreign exchange contract).

5.54 Accounting questions

• How is the cash settlement at maturity to be treated? Is it a one off profit or loss or should it be amortised?

• If no fee is paid but a margin is included in the specified rate in the FRA how should this be treated?

• Sections 5.140 to 5.173 at the end of this chapter set out the accounting treatment for FRAs in various countries in Europe.

5.55 Taxation questions

• Can a non-trading company (eg a holding company) obtain tax relief for the cost of a FRA?

• For tax purposes should the recipient recognise any fee as income upon receipt or spread it over the period of the agreement?

• Can the cash settlement be paid without withholding tax?

• See also questions on forward contracts in section 5.17.

5.56 Interest rate cap

An interest rate cap (or interest rate guarantee) is an agreement stating that on prescribed future date or dates if the prevailing interest rate, as determined by a pre-specified interest rate index (eg LIBOR), is above a strike rate specified in advance, the seller will pay the buyer an amount equal to the additional interest cost until the next reference date based on an agreed amount of notional principal. The writer of the cap receives a fee (or premium) which is paid up front by the purchaser. The purchaser specifies the interest rate index, the time period and the notional principal.

For example, Bank A sells a 3-year cap to Corporation B on a notional principal amount of $10 million where the underlying index is 3-month LIBOR and the strike rate is 10%. The agreement is effective from 1 January 19X1, with the strike rate fixed quarterly and payment made quarterly in arrears. Bank A will make payments to Corporation B in any quarter over the 3-year life of the agreement when 3-month LIBOR is greater than 10%. If on 31 March 19X2, 3-month LIBOR is 12%, Bank A will pay the following amount to Corporation B:

$$\$10 \text{ million} \times \frac{(12 - 10)}{100} \times \frac{91}{360} = \$50,556$$

Some of the more important general characteristics of the interest rate cap market are as follows:

● caps are mainly denominated in US dollars although markets exist in other currencies such as sterling and yen;

● caps are sold usually by banks to corporate customers. They are tailored for each customer and are not traded;

● caps have been sold with maturities ranging between three months to 12 years. The range of maturities was increased when investment banks arranged the issue of capped FRNs (see chapter 2 – Debt Instruments) and stripped the cap for sale to another customer;

● the underlying index which is most frequently used is 3-month LIBOR. However, rates based on other indices are widely available, including 1 and 6 month LIBOR, United States prime rate, US commercial paper rate, and the US Treasury bill rate.

● The up front fee payable to the seller is normally quoted in basis points of the notional principal. In the above example, if the price is 150 basis points, the fee payable will be $150,000 (1.5% × $10 million).

● The method for calculation of payment of interest over the strike rate will be specified in the agreement. The basis of calculation in the above example is actual/360.

• When interest rates are higher than the strike rate a cap is similar to an interest rate swap from floating to fixed rates interest.

Variations

Interest rate floor	The reverse of a cap. When interest rates fall below a pre-specified index the writer pays the difference in return for a fee received. The floor is effectively a series of European call options. A floor is generally more expensive than a cap as it exposes the bank to a credit risk. The buyer is protected from a fall in interest rates.
Deferred (or forward) cap	An agreement whereby a bank contracts to sell a cap to a customer with the commencement date in the future. They are useful if the customer has a fixed future commitment and finds the interest currently being offered attractive.
Options on caps or floors (Caption of Floortion)	An option to buy a cap (or floor) in the future. A caption is useful if a company is uncertain of future interest rates and is involved in a major tender and needs to be able to fix borrowing costs. A floortion is useful if a company wants to deposit funds at a floating rate while still leaving the potential for upward movements in rates.
Seasonal caps	A cap where the principal protected varies according to the purchaser's seasonal level of borrowings.
Cap with amortising/ accreting schedule	Cap where the notional principal is matched with the principal of, for example, a loan repayment, where the principal either diminishes or increases over the life of the loan.

459

5.57 Pricing of interest rate caps

An interest rate cap is effectively a series of European put options on the relevant futures contract (usually short term interest rates) which are written by the bank and purchased by the customer. The price of the cap should be equivalent to the sum of the prices of the options which can be determined by the use of an option valuation model. Factors which are relevant to the pricing of caps are:

● once the bank has received its up front fee, it is not exposed to any credit risk with regard to the customer. Therefore, the fee will not include any premium charged for such risk;

● the price of the underlying instrument. For interest rate caps with maturities of up to three years, this price can be determined by reference to the price of the appropriate interest rates futures contract. Where caps have maturities greater than three years, the appropriate forward interest rates can be calculated by interpolating and extrapolating from the futures prices with reference to swap rates.

5.58 Benefits

● The purchaser can limit exposure to adverse movements in interest rates.

● The selling bank is not exposed to any credit risk on an interest rate cap. Consequently a cap is a useful alternative to an interest rate swap for corporations with weak credit ratings who wish to fix their borrowing rates but either do not have access to the swap market or who would have to pay a prohibitive risk premium to obtain fixed rate funds.

● If interest rates remain below the strike rate for a substantial period over the life of the cap, the floating rate borrower would have obtained funds cheaper than by entering into an interest rate swap.

● An interest rate cap is tailored to the individual customer's requirements unlike traded option contracts which have standard terms.

● An interest rate cap can generally be purchased for longer maturities than is available for traded option contracts.

● There are no administration costs involved in monitoring and paying margins as with exchange traded options.

5.59 Risks and disadvantages

• The borrower has to pay an upfront fee to the bank. It would generally be cheaper for a floating rate borrower with access to the swap market to enter into an interest rate swap if interest rates are generally higher than the strike rate throughout the life of the cap.

• Caps and floors are not readily tradeable and once purchased cannot be resold, only cancelled with the counterparty. The market is relatively illiquid compared to the swap market so an offsetting transaction may not be economical.

5.60 Accounting questions

• Should the price (premium) be spread over the life of the instrument or written off at inception?

• How should payments received (or made) under the cap be treated?

• If the price (premium) is spread over the life of the instrument and interest rates move well outside the range of the instrument should any unamortised cost be written off?

• Is part of the price an arrangement fee rather than a premium and if so how should it be treated?

• Is the cost an expense or an adjustment to interest charges/credits?

• How should premium income be recognised?

5.61 Taxation questions

• Is the initial premium an allowable expense particularly for special category companies (eg holding companies)?

• Is the premium an allowable expense when paid or only as amortised over the life of the agreement?

• Is the premium an immediate taxable receipt of the writer or can it be amortised for tax purposes?

• See also general taxation questions in section 5.49.

5.62 Interest rate collar

An interest rate collar is a combination of a cap and a floor. If interest rates rise above the level stipulated in the contract, the seller of the collar will pay the purchaser an amount equal to the additional cost to the next reference date; however, if interest rates fall below another stipulated level, the purchaser will pay the seller. The purchase of the collar is an attractive alternative to a cap if the purchaser believes that interest rates are going to rise as the fee received for the floor offsets the price paid for the cap. Zero cost collars can be constructed whereby the fee paid to the bank for the cap is offset by the fee received for the collar, enabling the purchaser to hedge against a rise in interest rates at nil cost but with an exposure if interest rates fall below the floor price. The rates at which the premiums cancel is referred to as the forward band. In such a transaction the cap rate will typically be higher than the market level of fixed interest rates.

Variation

Participating Rate Agreement (PRA) or Participating Interest Rate Agreement (PIRA)	A collar where the purchaser agrees to pay the seller an agreed percentage of any difference between the strike rate and current market rates (while below the strike rate). As a result there is no up front premium. In effect the purchaser buys an interest rate cap and simultaneously sells a floor at the same strike rate but for a proportion of the notional principal on the cap, which creates a fee equal to the fee paid for the cap. The overall position of the buyer is similar to a collar except that, as the floor will typically be in the money at the inception of the contract, the purchaser will have to make payments (until and if interest rates rise above the strike rate), but based on a lower principal amount. Also called a Participating Cap.
Corridor	The simultaneous purchase and sale of a cap. The cap sold is for a higher interest rate than the one purchased. The premium on the cap sold is used to offset the cost of the purchased cap.

5.63 Benefits

- The fee receivable for the floor element of the collar reduces the overall cost to the purchaser of hedging against the rise in interest rates.
- Other benefits as for caps in section 5.58.

5.64 Risks and disadvantages

- If interest rates decrease to below the floor level, the purchaser will face additional costs as payments will have to be made to the seller for the difference between the strike rate and current interest rates.
- The inclusion of a floor in the agreement introduces credit risk to the seller as, if interest rates fall, the counterparty is committed to make payments.
- The value of the floor element may be very low if the prevailing yield curve is steeply positive, reducing the cost saving compared with the outright purchase of a cap.

5.65 Accounting and taxation questions

As for caps in sections 5.60 and 5.61.

5.66 Synthetic agreement for foreign exchange (SAFE)

Synthetic agreements for foreign exchange (SAFE) were introduced by Midland Bank and are the equivalent of forward rate agreements in the currency market. Initially these agreements were introduced by Midland Bank as Foreign Exchange Agreements (FXAs) and by Barclays Bank as Exchange Rate Agreements (ERAs) but the British Bankers' Association has drawn up standard terms for these type of agreements under the SAFE acronym. They can be used to hedge a foreign exchange exposure over a period of time in the future and are equivalent to a forward/forward currency swap but with no principal exchanged. The SAFE combines two forward currency contracts into a single transaction. There is no exchange of principal but instead the costs of a notional currency exchange in the future are agreed and at the settlement date the seller pays the purchaser any increase in the cost of the notional exchange. If the cost has fallen the purchaser pays the seller.

For example, Company A wishes to buy six months forward and sell twelve months forward $10 million against French francs on 11 April 19X1. The spot rate is $1 = Ffr 5.950. The forward discounts are Ffr O.20/$1 for six months and Ffr 0.50/$1 for 12 months. Company A buys an FXA 6 month against 12 month for notional principal of $10 million with the exchange rate at commencement of Ffr6.15 (being the current six month forward rate) and forward/forward points of Ffr 0.30/$1 (0.50–0.20).

At settlement date in six months time the actual spot rate is Ffr 7.00/$1 and the six month forward points rate is Ffr 0.25/$1.

The bank will pay the company the difference in the cost of setting up a swap and the notional swap of the FXA (the loss at the spot rate and the gain on the forward rate discounted at the French franc LIBOR rate (say 8%)).

	Ffr
$\$10 \text{ million} \times (7.00 - 6.15)$	8,500,000
$\$10 \text{ million} \times \left[\dfrac{(7.00 + 0.25) - (6.15 + 0.3)}{1 + \left(0.08 \times \dfrac{183}{360}\right)}\right]$	(7,687,380)
	Ffr 812,620

Variations

Exchange Rate Agreement (ERA)	A SAFE product marketed by Barclays Bank but which does not reflect changes in the spot rate, only in the forward spread (in the above example the change in the spot rate would be ignored).
Foreign Exchange Agreement (FXA)	A SAFE product marketed by Midland Bank which reflects changes in the spot rate and in the forward spread as in the above example.

Chapter 5

5.67 The SAFE market

• Like the FRA, the SAFE is traded on an OTC market mainly in London.

• The SAFE market is not widely developed being used mainly in the interbank market with few corporate participants.

• Transactions are quoted in three-sixes (a three month forward rate in three months time), six-twelves (a six month forward in six months time) as for FRAs.

• Transactions are typically in US dollars against sterling, deutschmarks, Swiss francs and yen and sterling against deutschmarks.

• The British Bankers' Association has drawn up guidelines and standard terms for the contract (SAFE BBA Master Terms). The SAFE BBA terms includes the following formula for the calculation of the settlement amount:

$$S = P2 \times \frac{[(OER - SSR) + (CFS - SFS)]}{1 + \dfrac{L \times D}{100 \times B}} - [P1 \times (OER - SSR)]$$

Where:

S   = Settlement amount

P1   = First notional principal

P2   = Second notional principal

CFS = Contract forward spread

SFS = BBA settlement forward spread

OER = Outright exchange rate

SSR = BBA settlement spot rate

L   = BBA Interest settlement rate for the secondary currency (expressed as a number and not as a percentage)

D   = Number of calendar days in the swap period

B   = 360, or, if interest rates in respect of the secondary currency are calculated on a 365 day year basis, 365

465

• As noted above an ERA is an agreement using the change in forward spread only. Therefore, the settlement formula above would not compensate for any change in spot rates. Accordingly, both OER and SSR are zero for ERAs. An ERA may only be contracted in equal amounts of primary currency on the settlement and maturity dates ie for ERAs P1 = P2.

• An FXA is an agreement regarding changes in both forward spreads and spot rates. This is effected by the use of outright exchange rates in the settlement formula (OER and SER).

5.68 Benefits

• Simple and flexible way of hedging future foreign exchange exposure.

• Use of a SAFE avoids the administrative cost of monitoring margin calls which is required for financial futures.

• Like FRAs there are no funding costs involved in using SAFEs and they do not require extensive credit lines as would the underlying forward foreign currency contracts.

• The instrument can be tailored to the user's precise requirements in terms of settlement date, maturity date principal and exchange rate to be hedged.

• Principal is not exchanged (only the settlement difference) so the credit risk is much reduced.

5.69 Risks and disadvantages

• There is no central market place so that liquidation is only by agreement to cancel or by purchasing a reverse transaction.

• There is a risk that the counterparty may not perform at maturity of the contract. Unlike financial futures contracts, there is no clearing house to guarantee performance.

5.70 Accounting questions

- As for FRAs in section 5.60.

5.71 Taxation questions

- Can a non trading company (eg a holding company) obtain tax relief for the cost of the SAFE.
- Can the cash settlement be paid without withholding tax.
- See also questions on forward contracts in section 5.17.

5.72 Range forward contract

A range forward contract is a forward foreign exchange contract that specifies a range of exchange rates within which the currencies will be exchanged at maturity. The contract was designed by Salomon Brothers. The user can take advantage of favourable currency movements to the upper end of the range and the risk is limited to the lower end of the range if the movement in exchange rates is unfavourable. If at maturity the exchange rate is inside the range, the contract will be settled at the spot exchange rate. If the rate at maturity is outside the range the exchange rate used is that at the end nearest to the actual rate.

When executing a range forward contract, the purchaser can specify either the upper end of the range or the lower end. The bank will then calculate the other end of the range (by reference to market conditions such as interest rate differentials).

For example, on 1 October 19X1 A Inc a United States corporation wishes to hedge a payment of £1,000,000 which it will have to make on 31 March 19X2. On 1 October 19X1 the 6 month £/$ rate is 1.65. A Inc's treasurer believes that sterling is unlikely to appreciate to any great extent above this level but that there is a considerable risk of significant depreciation against the US dollar. Therefore he enters into a range forward contract fixing the lower range at 1.60. The bank fixes the upper rate at 1.70. The profit profile will be as follows:

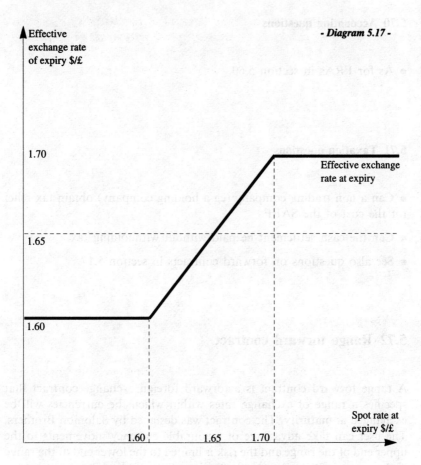

Diagram 5.17: Range forward contract

The dealer who offers the contract to the customer hedges his position using a zero cost option strategy which is explained in section 5.31 above. The dealer is therefore able to offer the customer a play on exchange rates without charging a premium.

Variations

Cylinder option

A cylinder is the purchase of an option and the simultaneous writing of a second option to the bank. The contract was designed by Citibank. The premium payable is offset against the premium earned with only a small net payment to the bank. The purchaser can select the degree of risk by adjusting the prices of the two options (the ceiling and floor of the 'cylinder') and it is possible to eliminate the premium. The effect is the same as range forward contract in that a range of exchange rates can be set but depending on the range set a premium may be payable.

Zero cost ratio option (ZECRO)

A currency option involving the simultaneous option purchase and sale of put and call options for different quantities of currencies at the same strike price. Marketed by Goldman Sachs the options are such that the premiums cancel.

5.73 Benefits

• The customer does not have to pay an up-front premium for a range forward contract.

• The range forward contract can be used to hedge foreign currency commitments. It is thus a substitute hedging vehicle for foreign currency forward contracts.

• The range forward contract is structured to limit downside currency risk while leaving some potential for profit; it therefore has some of the benefits of option contracts.

5.74 Risks and disadvantages

• A range forward contract is a binding contract, and, as with an outright forward contract, a risk of exposure may exist if the future commitment which is being hedged fails to materialise.

• The profit potential is limited to the size of the range offered by the bank. Purchasers who expect the currency to move significantly in their favour should buy currency options as options do not limit the upside potential for profit.

- Outright forward contracts should be preferred where purchasers believe that currencies will consistently move against them.

- This type of contract is available for only major currencies against the US dollar.

5.75 Accounting questions

- Which exchange rate should be used to value outstanding range forward transactions?

- Other issues are as for forward contracts, see section 5.16.

5.76 Taxation questions

- Questions are as for forwards contracts in section 5.17.

5.77 Break forward contract

This instrument is a conventional forward foreign exchange contract but allows the bank's customer to cancel (break) the contract at a specified exchange rate ('the break rate'). It is in effect a cancellable forward contract. If the spot rate at maturity is more favourable than the break rate specified in the contract, the customer uses the currency position resulting from the forward contract specified in the break forward contract to offset a contract with the bank at the break rate. The cost is limited to the difference between the agreed forward rate and the break rate. The customer then enters into the spot market to obtain the benefit of the favourable movement in exchange rates. The contract was designed by Midland Bank. The cost to the customer of having the ability to break the contract is reflected in paying a forward rate ('the fixed rate') above the market rate at the time of entering into the contact (ie the rate is worse than the forward rate ruling when the contract is executed).

For example, if a company buys US dollars forward using a break forward contract, and in the intervening period prior to maturity the US dollar weakens relative to the agreed forward rate, the dollars can be bought at the agreed forward rate and then sold to the bank at the break rate. The required US dollars are then repurchased at the spot rate. Thus, overall the US dollars will be cheaper than if the company had entered into a conventional forward contract but more expensive than if no cover was arranged or a currency option used (depending on the option premium). However, if the dollar strengthens the agreed forward rate restricts any loss. The following diagram illustrates the profit profile of the purchase of a break forward.

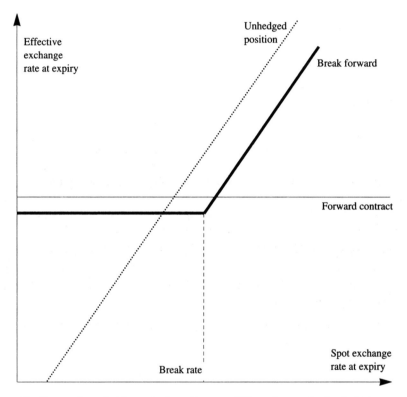

The diagram shows that the contract provides cover if the exchange rate at maturity is less than the break rate but allows a profit to be made if the rate moves favourably, albeit less than if the position was unhedged.

Diagram 5.18: Break forward contract

As can be seen from the profile the Break Forward contract is essentially a repackaged call option (a forward purchase and a put option are equivalent to a call option). The break rate is the strike price and the difference between the break rate and the fixed rate is, effectively, the premium, although of course this is payable at maturity and not at the

471

inception of the contract. The purchaser of a break forward can either choose the fixed rate or the break rate and the bank then calculates the other.

Variations

Forward with optional exit (FOX)   Hambros Bank version of a break forward.

Forward break   Citibank version of a break forward.

5.78 Benefits

• The use of a break forward contract enables a purchaser to retain some element of control in the event of movements in exchange rates prior to maturity while retaining protection from unfavourable movements. If the movement is favourable (ie, if purchasing a currency which depreciates in value, or selling a currency which appreciates in value), it is possible to take some of the profit arising on this movement.

• The purchaser can unwind the contract at any time by closing out the position at the break rate. Thus exposure to large fluctuations in exchange rates is minimised in the event of the future commitment which is being hedged not materialising.

• Unlike conventional options, no up front premium is payable.

5.79 Risks and disadvantages

• Although the purchaser can benefit from favourable movements in exchange rates, the profit will be lower than if no forward market transaction had been entered into and at the spot rate obtained at settlement date for the transaction.

• If the market does not move favourably, the purchaser will pay more than if a conventional forward foreign exchange contract had been used as the premium is reflected in the forward rate.

5.80 Accounting questions

● As for Range Forwards in section 5.75.

5.81 Taxation questions

● Does the break forward actually consist of a forward contract and an option?

● Is the excess of cost of the contract over current market price for a straightforward contract the cost of the option?

● If the break forward is not linked to a trading transaction, will the customer obtain tax relief for the unexercised option price?

● Other questions as for forward contracts in section 5.17.

5.82 Scouts

A Shared Currency Option Under Tender (SCOUT) is marketed by Midland Bank and is a form of contingent forward contract. The SCOUT is sold to the awarder of a large contract subject to tender by a number of parties and in which there is foreign exchange risk. The premium paid to the bank is shared among the tenderers. Such tenders are often large and exposure to movements in exchange rates in the period between the submission of a bid and the award of the contract (or rejection) is ideally suited to an option. However, as only one firm can be awarded the contract, the option premium would be a high sunk cost to each tenderer. By using a SCOUT all the tenderers are protected from foreign exchange movements and when the contract is awarded the successful tenderer is also awarded the option to give the required foreign exchange cover. If all the tenders are unsuccessful any profit which may arise on the SCOUT is shared between the tenderers.

Variations

Tender to Contract option (TTC)	A contract which allows tenderer to pay 10% of the option premium with the 90% payable on successful tender.

Export Tender Risk Avoidance (EXTRA)

Hambros Bank contract to hedge US dollar tender contracts. The contract is less flexible than the SCOUT as it is based only in US dollars for small amounts with fixed 3, 6, 9 or 12 month periods. A proportion of the fee is returnable if the tender is unsuccessful.

Compound option

This is an option on an option for a specific currency. It is the currency equivalent of captions/floortions. The option premium on the initial option is lower than a conventional option but if exercised the overall cost will be higher than the purchase of an outright currency option.

5.83 Benefits

• The cost of the premium is shared between tenderers but with full option cover of foreign currency exposure for the successful tenderer. The cost to an individual tenderer is therefore substantially less than a currency option.

• For the contract awarder the currency protection may result in more bids thus more competition.

• A tenderer may be willing to bid more aggressively as hedging costs are reduced while retaining full cover.

5.84 Risks and disadvantages

• For an unsuccessful bidder there is still a cost involved.

• As with an option contract if rates move favourably the contract will have proved (with the benefit of hindsight) unnecessary.

5.85 Accounting questions

● As for options in section 5.37.

5.86 Taxation questions

● Is the option a capital or income transaction for the awarder?

● Is the award of the option an arm's-length transaction?

● If the option is a capital transaction, will the awarder obtain any tax relief for the cost of the option?

5.87 Participating forward contract

The participating forward contract is a contract to buy or sell foreign currency, at a fixed future date, with a predetermined minimum or 'floor' exchange rate and unlimited profit potential if exchange rates move favourably. The contract was designed by Salomon Brothers. If the currency moves in the holder's favour, the benefit equals a percentage of the total currency move which is specified in advance. This percentage is called the participation rate.

The buyer of the participating forward contract pays for the downside protection and has unlimited upside potential but with less than 100% participation in favourable movements in exchange rates. The purchaser specifies either the minimum exchange rate or the participation rate, and the issuer determines the other rate. In the example used to describe the operation of range forward contracts, A Inc's treasurer believed that sterling is likely to depreciate against the US dollar. Suppose, however, that he thinks that sterling is likely to appreciate but he still wishes to limit the downside risk. He enters into a participating forward contract and sets the floor rate at 1.60. The Bank sets the Participation rate at 60%. The profit profile is as follows:

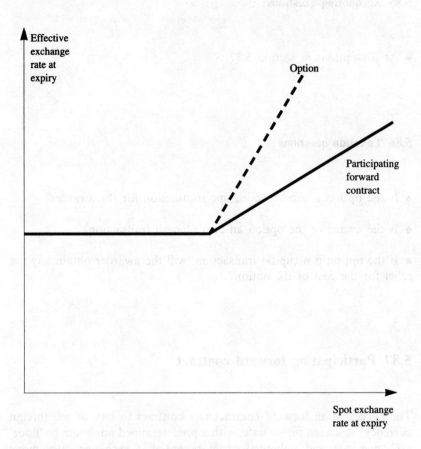

Diagram 5.19: Participating forward contract

The diagram compares the profit with what would be obtained with the purchase of a call option. However, no premium is payable on the participating forward contract and the downside risk has been eliminated at a rate below 1.60. The determination of the participation rate and the minimum exchange rate are inter-linked. A participating forward contract with a minimum rate set further from the forward rate will offer a higher participation rate than a contract with the minimum rate set closer to the forward rate.

Variations

Shared Option Forward Agreement (SOFA)	A forward foreign exchange contract whereby the floor exchange rate and a 'compensation rate' is agreed between the

bank and its customer at the inception of the contract. If the movement in the exchange rate is favourable to the customer, the customer will pay the percentage of its profit determined by the compensation rate back to the bank. To continue with the earlier example, where A Inc wishes to hedge a payment of £1 million, in 6 months time, a SOFA contract could be entered into with a rate set at 1.59 (compared to the conventional 6 month forward rate of 1.65) and a compensation rate of 25%. If in 6 months time the dollar has appreciated beyond 1.59 (for example, to 1.50), A Inc will buy sterling at the contracted rate of 1.59. However, if the dollar depreciates to, 1.70, A Inc will purchase sterling at that rate but pay 25% profit over the contracted rate of 1.59 to the bank. This product was developed by Barclays Bank.

Forward with rebate	Product similar to Participating Forward contract developed by Chase Manhattan
Citiplus	Similar product marketed by Citibank.

5.88 Benefits

● There is no up-front premium.

● The participating forward contract offers both downside protection and unlimited profit potential (subject to the participation percentage) if rates move favourably.

● The participating forward contract is suitable for hedging long term items if wide fluctuations in exchange rates are anticipated.

5.89 Risks and disadvantages

● The minimum rate will typically be less favourable than the rate for an equivalent outright forward contract, and will become less and less favourable for higher participation rates.

• As with forward contracts, the participating forward contract is binding and can therefore create an exposure (the floor exchange rate) if used to hedge a future commitment which does not materialise.

5.90 Accounting questions

• How much of the profit or loss accruing on the participating forward contract can be taken up at each balance sheet date?

• Otherwise as for forward contracts in section 5.16.

5.91 Taxation questions

• Questions as for forward contracts in section 5.17.

5.92 Convertible option contract

A currency option with a 'trigger' price at which the option will convert automatically into a standard forward foreign exchange contract. With a convertible call option contract the trigger will be activated if the exchange rate moves a predetermined amount below the strike price (and, conversely, a predetermined amount above the strike rate for a put option).

5.93 Benefits

• The user of the contract can fix the maximum amount he will pay or the minimum amount he will sell of the foreign currency but can still profit from any upside movement in exchange rates.

• The user will pay a lower premium for the option because of the possibility the contract may be converted into an outright forward.

5.94 Risks and disadvantages

• If foreign exchange rates move over the trigger price, the user will be committed to a binding contract. A risk of exposure arises if the contract is used to hedge a commitment which does not materialise.

5.95 Accounting questions

• Should convertible option contracts be accounted for as an option or forward contract?

5.96 Taxation questions

• See questions on options (section 5.38) and forward contracts (section 5.17).

Swaps and repurchase agreements

5.97 Swaps – overview

The swap developed during the 1980s as a tool to enable companies to vary the terms of their loans and therefore to manage their liabilities more effectively. More recently, swaps have been used in a similar way to manage assets. Swaps originally developed where each party to the swap could access a particular market on comparatively better terms than the other party. This comparative advantage would then be shared between the parties (and any intermediaries arranging the transaction) to lower their funding costs. The parties entered the markets where they had the advantage and agreed to exchange (swap) cashflows. This result gave the parties better terms in their preferred market than if they had entered it directly. The two basic types of swap are as follows:

Interest rate swap   The two parties to the transaction exchange the terms under which they pay interest on their liabilities. Typically, they will exchange interest paid at a fixed rate for interest paid at a floating rate, and vice-versa.

Currency swap   The two parties to the transaction exchange liabilities denominated in different currencies as well as the related interest payments.

These two basic swap structures (and the variations which have been developed from them) are described further in the following sections, together with examples which show how the parties to the swap can exploit the comparative advantages they possess and each reduce their funding costs. This is an example of arbitrage, the exploitation of inefficiencies between markets (in this instance, different perceptions of borrowers in different markets). The rapid growth of the swap market has reduced the inefficiencies existing between different capital markets and consequently has reduced the savings that can be made by borrowers by entering into a swap. Other factors have contributed towards the continuing development of the swap market including:

• avoidance of local regulation. If a company has surplus funds in a local currency, (for example representing the earnings of a foreign subsidiary) and due to either tax implications or currency restrictions, the cost of exporting those funds would be prohibitive, it could enter into a swap with a local company to obtain the funds in the currency which it requires;

• exploitation of local regulations. A company can issue securities to exploit local tax regimes, which will be attractive to local investors and can therefore be issued at low cost, and can then use a swap to obtain the type of funds it requires. For example, until recently Japanese tax regulations made zero coupon bonds attractive to Japanese investors. Foreign companies could issue zero coupon bonds denominated in yen and swap the proceeds (either into the currency they required, or the interest rate profile they required, or both);

• creation of new assets and liabilities. The flexibility of swaps has enabled the creation of assets and liabilities which were not previously available and which are attractive to both investors and borrowers. For example, if zero coupon bonds do not exist in a particular currency they can be created by linking a currency swap to zero coupon bonds issued in another currency.

An important recent development has been the use of swaptions (section 5.113), where borrowers take options written by financial intermediaries to enter into swaps in the future at current market rates.

5.98 The role of the intermediary

Swaps between two counterparties are usually arranged by a bank or other intermediary. The matching of counterparties will be achieved in either of two ways:

• the intermediary will act as broker and the counterparties will contract directly with each other to swap payments and receipts, with either or both parties paying an arrangement fee to the intermediary;

• the intermediary (usually a bank) will take a position. It will enter into a swap contract with each counterparty and will pass on payments between them. The intermediary may earn its profit by taking a 'turn' out of these payments and/or from fees. The intermediary will often enter into a swap with one party before it has found a counterparty for the other side of the swap. The intermediary will take this open position because it believes it will be able to find a counterparty at a later date and close out its position at a profit. When this is done regularly it is known as 'warehousing'. The intermediary can do this because it can use hedging techniques to reduce substantially its risk (particularly with interest rate swaps). Intermediaries will now frequently hedge their swap portfolios on a global basis. The development of warehousing has increased significantly the liquidity of the swap market.

5.99 Nature of the swap market

The swap market has been growing rapidly and while statistical information is difficult to obtain the International Swap Dealers Association (ISDA) estimated that, in the first six months of 1990, US$656 billion of interest rate and currency swaps were transacted (using notional principal). This was a 40% increase over the same period in the previous year and while volumes are likely to be lower in the second half of 1990 individual currency sectors are likely to be considerably in excess of 1989. US dollar denominated swaps account for some 57% of the total in the six months. The growth of the swap market has led to the development of two recognisably different markets:

- the short term, interbank market; and

- the long term market, linked to the issue of Eurobonds.

Short term market

The short term market (usually considered to be swaps with maturities of up to three years) is primarily a US dollar interest rate swap market, and exhibits the following features:

- it is largely an interbank market;

- the market is centred in New York, with significant activity also in London and Tokyo. There is also a growing market in Switzerland based on the many short term Swiss franc bonds issued by foreign corporations;

- the market is highly developed, with both market makers and brokers quoting prices;

- there is a substantial secondary market, which has greatly contributed to the liquidity of the market, by enabling market makers to close out their positions quickly. This reduction in risk for market makers has led to a narrowing of dealing spreads;

- the development of the secondary market has been assisted by the use of financial futures to hedge and unwind, and hence price, positions.

Long term market

The long term market is dominated by new issue activity in the Eurodollar bond market and is based in London. Some of the more important features of the long term market are as follows:

- pricing in the interest rate swap market is derived from the spread over United States Treasury bond rates for similar maturities;

- typically, a borrower will issue a fixed rate bond in the Eurobond market and will wish to swap into floating rate funds. Given the size of most Eurobond issues, the ability of banks to 'warehouse' a swap without a counterparty on the other side enables bond issues which are to be swapped to be made quickly and at a time which maximises the cost savings to the issuer;

- currency swaps are also linked to Eurobond issues, although warehousing occurs less frequently due to the difficulty in hedging interest rates in many currencies;

- there is a secondary market for long term swaps, but there is far less liquidity than in the short term market. This is in part due to the fact that longer dated swaps tend to be tailored to the needs of individual borrowers, which can lead to problems in closing out the position where there are non standard terms, either in the documentation of the contract or in the dates or terms of payment. However, liquidity has been aided by recent moves to standardise documentation. Both the ISDA and the British Bankers' Association (BBA) have issued standard contracts for interest rate swaps which have been widely adopted.

5.100 General accounting questions

The accounting questions to be considered by end users of swaps (which can include banks and other financial institutions) are different depending on whether the transaction is an interest rate or a currency swap. It also depends on whether the end user is a bank or intermediary actively involved in the swap market or a company using a swap to hedge its balance sheet liabilities or assets (such end users are referred to below as 'corporates' which is the term generally used in the markets). Questions relating to corporates are raised in the sections below which describe the particular type of swap. However, for financial intermediaries who may be arranging, broking or trading in swaps, the accounting questions to be considered are similar for both currency and interest rates swaps, and are set out below.

Financial intermediaries

Profit recognition

• When should the intermediary recognise the profit on matched swap deals? The main alternatives are:

– To accrue the profit evenly over the life of the swap.

– To accrue the profit on a 'cash basis' over the life of the swap.

– To recognise all or substantially all of the profit on the swap once the transaction has been arranged.

– To mark the individual swaps to market.

To the extent that swaps are loss making, provision should be made as soon as the loss is identified.

• Which of the above is the most appropriate is still a matter of debate and there is as yet no definitive generally accepted accounting principles for swaps in either Europe or the United States (although FASB Statement 52 on Foreign Currency Translation does deal with currency swaps). The matters to be considered in deciding between the alternatives are:

– Does the intermediary do most of its work (and therefore incur most of the costs associated with the revenue) at the inception of the deal or are there still considerable administrative costs to be incurred and other remaining risks over the life of the swap?

– Can the profit be determined with a sufficient degree of certainty?

– What is the effect of early termination by the counterparty or assignment by the intermediary?

– Is the cash flow of the swap even throughout its life or are there irregular flows or 'balloon' amounts?

– Is the profit earned by way of fee without further risk to the intermediary over the life of the transaction?

– Is the fee or profit received equally over the life of the swap or substantially up front or at maturity?

Credit risk

If swaps are marked to market or valued using net present value techniques an element of the value is dependant on the credit quality of the counterparty. This element may be deferred and taken to profit over the life of the swap. This is equivalent to lending margins offered to counterparties of different credit status which would be accrued evenly over the life of a loan. However, the exposure which results if a party to a swap defaults also needs to be considered particularly in the case of currency swaps. With currency swaps, where there is usually an exchange of principal at maturity, this can represent a significant risk if exchange rates have changed materially since inception. The assessment of the credit risk is not a question of profit recognition on the swap but an analysis of changes in credit risk. Credit risk should be assessed regularly (possibly using mark to market techniques) and, if there is any doubt as to the position of a counterparty, provision for any loss should be made.

Discounting and marking to market

If it is considered appropriate to recognise substantially all the profit or loss on the swap following the commencement of the swap, the following issues have to be considered:

● should the cash flows arising from the swap be discounted? Any profit on the swap will not be fully realised in cash until the transaction has been completed (usually many years later), and until that time any receivable will have to be funded. In the United Kingdom Exposure Draft 53 deals with the need to discount long term receivables and payables in the context of accounting for acquisitions. ED 53 states that discounting should be used for long term receivables or payables and that the discount rate should be that appropriate to the intermediary given the risk of the particular asset or liability;

- what will be the most appropriate rate to use to discount the swap? Should it be the marginal cost of capital, or average cost of capital? If so, how are these measures to be calculated? Should an external benchmark such as the United States Treasury bond rate for a similar maturity be used? Can the rates used be calculated consistently? A technical release (TR 773) from the Institute of Chartered Accountants in England & Wales contained recommendations on the use of discounting and states that the rate should be that related to the riskiness of the asset or liability. Consequently it would seem inappropriate to use the marginal or average cost of capital and the rates should be based on an external benchmark.

If the swaps are to be marked to market then:

- How is market value to be determined on a consistent basis?

- Are there sufficiently liquid markets for all the swaps in the portfolio (particularly non US dollar swaps)? A secondary market exists but how liquid is it for the particular swaps in a portfolio? How many quotations can be obtained from market makers?

- If there is not a liquid market, is it nevertheless reasonable to value the swap on a discounted cash flow basis?

- Are all the swaps sufficiently standard to be tradeable or are the terms too specific?

- If the cash flows are discounted to give a 'value' is this a true market value which could be realised?

In the United Kingdom, the British Bankers' Association Statement of Recommended Accounting Practice for Commitments and contingencies, currently published as an exposure draft, recommends:

- non hedging transactions be marked to market and profits and losses recognised immediately in full;

- in situations where the profit or loss is not immediately realisable an appropriate discount rate should be applied to anticipated cash flows and a proportion of the net present value so derived be spread over the life of the transaction the remainder being recognised immediately. The proportion deferred should take account of all likely future costs, including the cost of maintaining capital and of any continuing credit and other risks.

Unmatched swap positions

Where an intermediary holds an unmatched swap, this could either be a position to be held for trading purposes or to be 'warehoused' until a matching swap can be found. In these circumstances, should the swap be marked to market, or should the individual elements of the swap be accounted for on an accruals basis as if they were conventional banking transactions? If market prices are to be used, the considerations for marking to market in the above paragraph apply.

5.101 General taxation questions

• Are swap arrangement fees eligible for tax relief?

• Are periodic exchange fees eligible for tax relief?

• Are periodic exchange fees tax deductible on an accruals basis or only when paid?

• Should only the net fees paid or received be included in the computation of taxable profit?

• Must withholding taxes be deducted from the periodic exchange fees? Does the status of the counterparty (eg a bank) make any difference and is there any difference between long and short term swaps?

• Can exemption from any withholding tax requirements be obtained through the 'business profits' or 'other income' article of a double tax treaty?

• Can swap positions be regarded as inventory and so valued at lower of cost and market value? Does the type of company (eg bank or other financial services company) make any difference?

• Should the fee for taking over an 'off market' swap be recognised at inception on a mark to market basis or by amortising it over the life of the swap?

• Should profits and losses on unwound hedges on swaps be recognised immediately or over the remaining life of the swap?

• Are the periodic exchange fees a supply for VAT purposes and is such a supply exempt or zero rated if the counterparties are resident in different countries?

• See also specific questions on interest rate swaps (section 5.107) and currency swaps (section 5.112).

5.102 Interest rate swaps

'Plain vanilla' interest rate swaps (also called coupon swaps) occur where counterparties exchange payments of fixed and floating rates of interest on a specified principal amount ('the notional principal'). The cash flows are in the same currency and there is no exchange of principal.

Interest rate swaps developed where borrowers had comparative advantages in different capital markets. For example one party can raise floating rate funds fairly cheaply but wants fixed rate funds. The other party finds it easy to raise fixed rate funds, but wants floating rate funds at the lowest possible cost. Banks have been the major source of fixed rate funds as they can usually obtain fixed rate funds more cheaply than corporations. However, banks usually want floating rate liabilities to match their floating rate assets (eg bank overdrafts etc). Companies on the other hand can often raise floating rate funds almost as cheaply as banks but want fixed rate funds. Interest rate swaps exploit, to the advantage of both parties, the fact that investors in fixed rate debt are often more sensitive to credit ratings than investors in floating rate debt. The development of the swap market has tended to reduce this differential.

For example, suppose that borrower P is an AAA rated bank which can raise fixed rate funds at 10%. However, the bank wants floating rate debt to match its floating rate assets. It can obtain floating rate funds at 6 month LIBOR + 0.25%. Borrower Q is a BBB rated company which can raise floating rate funds at 6 month LIBOR + 0.75%. However, Q wants to obtain fixed rate debt to lock in its interest cost, but can only raise fixed rate debt at 11.50%. These differences are shown below:

	Bank P (Bank)	Company Q (Company)	Difference
Cost of issuing fixed rate debt	10%	11.50%	1.50%
Cost of issuing floating rate debt	LIBOR + 0.25%	LIBOR + 0.75%	0.50%

The net saving possible is therefore 1% and a typical structure involving an investment bank acting as intermediary might be as follows:

● Bank P will issue a $100 million 10% fixed rate Eurobond. Under the terms of a swap agreement, P will pay floating rate interest at LIBOR on the $100 million to an investment bank and in return receive 10.30% fixed rate interest.

● Company Q will raise a $100 million Euroloan from a syndicate of banks and pay floating rate interest at LIBOR + 0.75%. Under the terms of a swap agreement, Q will pay 10.40% fixed rate interest to the investment bank and receive floating rate interest at LIBOR.

The resulting cash flows between the parties to the swap agreement can be shown as follows:

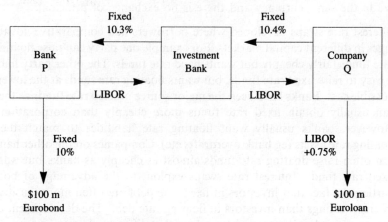

Diagram 5.20: Interest rate sw⁻ ⁻

⸰   ving for each party will be as follows:

Bank P

Payment on fixed rate bond	10%
Receipt from swap agreement	10.30%
Payment through swap agreement	LIBOR
Effective cost of borrowing	LIBOR – 0.30%
Cost of raising own floating rate debt	LIBOR + 0.25%
Saving	0.55%

Company Q

Payment on floating rate Euroloan	LIBOR + 0.75%
Receipt from swap agreement	LIBOR
Payment through swap agreement	10.40%
Effective cost of borrowing	11.15%
Cost of raising own fixed rate debt	11.50%
Saving	0.35%

The intermediary investment bank makes a turn of 0.10% by receiving fixed rate interest at 10.40% and paying on to bank P 10.30%.

Variations

Basis swap	A swap between two counterparties who have both raised floating rate debt, but based either on different indices or on different pricing periods. For example, a swap could be arranged between debt based on 6 month LIBOR and debt whose interest rate varies with the US prime rate or US commercial paper rate. Alternatively debt paying interest at 6 months LIBOR could be swapped for debt paying interest at 1 or 3 months LIBOR.
Zero coupon swap	A zero coupon swap allows a borrower who can issue cheap zero coupon debt to swap into conventional floating rate debt. However, this swap structure exposes the borrower to a greater credit risk with the swap counterparty than with a plain vanilla interest rate swap because of the reinvestment risk and the fact that the fixed rate interest is not received until maturity.
Deferred (or forward) swap	A swap the terms of which are fixed but with a commencement date in the future. In effect it is similar to an FRA but with a longer maturity than is available typically in that market.
Reset (or arrears) swap	A swap where the floating rate is paid at the end of each interest rate period based not on the index at the start of that period but on the index at the end of that period.
Accreting (or drawdown) swap	The notional principal increases over the life of a swap. Such an arrangement would be structured to mirror the drawdown of funds under a borrowing facility.
Amortising swap	The amount of the notional principal decreases over the life of the swap. This swap is structured to mirror borrowings

	where the principal is repaid in instalments (eg a bond with a sinking fund provision).
Mortgage swap	A contract to exchange the difference between a fixed rate payment and a floating rate payment on a notional principal amount which declines in proportion to the monthly payments and prepayments of an indexed pool of mortgage backed securities (see chapter 3 – Asset Backed Securities) for a specified period.

5.103 Pricing of interest rate swaps

The vast majority of interest rate swaps are transacted in US dollars. In the long term market the fixed rate side of the swap is usually priced by reference to United States Treasury bonds. The key features of the price quoted for a plain vanilla US dollar interest rate swap are as follows:

• the fixed rate side which is quoted in the market is against US dollar LIBOR;

• the fixed rate side of the swap is priced off the yield of the 'on the run' United States Treasury bond issue of equivalent maturity. The on the run United States Treasury bond issue is the most actively traded Treasury bond for that maturity. The size and liquidity of the United States Treasury bond market enables swap dealers to hedge swaps in that market, which accounts for its use in the pricing mechanism;

• the swap will be quoted as a 'spread' over the Treasury bond, expressed in basis points. Therefore, if a five year swap is quoted at 'Treasury + 75', and the yield on the five year United States Treasury bond is currently 9.75%, the price of the swap is 10.50% fixed against 6 months US dollar LIBOR;

• swap prices are quoted by market makers and quotations are readily available on dealing screens (eg Reuters). However, these prices are for transactions between $10 – $25m and are indicative only, as in practice, counterparty credit status will affect final pricing;

• the rate quoted by the market maker is quoted on the assumption that interest is calculated on an actual days/365 basis with semi-annual coupons (known as the 'Treasury Bond Basis'). The interest basis used in a particular swap can be an important factor in determining its cost, and this cost has to be calculated by converting all cash flows in a transaction onto an equivalent basis. For example, a swap may be linked to a fixed rate Eurobond issue, on which interest will be calculated on 30/360 basis assuming annual coupons;

- the dealing spread between bid and offer prices is typically 10 basis points. Thus, if 75 basis points is the mid-price in the example above, the actual quotation would be 70–80; that is, the market maker would pay a fixed rate at 10.45% and receive a fixed rate at 10.55%. Until recently, the dealing spread was typically 20 basis points and the narrowing of spreads is indicative of the increasing competitiveness of the market. However, the extension by regulators around the world of capital adequacy requirements to swap markets may lead spreads to widen again.

The use of the spread over United States Treasury bonds to price interest rate swaps has two important consequences:

- intermediaries are able to hedge against their interest rate risk by use of United States Treasury bonds (and bond futures and options). If, in the example above, the market maker had entered into a swap to pay a fixed rate at 10.45%, he could buy the equivalent Treasury bond (and thus receive fixed coupons) and sell the Eurodollar future maturing closest to the next floating rate refix date. It is the ability to hedge which has allowed intermediaries to warehouse swaps. However, intermediaries cannot hedge against the spread risk. The spread risk results from swaps being priced as a margin over a fixed rate index (such as the United States Treasury bond). The spread can move against an intermediary (eg by reducing) and unmatched swap positions can only be closed out at a lower spread than expected. Spread risk cannot be hedged easily and proper monitoring of the risk is important to manage this exposure;

- issuers of fixed rate Eurobonds will attempt to launch new issues maximising the 'spread window' which occurs when the differential between the United States Treasury bond rate (which determines the price at which the issue can be swapped) and the rates required in the Euromarket diverge. This can reduce significantly the cost of funds.

Non US dollar swaps are usually quoted at a fixed rate against LIBOR (or another appropriate floating rate index, such as PIBOR for French francs). This is quoted as an absolute rate, not a margin over government bonds. This is a reflection of the fact that other government bond markets are not as liquid as in the United States. The basis for the calculation of interest will vary according to the currency concerned, and will usually be the method commonly used for paying interest on bonds issues in that currency. For example, sterling swaps usually use an actual/365 basis except for those based on Eurosterling bonds which use 30/360.

5.104 Benefits

• Each party to the swap can obtain the interest profile required at a reduced cost.

• Swaps permit an active liability management as the interest profile of debt can be easily and rapidly changed in response to changing market conditions or the companies requirements, due to the ability to enter into, reverse or undo a swap.

• As interest rate swaps do not involve the exchange of principal, entering into a swap will not usually affect balance sheet footing or gearing ratios. However, regulators are now requiring inclusion of swaps in calculations of the adequacy of capital of banks and other financial institutions.

• If interest rates move favourably it may be possible to terminate or sell the swap for a substantial cash sum.

• As the counterparties to the swap do not exchange principal in an interest rate swap, the amount at risk is small relative to the size of the outstanding debt.

5.105 Risks and disadvantages

• The market risk to each counterparty is that interest rates may move against them. If interest rates fall, a floating rate borrower who has swapped into fixed rate will incur higher costs than if the original floating rate debt had not been swapped.

• If there is no intermediary, the counterparties are exposed to credit risk which may be difficult to monitor particularly if they lack the relevant experience. The use of an intermediary may reduce this risk but there is an exposure to the intermediary.

• It may not be possible, or it may prove expensive, to terminate the swap if market conditions change. If the swap has 'odd' payment dates it may

492

be more expensive or difficult to terminate. While an offsetting swap could be arranged this creates an exposure to another counterparty.

● An issuer of fixed rate bonds who swaps into floating may obtain cheaper funds, but in a plain vanilla swap the option of redeeming the bonds under the terms of any call coupon will be lost. The increased cost of a callable or extendible swap will reduce the potential savings.

● Administrative cost of calculating and making the swap payments.

● An intermediary holding unmatched swaps may be exposed to changes in the swap spread even if the position is hedged.

5.106 Accounting questions

Intermediaries

● See the general accounting questions in section 5.100.

Corporates

● Interest rate swaps are often described as off-balance sheet transactions. However, this is not an entirely accurate description of the transaction as the counterparties never exchange principal, and the swaps are not used to raise new funds but merely to modify the terms of existing obligations. Therefore the existence of the swap has no effect on the presentation of the debt on the company's balance sheet. The company should, however, consider whether the existence of the swap affects materially the terms of their debt and therefore whether the terms of the swap agreement should be disclosed. For a company actively involved in liability management the position may change during the period so disclosure of specific transactions may not be particularly meaningful.

● Should receipts and payments made under a swap agreement be shown gross, or would it be more appropriate to show them net (both on the balance sheet and in the profit and loss account) as an adjustment to interest payable, to reflect the fact that the swap has been entered into to modify the structure of the interest payments?

● Swap agreements will sometimes provide for 'balloon' payments often at either the commencement or the termination of the swap. How should these payments be recognised in the profit and loss account?

• Payments may be made up front as arrangement fees (to the intermediary) but, if large, they may in effect be yield adjustments (ie adjust the interest flows which accrue over the life of the swap into line with market rates). How should such payments be treated in the profit and loss account?

• If market conditions change, the company or the counterparty may unwind or terminate a swap. This will normally be effected by a single payment or receipt. Should this amount be taken to profit or loss immediately or should it be spread over the remaining life as a modification to the interest charge? To arrive at the most appropriate accounting treatment, the company will have to consider:

− Was the swap originally undertaken to hedge specific and determinable assets and liabilities?

− If it was, do these assets and liabilities still exist?

− Has the receipt or payment been made on a discounted basis, and if so, should this be taken into account in determining the period in which the amount should be taken to profit and loss?

• Sections 5.140 to 5.173 at the end of this chapter set out the accounting treatment for interest rate swaps in various countries in Europe.

5.107 Taxation questions

• Does an interest rate swap create any supplies for VAT purposes? Are any such supplies VAT exempt or zero rated?

• Should profits and losses on zero coupon swaps be recognised on a cash basis, on a straight line amortisation of discount, a constant rate of return, by marking to market or some other basis? Should the accounts treatment necessarily be followed for taxation? Does the status of the company (eg a bank or financial institution) make any difference?

• Are payments on a zero coupon swap tax deductible and should an end user recognise income and expense on a zero coupon swap on a paid or accruals basis?

• See also general questions on swaps in section 5.101.

5.108 Currency swaps

In a straight currency swap, two counterparties will exchange principal amounts of different currencies, usually at the prevailing spot exchange rate. This exchange of principal can be either notional or physical. On the maturity of the swap the principal amounts will be re-exchanged at the same exchange rate. Over the term of the swap the counterparties will make periodic exchanges of fixed rate interest in the different currencies.

The effect of this transaction is similar to the swap undertaken by foreign exchange dealers, i.e. a spot purchase and a forward sale of currency, or vice-versa, except that the interest rate differential is accounted for by periodic exchanges of interest as opposed to being expressed in the difference between the spot and the forward exchange rates. Companies will enter into currency swaps because it allows them to exploit their relative strength (comparative advantage) in different markets and reduce each party's funding costs.

For example, assume that US Inc., a United States Corporation, is about to start operations in Germany. It is well known in the United States debt markets, but relatively unknown in the deutschmark (DEM) market. The company can borrow at better rates in the US dollar than in the DEM market. If the company or its investment bank can find a German company with the opposite profile (i.e. G AG, a German company wanting to finance a United States subsidiary but is not well known in the United States credit markets), both parties can obtain funds in the currencies they want at cheaper cost by using a currency swap than if they raised them directly themselves as follows:

• US Inc. can raise $100 million from a 10 year bond issue in the domestic United States markets at 7.50%. It could raise DEM200 million in the Eurobond market at 4.25%;

• G AG can raise DEM200 million for 10 years in the Euromarket at 3.75%. It could raise $100 million at 8.20%;

• US Inc. will therefore issue a US dollar domestic bond and G AG will make a Euro-DEM bond issue. The two parties agree to swap the proceeds of these issues and to make periodic payments to reflect each other's interest liability in currency to the holders of the bonds. The swap will be reversed after 10 years when the bonds are due for redemption.

The cash flows can be shown diagrammatically as follows:

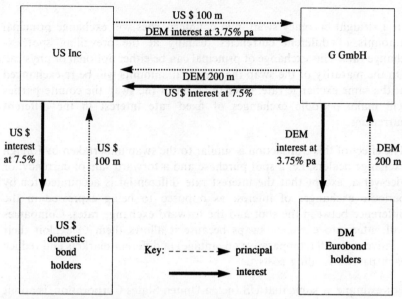

The principal cash flows at the inception of the transaction would be reversed at maturity

Diagram 5.21: Currency swap

The cash saving to US Inc. is the difference between the DEM interest paid on the swap and what would be payable if it made its own Euro-DEM issue calculated as 4.25 − 3.75 = 0.5% per annum. Similarly the saving to G AG is 8.20 − 7.50 = 0.7% per annum. It is possible that the rates would be adjusted so that both parties shared equally in the saving or the stronger party (in this case US Inc) receives more of the saving.

As in the interest rate swap example, an intermediary may take a position between the two counterparties and make a profit by taking a turn out of the funds paid on to one or both parties. Alternatively, the intermediary may act purely as a broker and charge a fee or commission to one or both parties.

Variations

Fixed rate currency swaps — An alternative name for the plain vanilla currency swap, described above.

Principal only swap — A transaction whereby there are periodic adjustments of principal between the parties based on two different exchange rates.

Currency coupon swap	This is a hybrid between a straight currency swap and an interest rate swap, whereby fixed rate interest in one currency is swapped for floating rate interest in another with an exchange and re-exchange of principal.
Circus swap	A currency coupon swap where the floating rate is US dollar LIBOR, which is swapped against fixed rate in another currency. Circus swaps are often used to facilitate a swap between fixed rate borrowings in two currencies where there is not active swap market. The use of the US dollar LIBOR as an intermediate link has greatly increased the liquidity of the currency swap market. For example, Company X can raise fixed rate debt in Canadian dollars but wants Danish kroner funds. It is unlikely that a counterparty could easily be found who had raised fixed Danish kroner debt but wanted Canadian dollars. However, given the size of the US dollar interbank market, Company X could probably enter into two swaps as follows (the arrows represent the initial flow of principal):

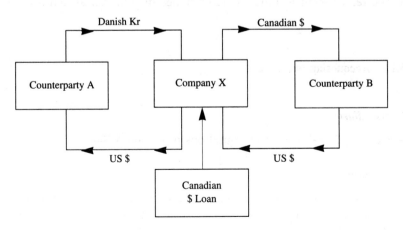

Diagram 5.22: Circus swap

497

5.109 Benefits

• Each party can obtain the funds it requires more cheaply than if it had raised them directly itself.

• Swaps permit an active liability management as the interest profile of debt can be easily changed.

• If exchange rates (or interest rates) move favourably it may be possible to terminate or sell the swap for a substantial cash sum.

5.110 Risks and disadvantages

• In the event of default by the counterparty, each party has a credit risk to the extent that the currency they have swapped into has depreciated against the currency they have swapped from. In the example of a currency swap, if G AG defaulted on the swap, and the US dollar has appreciated against the DEM, US Inc. would have to continue to service the interest payments on the US dollar domestic bond out of DEM assets which had depreciated in value. This risk can be reduced by using an intermediary although there is then exposure to the intermediary.

• It may not be possible or may prove expensive to terminate the swap if market conditions or the company's needs change.

• Administrative costs of calculating and making the swap payments.

• The requirement to fund the re-exchange of principal at maturity.

5.111 Accounting questions

Intermediaries

• See the general accounting questions in section 5.100.

Corporates

• A plain vanilla currency swap is in effect a spot purchase and forward sale of a foreign currency. The cash purchased spot (or the assets acquired with it) will be valued at the spot rate. How should the forward commitment be valued? With a conventional forward foreign exchange contract not taken out as a hedge, the commitment would be compared to the forward rate ruling at the balance sheet date for the remaining term of the contract and any losses accrued for. Would it be appropriate to use the forward rate for a swap? Does the fact that periodic payments are swapped to compensate for the interest differential mean that the spot rate would be more appropriate?

• Where a foreign currency loan is taken out to fund a new equity investment in a foreign subsidiary, or to hedge an existing equity investment, can any profits or losses arising on the revaluation of the loan be charged direct to reserves (or some other component of shareholders' funds) and set off against profits and losses arising on the revaluation of the investment? Should this principle apply to a currency swap (given that the original loan may not be denominated in a foreign currency)?

• Where the swap can be identified as a hedge, should the asset or liability being hedged be valued at the rate ruling in the swap?

• If currency swaps are used to hedge future costs or revenues instead of forward foreign currency contracts how should the interest differential be treated?

• Sections 5.140 to 5.173 at the end of this chapter set out the accounting treatment for currency swaps in various countries in Europe.

5.112 Taxation questions

• Does re-exchange at the end of a currency swap create taxable income or capital gains by reference to spot rates then ruling?

• Must a re-exchange by connected parties be deemed to take place at current spot rates regardless of the stated price?

• Is any gain or loss on re-exchange deemed to arise at inception of the swap, or only on re-exchange?

• Are periodic payments made under a 'principal only currency swap' income or capital?

• Does a currency swap to hedge foreign currency borrowing create a tax exposure if the reporting currency weakens, if the loss on the related borrowing is non-tax deductible?

• Does a currency swap create any supplies for VAT purposes? Are any such supplies VAT exempt or zero rated?

• Is the exchange of principal outside the scope of VAT?

• See also general tax questions on swaps in section 5.101.

5.113 Swaptions

A swaption (or an option on a swap) is an option to enter into an interest rate swap at a future date at a fixed interest rate determined by reference to current market rates. As with options, swaptions can be for American exercise (at any time until expiry) or European exercise (at expiry). The holder of a swaption is able to limit the risk in switching from floating interest rates to fixed interest rates (or vice versa) for the cost of the premium while still able to benefit from favourable interest rate movements. This provides a greater flexibility for liability (or asset) management than the swap market. Swaptions may be used by issuers of callable debt which has been swapped so that the swap can be reduced if the debt is called.

Swaptions are available on the OTC market from banks and intermediaries who hedge the risks using exchange traded options on interest rates. Swaptions being a combination of a swap and an option on interest rates are priced using traditional option pricing theories.

Floating rate borrower

A swaption usually involves an option on the fixed rate component of a swap at a rate linked to current market rates. Floating rate borrowers who wish to swap into fixed rate funds but who believe that interest rates may fall could enter into such a swaption. If interest rates rise, the borrower exercises the option and enters into the swap at the lower fixed rate than prevailing market rates. Alternatively, if market rates fall, the borrower allows the option to expire, and enters into the swap at the lower fixed rate.

For example, B AG has raised a 10 year floating rate $100m syndicated loan paying 1% above LIBOR to finance its United States subsidiary. It wishes to fix its interest cost and could currently enter into a swap to pay 9% fixed against LIBOR (an effective fixed rate of 10% being the swap rate of 9% plus the 1% margin over LIBOR). However, the treasurer feels that interest rates may fall in the next year but wants protection against a rise in interest rates. Accordingly a swaption to enter into a swap at 9% fixed against LIBOR in one year for the premium of $1\frac{1}{2}$% of notional principal ($1.5 million) is purchased.

When the exercise date is reached interest rates may have fallen or increased. the position would be as follows:

- if fixed interest rates have increased by 1% to 10% B AG will exercise the swaption and enter into a swap to pay 9% and receive LIBOR. This will enable B AG to fix its funding costs for 9 years at 10%. (9% fixed plus margin on LIBOR on original borrowing of 1%). In cash terms the effect of the swaption is:

Premium for swaption	(1,500,000)
1% × 9 years × 100m	9,000,000
Total cash saving	$7,500,000

However, to determine the effective overall cost it would be necessary to discount the cash flows back to the date of the premium payment.

The total cost is in excess of the overall effective cost available at the date the swaption was purchased (ie a swap at 9%) by the amount of the premium on the swaption but the treasurer has retained flexibility if interest rates should fall;

- if interest rates fall the swaption will not be exercised and a swap at the then market rates will be obtained. Interest rates have to fall by only a small amount to cover the cost of the premium. For example if rates fall by $\frac{1}{2}$% the position would be:

Premium for swaption	(1,500,000)
Saving on fixed borrowing $\frac{1}{2}$% × 9 years × 100 m	4,500,000
	$3,000,000

Once again the overall effective cost would be found by discounting the cash flows back to the date of the premium payment.

Clearly the cost is more than if the swaption had not been purchased and the treasurer had been unhedged. However, for a relatively small premium, flexibility is retained and there is protection against rising interest rates.

Fixed rate borrower

The purchase of a swaption may be attractive to a fixed rate borrower who wishes to swap into floating rate funds but who believes that interest rates may rise in the future. If interest rates remain at current levels or fall, the borrower will exercise the swaption and receive fixed rate interest at the contracted rate which is in excess of the then current market level and pay the then lower market level of floating rate. Conversely if market interest rates rise the swaption would not be exercised. For example, if a borrower has raised fixed rate funds at 9% and he could swap them into LIBOR + 1% (the current LIBOR being $7\frac{3}{4}\%$). If a swaption is taken out at 9% the position with current interest rates, a rise and fall at the swaption exercise date is shown diagrammatically below.

Current position

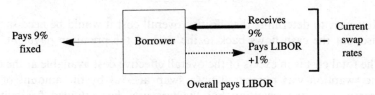

Interest rates fall

Swaption: 9% received against LIBOR + 1% exercised
Current rates: 8% fixed

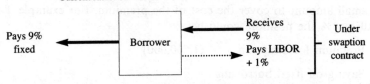

Interest rates rise

Swaption not exercised
Current rates: 10% fixed

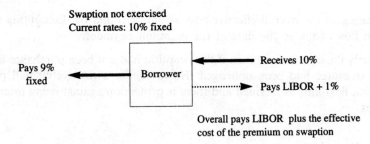

Diagram 5.23: Swaption

As with the floating rate borrower a fixed rate borrower can use swaptions to hedge against an unfavourable movement in interest rates for the cost of the premium.

502

Variations

Callable swap	Fixed rate payer to the swap has the right to enter into additional swaps at a fixed date or dates, at a pre-specified cost. The fixed rate payer usually compensates the counterparty to the swap by an upfront premium or an adjustment to the swap rate. Such a swap could be used in conjunction with an issue of debt with warrants (see chapter 2 – Debt Instruments) which had been swapped into floating rate funds. If the warrants are exercised (usually into fixed rate bonds at a lower coupon than the host bonds) additional floating rate funds can be called from the callable swap.
Puttable swap	The fixed rate payer to the swap has the right to terminate the swap at future specified date or dates. As with a callable swap the holder pays the provider a premium upfront or an adjustment to the swap rate. Such a swap could be used in conjunction with a callable bond (see chapter 2 – Debt Instruments).
Extendible swap	One of the parties to the swap has the option to extend the swap for a further pre-specified period at maturity date. To compensate for the granting of the option, the other party receives a more favourable rate.
Contingent swap	One party will receive a premium for agreeing to enter into a swap if some contingency occurs (for example, where investors exercise debt warrants issued with the counterparty's debt instrument).

5.114 Benefits – swaption purchaser

• The purchaser of a swaption has flexibility to react to favourable movements in interest rates but is insured against the effect of unfavourable movements.

• Swaptions can be tailored to the specific requirements of the purchaser.

• The purchaser can use a swaption in conjunction with a debt instrument (eg debt with warrants) to hedge interest rate risks and lock in a known funding rate.

5.115 Benefits – swaption writer

• The writers of swaptions are usually banks or other intermediaries. The benefits are similar to those of writing other types of OTC option – the writer will determine the premium on the basis of estimates of volatilities and other market factors where it believes that overall swaption writing will be profitable.

5.116 Risks and disadvantages – swaption purchaser

• As with other options, with hindsight the purchase of a swaption can be expensive. The purchaser of a swaption usually believes that interest rates will move in a particular way in the future but is not certain. If rates move as predicted, with hindsight it would be less expensive not to take out the swaption (which will expire unutilised). Alternatively, if rates move the opposite way, and the swaption is exercised, with hindsight it would have been less expensive to enter into a swap at the outset.

• The swaptions market is still relatively illiquid and it can be expensive or difficult for a purchaser to close out his position.

• The purchaser is exposed to a credit risk as the contract will only be exercised if rates have moved against the writer.

5.117 Risks and disadvantages – swaption writer

• As with swaps, swaptions may be difficult to hedge fully and in particular the writer may be exposed to changes in the swap spread.

5.118 Accounting questions

● Should the purchaser of the swaption amortise the premium over the life of the swaption, or should the cost be charged over the life of the related borrowing?

● Should the writer of the swaption recognise the premium as income evenly over its life or should it be deferred until expiry date?

● An active participant in the swaptions market could be both a purchaser and seller (or writer) of different swaptions. Is it appropriate for either the long or short positions to be marked to market by the use of pricing models?

5.119 Taxation questions

● See questions on options (section 5.38) and general questions on swaps (section 5.101).

5.120 Asset swaps

Asset swaps are similar to interest rate and currency swaps except that they are undertaken by holders of assets rather than liabilities. Asset swap is a general term for any repackaging of a debt instrument paying fixed interest into floating or vice versa or involving a change in currency of interest and/or principal. For example, an investor may be holding a fixed rate bond and may enter into a swap to convert the cash flows into floating rates as set out in the diagram below.

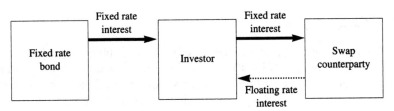

Diagram 5.24: Asset swap

The market for asset swaps exists due to the opportunity to arbitrage between interest rate structures or to create assets which would not otherwise exist (eg credit status of the issuer versus the interest rate structure). For such an asset swap the investor might use a fixed rate bond which is undervalued in the market (by reference to its coupon and credit status) to provide a 'high' yield FRN. This may occur where an investor holds a large amount of a bond issue and cannot easily sell it as investor demand is saturated and to sell would reduce significantly the price. However, interest rates are expected to rise which will reduce the value of the bond. In these circumstances, an asset swap can create a FRN with a yield significantly in excess of the yield on conventional FRNs. If interest rates do rise the yield of the asset swap will be in excess of the fixed rate bond. These swaps have been particularly attractive to banks who require medium to long term assets with floating rate returns and high yields.

Some of the most attractive asset swaps to investors have been as follows:

● zero coupon bond in a currency in which such bonds are unavailable created from a zero coupon bond in another currency using a long term foreign exchange contract;

● a floating rate bond issued by a government where the usual public issues are fixed rate bonds.

5.121 Other forms of asset swaps

Both the transaction structures referred to below involve the swapping of one form of asset for another. However, their structures (and the reasons why the counterparties enter into them) are different than the asset swap described above.

Debt/equity swap

Debt/equity swaps developed because of the difficulties faced by lesser developed countries ('LDCs') in repaying loans. In a debt/equity swap loans made to LDCs are exchanged for an alternative form of investment in the country concerned (eg an equity investment in local enterprise). The debt/equity swap was assisted by the developed secondary market in LDC debt. In the secondary market investment banks will quote indicative two way prices for LDC loans. The degree of discount to face value at which such debt will be quoted depends on the extent of the performance on its loans by the government concerned, as well as the future economic outlook for the country. Price quotes will range from 10% to 90% depending on the country and type of loans concerned.

A debt/equity swap usually involves a company which wishes to invest in a LDC country purchasing the debt of that country in the secondary market and agreeing with the country's government to exchange the debt for an agreed amount of the local currency, which it requires to make its investment in the local enterprise. The investing company will in effect redeem the debt at a higher value than the amount for which it was purchased in the secondary market (although still at a considerable discount to face value) but in local currency. The government of the country concerned will be prepared to purchase the debt for an amount greater than its secondary market value (which will still be below face value) because it is to be redeemed in local currency rather than the currency in which it is denominated and will therefore not use up currency reserves. A similar process can be used by multinationals to invest in subsidiaries located in LDCs. The investment could be in equity or a local currency loan to the subsidiary (so called debt conversion).

Commodity swap

A commodity swap is a transaction which allows users to fix the price of a commodity. Typically a commodity swap will involve an agreement between the producer and a consumer of a commodity to fix the price at which they will sell and purchase the commodity respectively for fixed future period. Although there are well developed markets for trading and hedging many commodities, these markets may not be appropriate for many producers or consumers and prices are not usually quoted far into the future. In a simple example of a commodity swap a consumer may agree to pay a fixed price for a pre-specified amount of commodity for a number of years in return for which the producer will pay an amount based on a floating index (eg the market price). The two parties would settle on a regular (eg six monthly) basis. Typically a bank will act as intermediary and bring together a producer who requires certainty of income and a consumer who wants to fix his costs.

The market in commodity swaps is currently growing very quickly, and its development has been assisted further by the decision in 1989 of the United States Commodity Futures Trading Commission (CFTC) that it would not regulate the commodity swap business of United States commercial banks (who have been amongst the largest participants in this market). Banks and other financial intermediaries have to date mainly restricted their involvement to acting as brokers in most transactions, although increasingly they are acting as principal and hedging their risks through the commodity futures and option markets. In addition, markets in commodity swaptions, collars and caps are developing.

A large number of commodity swaps are concluded in the oil market and they account for much of the long dated forward oil market which developed from the physical and futures markets in oil and petroleum products. Major consumers of petroleum products (eg airlines and transport companies) are amongst the users of oil swaps which allow the specific requirements of the consumer to be hedged. Such swaps provide more precise hedge over a longer period than would be the case with futures or option contracts. A typical oil price swap is constructed as follows:

An oil producer, GH Inc, wants to sell five million barrels of Brent crude oil over a five year period at a fixed price. PQ Limited, a user of Brent crude wants to buy the same volume at a fixed price. The two parties are brought together by an intermediary bank (B) using oil swaps. The transaction is agreed as follows:

Bank B and Producer GH Inc

Semi annual payments will be made by B to GH Inc on 500,000 barrels at a fixed price of US$19 per barrel in return for which GH Inc pays B a floating price based on average market prices in the period. GH Inc then sells its six monthly production of 500,000 barrels in the physical oil market. The overall effect is that GH Inc receives a fixed price of US$19 per barrel on 500,000 barrels of oil.

Bank B and User PQ Limited

Semi annual payments will be made by PQ Limited to B on 500,000 barrels at a fixed price of US$19.15 per barrel in return for which B pays PQ Limited a floating price based on average market prices in the period. PQ Limited then buys its oil requirements (500,000 barrels every six months) in the physical market. The overall effect is that PQ Limited pays US$19.15 per barrel for 500,000 barrels of oil.

At the end of each six month period the three parties would agree to settle only the difference between the fixed and floating prices. The intermediary makes a profit from the transaction from the difference in the two fixed prices (ie 15 cents a barrel). The transaction is shown diagrammatically below:

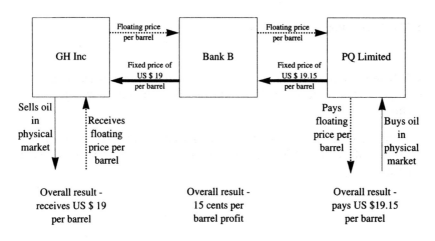

Diagram 5.25: Oil swap

5.122 Benefits

• The high yields on asset swaps are attractive to investors.

• Asset swaps offer a means of hedging bond portfolios in times of uncertainty over interest rate movements.

5.123 Risks and disadvantages

• The 'new' assets created by the swap are extremely illiquid. To liquidate a position, the investor would have to unwind the swap as well as sell the underlying security, which could be expensive.

• The use of the swap has exposed the investor to two credit risks; in addition to the risk of the issuer defaulting on the bond issue, the investor is exposed to the risk of default by the swap counterparty (although this risk is limited to the fixed/floating rate interest differential).

• The swap means that the investor has more cashflows to administer thereby increasing costs.

5.124 Accounting questions

• Where there is an exchange of principal (for example, where a bond is swapped between currencies), should this be reflected on the investor's balance sheet?

• If the securities are marked to market does the swap have to be marked also, and if so, how? Should the bond and the swap be considered separately?

5.125 Taxation questions

• See general taxation questions in section 5.101.

5.126 Synthetic securities

'Synthetic securities' is a general name for asset swaps which are packaged and marketed to a group of investors by investment banks rather than being 'home made' by the investors themselves. The cash flows may be constructed differently, but the resultant instrument is the same as an asset swap. There are two basic structures used to create a synthetic security as follows:

• direct sale of the synthetic security by the investment bank; and

• issue of synthetic security through a Special Purpose Vehicle (SPV).

In the description of asset swaps, there is an example of an underperforming fixed rate bond being swapped into a high yielding FRN. The same example describes the two ways of issuing a synthetic security.

Sale of synthetic security by investment bank

If the synthetic security was issued directly by the investment bank, the interest cash flows would be as follows:

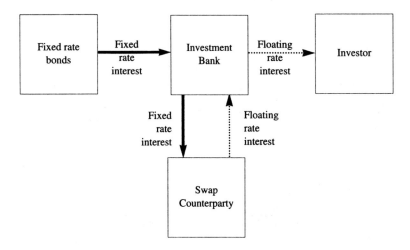

Diagram 5.26: Synthetic securities sold by investment bank

The investment bank will purchase the bonds and then swap the fixed rate coupons into floating rate interest (either direct with a counterparty or by using its own swap warehouse). Bonds will then be sold to investors with a floating rate of interest. Although the investment bank is entitled to the coupons on the fixed rate bond, for which it pays the investor the floating interest rate, the investor would have an equitable interest in the principal of the bonds. The investor is not a party to the interest rate swap, which will be on the books of the investment bank. However, the transactions will normally be structured so that the investor will suffer any costs incurred by the investment bank in respect of the swap (for example, as may occur if the swap counterparty defaults).

Issue of synthetic security by SPV

In this instance, the investor still purchases the asset through one contract, but the investment bank, instead of having the swap on its own books sets up a Special Purpose Vehicle (SPV), usually offshore in a jurisdiction with attractive tax treatment (eg the Channel Islands or Cayman Islands), whose sole function is to issue the 'synthetic securities'. The SPV will purchase the bonds and be the principal in the swap transactions. To fund the purchase of bonds the SPV will make a public issue of the synthetic securities which will be secured on the portfolio of bonds. The SPV will be administered by the investment bank, which will also lead manage the bond issue. The bonds are held by a custodian bank for the benefit of the holders of the synthetic securities. The cash flows are as follows:

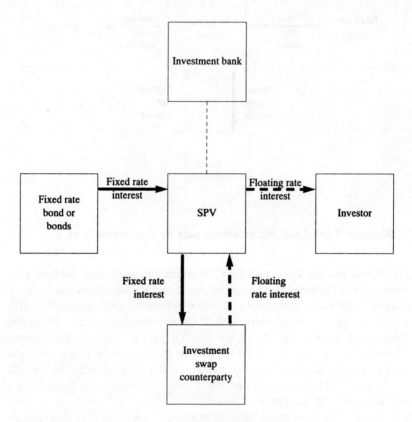

Diagram 5.27: Synthetic security issued by SVP

Under this structure, the investor would not take title to the principal of the original bond; his interest would be in the new bond issued by the SPV. As with the synthetic security issued by the investment bank, the investor is still indirectly exposed to the credit risk of the original bond issues and the swap counterparty. Most SPVs are only minimally capitalised, and therefore any defaults on its assets or by swap counter-parties would be passed on to investors in its bond issues in terms of lower yields.

Most of the early issues of synthetic securities involved purchasing seasoned securities in the secondary market but increasingly such swaps are being undertaken in the primary market, for example where bonds have proved difficult to place. This is particularly true in the Euromarkets in the case of Japanese ex warrants bonds. The strength of the Japanese equity market created demand for the bonds with equity warrants. These bonds were issued with very low coupons and were initially attractive because of the equity warrants and a rising stock market. However, the equity warrants are stripped from the bonds leaving very low coupon bonds to be traded separately. These low coupon bonds are not particularly attractive to investors and repackaging resulted in more attractive securities.

Amongst the more significant synthetic issues have been the following:

Trust Obligation Participating Securities (TOPS)	The first TOPS issue was an FRN backed by a fixed rate Eurobond issued by the Kingdom of Denmark swapped into a 2 year FRN. TOPS 2 was a much more complex transaction involving the issue of an FRN based on a package of Japanese ex warrant bank guaranteed bonds. There have since been a number of other issues in this series using the same structure.
Bearer Eurodollar Collateralised Securities (BECS)	Fixed rate US dollar denominated issue collateralised by a US dollar FRN issued in the Euromarket by the United Kingdom government. This issue was attractive because the British government has not issued directly any fixed rate US dollar denominated bonds.
Securities Transferred Repackaged (STARs)	This was an FRN denominated in deutschmarks backed by a US dollar Kingdom of Denmark FRN. The issue was made possible by the use of a currency swap.
Securities Transferred and Repackaged Into Pound Equivalent Securities (STRIPES)	This was issued in conjunction with STARs and was backed by the Kingdom of Denmark FRN referred to above. This portion of the issue was denominated in sterling and was also an FRN.

There have also been many other such issues under names such as LIVES (Latest Investment Vehicles for Ex–Warrant Swaps), SABRE, JETS, JEWEL, MECS and FLAGS some of which have a number of generations.

5.127 Benefits – investor

● Synthetic securities are more liquid than 'home made' asset swaps. The role of the investment bank in joining permanently the bond and the swap creates a tradeable package and the bank usually has a commitment to make markets. This makes it easier (and cheaper) for the investor to liquidate his position as the bonds are issued and traded in the same way as a normal issue.

● The cash flows are simplified when compared to an asset swap, as there is only the receipt of interest and principal and no swap payments.

● The investor will still have indirectly the credit risk to the swap counterparty but this will not use his credit lines.

● As with asset swaps, the yield on, say, a synthetic FRN will be significantly higher than for a conventional FRN.

● If the security is issued by an SPV based on a portfolio of bonds, the credit risk is reduced as the principal is spread among a number of issuers.

5.128 Benefits – investment bank

● By identifying underperforming assets, and repackaging them in a form which is more attractive to investors, the investment bank can make a profit by either taking a 'turn' out of the interest cash flows, by charging an administration fee to the SPV, or both.

5.129 Risks and disadvantages – investor

● Although synthetic securities are more liquid than asset swaps, they are generally less liquid than conventional securities. Typically, only the investment bank which repackaged the security will make a market in the issue.

● The investor is still indirectly exposed to the credit of the original issuer and the swap counterparties.

5.130 Risks and disadvantages – investment bank

● The investment bank may assume the credit risk which would be taken by the investor himself in an asset swap – that is, the bank may be exposed to the risk of default by both the bond issuer and the swap counterparty.

● There is a considerable amount of administration involved.

5.131 Accounting questions

● It may be difficult to obtain market prices but otherwise there are no specific accounting questions for the investor.

● For the investment bank, should profit be split between that which is a reward for any credit risk, that which is a reward for the administration cost and that which is an arbitrage gain? How should each part of the profit be accounted for?

● If the issue is made through an SPV which is a subsidiary, should this be consolidated in the accounts of the investment bank?

5.132 Taxation questions

● See general taxation questions in section 5.101.

5.133 Repurchase agreements (REPOS)

A repurchase transaction (repo) is an agreement whereby one party (known as the 'seller-borrower') sells a security to the other party (the 'buyer-lender') with a simultaneous agreement to repurchase the security at a fixed future date at a stipulated price. Whilst the legal form of the transaction is a sale and a repurchase, in substance the seller-borrower borrows the proceeds of the sale from the buyer-lender and deposits the securities he has 'sold' as collateral. The difference between the sale and repurchase price of the security is essentially interest cost to the seller-borrower.

The repo market in United States government securities is a very active market and forms a major part of the United States money market. While the agreements provide for the physical transfer of the security from the borrower to the lender this may not occur particularly in the very active overnight market. Such repos are called 'hold in custody repos' and clearly there is a much increased credit risk to the lender.

Variations

Reverse repo	A repo transaction from the buyer-lender's viewpoint.
Matched repos	A repo and exactly offsetting reverse repo.
Open repo	These have no fixed maturity date with either party having the right to terminate the agreement. Interest is agreed on a daily basis.
Gensaki	A repo using Japanese government bonds. The maturity can be from overnight to one year. As in the United States government bond repo market Gensaki is a very active market.

5.134 Benefits – seller-borrower

• For a securities trading company, the use of repos is a relatively cheap and flexible alternative to using credit lines or money market deposits to fund its portfolio of securities.

5.135 Benefits – buyer-lender

• The attraction of repos to corporations acting as buyer-lender is that they provide alternatives to commercial paper, certificates of deposit, treasury bills, and other short-term investments, with more flexibility in maturities which makes them an ideal place to 'park' funds on a temporary basis (usually overnight).

• Depending on the quality of the collateral (often Government stocks) this can be a relatively secure investment.

• For a securities dealing company acting as a buyer-lender, the securities held as collateral can be used to cover short inventory positions. This can be an alternative to stock borrowing.

5.136 Risks and disadvantages – seller-borrower

• The seller-borrower is exposed to the risk of loss if the counterparty defaults on the repurchase to the extent of the difference in value of the security deposited as collateral and the amount of the loan.

5.137 Risks and disadvantages – buyer-lender

• The buyer-lender is exposed to the risk of loss in the event of default by the seller-borrower if the market value of the collateral is less than the amount of the loan. In the case of a 'hold in custody repo' the exposure could be greater if the securities are not properly (and legally) transferred to the seller borrower.

• The buyer-lender needs to evaluate the creditworthiness of the seller-borrower since the securities will often not be physically or otherwise transferred into the custody of the buyer-lender but rather the securities are retained in safekeeping (custody) for the buyer-lender.

• The buyer-lender needs to monitor the market value of the security and make calls for additional security if the price falls.

5.138 Accounting treatment

The main accounting issue is whether the repo should be accounted for as a sale or a financing transaction. The main accounting questions to be addressed are as follows:

• In the accounts of the seller-borrower, should the repo be shown separately as a liability on the balance sheet, or treated as a sale of the securities and deducted from inventory?

• In the accounts of the buyer-lender, should the transaction be disclosed as a collateralised receivable, or should the securities purchased be included in security positions/investments?

In order to determine appropriate treatment it is necessary to consider whether, in substance, the transaction leaves the original owner with the principal benefits and risks of ownership? If so in substance, the transaction is a financing of the securities not a sale.

The following additional disclosure issues may need to be considered:

• the type and market value of assets which have been deposited as collateral;

• the maturity dates of repo transaction;

• further disclosure if a large proportion of these transaction are with one counterparty;

• the ratio of the value of outstanding repos to the company's total assets or shareholders' funds.

5.139 Taxation questions

• Is the initial transfer of assets a disposal for tax purposes crystallising a profit or loss based on original cost?

• Does repurchase at higher cost create a tax deduction for increase in price or is cost of repurchase merely the cost of inventory acquired?

• Should the profit on resale be taxed as income or capital gain in the hands of the 'investor'?

• Is the VAT supply the full value of the asset on each transfer or only the profit on resale ?

• Are any other duties payable on the transfer of the securities?

Hedging instruments – country accounting and taxation

United Kingdom

5.140 Accounting treatment

Introduction

With the exception of SSAP 20 'Foreign Currency Translation' the Companies Act 1985 and SSAPs do not deal with the accounting treatment of hedging instruments. SSAP 18 'Accounting for Contingencies' may be relevant to some hedging instruments but this SSAP would normally be encompassed by the fundamental accounting concept of prudence. Exposure draft ED 49 'Reflecting the substance of transactions in assets and liabilities' and Technical Release TR 677 'Accounting for complex capital issues' (as explained in chapter 6 – Country Accounting and Taxation Frameworks, technical releases are not mandatory) provide guidance on the accounting treatment of some hedging instruments. The International Accounting Standards Committee ('IASC') has issued an exposure draft called 'Accounting for Financial Instruments' which provides a framework accounting for most of the instruments in this chapter. The exposure draft provides guidance for developing accounting policies for recognising, measuring and disclosing financial instruments including options, forward contracts, futures contracts and swaps. The following paragraphs set out the matters which need to be considered in determining the appropriate accounting treatment.

General concepts

Financial statements should disclose sufficient information about a hedging instrument for a reader to appreciate its nature and impact. ED 49 and TR 677 state that where a transaction has a number of constituent parts the accounting treatment of each should be considered separately but having regard to the true commercial effect of the transaction taken as a whole. This principle is likely to be particularly relevant to hedging instruments used by companies to hedge assets, liabilities and current or future transactions.

The accounting treatment for hedging instruments will usually depend upon the type of organisation involved in the transaction and its purpose. Usually the economic rationale for entering into transactions involving hedging instruments will be different for entities involved in the financial services sector from non-financial service sector firms ('corporates').

Transactions involving hedging instruments can be analysed into trading, speculation and hedging. Usually corporates will be involved in hedging while financial services sector firms will usually be trading and/or hedging. In order to determine the appropriate accounting treatment it will be necessary to determine the purpose of the particular transaction.

To the extent that companies are involved in either trading or speculation the accounting treatment of all hedging instruments is relatively straightforward and will comprise:

- determining the appropriate valuation policy for the hedging instrument in the balance sheet, which should be consistent with the other accounting policies adopted by the company;

- the recognition of the profit or loss which arises on the valuation. Once again this must be consistent with the treatment adopted for other items in the financial statements.

If the company is following the principle of 'marking to market' for its current asset readily marketable investments (as proposed in ED 55 'Accounting for Investments') then hedging instruments held for trading or speculative purposes should be treated in the same way and valued at market prices.

If the hedging instrument is used for hedging purposes it will be necessary to ensure that it satisfies the conditions set out in section 5.6. Assuming that these conditions are satisfied then the appropriate accounting treatment will usually be to ensure symmetry between the underlying transaction and the hedging instrument using the accruals or matching concept.

Set out below is the accounting treatment for the various major types of instruments described in this chapter when they are used by corporates for hedging purposes. To the extent that anticipated transactions are hedged there must be reasonable certainty that the underlying transaction will occur before hedge accounting can be applied. Hedge accounting can apply only while the instrument is being used to hedge an identifiable risk and so long as it remains an effective hedge.

Forward contracts

Where a forward contract is used to hedge an asset or liability the contract price may be used to value the relevant asset or liability. This treatment is endorsed by SSAP 20 which states that for foreign exchange balances where there are related or matching forward foreign exchange contracts, the rates of exchange specified in the contracts may (not must) be used to translate monetary assets and liabilities denominated in foreign currencies. A similar treatment is proposed in SSAP 20 where an anticipated trading transaction is covered by a forward foreign exchange contract.

The IASC exposure draft on financial instruments notes that a forward contract constitutes a financial asset/liability separate and distinct from the underlying financial instrument (eg the foreign currency). The contracted right or obligation is contingent upon the passage of time and must be valued and that this value (not the underlying financial instrument) should be reflected in the accounts. This treatment is proposed as the contractual right or obligation is distinct from the underlying instrument and the risks and rewards associated with the underlying instrument remain with the holders of the instrument until maturity.

As well as hedging currency exposure, foreign currency forward contracts can effect the financing costs of a transaction particularly in treasury management. The effect of a forward foreign exchange contract on financing costs can perhaps be best illustrated by a simple example of treasury management.

Company A wishes to borrow £10 million for 6 months from 1 July 19X1 to 31 December 19X1. The United Kingdom interest rate is 10% but the US dollar interest rate is only 6%. Therefore Company A borrows $17.5 million and converts it at the spot rate to £10 million. At the same time the 6 months forward rate is 1.71667 and Company A enters into a forward contract to sell £10.5 million for $18.025 million to repay the US dollar loan and interest. The overall result is that Company A has incurred a cost of £500,000 in completing the transaction as it needs to have £10.5 million available at maturity to repay to US dollar borrowings having only raised £10 million in the original transaction. However, the interest cost at 6% for the period of the loan is only US$525,000 or £306,000. The difference in the total cost is an exchange loss of £194,000 which can be calculated by converting $17.5 million to sterling at the forward exchange rate and comparing the result to £10 million. If the company had borrowed £10 million at 10% the cost would have also been £500,000. Due to imperfections in the market it may be possible for Company A to achieve interest savings on such a transaction due to an arbitrage opportunity. However, any saving is likely to be small and market prices will move quickly back into line.

If Company A prepares its accounts at 30 September 19X1 (ie half way through the period covered by the forward contract) and adopts the accounting treatment suggested by SSAP 20 the position will be:

US dollar loan	$17,500,000
Interest	$262,500
	$17,762,500
Convert at forward contract rate of 1.7167	£10,347,000

Compare this with the position if the company had borrowed £10 million at 10% when the liability at 30 September 19X1 would be £10,250,000. The company appears to have made a loss of £97,000 when, as explained above, the overall cost of the transaction at maturity is equal whether US dollars or sterling was borrowed. This 'loss' arises because by using the exchange rate in the forward contract, the exchange loss of £194,000 has all been provided in the accounts to 30 September 19X1 rather than spreading this cost over the life of the loan as would be the case if the higher sterling interest costs had been incurred.

Consequently if Company A prepares its accounts at 30 September 19X1 it would not be appropriate to value the foreign currency liability (the US dollar loan) at the forward contract rate as this would recognise the loss of £194,000 in those accounts which would not match the costs and benefits of the transaction.

The financing effects of such transactions (ie both the interest and exchange gain/loss) should be taken into the profit and loss account over the life of the transaction as part of the company's financing activities rather than taking the foreign exchange gain or loss immediately. This is permitted by SSAP 20 which does not cover forward contracts and, in any case, is not prescriptive to such transactions. Treatment as part of the company's financing would be in accordance with the United States Statement of Financial Accounting Standards (SFAS 52) 'Foreign Currency Translation'. International Accounting Standard 21 'Accounting for the Effects of Changes in Foreign Exchange Rates' requires that the difference between the forward and spot rate on inception should be recognised over the life of the contract.

The effect of spreading financing costs should be distinguished from the fixing of the cost of a transaction and the settlement of the related asset or liability. Hedging an asset or liability is an alternative to selling or acquiring the foreign currency on the transaction date and borrowing or depositing these funds until settlement date. Thus the premium or discount associated with a forward foreign exchange contract represents the cost or benefit of using that instrument instead of a cash transaction. The approach suggested by SSAP 20 is of course much simpler and at the end of the hedging instrument's life there is (as shown above) no overall difference in the result. However, at an intermediate date, as shown in the above example, following the approach suggested by SSAP 20 will result in the premium or discount in the forward rate being recognised as soon as the transaction is recorded (or at least as soon as a balance sheet is drawn up). Consequently care must be exercised to ensure that anomalous results are avoided with forward foreign exchange contracts.

Futures contracts

Futures contracts are similar to forward contracts except that their standardised nature means that there is no delivery of the underlying financial instrument. The above paragraphs dealing with forward contracts are also relevant to futures contracts.

Futures contracts can be used for hedging existing assets and liabilities or anticipated transactions. The accounting treatment of assets and liabilities hedged with futures contracts will depend upon the accounting policies adopted for the underlying transaction. If the underlying asset or liability is carried at market value then the futures contract should be treated in the same way and any profit or loss included with that which arises on the underlying transaction (in the profit and loss account or revaluation reserve). If the underlying asset or liability is carried as the lower of cost and market value any profit or loss arising on the futures contract should be considered when determining the adjustments at the balance sheet date. The non symmetrical treatment of the underlying transaction will mean that a similar treatment will be required for the futures contract. For example:

• if the underlying transaction has a value which results in a profit which is not recognised then the loss on the futures contract would also be ignored;

• if the underlying transaction has a value which results in a loss, which would be provided (eg to write down an asset from cost to market value), then the profit on the futures contract would be recognised.

Where a futures contract is used to hedge an anticipated commitment the profit or loss should be carried forward and amortised to the profit and loss account over the period that the underlying transaction relates (eg the term of the loan if the interest rate has been hedged) or added to or deducted from the value of the underlying transaction (eg stock).

Daily margin payments between the corporation and its broker or clearing house should be accounted for as debtors or creditors. They should have no profit and loss account implications although they may provide a measure of the value of the futures contract.

Hedging instruments

Options

As noted in section 5.19 there are two basic types of option contracts; traded options and over the counter options. The accounting treatment for both types of option is the same but for traded options market prices can be obtained whereas it may be difficult to obtain values for OTC options. The accounting treatment of purchased options will be similar to that for futures contracts except that at inception it will be necessary to record the premium in the balance sheet as it represents the initial value of the option. Where options are used for hedging purposes and the underlying asset or liability is carried at market value a similar treatment should be adopted for the option. If the lower of cost and market value is the accounting policy adopted then the option should be valued at the higher of cost or market (market value of a purchased option can never be less than nil). Gains or losses on purchased traded options hedging anticipated commitments should be deferred until the commitment occurs. With OTC options the position is more complex because at any intermediate valuation date it may be difficult to value the option. Accordingly it may be necessary to design an accounting policy which ensures that the premium cost is matched with the underlying transaction.

Options can also be written to enhance income from existing assets (eg equities) or as a speculation. Where options are written to enhance income the premium income received should be taken to the profit and loss account over the life of the contract. However, the option and underlying transaction must also be valued and they must be treated in a consistent manner.

The accounting treatment for options can be complex and it is possible to account separately for the time value and intrinsic value. In such a case the time value is amortised over the period covered by the option or written off immediately. The change in the intrinsic value would be taken into account when valuing the related asset, liability or anticipated transaction. If the option is used to hedge an anticipated transaction it may be prudent to write off the whole premium at inception.

Warrants

Warrants will either be purchased or sold to hedge an underlying transaction in which case the accounting treatment is as outlined above (for options) or they will form part of a debt instrument. When issued as part of a debt instrument TR 677 states that since the bonds and warrants can be sold independently of each other the issuer should split the proceeds and account separately for the portion relating to the bond and the warrant. The bond will have a value independent of the warrant, which can be determined by considering the value of similar bonds in the market that do not have warrants attached. For example a bond with a redemption value of £100m and warrant exercisable into equity could be split.

	£m
Bond	95
Warrant	5
Total issue price	100

In this example, the bond is assumed to have a market value excluding the warrant of £95 million. The discount on the bond would be amortised to the profit and loss account over the life of the bond as part of the interest cost. In addition, the proceeds from the warrant would be treated as an advance payment for the issue of shares. It is debatable where in the balance sheet the amount paid for the warrant should be disclosed, but it is probably best to show it as part of shareholders' funds. If the warrant expires, its value (in the example £5 million) can be taken to the profit and loss account. On the other hand, if the warrant is exercised, its value should be treated as part of the proceeds received for the issue of shares and as such should be included in the share premium account or as part of share capital.

Forwards, futures and options products

Hedging with one of these 'third generation' products (such as range forwards, break forwards etc) will usually require a similar approach to those set out in the paragraphs above dealing with forwards and options. Typically the approach will follow that of hedging with options. The treatment of some of the particular types of instruments is set out below.

Forward rate agreements

Where a FRA is entered into as a hedge (by a corporate), the settlement amount received or paid should be treated as part of the interest cost and amortised over the interest period covered by the notional deposit. Any unamortised compensation amount outstanding at the company's year end would be carried forward as a debtor or a creditor. The arrangement fees for such a contract should normally be written off as incurred. The accounting policy note should explain the treatment adopted. In addition, any FRAs that exist at the balance sheet date should be referred to in the contingent liabilities note under financial commitments. If FRAs are entered into as a trade or speculation they should be marked to market and the resulting profit or loss treated consistently with other trading instruments.

Caps, floors and collars

For a corporate hedger the receipt or payment under a cap, floor or collar agreement should be treated as part of the interest cost. In addition, any fees incurred for arrangement of the transaction (for example, administrative costs) should be expensed when they are incurred. The premium paid for the instrument should be expensed (a corporate hedger would not normally be writing these instruments and receiving premiums) over the period of the arrangement. However, it may not be possible to split the fee into its constituent parts (the administration element and the premium). Consequently, a practical solution is to expense all of the fees incurred in the arrangement in equal instalments over the term of the agreement. The accounting policy adopted for such arrangements should be disclosed and details of the agreements should be given in the notes to the financial statements.

Interest rate swaps

The accounting treatment of interest rate swaps used by corporates to hedge against interest rate exposures are dealt with in TR 677. The parties to the swap will pay each other the difference between the amounts of interest swapped. Consequently, the net amount of the difference will be added to or deducted from the interest charge in the profit and loss account. There should be full disclosure of the arrangement in the notes to the accounts so that the true commercial effect is clearly explained. In addition, it will be necessary to consider whether the departure from the requirement of the Companies Act not to net income and expense needs explanation.

There are three other matters to consider:

● fees paid as part of the interest rate swap transaction. If the comparative advantage of one party to the swap is greater than the others this may be dealt with in the pricing of the swap or by way of a fee (usually paid upfront). In such circumstances the fee would be accrued evenly over the life of the swap. However, to the extent that fees are charged for setting up the swap (eg by an intermediary) they should be written off immediately;

● some interest rate swap transactions may have uneven payments, balloon payments or off market interest rates. In such circumstances, the payments should be spread evenly over the life of the swap using either a yield basis or, if the effect is small, a straight line apportionment;

● most interest rate swaps will permit early termination subject to a settlement amount. The settlement amount will reflect the net present value of the interest rate differential from the termination date until the original maturity date. Usually early termination is considered by a corporate only when the interest rate differentials have moved so that they receive a settlement amount. This 'profit' (or 'loss' if interest rates move in the other direction) represents the present value of the future cost (or benefit if it is a loss) to the corporate of no longer being hedged. The amortisation of the termination amount until the original maturity will normally be the appropriate treatment in such circumstances. Such a treatment will give the same result as if the corporate had entered into an offsetting swap at the new market rates for the remaining life of the swap (which is the alternative to termination). This can be seen from the following example:

> Three years ago when LIBOR was $9\frac{3}{4}\%$ Company A agreed to pay fixed rates of interest of 11% and receive LIBOR $+\frac{1}{2}\%$ for six years on a notional amount of £30 million. The transaction had the effect of transforming a floating rate loan of £30m to a fixed rate loan. Interest rates are now such that:
>
> (a) Company A can receive fixed rates of interest of $12\frac{3}{4}\%$ for three years and pay LIBOR $+\frac{1}{2}\%$; or
>
> (b) terminate the swap and receive a settlement amount of £1,260,961.
>
> LIBOR is now $11\frac{1}{2}\%$.

The position under scenario (a) is that for the next three years Company A will receive $(12\frac{3}{4}-11) \times$ £30m $=$ £525,000 but will be exposed to the risk of rising interest rates. The net present value (NPV) of the interest differential is calculated as follows:

Year	Cash receipt	NPV*
3	525,000	468,750
4	525,000	418,527
5	525,000	373,684
		£1,260,961

*Assuming annual payments and discount rate of 12% (being the current borrowing rate of LIBOR $+\frac{1}{2}\%$)

This is also the amount which would be paid to A to terminate the swap as it represents the cost to the counterparty of finding a replacement for A.

Currency swaps

SSAP 20 does not deal with the accounting treatment of currency swaps. The most authoritative guidance available is the United States standard FAS 52 ('Foreign Currency Translation') and the following paragraphs (which are concerned with the accounting treatment to be adopted by corporates) reflect substantially the conclusions reached in that standard.

A currency swap used by a corporate for hedging purposes will result in the funds of the corporate being exchanged into another currency. Following the first leg of the swap, each party to a currency swap will have purchased one currency, with a commitment to sell that currency at a future date. Unlike most other foreign currency commitments, the forward leg of the swap should be revalued by a corporate in the balance sheet at the spot rate, rather than the forward rate of exchange. This is because the effect of the interest rate differential between the spot and forward rates is already reflected in the periodic payments made between the parties. How the gain or loss arising on this revaluation should be accounted for will depend on the purpose of the transaction. Where the transaction is speculative or is undertaken to hedge a foreign currency position the gain or loss on the revaluation of the forward commitment should be reflected in the profit and loss account. If the transaction is a hedge, the gain or loss on the commitment should offset the gain or loss on the asset which is being hedged.

If the transaction is intended to hedge a foreign currency commitment (such as a future cost or revenue), the gain or loss on the commitment arising from the hedge should be deferred and recognised in the profit and loss account at the time the gain or loss on the commitment being hedged is recognised.

A currency swap may be used to hedge an investment in a foreign subsidiary in conjunction with a loan taken out in local currency as this may be a cheaper alternative to raising funds in the foreign currency. SSAP 20 states that where a company has used foreign currency borrowings to finance or provide a hedge against its foreign equity investments and certain conditions apply, the company may revalue these investments into the foreign currency at the balance sheet date. Where this treatment is adopted, the gain or loss on the revaluation of the investments and the borrowings should be reflected through retained earnings rather than through the profit and loss account. SSAP 20 does not address the issue of currency swap but it appears reasonable to adopt this treatment where a swap and local currency loan have been used as an alternative to creating a hedge by use of foreign currency borrowing, as the substance of the transactions is the same.

The periodic payments made between the parties should be reflected as an adjustment to interest expense, to reflect the fact that such payments adjust for the impact of the interest rate differential.

As with interest rate swaps there should be full disclosure of the arrangement in the notes to the accounts so that the true commercial effect is clearly explained. The treatment of (eg uneven payments and early termination) will follow the principles set out above for interest rate swaps.

Repos

The accounting treatment for repos is set out in the application notes to ED 49, as well as the explanatory notes. The exposure draft, which is not mandatory, must be regarded as best practice and the application notes are stated to be standard practice in relation to transactions 'fitting the circumstances they describe'. The application for repos note states that the assets subject to a repo transaction are usually individually large although this feature is not essential. The application note also discusses more complex arrangements than typical transactions involving the sale and repurchase of securities (repos) which are dealt with in the explanatory notes to the exposure draft. It is likely that the Accounting Standards Board (ASB) will issue a Financial Reporting Standard (FRS) to replace ED 49 which will become mandatory. The FRS is likely to confirm the treatment suggested by ED 49.

The explanatory notes state that 'A sale of goods with a commitment to repurchase may leave the original owner with the principal benefits and risks of ownership if the repurchase price is predetermined and covers the costs, including interest, incurred by the other party in purchasing and holding the goods'. This will usually be the case with a repo. The application of the exposure draft will result in repos being accounted for as a financing transaction rather than a sale of the securities. Accordingly the seller-borrower will retain the asset on balance sheet and record the borrowing as a liability. The buyer-lender will record the loan made as an asset not the underlying security which is merely held as collateral for the loan. For the seller-borrower the sale and any apparent profit will not be recorded as such. The proceeds of 'sale' will be classified as a loan analysed between long and short term, as appropriate. Interest on the loan (in whatever form) should be accrued in the normal way. The notes to the accounts and accounting policies would explain the treatment adopted.

5.141 Taxation treatment

The tax treatment of interest rate hedging instruments largely depends upon whether the profits or losses or costs incurred from such transactions are part of a company's trading activities or whether they are of a capital nature. Much depends upon the intention of a company when entering into the hedging transaction. Profits and losses are strictly taxable on a realisation basis but in practice, where short-term hedging transactions are involved, the Inland Revenue may accept the treatment adopted in the accounts if profits and losses are recognised on a consistent basis from one year to the next; in other words, an accruals or market valuation basis consistently applied is often accepted as reasonable.

Long-term hedging instruments such as swaps are treated in a similar way to the interest on the underlying loan. Consequently swap fees will normally be allowable on an accruals basis if payable by a United Kingdom trader to a United Kingdom bank (or United Kingdom swap dealer). If payable by a non-trader (ie, investment company), the swap fees will be deductible from total profits on a paid basis if payable to a United Kingdom bank or swap dealer (or if paid under deduction of basic rate tax as if an annual payment).

Certain instruments, such as futures and options, which are quoted on a recognised stock exchange, will fall to be capital assets giving rise to a capital gain or loss, if such gain or loss is not part of the company's normal trading activity.

Channel Islands

5.142 Accounting treatment

The accounting treatment follows closely best practice adopted in the United Kingdom.

5.143 Taxation treatment

Resident companies

The tax treatment of hedging instruments largely depends upon whether the profits or losses arising from such transactions are part of the company's trading activities or whether they are of a capital nature. This will usually be apparent and depends upon the intention of the company when entering into a hedging transaction. Currently hedging instruments are principally used in the financial services sector. Taxation treatment will invariably follow the accounting treatment.

Non-resident companies ('exempt' companies)

Exempt companies are treated as not resident for tax purposes and are exempt from local income tax except in certain very limited circumstances. Such companies merely pay a flat rate exempt company fee.

Isle of Man

5.144 Accounting treatment

The accounting treatment follows closely best practice adopted elsewhere in the United Kingdom.

5.145 Taxation treatment

The tax treatment of interest rate hedging instruments follows the accounting treatment. No special tax rules apply.

Republic of Ireland

5.146 Accounting treatment

The accounting treatment follows closely best practice adopted in the United Kingdom.

5.147 Taxation treatment

The treatment of interest rate hedging is at present unclear and no special tax rules apply. However, the tax authorities have indicated that payments under hedging transactions are considered to be annual payments and income tax may therefore need to be deducted at source and the payment treated as a charge against profits unless prior permission has been obtained to make such payments without deduction of tax and to treat such payments for tax purposes in accordance with accounting principles.

France

5.148 Accounting treatment

The *Plan Computable General* (see chapter 6 – Country Accounting and Taxation Framework) does not deal with the accounting treatment of hedging instruments. Nevertheless, the *Conseil National de la Comptabilite* (CNC) has defined a hedging transaction in its 1986 guideline dealing with accounting for transactions carried out on the MATIF and in its 1987 guideline dealing with accounting for interest rate options. According to CNC hedging transactions must meet the following four criteria:

• they must reduce the risk on the underlying transaction;

• there must be a correlation between the change in the value of the hedging transaction and the change in the value of the underlying transaction;

• the identification of the risk to be hedged must allow for all the existing assets, liabilities and commitments;

• hedging transactions must be identified and accounted for as a hedge from inception until maturity.

The accounting for hedging instruments will depend upon the accounting policy adopted for the underlying transaction. The objective of the accounting treatment should be to cancel or reduce the change in value which may be recognised on the underlying transaction. To meet this objective, it will usually be necessary to defer gains or losses incurred on the hedging instrument.

5.149 Taxation treatment

Special tax rules apply to financial futures transactions. Trading profits realised on quoted investments are taxed according to the mark to market value. Non-quoted investments are taxed at the end of the futures contract.

The mark to market basis does not apply to hedging operations where the profit or loss is carried over to the year following the hedging operation. Neither does the mark to market basis apply to symmetrical positions in which case, losses incurred on an instrument balanced by unrealised gains on other similar positions are not tax deductible. The 'symmetrical position' concept, applies both to quoted and non-quoted financial futures.

Interest rate swap contracts are not usually revalued at the end of the fiscal year and losses on existing contracts are not tax deductible.

Luxembourg

5.150 Accounting treatment

There are no specific rules for the accounting treatment of hedging instruments except in the banking industry where some basic principles to be followed have been established by the regulatory body, the *Instit Monetaire Luxembourgeois* (IML).

These rules, together with generally accepted accounting principles, are based on the following fundamental concepts:

• prudence – unrealised gains are generally not recognised;

• true and fair view – accounting treatment of the various components of a transaction should be assessed considering the true commercial effect of the transaction taken as a whole;

• matching of revenue and expenses – commissions, fees and margins are generally amortised over the life of the hedging instruments.

5.151 Taxation treatment

There are no special tax rules which apply to hedging instruments and the tax treatment normally follows the accounting treatment.

Belgium

5.152 Accounting treatment

The accounting treatment for hedging transactions is regulated by the provisions of the Royal Decree of 8 October 1986 and its amendments and by the guidelines issued by the Commission on Accounting Standards.

The general rules require that an appendix to the financial statements indicates the total commitment represented by outstanding hedging instruments. The rules also provide that the fundamental principle of prudence must be followed (ie that provisions for likely losses should be made but that gains should be deferred). Expenses should also be amortised over the life of the contract.

The Commission on Accounting Standards has issued a general position paper recommending how to treat foreign currency balances and transactions in financial statements which covers the treatment of forward foreign exchange contracts (see below). The recommendation is based on principles internationally accepted. However, the deferral of the gains is possible which is often selected by the users of hedging instruments other than forward foreign currency contracts.

The distinction between hedging and speculative transaction is determined and the basis set out in section 5.6.

Forward foreign exchange contracts

The Belgian Commission on Accounting has issued an opinion on the accounting treatment of forward foreign exchange transactions. This opinion does not deal with other hedging instruments. The opinion is not an accounting standard and is only technical advice for the treatment of foreign currencies and balances. It includes the following:

● to account for transactions in foreign currencies by converting monetary assets and liabilities at closing rate; and

● forward premiums and discounts on transactions should be accrued over the life of the contract.

The opinion does not deal with the accounting treatment for speculative contracts.

Other hedging instruments

Generally accepted accounting principles should be used for other hedging instruments:

- losses must be provided as soon as they are identified and gains deferred until they are realised;

- amounts should be recorded on an accruals basis;

- the accounting treatment will depend on whether the instruments are used for hedging or speculative purposes.

Swaps

The swap and the underlying transaction will be combined to determine whether there is a gain or loss on the position. Fees (when invoiced separately) may either be expensed immediately or amortised over the life of the swap.

Options

The premium may be recorded as a deductible expense or as a deferred charge. If the premium is recorded as an asset, its value must be amortised over the life of the option. Since the market value of the option can fluctuate, its balance sheet value should reflect such changes.

Financial futures

Gains or losses on a financial futures contract should be recorded as income or losses as from the moment the underlying transaction is executed. Gains and losses realised on the closing of a future contract before the sale of the underlying asset will be recorded as an adjustment to the value of the asset (provided the value of the asset adjusted in this way does not exceed its market value); this adjustment will be depreciated over the remaining life of the asset.

5.153 Tax treatment

The Belgian Income Tax Code does not include specific rules with respect to hedging instruments. The accounting rules with respect to valuation, depreciation, write-offs and allowances will apply for tax purposes.

The Netherlands

5.154 Accounting treatment

General

In general any hedging instrument must be treated in such a way that a true and fair view is given, allowing the reader of the statements to form an adequate opinion on the results, shareholders' equity, solvency and liquidity of the company. The general principle of 'substance over form' allows the offset of the results of the hedge instrument against the result of the underlying transaction. Valuation of hedging instruments may follow the rules for the underlying transaction.

If the transaction is purely speculative then the instrument should be included at market value at the balance sheet date and any unrealised gain, included in a 'constrained reserve'. This reserve forms a part of shareholders' equity, but it cannot be distributed to shareholders until the profit is realised. Losses must be provided in the profit and loss account.

Forward contracts and futures contracts

Any forward or futures contracts must be noted as off-balance sheet obligations. The accounting principles are similar to the general rule noted above.

Options

In so far as options are used to reduce the exposure to price fluctuations they may be valued in the same way as the underlying transaction. The premium should be amortised to the profit and loss account. Speculative positions should be valued at market price and the premium on that position can be taken as income or cost immediately. Losses on uncovered positions must be provided for immediately.

Warrants

Warrants should be valued separately using market prices. Unrealised profit should be entered into the constrained reserve, as described in the general rules above.

Swap transactions

There are no prescribed accounting standards for swap transactions. If the swap is properly matched, then it is common practice to denote the actual transaction at the swap rates.

Sale and repurchase transactions (repos)

The general rule for repos is to follow the economic risk. The economic risk is still with the original owner, if:

- the original owner still runs the risk of price fluctuations; and

- the original owner pays 90% of the value of the asset, regardless whether or not the asset is bought back.

As a result of that assessment, if the transaction is considered as a financing of the asset (rather than as a sale) the asset is kept on the balance sheet of the seller-borrower.

5.155 Taxation treatment

Taxation mainly follows the accounting rules. However, valuation will be allowed at cost or lower market price, with profits taken on a strict realisation basis. Short-term transactions can also be valued at market price, if applied on a consistent basis throughout the year.

Warrants held as investments by companies are taxed as shares. Receipts for warrants issued are treated as capital as soon as they are exercised. The value of the warrant will not be taxed in the issuing company. For individuals the value of the warrant will be taxed as income tax, if it is connected to a loan with a low interest rate.

Sale and repurchase transactions will mostly follow the accounting treatment. The 90% criterium will be applied to decide for fiscal purposes whether an asset is an investment of the company or a lease.

In cases where the objects of the tax laws are distorted by a transaction or series of transactions ('a construction') there are tax rules to ensure that substance goes before form. A construction is identified when its outcome is clearly economically unprofitable, and is only attractive because of its fiscal advantages.

Germany

5.156 Accounting treatment

There are no codified accounting principles for hedging instruments in Germany except for the new rules for foreign currency transactions undertaken by banks (section 340 in Commercial Code as amended in

October 1990). The accepted treatment of the main items included in this chapter is set out below.

Forward contracts

Profits and losses arising on forward contracts will be recognised only at maturity of the contracts. However, in accordance with the imparity principle any probable losses (based on knowledge at the balance sheet date) must be provided even though profits cannot be recognised. In respect of individually hedged positions it is acceptable not to provide for any losses (hedging on a 'macro' or overall basis is not allowed for accounting purposes). For banks, unrealised profits and losses from open forward foreign exchange contracts can normally be set off if in the same currency and they are within the same year. Except for such contracts, unrealised gains arising on valuations at the balance sheet date cannot be recognised.

Futures contracts

The generally accepted treatment for forward contracts is not generally applicable to all futures and there are no regulations or statements from professional bodies in relation to futures contracts. If stock index futures are used for hedging purposes they do not comply with the principles developed for forward contracts unless the underlying transaction (eg a portfolio of equities) exactly replicates the index. Consequently any profit or loss on the futures contract will be recognised only at maturity even if the contract is designated a hedge. Probable losses from these contracts must be provided in accordance with the imparity principle. For other futures contracts the treatment would be as for forward contracts.

Options

In 1987 the banking panel of the *Institut der Wirtschaftsprüfer* released a statement dealing with currency, stock and bond options. The statement provided that:

● option contracts must be valued at the lower of cost and market value;

● the premium paid is treated as an intangible asset and recorded in the balance sheet as an 'option right'. Premiums received on written options are recorded as liabilities;

● upon exercise of an option the acquisition cost of the underlying transaction comprises the settlement price plus the book value of the option. If the option lapses the book value must be written off;

● upon exercise an option writer must add premiums received to the sales proceeds of the underlying transaction. If the option lapses the premium is taken to income;

- any unrealised losses from uncovered written options must be provided.

The statement permits hedge accounting if a put option is purchased and the option is designated a hedge and matched to the underlying transaction. A write down of the underlying transaction is limited to the option's exercise price.

Hedge accounting is not permitted in respect of future commitments. Hedge accounting applies only to put options. According to the above principles the time value of an option would not be amortised.

Forward rate agreements

In general FRAs are treated like interest rate futures contracts. If a hedge of a particular underlying transaction can be identified then hedge accounting is permitted. As FRAs can be matched specifically to the underlying transaction and hedge accounting would be the usual treatment.

Interest rate caps

As interest rate caps are a series of put options, hedge accounting can be applied and the fee (premium) treated as an intangible asset.

Swaps – intermediaries

Following a statement from the German Bankers' Association, interest and currency receivables from matched swap deals should not be set off against each other but accounted for on an individual basis. Profits and losses from matched swaps should be accounted for on a cash basis over the life of the swap. Unmatched swaps should be treated in accordance with the imparity principle and provision must be made for any losses but profits may not be recognised. The individual elements of the swap should be accounted for as if they were conventional banking transactions.

Swaps – corporates

The treatment of swaps for corporates is currently the subject of much debate in Germany. In principle hedge accounting can be applied when swaps are matched exactly with the underlying transaction. Such matching involves the identification of specific transactions and matching of the maturity and amount. There must be no intention to terminate the hedge before maturity. Any profits or losses from the hedge are accounted for over the life of the swap. For currency swaps the asset or liability being hedged should be valued at the swap rate.

Repos

Accounting for repos distinguishes between unconditional repos (an outright sale and repurchase or 'echte' repos) and repos where the buyer is entitled (eg by an option) but not obliged to resell the securities ('unechte' repos). For banks the accounting principles for these transactions have recently been laid down in the Commercial Code.

For 'unechte' the purchaser records the securities while the seller is obliged to show the repurchase price at the bottom of the balance sheet.

In case of an unconditional repo ('echtes') the seller records the securities in the balance sheet together with a liability equivalent to the cash amount received. The purchaser records a receivable of the same amount. The difference between the sale and purchase price has to be amortised over the life of the repo.

5.157 Taxation treatment

The tax treatment of interest rate hedging instruments follows the accounting treatment.

Switzerland

5.158 Accounting treatment

General

The general accounting rules for Switzerland are set out in chapter 6 – Country Accounting and Taxation Framework which notes that the concept of overall valuation of the total position in a type of instrument, including any hedging transactions, is acceptable in Switzerland. This concept is important for hedging instruments as, for example, the net foreign exchange risk can be determined by accumulating the total of all positions (of the same currency) including anticipated future transactions. The net result can then be considered in the light of the imparity principle which does not permit unrealised gains to be recognised. There are no specific accounting rules in Switzerland for the accounting treatment of hedging instruments. Set out below is the generally accepted treatment for the instruments in this chapter.

Forwards and futures contracts

Forward and futures contracts cannot be treated as marketable securities and must therefore be valued in accordance with the principles set out above.

Options

Option premiums can be capitalised by the purchaser. The most appropriate heading in the balance sheet will usually be 'other assets'. The general accounting rules are then followed for their valuation. At expiry date the amount should be written off to the profit and loss account. If the option is exercised, the premium is treated as part of the acquisition/disposal amount. In case of a hedge where the market price is lower than the value of the underlying transaction the buyer of a put option can value the underlying assets at the strike price less the premium paid (and capitalised under other assets). The seller of an option needs to defer the premium received until either the option expires or the option is exercised. A provision is required for any contingent losses due to adverse market movements. Such a provision may be determined net of the option premium received and deferred.

Forward rate agreements

There are no accounting rules directly applicable to FRAs. In general the treatment will depend whether the transaction was designated as a hedge or is speculative. If the hedge criteria are met the accounting for the FRA should be related to the accounting of the underlying transaction. Any profit or loss on the FRA would, as a consequence, be amortised and spread as an adjustment to interest charges or income. Speculative FRAs should be valued and treated in accordance with the imparity principle.

Swaps

There is as yet little guidance of how swaps should be treated in Swiss financial statements. Receipts and payments under a swap agreement should be shown net, as an adjustment to interest. The valuation of swaps would depend on how the swap is structured and linked to other items in the accounts. If the underlying transaction is valued at cost (eg receivables, etc), then the swap should be treated on an accruals basis. If the underlying position is valued at market (eg securities) then the swap should be valued on a market value or present value basis.

5.159 Taxation treatment

The tax treatment of hedging instruments follows the accounting treatment.

Austria

5.160 Accounting treatment

There are no codified accounting principles for hedging instruments in Austria. Accounting practice for hedging instruments follows the imparity principle, ie any probable losses (based upon knowledge at the balance sheet date) must be provided and profits cannot be recognised. The treatment in the financial statements of a company of the hedging instruments in this chapter is not clear.

5.161 Taxation treatment

The tax treatment follows the accounting treatment. No special tax rules apply.

Sweden

5.162 Accounting treatment

General

The general accounting rules for Sweden are dealt with in chapter 6 – Country Accounting and Taxation Framework. There are no specific accounting and taxation rules for most hedging instruments which means that each transaction must be evaluated in light of its purpose and the underlying transaction. The net result then has to be considered in the light of the imparity principle, which as a general rule does not permit unrealised gains to be recognised. In the absence of specific accounting rules the comments below are based on the generally accepted treatment of the instruments in this chapter.

Forward contracts

The transaction does not normally have any balance sheet implications until the agreed future transaction date. At that date it is recorded and treated like any other on balance sheet transaction of the equivalent type. Any losses arising on a comparison to market rate of the total position at the balance sheet date will normally be reflected in the income statement in accordance with the imparity principle.

Futures contracts and FRAs

The total commitment under future contracts is normally recorded in a footnote in the annual accounts. If a market valuation of the total position shows a loss, the loss is normally recorded in the income statement. Actual gains or losses on FRAs are normally included in the interest income or the interest expense as the case may be.

Options

There are a number of different rules and interpretation of rules, depending on the type of option (OTC or standardised, equity, interest, foreign exchange, commodity etc) as well as the type of issuer or purchaser of the option. However, the following are the rules generally applied to most options:

• option premiums can be capitalised by the purchaser. This will most appropriately be done under the heading 'bonds and other investments'. Over the life of the option it is then valued in accordance with the general accounting rules. At maturity the amount should be written off to the income statement;

• if the option is exercised, the premium should be treated as part of the acquisition or selling price;

• if a put option is purchased as a hedge for a specific asset and the market price for this asset is lower than its original purchase price, then the holder can value the underlying asset at the strike price less the premium paid for the option;

• the seller of an option should defer the premium received until the option is exercised or expired. If adverse market price movements arise during the life of the option a provision should be made. Such a provision may be determined net of the option premium received and deferred.

Interest rate caps

As interest caps can be regarded as a hedge consisting of a series of put options a similar accounting treatment can be applied.

Swaps

Although a marking to market of interest and currency swaps would be appropriate for financial institutions, it is not common practice. One of the arguments for continuing the present practice of accrual accounting is that the underlying loan transaction is not subject to market valuation. At the balance sheet date currency swaps should be valued at the higher of the rate at the transaction date and the market rate for the currency received under the swap. For interest rate swaps, and the interest element of currency swaps interest income and expense is recorded on an accruals basis.

Repos

In Sweden there is no clear consensus of how to account for repos. The most common view is that it should be treated in the 'most conservative way' ie if a market valuation indicates a loss, then the loss should be accounted for and if the market valuation indicates a gain, then it should not be accounted for until the maturity of the repo. Repos are generally treated as a sale and the related securities are eliminated from the balance sheet. The commitment to repurchase is recorded as an off balance sheet item. If at a balance sheet date the repurchase price is higher than market the unrealised loss is provided. For buyer–lenders, reverse repos are treated as securities and are carried at the lower of cost or agreed resale price.

5.163 Taxation treatment

The tax treatment of hedging instruments does not differ from the accounting treatment for banks, insurance companies and other financial institutions holding them as current assets (stock in trade). For other companies and for individuals the following rules apply. It should be noted that the legislation assumes that the instruments generally are held for speculative purposes, but it is impossible to determine if the treatment would differ when the instruments are used for hedging.

Forwards and futures contracts

Taxation arises at the transaction date. The net result is treated as a capital gain or loss irrespective of whether the transaction is an actual delivery or a cash settlement.

Options

The premium is taxed at the date of offset, expiration or maturity, unless the option has a maturity exceeding 12 months, in which case the premium is taxed on receipt. The net result of the transaction is regarded as a capital gain or loss and, in applicable situations, as part of the result at the sale of the underlying asset. A loss is generally deductible from other capital gains and for companies also from ordinary income but only if the underlying asset is a debt instrument, a currency or a commodity.

Caps, swaps and repos

The taxation of these instruments should generally follow their accounting treatment, but there is considerable doubt as regards the deductibility of losses anticipated in the accounts by way of provisions. These instruments are assumed to be held only by companies, so their treatment for individuals is not dealt with in legislation.

Norway

5.164 Accounting treatment

Introduction

With the exception of Generally Accepted Accounting Standard No 11 'Foreign Currency Translation' the Companies Act of 1976 and Generally Accepted Accounting Standards do not deal with the accounting treatment of hedging instruments.

General concepts

The accounting treatment for hedging instruments will usually depend upon the type of organisation involved in the transaction and its purpose. Usually the economic rationale for entering into transactions involving hedging instruments can be analysed into trading and hedging. Usually corporates will be involved in hedging while financial services sector firms will usually be trading and/or hedging. In order to determine the appropriate accounting treatment it will be necessary to determine the purpose of the particular transaction.

To the extent that companies are involved in trading the accounting treatment of all hedging instruments is relatively straightforward and will comprise:

• determining the appropriate valuation policy for the hedging instrument in the balance sheet, which should be consistent with the other accounting policies adopted by the company;

• the recognition of the profit or loss which arises on the valuation. Once again this must be consistent with the treatment adopted for other items.

If the company is following the principle of 'marking to market' for its current asset readily marketable investments then hedging instruments held for trading purposes should be treated in the same way and valued at market prices.

If the hedging instrument is used for hedging purposes it will be necessary to ensure that it satisfies the conditions set out in section 5.6. Assuming that these conditions are satisfied then usually the appropriate accounting treatment will be to ensure symmetry between the underlying transaction and the hedging instrument using the accruals or matching concept. Set out below is the accounting treatment for the major types of instruments described in this chapter when they are used by corporates for hedging purposes. To the extent that anticipated transactions are hedged there must be reasonable certainty that the underlying transaction will occur before hedge accounting can be applied.

Forward foreign currency contracts

Where a forward contract is used to hedge an asset or liability the contract price should be used to value the relevant asset or liability. This treatment is endorsed by Generally Accepted Accounting Standard No 11 which states that for foreign exchange balances where there are related or matching forward contracts, the rates of exchange specified in the contracts should be used to translate monetary assets and liabilities denominated in foreign currencies. The discount or premium in the forward contract rate is financial income or expense.

Futures contracts

Futures contracts can be used for hedging existing assets and liabilities or anticipated transactions/commitments. The accounting treatment of existing assets and liabilities hedged with futures contracts will depend upon the accounting policies adopted for the underlying transaction. If the underlying asset or liability is carried at market value then the futures contract should be treated in the same way and any profit or loss included with that which arises on the underlying transaction (in the profit and loss account or revaluation reserve). If the underlying asset or liability is carried as the lower of cost and market value any profit or loss arising on the futures contract should be considered when determining the adjustments at the balance sheet date. The non symmetrical treatment of the underlying transaction will mean that a similar treatment will be required for the futures contract. For example:

● if the underlying transaction has a value which results in a profit which is not recognised then the loss on the futures contract should also be ignored;

● if the underlying transaction has a value which results in a loss, which would be provided (eg to write down an asset from cost to market value), then the profit on the futures contract should be recognised.

Where a futures contract is used to hedge a future commitment the profit or loss should be carried forward and amortised to the profit and loss account over the period that the underlying transaction relates (eg the term of the loan if the interest rate has been hedged) or added to or deducted from the value of the underlying transaction (eg stock).

Daily margin payments between the corporate and its broker or clearing house should be accounted for as debtors or creditors. They should have no profit and loss account implications.

Options

As noted in section 5.19 there are two basic types of option contracts; traded options and over the counter options. For a purchased traded option used by a corporate for hedging purposes the accounting treatment will be similar to that for futures contracts except that it will be necessary to record the premium in the balance sheet. If the underlying asset or liability is carried at market value similar treatment should be adopted for the option. If lower of cost and market value is the accounting policy then the option should be valued at the higher of cost and market value (market value can never be less than nil). Gains or losses on purchased traded options hedging future commitments should be deferred until the commitment occurs. With OTC options the position is more complex because at any intermediate valuation date it may be difficult to value the option. Accordingly it will be necessary to design an accounting policy which ensures that the premium cost is matched with the underlying transaction.

In addition options could be written by a corporate to enhance income from existing assets such as equities. The corporate will receive premium income which should be taken to the profit and loss account over the life of the contract. However it will be necessary to ensure that the underlying transaction and the option are not valued in an inconsistent manner.

Forwards, futures and option products

Hedging with one of these 'third generation' products (such as range forwards, break forwards etc) will usually require a combination of the approaches set out in the paragraphs above dealing with forwards and options. Typically the approach will follow that of hedging with options. The treatment of some of the types of instruments is set out below.

Interest rate swaps

The parties to the swap will pay each other the difference between the amounts of interest swapped. Consequently, the net amount of the difference will be added to or deducted from the interest charge in the profit and loss account. There should be full disclosure of the arrangement in the notes to the accounts so that the true commercial effect is clearly explained.

Currency swaps

In a currency swap used by a corporate for hedging purposes the funds lent to the corporate will have been exchanged into another currency. The most authoritative guidance available is the United States Standard FAS 52 ('Foreign Currency Translation') and the following paragraphs (which are concerned with the accounting treatment to be adopted by corporates) substantially reflect the conclusions reached in that standard.

Following the first leg of the swap, either party to a currency swap will have purchased one currency, with a commitment to sell that currency at a future date. Unlike most other foreign currency commitments, the forward leg of the swap should be revalued by a corporate in the balance sheet at the spot rate, rather than the forward rate of exchange. This is because the effect of the interest rate differential between the spot and forward rates is already reflected in the periodic payments made between the parties. How the gain or loss arising on this revaluation should be accounted for will depend on the purpose of the transaction. Where the transaction is speculative or is undertaken to hedge a foreign currency position the gain or loss on the revaluation of the forward commitment should be reflected in the profit and loss account. If the transaction is a hedge, the gain or loss on the commitment should offset the gain or loss on the asset which is being hedged.

If the transaction is intended to hedge a foreign currency commitment (such as a future cost or revenue), the gain or loss on the commitment arising from the hedge should be deferred and recognised in the profit and loss account at the time the gain or loss on the commitment being hedged is recognised.

5.165 Taxation treatment

There are no specific tax rules in these areas. There is currently limited practical experience on how to handle these problems.

Finland

5.166 Accounting treatment

Introduction

The accounting legislation in Finland is currently under review. The review committee published a proposal at the end of November 1990 for changes needed in the Finnish accounting legislation and practice which also took into consideration the requirements of the EC directives as far as possible.

The proposal contains general principles for the accounting treatment of hedging instruments. There have been no codified regulations for the accounting treatment of hedging instruments in Finland. Banking Supervision is also going to give new instructions for the accounting by Finnish banks in the near future.

The general principles for the accounting treatment of hedging instruments set out below is mainly based on the proposals of the accounting review committee and the prevailing practice adopted in Finland. It must be emphasised that the above mentioned proposals are not yet in force and changes are possible before the new legislation is prescribed in a few years time.

General principles of the accounting treatment of hedging instruments

When the hedging instrument is used for hedging purposes it is necessary for the conditions set out in section 5.6 to be met. If these conditions are met then the accounting treatment is symmetrical between the underlying transaction and the hedging instrument using the accruals or matching concept. When a financial instrument has been used for hedging purposes it has to be valued in compliance with the valuation of the underlying asset or liability.

When a financial instrument has been used for hedging purposes it is valued at market rates at the balance sheet date. The underlying transaction is valued similarly. However, the maximum gain on the hedging instrument which can be taken into the income statement is the amount of the loss arising on the valuation of the underlying transaction. Thus it is not permitted to take any unrealised gains into the income statement.

The gains or losses arising on a hedging instrument are taken into the income statement in the period when the contract is exercised or terminated. Any loss on a hedging instrument must be taken into the income statement at the balance sheet date.

If the hedging instrument relates to the acquisition of the underlying commodity, any gains or losses are added to or deducted from the acquisition cost of the underlying transaction. When a hedging instrument has been used to hedge the risk of another financial instrument, it is permitted to offset the loss on such contracts assuming that those contracts are matched exactly.

When the hedging instruments are used other than for hedging purposes they should be carried at the lower of cost and market value and the losses should be provided for as soon as they are foreseen. The gains are taken into the income statement in the period when the contract is exercised or terminated.

Forward foreign exchange contracts

The discount or premium in the forward contract rate serves a function of the interest differentials between the two currencies. Consequently where a forward foreign exchange contract is used to hedge an asset or liability it could be accounted for as if it were a financing transaction. The financing element could be taken into the profit and loss account over the life of the transaction.

Futures contracts

When a futures contract is used to hedge a futures commitment the profit or loss should be carried forward and amortised to the profit and loss account over the period that the underlying transaction relates to.

Options

Premiums paid for options are recorded as advance payments in 'liquid assets'. Premiums received on written options are recorded as advance payments in 'short term liabilities'. The premiums, received or paid, should be deferred until the exercise or termination of the option and taken into the profit and loss account in that period. If the option contract is exercised by purchasing the commodity or financial instrument, the premiums paid or received are added to or deducted from the acquisition cost of the underlying transaction. If an option contract has been purchased to hedge interest or exchange rate fluctuations on assets, liabilities or future commitments the option contract will be marked to market value at the balance sheet date. The underlying asset, liability or future commitment will be treated similarly at the balance sheet date. However as noted above no unrealised gain can be included in the income statement.

Forward rate agreements

When a FRA is used as a hedge, the settlement amount received or paid should be treated as part of the interest cost and amortised over the interest period covered by the FRA.

Interest rate swaps

The parties of the swap will pay each other the difference between the amounts of interest swapped. When an interest rate swap has been used to hedge liabilities or assets, the net amount of the difference will be added to or deducted from the interest charge or the interest income in the profit and loss account.

Currency swaps

Accounting for currency swaps has not been formalised in Finland but the treatment has to be in compliance with the treatment adopted for foreign currency transactions. If the transaction is a hedge, the gain or loss on the commitment should offset the gain or loss on the asset/liability which is being hedged.

Repos

Repos are accounted for as a financing transaction rather than a sale. Accordingly the seller-borrower will retain the asset on the balance sheet and record the borrowing as a liability. The buyer-lender will record the loan as an asset not the underlying security. The difference between the sale and repurchase price of the security is essentially in the interest cost to the seller-borrower. Interest on the loan (in whatever form) should be accrued in the normal way.

5.167 Taxation treatment

The taxation treatment of hedging instruments has not yet stabilised and there are differences between the accounting and taxation especially in regard to options. For taxation purposes the premiums received for options are regarded as income as they arise. The tax treatment of interest rate hedging instruments follows the accounting treatment. It will probably take a few years before the accounting and taxation treatments have been finalised and before that there are problems to be expected.

Greece

5.168 Accounting treatment

There are no laid down accounting principles for hedging instruments in Greece. Furthermore, the limited use of hedging instruments has resulted in a less than consistent treatment in practice. Generally speaking, the treatment follows the general rule of restating foreign currency balances at year end and taking the resulting gain or loss to the results for the period. However in the case of hedging instruments some companies account for the profit or loss only at the maturity of the contract while others take up the profit or loss up to the balance sheet date. Companies which are subsidiaries of foreign companies sometimes follow international accounting standard on instruction from their parent companies.

5.169 Taxation treatment

There are no specific tax rules relating to this area and generally the tax treatment follows the accounting treatment. However, there are certain tax peculiarities relating to foreign exchange gains and losses in general which would also apply in this case.

Cyprus

5.170 Accounting treatment

With the exception of IAS21 'Accounting for the Effects of Changes in Foreign Exchange Rates', the Cyprus Companies Law and IASs do not deal with the accounting treatment of hedging instruments. IAS10 dealing with contingencies may be relevant to some hedging instruments but this IAS would normally be covered by the fundamental accounting concept of prudence. Accounts, however, should disclose sufficient information about a hedging instrument for a reader to appreciate its nature and impact bearing in mind the need to reflect the substance of the transaction.

5.171 Taxation treatment

There is no established practice for the taxation of such instruments which are in any case not encountered very often. Their taxation treatment would normally be determined taking into account their accounting treatment and whether the results or costs incurred are part of the company's trading activities or whether they are of a capital nature.

Italy

5.172 Accounting treatment

General

In Italy there are presently no codified accounting principles for the treatment of hedging instruments, except for the treatment of foreign exchange contracts and currency swaps. This is because more recent instruments such as options (except those on shares) are not commonly used or do not yet exist in Italy (eg futures contracts). The codified or generally accepted treatment is set out below.

Forward contracts

For foreign exchange forward contracts established accounting principles state that the difference between the rate of exchange at the contract date and forward rate be recorded in the income statement over the life of the related contract. The commitment to sell or purchase currency must be recorded in memorandum accounts. If the contract is speculative the position must be evaluated at the balance sheet date; losses will be charged to the income statement, while profit will be deferred until maturity. Forward contracts relating to fixed income securities are normally recorded among memorandum accounts up to the date of the deferred settlement. At the balance sheet date, the transaction is evaluated on the basis of market value. Potential losses must be provided, while unrealised profits are deferred until the end of the transaction.

Options

For stock and bond options the premium corresponding to the purchase or sale of the option is accounted for in the financial statements at the time of payment or receipt as an asset or liability. In the event of the exercise of purchased options, the premium paid is added to the price of underlying securities; in the event of sale, it is added to the sale price of securities. In the event of the option not being exercised the premium is written off or taken to income. Transactions in progress at the end of the year, are recorded in the memorandum accounts. If a loss is foreseen at the balance sheet date, it must be provided for.

Swaps

As far as currency swaps are concerned, established accounting principles require that the difference between spot exchange rate and forward rate be recorded in the income statement over the life of the contract. The commitment to collect or deliver currency will be recorded in the memorandum accounts.

For interest rate swaps, the accounting treatment applied is to record net interest flows exchanged between the parties. The notes to the financial statements will include appropriate disclosure on the terms of the transaction.

Repos

For repurchase agreements of securities performed by banks and stock-brokers there are generally accepted accounting practices. The securities subject to the repo are retained in the accounts of the seller-borrower and amounts received are recorded as borrowings. For the buyer-lender the amount is shown as a loan. The difference between the purchase and the sale prices is accounted for over the life of the contract on an accruals basis and recorded in the income statement as interest receivable or payable. The amount of securities held or delivered as guarantee is noted in the accounts.

5.173 Taxation treatment

Under Italian tax legislation there are no specific regulations dealing with hedging instruments such as futures, options, swaps, largely due to the fact that they are not commonly used in Italy. Therefore, these trans-actions are taxed in accordance with the general principles of Italian tax law. Generally costs and income are taxable in the year that they become certain and of determinable amount. For the financial instruments in this chapter these requirements usually are not met until the end of the relevant contracts and thus any income/loss therefrom forms part of taxable income only at the end of the contract. The only exception to this general rule is the treatment of premiums on options which are taxed as a cost or income on an accruals basis from the moment at which the parties enter into the contract.

Table 5.1: London Metal Exchange - Futures Contracts

	Aluminium high grade 99.7%	Lead 99.97%	Copper Grade A	Nickel 99.80%	Tin 99.85%	Zinc Special High Grade 99.995%
Unit of trading	25 tonnes	25 tonnes	25 tonnes	6 tonnes	5 tonnes	25 tonnes
Delivery day	Daily for 3 months forward then every Wednesday for the next three months and then every 3rd Wednesday of the month for 21 months	Daily for 3 months forward then every Wednesday for the next three months and then every 3rd Wednesday of the month for 9 months	Daily for 3 months forward then every Wednesday for the next three months and then every 3rd Wednesday of the month for 21 months	Daily for 3 months forward then every Wednesday for the next three months and then every 3rd Wednesday of the month for 9 months	Daily for 3 months forward then every Wednesday for the next three months and then every 3rd Wednesday of the month for 9 months	Daily for 3 months forward then every Wednesday for the next three months and then every 3rd Wednesday of the month for 21 months
Last trading day	2 days before delivery day	2 days before delivery day	2 days before delivery day	2 days before delivery day	2 days before delivery day	2 days before delivery day
Trading months	Each delivery day	Each delivery day	Each delivery day	Each delivery day	Each delivery day	Each delivery day
Quotation	US$ per tonne	£ per tonne	£ per tonne	US$ per tonne	US$ per tonne	US$ per tonne
Minimum price fluctuation	$1.00	£0.25	£0.50	$1.00	$1.00	$0.50
Tick size	$25.00	£6.25	£12.50	$6.00	$5.00	$12.50
Initial margin	$2,750	£500	£3,000	$10,800	$2,500	$2,000
Delivery terms	Physical delivery, which calls for the receipt or delivery of an LME standard brand from or into an LME approved warehouse	Physical delivery, which calls for the receipt or delivery of an LME standard brand from or into an LME approved warehouse	Physical delivery, which calls for the receipt or delivery of an LME standard brand from or into an LME approved warehouse	Physical delivery, which calls for the receipt or delivery of an LME standard brand from or into an LME approved warehouse	Physical delivery, which calls for the receipt or delivery of an LME standard brand from or into an LME approved warehouse	Physical delivery, which calls for the receipt or delivery of an LME standard brand from or into an LME approved warehouse

Table 5.2: The London Futures and Options Exchange - Futures Contracts

	Cocoa No 7 contract	White Sugar No 5	Raw Sugar No 6	European Washed Arabica Coffee
Unit of trading	10 tonnes	50 tonnes	50 tonnes	37,500 pounds
Delivery day	First trading day of the contract month	Anytime during the next month	Last trading day of the contract month	Any day in the delivery month
Last trading day	Last working day of the month	15th day of the preceding month	Last day of the preceding month	Last day of the delivery month
Delivery months	March, May, July, September, December. Seven months quoted.	March, May, August, October, December. Seven months quoted.	March, May, August, October, December. Seven months quoted.	March, May, July, September, December. Seven months quoted.
Quotation	£ per tonne	$ per tonne	$ per tonne	$ per tonne
Minimum price fluctuation	£1 per tonne	$0.10 per tonne	$0.20 per tonne	$0.0005 per pound
Tick size	£10	$5	$10	$18.75
Initial margin	Variable, defined by ICCH	Variable, defined by ICCH	Variable, defined by ICCH	Variable, defined by ICCH
Delivery terms	Delivery to warehouse	Delivery FOB	Delivery FOB	Delivery FOB
Origins of commodity allowable	West Africa, South America, West Indies and other cocoa producing countries as defined in the Rules	White beet or cane crystal sugar or refined sugar of any origin from the current crop and subject to certain quality criteria	Raw Cane sugar, FAQ current crop minimum 96 degree polarisation at time of shipment from a producing country as defined in the Rules	Africa, South America, West Indies and producing countries as defined by the Rules
Price basis	£'s sterling per tonne ex warehouse UK or in warehouse Amsterdam, Antwerp, Bremen, Hamburg or Rotterdam	US$ and cents per tonne FOB stored designated ports	US$ and cents per tonne FOB designated port	US$ and cents per pound in warehouse London, Home Counties, Felixstowe, Hamburg, Bremen, Amsterdam Rotterdam, Antwerp, Le Havre, Barcelona and Trieste

Table 5.2 (continued): The London Futures and Options Exchange - Futures Contracts

	Robusta Coffee	MGMI metal index	Rice
Unit of trading	5 tonnes	US$ 100 per index point	50 tonnes
Delivery day	First trading day of the contract month	Monday prior to third Wednesday of expiry month	Any day in the month following contract month
Last trading day	Last working day of the month	Monday prior to third Wednesday of expiry month	10th day of month preceding delivery month
Delivery months	January, March, May, July, September, November. Seven months quoted.	First 3 months continuous, March, June, September, December, March (2).	October, December, March, May, July. Seven months quoted.
Quotation	$ per tonne	Index value	$ per tonne
Minimum price fluctuation	$0.2 per tonne	0.1 of an index point	$0.25 per tonne
Tick size	$1.00	$10	$12.50
Initial margin	Variable, defined by ICCH	Variable, defined by ICCH	Variable, defined by ICCH
Delivery terms	Delivery to warehouse	Cash settled	Delivery FOB
Origins of commodity allowable	Africa, India, West Indies, and other coffee producing countries as defined in the Rules	6 non-ferrous metals traded on the LME	High quality internationally traded long grain rice, current crop Thai 100B & US2/4
Price basis	US $ per tonne in warehouse London, Home Counties, Bristol, Hull, Amsterdam, Rotterdam, Le Havre, Hamburg, Bremen, Antwerp, Barcelona, Trieste and Felixstowe.	US $ per index point	US $ and cents per tonne, FOB (Kohsichang) or FAS (Houston, Lake Charles, New Orleans) FAS at 5% premium

Table 5.2 (continued): The London Futures and Options Exchange - Futures Contracts

	Commercial property futures	Commercial rent futures	Residential property futures	Mortgage interest rate futures
Unit of trading	£500 per index point	£500 per index point	£500 per index point	£500,000 per lot
Exercise day/ expiry day	Last Wednesday of calendar month one month following contract month expiry	Last Wednesday of calendar month one month following contract month expiry	Fifth business day of the calendar month following the contract month	Third Wednesday of the contract month
Last trading day	Last business day of contract month	Last business day of contract month	Third Friday of calendar month	11.00am on the expiry day
Trading months	First three consecutive months and the next four months in the March, June, September, December quarterly cycle	First three consecutive months and the next four months in the March, June, September, December quarterly cycle	First three consecutive months and the next four months in the March, June, September, December quarterly cycle	First three consecutive months and the next four months in the March, June, September, December quarterly cycle
Quotation	IPD Capital Growth Index	IPD Rental Growth Index	The new Nationwide Anglia house price index	100 minus the rate of interest
Minimum price fluctuation	0.05 of an index point	0.05 of an index point	0.05 of an index point	0.01 of an index point
Tick size	£25	£25	£25	£12.50
Initial margin	£600	£600	£1,500	£400
Delivery terms	Cash	Cash	Cash	Cash

(Currently suspended from trading)

559

Table 5.3: International Petroleum Exchange - Futures Contracts

	Gas Oil	Brent Crude	Heavy Fuel	Dubai Sour Crude	Naphtha
Unit of trading	100 tonnes	1,000 barrels (42,000 US gallons)	100 tonnes	1,000 barrels (42,000 US gallons)	100 tonnes
Delivery day	Between 16th and last calendar day of the delivery month	Not applicable due to cash settlement	Not applicable due to cash settlement	Not applicable due to cash settlement	Between 9th and 24th calendar day of the delivery month
Last trading day	2 days prior to the 14th calendar day of the delivery month	One business day prior to the first day of the delivery month becoming 'wet' or cargoes dated	2 business days prior to 14th calendar day of delivery month	15th day of month before delivery month	Last business day of calendar month prior to delivery month
Trading months	9 months including current month	6 months following current month	6 months including current month	6 months following current month	6 months following current month
Quotation	$ per tonne	$ per barrel	$ per tonne	$ per barrel	$ per tonne
Minimum price fluctuation	$0.25 per tonne	$0.01 per barrel	$0.10 per tonne	$0.01 per barrel	$0.25 per tonne
Tick size	$25	$10	$10	$10	$25
Initial margin	$1,500	$1,500	$5,000	$6,000	$1,500
Delivery terms	Physical delivery of gas oil into coaster from customs bonded installation in Amsterdam, Rotterdam or Antwerp	Cash	Cash	Cash	Physical delivery of naphtha into coaster from Customs bonded installation in Amsterdam, Rotterdam or Antwerp

Table 5.4: The Baltic Futures Exchange Limited - Futures Contracts

	Freight Index (BIFFEX)	EEC Wheat	EEC Barley	Pigs
Unit of trading	US$10 x index	100 tonnes	100 tonnes	3,250kg
First notice day/ settlement day	First business day after last trading day	Seventh day prior to the contract month of delivery	Seventh day prior to the contract month of delivery	First market day after last trading day
Last trading day	Last business day of contract month except December when it is 20th December	23rd day of the delivery month. (22nd for June)	23rd day of the delivery month	Last Tuesday of the delivery month
Contract months	Current and following month and January, April, July, October for two years ahead	January, March, May, June, September, November	January, March, May, September, November	Current month and succeeding nine months but excepting December
Quotation	$ per index point	£ per tonne	£ per tonne	pence per kg
Minimum price fluctuation	One index point	5 pence per tonne	5 pence per tonne	0.1 pence per kg
Tick size	$10	£5	£5	£3.25
Initial margin	$500 per contract (minimum)	£100 per lot (minimum)	£100 per lot (minimum)	£65 per lot (minimum)
Delivery terms	Cash	Physical delivery	Physical delivery	Cash

561

Table 5.4 (continued): The Baltic Futures Exchange Limited - Futures Contracts

	Potatoes (deliverable)	Soyabean Meal	Soya - Hi Pro
Unit of trading	20 tonnes	20 tonnes	20 tonnes
First notice day/ settlement day	4th business day of the contract month of delivery	22nd calendar day of delivery month	2 business days prior to 16th of delivery month
Last trading day	10th day of the delivery month or next business day	7 days before first business day of delivery month	2 business days prior to 16th of delivery month
Contract months	September, October, November, February, March, April, May, June (10 months quoted)	February, April, June, August, October, December	February, April, June, August, October, December
Quotation	£ per tonne	£ per tonne	£ per tonne
Minimum price fluctuation	10 pence per tonne	10 pence per tonne	10 pence per tonne
Tick size	£2	£2	£2
Initial margin	£400 per lot (minimum)	£100 per lot (minimum)	£100 per lot (minimum)
Delivery terms	Physical delivery	Physical delivery	Physical delivery

562

	Robusta Coffee (Traded in Paris and Le Havre)	White sugar (Traded in Paris)	Potatoes (50mm diameter) (Traded in Lille)	Potatoes (40mm diameter) (Traded in Lille)	Cocoa (Traded in Paris)
Unit of trading	5 tonnes	50 tonnes	20 tonnes	20 tonnes	10 tonnes
Delivery day/ exercise day/ expiry day	Cash: automatic daily clearing Delivery: between the first and the last of delivery month	Cash: automatic daily clearing Delivery: between the first and the last of delivery month	Cash: automatic daily clearing Delivery: between the first and the last of delivery month	Cash: automatic daily clearing Delivery: between the first and the last of delivery month	Cash: automatic daily clearing Delivery: between the first and the last of delivery month
Last trading day	6.30pm last day of trading month	7 pm 15th of trading month	4.30pm 2nd Thursday of the month	4.30pm 2nd Thursday of the month	6.30pm last day of trading month
Quotation	Price for 100g	Price per tonne	Price per 100kg	Price per 100kg	Price for 100kg
Minimum price fluctuation	Depends on the price of the tonne or the quintal	Depends on the price of the tonne or the quintal	Ffr 0.25	Ffr 0.25	Ffr 50
Tick size and value	Ffr 50	Ffr 50	Ffr 50	Ffr 50	Ffr 50
Initial margin	8 to 12% of the contract	8 to 12% of the contract	8 to 12% of the contract	8 to 12% of the contract	8 to 12% of the contract
Delivery terms	Physical delivery	Physical delivery	Physical delivery	Physical delivery	Cash or physical delivery
Trading months	January, March, May, July, September, November	March, May, August, October, December	November, February, April, May	November, April	March, May, July, September, December

Table 5.6: Amsterdam Pork and Potato Exchange - Futures Contracts

	Live Hogs	Potatoes
Unit of trading	10,000 kg	25,000 kg
Last trading day	Varies, published by exchange	Varies, published by exchange
Contract months	12 months forward every month	February, March, April, May, June, November
Quotation	Price per kg	Price per 100 kg
Minimum price fluctuation	NLG 0.05	NLG 0.10
Initial margin	15% of contract minimum NLG 2500	15% of contract minimum NLG 1750
Delivery terms	Cash	Cash

Table 5.7:   *London International Financial Futures Exchange - Stock Index Futures*

	FT-SE 100 Future	FT-SE Eurotrack 100 Future
Unit of trading	Valued at £25 per full index point	Valued at DM100 per index point
Delivery day/ exercise day/ expiry day	First business day after the last trading day	First business day after the last trading day
Last trading day	11.20am the last business day in the month	11.20am third Friday in delivery month
Quotation	FT-SE 100 Index points	Index points
Minimum price fluctuation	0.5	0.5
Tick size	£12.50	DM50
Initial margin	£1,500	DM 4,000
Delivery terms	Cash settlement at the exchange delivery settlement price	Cash settlement at the exchange delivery settlement price
Trading months	March, June, September, December	March, June, September, December

Table 5.8: London International Financial Futures Exchange - Futures Contracts on Eurocurrency Deposits

	Three Month Eurodeutschmark (Euromark) Interest Rate Future	Three Month Eurodollar Interest Rate Future	Three Month Sterling Interest Rate Future	Three Month European Currency Unit Interest Rate Future	Three Month Euro Swiss (EuroSwiss) Interest Rate Future
Unit of trading	DEM 1,000,000	$1,000,000	£500,000	ECU 1,000,000	Sfr 1,000,000
Delivery day/ exercise day/ expiry day	First business day after the last trading day	First business day after the last trading day	First business day after the last trading day	First business day after the last trading day	First business day after the last trading day
Last trading day	11.00am two days prior to the third Wednesday of delivery month	11.00am two business days prior to the third Wednesday of delivery month	11.00am third Wednesday of delivery month	11.00am two business days prior to the third Wednesday of delivery month	11.00am two business days prior to third Wednesday of delivery month.
Quotation	100 minus rate of interest	100 minus rate of interest	100 minus rate of interest	100 minus rate of interest	100 minus rate of interest
Minimum price fluctuation	0.01%	0.01%	0.01%	0.01%	Sfr 0.01
Tick size	DEM 25	$25	£12.50	ECU 25	Sfr 25
Initial margin	DEM 500	$500	£300	ECU 500	Sfr 500
Delivery terms	Cash settlement based on the exchange delivery settlement price	Cash settlement based on the exchange delivery settlement price	Cash settlement based on the exchange delivery settlement price	Cash settlement based on the exchange delivery settlement price	Cash settlement based on the exchange delivery settlement price.
Trading months	March, June, September, December	March, June, September, December	March, June, September, December	March, June, September, December	March, June September, December

Table 5.9: London International Financial Futures Exchange - Futures Contracts on Government Bonds

	Long Gilt Future	US Treasury Bond Future	German Government Bond (Bund) Future	Japanese Government Bond (JGB) Future	Italian Government Bond (BTP)	ECU Bond Future
Unit of trading	£50,000 nominal value notional gilt with 9% coupon	US$100,000 par value notional US Treasury Bond with 8% coupon	DEM 250,000 nominal value notional German Government Bond with 6% coupon	Y100,000,000 face value notional long term JGB with 6% coupon	ITL 200,000,000 nominal value 12% coupon	ECU 200,000 nominal value notional ECU Bond with 9% annual coupon
Delivery day/ exercise day/ expiry day	Any business day in delivery month (at seller's choice)	Any business day in delivery month (at seller's choice)	10th calendar day of delivery month. If this is not a working day then the next Frankfurt working day	First business day after the Tokyo Stock Exchange last trading day	10th calendar day of delivery month	20th calendar day of delivery month
Last trading day	11.00am two business days prior to last business day in delivery month	4.10pm seven CBOT working days prior to last business day in delivery month	11.00am (Frankfurt time) Three Frankfurt working days before delivery day	3.00pm one business day prior to the Tokyo Stock Exchange last trading day	4 working days prior to the delivery day	11.00am (Brussels time) Same last trading day as the LIFFE Bund contract
Quotation	Per £100 nominal	Per $100 par value	Per DEM 100 nominal value	Per Y100 face value	ITL 100 nominal value	Per ECU 100 nominal value
Minimum price fluctuation	£1/32	£1/32	DEM 0.01	Y0.01	ITL 0.01	ECU 0.01
Tick size	£15.625	$31.25	DEM 25	Y10,000	ITL 20,000	ECU 20
Initial margin	£500	$1,250	DEM 2,000	Y 600,000	ITL 2,000,000	ECU 2,000
Delivery terms	Invoiced amount in respect of each deliverable bond is to be calculated by the exchange delivery settlement price factor system. Adjustment is made for full coupon interest accruing at delivery day	Any US Treasury bond maturing at least 15 years from 1st day of contract. Must be capable of transfer by means of the US Federal Reserve wire	Any Bundesanleihe with 8.5 - 10 years until maturity remaining as at the tenth calendar day of the delivery month	Cash settlement based on the delivery settlement price of the Tokyo Stock Exchange JGB futures contract	Cash settlement at the exchange delivery settlement price	Invoiced amount in respect of each deliverable bond is to be calculated by the exchange delivery settlement price factor system. Adjustment is made for full coupon interest accruing at delivery day
Trading months	March, June, September, December	March, June, September, December	March, June, September, December	March, June, September, December	March, June, September, December	March, June, September, December

Table 5.10: *Marché à Terme International de France - Financial Futures Contracts*

	Notional bond (7-10 years)	PIBOR (3 months)	CAC 40 Index	Euro DEM (3 months)	4-year French Treasury notes	ECU
Unit of trading	Ffr 500,000 nominal value	Ffr 5,000,000	200 x Index	DEM 1,000,000	Ffr1,000,000 nominal value	ECU 100,000
Delivery day/ exercise day/ expiry day	Last day of the delivery month	15th of the delivery month	Last day of the delivery month	One day after last trading day	Last business day of delivery month	5 calendar days after last business day
Last trading day	4pm 4 business days before the delivery month	4pm 2nd business day preceding the 11th Thursday of each quarter	5pm last business day of the month	11am two business days prior to the third Wednesday of delivery month	Third to last business day of delivery month	Four days prior to last business day of delivery month
Quotation	Percentage of nominal	100% less interest rate	Index	Percentage of nominal index with 2 decimals 100% less interest rate	Percentage of par in minimum increment of 0.02% of contract	Percentage of par to two decimal places
Minimum price fluctuation	0.02%	0.01%	0.1 of an index point	Percentage of base point; 0.01%	0.02% of contract	0.02% of contract
Tick size	Ffr 100	Ffr 125	Ffr 20	DEM 25	Ffr 200	ECU 20
Initial margin	Ffr 25,000	Ffr 15,000	Ffr 30,000	DEM 1,000	5% of nominal	ECU 2,000
Delivery terms	Settlement by cash or delivery of equivalent bonds	Cash	Cash	Cash	Physical delivery	Physical delivery
Trading months	March, June, September, December	March, June, September, December	3 months and one quarterly expiry month	March, June, September, December	March, June, September, December	March, June, September, December

Table 5.11: *Irish Futures and Options Exchange - Financial Futures Contracts*

	IFOX Long Gilt	IFOX 3 month DIBOR contract	IFOX Short Gilt	ISEQ Index
Unit of trading	IR£50,000 nominal of a notional 8%, 20 year government stock	IR£100,000 3 month deposit	IR£100,000 nominal of a notional 8%, 5 year Irish Government stock	IR£10 per full point index
Delivery day/ exercise day/ expiry day	3rd Wednesday in delivery month	3rd Wednesday of settlement month	3rd Wednesday of delivery month	3rd Thursday of settlement month
Last trading day	11.00am 2 business days before delivery date	11.00am 2 business days before settlement date	11.00a.m 2 business days before delivery date	4.15pm 1 business day before settlement date
Trading months	March, June, September, December	March, June, September, December	March, June, September, December	March, June, September, December
Quotation	IR£'s per IR£100 nominal	100.00 minus rate of interest	IR£ per IR£100 nominal	Index points to one decimal point
Minimum price fluctuation	IR£0.01	IR£0.01	IR£0.01	IR£0.01
Tick size	IR£5	IR£2.5	IR£10	IR£1
Initial margin	IR£2,500	IR£3,000	IR£3,000	IR£1,300
Delivery terms	Nominal amount of deliverable stock whose value at delivery date is IR£50,000 on a semi-annual gross redemption yield equal to notional coupon (8%)	Cash only	Nominal amount of deliverable stock whose value at the delivery date is IR£100,000 on a semi-annual gross redemption yield equal to notional coupon (8%)	Cash only

Table 5.12: Deutsche Terminborse - Financial Futures Contracts

	Notional Government Bond (Bund Future)	German Stock Index DAX (DAX Future)
Unit of trading	DEM 250,000 notional value	DEM 100 x DAX index point
Trading delivery day	Tenth calander day of delivery month	Third Friday of settlement month
Last trading day	12.30pm two business days before delivery day	Last day before settlement day
Quotation	DEM per DEM 100 of nominal value	In DEM (1/10 of an index point)
Minimum price fluctuation	0.01	0.5
Tick size	DEM 25	DEM 50
Initial margin	Risk based margin 200 ticks; DEM 5,000	Risk based margin 50 ticks; DEM 13,500
Delivery terms	Cash	Cash
Trading months	March, June, September, December	March, June, September, December

Table 5.13: Stockholm Options Market - Financial Futures Contracts

	OMr 5 Interest Rate Future	OMr 10 Interest Rate Future	OMax Stock Futures	OMX Index Futures	OMVX Treasury Bill Future
Contract unit	SEK 1,000,000	SEK 1,000,000	100 shares	Index x SEK100	SEK1,000,000
Delivery day/ exercise day/ expiry day	Third Wednesday in expiration month	Third Wednesday in expiration month	Third Friday in expiration month	3 bank days after the fourth Friday in expiration month	Third Wednesday in expiration month
Last trading day	Expiration day (noon)	Expiration day (noon)	Bank day prior to expiration day	Bank day prior to expiration day	Expiration day (11.00am)
Trading months	Six month contracts introduced every three months	Six month contracts introduced every three months	Six month contracts introduced every three months	Three month contracts listed every month	Six month contracts introduced every three months
Quotation	Yield to maturity	Yield to maturity	Price per share	Per hundreth of the OMX index value	Per hundreth of the OMX index value
Minimum price fluctuation	SEK 0.01	SEK 0.01	SEK 0.01	SEK 0.01	SEK 0.01
Initial margin	OM's margin system	OM's margin system	OM's margin system	OM's margin system	OM's margin system
Delivery terms	Cash settlement against fixing yield. Thereafter, delivery of bonds of net position in futures contracts with the expiration month	Cash settlement against fixing yield. Thereafter, delivery of bonds of net position in all futures contracts with the expiration month	Physical delivery	Cash	Cash settlement against fixing yield. Thereafter, delivery of bonds of net all position in all futures contracts with the expiration month

Table 5.14: *Financiele Termijnmarkt Amsterdam - Financial Futures Contracts*

	FTO (8 - 10 year Government Bonds)	FT 5	FTI (EOE equity index)
Contract unit	NLG 2,500 x price of hypothetical bond with 7% coupon and NGL 250,000 nominal value	NLG 200 x EOE top 5 index	NLG 200 x EOE equity index
Delivery day	Same day as bonds	Same day as options	Same day as options
Last trading day	7th day of the month	Third Friday of the month	Third Friday of the month
Trading months	September, December, March, June	1,2,3 and 6,9,12 month series	1,2,3 and 6,9,12 month series
Quotation	Bond price (% basis)	Index	Index
Minimum price fluctuation	NLG 1 cent	NLG 10 cents	NLG 5 cents
Tick size	NLG 2,500 cents		
Initial margin	NLG 4,000	NLG 6,000	NLG 4,000
Delivery terms	Cheapest to deliver based on conversion factors. Minimum 8 yrs to maximum 10 yrs maturity with an issue size of at least NLG 1 billion.	Cash settlement at exchange settlement price	Cash settlement at exchange settlement price

Table 5.15: *Mercado Espanol de Futuros Financiers (MEFF) - Financial Futures Contracts*

	3 year notional Government Bond	90 day MIBOR Deposit
Unit of trading	10,000,000 Ptas of nominal value	10,000,000 Ptas 90 day deposit
Delivery day	Third Wednesday of delivery month	Third Wednesday of delivery month
Quotation	Ptas per 100 Ptas nominal value	Interest rate on 90 day time deposit
Minimum price fluctuation	One basis point	One basis point
Tick size	Pta 1,000	Pta 250
Initial margin	4% of nominal (400,000 Ptas)	0.3% of nominal (30,000 Ptas)
Delivery terms	Physical delivery	Cash
Trading months	March, June, September, December	March, June, September, December

Table 5.16:   *Guarantee Fund for Danish Options and Futures - Futures Contracts*

	KFX stock index	9% Annuity Mortgage Credit Bond 2006	Danish Government Bond
Unit of trading	1,000 DKr x index	1,000,000 DKr nominal value	1,000,000 DKr nominal value
Delivery day/ exercise day/ expiry day	First business day in expiry month	First business day in expiry month	Third business day in expiry month
Last trading day	One business day before expiry	One business day before expiry	One business day before expiry
Minimum price fluctuation	0.05%	0.05%	0.05%
Tick size	DKr 50	DKr 500	DKr 500
Initial margin	10%	4%	4%
Delivery terms	Cash	Cash	Cash
Trading months	March, June, September, December	January, April, July, October	March, June, September, December

Table 5.17: *London Traded Options Market - Options Contracts*

	Over 60 individual equities	FT-SE 100 Index (American exercise)	FT-SE 100 Index (European exercise)	Restricted life options
Unit of trading	1,000 shares	£10 x Index	£10 x Index	1,000 shares
Expiry day	Two days before last day of dealings for last complete Stock Exchange account	Last business day of contract month	Last business day of contract month. This is the only day on which that month's contracts can be exercised.	Two days before last day of dealings for last complete Stock Exchange account
Last trading day	As per expiry day	As per expiry day	As per expiry day	As per expiry day
Expiry cycles	4 monthly cycle or up to 9 months out	Nearest 4 months plus up to 2 additional months out to a maximum 12 months	4 months out to a maximum of 1 year on the March, June, September, December cycle	2,4,6 month expiry series
Quotation	Pence per share option	Index points	Index points	Pence per share option
Minimum price fluctuation	1/4p	1/2p	1/2p	1/4p
Delivery terms	By delivery of shares	Cash. Two business days after exercise day	Cash. Two business days after exercise day	By delivery of shares

Table 5.18: *The European Options Exchange - Options Contracts*

	Options on Dutch Equities	Option on GBP/NLG currency	Option on USD/NLG Currency	Option on Dutch Government Bonds one issue
Unit of trading	100 shares	£10,000	$10,000 and $100,000 (Jumbo Dollar)	NLG 10,000 nominal value
Last trading day	3rd Friday of the month	3rd Friday of the month	3rd Friday of the month	3rd Friday of the month
Quotation	Price per share	GB£/NLG	US$/NLG	Price percentage
Minimum price fluctuation	NLG 0.10	NLG 0.01	NLG 0.05 NLG 0.01 (Jumbo)	NLG 0.01
Initial margin	Calculated by the EOE with reference to daily published risk factors and the level of initial margin for the related futures contract which it cannot exceed	Calculated by the EOE with reference to daily published risk factors and the level of initial margin for the related futures contract which it cannot exceed	Calculated by the EOE with reference to daily published risk factors and the level of initial margin for the related futures contract which it cannot exceed	Calculated by the EOE with reference to daily published risk factors and the level of initial margin for the related futures contract which it cannot exceed
Delivery terms	Standard Amsterdam procedure	Physical delivery	Physical delivery, modified European style contracts not exercisable before expiry date	Standard Amsterdam procedure
Trading months	Cycle 1: October, January, April, July and 1,2,3,4 and 5 years Cycle 2: November, February, May, August	1,2,3 and 6,9,12 month series	1,2,3 and 6,9,12 month series	November, February, May, August + 1,2,3 years

Table 5.18 (continued): The European Options Exchange - Options Contracts

	EOE Stock Equity Index	Option on gold	Major market Index Option on US Stocks (also traded in Chicago)	Dutch top 5 Index Options	Options on Bond Future
Unit of trading	NLG 100 x Index	10 troy ounces	Index x $100	NLG 100 x Index	1 FTO future nominal NLG 250,000
Delivery day/ exercise day/ expiry day	N/A	N/A	N/A	N/A	N/A
Last trading day	3rd Friday of the month	3rd Friday of the month	3rd Friday of the month	3rd Friday of the month	3rd Friday of the month
Quotation	Index	$ per troy ounce	Index	Index	NLG per NLG 100 nominal value
Minimum price fluctuation	NLG 0.10	$0.10	$1/16 for premiums under $3 $1/8 for premiums over $3	NLG 0.10	NLG 0.01
Initial margin	Calculated by the EOE with reference to daily published risk factors and the level of initial margin for the related futures contract which it cannot exceed	Calculated by the EOE with reference to daily published risk factors and the level of initial margin for the related futures contract which it cannot exceed	Calculated by the EOE with reference to daily published risk factors and the level of initial margin for the related futures contract which it cannot exceed	Calculated by the EOE with reference to daily published risk factors and the level of initial margin for the related futures contract which it cannot exceed	Calculated by the EOE with reference to daily published risk factors and the level of initial margin for the related futures contract which it cannot exceed
Delivery terms	Cash	Physical delivery	Cash	Cash	Physical delivery
Trading months	1,2,3 and 6,9,12 months series	November, February, May, August	1,2,3 month series + 6 and 9 months	1,2,3,6,9 and 12 month series	3,6 months February, May, August, November

577

Table 5.19: Swiss Options and Financial Futures Exchange - Futures and Options Contracts

	Swiss market stock index futures contract	Swiss market stock index option contract	Options on Swiss equities
Unit of trading	SFr 5 x Index	SFr 5 x Index	5 shares
Delivery day/ exercise day/ expiry day	Saturday after the third Friday of a month	Saturday after the third Friday of a month	Saturday after the third Friday of a month
Last trading day	One day prior to expiration day	One day prior to expiration day	One day prior to expiration day
Quotation	Bid/ask	Bid/ask	Bid/ask
Minimum price fluctuation	SFr 5	Varies	Varies
Initial margin	SFr 5,000		
Delivery terms	Cash	Cash	Physical delivery
Trading months	First 3 months, January, April, July, October	First 3 months, January, April, July, October	First 3 months, January, April, July, October

Table 5.20: *Deutsche Terminborse - Options Contracts*

Options on German Equities

Unit of trading	50 shares
Delivery day/ exercise day/ expiry day	Exercise on any business day during trading hours; delivery two days after exercise day
Last trading day	Third Friday of every trading month
Quotation	DEM
Minimum price fluctuation	DEM 0.10
Tick size	DEM 5
Initial margin	Option price plus margin (based on volatility of underlying stock)
Delivery terms	Physical with the exception of cash settlement on Allianz options
Trading months	1,2 and 3 months and 6 months in March, June, September, December cycle

Table 5.21: **Stockholm Options Market - Options Contracts**

	Equity Options -16 stocks	OMX Index Options	OMR5 Interest rate Option
Unit of trading	100 shares	SEK100 x Index	SEK 1,000,000
Delivery day/ exercise day/ expiry day	Third Friday in expiration month	Normally fourth Friday in expiration month	Third Wednesday in expiration month
Last trading day	Day prior to expiration day	Day prior to expiration day	Expiration day at noon (local time)
Quotation	Prices per share	Per hundreth of an option	Per hundreth of an option
Minimum price fluctuation	SEK 0.01	SEK 0.01	SEK 0.01
Initial margin	OM's margin system	OM's margin system	OM's margin system
Delivery terms	Physical delivery	Cash	Automatic exercise of in-the-money options. Closing through cash settlement
Trading months	3 and 6 months	3 month contract every month	6 month contract introduced every 3 months

Table 5.22: *Marché à Terme International de France - Options Contracts*

	Option on Notional bond	Option on White sugar Contract	Option on 3 month PIBOR Contract	Option on 3 month EuroMark Contract
Unit of trading	One futures contract Ffr 500,000	One white sugar futures contract 50 tonnes	One Pibor futures contract Ffr 5,000,000	One Euromark futures contract DEM 1,000,000
Delivery day/ exercise day/ expiry day	End of each quarter	Last business day of the month preceding the delivery month	End of each quarter	On any business day until last trading day (American Option) by delivery or reception of futures contract
Last trading day	Last Friday of the month preceding the maturity month	Last business day of the month preceding the delivery month	Two business days prior to the third Wednesday maturity month (from June)	Two business days prior to the third Wednesday of the delivery month (11.00am)
Quotation	Percentage of the contract	Ffr per tonne	% of nominal value	% of nominal value to three decimal places
Minimum price fluctuation	0.01% of nominal value	Ffr per tonne	0.005% of the nominal value	0.005% of the nominal value
Tick size	Ffr 50	Ffr 50	Ffr 62.5	DEM 12.5
Initial margin	Computed on the global future-option position	8-12% of position	No initial margin but cross margin on the futures on options contracts	No initial margin but cross margin on the futures on options contracts
Delivery terms	Cash	Cash or physical delivery	Cash	Cash
Trading months	March, June, September, December	March, May, August, October	March, June, September, December	March, June, September, December

Table 5.23: *Marché des Options Negociables de la Bourse de Paris - Options Contracts*

	Options on equities quoted on the Bourse	Option on the CAC 40 index
Unit of trading	Generally 100 shares	Ffr200 x index
Delivery day/ exercise day/ expiry day	End of each quarter	Last day of the delivery month
Last trading day	Last business day of the month of maturity	Last business day of the month of maturity
Quotation	Percentage of the contract	Percentage of index
Minimum price fluctuation	Ffr0.01	Ffr0.01
Initial margin	No initial margin but for investors in a net sale position only, the margining is adjusted daily to cover the least favourable liquidation value	No initial margin but for investors in a net sale position only, the margining is adjusted daily to cover the least favourable liquidation value
Delivery terms	Cash or stock delivery	Cash
Trading months	March, June, September, December	3 consecutive nearest term and 1 quarterly

Table 5.24: **Guarantee Fund for Danish Options and Futures - Options Contracts**

	KFX stock index	9% Annuity Mortgage Bond 2006	Danish government bond	Options on Danish stocks
Unit of trading	1 x KFX future contract	1,000,000 DKr	1,000,000 DKr	100 underlying stocks
Delivery day/ exercise day/ expiry day	First business day in expiry month	First business day in expiry month	Third business day in expiry month	First business day in expiry month
Last trading day	One business day before expiry	One business day before expiry	One business day before expiry	One business day before expiry
Minimum price fluctuation	0.05%	0.05%	0.05%	2.5% to 5%
Tick size	DKr 50	DKr 500	DKr 500	
Initial margin	0% to 10%	0% to 4%	0% to 4%	15%
Delivery terms	Cash	Cash	Cash	Cash
Trading months	March, June, September, December	January, April, July, October	March, June, September, December	March, June, September, December

Table 5.25: *Finnish Options Brokers - Options Contracts*

	FOX index future	Options on FOX index	Stock futures
Unit of trading	Index x 100 FIM	Index x 100 FIM	200-1000 shares
Delivery day/ exercise day/ expiry day	The 4th Friday of the expiry month	The 4th Friday of the expiry month	The 3rd Friday of the expiry month
Last trading day	Trading day immediately prior to expiration day	Trading day immediately prior to expiration day	Trading day immediately prior to expiration day
Trading months	February, April, June, August, October, December	February, April, June, August, October, December	February, April, June, August, October, December
Minimum price fluctuation	0.01%	0.01%	0.01, 0.05 and 1.0 FIM
Tick size	1 FIM	1 FIM	
Initial margin	Approx. 15-20% of the underlying value	Approx.15-20% of the underlying value	Approx. 15-20% of the underlying value
Delivery terms	Cash delivery 5 days after the expiration	Cash delivery 5 days after the expiration	Cash delivery 5 days after the expiration

Table 5.26:   *The London Futures and Options Exchange - Options Contracts*

	No 7 Cocoa Traded Options	No 6 Raw Sugar Traded Options	No 5 White Sugar Traded Options	Robusta Coffee Traded Options	European washed Arabica Coffee	Option on the MGMI Metal Index Future
Unit of trading	10 tonnes	50 tonnes	50 tonnes	5 tonnes	37,500 pounds	$ 100 per index point
Exercise day/ expiry day	Close of business on the third Wednesday in the preceding month	Close of business on the third Wednesday in the preceding month	Close of business on the first business day in the preceding month	Close of business on the third Wednesday in the preceding month	12.30am on third Wednesday of the month preceding the delivery month	Monday prior to the third Wednesday of expiry month
Last trading day	Until trading in underlying future ceases	Until trading in underlying future ceases	Until trading in underlying future ceases	Until trading in underlying future ceases	Until trading in underlying future ceases	Until trading in underlying future ceases
Trading months	March, May, July, September, December	March, May, August, October, December	March, May, August, October, December	January, March, May, July, September, November	March, May, July, September, December	First three consecutive months and the next four months in the March, June, September, December quarterly cycle.
Quotation	£ per tonne	$ per tonne	$ per tonne	$ per tonne	$ per pound	$ per index point
Minimum price fluctation	£1 per tonne	$0.05 per tonne	$0.05 per tonne	$ per tonne	$0.0001 per pound	$ 5 per 5 basis points
Initial margin	Margining system is maintained by the ICCH. Margins depend on the volatility of the underlying futures contract.	Margining system is maintained by the ICCH. Margins depend on the volatility of the underlying futures contract.	Margining system is maintained by the ICCH. Margins depend on the volatility of the underlying futures contract.	Margining system is maintained by the ICCH. Margins depend on the volatility of the underlying futures contract.	Margining system is maintained by the ICCH. Margins depend on the volatility of the underlying futures contract.	Margining system is maintained by the ICCH. Margins depend on the volatility of the underlying futures contract.
Exercise/strike price increments	£50 per tonne	$10 per tonne	$10 per tonne	$50 per tonne	$0.05 per pound	5 MGMI Index points
Delivery terms	Underlying futures contract	Underlying futures contract	Underlying futures contract	Underlying futures contract	Underlying futures contract	Underlying futures contract

Table 5.27: International Petroleum Exchange - Options Contracts

	Gas Oil (American Style)	Brent Crude (American Style)
Unit of trading	100 tonnes	1,000 barrels
Exercise day/ expiry day	Any time up to 1 hour after cessation of trading on expiry day	Any time up to 1 hour after cessation of trading on expiry day
Last trading day	3rd Wednesday of month prior to delivery month	3rd day before cessation in underlying futures contract
Trading months	First three months of underlying futures contract	First three months of underlying futures contract
Quotation	$ per tonne	$ per barrel
Minimum price fluctuation	$ 0.05 per tonne	$ 0.01 per barrel
Tick size	$5	$10
Initial margin	$1,000	$1,000
Exercise/strike price increment	Multiples of US$ 5.00 per tonne	Multiples of US$ 0.50 per barrel
Delivery terms	IPE options are exercised into gas oil futures contracts	IPE options are exercised into Brent Crude oil futures contracts

586

Table 5.28: Baltic Futures Exchange - Options Contracts

	Wheat	Barley	Potatoes	Soyabean Meal	Soyabean Meal - Hi Pro	Pigs
Unit of trading	1 futures contract	1 futures contract	1 futures contract	1 futures contract	1 futures contract	1 futures contract
Exercise day/ expiry day	Next market day after last trading day	Next market day after last trading day	15th day of month preceding delivery month	Next market day after last trading day	Next market day after last trading day	Last business day of month preceding settlement month of futures contract
Last trading day	2nd Thursday of month prior to delivery month	2nd Thursday of month prior to delivery month	2nd Wednesday of month prior to delivery month	1st Market day of month prior to delivery month of underlying futures contract	1st Market day of month prior to delivery month	Subject to expiry of option
Trading months	January, March, May, November	January, March, May, November	April	February, April, June, August, October, December	February, April, June, August, October, December	Current month and succeeding nine months but excepting December
Quotation	Pounds per tonne	Pence per tonne	Pence per tonne	Pence per tonne	Pence per tonne	Pence per kg
Minimum price fluctuation	£0.05 per tonne	£0.05 per tonne	£0.10 per tonne	£0.10 per tonne	£0.10 per tonne	0.1 pence per kg
Tick size	£5	£5	£2	£2	£2	£3.25
Initial margin	One futures contract initial margin for granters	One futures contract initial margin for granters	Futures initial margin adjusted by delta factor	Futures initial margin adjusted by delta factor	Futures initial margin adjusted by delta factor	Futures initial margin adjusted by delta factor
Exercise/strike price increment	£1 per tonne	£1 per tonne	£5 per tonne	£1 per tonne	£1 per tonne	1 pence per kg
Delivery terms	Underlying futures contract	Underlying futures contract	Underlying futures contract	Underlying futures contract	Underlying futures contract	Underlying futures contract

Table 5.29: *London Metal Exchange - Options Contracts*

	Aluminium high grade 99.7%	Lead	Copper Grade A	Nickel	Zinc Special High Grade
Unit of trading	25 tonnes	25 tonnes	25 tonnes	6 tonnes	25 tonnes
Delivery day/ exercise day/ expiry day	1st/3rd Wednesday in each trading month	1st/3rd Wednesday in each trading month	1st/3rd Wednesday in each trading month	1st/3rd Wednesday in each trading month	1st/3rd Wednesday in each trading month
Last trading day	One month option, 1 day before delivery of futures 3 month option, 3 days before delivery	One month option, 1 day before delivery of futures 3 month option, 3 days before delivery	One month option, 1 day before delivery of futures 3 month option, 3 days before delivery	One month option, 1 day before delivery of futures 3 month option, 3 days before delivery	One month option, 1 day before delivery of futures 3 month option, 3 days before delivery
Trading months	January and every second month thereafter	February and every second month thereafter	January and every second month thereafter	February and every second month thereafter	February and every second month thereafter
Quotation	$ per tonne	£ per tonne	£ per tonne	$ per tonne	$ per tonne
Strike price increment	£25/$25 for strike price to $1725 US$50/tonne for strike price $1750-$2950 US$100/tonne for strike price $3000 or greater	£20/$20 per tonne	£25/$25 for strike price to $1725 US$50/tonne for strike price $1750-$2950 US$100/tonne for strike price $3000 or greater	£50/$50 per tonne	£20/$20 per tonne for strike price above $2000 per tonne
Delivery terms	Exercise calls for receipt or delivery of an LME standard brand from or into an LME approved warehouse	Exercise calls for receipt or delivery of an LME standard brand from or into an LME approved warehouse	Exercise calls for receipt or delivery of an LME standard brand from or into an LME approved warehouse	Exercise calls for receipt or delivery of an LME standard brand from or into an LME approved warehouse	Exercise calls for receipt or delivery of an LME standard brand from or into an LME approved warehouse
Initial margin	Margining system varies on a daily basis. Risk factors are calculated to give an indication of the potential change in the price of an option given a change in the price of the underlying commodity.				

Table 5.30: *London International Financial Futures Exchange - Option Contracts on Eurocurrency Deposits*

	Option on Three Month Eurodollar Interest Rate Future	Option on Three Month Sterling Interest Rate Future	Option on Three Month Euro Deutschemark (Euromark) Interest Rate Future
Unit of trading	1 Eurodollar futures contract $1,000,000	1 Three Month Sterling futures contract £500,000	1 Three Month Euromark futures contract DEM 1,000,000
Delivery day/ exercise day/ expiry day	Exercise by 5.00pm on any business day; delivery on the 1st business day after the exercise day. Expiry at 12.30pm on last trading day. Automatic exercise of in-the-money options on last trading day	Exercise by 5.00pm on any business day; delivery on the 1st business day after the exercise day. Expiry at 12.30pm on last trading day. Automatic exercise of in-the-money options on last trading day	Exercise by 5.00pm on any business day; delivery on the 1st business day after the exercise day. Expiry at 12.30pm on last trading day. Automatic exercise of in-the-money options on last trading day
Last trading day	11.00am Last trading day of Eurodollar futures contract	11.00am Last trading day of Three Month Sterling futures contract	11.00am Last trading day of Three Month Euromark futures contract
Quotation	Multiples of 0.01 (ie. 0.01%)	Multiples of 0.01 (ie. 0.01%)	Multiples of 0.01 (ie. 0.01%)
Minimum price fluctuation	0.01	0.01	0.01
Tick size	$25.00	£12.50	DEM 25
Initial margin	Calculated by clearing house with reference to daily published risk factors and the level of initial margin for the related futures contract which it cannot exceed	Calculated by clearing house with reference to daily published risk factors and the level of initial margin for the related futures contract which it cannot exceed	Calculated by clearing house with reference to daily published risk factors and the level of initial margin for the related futures contract which it cannot exceed
Delivery terms	Assignment of 1 Eurodollar futures contract for the delivery month at the exercise price	Assignment of 1 Three Month Sterling futures contract for the delivery month at the exercise price	Assignment of 1 Three Month Euromark futures contract for the delivery month at the exercise price
Trading months	March, June, September, December	March, June, September, December	March, June, September, December

Table 5.31: *London International Financial Futures Exchange - Option Contracts on Government Bonds*

	Option on Long Gilt Future	Option on US Treasury Bond Future	Option on German Government Bond (Bund) Future
Unit of trading	1 Long Gilt futures contract £50,000	1 US Treasury Bond Futures contract $100,000	1 Bund futures contract DEM 250,000
Delivery day/ Exercise day/ expiry day	Exercise by 5.00pm on any business day, 6.00pm on last trading day. Delivery on 1st business day after the exercise day. Expiry at 6.30pm on last trading day	Exercise by 5.00pm on any business day; extended to 8.30pm on last trading day. Delivery on the 1st business day after the exercise day. Expiry at 8.30pm on last trading day	Exercise by 5.00pm on any business day; extended to 6.30pm on last trading day. Delivery on the 1st business day after the exercise day. Expiry at 6.30pm on last trading day
Last trading day	4.15pm Six business days prior to the first day of the delivery month	4.10pm First Friday preceded by at least six CBOT working days before the first delivery day of the US Treasury Bond futures contract	4.00pm Six business days prior to the first day of the delivery month
Quotation	Multiples of 1/64	Multiples of 1/64	Multiples of DEM 0.01
Minimum price fluctuation	1/64	1/64	DEM 0.01
Tick size	£7.8125	$15.625	DEM 25
Initial margin	Calculated by clearing house with reference to daily published risk factors and the level of initial margin for the related futures contract which it cannot exceed	Calculated by clearing house with reference to daily published risk factors and the level of initial margin for the related futures contract which it cannot exceed	Calculated by clearing house with reference to daily published risk factors and the level of initial margin for the related futures contract which it cannot exceed
Delivery terms	Assignment of 1 Long Gilt futures contract for the delivery month at the exercise price	Assignment of 1 US Treasury Bond futures contract for the delivery month at the exercise price	Assignment of 1 Bund futures contract for the delivery month at the exercise price
Trading months	March, June, September, December	March, June, September, December	March, June, September, December

Chapter 6

Country accounting and taxation framework

Country accounting and taxation framework

Introduction

In most countries in Europe (and indeed, in the United States and Japan and other developed countries), specific accounting standards have not yet been developed to determine the accounting treatment to be adopted for the increasing number of complex financial instruments. The appropriate accounting treatment for a particular instrument can usually be determined by applying the general accounting concepts which have been adopted in the country concerned. To be able to do this, the economics and risks of the instrument have to be clearly understood. This chapter sets the general accounting and tax framework for each country within which the accounting treatment for each financial instrument would be determined. As noted in chapter 1 – Introduction, for members of the European Community this framework will be governed by the fourth and seventh directives. In addition, for banks and insurance companies there will be requirements imposed by directives specifically designed for such entities.

United Kingdom

6.1 Accounting

In the United Kingdom the general accounting requirements to be followed by United Kingdom corporations are set out in schedule 4 to the Companies Act 1985 (CA 1985). The CA 1985 has been amended by the Companies Act 1989 (CA 1989) but for accounting related matters this later Act inserts certain new requirements in CA 1985. Consequently CA 1985 remains the relevant legislation. CA 1985 sets out rules stipulating the format of, and the disclosure in, a company's accounts, and the methods by which profits, losses and assets and liabilities are to be calculated. For example, CA 1985 requires that current assets should be carried in the balance sheet at the lower of cost and net realisable value.

The overriding requirement of CA 1985 is that financial statements should give a true and fair view of the company's financial position and of its results for that period. The fact that this requirement is overriding has been used to justify the departure from specific accounting rules contained in Schedule 4 to CA 1985. For example, bond and security dealers generally rely on this requirement to justify carrying dealing assets in the balance sheet at market value, rather than at the lower of cost and net realisable value.

Fundamental accounting concepts

The 'true and fair override' is a requirement of the EC 4th Company Law Directive which has been implemented in the United Kingdom. However, the concept of 'true and fair' is well established and was central to United Kingdom company law prior to the implementation of the directive. No definition of a 'true and fair view' is given in statute, but it is generally accepted that accounts must:

● be prepared on the basis of the four fundamental accounting concepts of prudence, going concern, consistency and accruals;

● employ appropriate accounting policies which are to be consistently applied;

● disclose all information material to a proper understanding of the accounts;

● describe the amounts in the accounts in such a way that their true nature is explained unambiguously;

● strike a balance between completeness of disclosure and the summarisation necessary for clarity.

SSAPs and SORPs

The requirements of the Companies Act are supplemented by Statements of Standard Accounting Practice (SSAPs) and Statements of Recommended Accounting Practice (SORPs) issued by the professional accounting bodies.

SSAPs detail accounting principles and rules to be followed, unless otherwise stated, by all companies and any departure from these is required to be disclosed and explained. Before SSAPs are issued, they are circulated for comment from interested parties as exposure drafts (EDs). In particular, ED49, 'Reflecting the substance of transactions in assets and liabilities' which replaced ED42 'Accounting for Special Purpose Transactions' attempts to specify general characteristics of assets and liabilities. These characteristics,and the substance of the transaction, will help determine the accounting treatment for various complex financial transactions, including off-balance sheet financing transactions. To some extent the requirements of ED42 in relation to 'controlled non subsidiaries' have been covered by requirements in CA 1989 in respect of 'subsidiary undertakings'. However, ED49 goes further than CA 1989 by defining a 'quasi subsidiary' which, although not being a subsidiary undertaking, is a source of benefit or risks to the reporting company that in substance are no different to those of a subsidiary undertaking. In addition, ED49 has application notes dealing with specific types of transactions including sale and repurchase agreements and securitised mortgages. ED55 published in July 1990 'Accounting for Investments' recognises that readily marketable current asset investments should be valued at market values ('marking to market').

SORPs relate to particular industries and/or types of organisation (eg Pension Funds) and provide guidance on accounting principles and rules that are considered best practice for that industry. Compliance with the SORPs is not mandatory. The SORPs are initially prepared by bodies which represent the industry and were subsequently approved ('franked') and issued by the now disbanded Accounting Standards Committee (ASC). The British Bankers' Association has released a SORP on the Valuation of Securities and an exposure draft on Commitments and Contingencies. Other trade bodies are currently drafting SORPs dealing with other issues. The Accounting Standards Board (ASB) which has replaced the ASC has stated that it will not be franking industry SORPS in future. However, new SORPS will contain a statement that it contains no fundamental points of principle which are unacceptable to the ASB.

Technical Releases

In addition to statements setting out requirements and recommendations for accounting practice, the professional accounting bodies issue Technical Releases (TRs) which are discussion papers offering guidance on issues of current interest. In 1987 the Institute of Chartered Accountants in England and Wales issued TR 677 'Accounting for Complex Capital Issues' which attempted to set out general principles to be followed in accounting for new financial instruments and discussed the specific treatment to be adopted in respect of some of the instruments described in this book. The general principles set out in TR 677 form a reasonable basis for determining the accounting treatment of complex financial instruments. However, the conclusions reached on individual instruments are not mandatory and in some cases are controversial.

The future

The ASB is developing a number of Financial Reporting Standards (FRS) some of which will replace existing SSAPs and EDs. FRS1 'Cash flow statements' was published in September 1991 and a FRS to replace ED49 is expected by the end of 1991. As noted in chapter 3 – Asset

Backed Securities, this standard may impose significant new requirements on originators of such securities. In addition, the Urgent Issues Task Force of the ASB has been set up to issue pronouncements of best practice on topical issues. These pronouncements do not have the status of an FRS but should be viewed as mandatory. The recently created Financial Reporting Review Panel reviews company accounts for compliance with accounting standards and CA 1985. This panel has the power to require directors to amend accounts.

6.2 Taxation

For fiscal purposes, the United Kingdom comprises England, Scotland, Wales, Northern Ireland, United Kingdom territorial waters and other designated areas. Two main taxes are levied on income:

● corporation tax, which applies to bodies incorporated in the United Kingdom and foreign companies trading in the United Kingdom through a branch or agency;

● income tax, which applies to individuals, partnerships and trusts and is charged on a graduated basis dependent on income.

Corporate taxes

Corporation tax is levied on the profits of United Kingdom resident companies and foreign companies resident in the United Kingdom or trading in the United Kingdom through a branch or agency. A company resident in the United Kingdom is liable to tax on its worldwide profits, income and capital gains.

Income tax – the schedular system

Income tax is charged on the taxable income of the year of assessment. Corporation tax is charged on the company's income and gains of an accounting period. Income is taxable if it falls within one or other of the schedules of the Taxes Act 1988.

Schedule A   Taxes the annual profits or gains arising in respect of rent and similar payments from land in the United Kingdom.

Schedule B   Taxed the occupation of commercial woodlands in the United Kingdom. The charge to tax under this schedule is abolished with effect from 6 April 1988 subject to transitional provisions.

Schedule C   Taxes profits arising from public revenue dividends payable in the United Kingdom.

Schedule D   Taxes annual profits or gains arising from:
– any trade, profession or vocation;
– interest, annuities and other annual payments;
– non-United Kingdom securities and possessions;
– any other annual profits or gains not taxable under any other schedule.

Schedule E   Taxes emoluments from an office or employment.

Schedule F   Taxes distributions and dividends from companies resident in the United Kingdom.

Trading profits

The profit for tax purposes is based on the profits as shown by the accounts drawn up under ordinary principles of commercial accounting, but subject to specified adjustments. For example, the United Kingdom tax system allows tax depreciation on capital expenditure for only certain limited classes of asset.

Trading expenses

Expenses are only deductible if they are:

• incurred wholly and exclusively for business purposes;

• of an income rather than a capital nature.

Capital gains

Gains on the sale of capital assets are taxed separately. Non-corporate entities are chargeable to capital gains tax at income tax rates (currently 25% or 40%). Gains of a company are chargeable to corporation tax.

Other taxes include:

• inheritance tax;

• value added tax (VAT).

The tax legislation in the United Kingdom is complicated and subject to frequent change. The computation of taxable income while based on accounts, is calculated separately and the accounting policies do not necessarily reflect the taxation bases.

Administration

Income tax and corporation tax law is governed by parliamentary statute and case law. Each year a Finance Act is passed introducing new statute law and amending existing law. Case law is founded on the fundamental principle of the binding authority of precedent and has evolved and developed through the decisions of the judges in the Appeal Courts.

Channel Islands

6.3 Accounting

The disclosure requirements contained in the laws governing conduct of companies in the Channel Islands provide limited guidance with regard to the information to be disclosed in the financial statements to be presented to shareholders. The Societies of Chartered and Certified Accountants in both Jersey and Guernsey have agreed and issued a Statement of Channel Islands Accounting Practice which applies to all financial statements prepared in the Channel Islands for accounting periods commencing on or after 1 January 1989.

Financial statements of Channel Island incorporated companies should normally be drawn up in such a manner as to comply with Statements of Standard Accounting Practice issued by the accountancy bodies in the United Kingdom. The information to be disclosed in the financial statements is derived from the requirements of International Accounting Standard No. 5.

6.4 Taxation

Whilst the two principal Channel Islands, Jersey and Guernsey, are fiscally independent, taxes levied are substantially the same. There are no taxes on capital gains but income tax is levied on the profits of Channel Island resident companies and foreign companies resident in the Channel Islands or those trading through a branch or agency. Companies resident in the Channel Islands are liable to tax on their worldwide profits.

Since 1 January 1989, both Islands grant to companies which are incorporated in the Channel Islands but which are owned by non residents and which do not trade in the Islands the facility of Exempt

Company status. Such companies pay an annual fee (currently £500) regardless of their profits.

Other taxes include:

• customs and excise duties.

Administration

The administration of income tax is governed by Statute and where appropriate relevant United Kingdom case Law. Case Law is founded on the fundamental principle of the binding authority of precedent.

Isle of Man

6.5 Accounting

The accounting treatment in the Isle of Man follows closely that in the United Kingdom. United Kingdom SSAPs and SORPs apply in the Isle of Man.

6.6 Taxation

Taxation legislation in the Isle of Man is very brief and unsophisticated. It relates only to private and public companies which pay tax at 20% on their taxable profits. Income tax is payable by individuals based on their worldwide income less foreign tax (restricted to the local rate of tax) at the rate of 15% and 20%. In practice, contentious matters are dealt with by informal discussion with the taxation authorities and subsequently mutually agreed.

Republic of Ireland

6.7 Accounting

There are two principal sources of accounting requirements in the Republic of Ireland: legislation and the statements of the accounting bodies. Whilst the requirements of the legislation are mandatory for all limited liability entities preparing accounts, those of the accounting bodies vary from being guidelines or indicators of best practice up to being required in order for the accounts to show a true and fair view.

The basic companies legislation in the Republic of Ireland is the Companies Act 1963 (the 1963 Act). This legislation has been amended significantly by the Companies Amendment Act 1986 (the 1986 Act) which introduced the provisions of the EC 4th Directive into Irish company law. The 1986 Act does not apply in full to licensed banks or insurance companies which are exempted pending the introduction of equivalent EC legislation. The EC 7th Directive on group accounts has not yet been introduced into Irish law.

Irish companies legislation has the following general requirements which are of relevance to accounting for financial instruments:

● the accounts must give a true and fair view of the profit or loss for the period and of the financial position of the company at the year end. Whilst no definition of 'true and fair' is provided in the legislation, it is generally accepted to include:

– the use of the four fundamental accounting concepts (see section 6.1);

– appropriate accounting policies which are to be consistently employed;

– disclosure of all of the information relevant to a proper understanding of the accounts.

● the accounts must be prepared in a format which conforms with that set out in the Schedule to the 1986 Act. This involves a proper classification of assets and liabilities, the separation of short and long term assets and liabilities and the correct classification of provisions;

● assets and liabilities should be shown separately in the accounts and 'netting off' is not permitted except where a genuine right of set-off exists;

● assets should be stated at the lower of cost or net realisable value. There are, however, alternative accounting rules which can be applied in certain circumstances and permit the revaluation of fixed assets. The general requirement that accounts should show a true and fair view is often invoked to facilitate the carrying of dealing securities at market value;

● all material contingencies and commitments should be noted in the accounts;

● when shares are issued for a consideration greater than their nominal value a share premium must be recognised. The share premium account may be used only to issue new shares or set off expenses arising on the issue of shares and otherwise may be reduced only with the approval of the High Court.

The Irish accounting bodies subscribe to SSAPs and SORPs and they are issued simultaneously in the United Kingdom and Republic of Ireland. Hence the accounting requirements in the Republic of Ireland which arise from accounting standards and other pronouncements of the accounting bodies are similar to those in the United Kingdom.

6.8 Taxation

There are two taxes levied on income in the Republic of Ireland:

● corporation tax: this is payable on worldwide income of companies resident (ie managed and controlled) in the Republic of Ireland and on the profits attributable to an Irish branch or agency ('permanent establishment' in tax treaty cases) of companies not resident in Ireland. The basic corporation tax rate is 43% (40% from 1 April 1991) and there is a special 10% rate for profits from manufacturing. The 10% rate is also available to companies operating in the International Financial Services Centre in Dublin;

● income tax: this is payable at graduated rates on the income of unincorporated persons – individuals, partnerships and trusts.

Other taxes include:

● capital gains tax (CGT);

● capital acquisitions tax (CAT);

  –inheritance tax and gift tax;

● value added tax (VAT);

● stamp duty, including companies' capital duty;

● pay related social insurance (social security);

● customs and excise duties.

There are no local income taxes.

Tax legislation in the Republic of Ireland is complex and subject to frequent change. New and amended statute law is provided for in the Finance Act passed each year. Case law is founded on the fundamental principle of the binding authority of precedent and has evolved and been developed through judicial decisions of the Irish appeal courts.

France

6.9 Accounting

In France, general accounting requirements to be followed by the commercial companies are set out in the *Code de Commerce* (as contained in the law 83-353 of 30 April 1983 and the decree 83-1020 of 29 November 1983) and the *Plan Comptable General*, ie the General Counting chart of 27 April 1982. In addition, specific requirements applicable to banks and insurance companies are set out in standards issued by corresponding regulatory bodies. Further, the accounting bodies (such as the *Conseil National de la Comptabilite*), the French Stock Exchange Commission (*Commission des Operations de Bourse*, 'the COB') issue recommendations.

General accounting requirements cover the presentation and valuation of assets and liabilities as well as policies relating to the recognition of profits and losses. The accounts should present fairly the financial information which should be based on the four fundamental accounting concepts (prudence, matching (accruals), consistency and going concern).

Traditionally, the principle of prudence overrode the 'fairness' of presentation principle and unrealised profits were never recognised. Additionally, there has been no specific rule permitting commercial substance over legal form. In recent years, the development of new financial instruments and the increasing internationalisation of accounting practices have brought about an evolution in French accounting rules, as shown in the recent recommendations of accounting bodies. For example, the following rules are now followed:

● marking to market of certain trading activities in organised markets;

● the possibility of deferring realised profits and losses to allow a symmetric treatment for specific assets/liabilities and any corresponding hedging transactions.

To avoid possible controversial treatment for similar transactions, the COB in its 1988 annual report recommended that valuation rules be reviewed globally so that greater respect be paid to the economic substance of transactions. Accounting bodies are likely therefore to issue such recommendations in the near future; these recommendations will reflect collaboration between the general accounting bodies (the CNC), the Accountants Institute, the banks accounting bodies (represented by the *Commission Bancaire*) as well as large companies and banks themselves.

More generally, there is more and more pressure on large quoted companies to present general information in their financial statements on their risks and strategies in the field of interest rate sensitivity and in their use of new financial instruments.

6.10 Taxation

For fiscal purposes, France includes the Overseas Departments (states) (Guadeloupe, Guiana, Martinique et Reunion). For Overseas territories (New Caledonia, Polynesie, Wallis et Futuna, les Iles de l'Ocean Indien, les terres Australes et Antartiques, Mayotte et Saint Pierre et Miquelon), French tax rules do not apply unless expressly provided for.

In France two main taxes are levied on income:

● corporation tax – which applies to legal entities by reason of legal form (limited liability companies), business activity of a manufacturing nature (associations other than companies) or by reason of election (unlimited companies);

● income tax – which applies for individuals and unlimited companies. In the latter case, companies are not taxed in their own capacity and each partner is subject to individual tax or corporate tax on its prorata share of net taxable income.

Corporate taxes

Territoriality rules

According to territoriality rules, corporation tax is assessed on the profits of French resident companies as well as on the foreign corporation's profits derived from:

● a 'complete' cycle of transactions carried out in France (including the Overseas Departments);

● an establishment in France of a foreign corporation;

● activities performed by a dependent representative in France of a foreign corporation.

If a tax treaty applies, the taxable income in France is the income which is attributable to a permanent establishment located in France, within the meaning of 'permanent establishment' under the applicable double tax treaty. As a general rule French corporation taxes are not assessed on worldwide profits. However, some French companies may receive an authorisation from the Treasury to use a worldwide tax consolidation system.

Net taxable income

The net taxable income is the amount represented by the increase in a company's net worth from one financial year to the next. Determination of net taxable income begins with the computation of the current year's total gross income: whether related to the company's main business activities or not. For instance, capital gains are treated separately, and manufacturing profits, income from real estate and securities, and interest on loans are aggregated when determining taxable income. Deductible expenses are set off against gross income. As a general rule, in order to qualify as deductible, expenses must either be incurred for the company's own benefit, or necessary for normal business operations.

Tax rates

As from 1 January 1991 standard corporation rates are:

- 34% for retained earnings;
- 42% for distributed earnings.

Capital gains tax

Gains on fixed assets are included in income. They are divided into "short term' gains on fixed assets which were held for less than two years and 'long term' gains on the sale of assets which were held for at least two years. In addition, for depreciable fixed assets which have been held for at least two years, that part of the gain which corresponds with the depreciation charged on the assets (effectively a recapture of depreciation) is also taxed as a short term capital gain.

Long term capital losses are losses on the disposal of non-depreciable assets held for more than two years. Short term capital losses are those incurred on the disposal of all other fixed assets. Unrealised losses on investments in shares of companies may, under certain conditions, be treated as deductible long-term capital losses.

Short term gains are taxed at the standard corporate tax rate of 34%. Long term gains are taxed at 15%, 19% or 25% but only if the net balance is allocated to a special long term capital gain reserve. If this reserve is distributed, additional corporate tax and 'precompte' will have to be paid. The 25% tax rate is applicable to gains derived from the sale of some specific financial instruments (bonds and warrants, participating loan stock, units in investment funds, asset backed securities, etc) for the financial year beginning as of 1 November 1990.

Basis of computation

The computation of taxable income is based on accounts, is calculated separately and the accounting policies do not necessarily reflect the taxation bases.

Income tax on individuals

The annual French personal income tax (*'impot sur le revenu'*) is assessed on the worldwide income of individuals domiciled in France. It is assessed on their French source income when they are domiciled abroad. Individual income tax brackets are usually revalued each year by the French Parliament. The tax rates applicable for 1990 range from 0% to 56.8%. When an individual qualifies as a French resident, he (she) is generally liable to personal income tax on the aggregate of his (her), his (her) spouse's and dependent children's worldwide income. Tax exemptions, however, may be provided by certain countries' double tax treaties.

Definition of French tax resident status

According to French law, an individual is deemed to have his (her) fiscal domicile in France if:

● he (she) has his (her) home in France or he (she) has his (her) main abode in France;

● France is the place of his (her) principal activities;

● France is the centre of his (her) economic interests (ie his (her) income is principally derived from assets managed or located in France).

If an individual is domiciled in both France and another country, the laws of these countries and the double tax treaty signed with them, if any, must be referred to in order to determine the country in which the individual should be treated as resident.

Determination of taxable income

Taxable income is the aggregate of all income received by the taxpayer. Income is classified in different categories: manufacturing and trading profits, pensions, wages and salaries, income from professional activities, real estate income, and income from securities and similar sources. The taxable income of each category is determined and calculated separately by applying specific rules.

For example, salaries and other related benefits are taxed only after having deducted the employee's social security contributions and the following allowances subject to a threshold: a 10% business expenses allowance with a ceiling of Ffr 66,950 in 1990 and 20% additional allowance with a ceiling of Ffr 121,400.

For capital gains, a distinction is drawn between gains from fixed property and gains from financial investments. Gains from financial investments realised since 12 September 1990 may be taxed if the total amount of the annual sales of shares and bonds either listed or unlisted exceeds, during the relevant calendar year, an amount of Ffr 307,600. The tax rate is 17% on the sales of securities. The Ffr 307,600 threshold does not apply on the disposal of securities by an individual owning more than 25% of the share capital of a French company who are then taxable at 17% on any net capital gain realised.

Administration

There are four principal sources of tax law in France:

- tax treaties;

- laws and decrees;

- case law;

- regulations issued by the French tax authorities.

As regards case law, it should be noted that although the principle of 'stare decisis' is not operative in France the interpreation of tax laws issued either by *Conseil D'Etat* or *Cour de Cassation* are given great weight. As regards administrative regulations issued and published periodically in the *Bulletin Officiel des Impots*, such documents are not binding on the taxpayer but are binding on the tax administration provided the tax administration has taken a formal position with respect to the manner in which a provision of tax law is applied to a set of facts concerning the taxpayer.

Luxembourg

6.11 Accounting

In Luxembourg the general accounting requirements to be followed by companies are laid down in the law of 4 May 1984 which introduced the EC 4th Directive on company law into Luxembourg legislation. The law of 4 May 1984 is applicable to all corporations with the exception of banks, insurance companies and investment funds which are covered by specific laws and regulations.

The overriding requirement of the 4 May 1984 law is that financial statements must give a true and fair view of the company's financial position and results. Departure from the detailed provisions of the law is possible in order to comply with this overriding requirement.

It is generally recognised that the accounts must be prepared:

- on the basis of the four fundamental accounting concepts of prudence, going concern, consistency and accruals;

- avoiding the offsetting of assets and liabilities and of income and expenditure;

- disclosing all material information necessary to a proper understanding of the accounts.

There is no specific accounting standard for the treatment of financial instruments. The accounting treatment will thus be determined by reference to accounting treatments adopted by other countries (eg United States, United Kingdom, etc) provided these are in agreement with the accounting principles laid down in the law. These principles include:

- valuation of assets

Assets are generally valued at the lower of cost or market value except for the investments which can only be written down when there is a permanent diminution in value.

- revenue recognition

Unrealised losses should be recognised as soon as they are identified whereas unrealised gains are not generally required to be recognised. Specific accounting principles in the banking industry have been established by their regulatory body (IML).

6.12 Taxation

Luxembourg corporations are liable to the following taxes:

Income taxes

Income taxes are applied on the company's worldwide income and include:

- corporation tax

The basic rate amounts to 33% plus a surcharge of 1% of the tax to support the funding of unemployment relief. Reduced rates are applied to low incomes.

- municipal business tax on income

The rate of this tax is levied in favour of the municipalities and amounts to 9.09% for Luxembourg City. This tax is deductible for the calculation of the corporate tax and there is an abatement of Luxembourg francs 700,000.

The combined tax rate of these taxes is 39.39%.

Capital taxes

The following taxes are applied:

• net worth tax

Companies are subject to an annual net worth tax (*impot sur la fortune*) of 0.5%. Net worth is determined from the disclosed net assets of the company, although investments in affiliates and the value of foreign immovable property situated in treaty countries are excluded from the computation. The official value of real property situated in Luxembourg and the market values of securities are substituted for book values.

• municipal business tax on capital

An additional net worth tax on net assets is levied in favour of the municipalities. This differs from the comparable state tax in that the market value of movable assets rented from a non commercial entity and the official value of real property is deducted. There is an abatement of Luxembourg francs 1,800,000. The effective tax rate varies according to location. In Luxembourg City, the rate is 0.5%.

Branches of foreign corporations are subject to the above mentioned taxes.

Basis of computation of taxation

The taxable profit of a company is based upon the difference between net assets at the beginning and end of the financial year. Capital gains arising during the year are, therefore, included in profit and taxed at corporate income tax rates. There is in principle no difference between the commercial profit as per annual financial statements and the profit considered for taxation purposes.

Belgium

6.13 Accounting

Belgium is not traditionally a pioneering country for accounting and auditing. However in 1975 and 1976, Belgium was the first country in Europe to adopt the then still draft EC 4th Directive provisions and to implement these in respect of all large and medium sized businesses. The legal framework of the Belgian accounting legislation comprises:

- the Accounting Law of 17 July 1975;

- the Royal Decree of 8 October 1976 concerning the Annual Accounts of Business Enterprises;

- the Royal Decree of 7 March 1978 defining the minimum content and the presentation of a Standard Minimum Chart of Accounts;

- the Decree of 6 March 1990 concerning the presentation of consolidated accounts for Business Enterprises.

By law, a Commission for Accounting Standards has been organised and issues on request and upon its own initiative opinions on the practical interpretation of the legal provisions and on the appropriate treatment of specific transactions. The principles adopted for accounting legislation are those recommended by the EC Directives and cover the presentation and the valuation rules for assets and liabilities as well as the accounting policies to be adopted for the recognition of revenue and expenses. Among the basic principles underlying the preparation of accounts are prudence, matching, consistency and going concern. The first is often invoked to defer the inclusion of income wherever legally possible and particularly in the financial services area.

Tax returns are filed on the basis of the annual accounts, so companies generally defer, as far as possible, gains arising on the use of financial instruments and other transactions in order to improve cash flow by postponing the settlement of the corporation tax on such gains. Otherwise, in general and when transactions involve the use of financial instruments, disclosure of the commitments in the notes to the annual accounts is the treatment generally adopted together with provision for losses when these are likely to be incurred.

6.14 Taxation

Belgium levies four types of tax on income, according to the status of the beneficiary of the income:

- income tax is assessed on individuals who are considered Belgian resident for income tax purposes, ie having their domicile or the seat of their wealth in Belgium. Such individuals are taxed on their worldwide income at progressive tax rates. Foreign source income gives rise to either exemption (with the reserve of progressivity) to avoid double taxation of the income or to a reduced taxation in the absence of treaty protection;

• corporate income tax is assessed on incorporated bodies which are considered Belgian resident for tax purposes, ie having legal personality, having their registered office, main establishment or seat of management in Belgium, and carrying out operations of a profit making nature in Belgium. Belgian companies and foreign companies being Belgian tax resident are subject to the corporate income tax (at the rate of 43% for book years up to 31 December 1990, 41% up to 30 December 1991 and 39% thereafter, lower rates being available inter alia, for taxable income up to respectively BEF 16.6 million, BEF 14.8 million and BEF 13 million) on their worldwide income. Domestic tax provisions, as well as provisions of the tax treaties concluded by Belgium, aim to avoid double taxation on foreign source income;

• non resident income tax is assessed on individuals and bodies which are not considered Belgian residents for tax purposes. As a rule, such taxpayers are subject to the Belgian income tax only on the Belgian source income. The rates applicable are the rates of the individual income tax for non-resident individuals and 43% (subject to reduction according to tax treaties) for non-resident incorporated bodies. In practice withholding tax on income from personal property and from real property may be the actual tax liability for non-residents not having an establishment in Belgium;

• income tax on legal bodies is assessed on bodies which have activities of a non-profit making nature. The income tax for such legal bodies is, as a rule, equal to the withholding tax on the received income.

Other taxes include:

• value added tax (VAT);

• inheritance tax;

• registration duties (in particular, on transfer of real estate and on capital contributions);

• customs and excise duties;

• some minor direct and indirect taxes.

The Belgian legislation on the income tax system is subject to frequent change.

Corporate income tax

A Belgian corporate resident taxpayer is assessed on its worldwide income, as determined, in principle, from its accounting records (principle of the predominancy of the accounting on the income tax). For the purposes of assessing the taxable income of the corporate resident taxpayer, accounting results are, however, amended in order to take into consideration taxation effects. This may cause important differences between the accounting and tax results.

Withholding tax

Income from personal property is, as a rule, subject to withholding tax at 10% for interest (on loans concluded after 1 March 1990) and royalties and 25% for dividends. The Belgium tax rules and double taxation treaties can provide for a reduced rate.

Administration

All taxes and duties should, under the Belgian Constitution, be assessed by virtue of a law. Interpretation of the law is given by the Belgian tax authorities, in the form of administrative guidelines, which are an important source of information. Case law does not have the binding authority of precedent; it has, however, an important influence on the evolution of the administrative interpretation and the future modification of the tax legislation.

All Belgian taxpayers (except for some types of non-resident taxpayers) are obliged to file an income tax return. The income tax is, in principle, assessed on the basis of the income so declared.

The Netherlands

6.15 Accounting

In the Netherlands the general accounting requirements to be followed by Dutch corporations are set out in Title 9 of Book II of the Dutch Civil Code. There are also guidelines on annual reporting which supplement the law. For banks and other financial institutions certain requirements are prescribed by the Dutch Central Bank in its capacity as Credit System Supervisor.

Dutch law makes the requirement to give a true and fair view (*'getrouw beeld'*) of the financial position and the results for the period the overriding requirement. If it is necessary to depart from a principle contained elsewhere in law to achieve this requirement, compliance with that other principle is waived.

The Council for Annual Reporting in which the accounting profession participates has not issued specific accounting standards relating to financial instruments. In general terms accepted accounting principles require disclosure of equity and debt instruments so as to comply with the true and fair view requirement.

6.16 Taxation

Two main taxes are levied on income:

• corporation tax, which applies to entities incorporated in The Netherlands and foreign companies trading in The Netherlands through a branch or agency. The rate varies from 35% to 40%;

• income tax, which applies to individuals and partnerships of individuals and is charged on a graduated basis dependent on income. The rate varies from 40% to 60%.

The tax legislation in The Netherlands is complicated and subject to change. Interpretations of the tax law can be agreed in advance with the tax authorities and this method is frequently used in order to clarify the measurement of taxable income in cases of intercompany pricing, interest, royalties and dividends. Case law is founded on the fundamental principle of the binding authority of precedent and has evolved and developed through the decision of the judges in the appeal courts.

Dutch corporation tax laws gives tax exemption on dividends and capital gains arising from more than a 5% holding in investments whether foreign or Dutch. The Netherlands has taxation treaties with a large number of countries which gives international groups maximum flexibility. Double taxation and foreign withholding taxes can often be minimised by using a Dutch company.

Germany

6.17 Accounting

Not all accounting principles in Germany are codified but to a large extent they are laid down in the Commercial Code. The Commercial Code was changed in 1985 by adopting the EC Directives which resulted in new legal requirements effective for fiscal years beginning after 31 December 1986 except for consolidation requirements which must be applied for fiscal years beginning after 31 December 1989.

Following the incorporation of the EC Directives into German law, a number of accounting principles not codified before, have been codified by inclusion in the Commercial Code.

Commercial Code

The Commercial Code provides that every businessman (as defined by law) and all companies have a duty to keep accounts and to record in them all business transactions in accordance with the required accounting principles. Accounts must be maintained such that they provide to an expert third party, within a reasonable time, an insight into the business transactions and the financial position of the business. The business transactions must be traceable from their origin through to their settlement.

As well as these basic requirements, the Commercial Code includes general rules for the preparation of accounts and the valuation principles to be followed. Supplementary regulations for public limited companies, partnerships partly limited by shares and limited liability companies also derive from the Commercial Code.

Paragraph 264 of the Commercial Code states that the financial statements of the company (consisting of balance sheet, profit and loss account and notes) must, in compliance with required accounting principles, present a true and fair view of the net worth, financial position and results of the company. If special circumstances have the effect that the financial statements do not show a true and fair view, then corresponding additional disclosures must be given in the notes to the financial statements.

There are also principles set out by the declarations and recommendations of the *Institut der Wirtschaftsprüefer* (the professional institute of accountants).

General valuation principles

Amongst the basic general accounting principles which have precedence over the individual rules and regulations concerning valuation are the four fundamental accounting concepts of prudence, matching, consistency and going concern. Items included in the accounts must be valued on an item by item basis.

Profit can be taken into account only if it has been realised as at the balance sheet date. As a result, this principle determines the point at which the proceeds from sales arising from the company's activities may be taken into account. Realisation takes place upon delivery of goods or upon completion (performance) of a service. The prudence principle goes further than the realisation principle in that it treats proceeds and costs differently with all foreseeable risks and losses being taken into account even if they have not yet been realised. When losses become known after the period end the balance sheet figures must be revised accordingly.

Public companies and banks

In the case of an *'Aktiengesellschaft'* (public limited company) and a *'Gesellschaft mit beschraenkter Haftung'* (limited company), there are specific supplementary accounting principles and requirements for additional data to be included in the financial statements.

Banks are generally subject to the same accounting principles as all other companies but there are some exceptions which allow banks to have hidden reserves (for example by means of lower than normal valuations of securities or loans) and to avoid certain disclosure requirements by offsetting specified income against specified expenses.

The details are derived from banking law, tax law and from the banking supervisory board's regulations and declarations. These rules will be subject to amendment as a result of the European directive on bank accounting.

6.18 Taxation

The financial statements, prepared in accordance with German generally accepted accounting principles and complying with the terms of the German Commercial Code also provide the basis for tax purposes. For tax, separate financial statements are prepared.

There is a principle (*Massgeblichkeitsprinzip*) requiring consistency between commercial financial statements and those for tax purposes. This not only applies to the inclusion or non-inclusion of items, but also to the valuation of individual items, provided there is no compulsory valuation method required for tax purposes.

If there is a free choice of valuation methods for tax purposes the permissible valuation method chosen in the commercial balance sheet is at the same time the basis for valuation in the tax balance sheet.

Switzerland

6.19 Accounting

General

The Swiss Code of Obligations (SCO) specifies the Swiss accounting rules. In Article 957ff the general accounting rules are laid down whilst valuation and presentation principles are detailed in the 'corporation law' section.

The general rules require that proper books must be kept. Keeping proper books includes the presentation of 'complete', 'true' and 'clear' accounts. The accounts should be kept on a going concern basis, unless there are specific reasons not to; such as, if there are reasonable doubts as to the company's solvency. The overriding principle is clearly that of prudence. This can be subdivided into two other main principles which are:

- the lower of cost and market principle; and

- the principle of imparity.

The lower of cost and market principle is widely known and needs no further explanation. However, it does not apply to marketable securities for which article 667 of the Swiss Code of Obligations (SCO) states that 'marketable securities must not be valued at a price higher than their average stock exchange price during the month prior to the date of the balance sheet'. In practice a year end rate is acceptable if no major price movements occur and there is no major deviation to the average rate.

Imparity principle

The principle of imparity states that unrealised losses must be recognised (through the profit and loss account) whilst unrealised gains may not be. A key question in this respect is whether every position has to be looked at separately or in aggregate. There is consensus that within the same balance sheet category, losses and profits can be netted and the overall result considered in the light of the imparity principle.

As mentioned above marketable securities can be valued by law at average market rates but the situation is unclear for other instruments such as foreign currencies, metals, traded options and financial futures. These instruments have, in most cases, liquid markets. However, by their description they are not marketable securities and strictly speaking, the imparity principle would apply to such instruments. However, this has been challenged and as long as no major speculative positions are held, it is felt that market rates can be applied. This application is also favoured from an administration point of view as any other treatment is considered impracticable for banks with high trading volumes. However, as noted above, it is permitted to net profits and losses within the same balance sheet (or off balance sheet) caption. Consequently only the net gain or loss needs to be considered under the imparity principle.

It is generally accepted that a transaction which is a hedge does not have to be valued in isolation but can be looked at together with the underlying transaction. The imparity principle here will have to be applied on a combined basis.

Requirement of the SCO

The presentation of complete, true and clear accounts is required by Article 959 of the SCO. However, Swiss law allows unlimited undervaluations of assets or overvaluation of liabilities. Thus the balance sheet can be true and clear from only a prudent viewpoint (assets not overstated and liabilities not understated). The extent of this prudence can change year on year which will impact the profit and loss account which, as a result, may not give a true and clear picture. The descriptions in and the presentation of the accounts can be minimal but they must not be misleading.

Keeping proper accounts also encompasses the off-balance sheet items. A company must keep, at any point in time, proper records of such items in order to be aware of its contractual agreements and that, based thereon, any losses (gains) thereon can be determined.

At a minimum Swiss accounts consist of a balance sheet and a profit and loss account only with no footnote disclosure. Contingent liabilities in favour of third parties (guarantees and security interests) have, however, to be provided as supplementary information to the balance sheet (banks have more disclosure requirements).

6.20 Taxation

Direct taxes – corporate

Federal as well as cantonal and municipal income and capital taxes are levied in Switzerland. Broadly speaking the federal tax charge accounts for less than one third of the total tax burden of a Swiss entity. Each canton has its own tax law and different tax rates. There are some differences in tax legislation and considerable differences in tax rates between the various cantons.

Federal income taxes are levied on after tax profits whilst many cantons levy taxes on pre-tax profits. The computation and the tax periods are not necessarily identical. The tax rate depends mostly on the yield (ratio between taxable income and taxable capital). The maximum rate is generally reached when the yield exceeds 25% and the minimum rate if the yield is below 4%. This can, however, vary substantially. There is no general percentage as to what the minimum or maximum rates are since there exist considerable differences between the various cantons and municipalities. The minimum or maximum total income tax charge (federal and cantonal) can be expected to be between or near 10-14% or 20-35% respectively of pre-tax profits. Capital gains or losses are treated like any other income.

Tax basis – corporate

In Switzerland, the statutory accounts form the basis for the tax accounts. There are no separate accounts for tax purposes. Since accounting principles are governed by the overriding principle of presenting a prudent balance sheet, it is possible that the tax authorities will not accept certain (over prudent) accounting treatment which could lead to the creation of separate accounts for tax purposes.

Use of double taxation treaties

Swiss investors can claim the benefits of the double taxation conventions. There are special requirements that foreign controlled corporations must meet in order that their applications are considered justified and hence the applications are not considered an abuse of the convention. Such requirements relate to the financial structure, interest and royalty payments, minimum profit distribution as well as the writing off of intergroup assets purchased.

Direct taxes – individuals

As with corporations, individuals are subject to federal as well as cantonal and communal income taxes and the rate depends on the domicile of the individual and the taxation rates can vary substantially. There is also a state wealth tax. No federal income tax is charged on capital gains realised by an individual, provided he is not realising such gains as his business. Only very few cantons tax capital gains on movable property such as shares. Capital losses may be deducted from capital gains only if the latter are taxable.

Other taxes

There is a stamp duty on the issue of new shares of corporations (capital issue tax of 3%) and mutual funds (0.9%). A reduced rate of 1% is applied in merger or demerger situations.

A transfer tax of 0.15% on Swiss securities and of 0.3% on foreign securities is levied on securities purchased/sold through a Swiss professional securities dealer. The tax is lower on instruments issued for a period of less than three months. There are currently discussions considering a change in the transfer tax law as this tax is reducing the competitiveness of Switzerland in the global market place.

There is a 35% tax at source levied on dividends declared by a Swiss corporation. This tax is also levied on bond interest of Swiss domiciled issuers and on certain other interest payments.

Austria

6.21 Accounting

Financial statements must be prepared in accordance with generally accepted accounting principles. These requirements, together with those for the financial statements and the managing director's report, are codified in various ways, as follows:

● *Handelsgesetzbuch* (Commercial Code);

● *Aktiengesetz* (Joint Stock Companies Law);

● *Gesetz über die Gesellschaften mit beschränkter Haftung* (Private Limited Companies Law);

● *Bundesabgabenordnung* (Tax Procedural Law);

● *Fachgutachten der Kammer der Wirtschaftstreuhänder* (expert opinions of the Austrian Chamber of Accountants).

Generally accepted accounting principles include the four fundamental concepts (prudence, consistency, matching and going concern) as well as:

● offsetting of assets against liabilities and of income against expenses is prohibited;

● valuations at the balance sheet date have to be performed item by item;

● the valuation methods should not be changed;

● the purchase price or manufacturing cost of assets are normally maximum values (historical cost principle).

Commercial financial statements form an authoritative basis for the tax accounts (authoritative principle).

Every business enterprise, other than a small business is required to produce annual financial statements consisting of a balance sheet and a statement of profit and loss. Corporations are obliged to be audited and to have their financial statements published. They are also required to produce a managing director's report. There are certain industries such as insurance, banking and railways, which have to use special forms of financial statements.

Books and records are to be kept in Austria, in Austrian schillings and in chronological order. Financial statements have to be prepared at the end of every fiscal year, which must not exceed 12 months.

Depreciation rates are not fixed by law but have to correspond to the useful lives of fixed assets. A physical stock count has to be taken annually at the balance sheet date except where proper stock records are kept. Recognised statistical sampling methods may be used if the procedure is in accordance with required accounting principles.

Implementation of EC Directives

Austria has taken steps to modify Austrian Law so as to accord with EC Directives 4 (Accounting Directive), 7 (Consolidated Accounts Directive) and 8 (Auditor Directive) with the draft of a new Accounting Law published in 1988. The regulations corresponding with the 4th EC Directive (Accounting Directive) are expected to come into force as from 1991, the others some years later.

6.22 Taxation

Tax liability

Under domestic legislation individuals and companies resident in Austria are liable to Austrian tax on all their income, however and wherever it arises. However, income arising abroad may be exempted from Austrian tax by the terms of a double tax treaty. Austria charges income tax at progressive rates. Income exempt from Austrian tax is nevertheless taken into account in determining the rate of tax which will be charged on non-exempt income.

Business organisations such as corporations, cooperatives, associations and other foundations, endowments, and similar institutions ('*Anstalten*',

'*Stiftungen*') are liable to corporation tax, which is computed under the same rules as income tax except where otherwise provided.

Individuals are subject to income tax. Partnerships and other enterprises – not recognised as separate entities for tax purposes – are not separately liable, but their profit or loss is assessed on the partners or owners in proportion to their interest in the enterprise.

The tax law differentiates between two classes of taxable persons or legal entities: those subject to unlimited tax liability (fully liable) and those subject to limited tax liability (partly liable). A person is resident if he has any kind of habitation available for his own use in Austria (including a summer house, a rented room or a holiday flat).

Penal tax law

In Austria a penal tax law ('*Finanzstrafgesetz*') is in force. Any deliberate or negligent transgression of this law carries penalties which include imprisonment in severe cases, fines or forfeiture of property. The law is administered by common courts of justice or, in the case of minor matters, by special penal tax courts.

Sweden

6.23 Accounting

Most accounting principles are set out in the Accounting Act (*Bokforingslagen, BFL*) of 1976 and in the Companies Act (*Aktiebolagslagen, ABL*) of 1975. The Swedish Institute of Authorised Public Accountants (*Foreningen Auktoriserade Revisorer, FAR*) and the Swedish Accounting Standards Board (*Bokforingsnamnden, BFN*) have also issued accounting recommendations.

Since 1989 a new Swedish Financial Accounting Standards Board (*Redovisningsradet*) deals with accounting recommendations for public companies. The aim of the Board is to ensure that these recommendations are consistent, as far as possible, with international accounting standards. Gradually the FAR recommendations will be replaced by the *Redovisningsradet* recommendations.

Historically the Swedish accounting system has been influenced by the German system, where legislation has had a great importance in the development of financial statements. More recently Swedish accounting has been influenced by the United Kingdom and the United States and their accountancy standards are now of great importance. The concept of a true and fair view has begun to be adopted.

All private and public companies are required to present financial statements consisting of an income statement, a balance sheet and an administration report. Parent companies have to prepare consolidated accounts. The administration report includes information on matters significant to an evaluation of the results of the company's operations and its financial position which are not required to be disclosed in the income statement or in the balance sheet. The report also contains information on events of material significance to the company, including those occurring after the year end.

Specific valuation requirements

Inventories are stated at the lower of cost (FIFO) and market value. Either net realisable value or the replacement cost can be used as market value. Exceptionally a value in excess of cost but never in excess of market can be adopted. Long term construction contracts are usually accounted for on a completed contract basis.

Fixed assets are stated at original cost. If the asset declines in value annual depreciation must be provided using appropriate depreciation rates. Land and buildings and other fixed assets may be revalued.

Unrealised gains and losses on short term receivables and liabilities denominated in foreign currencies are included in the income statement. Unrealised gains on long term receivables and liabilities denominated in foreign currencies should be deferred and credited to a 'foreign currency reserve'. Movements on this reserve are reflected as an appropriation in the income statement and an untaxed reserve in the balance sheet. The untaxed reserve represents a 'hybrid' between equity and debt and may not be distributed to the shareholders.

As the income statement of Swedish companies forms the basis for taxation the prudence concept is frequently invoked reducing profits as far as permitted. The concept of deferred tax is not generally used. Appropriations for tax purposes are reflected as 'untaxed reserves' in the balance sheet between liabilities and stockholders' equity and 'appropriations to on taxed reserves' in the income statement.

The Accounting Act does not prohibit capitalisation of the cost of intangible assets like brands and franchise fees. However, with the exception of goodwill, intangible assets are unusual. Goodwill in consolidated balance sheets must be amortised over a maximum of ten years according to a recommendation by FAR. In practice however some companies use periods of 20-40 years.

The FAR has issued an exposure draft on accounting for financial instruments. The instruments dealt with are options, futures and interest rate and currency swaps.

The Companies Act provides that all companies should have at least one auditor. The auditors report to the general meeting of shareholders each financial year.

6.24 Taxation

From 1991 the Swedish system for taxation of corporations has been changed significantly.

Company taxes

The tax rate for companies has been lowered from 40-48%, to 30%.

Accounting and taxation

Swedish corporate taxation is based on the accounts of the company, and to compute the taxable income the profit according to the profit and loss statement is used as the basis from which various adjustments are made. High depreciation charges give the company the ability to amortise machinery, equipment and goodwill over five years.

Untaxed reserves

Companies have the right to allocate funds to a special tax equalisation reserve (SURV), up to a maximum of 30% of the company's equity capital.

The reserve is, in principle, based on the tax accounting values of various assets, less deductions for corporate liabilities as recorded in the balance sheet. A company utilising the SURV will have an effective tax burden on retained profits amounting to 23.7%. The tax rate on distributed profits will be the nominal 30%.

Companies with a small equity capital, especially companies in the services sector, may use an alternative method to compute the SURV based on a maximum of 15% of their payroll costs.

Capital gains

A reduction of the corporate tax rate to 30% has allowed uniform taxation of various types of income for companies. The previous practice of taxing capital gains arising on stock and property through a mix of taxes is replaced by full taxation of the gain at the time of sale.

Treatment of dividends

Sweden operates the classical system for taxation of companies and their shareholders, ie a double taxation. The lowering of corporate and personal income tax rates has also lowered the cumulative tax burden on the company and its shareholders. Since both pay tax at a 30% rate the effective tax rate on a distribution is 51%. Intercompany dividends are in many cases tax exempt in order to avoid a double (triple or more) taxation of company profits.

Personal tax

Taxation of individuals is based upon a classification of income as employment income, business income and income from capital. The two first classes (earned income) are subject to local at a rate of 27-32% and to national tax at a rate of 20% on the part of an income that exceeds SEK 180,300 (this limit is subject to annual adjustment).

Income from capital (primarily interest, dividends and capital gains) is subject to a national 30% tax. Such income is not subject to local tax. Interest expense is fully deductible unless it exceeds a certain limit, in which case the excess amount is deductible up to 70%. Capital gains are deductible up to 70% if certain conditions are met. If deductible expenses exceed taxable income the deficit entitles the individual to a tax credit amounting to 30% of the deficit. Credit is granted against tax on earned income and against property tax imposed in the same year. Excess credit cannot be carried forward.

Other taxes

Other taxes include:

• annual net wealth tax;

• VAT;

• gift and inheritance taxes;

• various indirect taxes (road tax, car excise, energy and fuel taxes alcohol and tobacco taxes etc).

Tax administration

All taxation is governed by Acts of Parliament. The tax legislation is independent from the state budget, although it is not unusual for the annual budget to include amendments of the Tax Acts, primarily concerning indirect taxes which are the major part of state revenues.

In addition to written law there are a number of precedents from the Supreme Administrative Court, which technically are not binding for authorities or lower courts but nevertheless can be regarded as binding for all practical purposes.

There is an annual assessment procedure under which most individuals and all companies have to file a tax return in which all taxable income and deductible expenses are reported. The companies report their income on a financial year basis. The majority of the individuals may file a summary tax return in which they primarily confirm that income statements issued by their employers and banks are correct and that they include all income during the fiscal year (calendar year).

Norway

6.25 Accounting

In Norway the main sources of accounting requirements are:

● the Companies Act to be followed by corporations. This came into effect in 1977;

● the Accounting Act to be followed by partnerships. This came into effect in 1978.

In addition interpretations of rules are available from the Official Interpretations of the Companies and Accounting Acts. There are also recommended accounting principles *'Anbefalinger om god regnskapsskikk'* ('Accounting recommendations') issued by The Norwegian Institute of State Authorised Public Accountants (NSRF) and The Accounting Standards Board (*'Norsk RegnskapsStiftelse'*).

As well as the four fundamental accounting concepts of prudence, matching, consistency and going concern, Norwegian financial statements are based on:

● current assets to be carried in the balance sheet at the lower of cost and market value. Capital assets normally to be stated at historical cost;

● amounts in the accounts and the principles adopted must be described by way of notes.

Norwegian accounting does not provide for deferred taxation and has an additional balance sheet category 'untaxed reserves' which is equivalent to deferred taxation and is placed between liabilities and stockholders' equity.

To date there are no specific rules or recommendations as to financial instruments in Norway. These are treated according to general accounting principles. The treatment adopted would tend to follow international best practice especially United States generally accepted accounting principles.

6.26 Taxation

Norway has the following taxes:

On corporations

- national income tax at 27.8%;
- local income tax at 21%;
- capital gains tax (included in taxable income and subject to both national and local taxes).

On individuals and partnerships

- national income tax (this tax is levied on a progressive basis with a ceiling);
- local income taxes at 26%;
- capital gains tax (a special national income tax of 40% is levied on gains from sales of shares. Other capital gains are – with few exceptions – included in taxable income).

Taxes on non-residents

- income derived by a non-resident corporation carrying on business in Norway, or by a non-resident individual, is taxed as though the non-resident were resident (permanent establishment);
- the withholding tax applies only to dividends at a rate of 25%;
- Norway has tax treaties with several countries to avoid double taxation.

Country accounting and taxation framework

Other taxes

Other significant taxes in Norway are:

- value added tax (20%);

- inheritance and gift taxes;

- taxes on payrolls (social security);

- land and property taxes;

- taxes on capital (corporations 0.3% – individuals at a progressive rate).

Proposed tax reform

In April 1991 the Norwegian Government proposed comprehensive tax reforms. The aim is that the new tax system will be effective from 1 January 1992. Tax rates are to be lowered and the tax base broadened. The government proposed to tax ordinary income, which includes capital income, at a common, flat rate of 28%. This will be the marginal tax rate on all types of capital income for all personal tax payers and companies. Moreover, various types of saving are to receive more equal tax treatment.

Restricted deductibility, including the introduction of more restrictive depreciation rules and the repeal of most tax credit arrangements, will broaden the tax base. Many enterprises have accumulated large tax credits on which tax would have become payable in the years ahead. As part of the reform the government proposes that, to a certain extent, such credits should qualify as equity capital and not be subject to tax.

The government proposes the introduction of a tax liability for gains on shares and deductibility in respect of losses incurred on the sales of shares. Share price rises up to 1 January 1992 will be taxed according to the previous rules regardless of whether or not the gain is realised. Share price rises after 1 January 1992 will be taxed at a rate of 28% upon realisation.

The income of self-employed persons will be split into capital income and personal income. The objective is equal tax treatment of the self-employed and wage earners.

Finland

6.27 Accounting

In Finland the general accounting requirements to be followed by Finnish corporations are set out in the Accounting Act 1973 (AA 1973). The AA 1973 is a skeleton law which sets out principles stipulating the format of and the disclosure in, a company's accounts and the methods by which profits, losses and assets and liabilities are to be calculated. The AA 1973 is complimented by the Companies Act 1978 and because the taxation of corporations in Finland is closely related to accounting treatment, also by the Business Income Tax Act.

Some authorities are also entitled to give legally binding accounting instructions for some business branches such as banks, security brokers, insurance companies and pension funds. Furthermore, the generally accepted accounting principles in Finland are influenced by the recommendations of the Accounting Board and the Association of Authorised Accountants.

The accounting legislation is currently under review and the committee undertaking this work has published proposals as to the changes needed to Finnish accounting legislation. The proposals also taken into account the requirements of EC directives. However a new Accounting Act is not expected to be in force until early 1993.

6.28 Taxation

In Finland two main taxes are levied on income:

• business income tax, which applies to bodies incorporated in Finland and foreign companies trading in Finland through a branch or agency;

• income and property tax, which applies to individuals and is charged on a graduated basis dependent on income.

Other taxes include:

• inheritance and gift tax;

• sales tax;

- customs and excise duties;
- stamp duty;

The tax legislation in Finland is subject to frequent change.

Greece

6.29 Accounting

In Greece, the general accounting reporting requirements to be followed by Greek corporations are set out in Law 2190/1920 as amended to comply with the requirements of the EC Directives. This law, which is the basic legislation relating to company law, stipulates the content of the financial statements and the notes thereto.

Aligned to the above legislation are the Uniform Charts of Accounts the use of which is compulsory for some types of specialised companies (banks and insurance companies) and recommended for all others. It is intended that the Uniform Charts of Accounts will become compulsory for all corporations as from 1 January 1991. The layout that the published financial statements must follow is given in the examples in the Uniform Charts of Accounts even if at present the companies do not use them for their accounting records.

As there is no formal recognised accounting body in Greece there are only very basic accounting standards. Most companies follow the requirements of tax legislation in preference to any other accounting methods. In some cases, tax legislation obliges companies to follow accounting policies which are not consistent with a true and fair view of the company's financial position, (eg additional depreciation). Furthermore, many companies do not make provision for doubtful debts, obsolete inventory, etc as such provisions are not tax deductible and they reduce the company's ability to transfer profits to tax free reserves. Accounting for deferred tax is unknown in published financial statements although some international companies include this in their internal reporting.

In general, extreme caution should be exercised in using Greek financial statements for purposes of any financial analysis. The lack of clarity or consistency in the definition of accounting concepts makes financial statements difficult to interpret and often seriously misleading for those who are unfamiliar with Greek accounting practices.

6.30 Taxation

Corporate tax

Greek corporations are subject to income tax on their net income derived from sources within or outside Greece, after deducting dividends and payments to directors and transfers to tax free reserves, where applicable. Corporate profits are taxed only once—either in the form of dividends or as retained earnings. If retained earnings that have been taxed in the hands of the corporation are subsequently distributed, the corporation is entitled to a tax refund.

Profits of corporations and foreign permanent establishments in Greece are taxed as follows:

- undistributed profits

  Unquoted companies
  - industrial, mining and quarrying companies   40%

    If the above come under investment incentive legislation
    (Law 1262/82)   35%
  - all other companies   46%

  Quoted companies
  - industrial, mining and quarrying companies   35%
  - other quoted companies   46%

- distributed profits (dividends)

  Unquoted companies
  - bearer shares   50%
  - registered shares   47%

  Quoted companies
  - bearer shares   45%
  - registered shares   42%

Reduced rates are applicable for dividends payable to shareholders residing in Belgium, Italy, Germany, Cyprus, Switzerland and Holland.

There are no state or provincial income taxes in Greece.

Capital gains

Capital gains are considered as income liable to tax when derived from:

(a) the concession of any right pertaining to the operation of an enterprise or to a profession;

(b) the concession of a commercial or other enterprise in its entirety, or of the firm's name, trade mark or goodwill, etc.

Gains referred to in (a) and (b) are taxable at a flat rate of 30% and 20% respectively. Similarly, gains resulting from the sale of fixed assets of an enterprise (except for property and ships) are considered as income derived from commercial activity. Such income is not taxable provided it is utilised for the additional depreciation of other existing machinery and industrial plant or new machinery and plant to be installed by the enterprise within two years. Alternatively, such income is not taxable if it is transferred to a reserve.

Capital gains resulting from the sale of securities (bonds and shares) are exempt from income tax. In the case of businesses such gains are to be credited to a special reserve fund intended to offset possible losses from the future sale of other securities. Should these gains ever be distributed, they are then subject to taxation.

Foreign business organisations trading in Greece are subject to Greek corporate tax (46%) on their total net income derived from Greek sources and/or from their permanent establishment in Greece.

Cyprus

6.31 Accounting

The general accounting requirement to be followed in Cyprus, as set out in section 141 of the Companies Law Chapter 113, is that every company must keep proper books of account which give a true and fair view of the state of the company's affairs and explain its transactions. The requirements in relation to the contents of final accounts are set out in the Eighth Schedule to the same legislation. The concept of 'true and fair' is well established in Cyprus and although not defined in the legislation the generally accepted definition is similar to that for the United Kingdom.

The requirements of the Companies Law are supplemented by the International Accounting Standards (IASs) issued to date which have been adopted by the local professional body, the Institute of Certified Public Accountants of Cyprus.

6.32 Taxation

Income tax in Cyprus is levied under the Income Tax Law 58 of 1981 as amended by subsequent legislation. Tax is levied on any income accruing in, derived from or received in Cyprus by any person in respect of profits from any trade, business, profession or vocation, or from any office or employment.

Tax on companies is levied at the rate of 42.5% while tax rates on individuals are progressive and reach a maximum of 60%. Revised legislation however, has now been prepared which if enacted will reduce these rates to 20% and 40% respectively coupled however with the introduction of VAT which does not exist at present.

Other taxes include:

• special contribution (to be abolished by the proposed revised legislation);

• capital gains tax (at a rate of 20%);

• estate duty.

Spain

6.33 Accounting

Traditionally Spanish accounting and financial reporting practices have been strongly influenced by French accounting conventions and by tax accounting principles. The requirements are expressed in various laws, the most important of which are the following:

• Commercial Code;

• business corporations laws;

• Limited Liability Companies law;

• General Accounting Plan.

With entry into the EC, Spain was required to modify its company law to bring it into line with the community directives. Act 19/1989 of July 27 incorporated the EC directives into Spanish law as follows:

• First Directive – company disclosure;

- Second Directive – formation of limited companies;
- Third Directive – mergers of limited companies;
- Fourth Directive – annual financial statements of limited companies;
- Sixth Directive – divisions of limited companies;
- Seventh Directive – consolidated accounts.

The changes arising as a result of the above law affect mainly the accounting, financial reporting and publication of information.

Report and accounts and accounting records

At the end of the year, the management must present to the General Shareholders' Meeting the director's report and the annual accounts which include:

- balance sheet;
- profit and loss account;
- notes to the accounts.

The financial statements must give a true and fair view of the financial position of the Company. The financial statements must be prepared in accordance with the four fundamental concepts of prudence, matching, consistency and going concern. Components of assets and liabilities must be valued individually.

Companies must keep their accounting records and present their financial statements in accordance with the government approved Chart of Accounts. The Chart of Accounts is classified into seven major groups as follows:

- Group 1 Basic financing – capital, reserves, long term loans;
- Group 2 Fixed assets – buildings, plant and machinery, patents, etc;
- Group 3 Current assets – raw materials, finished goods, etc;
- Group 4 Debtors and creditors from trade operations, suppliers, customers, etc;
- Group 5 Financial accounts – short term loans, cash and banks, short term investments;
- Group 6 Purchases and expenses;
- Group 7 Sales and revenues.

The special accounting and legal requirements of particular industries such as finance and insurance companies have resulted in separate Government approved charts of accounts.

Significant Spanish accounting practices

Group accounts

Consolidation of financial statements are not currently required under the Spanish law. However, if the parent company owns more than 25% of the share capital issued by the subsidiary, additional information about that investment must be provided in the parent company financial statements. As a rule the investments in subsidiaries are at cost. The preparation of consolidated financial statements is becoming a more common practice among large Spanish companies as they prepare to comply with the 7th EC directive. Consolidation will become compulsory in 1991.

Foreign currency translation

Foreign currency receivables and payables are translated at the exchange rate on the date the transaction was made. Translation gains or losses are not recognised until realised.

Deferred taxes

Deferred taxes are not generally provided for. Deferred tax is, in fact, an unfamiliar concept in Spain, since tax and book accounting are normally the same. However, this will probably change as Spanish companies move towards separate tax and financial accounting.

6.34 Taxation

Taxes in Spain are levied at national, regional, provincial and municipal levels, but those taxes levied at the national and regional levels, by the central and autonomous governments, are by far the most important.

Principal forms of taxation

At the national and regional levels, the principal taxes levied by the central and autonomous governments are as follows:

- corporate income tax;
- personal income tax;
- wealth tax;
- special taxes;

● value added tax.

Spanish tax legislation is based on general tax Law 230/1963, partially amended by Law 10/1985, and on annual general budget laws.

Corporate taxes

In general corporate income tax is currently levied at a rate of 35%. Rural savings banks, mutual insurance companies and cooperatives are taxed at 26%. There are tax incentives for investment and the creation of new jobs.

Taxable entities

All entities and organisations that have a separate legal status are subject to corporate income tax in Spain. The terms 'company', 'corporate', and 'corporation' are used to include all entities or organisations subject to income tax. Provided that certain conditions are met, holding companies and real estate companies, as well as professional firms, are not subject to tax at the corporate level. The income of such organisations is allocated between their shareholders or partners, in proportion to their ownership interest, and is subject to individual or corporate income tax depending on their personal status. Losses need not be attributed to the shareholders but may be carried forward and offset against the taxable income of the organisation during the next five years. This approach is referred to as 'tax-transparency'.

Foreign tax reliefs

Relief from double taxation is governed by tax treaties that Spain has entered into with other countries. In addition, a foreign tax credit may be allowed for foreign source income included on the Spanish tax return computed as the lesser of:

● the foreign tax paid on the foreign source income; or

● the Spanish tax attributable to the foreign source income.

Italy

6.35 Accounting

The regulations regarding the general accounting requirements and the preparation of the financial statements are set out in the Civil Code (*Codice Civile*). The rules in the Civil Code are general in nature and thus it does not specify accounting requirement for certain items. In view of this the Italian professional accounting bodies (*Consigli Nazionali del Dottori Commercialisti e dei Ragionieri*) have, in recent years, issued accounting principles, detailing the accounting requirements in respect of most items in financial statements. These accounting principles constitute an authoritative reference in so far as the interpretation of the Civil Code is concerned.

In cases not covered by the above accounting principles, reference is made to the accounting standards of the International Accounting Standards Committee.

Requirements of The Civil Code

The Civil Code stipulates that the Board of Directors have to submit the financial statements for approval by shareholders, within four months after the end of the accounting period. The minimum content of the balance sheet and the profit and loss account has been established but there is no prescribed format for the financial statements.

The Civil Code lays down the principal criteria for the valuation of tangible and intangible fixed assets, inventories, stocks and shares and amounts receivable. A Directors' report is filed with the financial statements. This report discloses among other things the criteria for valuation and accounting principles applied, comparative figures of the previous period, transactions with group companies and any significant post-balance sheet events.

Companies who have their financial statements audited must, in addition to the Directors' report, present the following statements:

● a balance sheet distinguishing between current and long term assets and liabilities;

● a profit and loss account presented in a vertical form in order to disclose gross profit, operating profit and net profit before taxation;

● a statement of changes in shareholders' equity;

● a statement of source and application of funds.

All the above statements must comply with the accounting principles stipulated by recognised professional accounting bodies.

The Civil Code has established the fundamental concept in that the financial statements should give a true and fair view of the company's financial position and of its results for the period. In addition to this the professional bodies have formulated other fundamental concepts in conformity with international standards (ie prudence, consistency, accruals and going concern).

There is no mention in the Civil Code about consolidated accounts for groups however the financial statements must disclose both the book value and the nominal value of any shareholding at balance sheet date. The holding company must include a copy of the financial statements of the subsidiaries under its control, whilst in the case of associated companies only the significant items in the financial statements are disclosed.

In conformity with international practice the professional accounting bodies provide for the presentation of the consolidated financial statements together with the Directors' Report. Major Italian group companies present consolidated financial statements. Moreover the *Commissione Nazionale per le Societa e la Borsa* (CONSOB), the stock exchange regulatory authority, expressly requires the presentation of consolidated financial statements in the case of quoted companies having controlling interests in subsidiaries of significant size.

EC Directives

The 4th and 7th EC Directive relating to financial statements, and consolidated group accounts respectively, are in the course of being introduced in Italy. A bill regarding the modifications necessary to bring Italian legislation in line with that of the EC has now been finalised. The above harmonisation procedures were approved in April 1991. The new legislation will be applicable from 1993 for financial statements and from 1994 for consolidated group accounts.

Under Italian tax legislation items deducted for tax purposes must be included in the financial statements. For example accelerated capital allowances in the earlier years of an asset life are included in the depreciation figures in the financial statements. Thus it can be said that at times tax legislation conflicts with company law.

6.36 Taxation

The main taxes in Italy are:

● corporation tax (IRPEG) which applies to all Italian business entities, associations, and non-resident entities deriving income from Italy. IRPEG is charged on all categories of income and capital gains;

• income tax which applies to individuals, is primarily charged on the income earned during the taxable period (eg cash basis). Capital gains are excluded unless they relate to gains on the disposal of development land or property which has been retained for less than five years;

• from 28 January 1991 for individuals and non-commercial enterprises capital gains realised on sales of equity holdings are subject to taxation which will be calculated depending on whether the taxpayer opts for a detailed or index based method of determining the capital gains. In the former case, the tax will be due once a year on filing the income tax return, at a rate of 25% applied to the total of capital gains realised by the person in the tax period, determined as the differences between the sales proceeds and the price paid on purchase net of any loss calculated according to the same criterion. In the latter case, the appointed intermediaries (stockbroker or bank) will apply a withholding tax of 15% on the capital gains deriving from each individual transfer, the determination of which varies according to whether the disposal concerns listed or unlisted shares;

• local income tax (ILOR) which applies to all persons and is charged on the same basis as IRPEF/IRPEG but with exemptions for wages, salaries, professional fees and dividend income.

Other taxes include:

• registration duties;

• property tax (INVIM) a tax on the increase in value of property over the period of ownership, charged at various rates depending on the rate of increase of value. The tax is also charged on the revaluation of the property every ten years in some circumstances;

• value added tax (IVA);

• a wide range of withholding taxes.

Administration

Tax law is governed by statute law. The system is based on self-assessment controlled by tax audits with heavy penalties for under declaration. Case law, although influential, is not binding.

Scope of taxes

Individual Italian resident companies are taxed on their worldwide income, whilst foreign subsidiaries of Italian companies are generally not subject to taxation in Italy. Tax regulations do not provide for group tax declarations. Foreign companies with a permanent establishment are subject to tax on all Italian source income.

Glossary of terms

AAA/Aaa	The highest credit rating given by the two main US rating agencies, Standard & Poors and Moody's.
Absolute rate	A bid made which is not expressed in relation to a particular funding base such as LIBOR or US treasury rates, ie 9.125% instead of LIBOR + 0.05%.
Accrued interest	Interest earned but not yet due and payable. The buyer of a bond, for instance, pays the seller the agreed price of the bond plus interest accrued since the last interest payment date up to and including the value date. The same computations are normally used in swap transactions.
Actuals	The physical or cash financial instrument, as distinguished from a futures contract.
After market	See 'Secondary market'.
After-tax yield	The internal rate of return of a debt instrument net of any income, withholding and capital gains taxes.
Agent	A person who acts on behalf of another person who is referred to as a principal.
AIBD	Association of International Bond Dealers.
All-in cost	Total cost of a financial transaction, including interest cost, periodic charges and and all front-end compensation, expressed as per cent per annum.
All or none	A condition that the full amount of an order to buy, or sell, securities be executed at an agreed price; a lesser amount is unacceptable.
Allotment	The amount of a new issue (ie number of bonds) given to a syndicate member by the lead manager.
American exercise	A call or put option which may be exercised at any time prior to expiration (see European exercise).
Amortisation	Gradual repayment of a debt over time, for example, through the operation of a sinking or purchase fund.

639

Announcement	In a new bond issue, the day on which a release is sent to prospective syndicate members, describing the offering and inviting underwriters and selling group members to join the syndicate.
Appreciation	A gradual increase in the value of currency, usually occurring over a period as the result of market forces of supply and demand in a system of floating exchange rates. By contrast, a devaluation is an official government act which produces a substantial decrease in an exchange rate, usually overnight.
Arbitrage	The simultaneous purchase and sale of similar financial instruments in order to profit from distortions from usual price relationships.
Asked	The price level at which sellers offer securities to buyers.
At or better	As regards a buy order for securities, purchasing at the specified price or under; for a sell order, selling at the specified price or above.
At the money	When the price of the underlying transaction equals the strike price of the option.
Average life	The weighted average of the maturities of all the bonds in a given issue after taking into account the amortisation provisions (ie reductions by sinking or purchase fund).
Balloon maturity	The last bonds of an issue maturing in a substantially larger amount than those of earlier maturities.
Basis	The difference between the cash price of a financial instrument and the price of a related financial futures contract.
Basis point	One one-hundredth of a percent (ie 0.01%), typically used in expressing bond yield differentials (7.50% − 7.15% = 0.35% or 35 basis points).
Basis risk	The risk of movement between two different interest rate profiles, eg LIBOR and US treasury rates.
BBAIRS	The British Bankers Association Interest Rate Swap containing standard conditions for UK swap arrangements.
Basket	A group of securities purchased or sold as a group in

some predefined ratio often a share index (eg FTSE 100).

Bear	A person who expects prices to fall.
Bear market	A period of generally falling prices and pessimistic attitudes.
Bearer bond	A bond for which the only evidence of ownership is possession.
Beneficial ownership	The ownership of securities or other investments through a nominee; a technique used to avoid revealing the identity of the ultimate owner.
Best efforts	1. Describes an offering which is not underwritten but sold according to what the market will bear. 2. Also used in the context of an institution undertaking to buy or sell a set number of securities at the best price available within a specified time period.
Bid	The price level at which buyers offer to acquire securities from sellers.
Bond	A negotiable certificate evidencing indebtedness. A legal contract sold by an issuer promising to pay the holder its face value plus amounts of interest at future dates.
Book entry system	Securities held in a computer system and either not represented by or not traded by actual certificates but by entries in the system.
Book value	The value of a financial instrument as shown by the accounting records but which is not necessarily identical to its market value.
Break	A sudden price change.
Broker	An individual or institution who introduces the two parties in a transaction to each other. The parties could be a buyer and a seller of foreign currencies or a borrower and a lender of a given currency or two swap counterparties with mirror interest rate or currency requirements. Brokers never take a position for themselves; they only arrange for transactions among other parties and charge a fee for this service.
Bull	A person who expects prices will move higher.

Bull market	A period of generally rising prices and optimistic attitudes.
Business day	In most international markets, any day excluding Saturdays, Sundays and legal or statutory holidays on which business can be conducted.
Buy in	A purchase to cover, offset or close a short position
Buy on close	To buy at the end of the trading session at a price within the closing range.
Buy on opening	To buy at the beginning of a trading session at a price within the opening range.
Call	The optional right of an issuer to redeem bonds before their stated maturity, at a given price on a given date. Also, a contract allowing the holder to buy a given number of a financial instrument from the granter of such a contract at a fixed price for a given period of time.
CGT	United Kingdom capital gains taxation
Capital market	The market for the purchase and sale of medium- and long-term financial instruments, including bonds, notes, swaps, and usually equities and commodities.
Cash commodity	The actual commodity or instrument as opposed to a futures contract based upon that commodity.
Cash market	The underlying currency or money market in which transactions for the purchase and sale of cash instruments to which futures contracts relate are carried out.
Cash price	A price quotation obtained or a price actually received in a cash market.
Cash settlement	A term typically used in money markets where settlement is immediate, usually within twenty four hours of the trade.
Cedel	One of the two major organisations in the Eurobond market which clears, or handles the physical exchange of, securities and stores securities. Based in Luxembourg, the company is owned by several banks and operates through a network of agents.
CHAPS	Clearing House Automated Payment System: an electronic system for settling accounts between the major clearing banks.

Cheapest to deliver	Refers to the selection of commodities or financial instruments used to deliver against a futures contract.
CHIPS	Clearing House Interbank Payments System.
Clean Price	The total price of a security less accrued interest.
Clear	The formal completion of a trade, brought about by proper delivery of securities by the seller and proper payment by the buyer.
Clearing day	Any business day except Saturdays, Sundays and legal holidays.
Clearing house	The organisation which registers, monitors, matches and guarantees trades on a futures market, and carries out financial settlement of futures transactions. It could be a division of the futures exchange, a separate subsidiary corporation of the exchange, or an independent body.
Clearing member	A member firm of the clearing house.
Clearing organisation	An organisation with which securities may be deposited for safe-keeping and through which purchase/sale transactions may be handled. The two foremost systems in the Eurobond market are Euroclear and Cedel.
Close	The period at the end of the trading session, officially designated by the exchange, during which all transactions are considered to be made 'at the close'.
Closing date	The date on which a new issue's proceeds are paid to the issuer by the lead-manager and the securities, in either a temporary or a definitive form, are delivered to the lead-manager by the issuer. In the case of Eurosecurities, this is generally 10 to 15 days after the signing of the issuers subscription agreement.
Closing price	The price at which transactions are made just before the close on a given day. Frequently there is not just one price, but a range of prices at which transactions were made just before the close.
Closing range	The high and low prices at which transactions took place during 'the close'.
Collateral	Assets pledged by a borrower to secure payment of a loan or bond issue in the event of default.

CMO	Collateralised mortgage obligation or The Central Moneymarkets Office of the Bank of England providing book entry settlement of sterling money market instruments.
Co-manager	A manager not running the books.
Commission	The one-time fee charged by a broker to a customer when a position is liquidated either by offset or delivery.
Commission broker	A member of a futures exchange who executes orders for members and non-members for the sale or purchase of financial futures contracts.
Commission des Operations de Bourse ('COB')	The French (Paris) Stock exchange.
Consortium bank	A bank with a group of other banks as shareholders, but where no one bank holds a disproportionate amount of the equity.
Contract grade	The type of cash instruments listed in the rules of the exchange that can be used when delivering cash commodities or instruments against futures contracts.
Contract month	The month in which futures contracts may be satisfied by making or accepting delivery.
Convergence	Movement of the price of a futures contract towards the price of the underlying cash commodity.
Conversion premium or discount	The ratio, expressed as a percentage, of a convertible bond's market value to its conversion value (ie its value if converted into equity). A premium occurs when the conversion value of the security is lower than the market value. A discount occurs when the conversion value is higher than the market value.
Conversion price	The share price at which the principal amount of a price convertible bond may be used to acquire common stock in or owned by the issuing company.
Conversion ratio	The number of shares which may be acquired upon the conversion of a convertible bond. The ratio is calculated as bond principal amount divided by conversion price.
Coupon	Generally, the nominal annual rate of interest expressed as a percentage of the principal value, which

the borrower promises to pay the holder of a fixed income security. The coupon is payable annually, semi-annually or, in some cases, quarterly, depending on the type of security.

Covenant
An agreement by a borrower included within the documents of a new issue which is legally binding upon the borrower over the life of an issue to carry out certain acts or to refrain from certain acts. Examples are to provide financial statements on a timely basis to maintain certain financial ratios and to refrain from incurring further indebtedness beyond a predetermined level.

Cover
To offset a previous futures transaction with an equal and opposite transaction. Short covering is a purchase of futures contracts to offset an earlier sale of an equal number of the same delivery month. Liquidation is the sale of futures contracts to offset the obligation to take delivery of an equal number of futures contracts of the same delivery month purchased earlier.

Cross-default
A covenant by a borrower or a swap counterparty in respect of itself and its subsidiaries, if any, whereby each party undertakes that, in the event of a default in a payment under its other borrowings, such an event will be considered to be an event of default in respect of the issue to which the cross default covenant applies.

Cross-hedging
The hedging of an open position in a futures contract of a different, but related, cash instrument.

Cross-rate
An exchange rate calculated from two other bilateral exchange rates (two different currencies compared to the same third currency).

Cum
Used in abbreviations cum div, cum rights etc. to indicate that the buyer is entitled to take part in the forthcoming dividend or rights issue. Also cum-warrants and cum-dividends.

CTD
See 'cheapest to deliver'.

Current yield
A measurement of return to a bondholder calculated as the ratio of coupon to market price expressed as a percentage.

Custodian	An institution holding securities in safekeeping for a client.
Day order	An order that is placed for execution, if possible, during only one trading session. If the order cannot be exercised that day, it is automatically cancelled.
Day trading	Refers to establishing and liquidating the same futures position or positions within one day's trading.
Dealer	An individual or institution which buys and sells financial instruments which it owns for its own account.
Debt ratio	The proportion of a company's long term debt to its capital which gives an indication of a corporation's reliance on long-term debt as a source of capital and its flexibility regarding future financing. See 'gearing'.
Debt service	Payments of principal and interest required on a debt over a given period.
Default	The non-performance of a stated obligation. The non-payment by the issuer of interest or principal on a bond or the non-performance of a covenant.
Delayed delivery	A provision in a new issue permitting certain individuals or institutions to acquire and take delivery of specified amounts of securities on a stated date(s) after the original offering is closed.
Delivery against payment (DVP)	A delivery of securities to a designated recipient only upon receipt of payment cf. free delivery.
Delivery risk	In any foreign currency transaction, there is delivery risk between currency settlement hours outside the country involved and the actual settlement hours in the country of the currency. This risk, the full principal amount of the transaction, is at risk at maturity regardless of the nature of the transaction.
Delta	The relationship between an option price and the price of the underlying transaction.
Depreciation	A gradual decline in the value of a currency, usually occurring over a period of time on account of market forces of supply or demand.

Depth of the market	The amount that can be dealt in the market at a given time without causing a price fluctuation. Thin markets are usually characterised by wide spreads and substantial price fluctuations during a short period of time. Strong markets tend to be characterised by relatively narrow spreads and stable prices.
Difference account	In the UK, an account given to a client by an LME broker when a position is closed.
Dilution	The reduction in a company's earnings and voting power per share caused by an increase in the number of shares in issue. In the case of an issue of options for shares (including convertible bonds), dilution is often calculated on a primary basis (ie initial) and a fully diluted basis (ie following exercise or conversion of all the options).
Dirty price	The total price of securities which includes accrued interest.
Discount	The difference between the stated par and the market price of an issue, for issues selling below par, or the difference between the spot exchange rate and the forward exchange rate when the latter is below the former.
Discount basis	A method for quoting the annualised return on non-interest bearing securities, which always sell at a discount, in which the amount of the discount from par represents the investor's income during the life of the securities.
Discount rate	The interest rate at which a central bank discounts government bills to financial institutions usually referred to as the official discount rate.
Discount yield	The yield on a note at issue date represented by the issue discount purchase price to face value.
Double taxation agreement	An agreement between two countries designed to avoid double taxation of income. Under the terms of such an agreement, a tax payer in both countries can either apply for a reduction of taxes imposed by one country, or can obtain credit for taxes paid in one country against the tax liabilities in the other.
Drawdown	The drawing of funds made available by a bank or

	other financial institution under the terms of a loan facility.
Drawdown period	The period of time after the introduction of a loan facility during which the borrower may drawdown funds.
Due date	The date on which payment of interest or principal becomes due and payable.
Due diligence	Detailed review of a borrower's overall position, conducted by representatives of the lead manager, often with the assistance of legal counsel. Due diligence is normally performed in conjunction with the preparation of the documentation for a new issue.
Dutch auction	A pricing mechanism in which buyers submit bids. The price for all buyers is the marginal price at which the entire issue can be sold.
ECU	European Currency Unit. A composite currency, the value of which is determined on the basis of a basket of European currencies
Euroclear	One of the two major organisations in the Eurobond market which clears, or handles the physical exchange of, securities and stores securities. Based in Brussels, the company is owned by several banks and operated under contract by Morgan Guaranty Trust Company of New York.
Eurocurrency	A freely convertible currency held outside the country in whose currency it is denominated eg US dollars held by the London branch of an American bank. Hence the terms Euromarkets, Eurodollars, etc.
Eurodollar	US dollars deposited in a US bank branch or a foreign bank outside the United States.
European exercise	A call or put option which may be exercised only on its expiration date (see American exercise).
Event of	An event which legally entitles an investor (or his default trustee) demand immediate repayment of a loan facility or debt instrument.
Ex	The opposite of cum, and used to indicate that the purchaser is not entitled to participate in whatever forthcoming event is specified. Ex dividend, ex rights, etc.

Face value	The amount, exclusive of interest or premium, due to a security holder at maturity and inscribed on the face of the security. Also referred to as par value.
Facility fee	The equivalent, in syndicated loan terminology, of a combined commitment fee (fee charged on undrawn amounts) and an underwriting fee (charged on drawn amounts).
Fail	The failure to deliver or receive payment or securities in proper form by the agreed settlement date of a trade.
Firm	A market where prices are increasing.
	A word used in markets (especially the foreign exchange market) where a 'firm' quote means that a dealer is willing to trade at the rate quoted.
Firm order	A buy or sell order for securities that can be completed without further confirmation during a given time period.
Fixed rate interest	Interest on a security which is calculated as a constant specified percentage of the principal amount and paid at the end of specified interest periods, usually annually or semi annually until maturity.
Fixing	The determination of the interest rate on a floating rate security or loan generally two business days before the beginning of each interest period.
Floating or variable rate interest	Interest on an issue of securities which is not fixed for the life of the issue but which is periodically calculated by an agent bank using a formula specified in the terms of the issue.
Floor broker	A member who is paid a fee for executing orders for clearing members and their customers.
Floor trader	An exchange member who executes his own trades by being personally present in the pit or place provided for futures trading.
Free delivery or free payment	Payment for securities which is not conditional upon the simultaneous delivery of the securities cf. delivery against payment.
Fungible securities	Identical securities which are kept in a clearing system where the book-keeping is such that no specific securities are assigned to customer accounts by their

serial numbers. Only the aggregate number of identical securities in the system and the total amount of customer holdings of such securities are controlled.

Gearing	The proportional relationship between debt capital and equity capital.
Global bond	A temporary certificate representing a whole of an issue of debt instruments, created to control the primary market distribution of the issue. This is done either to comply with particular legal restrictions or because definitive bond certificates are not immediately available.
Give-up	At the request of the customer, a brokerage house which has not performed the service is credited with the execution of an order.
Good delivery	A delivery of unmutilated securities in which all legal and procedural matters are in proper order and which will be accepted by a transfer/clearing agent.
Good value	A payment for securities in cash or immediately available funds.
GNMA	Government National Mortgage Association; a US government agency that approves the issue of mortgage-backed securities with repayment of principal and interest fully guaranteed by the US Treasury.
Grace period	The period between the primary market offering of an issue of securities and the first operation of its sinking fund or purchase fund.
Grey market	The market in a new bond issue prior to formal offering.
Gross spread	The sum of the management and underwriting fees and the selling concession on a bond issue, usually expressed in percentage terms.
GTC	Good till cancelled. Open orders to buy or sell at a fixed price that remain effective until executed or cancelled.
Haircut	A term which describes the percentage deduction from the valuation of a security in the context of capital adequacy calculations (usually in the US).
Hedging	A device used by traders and sophisticated investors to reduce loss due to market fluctuations. This is done

	by counter balancing a current sale or purchase by another, usually future, purchase or sale. The desired result is that the profit or loss on the current sale or purchase will be off-set by the loss or profit on the future sale or purchase.
ICAEW	Institute of Chartered Accountants in England & Wales.
Immediately available funds	Funds with immediate good value, such as cash.
Inter-bank rates	The bid and offered rates at which international banks place deposits with each other.
Interest coverage	Also called interest coverage ratio. A measure of a borrower's ability to make interest payments out of earnings or cashflow.
Interest rate differential	The difference in the rate of interest offered in two currencies for investments of identical maturities.
Intermediary	An institution acting between two or more other entities by assuming certain rights and obligations. For example, an intermediary in a swap transaction assumes the credit risk of the counterparties (or end-users) of the swap.
Internal rate of return	The interest rate which equates the present value of a future stream of payments with the initial investment, i.e. the yield to maturity.
In the money	A transaction showing a profit because of market movements.
Inverse yield curve	See 'yield curve'.
Investment bank	A financial institution engaged in the issue of new securities, including management and underwriting of issues as well as securities trading and distribution.
ISDA	International Swap Dealers Association
ISE	The International Stock Exchange of Great Britain and the Republic of Ireland.
Issue price	The gross price (before allowances or commissions) placed on a new bond issue, expressed as a percentage of principal amount and usually varying from 98% to 102%.

Glossary of terms

Issuer	Any corporation or governmental unit which borrows money through the sale of securities.
Kerb trading	The execution of transactions after the close of the official market.
Last trading day	The final day during which trading may take place on a day in a particular delivery month. Futures contracts outstanding at the end of the last trading day must be settled by delivery of the specified financial instrument, or settlement may be made in cash at the option of the buyer in certain contracts.
Lead-manager	In a new securities issue, the managing bank responsible for initiating the transaction with the borrower and for organising or designating another to organise the successful syndication and placement of the issue in the primary market.
LIBID	See 'LIBOR'.
Life	The period between a security's issue date and its final maturity.
Life to call	The period remaining before a borrower's first option to call or redeem a security cf. life to put.
Life of contract	Period between the beginning of trading in a particular future and expiration of trading in the delivery month.
Life to put	The period remaining before a borrower's first option to put or sell a security.
LIMEAN	See 'LIBOR'.
Limit move	The maximum fluctuation in price of a futures contract permitted during one trading session, as fixed by the rules of the exchange.
Limit order	An order given to a broker which has restrictions on its execution. The customer specifies a price, and the order is executed only if the market price equals or betters that price.
Listing	The acceptance of an issue of securities for trading on a Stock Exchange in accordance with its rules and regulations.
Liquidation	Any transaction that offsets or closes out a long or short position.

Liquidity	Cash or securities that are so marketable that they may be converted into cash at any time with minimal risk of capital loss.
Liquid market	A market where buying and selling can be accomplished with ease, due to the presence of a large number of interested buyers and sellers prepared to trade substantial quantities at small price differences.
London Inter-bank Offered Rate (LIBOR)	The rate of interest offered on deposits with commercial banks operating in the London Eurocurrency market. LIBID and LIMEAN refer to the bid side, and the mean of LIBOR and LIBID, respectively.
Long	To own financial instruments; held for investment purposes or in anticipation of future price rises, or because of temporary inability to sell. Also referred to as long position.
Long position	Ownership of a financial instrument.
Maintenance margin	The minimum margin which a customer must keep on deposit with a member at all times.
Making a market	Dealers who stand ready to buy and sell certain financial instruments and quote bid and offer prices are said to be 'making a market'.
Management fee	That portion of the gross spread earned by the managers of a new issue.
Management group	In relation to a securities issue the term refers to the group of financial institutions, managers and underwriters which liaise with the lead manager in the distribution and pricing of the issue.
Manager	One of the firms participating in the management group and taking actions on behalf of the underwriters in a new issue (synonymous with co-manager).
Mandate	Authorisation from a borrower to proceed with a new bond issue at terms agreed with the lead manager.
Margin	An amount of money deposited by traders of futures contracts as a guarantee of fulfilment of the futures contract.
Margin call	A demand for additional funds because of adverse price movement on an open futures position.

Mark to market	The daily adjustment of open positions to reflect profits and losses resulting from price movements occurring during the last trading session.
Market maker	Any trading firm making prices in financial instruments prepared to deal at that price. See 'making a market'.
Market order	An order to buy or sell that is to be executed at the best possible price and as soon as possible.
Matched	A forward purchase is said to be matched when offset by a forward sale for the same or nearly the same date or vice versa.
Maturity	The date on which a given debt security becomes payable to the holder in full.
Mezzanine debt	Debt that is subordinated to the claims of senior lenders. The term is usually applied to leverage buy-outs, where such funding occupies a place in seniority immediately above that of common stockholders.
Money market	The market for the purchase and sale of short-term financial instruments. The short term is usually defined as less than one year.
Naked	An unhedged long or short position in a financial instrument.
NASDAQ	National Association of Security Dealers Automated Quotations: a computerised quotation system dealt with in the US over-the-counter market, sponsored by the National Association of Securities Dealers.
Negative carry	The net loss incurred when the cost of carry is more than the yield on the securities being financed.
Nominal amount (or value)	The value stated on the face of a security.
Nominee	A person or institution holding a security in his own name for the benefit of the actual or beneficial owner, usually to ensure anonymity.
Non-callable	Cannot be redeemed by the issuer for a stated period of time from date of issue.
Note	A promise to pay. A written agreement, the issuer promising to pay the holder on a given date or on demand a certain sum of money. The difference

between notes and bonds is normally that of maturity, notes typically having a shorter life.

Odd-lot
Any block of securities, either bid or offered, that is smaller than the standard round-lot block for that type of security. General over-the-counter market practice dictates that prices for odd-lots are discretionary.

Offer
The price or terms under which a person is willing to sell.

Offering circular
A document giving a description of a securities issue, including a complete statement of the terms of the issue and a description of the issuer, as well as its historical and financial statements. Also referred to as a prospectus.

Offering date
The date on which an allotment in respect of a new issue is made.

Open contracts
Contracts which have been bought or sold without the transactions having been completed or offset by subsequent sale or purchase, or actual delivery or receipt of the underlying financial instrument.

Open interest
The cumulative number of futures contracts which have been purchased and not yet offset by opposite futures transactions, nor fulfilled by delivery.

Open order
An order which is good until cancelled or executed.

Open outcry
Method of dealing on futures markets involving verbal bids and offers which are audible to all other market participants on the trading floor or pit.

Opening
The period at the beginning of the trading session officially designated by the exchange during which all transactions are considered to be made 'at the opening'.

Opening price
The price or price range of transactions recorded during the period designated by the exchange as the official opening.

Option to double
A sinking fund provision, allowing the issuer to double the number of securities purchased by the fund at the call price.

Original margin
The initial deposit of margin money required to cover a specific new futures position.

Out of the money	A transaction showing a loss because of market movements.
Over the counter (OTC)	The purchase and sale of financial instruments not conducted on an organised exchange.
Par	Price of 100% of a security's face value. Principal amount at which an issuer of bonds agrees to redeem its bonds at maturity.
Pari passu	Generally used in the context of securities ranking pari passu, ie equally in right of payment with each other.
Participation	An invitation (together with the related documents) to underwrite a certain principal amount of a new issue. Also the size of the underwriting commitment.
Paying agent	One of a group of banks responsible for paying the interest and principal of an issue.
P/E ratio	The relationship between a company's stockmarket value and its after-tax profit. The ratio is most commonly used by investment analysts to determine a company's future growth. A high P/E indicates good growth whilst conversely a low P/E indicates poor profitability.
Paper	Jargon which refers to securities, commercial paper or market instruments, generally short term.
Perfect hedge	A hedge in which a change in the futures price exactly cancels out any change in the cash market price.
PIBOR	Paris Interbank Offered Rate. The French equivalent of LIBOR.
Pick-up	The gain in yield which follows the sale of a block of securities and the subsequent purchase of another block which has a greater yield.
Place	To sell securities to investors during their primary market-distribution.
Placing agent	A financial institution which either commits to place a security with investors or is requested to submit bids on an issuer's security.
Placing memorandum	A confidential document which is provided to a private placement syndicate and to its investor clients. It is written by the lead-manager and contains all the

relevant information about the borrower and the placement.

Placing power	Ability of a bank to sell or place a new issue of securities.
Point	The smallest increment of price movement possible in trading a given futures contract, equivalent to the minimum price fluctuation.
Portfolio	Collection of financial instruments or transactions denominated in various currencies.
Position	An interest in the market, either long or short, in terms of financial instruments.
Position trading	A type of trading involving the holding of financial instruments for an extended period of time.
Positive carry	The net gain earned when the cost of carry is less than the yield on the securities being financed.
Praecipium	That portion of the management fee attributable to the lead manager in respect of his services before division among the co-managers.
Premium	For debt instruments with issue prices greater than par value, the amount of the difference between par and the price.
Prepayment	A payment on a bond or loan made prior to the originally appointed date.
Present value	The current value of a given future cash flow stream, discounted at a given rate.
Price of security	The worth of a security expressed as a percentage of its a principal value.
Pricing	In a new security issue, the day when final terms are decided prior to formal offering.
Primary market	The market relating to the original issue or first sale of new securities.
Prime rate	An average of rates quoted by the major US banks on a given day.
Principal	Par value or face amount of a security, exclusive of any premium or interest. The basis for interest computations.

Prospectus or offering memorandum	A document giving a description of an issue of securities including a statement of the terms of the issuer and a description of the issuer along with its most recent and historical financial statements. The prospectus is circularised to the appropriate legal authorities, stock exchanges and prospective investors.
Public offering	An offering for sale of a new issue of securities to the general investing public.
Purchase fund	An arrangement under which an issuer undertakes to buy back or arrange to have bought back a certain principal amount of bonds if they are trading below a set price, usually par, during a specified period of time.
Push trade	A transaction on which a profit should arise but is not guaranteed.
Put	A contract allowing the holder to sell a given number of securities back to the issuer of such a contract at a fixed price for a given period of time.
Quote	The market price of a given security.
Range	The high and low prices, or high and low bids and offers, recorded during a specified period.
Rating	A letter grade signifying a security's investment quality. In the United States the chief rating agencies are Moody's and Standard & Poors.
Real rate of return	A term used to describe the rate of return calculated by subtracting the rate of inflation from the nominal rate of return.
Realised yield	The return a security earns over a given period calculated by assuming that the interest income is reinvested at a specified reinvestment rate.
Reallowance	That portion of a selling concession which a syndicate member is permitted to pass on to another securities dealer.
Redemption	Extinguishing a debt through cash payment. The contractual right of an issuer to exercise optional redemption is also known as a call.
Redemption date	The day on which the issuer will pay holder capital and any accrued interest due under the security.

Redemption price	A price at which bonds may be redeemed, or called, at the issuer's option, prior to maturity (often at a slight premium over par).
Redemption yield	The current quoted yield on a security, adjusted to include the capital gain or loss on redemption.
Reference agent	In the case of floating rate securities and borrowings, a bank active in the Eurocurrency deposit market appointed to determine the rate of interest payable during the next interest period, on the basis of deposit rates quoted to it by other appointed reference banks and, in some cases, to publish this rate.
Reinvestment rate	The rate of reinvestment assumed for cash payments during an issue's or other investment's life.
Retire	To eliminate a debt obligation, either by repayment or prepayment, or redemption.
Rollover	The process of an issuer repaying a certain amount of an interest bearing security and immediately reissuing them in the same amount.
Round lot	A transaction which constitutes the acceptable minimum unit of trading for a particular issue or type of security.
Running the books	In a new securities issue, the function of a lead manager in preparing documentation, administering the offering (e.g., giving protection and making allotments), organising the syndicate and arranging for payment and delivery of the new securities.
Running yield	The ratio of coupon to market price expressed as a percentage. Also referred to as current yield.
Same-day settlement	A UK domestic market term used to describe cash settlement.
Scalp	Trading for small gains within a short time period (normally less than one day) rather than position trading.
SEAQ	Stock Exchange Automated Quotation System.
Seasoned securities	Refers to a securities issue which has been traded in the secondary market for some time; as opposed to newly offered securities. In the context of SEC regulations, securities qualify as seasoned only after they have been traded for between 90 and 360 days. Most

Eurobonds are not registered with the SEC and cannot be sold to US persons until they are seasoned.

SEC — Securities and Exchange Commission. A US government agency created with the aim of investor protection regarding securities transactions by the administration of securities legislation.

Secondary market — The market for bond securities which have already been offered, i.e. their initial distribution has ended. Such securities are also referred to as 'seasoned'.

Selling concession — In a new issue, that part of the gross spread paid to managers, underwriters and selling group members for each security actually purchased by them. Expressed as a percentage of face value.

Selling group — In a securities offering, the dealers acting only as sellers of the securities and not as underwriters. Underwriters and managers also participate in the selling group to the extent that they place securities in a new offering.

SEPON — A nominee company used by the International Stock Exchange of the United Kingdom and the Republic of Ireland (Stock Exchange Pool Nominees).

Settlement — The consummation of a trade involving the exchange of securities and the related payment.

Settlement date — The date on which a transaction is completed and cleared, i.e. payment is effected and securities are delivered. In the case of Eurobonds, including floating rate notes, the settlement date is usually seven days after the trade date and it is usually two days after the trade date in the case of CDs and FRCDs.

Short — To sell financial instrument not owned at the time. Usually done in anticipation of a price decline, in which case the seller can make delivery on the short sale with bonds purchased at a discount. The difference would be the seller's profit. Also referred to as short position.

Short covering — The purchase of securities previously sold short by a professional or retail investor in order to deliver them and thus close out a short position.

Short hedge — The sale of securities not owned by the seller in the expectation that the price of the securities will fall or

	as part of an arbitrage. A short sale must eventually be covered by a purchase of the securities sold.
Short-term security	Generally an obligation maturing in less than one year.
SIB	Securities and Investments Board. The chief regulatory body under the UK Financial Services Act 1986.
SIBOR	Singapore Interbank Offer Rate (SIBOR). The Singaporean equivalent of LIBOR.
Sinking fund	Repayment of debt by an issuer at stated regular intervals through purchases in the open market or drawings by lot.
Special drawing right (SDR)	A composite currency unit introduced by the International Monetary Fund and based upon a standard basket of currencies.
Specialistes des Valeurs du Tresor ('SVT')	Primary dealers in French government bonds.
Speculation	The assumption of a long or short position in a financial instrument or a currency in anticipation of a favourable market movement which should result in a gain when the position is covered.
Spot	Cash or current, i.e. the spot price is the immediate cash price; the spot market is the market for current transactions.
Spot rate yield curve	The yield curve where every point is the yield to maturity of a zero coupon bond of that maturity. Also known as the zero coupon yield curve.
Spread	In trading or the quotation of financial instruments, the difference between the bid and the asked price is the spread.
SDRT	Stamp duty reserve tax
SSAP	UK – Statement of Standard Accounting Practice.
Stop order	An order to sell or acquire securities when a pre-stated price level is reached or exceeded.
Subscription agreement	An agreement for the underwriting of a new issue between the issuer and the collective managers (or managers acting on behalf of the underwriters), describing certain terms and conditions of the issue and

the obligations of the parties to it. Also referred to as an underwriting agreement in syndicates arranged by US banks.

Subscriptions
In a new bond issue, the buying orders from the lead manager, co-managers, underwriters and selling group members for the securities being offered.

Switch
The exchanging of one security for another.

Syndicate
A group of banks which act together in underwriting and distributing a new securities issue.

Tap issue
A financing where only a portion of the full principal amount is initially placed on offer. The remainder is retained pending favourable market conditions or the need of the issuer for additional funds. Also referred to as a multiple tranche issue.

Tender offer
The sale of securities where the seller sets a tender price at which he is prepared to sell the securities. Tenders are made where the applicants state the price they are prepared to pay. The securities are subsequently allotted to the highest bidders.

Terms
For a new securities issue, the characteristics of the securities on offer: coupon, amount, maturity, etc.

The Stock Exchange
The International Stock Exchange of the United Kingdom and the Republic of Ireland.

Tick
Refers to the minimum possible changes in prices, either up or down.

Tombstone
An advertisement for an offering of new securities. Typically gives the terms of the issue and lists the managers and underwriters.

Trade date
The date on which a transaction is executed.

Trader
An individual who buys and sells securities with the objective of making short-term gains.

Tranche
Part of a single financing which is split into different maturities or principal amounts (or sometimes different currencies).

Trust deed
In a new bond issue, a contract defining the obligations of an issuer and appointing a trustee to represent the interests of bondholders. Also known as a trust indenture in the United States.

Underwrite	An arrangement under which banks agree to each buy a certain agreed amount of securities of a new issue on a given date and at a given price, thereby assuring the issuer of the full proceeds of a financing.
Underwriter	An institution engaged in the business of underwriting securities issues.
Underwriting fee	That share of the gross spread of a new issue accruing to members of the underwriting group after the expenses of the issue have been paid.
Value date	The date up to and including which accrued interest is calculated. The value date and the settlement date generally coincide as transactions are normally negotiated for value on a business day.
Volatility	The susceptibility of a price to rapid changes including exchange and interest rates. Volatility is frequently measured in standard deviations.
Wash trade	A matched deal producing neither gain nor loss.
When Issued	See grey market.
Withholding tax	A tax deducted at source which a paying agent is legally obliged to deduct from its payments of interest or dividends. However, persons or institutions residing outside the country levying the tax are not subject to payment of it.
Yield	Rate of return on a security as determined by its coupon and other characteristics, expressed as a percent and annualised.
Yield curve	A graphic illustration of the relationship between yield and maturity for a given range of securities.
Yield to average life	The yield calculated by using the average life of a debt instrument rather than its stated maturity, computed by assuming that the issue is redeemed in accordance with the amortisation schedule for the issue, and therefore has a theoretical maturity equal to the average life.
Yield to call	The yield of a given security when the next call date is substituted for its final maturity. Yield is also determined with reference to the next put date when

	the investor can require a borrower to redeem its securities.
Yield to maturity	The return earned on a bond at a given price if held to maturity.
Yield-to-Put (YTP)	The return a security earns assuming that it is held until a certain date and put to the borrower at the specified put price.
Zero coupon yield curve	See spot rate yield curve.

Alphabetical index

Alphabetical index

Acronym	Description	Category	Page
	Currency Swap	Hedging instrument	480, 495
	Currency – change Bond	Debt instrument	77
	Currency/Interest Rate /Commodity Warrant	Hedging instrument	448
	Cylinder Option	Hedging instrument	468
	Debt with Debt Warrants	Debt instrument	119
	Debt With Equity Warrant	Equity and Equity Linked	295
	Debt With Premium Put	Equity and Equity Linked	289
	Debt/Equity Swap	Hedging instrument	506
	Deep Discount Stepped Interest Loan Stocks	Debt instrument	98
	Deep Discounted Bonds	Debt instrument	96
	Deferred Coupon Bond	Debt instrument	98
	Deferred Coupon FRN	Debt instrument	43
	Deferred Interest Bond	Debt instrument	98
	Deferred Payment Bond	Debt instrument	106
	Deferred Premium Option	Hedging instrument	418
	Deferred Share	Equity and Equity Linked	246
	Deferred (or Forward) Cap	Hedging instrument	459
	Deferred (or Forward) Swap	Hedging instrument	489
	Depository receipt	Equity and Equity Linked	242
	Detachable Warrants	Hedging instrument	446
	Double Option	Hedging instrument	419
	Drop – lock FRN	Debt instrument	43
	Dual Currency Bond	Debt instrument	74
	Dual Option Bond	Debt instrument	82

Alphabetical index

670

Financial instruments

Acronym	Description	Category	Page
	Fixed Rate Bonds	Debt instrument	34
	Fixed Rate Currency Swap	Hedging instrument	496
	Flip Flop Notes	Debt instrument	123
FRCD	Floating Rate CDs	Debt instrument	64
FRENDS	Floating Rate Enhanced Debt Security	Asset backed security	196
FRN	Floating Rate Notes	Debt instrument	41
	Floating Rate Preferred Stock	Equity and Equity Linked	281
	Floortion (see Caption)	Hedging instrument	459
	Foreign Currency Bond	Debt instrument	76
FXA	Foreign Exchange Agreement	Hedging instrument	464
FIPS	Foreign Interest Payment Security	Debt instrument	77
	Foretagscertifikat	Debt instrument	57
	Forward Break	Hedging instrument	472
	Forward Commodity Contracts	Hedging instrument	395
	Forward Contract	Hedging instrument	389, 394, 520
	Forward Foreign Exchange Contracts	Hedging instrument	395
FRA	Forward Rate Agreement	Hedging instrument	453
	Forward Reverse Option	Hedging instrument	418
FSA	Forward Spread Agreement	Hedging instrument	454
FOX	Forward with Optional Exit	Hedging instrument	472
	Forward with Rebate	Hedging instrument	477
	Forward/Forward Deposit	Hedging instrument	454
	French Commercial Paper	Debt instrument	55
	French Treasury Bills	Debt instrument	23

Acronym	Description	Category	Page
	Interest Rate Floor	Hedging instrument	459
	Interest Rate Future	Hedging instrument	454
	Interest Rate Futures	Hedging instrument	410
IRG	Interest Rate Guarantee	Hedging instrument	455
	Interest Rate Options	Hedging instrument	420
	Interest Rate Swap	Hedging instrument	480, 487
	Inverse FRN	Debt instrument	45
IC	Investment Certificate	Equity and Equity Linked	267
	Irredeemable Gilts	Debt instrument	19
	Junk Bonds	Debt instrument	111
	Kassenobligationen	Debt instrument	25
	Kommunalobligationen	Debt instrument	29
	Lehman Investment Opportunity Notes	Debt instrument	102
LIONs	Liquid Yield Option Note	Equity and Equity Linked	257
LYON	Long Dated Forward Rate Agreement	Hedging instrument	455
LDFRA	Long Straddle	Hedging instrument	430
	Lookback Option	Hedging instrument	419
	Marginal Reverse Forex Linked Bonds	Debt instrument	78
	Market Auction Rate Preferred Stock	Equity and Equity Linked	283
MARPs	Matched REPOs	Hedging instrument	516
	Maturing Adjustable Preferred Stock	Equity and Equity Linked	283
MAPs	Medium Term Note	Debt instrument	66
MTN	Mini – Max FRN	Debt instrument	45
	Mismatch FRN	Debt instrument	46

Acronym	Description	Category	Page
	Participating Preference Share	Equity and Equity Linked	253
PRA	Participating Rate Agreement	Hedging instrument	462
	Participation Certificate	Asset backed security	160
	Participation Certificates	Equity and Equity Linked	266
	Partly Paid Bonds	Debt instrument	105
	Partly – paid Dual Currency Bond	Debt instrument	76
	Pass Through Certificate	Asset backed security	164
	Pass Through Security	Asset backed security	160
PIK	Pay in Kind Debenture	Debt instrument	121
	Pay Through Bond	Asset backed security	164
PIPs	Performance Indexed Paper	Debt instrument	94
	Perpetual Bonds	Debt instrument	113
	Perpetual FRNs	Debt instrument	114
	Pfandbriefe	Debt instrument	29
PAC	Planned Amortisation Class	Asset backed security	181
	Preferred Share	Equity and Equity Linked	252
	Preferred Stock with a Dividend Holiday	Equity and Equity Linked	254
	Premium Put Convertible	Equity and Equity Linked	289
PERLS	Principal Exchange Rate Linked Securities	Debt instrument	78
POs	Principal Only Mortgage Backed Security	Asset backed security	185
	Principal Only Swap	Hedging instrument	496
PINCs	Property Income Certificate	Asset backed security	191
PARRs	Purchased Accelerated Recovery Right	Asset backed security	197
	Purgatory and Hell Bond	Debt instrument	78

Acronym	Description	Category	Page
	Rights Issue	Equity and Equity Linked	244
	Rolling rate FRN	Debt instrument	46
	Schuldscheine	Debt instrument	29
	Scrip Issue	Equity and Equity Linked	245
	Seasonal Caps	Hedging instrument	459
	Secured bonds	Debt instrument	15
STRIPES	Securities Transferred and Repackaged into	Hedging instrument	513
STARs	Securities Transferred Repackaged	Hedging instrument	513
SNCF	Securitised Note Commitment Facility	Debt instrument	61
STRIPs	Separate Trading of Registered Interest and Principal	Debt instrument	102
	Serial FRN	Debt instrument	46
	Serial Zero Coupon Bonds	Debt instrument	99
	Serial (or Strip) FRA's	Hedging instrument	455
	Share Warrant	Equity and Equity Linked	245
SCOUT	Shared Currency Option Under Tender	Hedging instrument	473
SOFA	Shared Option Forward Agreement	Hedging instrument	476
	Short Straddle	Hedging instrument	431
	Short Term Debt Instruments	Debt instrument	50
STARs	Short – Term Auction Rate Preferred Stock	Equity and Equity Linked	283
SNIF	Short – Term Note Issuance Facility	Debt instrument	61
	Simple Hedge	Hedging instrument	426
SAPCO	Single Asset Property Company	Asset backed security	192
SPOTs	Single Property Ownership Trust	Asset backed security	191
SPIN	Standard and Poors Indexed Notes	Debt instrument	87

Contact names and addresses

Country	Contact	Address
Austria	Hans Wessely	Coopers & Lybrand Berggasse 31 PO Box 161, A-1092 Vienna Telephone: (43) (1) 31 86 10-0 Fax: (43) (1) 31 86 10-6
Belgium	Raymond Eeckhout	Coopers & Lybrand Avenue Marcel Thiry, 216 B-1200 Brussels Telephone: (32) (02) 774 42 11 Fax: (32) (02) 774 42 99
Channel Islands	David Hill	Coopers & Lybrand Deloitte La Motte Chambers St Helier, Jersey CI, JE1 1BJ Telephone: (44) (0534) 602000 Fax: (44) (0534) 602002
	John Hallam	Coopers & Lybrand Deloitte National Westminster House PO Box 626, Le Truchot St Peter Port, Guernsey CI Telephone: (44) (0481) 726921 Fax: (44) (0481) 711075
Cyprus	Michael Zampelas Dinos Papadopoulos	Coopers & Lybrand 3 Themistocles Dervis Street PO Box 1612, Nicosia Telephone: (357) (02) 453053 (357) (02) 475194

Contact names and addresses

Country	Contact	Address
Finland	Mauno Tervo	Salmi, Virkkunen & Helenius Oy Coopers & Lybrand Oy PO Box 1015 (Keskuskatu 3) 00101 Helsinki Telephone: (358) (0) 658 044 Fax: (358) (0) 174 102
France	Phillipe Garnier Robert Magnan (Tax)	Coopers & Lybrand 56 Rue de Ponthieu 75008 Paris Mailing address: BP 451-08, 75366 Paris, Cedex 08 Telephone: (33) (1) 44 20 80 00 Fax: (33) (1) 45 62 74 96
Germany	Peter Schauss (Accounting) Horst Rattig (Tax)	Coopers & Lybrand Postfach 170 552 DW-6000 Frankfurt 1 Telephone: (49) (069) 711 00 Fax: (49) (069) 711 04 66
Greece	Andreas Acavalos	Coopers & Lybrand Abacus House 9 Semitelou Street GR-11528 Athens Telephone: (30) (01) 7710 112 Fax: (30) (01) 7777 390
Ireland	Bill Cunningham	Coopers & Lybrand PO Box 1283 Fitzwiltan House Wilton Place, Dublin 2 Telephone: (353) (01) 610333 Fax: (353) (01) 601782

Contact names and addresses

Country	Contact	Address
Isle of Man	Chris Talavera	Coopers & Lybrand 12 Finch Road, Douglas Isle of Man Telephone: (44) (0624) 626711 Fax: (44) (0624) 626712
Italy	Alfonso Lavanna	Coopers & Lybrand Consulenti di Direzione SpA Via Vittor Pisani 19, 20124 Milan Telephone: (39) (02) 66984987 Fax: (39) (02) 6693131
	Paolo Bovone	Coopers & Lybrand Consulenti di Direzione SpA Via Del Quirinale 26, 00187 Rome Telephone: (39) (06) 4828558 Fax: (39) (06) 4828578
Luxembourg	Didier Mouget	Coopers & Lybrand 15 rue des Scillas L 2529 Luxembourg-Howald Telephone: (352) 40 35 66 Fax: (352) 40 35 78
Netherlands	Ton Huisman Piet Oldenziel	Coopers & Lybrand Dijker Van Dien PO Box 4200 1009 AE Amsterdam Telephone: (31) (20) 56 86 666 Fax: (31) (20) 69 35 601
Norway	Einar Westby	Coopers & Lybrand AS Havnelageret, N-0150 Oslo 1 Telephone: (47) 02 40 00 00 Fax: (47) 02 42 50 91
	Per Kare Furnes	Coopers & Lybrand AS C Sundtstg 10, N-5004 Bergen Telephone: (47) 05 32 40 50 Fax: (47) 05 23 26 40

Contact names and addresses

Country	Contact	Address
Spain	Colin Blessley	Coopers & Lybrand SA Apartado de Correos 36-191 28080 Madrid Telephone: (34) (1) 572 02 33 Fax: (34) (1) 270 00 42
Sweden	Sigvad Heurlin	Coopers & Lybrand Tegeluddsvagen 31 PO Box 27318, 102 54 Stockholm Telephone: (46) (8) 666 80 00 Fax: (46) (8) 662 19 83
Switzerland	Willi Grau Bernhard Ueberwasser (Tax)	Coopers & Lybrand Stampfenbachstrasse 73 Postfach, CH 8035 Zurich Telephone: (41) (01) 365 88 11 Fax: (41) (01) 365 82 82
Turkey	Michael Clarke	Coopers & Lybrand Buyukdere Caddesi No 111, Kat 2-3 Gayrettepe 80300, Istanbul Telephone: (90) (1) 175 2840 Fax: (90) (1) 173 0493
United Kingdom	Phil Rivett Alastair Wilson Paul Reyniers	Coopers & Lybrand Deloitte Plumtree Court London EC4A 4HT Telephone: (44) (071) 583 5000 Fax: (44) (071) 822 4652

Dialling procedure

Most international telephone calls can now be made by means of the International Direct Dialling system (IDD). To dial direct, use the following sequence - International Access code, followed by country code, followed by area or city code, followed by local telephone number.

In many countries the area codes start with a zero. The zero is needed when telephoning from another area within that country but for most countries must be omitted when telephoning from another country.